HISTORY OF THE UNITED STATES

FROM THE COMPROMISE OF 1850

TO

THE McKINLEY-BRYAN CAMPAIGN
OF 1896

VOL. III

HISTORY

OF THE

UNITED STATES

FROM

THE COMPROMISE OF 1850

TO

THE McKINLEY–BRYAN CAMPAIGN OF 1896

BY

JAMES FORD RHODES, LL.D., D.Litt.

In Eight Volumes

VOL. III
1860-1862

KENNIKAT PRESS, INC./PORT WASHINGTON, N. Y.

HISTORY OF THE UNITED STATES

Volume 1 copyright 1892 by James Ford Rhodes
Volume 2 copyright 1892 by James Ford Rhodes
Volume 3 copyright 1895 by James Ford Rhodes
Volume 4 copyright 1899 by James Ford Rhodes
Volume 5 copyright 1904 by James Ford Rhodes
Volume 6 copyright 1906 by James Ford Rhodes
Volume 7 copyright 1906 by James Ford Rhodes
Volume 8 copyright 1919 by James Ford Rhodes

The eight volumes reissued by Kennikat Press in 1967
by arrangement with the estate of James Ford Rhodes

Library of Congress Catalog Card No: 67-27637

Manufactured in the United States of America

Note: Volume Nine of the History of the United States
       also published by Kennikat Press under the title
       "The McKinley and Roosevelt Administrations
       1897-1909" and may be ordered separately.

CONTENTS

OF

THE THIRD VOLUME

CHAPTER XIII

CHAPTER XIV

CHAPTER XV

CHAPTER XVI

CONTENTS

CONTENTS

LIST OF MAPS

CHAPTER XIII

IN the election of Lincoln the North had spoken. Because slavery was wrong, the majority of the Northern people had declared against its extension. South Carolina quickly made answer. Before the October elections, men in that State believed the choice of Lincoln probable,[1] and after Pennsylvania and Indiana had gone Republican, only a lingering hope remained that the issue could be other than that dreaded by the South.[2] The minds of men were preparing for action in case the event should actually take place. It was argued that honor and pecuniary interest alike demanded disunion.[3] There seemed little doubt that public opinion would support the political leaders of the State in promptly taking measures to put in force the long-threatened remedy of secession. Gist, South Carolina's governor, shaped with alacrity his official action in conformity to the sentiment of his State. Before the October elections he had sent a confidential letter to each of the governors of the cotton States, with the exception of Houston of Texas, saying that South Carolina would unquestionably consider her course in convention and asking for co-operation on the part of her sister States.[4] October 12, three days after Pennsylvania and Indiana had virtually decided the presidential contest, Gist called the usual session of the legislature for the purpose of appointing presidential elec-

---

[1] See Charleston *Mercury*, Oct. 2, 5, 8 ; Governor Gist's circular letter, Oct. 5, cited in Nicolay and Hay, vol. ii. p. 306.

[2] Ibid., Oct. 17 to 31; Charleston *Courier*, Oct. 13.

[3] See Charleston *Mercury*, Oct. 11, 17, 23, 31.

[4] MS. Confederate Archives, cited by Nicolay and Hay, vol. ii. p. 306.

tors; but at the same time he gave the unusual intimation
that some action might be necessary "for the safety and
protection of the State." [1]   November 5, the day before
the election, the legislature assembled at Columbia.   Governor Gist recommended that in case Lincoln was elected
provision should be made immediately for the holding of a
convention with a view to severing the connection of South
Carolina with the Federal Union. [2]

While Republican success was deemed almost certain, the
actual event caused a shock little lessened by the fact that
it had been long impending.   On election night the city of
Charleston anxiously awaited the news of the result, and
when it was known that a majority of Lincoln electors had
been chosen, the crowd broke forth in cheers for a Southern
confederacy. [3]   The excitement over what was called "the
fatal result" [4] did not cease with the morrow's sun.   The
morning despatches confirmed the news of the previous
evening, and doubt could no longer exist that the hated Republican party had carried the day.   Business was neglected.
The streets were crowded with people.   So well had the
public mind been educated and prepared that the proper
course to pursue was neither a matter of argument nor of
hesitation.   Disunion sentiment had made its appearance
in South Carolina in 1832 with powerful manifestation; it
slept for a while, but eighteen years later came again to
the surface, and though not then prompting the people to
overt acts, [5] it had not been stifled, but only awaited sufficient provocation to break out with renewed vigor.   At almost any time since 1851, on a proper showing and a fair
justification, it would have received the assent of a majority of voters.   It had strong support in the press; it had
the advocacy of the literary coterie of Charleston; [6] it had
rooted strength with the people; it had already begun to

[1] Charleston *Mercury*, Oct. 17.   [2] Ibid., Nov. 6.
[3] Ibid., Nov. 7.   [4] Charleston *Courier*, Nov. 7.
[5] See vol. i. pp. 45, 226.   [6] See Life of W. G. Simms, Trent, chap. vi.

dominate and shape the course of South Carolina's statesmen and politicians, who, because on them devolved the
responsibility of action, were less vehement in their expressions than editors of newspapers and writers for magazines;
and it was gaining slowly on the business men of Charleston and the large proprietors of the State, by arguments
addressed to their interest as well as to their honor.   The
disunion majority of the decade suddenly expanded to unanimity on the seventh day of November, 1860.   It did not
seem to a certain keen observer, on his visit in 1855 and
1856, that all South Carolinians were disunionists; but no
doubt on this point remained in his mind after his sojourn
at Charleston in January, 1861.[1]

The crowd that thronged the streets of Charleston on the
morning of November 7th were of one mind.   From their
point of view they had an undoubted grievance; consequently their complaint was just.   With one accord they invoked
secession as the remedy.   When the resignations of the
judge and the district attorney of the United States Court
were announced the excitement grew.   At noon the palmetto and lone star flag was stretched across the street from
an upper window of the Charleston *Mercury* office, and was
hailed with cheers and expressions of passionate attachment.[2]   No light spirit of bravado characterized the people.
There were, indeed, "symptoms of ill-advised demonstrations," but these were frowned upon.[3]   Charleston men of
family and property gave the tone to the sentiment of the
day.   But notwithstanding their belief in the probability
of peaceable secession, they could not ignore the fact that
the breaking up of a government was a serious affair; that
the process of dissolution was certain to be attended with
commercial depression, perhaps financial panic; and they
also felt that there was a possibility of their having to fight
for the cause of Southern rights.   So, in spite of the cheers

---

[1] See article of J. W. De Forest, *Atlantic Monthly*, April, 1861, p. 495.
[2] Charleston *Mercury*, Nov. 8.   [3] Charleston *Courier*, Nov. 9.

at welcome events, in spite of countenances brightened by enthusiastic personal contact, there was anxiety for the future, and on the whole the feeling was stern and deep, as befitted an Anglo-Saxon community on the eve of revolution.[1] "The tea has been thrown overboard—the revolution of 1860 has been initiated," said the Charleston *Mercury*.[2] The comparison of events in Charleston to the Boston "tea-party" occurs more than once in the agitation that immediately preceded the act of secession. It was a welcome assertion to the people that they were animated by the spirit of 1776.[3] Although the Massachusetts of Sumner and Garrison was hated, her example in the early days of the Revolution was constantly brought up to urge forward South Carolinians in the path that should lead to independence.[4] But of course the parallel could not be carried far. In the spirit of the people and its manifestations there was indeed a striking likeness, but when the underlying motive came to be considered the resemblance failed. There was a considerable difference between that early protest accompanied by deliberate action against unjust taxation and this precipitate movement to break the bonds with States whose offence lay in the declaration that slavery was wrong and should not be extended.

After having appointed presidential electors, who were instructed to vote for Breckinridge and Lane, the legislature did not, as had heretofore been the custom, adjourn. It continued in session in order to be ready to act as the situation demanded. Its members had been chosen in October when Lincoln's election was deemed probable, and at that time, in the feeling that "the irrepressible conflict is about to be vis-

---

[1] Charleston *Mercury* and *Courier;* conversation with Samuel Shethar, a New York merchant who had large business and social connections in Charleston, and who went there immediately after Lincoln's election to look after his interests.   [2] Nov. 8.

[3] See speech of S. L. Hammond at the business men's meeting, Charleston *Mercury*, Nov. 19.

[4] Speech of Mr. Bilbo at Charleston Hotel, ibid., Dec. 3.

ited upon us through the Black Republican nominee (Lincoln) *and his fanatical, diabolical Republican party,*" [1] men were elected who would translate into action the sentiment of their communities. It was a body which fully and fairly represented the State. The main question before the legislature was whether a convention should be immediately called. Trenholm, a member from Charleston, offered a resolution looking towards co-operation with Georgia, and the assembling of a convention of the Southern States. This move in the interest of delay was not received with favor by the legislature or by the city of Charleston.[2] A large and enthusiastic meeting of the citizens of Charleston was held, and prompt action was demanded from the legislature.[3] On Saturday, November 10, the legislature passed unanimously a bill which provided for a convention of the people of South Carolina, to be held December 17, for the purpose of considering the relations of the commonwealth " with the Northern States and the government of the United States." On the same day Chesnut sent to the legislature his resignation of his position of United States senator, and the reading of his letter was received with applause. Action was also taken towards putting the State on a military footing. Columbia rejoiced over these events, and willingly listened to words of praise for the prompt and resolute action of Charleston, " which has at times been considered lukewarm and, by virtue of her commercial interests, conservative in an eminent degree." [4]

Charleston itself went wild with delight over the action of the legislature. Men showed their intense feeling when they met in the streets by hand-shakings, and by thanking God that at last their destinies were in their own hands.[5]

---

[1] Statement in advocacy of a legislative ticket signed " Many Planters," Charleston *Mercury*, Oct. 2.

[2] See a careful editorial of the Charleston *Mercury*, Nov. 9; also speech of Mr. Lesesne, Nov. 15.   [3] Charleston *Courier*, Nov. 10.

[4] Speech of Conner at Columbia, Charleston *Mercury*, Nov. 12.

[5] Charleston *Mercury*, Nov. 12.

On Monday night, November 12, a meeting was held in Institute Hall to endorse the action of the legislature. The solid men of the city and ladies of high social position were present. Never had there been a larger gathering, never had such enthusiasm prevailed. Fireworks and illuminations testified to the general joy. During the week the feeling kept up to fever heat. Palmetto flags were flying everywhere. Minute-men paraded the streets.[1] On Tuesday, Hammond's resignation as United States senator was submitted to the legislature and accepted. On Thursday evening another large meeting was held at Institute Hall to receive the Charleston members of the legislature, which had completed its labors and adjourned. It was a recognition of the well-doing of faithful servants.

If any one is inclined to doubt that there was other than a single cause for secession and the war that ensued; if he feel himself almost persuaded by the earnest and pathetic statements of Southern writers since the war, who naturally have sought to place the four years' devotion and heroism of the South on a higher basis than that of a mighty effort to conserve an institution condemned alike by Christianity and by ethics, let him read the speeches and the newspaper articles of the early days of the secession movement in South Carolina. It cannot be denied that the South Carolinians looked the matter squarely in the face, and that sincerity characterized their utterances. "The first issue," said Trenholm, "was made upon the question of a tariff in which the sympathies of the world were with the South. Now we are joining the issue with the prejudices and the sympathies of the world against us." "The question is," declared a preacher in a Sunday sermon, whether slavery "is an institution to be cherished," or whether it "must be dispensed with."[2] While South Carolinians

---

[1] Charleston *Mercury*, Nov. 13; Charleston cor. New York *Tribune*, Nov. 12.

[2] Charleston *Mercury*, Nov. 16, 21. "Upon the subject of this institution [African slavery] we are *isolated* from the whole world, who are not only

did not for a moment doubt the right of secession, they were not ignorant of the fact that their movement might be called revolution. "It is not a legislative revolution, but a popular revolution," truly said a member of the legislature at the Thursday meeting; and a similar manner of expression is common in the political literature of the time.[1]

On Saturday, November 17, the business men of the city made manifest that their hearts were in the cause. At an immense meeting they raised a liberty-pole. When the palmetto flag was hoisted, cannon roared, the bands played the Marseillaise, and thousands cheered. The religious feeling of this religious community sanctioned the proposed

---

indifferent, but inimical to it." — McGowan in South Carolina Legislature, Nov. 9, cited in Greeley's American Conflict, vol. i. p. 334. "We have regarded the North as fatally hostile to the interests and the institutions of the South."—Extract from a resolution of the meeting of Nov. 12, endorsing the action of the legislature. "Our Confederacy must be a slave-holding Confederacy. We have had enough of a Confederacy with dissimilar institutions." — R. B. Rhett, at same meeting. "Three thousand millions of property is involved in this question."—Speech of O'Connor, Nov. 15. The foregoing are cited from the Charleston *Mercury:* Why do we mean to tear down this government "from the foundation to the turret?" asked Keitt. Because "its powers are about to pass into the hands of a sectional majority, which majority declares slavery shall die."— New York *Tribune,* Nov. 26. "Upon the great question involved we have not only the fanaticism of the North, but the sentiment of Europe arrayed against us."—Sermon of Rev. Jas. H. Elliott, St. Michael's Church, ibid., Nov. 27. "The institution of slavery must be under the exclusive control of those directly interested in its preservation, and not left to the mercy of those that believe it to be their duty to destroy it."—Message of Gov. Gist to the regular session of the legislature, ibid., Nov. 30. "Slavery was the corner-stone of the Republic, and in proportion as it strengthened, so strengthened the Republic. As it became contracted and feeble, so soon began the decay of the Commonwealth."—Speech of B. J. Whaley, Dec. 1, ibid., Dec. 7. See action of Presbyterian Synod of South Carolina, ibid., Dec. 4, 7 ; also Charleston *Mercury, passim.*

[1] See Charleston *Mercury,* Nov. 16. This journal entitled its account of events "March of the Revolution "—issue of Nov. 19. "We are in the midst of a revolution. . . . Momentous remedy to redress momentous wrongs !"—Speech of R. A. Pringle, ibid. "We are on the steady march of a great revolution."—Speech of Mayor Macbeth, ibid., Dec. 3.

political action. Whenever a liberty-pole was raised or a palmetto banner dedicated, the proceedings were opened with prayer. " May our State and our sister States in this great crisis," prayed a clergyman, at the business men's meeting, " act as becomes a moral and religious people." " It is my settled conviction," declared a preacher, " that the course this State is at present pursuing is the one that God approves of." [1] The legislature set apart November 21 as a day for prayer and preparation, so that " a Christian people, struggling in a good cause, should invoke Providence for its success." [2]

Charleston and South Carolina people felt that secession was no longer a choice, but a necessity; that they had submitted to as much aggression from the North as a free people could endure and preserve their liberties. It is a striking evidence of the mutual misunderstanding between the two sections that, while eleven twelfths of the Northern voters thought the South had lorded it over the North since the annexation of Texas, South Carolinians, almost to a man, and the majority of the men of the cotton States, were equally convinced that they had suffered grievous wrongs from the North. This sentiment was now strong in South Carolina. When her people acknowledged the greater prosperity of the North, they asserted that it had been obtained at the expense of the South by protective tariffs. In the event of separation, the South Carolinians had dreams of unrestricted direct trade with Europe, which would redound to the advantage of their agricultural interests, and would make Charleston rival Boston and New York in commercial importance. They considered the admission of California in 1850 as a free State an outrage, and asserted that insult was added to injury in the resistance by State legislation and by mobs to the enforcement of the Fugitive Slave law, when that law had been conceded by the North as an offset for the gain which destroyed the equilibrium

---

[1] Charleston *Mercury*, Nov. 19, 21.   [2] Ibid., Nov. 21.

between the two sections.[1] The urging of the commercial question, the assertion that the South suffered grievously from the tariff acts, was a survival from 1832, and was one of those lesser arguments that are popularly supposed to add somewhat of strength to the main cause ; but it did not touch the vital matter. The grievance regarding slavery resolved itself into a fierce resistance to the virtual reproach of the Republican party that the South Carolinians were living in the daily practice of a heinous wrong.

If the negro had never been brought to America and enslaved, South Carolina would not have seceded. Nothing in all history is plainer than that the ferment of which I have been speaking was due solely to the existence of slavery. That the North had been encroaching upon the South, that it had offered an indignity in the election of Lincoln, was for South Carolinians a feeling perfectly natural, and it was absolutely sincere. The President-elect believed that slavery should ultimately be done away with, while they were convinced that it was either a blessing, or else the only fit and possible condition of the negro in contact with the white. That their cause was the cause of life, liberty, and property seemed, from their point of view, beyond question. No South Carolinian would have maintained that any overt act of oppression had yet been committed, but he would have asserted that a free people must strike at the first motion of tyranny, while for an example he might have pointed to the sons of Massachusetts in the years that preceded the American Revolution.[2] It soon began to be apparent that the course on which the State was entering with such enthusiasm involved a great sacrifice. Business grew bad, merchants found it difficult or even impossible to pay their debts, and, before the end of November, the banks of Charleston were forced to suspend specie pay-

---

[1] The feeling as to the destruction of the equilibrium, which Calhoun had powerfully expressed in 1850 (see vol. i. p. 129), was now strong in South Carolina.

[2] See The American Revolution, John Fiske, vol. i. p. 71.

ments.[1] But the people showed no signs of faltering.
During the month of November there was a round of
meetings, pole-raisings, dedications of banners, fireworks,
and illuminations ; and the music of this nascent revolution
was the Marseillaise.

Interest now became centred on the next formal step
to be taken in the march of secession. December 6 had
been fixed as the day on which delegates to the convention
should be chosen. Voters did not divide on party lines.
Indeed, since 1851, political divisions, such as were seen in
the other Southern States, did not exist in South Carolina.
Had the popular vote for President obtained there as elsewhere, the voice for Breckinridge would undoubtedly have
been almost unanimous. The lines of 1851, of separate
State action or co-operation,[2] were sometimes referred to,
but they were obliterated by the actual unanimity of sentiment. Had there been a union party or a party of delay, a
contest would have been natural, but no such parties existed. It was a favorite notion of some Northern observers
that a latent union sentiment existed in South Carolina, but
that it was kept under by intimidation. Anonymous letters
may be found scattered through the Northern journals of
this period, which, were they representative, would go to
substantiate this belief. But all other contemporary evidence points to the view that I have taken. It is almost certain that the non-slaveholding whites were as eager for
secession as the slave-owners. The antipathy of race, always strong, had been powerfully excited by assertions that
submission meant the freeing of the negroes and the be-
stowal on them of civil rights, and by the statement, often
repeated and currently believed, that Vice-President-elect
Hamlin was a mulatto.[3]

The fact that the South, in its sentiment on slavery, was

---

[1] Charleston *Mercury*, Nov. 30.   [2] See vol. i. p. 226.
[3] The most authoritative statement came from R. B. Rhett, who had served
with Hamlin in both the National House and the Senate. See his speech
of Nov. 10, New York *Tribune*, Nov. 17.

at war with the rest of the civilized world, undoubtedly lent arrogance to assertions of South Carolinians and intolerance to their acts.   They were especially severe on Northerners suspected in any way of propagating abolition opinions.[1] An example of this is seen in the action of the book-shops of Charleston, in closing their accounts with the publishers of *Harper's Weekly* and *Magazine*, and returning all the copies on hand, because the *Weekly* had published a bio- graphical sketch and full-length portrait of Abraham Lin- coln.[2]   Yet the experience of Petigru would seem to show that a union party headed by South Carolinians of charac- ter and position would have obtained a hearing and been permitted to advocate unmolested their views.[3]   The elec- tion of delegates to the convention did not turn on any party differences, nor were the candidates nominated by parties.   In some places they were put up by public meet- ings; in Charleston the nominations were made through the advertising columns of the newspapers.   The election turned on the personal standing and ability of the candi- dates, and, in the main, the most distinguished men of the State were chosen.   Of the twenty-two delegates elected from the Charleston district, seventeen had declared for prompt secession and forever against reunion, three favored secession as soon as practicable, and two did not respond to

---

[1] See the recommendation of Governor Gist for legislation "to dispense with the necessity, as much as may be possible, of resorting to Lynch law and illegal executions."—New York *Tribune*, Nov. 30.

[2] Charleston *Mercury*, Nov. 12.

[3] Memoir of James Louis Petigru, William J. Grayson, written at Charles- ton in 1863.   "Mr. Petigru was not of a complexion to be moved from his firm devotion to the cause of the Union" (p. 14).   "He seemed to stand almost alone in the community in which he lived" (p. 15).   See also p. 146.   "The people understood and appreciated Mr. Petigru.   They elect- ed him during the tumult and dissension of secession to the most important trust and the largest salary in their gift. . . . His freedom of speech never shook the confidence of the people for a moment, nor was their favor able to stop or restrain the freedom he was accustomed to exercise" (p. 150). See Forts Sumter and Moultrie, Doubleday, p. 56 ; also article of J. W. De Forest, *Atlantic Monthly*, April, 1861, p. 496.

the inquiries of the Charleston *Mercury;* but one of these was C. G. Memminger, afterwards Secretary of the Treasury of the Southern Confederacy, and he had declared in a speech that "secession is a necessity, not a choice." [1]

After the October elections, Northern Democrats and Northern supporters of Bell deemed the secession of South Carolina probable, in the event of Republican success; [2] that the President and his cabinet shared this belief is undoubted. General Scott, whose position at the head of the army, and whose knowledge of the Southern people gave him the right to make suggestions, wrote the President, October 29, adverting to the threatened secession of some of the Southern States, and advising that the nine important sea-coast forts in their borders "should be immediately so garrisoned" that it would be impossible to take any one of them by surprise. The self-sufficiency of the general led him, in this letter, to go beyond merely military considerations, and to enter upon a political argument with suggestions of state looking to peaceable disunion that were both inopportune and unwise. Buchanan probably met the general's counsel in his mind much as he afterwards discussed it in his book. [3] Seeing the

---

[1] New York *Tribune,* Nov. 30. The total vote of Charleston for delegates to the convention was 3721, against 3879 for members of the legislature in October. It was called a "heavy vote." Fourteen of the Charleston delegates were of the old secession party, seven of the old co-operation party. —Charleston *Mercury,* Dec. 7, 8. William Gilmore Simms wrote a friend at the North, Nov. 20 : "South Carolina will be out before Christmas. Her legislature was unanimous, and every member of the convention nominated is for secession unreservedly."—Trent's Simms, p. 253.

It is impossible for me to mention all the authorities from which I have derived this view of South Carolina sentiment between the election of Lincoln and the passage of the ordinance of secession.

[2] See vol. ii. p. 488.

[3] Buchanan's Administration on the Eve of the Rebellion, written by Buchanan, ch. v. I shall refer to this work hereafter as Buchanan's Defence. It was written soon after the outbreak of the war. A large part of Scott's letter is quoted in this chapter. Scott, in his Autobiography, written in 1863, cites only his military recommendations. See vol.

futility of Scott's political scheme, he preferred to expose its weakness with the art of a cunning logician rather than to concentrate his attention on that part of the letter in which the experience and knowledge of the veteran commander shone as a beacon to guide the President. For the tenor of General Scott's advice in regard to the garrisoning of the forts was far-seeing and wise. It was certainly high time that the President, the war and the navy departments, and the general of the army should begin to make preparations secretly, so that troops could be sent on short notice to any of the Southern forts which the logic of the situation might demand to be garrisoned or reinforced. The general was ready to execute orders with discretion and zeal, but the President did not speak the word. The forts in Charleston Harbor were Moultrie, Sumter, and Castle Pinckney. Moultrie was the only one garrisoned by troops,[1] but the other two were the important positions; Sumter commanded the harbor, and Castle Pinckney commanded the city of Charleston.

The presidential election took place November 6; the South Carolina legislature passed the act calling a convention November 10. No man of judgment and public experience could now longer doubt that South Carolina would secede soon after December 17, the day fixed for the assembling of the convention. November 8 the war department received a letter from Colonel Gardner, then in command at Fort Moultrie, advising that the garrison be strengthened in Moultrie, and that a company of soldiers be sent to Fort Sumter and another to Castle Pinckney.[2] November 9, if Floyd's diary

---

ii. p. 609. The letter was published entire in the *National Intelligencer*, Jan. 19, 1861.

[1] The garrison had 64 men.—Report of F.-J. Porter, Assistant Adjutant-General, The War of the Rebellion: A Compilation of the Official Records of the Union and Confederate Armies, Series I., vol. i. p. 70. I shall refer to this work as Official Records, and Series I. will be understood unless otherwise specified.

[2] Official Records, vol. i. p. 69. F.-J. Porter, however, Assistant Adjutant-General, after a personal inspection of the forts and troops in Charles-

is genuine and correct, Attorney-General Black, in cabinet
meeting, earnestly urged "sending at once a strong force
into the forts in Charleston Harbor"; and Secretary Cass
substantially agreed with him.[1] Never in our history in a
trying time has the course which the executive should pursue been less open to doubt than in the situation which now
confronted President Buchanan. In addition to the actual
facts clearly indicating the correct policy, a precedent of the
highest value existed. In every step which he ought to have
taken, he had before him the example of President Jackson, the great hero of his own party, whose action had been
supported by all but four States of the country. Moreover, Jackson had been Buchanan's trusted political leader,
and had written him while he was in Russia a confidential
letter, giving him some account of the trouble of 1832–33,
and saying, "I met nullification at its threshold."[2] Before
the South Carolina convention of 1832, which passed the
ordinance of nullification, met,[3] Jackson sent for General
Scott and asked his advice as to what should be done to
carry out his determination that "The Union must and
shall be preserved." The counsel of Scott was: Garrison
strongly Fort Moultrie and Castle Pinckney ("Sumter was
not quite above ground"); have a sloop-of-war and some
revenue-cutters in Charleston "to enforce the collection
of duties." "Proceed at once," was the prompt reply of
President Jackson, "and execute these views. You have
my *carte blanche* in respect to troops; the vessels shall be
there."[4]

It was gross dereliction of duty on the part of President
Buchanan that he did not at once send for General Scott,

ton Harbor, reported, Nov. 11, against the occupation for the present of
Sumter and Castle Pinckney, but he did advise the strengthening of the
garrison at Moultrie.—Official Records, vol. i., p. 70.
  [1] Life of Robert E. Lee and His Companions in Arms, by a distinguished
Southern journalist (Pollard), p. 792 ; Nicolay and Hay, vol. ii. p. 360.
  [2] Life of Buchanan, Curtis, vol. i. p. 185.   [3] See vol. i. p. 45.
  [4] Autobiography of Lieutenant-General Scott, vol. i. p. 235.

and discuss with him in detail the action of Jackson, and then decide to carry out a similar policy. For—in spite of the verbose reasoning with which Buchanan and his defenders have confused the question, by insisting that what was involved was really the coercion of a State, and then proceeding to discuss the right and the expediency of such action, and his lack of authority—the course that the executive should have pursued is as clear as day. Buchanan denied the right of secession, and acknowledged that it was his duty to enforce the laws in South Carolina in so far as he was able. November 17 he asked for an opinion of his attorney-general. This move was proper, but, like most of his proper actions in this crisis, tardy. Yet when the opinion came giving him warrant for the Jacksonian policy, it was not too late to follow it. Attorney-General Black, as sound a jurist as ever advised a President, replied in three days to his request. "You can now," he wrote Buchanan, "if necessary, order the duties to be collected on board a vessel inside of any established port of entry. . . . Your right to take such measures as may seem to be necessary for the protection of the public property is very clear." [1] When we brush away all extraneous considerations, when we isolate the question of executive duty from party disputes and constitutional theories, it is surprising what unanimity existed at the North in regard to the matter of the greatest practical moment. Not a lawyer in the North would have denied the powers of the President as thus laid down by Black. Had Buchanan decided promptly to act with energy on that line of duty, every Northern man who had voted for Lincoln, Douglas, or Bell, and nearly every Northern man who had voted for Breckinridge would have sustained him with enthusiastic zeal. No more scathing criticism on the President can be pronounced than that of Black himself who, forty days later, spoke of "the fatal error which the administration have committed in not sending

---

[1] Life of Buchanan, Curtis, vol. ii. p. 321.

down troops enough to hold *all* the forts" in Charleston Harbor.[1]

The means at the President's command to carry out a Jacksonian policy may be gathered from the controversy between him and General Scott, which was printed in the columns of the *National Intelligencer* in 1862, and continued in their respective books. It appears, according to Scott, that 1000 soldiers of the regular army were disposable,[2] and, while this is denied by Buchanan,[3] we shall have no difficulty in believing Scott's statement to be correct, when we remember that the army had 16,000 effective men.[4] It is true that the American army was then, as it always has been in time of peace, small for the duty imposed upon it; but we may be sure that if the will to do so had existed, there would have been no great difficulty in placing 1000 men during the month of November in Southern forts where they were most needed. That there were 400 soldiers ready October 29 every one admits;[5] and it would have been a good beginning of a policy of action had the President, after the South Carolina legislature called the convention, sent these troops to Charleston.

That to garrison the Southern forts would have increased the irritation of South Carolina and would have driven the other cotton States onward in the path of secession, as the defenders of the President maintain,[6] is possible. On the other hand, a determination on the part of the administration to protect the public property and collect the duties, accompanied by the proposal of a compromise to allay the disaffection of the South, might have caused the remainder of the Southern States to delay their movements. For it must

---

[1] Memorandum for the President on the subject of the paper drawn up by him in reply to the Commissioners of South Carolina, Dec. 30, Essays and Speeches of J. S. Black, C. F. Black, p. 16.

[2] Letter of Nov. 8, *National Intelligencer*, Nov. 13, 1862.

[3] Letter of Nov. 17, ibid., Nov. 25, 1862.

[4] Buchanan's Defence, p. 104.   [5] Ibid., p. 103.

[6] Ibid., p. 106; Curtis, vol. ii. p. 304.

be borne in mind that this matter of plain executive duty
had not in November become confounded in the Southern
mind with the coercion of a State, as it did two months
later. Yet, whatever may have been the weight of probability as to the effect of such a vigorous step, the case was
one of those where the executive officer should have done
his duty regardless of the consequences.

It is true that the crisis was a much greater one than that
which Jackson had to meet. Then, although the disunion
party had a large majority in South Carolina, and she had the
tacit sympathy of three sister States, the case was vastly different from the present situation where unanimity prevailed
within her confines, and she had the avowed sympathy of all
the cotton States. In 1832, Louisiana and the border States
were against South Carolina; now Louisiana was getting
ready to follow her, while the border States, though deprecating her precipitate movement, shared her feeling as to
the aggression of the North.[1] Yet, if the crisis was greater,
greater would have been the glory to him who met it in the
way unerringly pointed out by precedent, law, and devotion
to the Union. It was a pregnant opportunity for an executive gifted with singleness of purpose, a dauntless temper of
mind, and a wisdom to guide his valor to act in safety. But
on such a man as Buchanan fortune lavishes her favors in
vain. Vacillating and obstinate by turns, yet lacking firmness
when the occasion demanded firmness, he floundered about in
a sea of perplexity, throwing away chance after chance, and,
though not wanting in good intentions and sincere patriotism, he laid himself open to the undisguised contempt of all
sections and all parties. In but one respect has the later differed from the contemporary judgment of him. From an
oft-repeated Northern charge that he was actuated by treachery to his own section, he has been fully absolved. When,
however, we compare what he did with what he ought to

---

[1] See Richmond *Enquirer, Whig, Dispatch,* the Baltimore *Daily Exchange,*
and the *National Intelligencer.*

have done, we may affirm with reason that of all of our Presidents, with perhaps a single exception, Buchanan made the most miserable failure. He had been so long under Southern domination that he could not now throw it off. Common prudence required that he should keep in his cabinet none but stanch Union men; this test would have resulted in the retirement of Cobb and Thompson, and probably a reconstruction of the whole cabinet in the middle of November, such as took place late in December and in January. According to Floyd's diary, a difference developed itself in cabinet meeting as early as November 10, on the question of the South's submission to Lincoln's election and the right of secession, in which dispute Cobb, Thompson, and Floyd ranged themselves on one side, and Cass, Toucey, Black, Holt, and the President on the other.[1]

At a time when a plan of resolute action should have been the daily and nightly thought of Buchanan, he sat himself down to write an essay on constitutional law, which he sent to Congress as his annual message. While engaged in this work, the War Department received a letter from Major Robert Anderson, who, on account of his high reputation, had been selected to command Fort Moultrie. The recommendations in this letter, in addition to previous advice and entreaties, should have come to the President with such a cumulative force that even he could no longer fail to appreciate that which nearly every Union man in the country saw as an imperative necessity. November 23, Anderson suggested that Moultrie be reinforced. He added: "Fort Sumter and Castle Pinckney *must* be garrisoned immediately, if the government determines to keep command of this harbor." This native of Kentucky, who had taken a wife from Georgia, then went on: "I need not say how anxious I am—indeed, determined, so far as honor will permit—to avoid collision with the citizens of South Carolina. Nothing, however, will be better calculated to prevent

---

[1] Life of Lee, Pollard, p. 794. Holt was Postmaster-General.

bloodshed than our being found in such an attitude that it would be madness and folly to attack us.   There is not so much of feverish excitement as there was last week, but that there is a settled determination to leave the Union, and to obtain possession of this work, is apparent to all." [1] Before the President's message went to Congress, Anderson iterated these suggestions, and in this last letter he showed that the administration could depend on him to act with moderation as well as firmness.   Making a requisition for howitzers, heavy revolvers, and muskets, he added, "God forbid, though, that I *should*" have to use them. [2]

But the President, instead of accepting the advice of Major Anderson, was taking counsel with Jefferson Davis in regard to the message, and modifying it in deference to his suggestions. [3]   The original draft of it was read to the cabinet, receiving in the main the approval of all but Cobb and Thompson, who objected to the denial of the right of secession. [4]   Four days after the President sent his message to Congress, Secretary Cobb resigned his position, and, in honor, Thompson should have done likewise, but he clung to his place a month longer.   A President made of sterner stuff would certainly have demanded his resignation.

The annual message was read to Congress, December 4. We may pass over without criticism the assertion therein

---

[1] Anderson to Cooper, Official Records, vol. i. p. 75.   Cooper was Adjutant-General of the Army.

[2] Anderson to Cooper, Nov. 28, Official Records, vol. i. p. 79.

[3] Rise and Fall of the Confederate Government, Jefferson Davis, vol. i. p. 59.   The author adds: "The message was, however, somewhat changed, and . . . I must say that in my judgment the last alterations were unfortunate—so much so that when it was read in the Senate I was reluctantly constrained to criticise it."

[4] Curtis, vol. ii. p. 333.   C. F. Black, Essays and Speeches of J. S. Black, p. 11, states that Cass objected to it and "impressively demanded that the right of Congress to make war against a State should be denied in more forcible terms than the President had used.   It was so modified solely to meet his views."

contained that the Southern discontent was due to the Northern agitation of slavery. Because Buchanan was Buchanan, it would have been sinning against his nature and the convictions of many years had he neglected this occasion to tell the North how much it had been in the wrong. Nor can fault be found with the expression of his hope that the Northern States which had offended would repeal their Personal Liberty laws. The parts of the message that we may commend set a standard to which we can hold the President, and they indicate a policy which, carried out logically in word and deed, would have made the name Buchanan in America a far different household word. He denied the right of secession. The framers of this government, he said, "never intended to implant in its bosom the seeds of its own destruction, nor were they at its creation guilty of the absurdity of providing for its own dissolution. . . . Secession is neither more nor less than revolution."[1] Congress had not encroached upon a right of the South, and the threatened dissolution of the Union proceeded from an apprehension of future danger, which was no just cause of revolution. He asserted the unquestioned right of property of the United States in the forts, magazines, and arsenals in South Carolina; "the officer in command of the forts has received orders to act strictly on the defensive;" if the forts are attacked, "the responsibility for consequences would rightfully rest upon the assailants." Then the President began to falter, entering upon an extended argument to prove that Congress had no right to coerce a State. While in this reasoning he had the support of his attorney-general, and undoubtedly that of many of the best lawyers in the North, irrespective of their party attachment, the introduction of the subject was unwise, for, as Black pointed

---

[1] Of course these ideas came from Webster (see vol. i. p. 51), but Buchanan could not have had a better guide. So much of the message as referred to internal affairs is printed in Curtis's biography, vol. ii. p. 337.

out,[1] the coercion of a State, as jurists understood it, would be
apt to become confounded in the popular mind with the enforcement of the laws. This was actually the case, and became the source of much mischief. The discussion of coercion was, moreover, irrelevant to the emergency. No one
of any political standing or following called for such a policy.

When on the subject of the forts, the President should
have stated that it was his firm intention to hold them;
and, when announcing that " the revenue still continues to
be collected as heretofore at the custom-house in Charleston " — knowing that the collector had determined to resign when South Carolina passed the ordinance of secession[2]
— he should have asserted emphatically that, no matter
what took place, he should collect the duties in the custom-
house, on board of a revenue-cutter in the harbor, or, as
Jackson had done, in Castle Pinckney. Had the forts in
Charleston Harbor been properly garrisoned, the declaration
of such a policy could only have been received in South
Carolina, and in the communities that sympathized with her,
as the assertion of a solemn duty; it might have met with
the approval of a considerable minority in the border States,
and it surely would have caused a thrill of patriotism at the
North that could not have failed to unite it almost to a man.
The great need of the time was the assertion of a vigorous
nationality on some point that people could rally around without being hampered by constitutional quibbles and legal tech-
nicalities. The President should further have indicated to
Congress with some detail what additional legislation he
needed for the present exigency. Hand in hand with the
recommendation of some action for the purpose of allaying
Southern discontent should have gone the express determination to use all the power at his command to defend the

[1] See Curtis, vol. ii. pp. 352, 382.
[2] See letter of Wm. F. Colcock, collector of Charleston, stating his intention of giving up his office, Charleston *Mercury*, Nov. 8.

public property and collect the duties. Had the President thus acted as became a sterling Union man, the country would have forgiven his bootless suggestion of compromise —his proposal to have incorporated into the Constitution what was substantially the important article of the Breckinridge platform, an article which had been resisted by the Douglas Democrats in the Charleston convention to the disruption of their party, and had been declared against by every Northern State.

That Buchanan deserves historical censure for not having pursued the Jacksonian policy seems to me beyond question; for the path of duty was so plain that he should have walked in it, and accepted whatever consequences came from right-doing. Yet what the consequences might have been is a fair subject of historical inquiry. That firm and prompt action on the part of the President would have been alone sufficient to nip secession in the bud, as it did nullification in 1832, I cannot bring myself to believe, although it so appeared to some contemporary actors,[1] and although such a view has been urged with persistence by later writers. It does, however, seem possible that such vigor might have led, in December, to a compromise of a sort to prevent the secession of any State but South Carolina. Yet those of us who hold to the idea of the irrepressible conflict can see in the success of such a project no more than the delay of a war that was inevitable, a postponement proper indeed, if the compromise were not dishonorable—for the stars in their courses were fighting on the side of the North. Yet the weight of probability tends to the view that the day of compromise was past, and that the collision of sentiment, shaping the ends of the North and the South, had now

---

[1] "One single hour of the will displayed by General Jackson would have stifled the fire in its cradle."—Charles Francis Adams's Address on Seward, Albany, April 18, 1873, p. 44. See Trumbull's speech in the Senate, March 2, 1861. "If we could have held Fort Sumter, there never would have been a drop of blood shed."—Montgomery Blair, May 17, 1873. Lincoln and Seward, Welles, p. 67.

brought them both to the last resort of earnest men. That
Buchanan feared a conflict is evident : the mainspring of his
wavering course was his feverish desire that the war should
not begin under a Democratic administration, nor while he
was in the Presidential chair. His policy was guided by
the thought of after me the deluge, and must be classed
among the wrecks with which the vacillation of irresolute
men have strewn the coasts of time.[1] Assuming that war
was probably inevitable in 1861, and that Buchanan believed it to be so, a grave indictment against him is that he
threw away many of the advantages which the North had
in the possession of the national government and in an
established administrative system. During the last four
months of his presidency, inaction was the course pursued
by the North, busy preparation that pursued by the South.
Since destiny pointed to certain war and the doom of the
Southern cause, the better the preparation of the North
the shorter would have been the conflict and the less
the suffering. But Buchanan could not forget his party
interests when he should have sunk all else in the feeling
that he was an American and a disciple of Jackson and of
Webster. Had he risen to that height the war might
have begun under his presidency, but he would have had
a united North at his back ; and when he retired to private
life with the approval of a grateful people, he might have
handed over to his successor, with the advantage of a con-
tinuity of administration, a well-defined policy.

Buchanan's message, like all non-committal executive
papers in a crisis of affairs, failed to satisfy positive men in
either section. His subserviency to the South had so alienated most of the Northern people from him[2] that only a
most decided revolt against those who had been his masters—
such as Douglas had achieved in 1857—would have brought

[1] In his speech in the House, Feb. 7, 1861, Henry Winter Davis spoke of
the President as muttering : "Not in my time, not in my time ; after me
the deluge !"   [2] See vol. ii. p. 476.

him their hearty support. Seward's criticism was made in a private letter, but the substance of it got into the newspapers, and struck the popular note. The message, he said in writing to his wife, "shows conclusively that it is the duty of the President to execute the laws — unless somebody opposes him ; and that no State has a right to go out of the Union — unless it wants to." [1] As was foreseen by Black, the President entangled the general understanding by his unnecessary attempt to make clear the difference between the coercion of a seceding State and upholding within her limits some striking symbol of national authority. Yet there were many men at the North who could appreciate the distinction that he made, and who felt that the message was by no means an entire surrender to Southern demands; there were also timorous souls, with anxiety reasonable and just, who saw in the President's course a possible chance of averting civil war : these wrote him letters of approbation.[2]

On the first of November, 1860, Buchanan was popular at the South, and his administration received a certain measure of approval. He had served that section well, and his name ought to have inspired enthusiasm; but he had suffered in its estimation because his policy of making Kansas a slave State had not been a success. His message failed to satisfy the South. The Disunionists did not like the denial of the right of secession.[3] Yet some so-called Unionists in

---

[1] Letter of Dec. 5, Life of Seward, F. W. Seward, vol. ii. p. 480; correspondence New York *Evening Post*, Nicolay and Hay, vol. ii. p. 371; The *Liberator*, Dec. 14.   Seward undoubtedly made the same or a similar statement to the correspondent of the New York *Evening Post*. He wrote, Dec. 6 : " I have talked with Thayer, reporter for the *Evening Post*."—Life, vol.ii. p. 480.   James Russell Lowell, in the *Atlantic Monthly* for Jan., 1861 (p. 118), spoke of Buchanan as one " who knows no art to conjure the spirit of anarchy he has evoked but the shifts and evasions of a second-rate attorney, and who has contrived to involve his country in the confusion of principle and vacillation of judgment which have left him without a party and without a friend."   [2] Curtis, vol. ii. pp. 353, 357.

[3] Ibid., p. 358; Richmond *Enquirer*, Dec. 11.

the cotton States were pleased with the position he had taken.[1]   There were steadfast Union men in the border States—and these may have been many—to whose idea of nationality the President's abnegation of his own authority and his denial of the power of Congress came with a shock.[2] The pity of it was that he made no ringing declaration of what he proposed to do in the way of executing the laws—such a declaration as would have served as a common rallying-point for them and for the people of the North.

Immediately after the election the Republicans were in high glee at their success. Their companies and battalions of Wide-awakes lent themselves handily to the enthusiastic demonstrations. For the moment it seemed as if nearly every one at the North was of their party.[3] But their joy was short-lived, for it began to be apparent that the Republican contest for the possession of the government had only begun. In less than a week men who were not blinded by preconceived ideas were convinced that South Carolina would certainly secede, and that there was danger of the other cotton States following her example. The question arose, What would the Republicans do to prevent disunion? They were the arbiters of the situation, and—assuming

---

[1] Curtis, vol. ii. p. 358.

[2] "To say that no State has a right to secede, that it is a wrong to the Union, and yet that the Union has no right to interpose any obstacles to its secession, seems to me to be altogether contradictory."—Crittenden of Kentucky in the Senate, Dec. 4. Crittenden's devotion to the Union was like that of Clay. "But if secession is revolution, it seems to us that the general government has the inherent and undeniable power to suppress it. It might be unwise to exercise that power, and, as against the contemplated movement at the South, it certainly would be injudicious and ruinous to do so; but that the President and Congress have the mere legal right to put down a revolution, insurrection, or rebellion in a State we cannot doubt."—Baltimore *Daily Exchange*, Dec. 5. This paper had supported Breckinridge.

[3] Lincoln's majority over Douglas, Breckinridge, and Bell at the North was 293,769.—Greeley's American Conflict, vol. i. p. 328.

what was undoubted, that the sentiment of South Carolina would drive her to secession — on their action depended whether the outcome should be disunion, and, in case of disunion, whether it should be war or peace. There were some who blinked the fact, and asserted stoutly that the declarations of the Southerners were idle threats, but a disposition to look matters squarely in the face prevailed. When men met on the streets, in public places, or in society, the common salutation of the day and the usual talk gave way to the question that rose in every mind, "Do you think the South will secede?"[1] Not many answered as Beecher did this question: "I don't believe they will; and I don't care if they do."[2]

Opinion of the way in which the crisis should be met formed on three distinct lines. A spontaneous feeling existed that the election had been fair, that the decision had been reached in a constitutional manner, and that it was the duty of the South to submit to the election of Lincoln as the Northern Democrats were submitting to it, and as Republicans had acquiesced in the election of Buchanan. This seemed especially incumbent upon the Southern people, for, to the pro-slavery policy of the present administration, carried out at their dictates, was due the Republican success of 1860.[3] Many of those belonging to the victorious party,

---

[1] See H. W. Beecher's address in Boston, Nov. 27, New York *Tribune*, Nov. 30; Washington correspondence New York *Tribune*, Nov. 29.

[2] Ibid.

[3] "The chief virtue of Republican success was in its condemnation of the narrow sectionalism of Buchanan's administration, and the corruptions by which he attempted to sustain his policy. Who doubts but that if he had been true to his promises in submitting the controversy in Kansas to its own people, and had closed it by admitting Kansas as a free State, that the Democratic party would have retained its power? It was his infernal policy in Kansas . . . that drove off Douglas and led to the division of the Democratic party and the consequent election of Lincoln."—Letter of John Sherman to General Sherman, Nov. 26, 1860, *Century Magazine*, Nov. 1892, p. 92. "We owe the election of Lincoln only to the misrule of the present administration, and to the unfortunate dissensions in our own party."—August Belmont to John Forsyth of Alabama, Dec. 19, Letters of Belmont, privately printed, p. 21.

who held decidedly the belief that submission was a moral
and political obligation resting on the South, and that the
United States was a nation, went the whole length which
their position logically required.   To secede and do any act
of violence was, in their view, treason, and men who engaged in such work were traitors.   Those who were reading
men—and the majority of Republicans in 1860 were such—
fed on literature adapted to sustain this opinion.   Jackson's proclamation against the nullifiers and Webster's
speech advocating the Force bill[1] were published in a con-
venient form to supply a popular demand.   About this time
appeared the last volume of Parton's picturesque " Life of
Jackson,"[2] and the graphic story of the way in which the
sturdy general met nullification at the threshold had an effect in shaping public sentiment.   Dwelling upon this epi-
sode of our history and despairing because of the imbecility
of Buchanan prompted the North to burst forth almost in
one voice : " Oh, for an hour of Andrew Jackson !"

Another phase of opinion was both represented and led
by Horace Greeley.   Three days after the election the New
York *Tribune*, in a leading article, said : " If the cotton
States shall decide that they can do better out of the Union
than in it, we insist on letting them go in peace.   The right
to secede may be a revolutionary one, but it exists nevertheless. . . . Whenever a considerable section of our Union
shall deliberately resolve to go out, we shall resist all coercive measures designed to keep it in.   We hope never to
live in a republic, whereof one section is pinned to the resi-
due by bayonets."[3]   The *Tribune* was the most influential

---

[1] See vol. i. pp. 46, 50.

[2] See J. R. Lowell's criticism of this book, *Atlantic Monthly*, March, 1861,
p. 381 ; also notice in *Harper's Magazine*, Jan., 1861, p. 260.

[3] Issue of Nov. 9.   The article is also printed in Greeley's American
Conflict, vol. i. p. 358.   Nov. 16, the leading article in the *Tribune* said :
" If the fifteen slave States, or even the eight cotton States alone, shall
quietly, decisively, say to the rest, ' We prefer to be henceforth separate from
you,' we shall insist that they be permitted to go in peace.   War is a hideous necessity at best, and a civil conflict—a war of estranged and embit-

journal of the Republican party, and, next to Seward and Lincoln, Greeley was the most powerful leader of opinion in that party. This view had its greatest popularity in November and in the first part of December, 1860; it received the countenance of other Republican newspapers;[1] it prevailed with Henry Ward Beecher, whose consummate oratory swayed many audiences;[2] it won, also, a certain adherence from the Garrison abolitionists, who saw in the accomplishment of it the realization of their dream of many years.[3] The tendency of Southern and Democratic writers has been, not unnaturally, to overrate the strength of this opinion at the North; on the other hand, because of its speedy decline in public estimation after the middle of December, as well as for the further reason that the war was prosecuted on a theory diametrically opposed to it, we are liable to fall into the error that it was merely the erratic outburst of an eccentric thinker, having no root in public sentiment. It seems clear to me, however, that a respectable minority of Republicans were inclined to a similar view in the last months of 1860. That Greeley came near being nominated United States senator by the New York Republican caucus in February, 1861, and that his strength forced the followers of Seward and Weed to drop their candidate,

---

tered fellow-countrymen—is the most hideous of all wars." I do not feel quite certain that the article of Nov. 9 was written by Greeley; but Nov. 19 an article appears, obviously by Greeley, which goes over the same ground, and reiterates what was said Nov. 9 and 16.

Nov. 30 the *Tribune* said, in an editorial : "If the cotton States generally unite with her [South Carolina] in seceding, we insist that they cannot be prevented, and that the attempt must not be made. Five millions of people, more than half of them of the dominant race, of whom at least half a million are able and willing to shoulder muskets, can never be subdued while fighting around and over their own hearth-stones. . . . Those who think to salve over the widening chasm between the free and the cotton States are utterly unaware of the seriousness of the matter in issue."

[1] Greeley's American Conflict, vol. i. p. 359.

[2] See address in Boston, before cited. "In so far as the free States are concerned," he said, "I hold that it will be an advantage for the South to go off."   [3] See the *Liberator* for Nov. and Dec.

Evarts, and unite on Harris as the only means of defeating Greeley,[1] shows that advocating acquiescence in peaceable secession did not forfeit a leader's standing in the Republican party. Yet it is also true that, after January 1, the *Tribune* in a measure recanted,[2] and it is quite possible that its articles of November, 1860, cost Greeley the senatorship. For peaceable disunion, when it came to be thoroughly discussed, was seen to be a geographical and military impossibility; it did violence to the Union feeling, the strongest political sentiment at the North; it wounded those who had a strong idea of nationality, and who loved to boast of the country which extended from ocean to ocean, from the Lakes to the Gulf, and whose great river rose amid the snows of the North to end its course in the land of the sugar-cane.

What we may properly call the Greeley policy obtained its strength largely on account of a general repugnance to the coercion of a State. If South Carolinians were almost unanimous for secession, the impracticability of any plan of coercion seemed manifest whenever the enforcement of it came to be discussed. One strong tie that bound the States together, a daily reminder of the federal authority, was not at this time in question. The government duly transmitted the mails to South Carolina, and to the other States bent on secession, until Fort Sumter was fired upon; the Southern postmasters did not resign, but continued to account to the post-office department at Washington. The resignations of the United States judge and district attorney, at Charleston, prevented the holding of the federal courts, but this was not a matter requiring instant remedy. Even if successors were appointed, they could not conduct the judicial business without juries, and on these no South Carolinian would serve. Did coercion mean the sending of

---

[1] New York *Tribune*, Feb. 4, 1861; Life of Thurlow Weed, vol. ii. p. 322.
[2] See *Tribune* of Jan. and Feb., 1861, especially Greeley's article of Jan. 14 and the editorial of Feb. 2.

troops to Charleston to force men to do jury duty, to con-
strain the legislature to choose United States senators, to
tear down the palmetto flags flying in the streets of Charleston, and to prevent the assembling of the convention that
would surely adopt an ordinance of secession? The moment
these questions were asked it was seen that coercion was
neither possible nor desirable. Yet there existed the clear
distinction drawn by Attorney-General Black between the
collection of the revenue and the protection of public property, and what he termed "an offensive war to punish the
people for the political misdeeds of their State government,
or to enforce an acknowledgment that the government of
the United States is supreme." Buchanan's policy of letting I dare not wait upon I would encouraged the dogmatic
assumptions of the secessionists to the point of maintaining
that any move towards the collection of the duties or the reinforcement of the forts would be coercion; while the Northern advocates of an heroic course, thinking perhaps there
was virtue in a name that implied physical force, continued
to employ the word coercion when, according to the distinction of Black, they meant no more than the use of that
authority which he had without reservation ascribed to the
President.[1] The progress of events gave a certain justification to this confusion of thought. An act of executive duty,
which would have occasioned only an emphatic protest from

---

[1] This is illustrated by J. R. Lowell's article, "E Pluribus Unum," in
the *Atlantic Monthly* for Feb., 1861. He wrote: "The United States are
a nation, and not a mass-meeting. . . . In the present case the only coercion called for is the protection of the public property and the collection of the federal revenues. If it be necessary to send troops to do this,
they will not be sectional . . . but federal troops, representing the will
and power of the whole Confederacy" (pp. 238, 239). This article is reprinted in Lowell's Political Essays. Dec. 21 the New York *Tribune*, which,
by this time, had become an advocate of what was known as the coercion
policy (*infra*, p. 166), said, in commenting upon the secession of South
Carolina: "Only let the State continue to pay the regular duties on imports, and keep her hands off the forts, and she can secede as long as
she pleases."

South Carolina in November, caused a demonstration of war in January. This perplexity would not have arisen at the North had Buchanan seized his great opportunity and made himself the national hero.

A third phase of Republican opinion found expression in the advocacy of a compromise. Many who had voted for Lincoln, believing with the generality of their party that the Southern menaces of disunion were largely gasconade,[1] were now, since they had awakened to the seriousness of the situation, frightened at the result of their own work. August Belmont, in writing to John Forsyth of Alabama in November, spoke of "the reaction which has already taken place among thousands who voted for Lincoln," and in December he wrote: " I meet daily now with men who confess the error they have been led into, and almost with tears in their eyes wish they could undo what they helped to do." [2] There were, indeed, Republicans who felt that they might offer without dishonor a compromise that would retain the cotton States excepting South Carolina, yet who had no craven regrets at the election of Lincoln, and who were willing, if need were, to fight for the Union. The most eminent exponent of such an opinion was Thurlow Weed, whose adroitness in practical politics had hitherto been his chief distinction, but who now rose almost to the height of statesmanship. With judicial purpose he brought himself to look upon the Southern side of the question, and with magnanimity he urged, " They who are conscious of least wrong can best afford to manifest a spirit of conciliation." [3] Weed was now sixty-three years old ; he had that intense love for the Union characteristic of Whigs whose ideas had been moulded by Webster and Clay. The danger of disunion and how to avert it were his daily and nightly thoughts. By the

---

[1] See vol. ii. p. 488.

[2] Letters of Belmont, privately printed, pp. 6, 21.

[3] He added: " In the present controversy the North is nearest right, though not wholly blameless. There are motes, at least in ours, if there are beams in our neighbors' eyes."—Life of Thurlow Weed, vol. ii. p. 307.

end of November he had matured in his mind a plan of compromise, which he suggested in his newspaper, the Albany *Evening Journal*—at this time, probably, the most powerful organ of public opinion outside of New York City. He proposed, in the place of the actual "vindictive Fugitive Slave law," one that should provide for the payment for rescued slaves by the counties in which the violation of the law had taken place. In regard to the "vexed" territorial question, he asked, "Why not restore the Missouri Compromise line?"[1] By this he meant the extension of that line to the Pacific Ocean, allowing slavery south and prohibiting slavery north of it. In an article which he wrote advocating this plan of conciliation, Weed showed a rare comprehension of Southern sentiment; he urged his plan with cogent reasoning, the result of profound reflection irradiated by his long public experience.[2] It was a bold step for a partisan Republican to take, and this he appreciated; he thought the suggestions would at first be unpopular with his political friends, but he deemed it his duty as a leader of opinion to express his views frankly, hoping that his party would come to regard the situation as he did, or, at all events, that from the discussion to which his articles would give rise, the Republicans might work out a plan to ward off disunion.[3]

To Greeley and to Thurlow Weed, the great journalist and the great politician, praise is due because, at a crisis when it was easier and safer to criticise and object, they did not hesitate to express their positive convictions. Greeley's policy, when ventilated, was seen to be impossible. Yet at first it appeared to be a solution worthy of consideration; and, had a sea as wide as that between England and Ireland flowed between the cotton States and the rest of the Union,

---

[1] Albany *Evening Journal*, cited in the New York *Tribune*, Nov. 27.

[2] See his article of Nov. 30, cited in Greeley's American Conflict, vol. i. p. 360, which deserves a careful reading.

[3] See article in *Evening Journal*, Dec. 1, cited in the New York *Tribune*, Dec. 3.

it might have been a wise settlement of the difficulty. Thurlow Weed's policy gained strength with the discussion of it in the light of the progress of events. The general tendency being towards the effacement of former party lines, this policy received the approval of those at the North who voted for Douglas, Breckinridge, and Bell. Douglas, beginning now that last and most glorious portion of his career, on which his admirers love to dwell, spoke at New Orleans, two days after the election, against secession;[1] November 13, he wrote a formal letter to the business men of New Orleans, showing from the Southern point of view the folly of it;[2] and on the way north he addressed with the same purpose a Virginian audience.[3] His course was calculated to foster among the Southern people a sentiment that should induce them to meet half-way the overtures of Republicans disposed to follow Thurlow Weed.

Thus stood affairs on December 3, when Congress met. South Carolina was practically unanimous for secession; the President had failed utterly to rise to the emergency, while at the North there existed an overwhelming desire to preserve the Union. All eyes were directed towards Congress. Would it avert the threatened danger? As the persistent attitude of South Carolina and the warm sympathy with her of her sister States were fixed facts, the question was, What would the Republicans in Congress be willing to do to satisfy the South? Compromise had solved the difficulty in 1820, in 1833, and in 1850; and it was now apparent that the border State men and the Northern Democrats could unite on a plan which would prevent the secession of all the States except South Carolina. Would the Republicans go as far as that? Properly to judge their action in this crisis, we must first inquire, what were the grievances of the South as made known to Congress?

The tangible grievances were the interference with the

---

[1] New York *Tribune*, Nov. 15.   [2] *National Intelligencer.*
[3] New York *Tribune*, Dec. 3.

execution of the Fugitive Slave act by the Personal Liberty laws,[1] and the denial by the North to the owners of negro slaves of the common rights of property in the territories. The wrong done the South by the Personal Liberty laws was dwelt upon by men who were opposed to secession, and who, taking an impregnable position, were willing to rest their case upon a remediable complaint. Their conspicuous exponent was Alexander H. Stephens. In the famous speech which he made before the Georgia legislature, November 14, he thrust this view into prominence.[2] His words gave rise to much discussion. It may be positively affirmed that, if the sole grievance of the South had been the alleged nullification of the Fugitive Slave act by many Northern States, there would have been no secession but that of South Carolina. For this grievance would certainly have been redressed. Vermont, the pioneer in this sort of legislation, had already taken steps towards the revision of her Personal Liberty act.[3] On December 17 the national House of Representatives, in which the Republicans and anti-Lecompton Democrats had a clear majority, earnestly recommended, by a vote of 153 to 14, the repeal of the Personal Liberty laws in conflict with the Constitution. These facts, with others that will be mentioned later, show that, if it would have appeased the South, every State, with the possible exception of Massachusetts, either would have rescinded this legislation, or so modified it that it no longer would have been an offence. Early in the session of Congress, however, the Republicans were told that this would not settle the difficulty. "You talk about repealing the Personal Liberty bills as a concession to the South," said Senator Iverson of Georgia. "Repeal them all to-

[1] See vol. ii. p. 73.
[2] The War Between the States, Stephens, vol. ii. p. 294. The Personal Liberty acts, Stephens wrote in a confidential letter of Jan. 1, 1861, "constitute the only cause, in my opinion, which can justify secession."—Johnston and Browne, p. 376.
[3] See remarks of Collamer, Dec. 18, *Globe*, p. 120; Speech of Morrill, Feb. 18, 1861, ibid., p. 1006.

morrow, sir, and it would not stop the progress of this
revolution." [1] Iverson spoke for a large party in the empire State of the South. Since the secession of South Carolina had become a foregone conclusion, the action of
Georgia was awaited with breathless interest, and every indication of her sentiment was scanned with care. "What
though all the Personal Liberty bills were repealed," asked
Jefferson Davis, the leader of the cotton States; "would
that secure our rights?" [2]

The other tangible grievance—the refusal of the North
to recognize that the slaveholder's human chattels had the
common attributes of other property in the territories—was
urged with emphasis by Davis and by Toombs. [3]   It was indeed replied that the Dred Scott decision gave them all that
they claimed, but to this it was naturally rejoined that the
President-elect did not accept as binding the general principle in regard to slave property as asserted by Chief-Justice
Taney. [4] The experience of the last seven years had made
patent to each party the importance of a friendly executive,
when the issue of freedom and slavery should come to be
fought out in the territories.

The intangible grievance of the South was the sentiment
of the North in regard to slavery. In most of the public
declarations and confidential letters one is struck with the influence which the stigma cast by Republicans upon the slave-
holders had on the Southern mind. This sensitiveness proved
to be a heavy obstacle in the way of compromise. Between
the idea that slavery was right, or, at least, the only suitable
condition of the negro, and the idea that slavery was a blot
upon the nation, it seemed wellnigh impossible to hit upon
the common ground of opinion which was a necessary an-
tecedent to compromise. "The true cause of our danger,"

---

[1] Senate, Dec. 5, *Globe*, p. 11.   [2] Senate, Dec. 10, *Globe*, p. 29.
[3] Speeches of Davis, Dec. 10 and Jan. 10, 1861, *Globe*, pp. 29, 311; resolutions of Toombs and Davis, Journal of Committee of Thirteen, pp. 2, 3;
Speech of Toombs, Jan. 7, 1861, *Globe*, p. 268.
[4] See Senate speech of Toombs, Jan. 7, 1861, *Globe*, p. 269.

declared Jefferson Davis, "I believe to be that a sectional hostility has been substituted for a general fraternity. . . . Where is the remedy?" he asked. "In the hearts of the people" is the ready reply.[1]

The election of Lincoln seemed to the Southerners a declaration of hostility to their institution by the Republican party. When they read his speeches in the Lincoln-Douglas debates, they saw that he clearly stood for the conviction that slavery is wrong, and that the government could not endure permanently half slave and half free. Yet, despite the misunderstanding of one section by the other, a com-

---

[1] Senate, Dec. 10. *Congressional Globe*, p. 29. Davis continued: "I call upon you, the representatives of the majority section, here and now to say so, if your people are not hostile ; if they have the fraternity with which their fathers came to form this Union ; if they are prepared to do justice ; to abandon their opposition to the Constitution and the laws of the United States ; to recognize and to maintain and to defend all the rights and benefits the Union was designed to promote and to secure. Give us that declaration, give us that evidence of the will of your constituency to restore us to our original position, when mutual kindness was the animating motive, and then we may hopefully look for remedies which may suffice; not by organizing armies, not so much by enacting laws, as by repressing the spirit of hostility and lawlessness, and seeking to live up to the obligations of good neighbors and friendly States united for the common welfare."

It is interesting to compare with this Lowell's view, written at about the same time. (*Atlantic Monthly*, Jan., 1861, p. 120.) "The fault of the free States in the eyes of the South is not one that can be atoned for by any yielding of special points here and there. Their offence is that they are free, and that their habits and prepossessions are those of freedom. Their crime is the census of 1860. Their increase in numbers, wealth, and power is a standing aggression. It would not be enough to please the Southern States that we should stop asking them to abolish slavery : what they demand of us is nothing less than that we should abolish the spirit of the age. Our very thoughts are a menace. It is not the North, but the South that forever agitates the question of slavery. The seeming prosperity of the cotton-growing States is based on a great mistake and a great wrong; and it is no wonder that they are irritable and scent accusation in the very air. It is the stars in their courses that fight against their system, and there are those who propose to make everything comfortable by act of Congress."

These two quotations show, as clearly as anything that I know, the underlying reasons of the war between the North and the South.

promise on the lines laid down by Thurlow Weed was possible in December. Many schemes were proposed, but the most famous of them is that of Senator Crittenden of Kentucky; of those which would have been acceptable to the cotton States other than South Carolina, this plan was the one fairest to the North. Crittenden had now reached the age of seventy-three. An old Whig and a lover of the Union of the Henry Clay sort, actuated by sincere patriotism, having the confidence of all parties in the Senate, adapted by the character of his mind and by his residence in a Union-loving border slave State to look in some degree upon both sides of the question, it was fitting that in his last years of public service he should do all in his power to cure the breach between the two sections. He introduced his plan of compromise in the Senate, December 18. Its salient feature was the disposition of the territorial question. Could that have been agreed to, an accommodation on the other points of difference would not have been difficult. Crittenden proposed as a constitutional amendment that slavery should be prohibited "in all the territory of the United States now held, or hereafter acquired, situate north of latitude 36° 30′. . . . In all the territory south of said line of latitude . . . slavery is hereby recognized as existing, and shall not be interfered with by Congress, but shall be protected as property by all the departments of the territorial government during its continuance." States should be admitted from the territory either north or south of that line with or without slavery, as their constitutions might provide.[1]

---

[1] This was called Article 1. The Crittenden compromise provided for other constitutional amendments :

Article 2. "Congress shall have no power to abolish slavery in places under its exclusive jurisdiction, and situate within the limits of States that permit the holding of slaves."

Article 3. Congress shall have no power to abolish slavery in the District of Columbia without compensation, and without the consent of its inhabitants, of Virginia, and of Maryland.

On the same day that Crittenden proposed his compromise, the Senate adopted the resolution of Powell of Kentucky, which provided for a special committee of thirteen to consider " the grievances between the slave-holding and the non-slave-holding States," and to suggest, if possible, a remedy. Two days later the Vice-President named as the committee : Powell of Kentucky, Hunter of Virginia, Crittenden of Kentucky, Seward of New York, Toombs of Georgia, Douglas of Illinois, Collamer of Vermont, Davis of Mississippi, Wade of Ohio, Bigler of Pennsylvania, Rice of Minnesota, Doolittle of Wisconsin, Grimes of Iowa. Three of the senators were from the border slave States, two from the cotton States, three were Northern Democrats, and five were Republicans. The constitution of the committee was eminently fair, the distribution according to parties and sections just. In ability, character, and influence all the senators stood

---

Article 4. Congress shall have no power to prohibit or hinder the transportation of slaves between slave-holding States and territories.

Article 5. A provision for the payment of the owners by the United States for rescued fugitive slaves.

Article 6. "No future amendment of the Constitution shall affect the five preceding articles . . . and no amendment shall be made to the Constitution which will authorize or give to Congress any power to abolish or interfere with slavery in any of the States by whose laws it is or may be allowed or permitted."

Resolutions were also offered :

1. That the slave-holding States are entitled to the faithful observance and execution of the Fugitive Slave laws.

2. That Congress should earnestly recommend the repeal of the Personal Liberty laws to the several States that had enacted them.

3. That the Fugitive Slave law of 1850 should be so amended as to make the fee the same, whether the alleged fugitive was sent back to slavery or released, and limiting the powers of the marshal in summoning to his aid the *posse comitatus ;* thus taking from the law two features that had been peculiarly obnoxious to the North.

4. That the laws for the suppression of the African slave trade " ought to be made effectual and ought to be thoroughly executed." As the full text of the proposed Crittenden compromise is part of the history of this time, I give references where it may be readily found : Journal of the Committee of Thirteen, p. 3 ; *Congressional Globe,* p. 114 ; Life of Crittenden, Coleman, vol. ii. p. 233 ; Greeley's American Conflict, vol. i. p. 376.

high; three of them were leaders of public sentiment. There was warrant for believing that, if the Union could be saved by act of Congress, these senators would discover the way. On the day that they first met in committee, December 21, the news recently received must have heightened their impression of the gravity of the situation and added to their sense of responsibility. December 20, the South Carolina convention had unanimously adopted the ordinance of secession, an action which kindled enthusiasm in the cotton States, and awakened some demonstrations of approval in North Carolina and Virginia. It was believed that unless a composition could be effected, Georgia, Florida, Alabama, and Mississippi would certainly secede, and that Louisiana and Texas would probably follow their example. The stake which the North had to play for was these six cotton States. If they were not won, might not the game be shifted to a contest where the border slave States would be at hazard? This was well understood by the Northern senators when the members of the committee came together and conversed informally on their first day of meeting. The people of the North for the most part had some notion of the peril in which the Union lay; but they felt that if these thirteen men could not agree on an acceptable compromise, there was not elsewhere in the country wisdom to devise a plan and influence to get it adopted. On one day they read of the secession of South Carolina; on the next, that there had been "a free interchange of opinion" among the members of "the select committee of the Senate on the crisis;"[1] and it might have seemed to augur well that these gentlemen who met on a high social footing could begin their proceedings by a sincere endeavor to understand one another's position, rather than by presenting cut-and-dried ultimatums. This fact was the more noteworthy, as the session had been remarkable for an almost complete cessation of social intercourse between Northern and Southern

---

[1] Associated Press despatch, Dec. 21.

senators.[1] It was, indeed, a rare committee. On election day no two men in public life had stood for sentiments so diametrically opposed as Seward and Jefferson Davis, and yet they were on friendly social terms and had been intimate. The incessant and bitter party and factional warfare of seven years could not sour the genial nature of Douglas, who was disposed to extend the right hand of fellowship to every man on the committee, with the possible exception of Davis. In addition to a willingness to sink any personal animosities, he also stood ready to yield somewhat of his political views for the purpose of avoiding disunion.[2] Crittenden was the Nestor of the Senate. Collamer, Grimes, and Doolittle were Republicans of sound judgment, and, we may believe, loved their country better than their party. Union-loving Kentucky had both of her senators on the committee, Union-loving Virginia had one.

December 22, the committee got fairly to work. On the motion of Davis, it was decided that no report should be adopted unless it had the assent of a majority of the Republican senators, and also a majority of the other eight members of the committee. This was a wise and even necessary arrangement. It was reasonably certain that no compromise could be carried through Congress without the concurrence of at least three of the Republican members of the committee; and as the different propositions comprised constitutional amendments which required the approval of three fourths of the States, time would be wasted in presenting to the country any compromise not sustained in the manner called for by the Davis resolution. Crittenden now introduced his compromise, and the committee with praiseworthy speed proceeded to vote upon it. On the first article of the proposed constitutional amendment—the one having for its scope the settlement of the slavery question in the

---

[1] Article of Frederic Bancroft, *Political Science Quarterly*, Sept., 1891, p. 402 ; *Congressional Globe*, p. 12.

[2] See Associated Press despatch, Dec. 21 ; Douglas's speech in the Senate, Jan. 3, 1861.

territories, of which an abstract has been given in the text[1]—
the vote stood : Yeas, Bigler, Crittenden, Douglas, Hunter,
Powell, Rice—6. Nays, Collamer, Davis, Doolittle, Grimes,
Seward, Toombs, Wade—7. The senators from the border
slave States and the Northern Democrats voted for it;
the senators from the cotton States and the Republicans
against it. All the Republicans of the committee voted
against the rest of the proposed articles amending the Constitution ;[2] all the other members of the committee voted for
them. On the first and second resolutions,[3] the Republicans
are recorded in the negative ;[4] the Democrats and Crittenden, in the affirmative. The third and fourth resolutions,
which were favorable to the North, had the unanimous vote
of a full committee.[5]

The first article of the proposed constitutional amendment, the one devoted to the territorial question, was of all
by far the most important. Unless an agreement could be
reached on this point, no compromise was possible. As
Davis and Toombs voted with the Republicans against
that proposition, it is often asserted that they, jointly with
the Republicans, are responsible for the defeat of the
Crittenden compromise; but this is a mistake, for the evidence is undoubted that, if a majority of the Republican
members of the committee had indicated their intention
to accept that as a settlement, Davis and Toombs would
also have supported it.[6] No fact is clearer than that the

---

[1] See p. 150.

[2] On article 6, Grimes's vote is not recorded. For the articles, see note
1, p. 150.   [3] Ibid.

[4] On the first resolution the names of Seward and Collamer are not recorded; neither Hunter nor Grimes voted on the second.

[5] See Journal of Committee of Thirteen, pp. 5-7.

[6] "In the committee of thirteen, a few days ago, every member from the
South, including those from the cotton States [Davis and Toombs], expressed their readiness to accept the proposition of my venerable friend
from Kentucky [Crittenden] as a final settlement of the controversy, if
tendered and sustained by the Republican members." — Douglas in the
Senate, Jan. 3, 1861, *Globe*, Appendix, p. 41. "I said to the committee of
thirteen, and I say here, that, with other satisfactory provisions, I would ac-

Republicans in December defeated the Crittenden compromise; few historic probabilities have better evidence to support them than the one which asserts that the adoption of this measure would have prevented the secession of the cotton States, other than South Carolina, and the beginning of the civil war in 1861.[1] It is worth while, therefore, to

---

cept it" [the territorial provision of the Crittenden compromise].—Toombs in the Senate, Jan. 7, 1861, *Globe*, p. 270. "I can confirm the senator's declaration that Senator Davis himself, when on the committee of thirteen, was ready, at all times, to compromise on the Crittenden proposition. I will go further and say that Mr. Toombs was also."—Douglas in the Senate, March 2, 1861, *Globe*, p. 1391; see also remarks of Pugh, same day, ibid.. p. 1390. "Davis, Toombs, and others of the Gulf States would have accepted it [the Crittenden compromise]. The author talked with Mr. Crittenden frequently on this point. Not only did he confirm the public declarations of Douglas and Pugh, and the speech of Toombs himself to this effect, but he said it was so understood in committee. At one time while the committee was in session Mr. Crittenden said: 'Mr. Toombs, will this compromise, as a remedy for all wrongs and apprehensions, be acceptable to you?' Mr. Toombs with great warmth replied, 'Not by a good deal; but my State will accept it, and I will follow my State.'"—Three Decades of Federal Legislation, S. S. Cox, p. 77, see also p. 69; Clingman's Speeches and Writings, p. 523; Life of Davis, Alfriend, p. 214; Greeley's American Conflict, vol. i. p. 383; Associated Press despatch of Dec. 22; interview with Toombs, 1880, Life of Seward, vol. ii. p. 486. I do not find a distinct statement from Davis similar to that of Toombs, but it seems apparent from his speech of Jan. 10, 1861 (see *Globe*, p. 310), that he would have accepted the Crittenden compromise. The only contemporary evidence I have found suggesting that the expressions of Davis and Toombs might have been insincere is a letter from Seward to Lincoln of Dec. 26, in which he says: "I think that they [Georgia, Alabama, Mississippi, and Louisiana] could not be arrested, even if we should offer all you suggest, and with it the restoration of the Missouri Compromise line. But persons acting for those States intimate that they might be so arrested because they think that the Republicans are not going to concede the restoration of that line."—Nicolay and Hay, vol. iii. p. 263. I do not think that this suspicion weakens the other evidence; it is not consistent with the characters of Davis and Toombs. They were men whose position on any important question it was never difficult to know.

[1] I will cite four contemporary expressions of opinion to this effect. Trumbull asks Crittenden, Jan. 7, 1861, "if he has any assurance that civil war is to be averted by his resolution." Crittenden replied: "I believe it will. Of course I cannot say for certain; I may be mistaken. . . .

inquire by what influences the Republicans were led to take this position, and to consider whether their course can be justified at the judgment-bar of history.

To answer the first part of this proposed inquiry the course of Seward and of Lincoln, the leaders of the Republican party, demands our attention. On the day after that on which Lincoln was elected, Seward possessed a more powerful influence than any one in the Republican party This influence became somewhat weakened with the Republican senators and representatives by the time that Congress met, for Seward was naturally supposed to favor the compromise suggested by his faithful friend and political partner, Thurlow Weed. That supposition had received much credence from the sanction of the plan by the New York *Times* and the New York *Courier and Enquirer*, journals which had steadily supported Seward, and the editors of which were his warm personal and political friends.[1] Moreover, Dana had told some Republican members, who called at the *Tribune* office on their way to Washington, and expressed regret at the overtures of Weed, that the arti-

It may not satisfy South Carolina. Hers is a peculiar case; but I believe it will satisfy almost all the Southern States; at any rate, to such an extent that there will be no further proceeding in this revolution, no further secession, no further revolution."—*Globe*, p. 267. Pugh said in the Senate, March 2: "At any time before the 1st of January a two-thirds vote for the Crittenden resolutions would have saved every State in the Union but South Carolina."—Ibid., p. 1390. If Duff Green reports his interview with Lincoln accurately, Lincoln may be cited in support of this view. Green wrote to President Buchanan on the day of the interview, Dec. 28: "I brought with me a copy of the resolutions submitted by Mr. Crittenden, which he [Lincoln] read over several times, and said that he believed that the adoption of the line proposed would quiet, for the present, the agitation of the slavery question, but believed it would be renewed by the seizure and attempted annexation of Mexico."—Life of Buchanan, Curtis, vol. ii. p. 426. If the propositions of Mr. Crittenden, wrote August Belmont to Douglas, Dec. 26, "could but receive the unanimous support of the senatorial committee of thirteen, the Union might be saved; otherwise I cannot see one ray of hope."—Letters of Belmont, privately printed, p. 23.

[1] New York *Times*, Nov. 26, Dec. 4 ; New York *Courier and Enquirer*, Nov. 28, Dec. 1 ; Seward to Weed, Dec. 3, Life of Weed, vol ii. p. 308.

cles were Seward's, and that he "wanted to make a great
compromise like Clay and Webster." [1] The first part of
Dana's statement we must regard as a mistake; [2] and, while
the evidence is not positive that Seward contemplated head-
ing a movement of Republicans that would have resulted in
the acceptance by them of a plan similar in essence to the
Crittenden compromise, yet his private correspondence from
December 1 to December 13 shows that he was wavering,
and gives rise to the belief that the pressure of Weed, Raymond, and Webb, backed as they were by powerful New
York men of their party, [3] would have outweighed that of
his radical Republican colleagues if he had not been restrained by the unequivocal declarations of Lincoln. "No
one has any system, few any courage or confidence in the
Union in this emergency," he wrote home December 2 ; "I
am engaged busily in studying and gathering my thoughts
for the Union." [4] I told the Republican caucus of senators,
he wrote Weed, that "they would know what I think and
what I propose when I do myself. . . . The Republican party
to-day is as uncompromising as the Secessionists in South
Carolina. A month hence each may come to think that
moderation is wiser." [5] "Our senators," he said, in a letter

[1] Seward to Weed, Dec. 3, Life of Weed, vol. ii. p. 308.
[2] "You will see that Mr. Weed lets me out of responsibility for his well-
intentioned but rather impulsive movements. He promised me to do so."
—Letter of Seward to his wife, Dec. 2, Life of Seward, vol. ii. p. 479.
[3] August Belmont wrote Governor William Sprague of Rhode Island,
Dec. 13 : "I can assure you that all the leaders of the Republican party in
our State and city, with a few exceptions of the ultra radicals, are in favor
of concessions, and that the popular mind of the North is ripe for them";
and Dec. 19: "Last evening I was present at an informal meeting of about
thirty gentlemen, comprising our leading men, Republicans, Union men,
and Democrats, composed of such names as Astor, Aspinwall, Moses H.
Grinnell, Hamilton Fish, R. M. Blatchford, etc. They were unanimous in
their voice for reconciliation, and that the first steps have to be taken by
the North."—Letters of August Belmont, privately printed, pp. 15, 16.
[4] Life of Seward, vol. ii. pp. 478–79.
[5] Life of Weed, vol. ii. p. 308. "The real object of the caucus was to
find out whether I authorized the *Evening Journal, Times,* and *Courier* ar-

to his wife, December 7, "agree with me to practice reticence and kindness. But others fear that I will figure, and so interfere and derange all." "The debates in the Senate," he wrote, three days later, "are hasty, feeble, inconclusive, and unsatisfactory; presumptuous on the part of the ill-tempered South; feeble and frivolous on the part of the North."[1]

Lincoln's influence on the march of events must now be taken into account. A letter tendering Seward the position of Secretary of State was delivered to him December 13. In it the President-elect said that this had been his "purpose from the day of the nomination at Chicago," and he had "the belief that your position in the public eye, your integrity, ability, learning, and great experience all combine to render it an appointment pre-eminently fit to be made."[2] Seward did not immediately accept the offer. In a polite and considerate letter he replied that he should like time for reflection and to consult his friends;[3] of all persons, he desired most the counsel of his wife and of Thurlow Weed.[4] Leaving Washington December 14, he arrived at Albany the next day, and remained there long enough to have a full consultation with Weed, in which we may be sure that his probable colleagues in the cabinet, as well as the affairs of the country, were discussed. Much as he wished to, he had not deemed it prudent to visit Lincoln,[5] but while at Albany he either suggested or fell in with the idea that Weed should go to Springfield on his behalf. He and Weed conferred together December 15 and 16. December 17, the Albany *Evening*

---

ticles, and to combine the whole influence of the Senate to bring these papers to better judgment. I kept my temper. I told them . . . as for influencing those three editors, or any one of them, they would find them as independent as the Senate itself and more potential."—Ibid.

[1] Life of Seward, vol. ii. pp. 480–81. See also the whole of the letter to Weed of Dec. 3, Life of Weed, vol. ii. p. 308; and the correspondence from Dec. 1 to Dec. 13, Life of Seward, vol. ii. pp. 478–81.

[2] Nicolay and Hay, vol. iii. p. 349. The letter was dated Dec. 8.

[3] Ibid., p. 350. The letter was dated Dec. 13.

[4] Life of Seward, vol. ii. p. 481.   [5] See his letter of Dec. 13.

Journal had a carefully studied editorial, in which, asserting that the " question must have a violent or peaceful solution," it urged the Republicans to accept as a settlement of the dispute regarding the territories what was substantially the Crittenden proposition.[1]   Weed then went to Springfield ; Seward went to his home at Auburn, there to await the return of his friend. Weed's consultation with Lincoln took place December 20.   His article in the *Evening Journal* having reached there at about the same time, served as a fitting text for a discussion of the critical state of affairs, and, before the conference ended, the news that South Carolina had passed the ordinance of secession furnished important material for it.[2]

Lincoln's mind was made up.   Naturally, no man in the

---

[1] Cited in the New York *Tribune*, Dec. 19.   The *Tribune* in the same issue remarked in an editorial : "*The Atlas and Argus* [the celebrated Albany Democratic newspaper] warmly praises the last new compromise of the Albany *Evening Journal*.   Praise from such a quarter is at least suspicious.   *The Atlas and Argus* also intimates that Mr. Seward was consulted in devising the new compromise.   This we judge to be malicious and untrue."

The Albany *Evening Journal* of Dec. 19 had the following article : " 'It is susceptible of proof that Senator Seward aided in preparing the leader of last evening's *Journal*.'—Albany *Evening Standard*.   There is not the shadow of foundation for this statement.   The following paragraph was originally appended to the article referred to, but, to avoid seeming ostentation, was omitted : ' To avoid possible misconstruction, it may be proper to say that the senior editor of the *Journal*, consulting his own sense of duty and right, speaks for himself only.'   Telegraph reports having assumed Mr. Seward's acquiescence in the article, the Auburn *Advertiser* of Tuesday evening [Dec. 18] publishes the following paragraph : ' Mr. Seward, in conversation, fully repudiates the telegraph and newspaper assumptions of his authority for or concurrence in the Albany *Journal's* article of yesterday.   He says he wonders how long it will take newspapers to learn that, when he desires to be heard, he is in the habit of speaking in his proper place for himself.' "—Cited in the New York *World* of Dec. 20.

[2] Life of Thurlow Weed, vol. i. p. 604 *et seq.*   Weed gives a much fuller report of the discussion in regard to the cabinet than of that on the state of the Union.   The question of the New York patronage was hardly touched upon, and then was brought up by Lincoln (see p. 612).   For the date of the consultation, which is not given by Weed, see Springfield despatch to the New York *Tribune* of Dec. 20.

country had watched with greater anxiety than he the
course of events in South Carolina, or had studied more carefully the trend of Northern sentiment and the disposition
to compromise. His first belief, " that this government possesses both the authority and the power to maintain its own
integrity," was confirmed by his mature thought ; but, in
holding to this legitimate conviction, he did not lose sight
of an equally important fact. " The ugly point," he said,
in private conversation, " is the necessity of keeping the
government together by force, as ours should be a government of fraternity." [1] A statesman at such a crisis would
naturally cast about for a policy that might peacefully preserve the Union ; and a statesman such as was the President-elect, who had been devoted to peaceful pursuits, would
have deemed it wicked to conjure up visions of military
power and glory, and would shrink from beginning his administration with a civil war on his hands. There is no
doubt that, if the Crittenden compromise had been put forward as an ordinary congressional enactment instead of a
constitutional amendment, Lincoln would have accepted
every article of it except the one that proposed the settlement of the territorial question. [2] Touching the cardinal
principle of the Republican party, the principle that explained the reason of the party's existence, he was firm.
" Entertain no proposition for a compromise in regard to
the extension of slavery," he wrote, December 11, to Kellogg, the Illinois member of the House committee of thirty-
three on the crisis. " The instant you do, they have us
under again : all our labor is lost, and sooner or later must
be done over. . . . The tug has to come, and better now
than later. You know I think the Fugitive Slave clause of

---

[1] Conversations of Nov. 15 and Dec. 13, Nicolay and Hay, vol. iii. pp.
247–48.

[2] I think that this is clear from the whole tenor of his correspondence,
and especially from his letter of Dec. 15 to John A. Gilmer of North Carolina, to whom he afterwards offered a cabinet appointment. Nicolay and
Hay, vol. iii. p. 284.

the Constitution ought to be enforced — to put it in its
mildest form, ought not to be resisted." ¹ Two days later,
in a letter to E. B. Washburne, also a member of Congress
from Illinois, he repeats the same idea and objects to the
scheme for dividing the territory between slavery and
freedom by the Missouri line. "Let that be done," he
writes, "and immediately filibustering and extending slavery recommences. On that point hold firm as a chain
of steel." ² Lincoln's letter to John A. Gilmer of North
Carolina, written December 15, shows not only judicious
constancy, but a largeness of political comprehension that
is admirable. "On the territorial question I am inflexible," he said. "On that there is a difference between you
and us ; and it is the only substantial difference. You think
slavery is right and ought to be extended; we think it is
wrong and ought to be restricted. For this, neither has any
just occasion to be angry with the other." ³ In his communication to Thurlow Weed of December 17, he is less
positive than in the preceding letters referred to ; he intimates where before he had asserted ; he thinks it probable
where before he had been absolutely sure : but this indicates
no wavering of opinion ; he undoubtedly wrote in a less
confident tone out of respect to Weed, who had earnestly
advocated a policy to which he himself was opposed.⁴

On leaving Springfield, after a free and full interchange
of views with Lincoln, Weed brought away for the consideration of the Republican members of Congress a written
proposition from Lincoln, which embodied his views essen-

¹ Nicolay and Hay, vol. iii. p. 259.
² Reminiscences of A. Lincoln, North American Publishing Company, p.
30 ; Nicolay and Hay, vol. iii. p. 259. While Crittenden did not introduce
his plan into the Senate until Dec. 18, a compromise involving the division
of territory on the Missouri line began to be discussed soon after the opening of Congress, and the essential part of his own plan was foreshadowed
at least one week before he offered it to the Senate. See Washington correspondence New York *Tribune*, Dec. 7, and editorial in New York *Tribune*,
Dec. 12.   ³ Nicolay and Hay, vol. iii. p. 285.
⁴ Life of Weed, vol. ii. p. 310 ; Nicolay and Hay, vol. iii. p. 253.

tially as they have been here indicated.[1] There was now urgent need for Seward's presence at Washington, and, on his journey thither, travelling December 22 with Weed from Syracuse to Albany, he learned Lincoln's emphatic position in regard to slavery in the territories. Arriving late that evening at the Astor House, New York, he found in progress the annual dinner of the New England Society, celebrating Fore-fathers' Day. The distinguished and influential men gathered around that banquet board shared the common desire of the whole country to hear from Seward some expression of opinion on the existing crisis, some outline of policy to be pursued. He was the leader of the Republican party in Congress. Though it had not yet transpired that a position in the cabinet had been offered him, yet common report ran that he would be the Secretary of State of the incoming administration. This meant to most of those New York gentlemen that he would practically be the President. It was known that Weed had been at Springfield, and that Seward had seen him since his return. Since the election, the New York senator had not opened his mouth in public. When, therefore, he consented to speak to the banqueters, we may easily imagine with what intense, even anxious, interest these eminent representatives of literature, of the bar, and of the business of the metropolis hung upon his words. Since the disunion movement began, they had been distracted by the disturbed condition of financial affairs,[2]

---

[1] This appears from Seward's letter to Lincoln of Dec. 26, Nicolay and Hay, vol. iii. p. 262. The proposition itself is not printed by Nicolay and Hay, and does not appear in the Life of Weed or the Life of Seward. My friend Colonel Hay writes me that it is fair to presume it has been destroyed.

[2] "The country is at this moment convulsed with excitement, and its commercial affairs disarranged and sacrificed."—New York *Tribune*, Nov. 23. "We are suffering from a panic, and no man can see the end thereof." —Ibid., Dec. 8. "Three months ago the material condition of the country was healthy and prosperous. Careful trading and close economy had relieved it from the pressure which, during the four previous years, had weighed upon its energies and had restricted its resources. The magnifi-

but just now, despite South Carolina's ordinance, they were feeling cheered by a gleam of light reflected in an advance of stocks, and in the brightening up of the commercial skies.[1] Such was the estimate in New York City of Seward's greatness that it is likely every one present expected to hear this pale, slight man utter words of national salvation.

It does not ordinarily come within the province of an historian to criticise after-dinner oratory, but I can have no hesitation in saying that this speech of Seward's, full as it was of levity and unseemly jest, was unworthy of the man, of his position, and of the critical juncture of affairs.[2] Yet, touching the serious part of the discourse, it must be admitted that he probably did as well as any man under the existing circumstances could have done. There had been reason for thinking that Seward might support the Crittenden compromise; it was a fair inference from this speech that he would not do it. Strong in his advocacy of the Union, he urged that the question at issue be considered in a conciliatory temper, and he ended in the optimistic vein so frequently characteristic of his thought.

---

cent crops of the Northwestern States, when taken in connection with the steadily-increasing demand for the cotton of the South, warranted the belief that our commercial and industrial interests were about to enter upon a career of activity almost without parallel in the history of the republic. These well-grounded expectations have been scattered to the winds. Banks have suspended ; commerce languishes ; trade is paralyzed ; the Federal government has been brought to the verge of bankruptcy, and the prospect in the future is gloomier still. The depreciation in values is general and all - pervading." — Baltimore *Daily Exchange*, Dec. 8, see also editorial of Dec. 11. "The panic which is toppling down great business interests in the centres of trade and prostrating them in the dust."—New York *World*, Dec. 19.

[1] Life of Seward, vol. ii. p. 483 ; money article of New York *Tribune* for Saturday, Dec. 22.

[2] I refer to the speech as reported in the New York *Tribune* of Dec. 24, in the New York *Evening Post* of the same date, and as published in Moore's Rebellion Record, vol. i, Docs., p. 4. In the speech as printed in Seward's Works, vol. iv. p. 644, the jocose and familiar expressions are omitted.

On Monday, December 24, Seward was at Washington, in
attendance upon the committee of thirteen. It must be
called to mind that, on the Saturday previous, the committee voted on the Crittenden compromise, and that Seward's
name is recorded in the negative on all the articles of the
proposed amendment to the Constitution.[1] But he was not
present at the meeting of that day ; as we have seen, he was
on the way from Auburn to New York City. On account
of his absence, the Republicans were unwilling to have a vote
taken; but, since they could give no assurance as to when he
would return, the other senators refused to defer action.[2]
Monday, the committee permitted Seward to record his vote
on the several propositions that had been considered at the
previous meeting.[3]

It is a fair historic probability that Seward would have
favored in committee a compromise on the basis of the Crittenden plan, had he not already in a measure submitted himself to the leadership of Lincoln by entertaining the offer of
the State department. It is certain that if Lincoln, in the
interview with Weed, had given his adhesion to the Albany
Journal proposition, Seward would have championed it in
committee and in Congress ; and it seems almost certain that,
with such support, the Crittenden compromise in essence
would have been reported by the committee and adopted by
Congress. It has been seen that Lincoln's influence was exerted against the proposal for the division of territory on
the Missouri line. While, in spite of earnest requests from
many quarters,[4] he had refused to make a public declaration of his views, the letters to Kellogg and to Washburne[5]
were obviously written with the design of having their contents made known to Republican members of Congress on
whom rested any responsibility. Following these letters
came an important avowal. Greeley, who had been corre-

[1] See p. 154.	[2] Associated Press despatch, Dec. 22.
[3] Journal of committee of thirteen, p. 8.
[4] See Nicolay and Hay, vol. iii. chap. xviii.	[5] See pp. 160–61.

sponding with Lincoln,[1] made, on December 22, at the head of his editorial columns, in leaded type, this declaration: "We are enabled to state, in the most positive terms, that Mr. Lincoln is utterly opposed to any concession or compromise that shall yield one iota of the position occupied by the Republican party on the subject of slavery in the territories, and that he stands now, as he stood in May last, when he accepted the nomination for the presidency, square upon the Chicago platform."

What would have been the effect on the Republican members of the committee of thirteen if the weight of Lincoln's influence had been put in the other scale, if it had been exerted for instead of against the division of territory on the Missouri line? Collamer would likely have gone with Seward. At the beginning of the session he had said, in conversation with Clingman: "You must let us know your terms, for we do not want to part with you."[2] Wade, we may be sure, would have agreed to no compromise acceptable to the cotton States. He had declared in the Senate, "So far as I am concerned, I will yield to no compromise."[3] This remark was made in his speech of December 17—a speech which advanced him to the leadership of the radical Republicans, and which undoubtedly at that time had the approval of a majority of his party.[4] Greeley had ceased

---

[1] See Nicolay and Hay, vol. iii. p. 258.

[2] Speeches and Writings, Clingman, p. 523.

[3] *Congressional Globe*, p. 103.

[4] An editorial of Dec. 19, in the New York *World*, then an independent journal, reflects so well in the main Republican sentiment in the middle of December, that I give a long extract from it : " Wade is the Republican senator from the agricultural State of Ohio, and his speech is probably a very exact reflex, not merely of the Republican sentiment of his State, but of all the great agricultural communities of the North. The strength of the Republican party lies in the rural districts. In rural communities the moral element has more influence in politics than it has in towns, where the quick succession of events and ideas keeps the mind more alert, and does not allow that immobility of mental attitude which is favorable to a persistent contemplation of fixed principles. The slower perceptions of the agricultural

the advocacy of his own policy of letting the Southern States go in peace, partly for the reason that it met no hearty response from Northern sentiment, and partly out of deference to Lincoln.[1] The *Tribune* now came to the support of the policy laid down by Wade as " the only true, the only honest, the only safe doctrine." [2] This doctrine could be summed up in the two words, " no compromise."

What would have been the course of Grimes and of Doolittle in this supposable case is not so clear. That they sincerely objected to the Crittenden compromise as presented to the committee is undoubted ; [3] but if the plan had been mod-

---

mind do not enable it readily to keep up with the rapid pace of movements in revolutionary times. It seems incredible to those who are not in the thick of events that the great changes which we witness should have taken place in the six weeks since the presidential election. The panic, which is toppling down great business interests in the centres of trade and prostrating them in the dust, is unfelt and unappreciated in the homes of our farmers. The sudden blight which has fallen on all other interests has hardly yet come near to them. As to the cry of disunion, they have heard that raised so often, when it meant nothing, that they are now skeptical when disunion is close upon us. It is the old story of crying ' wolf,' till the cry has lost its effect when the danger is real.

" Wade's speech derives its significance from the circumstance that it may be taken as a pretty accurate index of the sentiment of the great mass of the Republicans in respect to the crisis. The tone of their press for the last ten days accords with the anti-compromise tone of this speech. The current, indeed, seems setting more and more strongly in that direction. The ground on which a majority of the Republican party stands to-day is earnest opposition to any further compromises, combined with entire willingness to accord to the South every right guaranteed to it by the Constitution. . . .

" Mr. Weed's quickness of perception and intimate personal relations with prominent business men in New York and other cities give him a full appreciation of the destruction to business interests that attends on the panic, and of the disasters and ruin that would accompany a dissolution of the Union. He occupies a different position from the great body of his party because, as his supporters will say, his mind takes a quicker grasp of the condition of affairs. He advocates compromise because he is convinced that the emergency can only be met by compromise or civil war."

[1] Nicolay and Hay, vol. iii. p. 258.   [2] Dec. 19.

[3] See Grimes's letters of Dec. 16, 1860, and of Jan. 28, 1861, Life of

ified, and if the altered proposition had been urged by Lincoln and championed by Seward, it is a fair presumption that neither Grimes nor Doolittle would have taken the responsibility of defeating such a compromise. It is unquestionable, as I have previously shown, that in December the Republicans defeated the Crittenden proposition;[1] and it seems to me likewise clear that, of all the influences tending to this result, the influence of Lincoln was the most potent. While it is true that a considerable majority of the Republican members of Congress were opposed to this scheme, it is also true that a public sentiment in its favor was rising and steadily growing at the North, and that if this opinion had been given direction and form by Republican leaders holding the positions of Seward and of Lincoln, it would have shaped the legislation of the existing Congress.[2]

Upon what grounds may the Republicans and Lincoln be justified for refusing their assent to this compromise? Every article of Crittenden's amendment to the Constitution mentioned "slavery" or "slaves." What the fathers with ingenious circumlocution had avoided[3] was here obtrusively asserted. To introduce that phraseology into the organic instrument of the land was to take a step backward, to run counter to the spirit of the age. True, it might be urged, as Taney had maintained in the Dred Scott decision, that "the right of property in a slave is distinctly and expressly affirmed in the Constitution,"[4] and that the Crittenden amendment asserted no more; but to Republicans who venerated the Constitution it had been a consoling circumstance that the word "slavery" or "slaves" did not occur

James W. Grimes, Salter, pp. 132, 133; see letter of Doolittle, Nov. 16, *Globe*, p. 9, speech of Dec. 27, ibid., p. 195.   [1] See p. 154.

[2] "The reported recent declaration of the President-elect, that he will strictly adhere to the Chicago platform, has confirmed the wavering Republicans to that policy, and increased the intensity of Southern feeling."
—Associated Press despatch, Dec. 23.

[3] See vol. i. p. 17.   [4] See vol. ii. p. 257.

in it. Lincoln, in his debates with Douglas, had given utterance to this feeling in impressive words,[1] and he was now
undoubtedly conscious of its full force. " The main point at
issue between the two sections of our Confederacy," said
Brown of Mississippi in the Senate, is, that " we claim that
there is property in slaves and they [the Northern senators]
deny it." [2] Coming after the Dred Scott decision and the
different constructions of it, the Crittenden amendment,
had it been made part of the Constitution, would have settled the question whether that instrument distinctly recognized slaves as property. This was undoubtedly the reason
why the Southern senators were strenuous to have the Crittenden compromise in the form of a constitutional amendment; [3] but, on the other hand, this was necessary in order
to prohibit slavery in the territories, as the Supreme Court
had denied to Congress that power.

Another objection to the Crittenden compromise, more
serious and perhaps insurmountable, lay in the fact that,
except on the understanding that the protection to slavery
south of the Missouri line should apply to all future acquisitions of territory, it would not be acceptable to the senators from the cotton States. The phraseology of the article
was misleading. In territory " now held or hereafter acquired" north of latitude 36° 30', slavery should be prohib-

---

[1] See vol. ii. p. 335.   [2] Speech of Dec. 27, *Globe*, p. 201.
[3] J. S. Pike wrote the New York *Tribune* under date of Dec. 22 : "I
think the case turns upon the question of whether an agreement can be
made to a partition of territory between the slave and free States. This is
the nub of the controversy when winnowed from its chaff. All the other
points, I fancy, can be managed. But the concession on the main one, of
a partition of territory after the plan of the Missouri Compromise, is the
sticking place. The revolutionists in the Gulf States don't want to be satisfied with this, but the other slave States, or those in them who are opposed
to dissolving the Union, consider that the concession would force the secessionists to desist. The partition is demanded under the form of a constitutional guaranty. No ordinary legislation will satisfy the slaveholders.
As Mr. Toombs says, it must take the shape of positive constitutional guaranty, or he would not give a fig for it, for the abolitionists are treacherous,
and would repeal the settlement to-morrow if they had a chance."

ited, while the protection to slavery apparently applied only to actual territory. Crittenden himself admitted that the article was ambiguous.[1] The speech of Toombs, however, in the Senate, January 7, 1861,[2] shows that he and Davis understood that, as regards that provision, the South and the North were on a par; and it is probable that, before accepting the compromise for their States, they would have demanded that their understanding of it should be expressly stated, as was afterwards done in the Powell amendment.[3] With this implication a part of the scheme, and with the annexation of Texas, the Mexican War, the attempts to get Cuba, and the filibustering in Central America fresh in the minds of the Republicans, it is easy to see why they objected to the first article of the Crittenden compromise. True, as Thurlow Weed might have argued, such things cannot take place under a Republican administration; against them we are insured for the next four years, and the spirit of the age is working constantly and powerfully for us. But Lincoln did not take this view. "Filibustering for all south of us and making slave States of it would follow in spite of us," he wrote Thurlow Weed.[4] "A year will not pass," he declared, "till we shall have to take Cuba as a condition upon which they will stay in the Union."[5]

After weighing with care the considerations on each side, it will appear that the Republicans and Lincoln may be justified in having refused to accept the Crittenden com-

---

[1] See letter of Crittenden, Feb. 4, 1861, to a gentleman in Trenton, N. J., New York *Times*, Feb. 21, 1861.   [2] *Globe*, p. 270.

[3] Powell's amendment was offered Jan. 9, 1861, and accepted by Crittenden. It was adopted by the Senate Jan. 16. In reply to a question of Pugh, Powell said: "I will say to the senator that I do think it material, and that was the intention of my colleague in presenting the resolutions. I put this amendment in to make it clear and distinct. I understand my colleague to accept it, as it carries out his original design."— *Globe*, p. 403.

[4] Letter of Dec. 17, Life of Weed, vol. ii. p. 311.

[5] Letter to J. T. Hale, Jan. 11, 1861, Nicolay and Hay, vol. iii. p. 288.

promise. A similar proposition was defeated by the Northern Whigs and Democrats in 1848.¹ Clay and Webster
in 1850 refused to entertain such a plan proffered by
Jefferson Davis and the Nashville convention.² Yet in
coming to the conclusion that the project of Crittenden
ought not at this time to have been agreed to by the
Republicans, I must express that judgment with diffidence.
An important fact in opposition to such a view is that
public sentiment in favor of this compromise was now
beginning to arise at the North. The manifestations of
this opinion are clear after the 1st of January, 1861, and
will be mentioned in the proper chronological order. For
the present it is desirable to refer to the expressions of
certain men as indicative of the growing sentiment of the
community. " I would most cheerfully accept your proposition," was the word Crittenden received from John A.
Dix, a Breckinridge Democrat, but more of a patriot than a
partisan. " I feel a strong confidence that we could carry
three fourths of the States in favor of it as an amendment
to the Constitution." ³ " I saw with great satisfaction your
patriotic movement," wrote Edward Everett, " and I wish
from the bottom of my heart that it may succeed." ⁴ Elisha
Whittlesey, a Republican living in northern Ohio, hoped
that Crittenden's efforts would succeed in preventing dis-

¹ See vol. i. p. 96.   ² Ibid., pp. 168, 174.
³ Letter of Dec. 22, Life of Crittenden. Coleman, vol. ii. p. 237.
⁴ Letter of Dec. 23, ibid., p. 237. He added : " There is nothing in
your resolutions for which I would not cheerfully vote, if their adoption as
amendments of the Constitution would save us from disunion, and, what
I consider its necessary consequences, civil war, anarchy, desolation at
home, the loss of all respectability and influence abroad, and, finally, military despotism. . . . I could wish that our Southern brethren would be
contented without inserting the word *slave* in the Constitution, it having
been *studiously* omitted by the framers, and also that the right of holding
slaves south of the 36° 30' had been left to inference, as it was in the Missouri Compromise, and not expressly *asserted*. Both these points will be
stumbling-blocks with many conservative members of the Republican
party. . . . Cannot our Southern friends be persuaded to proceed more deliberately ?"

union.[1] Robert C. Winthrop, an old Whig, thought some
features of the plan ought to be modified, but he wrote
Crittenden: "I should try hard to sustain you in such measures as were essential to rescue us from disunion and civil
war."[2]   August Belmont, representing the commercial interests of New York City, gave assurance of the anxiety
that prevailed regarding the success of what was regarded
as so fair a settlement of the difficulty.[3]

Before Crittenden had formally introduced his plan into
the Senate, there were many indications that Northern sentiment was ripe for a compromise that should accord generous terms to the South.   This sentiment was fostered by
the gloomy state of trade.   Since the secession movement
began, the New York stock market had been in a feverish
condition, resulting twice in panic.   The Charleston, Washington, Baltimore, and Philadelphia banks had suspended

---

[1] He wrote, Dec. 24: " My conservative neighbors express their high gratification in your able and patriotic effort to arrest the *mad designs* of those
who wish the dissolution of the Union. . . . We bless you as a peace-
maker."—Life of Crittenden, Coleman, vol. ii. p. 238.

[2] Letter of Dec. 24. He added: "And yet one hardly knows how to
hope for anything good while there is so much passionate and precipitate
action at the South."—Ibid., p. 239.

[3] He wrote Crittenden, Dec. 26: "I have yet to meet the first conservative Union-loving man, in or out of politics, who does not approve of your
compromise propositions, and consider them a most efficacious, if not the
only, remedy which can save this great country from ruin and destruction.
. . . I am afraid that no human power can stay the evil, since the Republican leaders by their vote in the committee of thirteen, have proved that
they are determined to remain deaf to the dictates of justice and patriotism.
Will the American people permit their country to be dragged to ruin by a
handful of puritanical fanatics and selfish politicians ?"—Letters of Belmont, privately printed, p. 24.   Belmont wrote Herschel V. Johnson of
Georgia, Dec. 30 : " Though the Republican leaders in Congress have thus
far disappointed my expectations, I have strong hopes that they will be
compelled to yield under the pressure of public opinion. In our own city
and State some of the most prominent men are ready to follow the lead of
Weed, and active agencies are at work to bring about a compromise. . . . In
regard to the territories, the restoration of the Missouri line, extended to
the Pacific, finds favor with most of the conservative Republicans, and
their number is increasing daily."—Ibid., pp. 26, 27.

specie payments; the New York banks had been forced to
issue clearing-house certificates.   The apprehended repudiation of debts due the North by Southern merchants was an
important factor in the situation.[1] Financial distress seemed
to be staring the country in the face.   Municipal elections,
taking place early in December in Boston and other New
England cities, and at Hudson, N. Y., showed a marked
falling - off in Republican strength since the presidential
vote.[2]   Among the Northern people there existed a wide-
spread belief that the abolitionists were largely answerable
for the present troubles, and this belief now began to show
itself in public demonstrations.   An anti-slavery convention
held December 3 at Tremont Temple, Boston, to commemo-
rate the anniversary of John Brown's execution, was broken
up by a mob largely composed, it is said, of Beacon Street
aristocrats.   A number of business men took possession of
the meeting, elected a chairman, and passed resolutions condemning John Brown, expressing their sense of the value of
the Union, and declaring the assemblies of certain "irresponsible persons and political demagogues" of Boston "a
public nuisance which, in self-defence, we are determined
shall henceforward be summarily abated."[3]   Thirteen days

---

[1] See money articles, New York *Tribune*, Nov. 19, 21, 22, Dec. 6, 7;
New York *Independent*, Nov. 15, cited by Von Holst, vol. vii. p. 250 ; New
York *Tribune*, cited on p. 269.

[2] See Greeley's American Conflict, vol. i. p. 362.

[3] New York *Tribune*, Dec. 4.   The anniversary of John Brown's execution coming on Sunday, this meeting was held Monday, Dec. 3.   Richard
Grant White, writer in 1862 of the first number of Harper's Pictorial
History of the Great Rebellion, thus spoke of this attempted meeting of the
abolitionists: ''The organizers of so flagrant an affront to public decency
were doomed to disappointment.''   The breaking up of the meeting is
characterized as ''proceedings somewhat irregular, but, under the circumstances, not quite unjustifiable.''—Part i. p. 21.   Per contra, see the indignant remarks of Carl Schurz in his address on '' Free Speech '' in Tremont
Temple, Boston, Dec. 11, 1860, Speeches, p. 222.   For the sentiment largely
prevailing in the commercial circles of Boston, see letter of Nathan Appleton of Dec. 15, 1860, printed in the *National Intelligencer*, Jan. 1, 1861.   He

later, on a Sunday morning, Wendell Phillips spoke at Music
Hall, bitterly condemning the disturbers of the Tremont
Temple convention. The audience being largely made up
of his friends, he delivered his speech without formidable
interruption, but, at the close of the meeting, it was necessary for a hundred policemen to escort him home, to protect him from a hooting mob of a thousand.' George William Curtis had engaged to deliver a lecture before the
People's Literary Institute of Philadelphia on "The Policy
of Honesty," but, owing to his connection with the anti-
slavery movement, the mayor of the city thought it would
be unwise for him to appear, and regretted the lack of lawful power to prevent such an orator from speaking in the
present state of public feeling. The owner of Concert Hall,
having been officially informed that, should the lecture be
given, there would be danger of a riot, cancelled the engagement he had made to let the hall for that occasion.' A
great union meeting called by Mayor Henry, a supporter
of Lincoln, was held in Independence Square, December 13,
the date on which Curtis had expected to lecture. The
speeches and the resolutions showed that, if the Crittenden
compromise had then been before the public, it would have
received the hearty approval of this assembly.' The same
may be said of the Pine Street meeting in New York City,
a private gathering of one to two hundred gentlemen of

---

wrote: "It is sad to see this powerful, glorious nation, in the midst of un-
paralleled prosperity, shattering itself into fragments, and all out of an impracticable idea, a nonentity, connected with the institution of slavery. . . .
The South is in a state of great excitement, a feeling of extreme indignation
towards the North. . . . The more extreme of our politicians " do not "represent the feelings of the masses in the North, even in New England."

  [1] New York *Tribune*, Dec. 17 ; see article of George W. Smalley, *Harper's
Magazine*, June, 1894.

  [2] Greeley's American Conflict, vol. i. p. 367 ; New York *Tribune*, Dec. 13.
Trouble had occurred the previous spring when Curtis had spoken in Philadelphia.

  [3] For the speeches and resolutions, see Greeley's American Conflict, vol.
i. p. 362 *et seq.*

high position and great influence, who had in the presidential canvass supported Douglas, Bell, or Breckinridge.[1]

Seward did not appreciate the danger in which the country lay. "Sedition," he wrote Lincoln, "will be growing
weaker and loyalty stronger every day from the acts of
secession as they occur."[2] Nor did Lincoln comprehend the
peril which menaced the nation should a settlement not be
reached, as did Everett, Winthrop, and August Belmont.
Lincoln knew plainly enough the worst that might happen
if the demands of the South were submitted to, but he did
not look upon the darkest side of the future in case of a
failure to make a compromise.[3] But there were representative men among the Republicans who predicted what would
come, and yet opposed the Crittenden plan. "War of a
most bitter and sanguinary character will be sure to follow
in a short time," wrote Grimes to his wife.[4] "The heavens
are indeed black," said Dawes, in a letter to an anxious
constituent, "and an awful storm is gathering. . . . I see no
way that either North or South can escape its fury. . . . I

---

[1] This meeting was held Dec. 15, Memoirs of J. A. Dix, Morgan Dix,
vol. i. p. 347 et seq.; New York Tribune, Dec. 17, 18; New York Times,
Dec. 17; New York World, Dec. 17. Among the signers of the call for the
meeting were: W. B. Astor, John J. Cisco, W. G. Hunt, James W. Beek-
man, John A. Dix. The chairman was Charles O'Conner. Ex-President
Fillmore sympathized with the object of the meeting. On the committee
of resolutions were: John A. Dix, James T. Soutter, E. Pierrepont, Samuel J. Tilden, William H. Aspinwall, Edward Cooper, Richard Lathers.

[2] Letter of Dec. 26, Nicolay and Hay, vol. iii. p. 264.

[3] See Herndon's Life of Lincoln, edition of Belford, Clarke & Co., p. 473;
Don Piatt's Memories of the Men who Saved the Union, p. 30. Many Republicans took the same view as Seward and Lincoln. J. S. Pike, whom
I have had occasion to quote many times, who was always sincere, and
who really was a representative man, asks, in a vehement argument written Dec. 18 to the New York Tribune: "Wherefore, then, this idle gabble,
this monstrous gassing about revolution and civil war?" Three days before he had written: "The talk of civil war is idle and childish."

[4] Letter of Dec. 16, Life of Grimes, Salter, p. 132. He added: "This
is certainly deplorable, but there is no help for it. No reasonable concession will satisfy the rebels."

am wellnigh appalled at its awful and inevitable consequences." [1]

The Republicans, however, did not merely object; they
proposed a compromise of their own. Seward, with the
unanimous consent of the Republican members, offered in
the committee, December 24, three propositions:

"1. That the Constitution should never be altered so as to
authorize Congress to abolish or interfere with slavery in the
States. (This to be enacted as a constitutional amendment.)

"2. That the Fugitive Slave law should be amended by
granting a jury trial to the fugitive.

"3. That Congress recommend the repeal by the States
of their Personal Liberty acts which contravene the Constitution or the laws." [2]

Only the first of these articles was determined in the
affirmative. [3] December 26, Seward offered a resolution
that "Congress should pass an efficient law for the punishment of all persons engaged in the armed invasion of any
State from another." [4] On that evening the Republican

---

[1] Printed in the New York *Tribune*, Dec. 24. He added: "And now that
the yawning jaws of destruction have been opened, I am called upon to
betray both the Constitution and the Union. . . . Discomfiture, disgrace,
destruction wait on timidity, vacillation, and concession. While safety, if
it come at all, comes only through moderation, calmness, and *firmness*."

[2] See letter of Seward to Lincoln, Dec. 26, Nicolay and Hay, vol. iii. p.
262; Journal of Committee of Thirteen, p. 10. The Washington correspondent of the New York *Tribune* said that this proposition was drawn
up by Collamer and Grimes. This is probable, as Seward did not arrive
at Washington until the morning of the 24th.—Life of Seward, vol. ii. p.
483. As the Southern Democrats, in committee, voted against the third
article on the ground that it would affect their laws imprisoning colored
seamen (Washington cor. New York *Tribune*, Dec. 24; New York *World*,
Dec. 26), I give it entire: "The legislatures of the several States shall be
respectfully requested to review all their legislation affecting the right of
persons recently resident in other States, and to repeal or modify all such
acts as may contravene the provisions of the Constitution of the United
States, or any laws made in pursuance thereof."

[3] For the amendments and the several votes, see Journal of the Committee, p. 11; Seward's letter of Dec. 26.

[4] Journal of the Committee, p. 13. This resolution was amended by the

members of the committee met at Seward's house, with
Trumbull and Fessenden, to consider the written suggestion Lincoln had given Thurlow Weed. The President-
elect was obviously willing to state the duty of enforcing
the Fugitive Slave law in stronger terms than had been
employed in the proposition of the Republicans, but, as they
thought the ground had been already covered, they offered
nothing further on this point.[1] It appears, however, from
a letter of Grimes to Governor Kirkwood, that the Iowa
senator assented to another proposition, viz.: "To admit
Kansas into the Union under the Wyandotte Constitution,[2]
and then to admit the remaining territory belonging to the
United States as two States, one north and one south of the
parallel of 36° 30', with the provision that these States might
be subdivided and new ones erected therefrom whenever
there shall be sufficient population for one representative in
Congress upon sixty thousand square miles."[3] The adoption of this would have given the Southerners a slave State,
for political purposes, in New Mexico.[4] While the machi-
nations of man had not overcome "an ordinance of nature"
and "the will of God"—for there were now but twenty-two
slaves in the territory[5]—New Mexico would have remained
for a while a pro-slavery pocket borough, as was Oregon on
her admission.[6] Although the Journal of the Committee of
Thirteen does not disclose the fact, it is apparent from the
context of Grimes's letter that the Republicans were ready
to agree to this proposal.

These propositions, then, were the Republican offer of

Democrats in a way unacceptable to the Republicans, and then lost by the
Republican votes.

[1] See Seward's letter of Dec. 26. While Seward heard from Weed, on
the 22d, the substance of Lincoln's suggestion, he did not receive it in written form until the morning of the 26th.   [2] See vol. ii. p. 475.

[3] Life of Grimes, Salter, p. 137.

[4] New Mexico comprised what is now New Mexico and Arizona.

[5] "Of these only twelve are domiciled ; the remainder are but transient
residents."—C. F. Adams, Speech, Jan. 31, 1861.

[6] See vol. ii. p. 417.

compromise. Considering that the slavery question had been submitted to the people at the presidential election, and that the anti-slavery party had won, was it not a fair offer? Did not the Republicans meet the cotton States half-way? Should not Davis, Toombs, and Hunter have agreed to the proposition? Could they not have done so without dishonor? As players in the political game, fault cannot be found with the Southerners for making extreme demands, but when they had ascertained the furthest concession the Republicans were willing to make, ought they not to have accepted it rather than run the risk of involving the country in civil war? For, while it was a prevalent idea at the South that the North would not fight, Jefferson Davis did not share that illusion, and was alive to the actual peril.

Jefferson Davis had taken, or had been forced into, a position that must now have embarrassed him if he made a sincere attempt to reach a settlement. In the House of Representatives, on December 6, a select committee of thirty-three on the crisis had been appointed. December 13, the committee adopted, by a vote of 22 to 8, a pacific resolution of Dunn, a Republican of Indiana, which had been offered as a substitute for one proposed by Rust, a Democrat of Arkansas, and which had been accepted by Rust.[1] Strangely enough, the next day after the adoption of this resolution—and, according to Reuben Davis of Mississippi, one of the committee of thirty-three, because of it—a number of Southern members of Congress met at

---

[1] This was the resolution : "*Resolved,* That, in the opinion of this committee, the existing discontents among the Southern people, and the growing hostility among them to the federal government, are greatly to be regretted ; and, whether such discontents and hostility are without just cause or not, any reasonable, proper, and constitutional remedies, and additional and more specific and effectual guarantees of their peculiar rights and interests as recognized by the Constitution, necessary to preserve the peace of the country and the perpetuation of the Union, should be promptly and cheerfully granted."—Journal of the Committee of Thirty-three, p. 7. The votes against this resolution were all Republican. Reuben Davis did not vote.

his rooms and prepared an address to their constituents which asserted: "The argument is exhausted. . . . In our judgment the Republicans are resolute in the purpose to grant nothing that will or ought to satisfy the South. We are satisfied the honor, safety, and independence of the Southern people require the organization of a Southern Confederacy—a result to be obtained only by separate State secession."[1] This manifesto was untimely and unjust. Even from the Southern point of view, it was at that time premature to assert that the Republicans would refuse a satisfactory compromise. Jefferson Davis, in signing the address, committed a grave indiscretion. It is charitable to suppose that he was induced to give it his sanction by the zealous persuasion of his more precipitate associates; and it is also due to him to say that, when first asked to serve on the Senate committee of thirteen, he declined, on the score of propriety, and that it was only at the request of Southern senators, holding views similar to his own, that he consented to do so.[2]

The committee of thirteen considered several other propositions besides those of Crittenden and the Republicans, but could come to no agreement. December 28, they adopted a resolution that they "had not been able to agree upon any general plan of adjustment, and report that fact to the Senate."[3] It was evident that the cotton States would ac-

---

[1] Washington *Constitution*, Dec. 15, cited by Nicolay and Hay, vol. ii. p. 436. See Recollections of Mississippi, Reuben Davis, p. 398. Davis says the action was taken on account of the resolution of Rust, but he does not state the resolution of Rust correctly. The signers of this address were : Five representatives of Alabama ; five representatives of Georgia; Iverson, senator from Georgia ; the representative from Florida ; one representative from Arkansas ; Jefferson Davis and Brown, senators from Mississippi ; three representatives from Mississippi ; two representatives from North Carolina; Slidell and Benjamin, senators from Louisiana ; one representative from Louisiana; Wigfall and Hemphill, senators from Texas; one representative from Texas ; four representatives from South Carolina.

[2] *Congressional Globe*, pp. 158, 182.

[3] Journal of Committee of Thirteen, p. 18.

cept nothing less than the Crittenden compromise; it was not so clear that the Republicans would do no more than they had offered. Yet it is a fact, which I hope to make clear as the story goes on, that, when the committee of thirteen failed to agree on a report, almost the last, if not the very last, chance of a compromise that could retain the cotton States was gone, although this was not generally appreciated, except by the cotton States themselves. If it had been fully comprehended, the pressure from the North on Congress and on the committee would probably have been so great as to lead to the adoption of the Crittenden compromise pure and simple.

While the leaders of parties and of factions in Congress were trying to effect a composition, Lincoln, in a quiet way and on other lines, endeavored to do something to retard the tide of secession. The Union speech which Alexander H. Stephens delivered November 14 before the members of the Georgia legislature[1] attracted Lincoln's attention, and led to a correspondence which began by his request for a revised copy of the speech.[2] This letter did not reach Stephens for two weeks; when it came, he immediately replied, ending with: "The country is certainly in great peril, and no man ever had heavier or greater responsibilities resting upon him than you have in the present momentous crisis." Lincoln's answer was an honest attempt to allay Southern apprehensions. He wrote: "I fully appreciate the present peril the country is in, and the weight of responsibility on me. Do the people of the South really entertain fears that a Republican administration would *directly* or *indirectly* interfere with their slaves or with them about their slaves? If they do, I wish to assure you . . . that there is no cause for such fears. The South would be in no more danger in this respect than it was in

---

[1] The War between the States, Stephens, vol. ii. p. 278.
[2] Letter of Lincoln to Stephens, Nov. 30, Letters and Speeches, Cleveland, p. 150.

the days of Washington. I suppose, however, this does not
meet the case. You think slavery is *right* and ought to be
extended, while we think it is wrong and ought to be restricted. That I suppose is the rub. It certainly is the only
substantial difference between us." [1]   Nevertheless, Lincoln
was clear that he could not give the faintest expression of
approval to the Crittenden compromise. Duff Green—
a Georgian, a prominent politician and editor, born before
the Constitution was adopted and loath to die with his eyes
resting on a dissevered Union—believing that deliverance
lay in the Crittenden project, went at President Buchanan's request to Springfield, in the hope of winning Lincoln's
support to this plan. Green and Lincoln had a long conversation on the Crittenden compromise. The President-
elect read the proposition over several times, but neither
in the conversation nor in the formal letter he afterwards
prepared for Green did he depart from the conviction he
had arrived at and had several times before expressed. [2]

Leading Republican senators and representatives, some
of whom held radical opinions, pressed Lincoln to call to
his cabinet Southern men of position and character who
had been adverse to his election. Thurlow Weed, on the
occasion of his visit to Springfield, had urged this with per-
tinacity. Lincoln was willing to do this provided it could
be done without sacrifice of principle, and with this end in
view he wrote an editorial, which appeared in the Springfield *Journal* on the morning of December 13, in which the
question was asked whether there were two or three Southern gentlemen, opposed to him politically, who would accept
a place in the cabinet; and, if so, whether this could be accomplished without the surrender of principle on either side

---

[1] Letter of Dec. 22. These three letters mentioned are given in fac-simile
in Cleveland, p. 150; Nicolay and Hay print Lincoln's letter of Dec. 22 in
full, vol. iii. p. 271.

[2] See letter of Green to Buchanan, Springfield, Dec. 28, Life of Buchanan, Curtis, vol. ii. p. 426; Letter of Lincoln to Green, Dec. 28, and
to Trumbull, same day, Nicolay and Hay, vol. iii. pp. 286–87.

and with due regard to the public service. While it was not known that Lincoln had actually written the article, it was well understood that he had inspired it.[1] It was, in fact, a tentative inquiry on the part of the President-elect whether there existed common ground on which he and Southern supporters of Bell or Douglas could meet. Afterwards an indirect offer was made to one such man,[3] and others were sounded with the purpose of carrying out this policy, but nothing came from any of these attempts.[4]

While Buchanan would have been glad to see the Crittenden compromise adopted,[5] he became, through his wavering course, unwittingly a bar to a settlement. Firmness in the execution of the laws and conciliation in the way of the removal of grievances should have been the key to his policy. Firmness makes compromise possible; willingness to conciliate justifies resoluteness. The President was ready to yield more to the South than the Crittenden plan,[6] but he shrank from the smallest assertion of the power of the government. The constitutional essay which he sent to Congress as his message led to nothing; it had not the slightest effect towards disentangling affairs in South Carolina. The people of Charleston, misled by their prejudices on slavery and State-rights, sincerely thought that they had begun another glorious revolution. Major Anderson, believing that

---

[1] Nicolay and Hay, vol. iii. p. 348 ; Springfield despatch of Dec. 13 to New York *Tribune*.

[3] After stating that the editorial "appeared at the head of this morning's *Journal*, Lincoln's organ," the Springfield despatch of Dec. 13 to the New York *Tribune* went on to say : "It is known to have emanated directly from the President."

[3] To John A. Gilmer, Nicolay and Hay, vol. iii. pp. 283, 363. Gilmer was a representative from North Carolina, classed by the *Tribune Almanac* as a South American, presumably a supporter of Bell.

[4] See Nicolay and Hay, vol. iii. p. 361 *et seq.;* Herndon, pp. 473, 477.

[5] See letter to James G. Bennett, Dec. 20, and special message of Jan. 8, 1861, Curtis, vol. ii. pp. 431, 435.

[6] See his annual message.

the South was at least half right in the controversy,[1] but having an eye single to his duty as a soldier, had implored his government to adopt some definite line of policy, and, if it were decided to hold the forts in Charleston harbor, he urged that troops or vessels of war be instantly sent. " I shall go steadily on," he wrote, " preparing for the worst, trusting hopefully in the God of battles to guard and guide me in my course."[2] General Wool, who had served with distinction in the War of 1812 and in the Mexican War, and who now commanded the military department which included South Carolina, Georgia, Florida, Alabama, and Mississippi, was eager to bear an active part. This veteran, now seventy - two years old, wrote, December 6, a private letter to his old friend, Secretary Cass. " If I can aid the President," he said, " to preserve the Union, I hope he will command my services. It will never do for you or him to leave Washington without every star in this Union is in its place. . . . It seems to me that troops should be sent to Charleston to man the forts in that harbor. You have eight companies at Fort Monroe, Va. Three or four of these companies should be sent, without a moment's delay, to Fort Moultrie."[3]

December 8, the very day on which General Wool's letter should have reached Washington, several of the South Carolina members of Congress who had not, in accordance with the example set by their senators, resigned their seats called to see the President. Knowing that the subject of the reinforcement of the Charleston forts was frequently and earnestly discussed in the cabinet, and that the rumor

---

[1] See Life of Buchanan, Curtis, vol. ii. p. 371; private letter of Dec. 11 to R. N. Gourdin, of Charleston, The Genesis of the Civil War, Crawford, p. 69.

[2] Anderson to Adjutant-General Cooper, Dec. 1, Official Records, vol. i. p. 82. Captain Foster, of the Engineers, sent through the proper channel a similar recommendation. See his letter of Dec. 4, ibid., p. 84.

[3] Troy *Times*, Dec. 31, cited in Moore's Rebellion Record, vol. i., Documents, p. 11.

ran that General Cass and Holt [1] were strenuous for such a policy,[2] these men sought information, and, should the occasion demand it, were ready to enter their protest. The President came from a cabinet council to see them in the ante-room. When they opened the matter, he was seemingly "much disturbed and moved," and spoke of a conversation he had had with the wife of Major Anderson, who had come from New York for the purpose of making known to him her alarm at the situation of her husband, whom she considered " in momentary danger of an attack from an ex-

---

[1] Joseph Holt, of Kentucky, postmaster-general, appointed in 1859 in the place of Brown, deceased.

[2] Assistant Secretary of State Trescot, of South Carolina, says: " General Cass and Judge Black were urgent that the forts should be reinforced." A short while before the President sent his message to Congress, continues Trescot, " Governor Floyd called upon me, evidently much excited. He said that just after dinner the President had sent for him (at the room in the State department, which he occupied while preparing his message); that when he reached him he found General Cass and Judge Black, who retired immediately upon his entrance. The President then informed him that he had determined to reinforce the garrisons in Charleston harbor, upon which a very animated discussion arose. The President finally consented to suspend his decision until General Scott could reach Washington, and he had been telegraphed to come on immediately." Trescot thereupon wrote Governor Gist of South Carolina, Nov. 26, asking him to assure the President that the forts would not be taken unless they were reinforced. Governor Gist replied, Nov. 29, that they probably would not be attacked, and added: "If President Buchanan . . . sends on a reinforcement, the responsibility will rest on him of lighting the torch of discord, which will only be quenched in blood." Trescot saw the President Dec. 2, two days before he sent his message to Congress, and communicated to him the tenor of this letter of Governor Gist. See Trescot's narrative, in Crawford's Genesis of the Civil War, pp. 26, 28, 30, 31, 34. I should have included part of this note in my narrative which led up to the President's message had not Floyd's statement that Buchanan had, in the latter part of November, determined to reinforce the forts seemed inconsistent with the other evidence. Trescot's narrative was written, says Crawford, in Feb., 1861 (see p. 21). In April, 1893, Mr. Trescot kindly showed me the original MS. from which Crawford has so largely cited. It is a straightforward .and truthful story, and in conversation Mr. Trescot assured me that he had no doubt that Floyd represented faithfully the President's determination. If Floyd was exact, it is simply added proof of Buchanan's vacillation.

cited and lawless mob." The President stated that he ought to take all measures possible to protect the lives of Major Anderson and his command. The South Carolina congressmen assured him that the State opposed any decided step before the convention met,[1] and that, unless reinforcements were sent or the existing status in Charleston harbor was in some way altered, there was no danger of an attack on the fort. If either of these things were done, they told the President emphatically, a collision could not, on account of "the excited state of feeling at home," be prevented. "The impression made upon us," relate Miles and Keitt, two of the delegation, "was that the President was wavering, and had not decided what course he would pursue." Pleased, however, that they had called, he desired that the substance of their statement be reduced to writing. Two days later[2] McQueen, Miles, and Bonham called, and gave him a memorandum, signed by themselves and two of their colleagues, which expressed their strong conviction that no attack would be made on the forts, provided the military status should "remain as at present." "I objected to the word 'provided,'" says Buchanan, "as this might be construed into an agreement on my part which I never would make." "We do not so understand it," replied the South Carolinians, and then they repeated what they had said at the first interview. "When we rose to go," relate Miles and Keitt, "the President said in substance: 'After all, this is a matter of honor among gentlemen. I do not know that any paper or writing is necessary. We understand each other.'" Later, McQueen and Bonham went to the White House in behalf of the delegation, and assured the President that, even after the ordinance of secession should be adopted, the forts would not be molested unless the negotiations between the federal government and commissioners appointed to treat for the public property should fail.

---

[1] Dec. 17 was the day appointed for the meeting of the convention.
[2] Dec. 10.

"I informed them," says Buchanan, "that what would be done was a question for Congress, and not for the executive. That, if the forts were assailed, this would put them completely in the wrong, and making them the authors of the civil war."[1]

At last Major Anderson's entreaties received some attention from the War department. Don Carlos Buell, assistant adjutant-general, was sent to Charleston to give him verbal instructions. "The great anxiety of the Secretary of War" to avoid "a collision of the troops with the people" of South Carolina was impressed upon Anderson. On account of his concern to steer clear of a course that would increase the irritation of the public mind, he had not sent reinforcements. Nevertheless, he felt confident that South Carolina would make no violent attempt "to obtain possession of the public works." "But," Buell continued, "as the counsel and acts of rash and impulsive persons may possibly disappoint those expectations of the government, the Secretary of War deems it proper that you should be prepared with instructions to meet so unhappy a contingency. . . .

"You are carefully to avoid every act which would needlessly tend to provoke aggression; and for that reason you are not, without evident and imminent necessity, to take up any position which could be construed into the assumption of a hostile attitude. But you are to hold possession of the forts in this harbor, and, if attacked, you are to defend yourself to the last extremity. The smallness of your force will not permit you, perhaps, to occupy more than one of the three forts, but an attack on or attempt to take pos-

---

[1] My authorities for these interviews are the Statement of Miles and Keitt to the South Carolina convention, Official Records, vol. i. p. 125; the correspondence, late in Dec. and Jan. 1, 1861, between the President and the South Carolina commissioners, ibid., pp. 109, 115, 120; the memorandum of Buchanan endorsed on the letter of the South Carolina congressmen, the endorsement being made soon after the last interview, Life of Buchanan, Curtis, vol. ii. p. 877.

session of any one of them will be regarded as an act of hostility, and you may then put your command into either of them which you may deem most proper to increase its power of resistance. You are also authorized to take similar steps whenever you have tangible evidence of a design to proceed to a hostile act." [1]

These instructions were not seen by the President until ten days later, [2] nor were they known as late as December 28 to General Scott; [3] they were given on the sole authority of Floyd, the Secretary of War. Yet, so long as the government would neither strengthen the garrison nor withdraw the troops, it is difficult to see how the instructions could be improved upon. [4]

Trouble in the cabinet now testified to the difficulty an executive must labor under while endeavoring in a crisis of affairs to pursue a middle and negative course. December 8, Cobb, the Secretary of the Treasury, in some respects the ablest man in the cabinet, but one whose ability did not run in the direction of finance, [5] formally resigned his posi-

---

[1] Fort Moultrie, S. C., Dec. 11, 1860. Memorandum of verbal instructions to Major Anderson, First Artillery, commanding at Fort Moultrie, S. C., D. C. Buell, assistant adjutant-general. Official Records, vol. i. p. 89.

[2] See his letter of Dec. 31, Official Records, vol. i. p. 117.

[3] Letter of Lay to Twiggs, ibid., p. 580.

[4] I cannot agree with the criticism which Nicolay and Hay, vol. ii. p. 388, make of these instructions, but their view and the authorities cited are worthy of careful consideration. As confirming the statement in the text, see Official Records, vol. i. pp. 103, 182.

[5] "The other night, in high glee, Toombs told Cobb in company that he had done more for secession than any other man. He had deprived the enemy of the sinews of war, and left them without a dollar in the treasury. He did not even leave old 'Buck' two quarters to put on his eyes when he died. This is a sore point with Cobb."—Letter of Alexander H. Stephens to his brother, Feb. 17, 1861, Johnston and Browne, p. 386.

Cobb had the Treasury department at an unfortunate time. The panic of 1857 burst upon the country soon after he began its administration, and the political troubles checked the natural recovery which began in 1860. (See p. 56.) Cobb, however, had a high idea of pecuniary honor. He was a good lawyer and a man of property; he owned 1000 slaves. See Memorial of Howell Cobb, Boykin, pp. 47, 98, 221.

tion. "A sense of duty to the State of Georgia," he wrote,[1] makes it improper for me to remain longer in your cabinet Hard upon the resignation of Cobb followed that of Secretary of State Cass. Apprising the President of his determination on December 11, he sent four days later a formal letter confirming his purpose and giving his reasons: which were that the President had refused to reinforce the Charleston forts; to send an armed vessel to aid in defence and in the collection of revenue; and because he had declined to remove the custom-house at Charleston to one of the forts in the harbor, and to make arrangements to compel the payment of duties when the present collector should give up his commission.[2]   On account of the long and honorable public career of Cass, his evident friendliness to the South, and his disposition to mediate whenever the sectional quarrel arose, this resignation caused, as the reasons for it became understood, a profound sensation.   The way it was received at the North would have made plain to President Buchanan, had he been in the mood to comprehend it, how ready were the Republicans in this crisis to take up with a Democratic leader who would stand as a champion for the Union and for the enforcement of the laws.[3]   General Scott

---

[1] See correspondence between Cobb and Buchanan, Washington *Constitution*, Dec. 12.

[2] For the correspondence between Secretary Cass and the President, see Curtis, vol. ii. p. 397.   The Buchanan comment on the resignation is interesting, see p. 399; also Essays and Speeches of J. S. Black, p. 11.   In this connection the remarks of McLaughlin should be read, Life of Cass, p. 337 *et seq.*   Trescot relates: "Not recognizing any right in a State to secede except as a revolutionary measure, General Cass would have resisted the attempt at the commencement, and, as the sworn officer of the United States, he would have done his utmost to preserve its integrity.   'I speak to Cobb,' he would say, 'and he tells me he is a Georgian; to Floyd, and he tells me he is a Virginian; to you, and you tell me you are a Carolinian. I am not a Michigander: I am a citizen of the United States.   The laws of the United States bind you, as they bind me, individually; if you, the citizens of Georgia or Virginia or Carolina, refuse obedience to them, it is my sworn duty to enforce them.'"—The Genesis of the Civil War, Crawford, p. 23.

[3] Washington correspondence New York *Tribune*, Dec. 14; *Tribune* edi-

had been ill most of the time since October 29, when he urged his views upon the President, but now, tortured by anxiety, he rose from his sick-bed in New York and came to Washington to relieve his mind of its burden, even if an old soldier's counsel should be set at naught.   December 13 he saw the Secretary of War and earnestly requested that the garrisons in the southern forts be strengthened, pointing out the organized companies and recruits available for that purpose.   Floyd opposed such a policy, but, at the request of the general, procured for him an interview with the President.   This took place two days later.   Scott argued strenuously for the reinforcement of Fort Moultrie and the sending of troops to Sumter, but Buchanan refused to do either.[1]   On this same December 15 he had a chance partially to repair his former mistakes.   Cass, Generals Scott and Wool, Attorney-General Black, and Joseph Holt, advised a Jacksonian policy.   General Scott, moreover, took especial pains to relate for the behoof of the President how Jackson had met a similar crisis, giving with circumstantial detail the steps that he had taken, and the reasons therefor.[2]   This clearly indicated a plan for Bu-

---

torial, Dec. 15; J. S. Pike to New York *Tribune*, Dec. 19; McLaughlin's Cass, p. 338.

[1] Scott's Autobiography, p. 615; Life of Buchanan, Curtis, vol. ii. p. 365; Buchanan's Defence, p. 175; Scott's letter of March 30, 1861, published in the *National Intelligencer*, Oct. 21, 1862.   Floyd in a speech, Jan. 11, 1861, at a complimentary banquet tendered him at Richmond after his resignation, refers to a time when the President was strongly inclined to send troops to Charleston, and says that he, Davis, Mason, and Hunter by their persuasions caused the project to be abandoned.   Floyd is apparently so oblivious of dates and the sequence of events that I cannot with any satisfaction use this speech as evidence, but the conversation he reports between the President and himself is interesting.   He does not give the date of it, but we may infer that it took place between the interview with the South Carolina congressmen and the visit of General Scott.   For the speech, see New York *Herald*, Jan. 17, 1861, and for a report of most of this conversation, see Nicolay and Hay, vol. ii. p. 394.

[2] This letter of General Scott's is so important that I give it entire: "Lieutenant-General Scott begs the President to pardon him for supplying,

chanan so full of wisdom, so strictly in conformity to law, so well adapted to win the approval of Europe, that, forti fied as he was by the opinion of prudent and trustworthy counsellors, and backed as he would have been by public opinion at the North, the wonder must ever remain that he did not nerve himself for one great effort and make that policy his own. But, with the curious obstinacy which vacillating men occasionally exhibit, no amount of persuasion was at this time sufficient to impel him to the performance of his bounden executive duty. "It is well known," he wrote, December 31, "that it was my determination, and this I freely expressed, not to reinforce the forts in Charleston harbor, and thus produce a collision, until they had been actually attacked, or until I had certain evidence that they were about to be attacked."[1] This feeling induced him on December 21 to modify the instructions which the Sec-

---

in this note, what he omitted to say this morning, at the interview with which he was honored by the President. 1. Long *prior* to the *Force bill* (March 2, 1833), prior to the issue of his proclamation, and, in part, *prior* to the passage of the ordinance of nullification, President Jackson—under the act of March 3, 1807, 'authorizing the employment of the land and naval forces'—caused reinforcements to be sent to Fort Moultrie, and a sloop-of-war (the *Natchez*), with two revenue cutters, to be sent to Charleston Harbor (all under Scott), in order to prevent the seizure of that fort by the nullifiers, and, 2, to insure the execution of the revenue laws. General Scott himself arrived at Charleston the day after the passage of the ordinance of nullification, and many of the additional companies were then en route for the same destination.

"President Jackson familiarly said at the time : 'That, by the assemblage of those forces, for lawful purposes, he was not making war upon South Carolina; but that if South Carolina attacked them, it would be South Carolina that made war upon the United States.'

"General Scott, who received his first instructions (oral) from the President (Jackson) in the temporary absence of the Secretary of War (General Cass), remembers those expressions well.

"Saturday night, Dec. 15, 1860."

Buchanan and Curtis speak of this letter (Defence, p. 179; Curtis, vol. ii. p. 376), and dismiss the wise and prudent advice of Scott by affirming that the times were different.

[1] Official Records, vol. i. p. 117.

retary of War had ten days earlier given Anderson.[1] Just
what were the Southern influences, if any, which now dominated the mind of Buchanan I have not been able to ascertain.[2] I feel quite sure that they did not emanate from his
cabinet. Cobb, whose sway had been potent,[3] had not only
resigned, but had left Washington to persuade his State of
Georgia that secession was the remedy she ought to employ.[4] Thompson, the Secretary of the Interior, not only

---

[1] The President having observed that Major Buell, in reducing to writing
at Fort Moultrie the instructions he had verbally received, required Major
Anderson, in case of attack, to defend himself to the last extremity, immediately caused the Secretary of War to modify this instruction."—Buchanan's Defence, p. 166.

The new order ran thus : " In the verbal instructions communicated to
you by Major Buell, you are directed to hold possession of the forts in the
harbor of Charleston, and, if attacked, to defend yourself to the last extremity. Under these instructions, you might infer that you are required
to make a vain and useless sacrifice of your own life and the lives of the
men under your command, upon a mere point of honor. This is far from
the President's intentions. You are to exercise a sound military discretion
on this subject.

"It is neither expected nor desired that you should expose your own
life or that of your men in a hopeless conflict in defence of these forts. If
they are invested or attacked by a force so superior that resistance would,
in your judgment, be a useless waste of life, it will be your duty to yield
to necessity, and make the best terms in your power. . . . —John B. Floyd."
—Official Records, vol. i. p. 103.

[2] If I felt warranted in following Floyd, I should say that Davis, Mason,
and Hunter still had influence at the White House, see note p. 188 ; see
also Davis's Rise and Fall of the Confederate Government, vol. i. p. 214.
Blaine states that, up to about the last of December, Davis, Toombs, Benjamin, and Slidell were "Buchanan's intimate and confidential advisers,"
Twenty Years of Congress, vol. i. p. 233. Owing to the former personal
and political friendship (see vol. ii. pp. 170, 171), I should be ready to believe this was correct, at any rate as far as Slidell is concerned, were it not
for Buchanan's distinct statement that the intercourse " between the revolutionary senators and the President . . . had been of the coldest character ever since the President's anti-secession message at the commencement of the session of Congress."—Buchanan's letter in the *National Intelligencer*, Nov. 1, 1862.   [3] See vol. ii. p. 280.

[4] Washington despatch to New York *Tribune*, Dec. 13; Memorial of
Howell Cobb, p. 30.

favored the secession of his own State, Mississippi,[1] but he openly went on a mission to win over North Carolina to the cause of disunion;[2] and, while Buchanan shirked from demanding his resignation, we may safely presume that after the middle of December, Thompson's opinion had no such weight with the President as had that of Jeremiah Black. Of all the cabinet officers Floyd's influence was the least.[3] It is more than probable that, as Buchanan had served the South since he lent himself to the scheme of making a slave State out of Kansas,[4] he could not now, owing to his sluggish nature, throw off at once the well-worn habit of that domination, and nothing less than a shock to his dignity by a question of his honor, coming from an accredited Southern source,[5] would enable him to shake himself loose and take the stand demanded by his Northern birth and breeding.

The gloom at the North on account of the President's course was deepened by rumors about his mental condition and moral courage. " The President is pale with fear," said Cass.[6] " Buchanan, it is said," wrote Grimes to his wife, " about equally divides his time between praying and crying. Such a perfect imbecile never held office before."[7]

---

[1] " Jacob Thompson openly avows that he regards the call of Mississippi as more imperative than his duty to the Union."—Leaded editorial, New York *Tribune*, Dec. 17.

[2] Journal of State Convention of Mississippi, p. 186; Clingman's Speeches and Writings, p. 526; Associated Press despatch from Washington of Dec. 17; letter of Secretary Thompson to Governor Ellis of North Carolina, dated Raleigh, N. C., Dec. 20, New York *World*, Dec. 27.

[3] " Certain it is that, during the last six months previous to the 29th Dec., 1860, the day on which Floyd resigned his office, after my request, he exercised less influence on the administration than any other member of the cabinet."—Buchanan's letter of Oct. 28, 1862, in the *National Intelligencer*, Nov. 1, 1862.

[4] See vol. ii. p. 280.

[5] To anticipate : this was furnished by the communication of the South Carolina Commissioners, dated Jan. 1, 1861, Official Records, vol. i. p. 120.

[6] To B. J. Lossing, Dec. 20, Pictorial History of the Civil War, cited in McLaughlin's Cass, p. 339.

[7] Letter of Dec. 16, Life of Grimes, Salter, p. 132.

A report got about that he was insane.[1] Such expressions were natural, and bear witness to the impatience and concern with which the Northern people followed from day to day the course of a policy that seemed an abandonment of a legitimate national authority. But a confidential letter from Buchanan furnishes a denial to all of these statements. "I have never enjoyed better health or a more tranquil spirit than during the past year," he wrote, December 20. "All our troubles have not cost me an hour's sleep or a single meal, though I trust I have a just sense of my high responsibility. I weigh well and prayerfully what course I ought to adopt, and adhere to it steadily, leaving the result to Providence."[2]

December 17, Pickens, the newly elected governor of South Carolina, wrote to the President a request that he should be permitted to take possession of Fort Sumter with a small body of men.[3] This letter was delivered to Buchanan December 20, the same day on which Caleb Cushing, whom he had sent to South Carolina to delay if possible her adoption of an ordinance of secession, reached Charleston. Cushing's errand proved bootless; but his conversation with the governor undoubtedly added weight to the telegram sent to Pickens by two of the South Carolina congressmen and Trescot, suggesting that the demand for Fort Sumter be withdrawn. This was accordingly done.[4]

In that part of the story which centres on the events taking place in Charleston, I had proceeded as far as Decem-

---

[1] See a double-leaded editorial in the New York *Tribune*, Dec. 17.

[2] Curtis, vol. ii. p. 355. "Occasional" (probably J. W. Forney) wrote the Philadelphia *Press:* "Those who pretend to know Buchanan's condition insist that his health was never better, and that during all the troubles he has been instrumental in creating he affects a gay and lightsome deportment."—Cited by the New York *Evening Post*, Dec. 20.

[3] South Carolina House Journal, cited by Nicolay and Hay, vol. iii. p. 2.

[4] Curtis, vol. ii. pp. 368, 383; The Genesis of the Civil War, Crawford, p. 83; Nicolay and Hay, vol. iii. p. 4.

ber 6, the day on which delegates to the South Carolina Convention were chosen. The President's message had been received and weighed.[1] From its positions, declared the Charleston *Mercury*, " we infer that the military power of the United States will not be used by Mr. Buchanan to coerce South Carolina after she goes out of the Union. This bugbear is therefore at an end." [2] The revolution marched on. Interest and expectation were aroused, not as to what the convention would do, for its action was certain, but as to the manner in which it would sever the bonds between the sovereign State and the Federal Union. A lull in public demonstrations might be noted, but there was no turning back. While an ardent desire for peace prevailed, preparation was making for war. Two thousand soldiers were drilling in Charleston ; it was thought South Carolina could put into the field, on short notice, ten thousand.[3] A fear of negro risings increased the tension.[4] Business grew worse. Plantation slaves could be sold for only half what they would have brought before the election of Lincoln.[5] In Charleston the value of all kinds of property except cot-

<hr/>

[1] It was published in full in the Charleston *Mercury* of Dec. 5.

[2] Charleston *Mercury*, Dec. 6.   As I have had frequent occasion to cite this journal as an index of opinion, and as the notion widely prevailed that it only represented the views of certain extremists (this is well stated by the Montgomery correspondent of the Mobile *Register*, cited in the *National Intelligencer* of Feb. 26, 1861 ; see also Trent's Simms), it is proper perhaps that I should say, while it had long been in advance of South Carolina sentiment, that sentiment, by 1860, had caught up with it.   Nov. 9 it spoke of its rapidly increasing subscription list ; Jan. 1, 1861, it asserted it had the largest circulation of any newspaper at the South ; Feb. 18, 1861, it said the circulation had kept gaining until it was impossible to supply the demand.   "We have bought a new Hoe press.   We print more dailies than any newspaper in this part of the South."   The *National Intelligencer* of Feb. 26, 1861, speaks of the *Mercury* as "the traditional organ of that public sentiment which has recently triumphed in South Carolina."

[3] Charleston correspondence of the New York *Tribune*, Dec. 8, 15.

[4] J. W. De Forest, *Atlantic Monthly*, April, 1861, p. 495 ; Charleston correspondence New York *Tribune*, Dec. 22 ; letter of a wife of a South Carolina planter to a relative in New York, New York *Tribune*, Dec. 10.

[5] Ibid.

ton had fallen fifty per cent. ; it was said that the railroads were not paying their running expenses; the hotels were not, as usual, full of strangers from the North, seeking a genial climate or looking after their business interests. Northern merchants could not make collections, and were disinclined to open new accounts.[1] The luxury-loving people of Charleston began making sacrifices of their taste for adornment and their love for display. Economy became the fashion. The patrician ladies bought no new gowns; superb silks were no longer seen. The scions of their rich houses laid aside their dandified suits for soldiers' uniforms, and were proud to carry a musket at the beginning of this war of independence. There were no concerts, no balls, and no weddings.[2] The priests of the Episcopal Church, in the prayer for all in civil authority, omitted the usual supplication for the President of the United States. On the first Sunday that Petigru noted this, he rose from his seat and left the church. The stars and stripes floated over Fort Moultrie, but were nowhere else to be seen; palmetto flags had taken the place of the national ensign.[3]

A new governor of South Carolina was to be elected. The legislature, on whom this duty devolved, began balloting December 11, but did not reach a choice until the seventh ballot, three days later, when Francis W. Pickens received a bare majority of the votes cast.[4] Pickens, a grandson of the general of Revolutionary fame, was a man of distinguished family, a wealthy planter, a classical scholar, and a lawyer of wide culture. Now fifty-five years old, he had, before attaining to the age of forty, served his State ten years in Congress; declining the mission to France offered him by Tyler, and the mission to England tendered him by Polk, he had, under Buchanan, represented his coun-

---

[1] Charleston correspondence New York *Tribune*, Dec. 7.

[2] *Atlantic Monthly*, April, 1861, pp. 490, 496, 502.

[3] Charleston correspondence New York *Tribune*, Dec. 8, 13, 14, 16.

[4] Pickens, 83 ; B. J. Johnson, 64 ; scattering, 16. See Charleston *Mercury*, Dec. 11 to Dec. 15.

try for two years at the court of St. Petersburg, but now, feeling that his talents and his life were due to his State, he had recently returned home to devote himself to her cause. A disciple of Calhoun, a nullifier of 1832, a delegate to the Nashville Convention of 1850, he had nevertheless inclined, upon his return from Russia, to oppose precipitate action on the part of South Carolina; but, carried along with the tide, he had, in a speech at Columbia before the election for governor, set himself in line with the sentiment of his State. The moderates supported him, but this was rather on account of a former feeling and because the extremists voted for Rhett, the owner of the Charleston *Mercury*,[1] than from any existing difference of opinion. For every one was agreed upon immediate secession and on war, should the forts be reinforced. No man could have been chosen who represented better than Pickens the actual sentiment, aim, and genius of South Carolina; and no one of her sons who came to the front in these parlous times showed greater aptitude for the direction of affairs.[2]

Pickens was inaugurated December 17, and in his address he averred that "the *great overt act* of the people of the Northern States" was the election of a chief magistrate "upon issues of malignant hostility and uncompromising war to be waged upon the rights, the interests, and the peace of half the States of this Union. . . . We have now no alternative left but to interpose our sovereign power as an independent State to protect the rights and ancient privileges of the people of South Carolina." Then, after asserting the Calhoun doctrine, and that their interests would impel them

---

[1] This was R. B. Rhett, Sr. He received on the fourth ballot 41 votes, while Pickens received 58, and Johnson 55. His son was then the editor of the Charleston *Mercury*.

[2] See The Genesis of the Civil War, Crawford, p. 79; Charleston "Fire-eating correspondent" of the New York *Evening Post*, Dec. 18; Charleston correspondence New York *Tribune*, Dec. 14; editorial in Charleston *Mercury*, Dec. 15; Diary of Floyd, Life of R. E. Lee, p. 794; editorial in New York *World*, Dec. 20.

to adopt the policy of free trade, he went on : " South Carolina is resolved to assert her separate independence, and, as
she acceded separately to the compact of union, so she will
most assuredly secede separately and alone, be the consequences what they may ; and I think it right to say with
no unkind feeling whatever, that on this point *there can be
no compromise, let it be offered from where it may.* . . . It is
our sincere desire to separate from the States of the North
in peace, and leave them to develop their own civilization
according to their own sense of duty and interest.   But
if, under the guidance of ambition and fanaticism, they decide otherwise, then be it so.   We are prepared for any
event, and, in humble reliance upon that Providence who
presides over the destiny of men and of nations, we will
endeavor to do our duty faithfully, bravely, and honestly." [1]
In his letter of the same day to the President, asking the
possession of Fort Sumter,[2] Governor Pickens showed his
comprehension of the feeling in his State.   " The excitement of the great masses of the people," he declared, " is
great under a sense of deep wrongs." [3]

On the same day that the governor was inaugurated the

---

[1] Charleston *Mercury*, Dec. 18.   There can be no doubt about the sentiment of the State on the reinforcement of the forts.   " Just so soon as
more troops are sent to the forts in Charleston, that moment will the sword
be drawn ; South Carolinians will consider the movement a *casus belli.*"—
Charleston *Courier*, cited in Charleston correspondence New York *Tribune*,
Dec. 8.   " The reinforcement of the forts at this time and under the present circumstances means coercion—war."—Charleston *Mercury*, Dec. 19.
In regard to the fear of an attack on the forts by a mob (*ante*, p. 183 ; see
Captain Foster's letters of Dec. 18, Official Records, vol. i. pp. 96, 97), the
Mercury said, Dec. 19 : " As to the bugaboo of mobbing the forts and slay-
ing the officers and troops, our amiable friends need not excite their phil-
anthropic sensibilities or roll up their eyes.   We are not a mobocracy
here, and believe in law, order, and obedience to authority, civil and military.   No mob will attack the forts.   In South Carolina we do not act by
mobs."

[2] See p. 192.

[3] Letter of Dec. 17, cited in The Genesis of the Civil War, Crawford,
p. 82.

convention met in the new Baptist church at Columbia.
Every member of it was present. A small-pox epidemic
raged in the capital city. Such has been the progress in
sanitary science since that time, that only men whose memories of 1860 are vivid will estimate aright the apprehension
of the delegates as they heard that morning of fourteen new
cases of the virulent and loathsome disease. On account
of the epidemic the convention adjourned, to meet the next
day in Charleston. There in secret session it deliberated.
It was a body worthy of the momentous action about to be
taken. The predominance of white-haired men attracted
the attention of all observers, and nearly all of the delegates had passed life's prime. Among them were many
who had represented South Carolina with ability in the
national Senate and House; five had been governors of
the commonwealth; many members of that dignified judiciary whose title came from legislative election, and whose
places, bearing ample compensation, were of life tenure, had
come forward to lend their guiding hands to their State
when she was on the point of taking a step fraught with
far-reaching consequence. Magrath, who had resigned his
position of United States judge the day after the election
of Lincoln,[1] was a delegate looked to for wise and energetic
counsel; the leading lawyers of the State were present,
while prominent Methodist and Baptist ministers, railroad
presidents, men of business, and influential planters completed the roll of this convention.[2]

Yet the important office of the convention was but to
register the will of the people. Hardly a difference of
opinion existed among South Carolina's citizens; none
manifested itself among their representatives. Only such

---

[1] See p. 116. The resignation of Judge Magrath, said Judge Black to
Crawford, "caused more anxiety to Mr. Buchanan than any other event
that occurred, except Anderson's movement from Moultrie to Sumter."—
The Genesis of the Civil War, p. 16.

[2] For the personnel of the convention more in detail, see Crawford,
p. 46.

delay obtained as was necessary to accomplish this organic act decently and in order. The convention met the fourth day of its session at twelve o'clock in St. Andrew's Hall. Chancellor Inglis, Judge of Chancery, a silver-haired gentleman, a large planter and slave-holder, and a man of parts, reported the ordinance of secession. Explaining that the committee had used the utmost brevity, he read with flashing eyes the burning declaration, " We, the people of the State of South Carolina, in convention assembled, do declare and ordain . . . that the union now subsisting between South Carolina and other States under the name of 'The United States of America' is hereby dissolved." [1] December 20, at a quarter-past one, this ordinance was unanimously passed. [2] It was known in the city that on this day the convention would take decisive action, and an excited throng had gathered about the hall eager for the first announcement of what its representatives, sitting in solemn and secret conclave, had done. Immediately on the declaration of the vote the door-keeper was apprised. He gave the word to the policeman nearest him. It 'was passed from mouth to mouth until it reached the sentinel at the tall iron gate at the entrance, and by him was proclaimed to the impatient crowd. Cheer after cheer rent the air. In less than fifteen minutes the Charleston *Mercury* had issued an extra giving the text of the ordinance, and the news that it had been unanimously adopted; [3] six thousand of these were soon sold, and the whole city knew that South

---

[1] The act was entitled "An Ordinance to dissolve the Union between the State of South Carolina and other States united with her under the compact entitled 'The Constitution of the United States of America.'" The part of it elided in the text is, "and it is hereby declared and ordained that the ordinance adopted by us in convention on May 23, 1788, whereby the Constitution of the United States of America was ratified, and also all acts and parts of acts of the General Assembly of this State ratifying amendments of the said Constitution are hereby repealed."

[2] Yeas 169, nays none.

[3] A fac-simile of this may be found in Nicolay and Hay, vol. iii. p. 14.

Carolina had, as she would wish it expressed, resumed her sovereign powers. The chimes of St. Michael's pealed an exultant note; the bells of all the other churches were loudly rung. The gun by the post-office, christened "Old Secession," and on which a copy of the ordinance had been pasted, belched forth the thunder of celebration; the cannon in the citadel echoed the glad tidings. Houses and shops were emptied; the streets were full of people. The cares of business and of family were forgotten; all faces wore smiles; all as they walked seemed to tread in air; joy was unconfined. Old men ran shouting down the streets. When friend met friend there was the hearty grasp of the hand as one said, "Thank God, they have put her out at last!" and as the other replied, "I breathe free now." Then they congratulated one another on the change of weather. For three days the sky had frowned and poured down rain. On this December 20 the sun had risen full and clear, and it pleased these men to say that Heaven smiled on their action. Volunteers donned their uniforms and hastened to their armories. New palmetto flags everywhere appeared. Every one wore a blue cockade in his hat. Great enthusiasm was shown at the unfurling of a banner on which blocks of stone in an arch typified the fifteen Southern States; these were surmounted by the statue of Calhoun with the Constitution in his hand, and the figures of Faith and Hope; at the base of the arch were blocks broken in fragments representing the Northern States. A scroll interpreted the allegory: a "Southern republic" was "built from the ruins" of the other half of the country. The sentiment of the community was shared by the boys firing noisy crackers, and, as it grew dark, Roman-candles — a spontaneous testimony to the general joy. That day the patricians of Charleston drank champagne with their dinners.

It was decided to make the signing of the ordinance an impressive public ceremony. The governor and the legislature, who had followed the convention to Charleston, were invited to assist in the proceedings that evening. At half-past six the members of the convention came together at the place of their deliberations, and, forming in files of two with locked arms, they marched silently, lighted by the flare of bonfires, to Institute Hall, which had been selected because it was the largest assembly-room in the city. At the foot of the staircase they were joined by the State senators and representatives. The hall was packed with spectators. The galleries were filled with ladies, dressed with what elegance the last year's wardrobe afforded. But dearer now to the Southern heart than trappings and show were the bright eyes and interested, encouraging looks of those women, who little recked that they were then beginning a course of devotion and heroism which has justly won the admiration of the world. On the floor the brilliant uniforms of the officers of the new-born army made a picturesque and suggestive contrast to the conventional broadcloth of the Carolina gentlemen.

The audience had not long to wait. The cry, " The convention is coming !" drew every one's regard. Its president, leaning on the arm of the clerk, entered by a door in the rear of the hall and took his place upon the rostrum. Following him came the President of the Senate and the Speaker of the House clad in their robes of office, with the clerks of both bodies in their black silken gowns. The delegates, the senators, and the representatives made their entrance by another door and took the reserved places in the body of the hall. A clergyman with bowed form and hair as white as snow advanced to the front of the platform with upraised hands, the whole assembly rising to their feet in reverent attitude while he invoked the blessing and favor of Almighty God on this great act of his people about to be consummated. The president of the convention, holding in his hand the parchment with the great seal of the State, read slowly and solemnly therefrom the Ordinance of Secession. As the last word " dissolved " left his lips the audience broke forth into cheers and shouts and roars that lasted until physical exhaustion made silence a necessity. The delegates sat grave and silent. They were now asked by the president to step forward and sign the ordinance. This ceremony took two hours, but the audience remained to witness it. When R. B. Rhett, who had been a disunionist since 1832, advanced to the rostrum, there were thunders of applause; cheers greeted Delegate Spratt, whose vehement advocacy of the reopening of the African slave-trade singled him out for notice; and ex-Governor Gist, who had been the official mouth-piece of the beginning of this secession movement, also inspired demonstrations of popular favor. To many of the people looking on there must have come the thought of that other signing of a Declaration of Independence, of that new era ushered in July 4, 1776; and their feeling grew stronger that now was beginning a second glorious revolution, which, if successful, would, on account of a securer basis, be more lasting.[1]

Those who knew that Caleb Cushing, now regarded as the envoy of a foreign power, had been solicited by a committee of the legislature to attend this ceremony,[2] might have imagined a likeness between this invitation and the request for assistance which another representative body— the French National Assembly of 1789—had preferred to Jefferson; and prophetic souls, to whom came the picture of the greatest of revolutions, must have seen beyond this present pledging of faiths an era of blood. It cannot but have occurred to all that in this very hall, eight months before, had been played the first act of the drama of secession, when the delegates from the cotton States withdrew from the national Democratic convention.[3]

When all the signatures had been affixed to the instru-

---

[1] Struck with the resemblance, it was said that a committee of the convention endeavored to borrow for this occasion, from a lady of Charleston, the table on which the immortal paper, drawn by Jefferson, had been signed ; but the lady told these gentlemen that rather than have it used for the Ordinance of Secession she would burn the table to ashes.

[2] Of course, Cushing declined the invitation.

[3] See vol. ii. p. 451.

ment¹ the president said, " I proclaim the State of South
Carolina an independent commonwealth." And then the
enthusiasm and the joy knew no bounds. Such cries of
exultation, such shouts of gladness had never before been
heard in Charleston. The scene in the streets was impressive, the avenues to the hall being filled with an ardent
throng. Military companies marched and countermarched
to the strains of martial music. The hurrahs above were
taken up by the crowd below. Before the response to the
cheers over the final declaration of the president had died
away, the clerk of the convention mounted a chair in the
streets and, holding aloft the parchment, besought silence.
When he had finished reading the ordinance to the people
wild gladness reigned. Bonfires were lighted; pistols and
fireworks were shot off. The liberty-pole at the head of
Hayne Street was brilliantly illuminated. Patricians and

---

¹ In the Athenæum in Boston is a fac-simile of the Ordinance of Secession, signed; also an illuminated broadside published at the time, headed :

1776   1860

DECLARATION OF INDEPENDENCE

IN CONVENTION, AT THE CITY OF CHARLESTON, DECEMBER 20, 1860

OF THE STATE OF   SOUTH CAROLINA

AN ORDINANCE

To dissolve the Union between the State of South Carolina and
other States united with her under the compact entitled the
" Constitution of the United States of America."

We, the People of the State of South Carolina, in Convention assembled,
do declare and ordain, and it is hereby declared and ordained

(Here follows the Ordinance of Secession, with signatures.)

plebeians, planters and poor whites of the country, rich merchants and laborers of the city mingled in a common throng and blended their voices in hailing the new era of independence. With truth could an organ of public opinion two days later say, " The most impressive feature in the action of South Carolina is the concentrated unanimity of her people." [1]

Four days after the passage of the ordinance a decent respect to the opinions of mankind prompted the convention to adopt a " Declaration of the immediate causes which induce and justify the secession of South Carolina from the Federal Union," and to publish it to the world. This Declaration recited the history of the colonial struggle for self-government, of the league known as the Articles of Confederation, and of the adoption of the Constitution to show that the States were sovereign and that the country's organic instrument was a compact between them. By the Personal Liberty acts the non-slaveholding States had deliberately broken the constitutional compact, "and the consequence follows that South Carolina is released from her obligation." The debate in the convention on the Declaration showed that while all were at one regarding the legal right of secession, this grievance touching the infraction of the Fugitive Slave law was but a lawyer's plea. But the hearts of all South Carolinians beat in unison with the writer of the Declaration when he spoke of the injustice of the North in excluding the South from the common territory, and when he affirmed in bitter complaint that the Northern States "have denounced as sinful the institution of slavery," and elected a man for President " because he has declared that 'this government cannot endure permanently half slave and half free.'" On the same day that

---

[1] Charleston *Mercury*. My authorities for this description are : Journal of the South Carolina Convention, Charleston, 1861; Columbia and Charleston correspondence New York *World;* Charleston *Mercury;* " Fire-eating correspondent" New York *Evening Post* from Charleston ; Crawford's The Genesis of the Civil War.

this declaration was adopted the convention voted an Address to the people of the slave-holding States. The Address drew an ingenious comparison between their present position and that of their ancestors in the colonies towards Great Britain ; it declared that " all confidence in the North is lost in the South ;" it asserted State sovereignty ; it closed with what the South deemed an adequate defence of slavery, and a generous and pathetic appeal to their sisters " to join us in forming a confederacy of slave-holding States." It was a franker paper than the Declaration. Yet one part of it was much criticised in the convention, and it was indeed an uncandid plea when, in the list of grievances, the North was charged with gross injustice for the tariff legislation of the country. As a matter of fact, both the senators and all the representatives of South Carolina had voted for the existing tariff of 1857 ; and since 1846 the United States had practically enjoyed a revenue tariff and one of a lower scale of duties than had been in force since 1816.[1] But the Address was drawn up by R. B. Rhett, a rigid doctrinaire and a disciple of Calhoun, and he maintained that since 1832, when the cause of the trouble was avowedly the revenue policy of the government, South Carolina had suffered, without interruption, a grievous wrong. Yet there was method in his adherence to a one-sided theory, and in his speech in convention defending the Address he argued truly that to get the confidence and sympathy of England, France, and Germany, it was wiser to go to the world with a protest against a high protective tariff than with a protest against the non-execution of the Fugitive Slave law.[2]

---

[1] See chap. xii.

[2] For the Declaration and Address, see Appendix to the Journal of the South Carolina Convention, pp. 325, 340. I would urge students of history to read both of these papers. The Declaration is printed in Moore's Rebellion Record, vol. i. Docs., p. 3, and in McPherson's Political History, p.15. McPherson also prints the Address, p. 12, and gives the debate in the convention, p. 16. The Declaration and the Address were published in the New York *Tribune*, Dec. 27. The Declaration, the Address, and the debate are published in the Charleston *Mercury* of Dec. 22 and 25. A mo-

Whether doctrinarianism or crafty policy predominated in
the mind of Rhett, the complaint of the tariff was inconsistent then, and became more inconsistent later when the
Southern Confederacy enacted the United States revenue
laws of 1857, and South Carolina consented to that policy
by her ratification of the provisional Constitution.[1]

Neither the Declaration nor the Address was equal to the
occasion ; nor were they worthy of a convention which had
at its disposal so much real ability and valuable public experience. An impartial observer must conclude that they
do not make out a case to justify setting on foot a revolution.[2] South Carolina's manifesto, owing in some degree to
the difference of theoretical opinion which displayed itself
when her sons came to set down the reasons for secession,
seems weak beside her action. In practice, those sons fully
agreed; in theory, they differed ; and this difference cropped
out when Rhett, a nullifier of 1832, prepared one paper,
and Memminger, a Unionist of 1832, reported another. A
consideration of these papers is, moreover, instructive, in
that it evidences how difficult it is for enlightened men to
formulate a justification of a cause which the rest of the
civilized world condemns. One point is common to the
Declaration and the Address, and of all reasons given for
secession it is the most significant. The convention asserted in both of these manifestoes that the Northern States
had violated the Constitution ; that they had not respected
its limitations, but had construed it in their own selfish
interests. There can be no doubt that every member of
that convention sincerely believed those assertions ; and if

---

tion to lay the Declaration on the table was defeated. Ayes 31, nays 124.
Journal of the Convention, p. 82.

[1] The vote on the ratification was 138 to 21. The Charleston *Mercury*
made a protest against the tariff legislation (see editorial of Feb. 12, 1861);
and there was some objection in the convention (see Journal, p. 227).

[2] See Alexander Stephens's caustic remarks on the Address. Private
letter to his brother, Johnston and Browne, p. 375. Stephens's argument
against secession is unanswerable.

we would understand the devotion of the South to what it called a sacred principle for the four years of the Civil War, this honest belief must be borne in mind.

The adoption of the ordinance of secession by South Carolina produced a profound impression at the North. While such action had been expected, there was hoping against hope that something might turn up to prevent it. In Baltimore the feeling was painful.[1] At some places in Virginia there were demonstrations of joy.[2] In the cotton States much enthusiasm characterized the reception of the news and satisfaction prevailed.[3] A particular interest centred on New Orleans, for the reason that Louisiana and Texas were comparatively tardy in the secession movement. The intelligence came there in the evening. An actor announced it from the stage of the Varieties Theatre. Wild enthusiasm prevailed; the play could not go on. The audience, after venting its glee in the theatre, rushed into the street and assisted at an impromptu meeting, at which the Marseillaise was played, zealous speeches in favor of the secession of Louisiana were delivered, and a bust of Calhoun, decked with the cockade, was exhibited.[4]

Public sentiment in the other cotton States[5] decidedly favored following South Carolina in the policy of secession, unless their grievances were redressed by the North.[6] Be-

---

[1] Baltimore *Daily Exchange*, Dec. 22.

[2] At Richmond, Norfolk, and Portsmouth, New York *World*, New York *Tribune*, Dec. 22.   [3] Ibid., Charleston *Mercury*, Dec. 21.

[4] Charleston *Mercury*, New York *Tribune*, Dec. 22.

[5] I include in the term cotton States, South Carolina, Georgia, Florida, Alabama, Mississippi, Louisiana, and Texas. This classification is not scientific, but I know of no better way to designate the seven States that first seceded. Between them the political sympathy was so close that it is at times necessary to speak of them as one community.

[6] The best evidence of this is that five conventions elected by the popular vote passed ordinances of secession in January, and Texas did likewise early in February. But trying for the moment to eliminate "this knowledge of the end," which Sir Arthur Helps put down as "one of the most dangerous pitfalls which beset the writers of history," I made a study of public opinion in the cotton States as it might be gathered from their news-

tween November 18 and December 11, conventions to consider a line of action in the present crisis had been called in all of them except Texas, whose Governor, Samuel Houston, a sturdy Union man, for a while blocked the movement. It will advantage us to consider somewhat in detail the course of opinion in Georgia, for the reason that she was the empire State of the South, and on her action depended whether the government of the Confederate States should be formed; and further for the reason that while the so-called Union party was possibly no stronger than in Alabama and Louisiana, it made in Georgia a better fight against secession. This contest has for us a particular interest in that it was prosecuted under the leadership of one of the truly representative men of the South, Alexander H.

---

papers, and those of the border and Northern States of November and December, fortifying these authorities with a careful reference to the other political literature of the time; and the conclusion I arrived at, which I have stated in the text, seems to me beyond dispute. As it is an important fact that this might have been appreciated while the Senate committee of thirteen was considering the Crittenden Compromise, I quote from two acute judges of popular feeling. " The disunion sentiment is paramount in at least seven States."—Thurlow Weed in his famous article of Nov. 30. " The secession of South Carolina, which must be looked upon now as an accomplished fact, will *inevitably* very soon be followed by the secession of all the cotton States . . . unless prompt and energetic measures are taken by the leading men of the North. . . . At this moment the patriotic men in the Gulf States are using every effort in order to bring about a joint convention. In this they are violently opposed by the disunionists, who are for immediate and separate action. The latter are undoubtedly in the ascendency."— Letter of August Belmont to Governor Sprague of Rhode Island, Dec. 6. Letters of August Belmont privately printed, p. 12. " The secession movement of the South has lost all the character of bluster and threat, which our Northern friends supposed too long was its principal element. The most conservative men have joined in it, right or wrong; they feel that their institutions and property are not any longer safe with the Union, and that self-preservation commands action before the Federal power passes into hands which they take for granted are hostile to their section. They do not threaten, but they want to be allowed to go out peaceably. The great majority are for immediate action, but the Union men are striving to postpone secession if possible until the 4th of March."—Belmont to Sprague, Dec. 13, ibid., p. 14.

Stephens. Yet the story of his career is not that of the typical Southerner who in those days reached political eminence. Although of good family, he was born to poverty, and his life from the age of six to fifteen was that of many a New England country lad. He did the chores of the farm and of the house, tended the younger children, fed the loom, was general errand-boy, and planted and ploughed the corn. The duties that were put upon him he discharged conscientiously. Of play he had none, of schooling in early life but little. At fifteen he had had perhaps in all two years of school; he could read well, could spell almost every word in Webster's spelling-book, and in arithmetic had advanced as far as the rule of three. At that time becoming an orphan by the death of his father, his deep religious convictions and habitual melancholy attracted the attention of some good and pious men who, thinking they saw in him the material of a Christian preacher, assisted him to a school and college education. But he chose the profession of law, at twenty-two was admitted to the bar, and in six years became one of the ablest lawyers of Georgia. Serving an apprenticeship in the legislature of his State, he was in 1843 sent to the national House of Representatives, and was continually re-elected until 1859, when, having served sixteen years, and reached the age of forty-seven, he voluntarily retired. He had a small and slender frame, weighing eighty-four pounds when he began the practice of law, and ninety-two pounds at the age of forty-eight. This diminutive physique, combined with youthful appearance, told against him in the struggle of life. In the first canvass he made for Congress the Whigs frequently mistook their candidate for a mere stripling, but his effective manner of speaking and his thorough knowledge of his subject soon dispelled the illusion. Frail and sickly from his birth, in manhood he became a victim to dyspepsia, and often brought to his labor an aching head and a body tormented by pain. Wonder might indeed be ours at the place he fills in his country's history, did we not remember

that much of the world's conspicuous work has been done
by men whose brains throbbed with distress, and whose
bodies were on the rack. The faith of the boy developed in
the man into deep-souled piety and a godly walk. Yet he
was given to morbid introspection, and took of human affairs a gloomy view; his thoughts, sometimes tinged with
superstition, and at other times with the moralizing of the
melancholy Jaques, dwelt constantly on the brevity of life.
Such feelings were heightened by his lack of companion-
ship, for until he had reached the age of twenty-four, when
began his warm and lasting friendship with Toombs, he
had not a sympathetic associate, and he never married. No
Puritan was more austere. The first time he saw the waltz
he wrote, " Oh, the follies of man, and how foolish are some
of his ways!" A witness to the coquetry of a handsome
young woman, he exclaims, " Alas the world!" [1] and with
the purity of thought and sensitiveness of soul of a girl
he shrunk from obscenity. Yet in physical courage he was
a true Southerner. Twice, at least, he was eager to fight a
duel; on one occasion, in an affray, the gleaming blade of
his adversary's knife descending towards his throat failed
to extort a word of retraction. Apparently free from any
desire to make money, he was economical, yet kind-hearted
and generous. In his Georgia home he dispensed an open
and frank hospitality after the fashion of his peers. As
early as 1834 Stephens had arrived at the conviction of the
sovereignty of the States and the right of secession. In the
troubles of 1850 he was a prominent figure, ardently upholding the rights of the South.[2] "I tell you," he then
wrote his brother, " the argument is exhausted. . . . *We
have ultimately to submit or fight.*" [3]

---

[1] Johnston and Browne, pp. 86, 95.   [2] See vol. i.
[3] Jan. 21, 1850, Johnston and Browne, p. 245. This characterization I
have drawn mainly from their admirable biography of Stephens. Some
touches I have derived from Cleveland's Stephens, from his sketch in
Appleton's Cyclopædia of American Biography, and from Stephens's The
War Between the States.

Such was the man who, flinging popularity to the winds, now emerged from his retirement in an endeavor to stem the tide which in his State was setting towards secession. His description of the irrepressible conflict, given in answer to the inquiry of a friend why he had withdrawn from public life, shows that he had long been alive to the danger against which the country was running. "When," he said, "I am on one of two trains coming in opposite directions on a single track, both engines at high speed, and both engineers drunk, I get off at the first station."[1] Inconsistencies there had been in the public utterances of Stephens, but no one doubted his sincerity or his devotion to principle. An expression in a private letter, when he was urged to correct a misconception in the public mind about a personal matter, manifests a noble self-assurance that came from treading in a straightforward course. " So I am right with myself," he wrote, " I care but little for the opinions of others." [2] It would be difficult, perhaps impossible, to name another man who had such respect from all sections of the country as Alexander H. Stephens at this time enjoyed. His speech, therefore, of November 14 before the legislature of Georgia attracted immense attention.[3] He did not deem the election of Lincoln a sufficient reason for secession, nor did he believe that the Southern people had been "entirely blameless." Lincoln would be "powerless to do any great mischief;" the Senate and the House were against him. The revenue policy of the national government was no reason for secession. "The present tariff," he declared, " was voted for by Massachusetts and South Carolina. The lion and the lamb lay down together." The only tangible present grievance that the South had was the Personal Liberty acts of certain Northern States, which aimed at nullifying the Fugitive Slave law ; but redress for this should first be demanded in the Union. He earnestly asked for delay ; he

---

[1] Johnston and Browne, p. 353; see also vol. ii, pp. 453, 490.
[2] Johnston and Browne, p. 354.
[3] Ibid., pp. 368, 369; *ante*, pp. 147, 179.

advised that all other means should be exhausted before trying the remedy of secession; and he suggested a conference with all the other Southern States.[1]

From the point of view of a man who believed that a State had the right to withdraw from the Union and who was in full sympathy with the South, this speech was an irrefragable argument against the expediency of immediate secession. Had cogent reasoning and policy prevailed with the Georgia people, they would have put themselves under the guidance of Stephens instead of yielding to the impulse of that disunion sentiment which, beginning at least as early as 1849, had, since the formation of the Republican party, been waxing strong. The dominant feeling found fit and able leaders in Toombs and Governor Brown. The night before Stephens's celebrated speech, Toombs had addressed the legislature, urging immediate secession.[2] November 18 the legislature unanimously passed the bill calling a convention, and fixed upon January 2, 1861, as the day for the election of delegates. A spirited canvass ensued. Stephens, his brother, and others exerted themselves to get men chosen who would favor co-operation with the other slave States, a policy that meant delay. This programme provided for a conference with the border as well as with the cotton States,[3] and fifty-two members of the legislature united in an address to the conventions of South Carolina,[4] Alabama, Mississippi, and Florida, asking them to defer final State action until a general convention of the Southern

---

[1] I would urge the historical student to read this speech. Most of it is printed in The War Between the States, vol. ii. p. 279; it may also be found in Johnston and Browne, p. 580, and Cleveland's Letters and Speeches, p. 694. The speech was published in the New York *Tribune* of Nov. 23.

[2] Stephens's War Between the States, vol. ii. p. 234.

[3] See letter of Linton Stephens, Nov. 29, which Alexander H. Stephens says represented the prevailing views of the Co-operationists, ibid., p. 317.

[4] See report of De Saussure explaining why the request could not be complied with, Journal of South Carolina Convention, Appendix, p. 345.

States could be held.[1]   Alexander H. Stephens, however,
had little hope of success.   November 30 he wrote George
Ticknor Curtis that he feared Georgia, Alabama, Florida,
and Mississippi would follow the example of South Carolina
and secede.   Speaking for his own State he said, " There
are a large number of people who will sustain my position;
but I feel that the odds are against us."[2]   His speech had
brought him letters from many parts of the country, all
but one of which showed a yearning for the preservation of
the Union;[3] that speech had, as we have seen, formed Lincoln's motive for opening a correspondence with him;[4] and
it made him the focus of the sentiment in Georgia which
favored delay.   In spite of the effort to restrain the people
of his State, and in spite of the words of encouragement
that came to him from the border States and the North, he
was in despair.   "I fear," he wrote December 3, "it will
all come to nought; that it is too late to do anything; that
the people are run mad.   They are wild with passion and
frenzy, doing they know not what."[5]

Immediately after his resignation of the Treasury Department, Howell Cobb issued an address in which he declared
that there was "no other remedy for the existing state of
things but immediate secession."[6]   But the dominant sentiment of Georgia needed no fostering from the leaders who
had been her representatives in the national arena.   The

---

[1] This address was issued from a meeting held Dec. 14.   See *National Intelligencer*, Dec. 22; New York *Tribune*, Dec. 21.

[2] Cleveland, p. 159.   The same day he wrote confidentially to his brother: "I am daily becoming more and more confirmed in the opinion that
all efforts to save the Union will be unavailing.   The truth is, our leaders
and public men who have taken hold of this question do not desire to continue it on any terms.   They do not wish any redress of wrongs; they are
disunionists *per se*, and avail themselves of present circumstances to press
their objects; and my present conviction is that they will carry the State
with them by a large majority."—Johnston and Browne, p. 369.

[3] Ibid.   [4] *Ante.*   [5] Johnston and Browne, p. 370.

[6] Howell Cobb Memorial Volume, p. 32; see also synopsis of his speech
at Macon, Augusta correspondence New York *Tribune*, Dec. 21.

middle of December Toombs wrote a public letter, in which, after reciting that " upon the questions that we have wrongs and that we intend to redress them by and through the sovereignty of Georgia, the State is unanimous," and that all look to " separation from the wrong-doers as the ultimate remedy," he said that the only difference of opinion which came to the surface was in regard to the time at which secession should be decreed.   To immediate action or indefinite postponement he was equally opposed; but he did favor secession on the 4th day of March, 1861.   Yet he went on to say : " *I certainly would yield that point to correct and honest men who were with me in principle*, but who are more hopeful of redress from the aggressors than I am, especially if any such active measures should be taken by the wrongdoers as promised to give us redress *in the Union*." [1]   This letter was not well received by the precipitators.[2]   The minute-men in Augusta, wrote Stephens, " are in a rage at Toombs's letter.   They say that he has backed down, that they intend to vote him a *tin* sword.   They call him a traitor. . . . I see that some of the secession papers have given him a severe railing."   The fire-eaters are generally discussing the letter, " saying that they never had any confidence in him or Cobb either. . . . These are," moralized Stephens, " but the indications of the fury of popular opinion when it once gets thoroughly aroused.   Those who sow the wind will reap the whirlwind." [3]   By December 23 Toombs had changed his tone.   This was, without doubt, partly owing to the action upon him of the public sentiment of his State, and to the hearty acclaim with which the secession of South Carolina had been received in the cotton States ; but the occasion which prompted his emphatic telegraphic despatch to Georgia — the rejection the day before of the Crittenden

---

[1] This letter was published in the Savannah *Republican* of Dec. 17, cited in the New York *Tribune*, Dec. 21.

[2] Letter of Stephens, Dec. 22, to R. M. Johnston, Johnston and Browne, p. 370 ; Macon, Ga., correspondence New York *Tribune*, Dec. 20.

[3] Letter to Linton Stephens, Dec. 22, Johnston and Browne, p. 370.

Compromise by the Republican members of the committee of thirteen — had much to do with it. " I tell you,"
he declared, " upon the faith of a true man, that all further
looking to the North for security for your constitutional
rights ought to be instantly abandoned. . . . Secession by
the 4th day of March next should be thundered from the ballot-box by the unanimous voice of Georgia on the 2d day
of January next." [1]

There were at this time in the border slave States of
Virginia, Maryland, Kentucky, and Missouri unconditional
secessionists and unconditional Union men ; but the great
body of the people, although believing that the wrongs of
the South were grievous and cried for redress, deemed secession inexpedient ; they thought that South Carolina had
been precipitate, and that the other cotton States, in making
preparation to follow her, were unwise.   In this mass of
public sentiment shades of difference existed.   Those who
leaned to the South were emphatic in asserting the right of
secession ; those who leaned to the North were ardent in
professing their attachment to the Union.   All denied either
the right or the feasibility of coercion ; all thought that the
troubles were susceptible of a peaceful settlement.   Again,
differences obtained among these States and in different
parts of the same State concerning the strength of the Union
and secession sentiments and the bias towards the South or
the North ; but in all of them the Crittenden Compromise
would have commanded a large majority, and its adoption
would almost universally have given heartfelt satisfaction.
North Carolina, Tennessee, and Arkansas partook more of
the feeling of these communities than of the feeling which
was carrying everything before it in the cotton States. [2]

---

[1] This telegram of Dec. 23 is printed in Greeley's American Conflict,
vol. i. p. 384 ; it was published in the Charleston *Mercury* of Dec. 24 and
presumably in all of the Southern newspapers.

[2] See editorial in Richmond *Enquirer*, Nov. 16 ; public letters of ex-Governor Wise (Nov. 19), H. L. Hopkins (Nov. 22), Senator Mason (Nov. 23),
published in Richmond *Enquirer* of Nov. 30, also editorial of Dec. 25 ;

At the first session held after the adoption of the ordinance of secession by South Carolina, the national House
of Representatives received a communication from her congressmen formally dissolving their connection with that
" honorable body." [1]   December 22 the South Carolina Convention elected by ballot three commissioners, Robert W.
Barnwell, James H. Adams, and James L. Orr, who were
sent forthwith to Washington, " empowered to treat with
the government of the United States for the delivery of the
forts, magazines, light - houses, and other real estate . . .
within the limits of South Carolina."   The convention proceeded on the theory that the partnership known as the
Union was now dissolved by the withdrawal of one of its
members; that while the real estate on which the public
works had been erected reverted to the sovereign State, the
works themselves, having been constructed at the common
cost, should be paid for by the retiring partner.   It was
also a logical sequence from this hypothesis that an ac-
counting should be had, to determine South Carolina's share
of the public debt and her share of the assets, " held
by the government of the United States as agent of the
confederated States, of which South Carolina was recently
a member."   Then a balance should be struck, and if the
value of the property which South Carolina took within
her boundaries was greater than her credit on the books of
the concern, she would pay the difference in money. [2]   The

---

Baltimore *Daily Exchange*, Nov. 12, Dec. 1, 10, and 12 ; New York *Trib-
une*, Nov. and Dec., especially the citations from the press of the border
States ; Letters and Times of the Tylers, vol. ii. p. 574 *et seq.; * Shaler's
Kentucky, chap. xv. ; Carr's Missouri, chap. xiii.

[1] This was Dec. 24.   The letter was dated Dec. 21, and signed by but
four of the members, McQueen, Bonham, Boyce, Ashmore, *Congressional
Globe*, p. 190.

[2] See the credentials of the commissioners, Official Records, vol. i. p. 111 ;
for this theory well stated see Rise and Fall of the Confederate Government, Davis, vol. i. p. 209; also letter to the President of Isaac W. Hayne,
Attorney - General of South Carolina and special envoy, Jan. 31, 1861,
House Committee Report No. 91, p. 66.

commissioners arrived at Washington the afternoon of December 26, and the next day they received the startling intelligence that Major Anderson had secretly removed his force
to Fort Sumter, had dismantled Fort Moultrie, spiked the
cannon, burned the gun-carriages, and cut down the flag-staff.

Anderson had chafed at the difficulties of his position.
The responsibility which the President should have assumed
was thrust upon a major of the army, who had been enjoined not to irritate the people of Charleston, and yet had
been directed to hold possession of the forts in the harbor,
which of itself was a constant and increasing source of irritation. It was, moreover, apparent that a single misstep on
his part might lead to the shedding of blood and the commencement of civil war; and no army officer ever had a
keener sense of a soldier's duty or felt a more loyal devotion
to his flag than Anderson. He soon saw that Sumter was
a better coign of vantage than Moultrie, and that the possession of it by the Charlestonians would make his own position untenable.[1] The expression of a desire for Fort Moultrie, which had been frequent in Charleston since the State
began making ready for secession, developed after the passage of the ordinance into an utterance of threats to take
it.[2] Anderson kept himself well informed of the public
feeling and of the probability of its taking shape in official
action, and when the commissioners departed, December 24,
for Washington, he became convinced that if they were not
successful in their negotiations, an attack on him would be
made.[3] He was equally convinced that Fort Moultrie was a

---

[1] Anderson to Cooper, Nov. 28, Dec. 9, 22, Official Records, vol. i. pp. 79,
89, 105. In Sumter at this time there was a gang of workmen under the
charge of Captain Foster of the Engineers engaged in completing and
strengthening the work.

[2] Anderson to Cooper, Dec. 6, Official Records, vol. i. p. 87; see also Foster
to De Russy, Dec. 18, ibid., p. 96; Crawford's The Genesis of the Civil
War, p. 100; Charleston correspondence New York Tribune, Dec. 11, 22.

[3] Anderson to Cooper, Dec. 22, Official Records, vol. i. p. 105; Charleston
correspondence New York Tribune, Dec. 22; Crawford, p. 101.

position he could not defend.[1] This, indeed, had been the
subject of his daily and nightly thoughts ever since he came
into command, and he had determined to make the removal
several days before it was actually accomplished.[2] Taking
counsel with no one, and intrusting the secret only to the
officers under him when it became necessary to do so for
the execution of his plan, he decided to transfer his force to
Sumter the evening of December 26. He had carefully and
prudently worked out all the details of his project, and, no
suspicion of it being excited in Charleston, he executed
it without any interference.[3] When Charleston woke up
the next morning and looked out on the bay, it saw, instead of the stars and stripes waving over Moultrie, a cloud
of smoke hanging about it, indicating that some strange
event had happened. When the truth became known, the
city was filled with excitement, indignation, and rage.[4] The
convention went into secret session. Governor Pickens
acted with promptness.

The South Carolina congressmen, in their interview with
Buchanan early in December,[5] understood him to pledge
himself that the military status in Charleston harbor should

---

[1] "When I inform you that my garrison consists of only sixty effective
men, that we are in a very indefensible work, the walls of which are only
about fourteen feet high, and that we have within 100 yards of our walls
sand-hills which command our work, and which afford admirable sites for
their batteries and the finest covers for sharp-shooters, and that besides this
there are numerous houses, some of them within pistol-shot—you will at once
see that if attacked in force, headed by any one not a simpleton, there is
scarcely a probability of our being able to hold out long enough to enable
our friends to come to our succor."—Private letter of Anderson published in Richmond *Whig*, Dec. 24, cited by Crawford, p. 100 ; see also
Anderson's letter, ibid., p. 70 ; Anderson to Cooper, Nov. 28, Dec. 1, 6,
Official Records, vol. i. pp. 78, 81, 87, Cooper to Anderson, Dec. 14, ibid.,
p. 92.
[2] See letter to his wife, cited by Nicolay and Hay, vol. iii. p. 47, note.
[3] See Crawford, p. 102 *et seq.;* Doubleday's Sumter and Moultrie, p. 59
et seq.
[4] Charleston *Mercury*, Dec. 28 ; Charleston correspondence New York
Tribune. Dec. 27; Crawford, p. 108.   *Ante*, p. 182.

not be changed without giving them due notice.[1] From this
and from quasi-negotiations carried on between Gist and the
President through the intermediary of Trescot,[2] then Assistant Secretary of State and afterwards agent of South Carolina, Pickens believed that Buchanan had promised to maintain the situation unchanged until the commissioners should
arrive at Washington to treat for the possession of the forts
and other property of the United States.[3] Indignant at
what he considered a violation of this agreement, he sent
Colonel Pettigrew to Sumter to recite the understanding to
Anderson and to demand " courteously but peremptorily "
that he should return to Fort Moultrie.   Anderson replied :
I knew nothing of an agreement between the President and
the governor.   My position was threatened every night by
the troops of the State.   One hundred riflemen on the sand-
hills which commanded the fort would make it impossible
for my men to serve their guns.   " To prevent this I removed
on my own responsibility, my sole object being to prevent
bloodshed."   Being in command of all the forts in the harbor, I had the right to transfer my force from Moultrie to
Sumter.   " In this controversy," he continued, " between
the North and the South, my sympathies are entirely with
the South.   These gentlemen [turning to the officers of the
post who stood about him] know it perfectly well.   But
my sense of duty to my trust is *first* with me, and this
rules my action."   Anderson met the demand which Colonel
Pettigrew had brought with this answer: " Make my com-
pliments to the governor, and say to him that I decline to
accede to his request ; I cannot and will not go back."[4]

---

[1] See statement of Miles and Keitt to the convention, Official Records, vol.
i. p. 125.   [2] Crawford, p. 31.
[3] See the governor's communication to the convention, Dec. 28, Official
Records, vol. i. p. 252 ; also his message, Journal of the S. C. Senate, Jan.
4, 1861, Crawford, p. 41.
[4] Crawford, pp. 110, 111; Anderson to Cooper, Dec. 27, Official Records,
vol. i. p. 3. On Anderson's sympathy with the South, see also Davis's Rise
and Fall of the Confederate Government, vol. i. p. 216.

At a quarter before noon the command at Fort Sumter was drawn up near the flag-staff, forming one side of a square; the workmen, one hundred and fifty in number, formed the other three sides; as all uncovered, the chaplain thanked God for their safe arrival at the fort, praying that the flag might never be dishonored and that it might soon wave again over a united people. At the end of the prayer Major Anderson rose from his knees, and as the battalion presented arms and the band played the Star-Spangled Banner, he raised the flag to the masthead and led the cheer that saluted the glorious ensign.[1] Three days later he wrote his former pastor: "Unwilling to see my little band sacrificed, I determined, after earnestly awaiting instructions as long as I could, to avail myself of the earliest opportunity of extricating myself from my dangerous position. God be praised! He gave me the will and led me in the way. How I do wish that you could have looked down upon us when we threw the stars and stripes to the breeze at twelve o'clock on the 27th! . . . I am now, thank God, in a place which will, by His helping, soon be made so strong that the South Carolinians will be madmen if they attack me. . . . You see it stated that I came here without orders. Fear not! I am sure I can satisfy any tribunal I may be brought before that I was fully justified in moving my command."[2]

Immediately after Governor Pickens received Anderson's answer refusing to return to Fort Moultrie, he gave orders to have his troops take possession of that post and of Castle Pinckney: this was done, and over them the palmetto flag soon waved.[3] On the same day, December 27, in obedience to an ordinance passed by the convention the day previous, the collector of the port and all the officers

---

[1] Crawford, p. 112 ; Doubleday, p. 71.

[2] Crawford, p. 130 ; see also Anderson's official report, Dec. 27, Official Records, vol. i. p. 3 ; also letter of Dec. 28, ibid., p. 112.

[3] Crawford, p. 113 ; letter of Foster, Dec. 27, Official Records, vol. i. p. 108; letter of Anderson, ibid., p. 3.

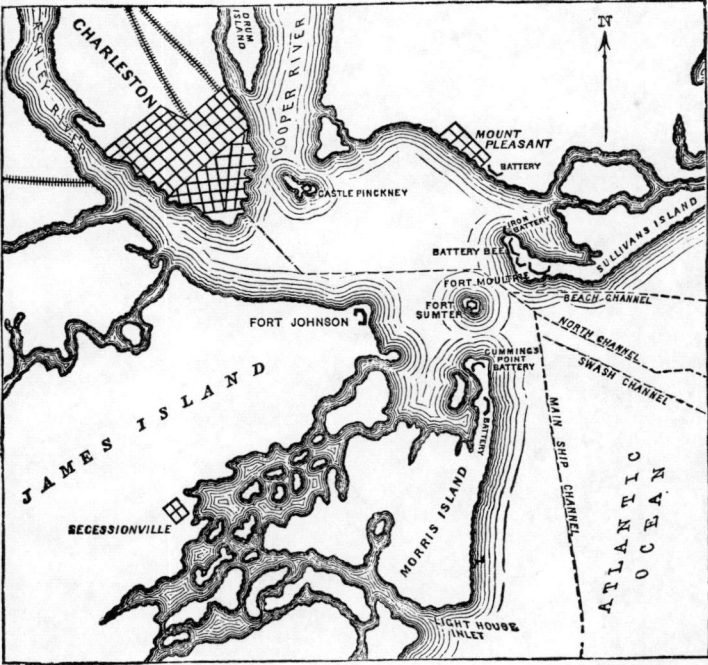

MAP OF CHARLESTON HARBOR

of the custom-house entered into the service of South Carolina ; the collector received duties and transacted all other
business in her name, depositing the funds remaining, after
the payment of salaries and expenses, in the Treasury of the
State.[1] Over the custom-house he raised the flag of South
Carolina.[2] December 30, the United States arsenal, with
a large quantity of arms and ammunition, was seized by the
order of the governor.[3] All the property of the national
government in the city and harbor of Charleston, except
Fort Sumter, was now under the protection of the palmetto
standard. The flag on the post-office indicated a new and
foreign power, but this one bond with the common country had not yet been severed ; the mails were delivered and
sent the same as before the ordinance of secession was
passed, United States postage-stamps were necessary to
insure the forwarding of letters, and the postmaster of
Charleston continued to account to the department at Washington.[4]

In ability and character the South Carolina commissioners were worthy of the important trust confided to them.
Robert W. Barnwell was a Harvard graduate and a lawyer, who had represented his State in the national House
and Senate, and had been president of the South Carolina
college ; more of a student than a politician, he especially
delighted in the study of theology ; he was a gentleman of
elegant manners, and when at Washington had been noted
for his religious walk, his urbanity and manliness. At first
opposed to immediate secession, he had now full sympathy

---

[1] See letter of Colcock, collector, to the convention Dec. 28, Journal of
South Carolina Convention, p. 128 ; see also pp. 95, 171.

[2] Crawford, p. 116 ; Official Records, vol. i. p. 109.

[3] Report of Humphreys, store-keeper to ordnance bureau, Official Records, vol. i. p. 6 *et seq.;* for quantity of arms in the arsenal and of ordnance
in Castle Pinckney and Fort Moultrie, see report of Maynadier, captain
of ordnance, ibid., p. 130.

[4] See Report of the Post-office Department, March 26, 1861, Journal of
Convention, Appendix, p. 403.

with the purpose of his State.[1]   James H. Adams was a
Yale graduate, an anti-nullifier of 1832, had served several
sessions in the legislature, and had once been governor.
James L. Orr had been a member of the national House
ten years, and once its speaker; while ready at this time to
defend with ardor the action of South Carolina, he impressed an old friend as being a Union man at heart.[2]   Abler
and better members of the convention could not have been
selected for this mission.   On their arrival at Washington,
Wednesday, December 26, they found that an interview
with the President had been arranged for them by Trescot[3]
at one o'clock on the next day.   Trescot was at their house
early on this Thursday morning when Senator Wigfall of
Texas entered and gave them the news of Major Anderson's removal to Fort Sumter.   All expressed their disbe-
lief in the intelligence, and when Floyd, who had just been
announced, came into the room, Trescot remarked: "Governor,[4] Senator Wigfall has just brought us this news [re-
peating it], and as you were coming up-stairs I said I would
pledge my life this movement was without orders."   "You
can do more," Floyd replied; "you can pledge your life
that it is not so.   It is impossible.   It would be not only without orders, but in the face of orders."[5]   Trescot took Floyd's

---

[1] See Charleston correspondence New York *Tribune*, Dec. 22 ; Jefferson
Davis's remarks in the Senate, Jan. 9, 1861.

[2] See Diary of a Public Man, entry Dec. 28, 1860, *North American Review*, Aug. 1879, p. 129.   [3] Now the agent of South Carolina.

[4] Floyd had been governor of Virginia and was generally addressed by
this title.

[5] This conversation is reported by Trescot (Crawford, p. 143); and I
have no doubt of its substantial correctness.   See Buchanan's Defence, p.
185 ; Diary of a Public Man, Dec. 28.   But Floyd's statement that the removal to Sumter was "in the face of orders" is incomprehensible.   Crawford thinks it probable that Floyd never read the Buell memorandum until it was called for by the President, p. 74.   I have not seen any evidence
to substantiate Floyd's statement in his Richmond speech of Jan. 17, 1861:
"Major Anderson, . . . after receiving these instructions (the Buell memorandum) wrote to the Secretary of War, 'I could not change my position,
for I have no authority to do so.'"

carriage, hastened to his home, and soon returned with two telegraphic despatches for Barnwell; these Barnwell read and handed them to Floyd, saying, "I am afraid it is too true." Floyd hurried to the department and sent his famous telegraphic inquiry,[1] receiving immediately from Anderson the more famous reply: "I abandoned Fort Moultrie because I was certain if attacked my men must have been sacrificed and the command of the harbor lost. . . . If attacked, the garrison would never have surrendered without a fight."[2]

In the meantime Trescot had driven to the Capitol, had communicated the news to Jefferson Davis and Senator Hunter, and had induced them to go with him to see the President. The President saw them after a short delay. "Have you received any intelligence from Charleston in the last few hours?" asked Davis. "None," was the reply. "Then," said Davis, "I have a great calamity to announce to you." After stating the facts, he continued, "And now, Mr. President, you are surrounded with blood and dishonor on all sides."[3] Buchanan was amazed at the news.[4] "My God!" he exclaimed, "are misfortunes never to come singly? I call God to witness, you gentlemen, better than anybody, *know* that this is not only without but against my orders. It is against my policy." The visitors urged the President to act immediately and order Anderson back to Fort Moultrie, and this indeed was his first impulse,[5] but he finally decided that he must consult his cabinet, and await further information.[6] It was a heated cabinet session that

---

[1] "Intelligence has reached here this morning that you have abandoned Fort Moultrie, spiked your guns, burned the carriages, and gone to Fort Sumter. It is not believed, because there is no order for any such movement. Explain the meaning of this report."

[2] For the full text of this despatch see Official Records, vol. i. p. 3.

[3] Trescot's narrative, Crawford, p. 143.

[4] Buchanan's Defence, p. 180; Curtis, vol. ii. p. 371.

[5] Trescot's narrative, Crawford, p. 144; Buchanan's letter of Dec. 31 to the commissioners, Official Records, vol. i. p. 118.

[6] Crawford; Davis's Rise and Fall of the Confederate Government, vol. i. p. 215.

day. Two decided opinions were revealed. Floyd asserted that nothing in Anderson's orders justified his movement, and the President was inclined to agree with him. Judge Black, who was now Secretary of State, sent for the Buell memorandum and the President's modification of it, read them, and then stoutly maintained that Anderson had acted in perfect accordance with his instructions, and that he deserved high praise.[1] We may without hesitation accept this opinion of Black as a right historical judgment.

This cabinet meeting furnished Floyd an opportunity to extricate himself with a shadow of honor from an ignominious situation. Found out in irregular and apparently corrupt financial transactions, for he had used the credit of the government in the attempt to prop the failing fortunes of some unscrupulous contractors, word had been sent to him on December 23 by the President, through their common friend Breckinridge, that he could no longer remain in the cabinet, and that he ought to resign.[2] Buchanan hourly expected his resignation, yet he came uninvited to the cabinet meeting of December 27, and his unusually peremptory manner made it clear that he was using this movement of Anderson to make an issue on which he might resign without disgrace. At the evening session he read "in a discourteous and excited tone" a paper asserting that the solemn pledges of the government had been violated, and that the only remedy left to avoid civil war was to withdraw the garrison from Charleston harbor. Two days later he formally resigned: the President promptly accepted his resignation, and placed Postmaster-General Holt in charge of the War Department.[3]

Owing to the stir caused by the removal of Anderson to Fort Sumter, the President's interview with the South Caro-

---

[1] Essays and Speeches of J. S. Black, C. F. Black, p. 12.
[2] Buchanan's statement, Curtis, vol. ii. p. 408 ; Buchanan's Defence, p. 185 ; see also C. F. Black, p. 13. For a fuller consideration of this matter, see note at the end of the chapter.
[3] At first *ad interim*, afterwards as full Secretary, ibid.

lina commissioners had been adjourned to the next day; it
then took place. At the beginning of it Buchanan gave the
commissioners formal notice that he could receive them only
as private gentlemen, and not as envoys from a sovereign
State. They maintained that the faith of the President given
early in December to the South Carolina congressmen had
been broken, and they pressed him with earnestness to order
Anderson back to Fort Moultrie. Buchanan fenced. " But,
Mr. President," urged Barnwell, "your personal honor is
involved in this matter; the faith you pledged has been violated; and your personal honor requires you to issue the
order." "You must give me time to consider," he replied;
"this is a grave question." "But, Mr. President," said Barnwell for a third time, "your personal honor is involved in
this arrangement." Buchanan, annoyed at this persistence,
answered: "Mr. Barnwell, you are pressing me too import-
unately; you don't give me time to consider; you don't
give me time to say my prayers. I always say my prayers
when required to act upon any great State affair." [1] The
commissioners were unable to obtain any promise from the
President. Considerable pressure had been brought to bear
upon him to induce him to yield,[2] and now an effort was
made by Orr to get Seward to use his influence and position
in favor of the restoration of the status in Charleston harbor.[3]
On the other hand, General Scott begged that Fort Sumter
should not be evacuated, but that troops, ammunition, and
provisions should be sent.[4] A letter from the commissioners, dated December 28, was sent to the President. It went
over the ground of the interview more formally, asserted
that until the Anderson movement was explained the commissioners would be forced to suspend negotiations, and

---

[1] Crawford, p. 148 ; Buchanan's Defence, p. 181 ; reply of the commissioners, Official Records, vol. i. p. 122.
[2] Ibid., p. 144 ; reply of the commissioners, Official Records, vol. i. p.
123.
[3] Diary of a Public Man, entry Dec. 28.
[4] Official Records, vol. i. p. 112.

ended with urging that the troops be immediately withdrawn from Charleston harbor.[1]

The difference between Buchanan and the South Carolinians in regard to the interpretation put upon the interview with the congressmen amounts to nothing. They held that there was on his part a pledge. This he denied, but he affirmed with truth that he had acted in the same manner as he would have done had he entered into "a positive and formal agreement."[2] South Carolina had indeed no reason to complain of President Buchanan. Rarely had a people played at revolution with less hinderance from an essentially strong government. The North, however, had abundant grounds of complaint that the executive of the nation had not asserted its legitimate authority and acted in accordance with the dominant sentiment of the country. If Buchanan had known that Anderson contemplated the occupation of Sumter, he would have peremptorily forbidden any such movement. It is one of many indications of his lack of ability to deal with the business in hand that when, December 21, he read the Buell memorandum, he failed to see any good reasons for thinking that the event in which Anderson was authorized to transfer his force had already happened. In trying times, when events come crowding fast, when every day seems too short for what there is to do, when yesterday's neglect encroaches on to-day's duty, and when to-day's indecision lends trouble to the morrow's plans, men who possess executive ability have so disciplined their minds that they let their routine work go, refusing to consider the unimportant things in order that their time may be employed in concentrating their attention upon the weighty matters, in the decision of which are bound up the welfare of their country and their own fame; and, when a conclusion must be reached in an affair of moment, they are ready

---

[1] For this letter see Official Records, vol. i. p. 109.
[2] Letter of Buchanan to the commissioners, ibid., p. 117.

to give hours, and, if necessary, a day, wholly to its consideration, sleeping over it, if the case admits; and finally,
when the decision is to be set down in writing—as this is
the shape that in modern times most far-reaching executive
acts take — every word is weighed, and every sentence is
analyzed in order that the paper may convey distinctly the
meaning of the author. Buchanan wasted his time and
strength in quibbles; he had neither for a matter of tran-
scendent consequence.[1] In November and December, 1860,
the most important spot in the country under his management was Charleston; the most important executive order
that went out was that left by Buell at Fort Moultrie: this
Buchanan did not see until several days after it was placed
on file in the War Department, and when at last he read it,
he failed to understand its scope or to grasp the situation
that confronted Major Anderson.

South Carolina and the North disagreed in the constructions they respectively put upon the acts of the last days of
December, even as the Calhoun and Webster theories of
the Union and the Constitution differed. South Carolina
maintained that Major Anderson, in removing his force
from one position in the State which he occupied only on
sufferance, pending negotiation, to another position within
her jurisdiction, solely for the purpose of being able to retain the stronghold for a foreign power against the will
of South Carolina, had " waged war," and that her conse-

---

[1] Lowell's criticism of Buchanan's course in November was hardly too
severe. He spoke of him as " a so-called statesman. . . who knows no art
to conjure the spirit of anarchy he has evoked but the shifts and evasions
of a second-rate attorney, and who has contrived to involve his country in
the confusion of principle and vacillation of judgment which have left
him without a party and without a friend ; for such a man we have no
feeling but contemptuous reprobation. . . . There are times when medioc-
rity is a dangerous quality, and a man may drown himself as effectually in
milk and water as in Malmsey."—*Atlantic Monthly*, Jan., 1861. This magazine appeared late in December. Although the names of the contributors
were not given in the magazine, it was known that Lowell wrote this article. See New York *Tribune*, Dec. 29.

quent acts were "simple self-defence." [1] The North, on the
other hand, held that all the forts belonged to the United
States; that its troops had the right to occupy any and
all of them; that Anderson's movement was not only right
but expedient, being a proper and necessary measure of
self-defence; that acts of war had indeed been committed,
but that these acts were the occupation of Fort Moultrie
and Castle Pinckney, the taking possession of the arsenal
and the custom-house, and that in all this South Carolina
had been the aggressor. Which was right? Had the question been submitted to the ballot, the voice of the people,
taking the country as a whole, would have been with the
North. The "God of Justice" and the "God of Hosts"
whom South Carolina invoked, [2] when the question was appealed to the last resort, decided that the voice of the people was the voice of God. As an historian has no choice
in a case of this kind but to accept the decision of the
event, [3] we may therefore affirm without hesitation that

---

[1] Letter of the commissioners to the President, Official Records, vol. i.
p. 124.   [2] Ibid.

[3] This view is so well stated by General J. D. Cox, in a review of Crawford's The Genesis of the Civil War, in the *Nation* for Jan. 8, 1888, that I
quote from it as support for the assertion in the text. "The war itself
settled some things by the complete assent of all intelligent men of the
South. The appeal to arms in this case as in others was the submission of
a controversy to the *ultima ratio regum* and its decision. We believe that
every statesman of the Southern States, who to-day claims to be a citizen
of the United States, distinctly and unequivocally holds that this contention was decided by the war in favor of the national view, and that, by virtue of such decision, the national view is determined to be and is the constitutional law of the United States. . . . We do not say that they were not
sincere and earnest in their own contention. We do not say that they now
admit that they were morally or even theoretically wrong in their position, . . . but . . . they agree with us that the constitutional principle is settled. In their anxiety to avoid strife, the officers of the United States often
fell short of the national claim that the ordinance of secession was revolutionary, and that the first shouldering of a musket or opening of a trench
was an act of war. He who writes history now has the great advantage
that this principle is settled," and he should "logically and clearly stick
to it in his analysis of events."

South Carolina's revolution had proceeded to overt acts of war.

The South Carolina commissioners awaited an answer. The President wavered, but in the end, following the bent of his sympathies, he prepared a reply favorable to their cause. The draft of this paper is not in existence,[1] but, from Judge Black's criticism of it, we know that it was a pusillanimous answer, and that in uttering it Buchanan made a further descent in that path of abasing his country which he had trod since the November election. I feel quite sure that he did not design to withdraw the troops from Charleston harbor, or agree formally to order Anderson back to Moultrie, but it seems clear that the restoration of the *status quo* was a legitimate consequence of the position which he took.[2] Late on Saturday evening, December 29, the President submitted to his cabinet the draft of his proposed answer. Toucey alone approved it. Thomas of Maryland, who was now Secretary of the Treasury, and Thompson did not deem it sufficiently favorable to the claim of South Carolina, while Black, Holt, and Edwin M. Stanton, now Attorney - General, opposed it on the ground that it conceded too much. No conclusion was reached.

---

[1] Curtis, vol. ii. p. 380.

[2] In spite of Seward's authority, and he had undoubtedly good channels of information, I do not think the President entertained the idea of withdrawing the troops. Seward wrote Weed, Dec. 29 : " The South Carolina interest demands the withdrawal of Anderson and abandonment of the forts. . . . The President inclines to yield. . . . I am writing you not from rumors, but knowledge."—Life of Seward, vol. ii. p. 487 ; see also letter to Lincoln, ibid., p. 488. Buchanan distinctly stated in his letter of Dec. 31 to the commissioners, Official Records, vol. i. p. 118, " Such an idea was never thought of by me in any possible contingency." I think most of the evidence tends to confirm that statement. On the contrary, see reply of the commissioners, ibid., p. 123. The commissioners would have been satisfied with the restoration of the *status quo*, see Trescot's narrative, Crawford, p. 159; Diary of a Public Man, entry Dec. 28. And, indeed, they might well be, as it would have led to the eventual abandonment of the forts by the United States. This certainty makes the point discussed in this note of little importance.

That night Judge Black spent in deep reflection. His feeling of personal devotion to Buchanan and his sentiment of duty to the country wrestled together. He had put up with the President's sins of omission, but could he be a party to the almost complete surrender of the national authority? In the morning his mind was made up. He told Stanton, Holt, and Toucey that, regarding the President's purpose as fixed, he had determined to resign. Stanton, and perhaps Holt, would have followed his example. Although it was Sunday,[1] Toucey hastened to the White House and informed Buchanan, who sent for Black. The interview was painful to Black, on account of the conflict between his loyalty to the President and his conviction that the course proposed meant disaster and ruin to the country; while it was unpleasant to Buchanan, since he had to choose between giving up Black and giving up his policy. The balance turned in favor of Black. The President gave him the draft of the proposed answer, and asked him to modify it in conformity to his views. Black went to his office and, with his feelings at white heat, wrote the celebrated memorandum. Stanton was with him and copied the sheets as fast as they were written.[2] Black showed a perfect comprehension of all the points involved; he understood thoroughly the rights and duty of the federal government; he saw with unerring sagacity the correct policy to be pursued: and all this he expressed with such cogency that this memorandum, constituting as it did the turning-point of Buchanan's policy, and preventing an abject compliance with arrogant demands, is worthy of the most careful consideration and the highest praise.[3] In unanswerable

---

[1] Dec. 30.

[2] Essays and speeches of J. S. Black, C. F. Black, p. 13 *et seq.;* see also Lincoln and Men of War Times, McClure, p. 277.

[3] The great importance of this memorandum induces me to quote a large part of it: The President having seemed to admit by implication that South Carolina was an independent nation, Black said:

"1. I think that every word and sentence which implies that South Car-

logic he vindicated the national doctrine, justified and commended Major Anderson in the strongest terms, refuted with crushing force the claim of South Carolina, and ended

---

olina is in an attitude which enables the President to 'treat' or negotiate with her, or to receive her commissioners in the character of diplomatic ministers or agents, ought to be stricken out, and an explicit declaration substituted, which would reassert the principles of the message. It is surely not enough that the words of the message be transcribed, if the doctrine there announced be practically abandoned by carrying on a negotiation.

"2. I would strike out all expressions of regret that the commissioners are unwilling to proceed with the negotiations, since it is very clear that there can be no negotiation with them, whether they are willing or not.

"3. Above all things, it is objectionable to intimate a willingness to negotiate with the State of South Carolina about the possession of a military post which belongs to the United States, or to propose any adjustment of the subject or any arrangement about it. The forts in Charleston harbor belong to this government—are its own, and cannot be given up. It is true they might be surrendered to a superior force, whether that force be in the service of a seceding State or a foreign nation. But Fort Sumter is impregnable and cannot be taken if defended as it should be. It is a thing of the last importance that it should be maintained, if all the power of this nation can do it; for the command of the harbor and the President's ability to execute the revenue laws may depend on it.

"4. The words 'coercing a State by force of arms to remain in the confederacy—a power which I do not believe the Constitution has conferred on Congress,' ought certainly not to be retained. They are too vague, and might have the effect (which I am sure the President does not intend) to mislead the commissioners concerning his sentiments. The power to defend the public property—to resist an assailing force which unlawfully attempts to drive out the troops of the United States from one of the fortifications, and to use military and naval forces for the purpose of aiding the proper officers of the United States in the execution of the laws—this, as far as it goes, is *coercion*, and may very well be called 'coercing a State by force of arms to remain in the Union.' The President has always asserted his right of coercion to that extent. He merely denies the right of Congress to make offensive war upon a State of the Union such as might be made upon a foreign government.

"5. The implied assent of the President to the accusation which the commissioners make of a compact with South Carolina by which he was bound not to take whatever measures he saw fit for the defence of the forts, ought to be stricken out, and a flat denial of any such bargain, pledge, or agreement inserted.

"6. The remotest expression of a doubt about Major Anderson's perfect

with : "I entreat the President to order the *Brooklyn* and
the *Macedonian*[1] to Charleston without the least delay, and
in the meantime send a trusty messenger to Major Anderson to let him know that his government will not desert
him. The reinforcement of troops from New York or Old
Point Comfort should follow immediately. If this be done
at once all may yet be not well, but comparatively safe.
If not, I can see nothing before us but disaster and ruin
to the country."

There was entire consistency between this memorandum
of Black, Secretary of State, and the opinion of November
20 of Black, Attorney-General.[2] In the memorandum he
appreciated and reflected the difference in meaning now at-

---

propriety of behavior should be carefully avoided. He is not merely a
gallant and meritorious officer who is entitled to a fair hearing before he
is condemned. He has saved the country, I solemnly believe, when its
day was darkest and its perils most extreme. He has done everything that
mortal man could do to repair the fatal error which the administration
have committed in not sending down troops enough to hold *all* the forts.
He has kept the strongest one. He still commands the harbor. We may
still execute the laws if we try. . . .

"7. The idea that a wrong was committed against South Carolina by moving from Fort Moultrie to Fort Sumter ought to be repelled as firmly as
may be consistent with a proper respect for the high character of the gentlemen who compose the South Carolina Commission. It is a strange assumption of right on the part of that State to say that our United States
troops must remain in the weakest position they can find in the harbor.
It is not a menace of South Carolina or of Charleston, or any menace at all.
It is simple self-defence. If South Carolina does not attack Major Anderson, no human being will be injured, for there certainly can be no reason
to believe that he will commence hostilities. The apparent objection to
his being in Fort Sumter is that he will be less likely to fall an easy prey
to his assailants.

"These are the points on which I would advise that the paper be amended. I am aware that they are too radical to permit much hope of their
adoption. If they are adopted, the whole paper will need to be recast."
—Essays and Speeches of J. S. Black, C. F. Black, p. 15.

[1] The *Brooklyn*, a steam sloop-of-war, "a new and formidable vessel of
twenty-five guns ;" the *Macedonian*, a war vessel of twenty-two guns, Nicolay and Hay, vol. ii. p. 382, vol. iii. p. 164 ; they were at the Norfolk navy
yard.   [2] *Ante.*

tached to the word coercion from that which it implied in November;[1] and he felt that the tone of the paper should be modulated to the progress of events; that, South Carolina having seceded and committed acts of war, the words of the executive addressed to her should be more forcible than the message to her when she was preparing to withdraw from the Union.

The memorandum, which embodied also the sentiments of Stanton and Holt, went to the President and caused him to modify the answer to the commissioners which he had prepared. The altered paper was delivered to them Monday, December 31. It has by no means the ring of Black's logic; yet the President, forced to eat his own words, did it with ready skill, and he indicated a policy that suffered Black, Stanton, and Holt to remain in his cabinet without prejudice to their national views. In answer to the request of South Carolina that he should withdraw the troops from Charleston harbor, he said, "This I cannot do; this I will not do;" and he announced, "It is my duty to defend Fort Sumter."[2] Buchanan's action tallied with his word. December 30, General Scott, not knowing of Floyd's resignation, had asked the President's permission to send a reinforcement to Fort Sumter;[3] this was immediately granted, and the general made out an order to have the *Brooklyn* ready, and to put on board of her at least 200 men from Fortress Monroe, with arms, ammunition, and supplies.[4] The President then suggested that, out of courtesy, it would be well to defer sending the order until he should receive a reply from the commissioners, and in this Scott promptly

---

[1] *Ante*, p. 133.

[2] For this letter of the President, see Official Records, vol. i. p. 115 ; Curtis, vol. ii. p. 386.

[3] Scott to the President, Official Records, vol. i. p. 114.

[4] The date of the order is Dec. 31, ibid., p. 119. The President received the request of General Scott the evening of Dec. 30, and gave the permission the morning of Dec. 31, Buchanan in the *National Intelligencer*, Nov. 1, 1862 ; Buchanan's Defence, p. 188.

concurred.[1] January 2, 1861, their answer came. It presented the South Carolina argument with force, but it was arrogant in manner and insolent in tone.[2] Appreciating that men of national views were now in the ascendency in the cabinet, knowing that Anderson would not only be sustained, but that an order to send him reinforcements had been issued,[3] they smarted from a sense of failure of their mission, and let their bitter disappointment get the better of their native courtesy.[4] The reading of this reply in cabinet meeting excited general indignation. Buchanan, feeling keenly the insult to the dignity of his office, wrote, "This paper, just presented to the President, is of such a character that he declines to receive it," and ordered that the letter with these words endorsed upon it be sent back to the commissioners.[5] He then turned to the Secretary of War, Holt, and said, emphatically, "It is now all over, and reinforcements must be sent."[6]

Anderson's removal of his force to Fort Sumter had electrified the Northern people, but, before venting their feeling of joy, they waited with breathless suspense to see whether he would be supported by the administration. During the days of gloom and humiliation since the November election they had searched in vain for a hero. It now seemed as if one had been found,[7] but for a happy fate

---

[1] As "the delay could not continue more than forty-eight hours," *National Intelligencer*, Nov. 1, 1862; Buchanan's Defence, p. 190.

[2] It is printed in Official Records, vol. i. p. 121, and Davis's Rise and Fall of the Confederate Government, vol. i. p. 597. The letter is dated Jan. 1.

[3] Trescot's narrative, Crawford, p. 159.

[4] Although Jefferson Davis defended the commissioners and criticised the President, he admitted that their reply was "harsh in some of its terms," remarks in the Senate, Jan. 9, 1861. It is said that Orr objected to sending any reply, Diary of a Public Man, entry Jan. 1, 1861.

[5] This was done. See Curtis, vol. ii. p. 392; Buchanan's Defence, p. 183. The commissioners left Washington the afternoon of January 2. They had in their letter stated that to be their purpose.

[6] Buchanan to Thompson, Jan. 9, 1861, Curtis, vol. ii. p. 402.

[7] "The feeling of the country has been unmistakably expressed in regard to Major Anderson, and that not merely because he showed prudence and

he needed the backing of the President. Despite the secrecy of the cabinet meetings, public rumor, though incor-
rect in detail, reflected passing well what was going on in
the inner councils of the nation. On the last day of the
year it became known that the troops would not be withdrawn from Charleston harbor, and that Anderson would
not be ordered back to Moultrie. The North had passed a
dismal Christmas; a merry New Year's now made amends.
Every one breathed freer and held up his head. All hearts
beat high; all breasts heaved with patriotic emotion; all
felt that their country and their flag meant something. A
salvo of artillery, beginning with the New Year, resounded
throughout the Northern cities, continuing until Saint
Jackson's Day,[1] when cheers for " Old Hickory " mingled in
fit unison with cheers for Major Anderson.[2] The House of
Representatives, by an imposing majority, voted approval
of his " bold and patriotic act." [3] No one imagined that the
difficulty was solved, but all felt that their government had
adopted a manly tone, and that they need no longer hang
their heads with shame as they gave heed to the opinion of
Europe. For the change of policy that caused this revulsion of feeling, for the vigorous assertion at last in word
and in deed that the United States is a nation, for pointing
out the way in which the authority of the federal government might be exercised without infringing on the rights
of the States, the gratitude of the American people is due
to Jeremiah S. Black.

NOTE.—The irregular financial transactions of Floyd attracted so

---

courage, but because he was the first man holding a position of trust who
did his duty to the nation."—Lowell's " E Pluribus Unum," *Atlantic
Monthly*, Feb., 1861, p. 239.

[1] January 8, the anniversary of the battle of New Orleans.

[2] Editorials and Washington despatches, New York *Tribune*, Dec. 28,
29, 31 ; ibid., Jan. 3, 9, 1861 ; Moore's Rebellion Record, vol. i., Diary,
pp. 9, 10, 11, 14. " The marked change in the policy of the administration
is felt in the very air to-day."—" S " to the New York *Times*, Washington,
Jan. 2, 1861.   [3] By a vote of 124 to 56, *Congressional Globe*, p. 281.

much attention at the time that, although not strictly necessary for a full understanding of the progress of events, I cannot pass them over with only the allusion in the text (*ante*, p. 225). Russell, Majors & Waddell, a firm who had large contracts with the War Department for transportation of army provisions over the Western and Southwestern plains, becoming embarrassed after the panic of 1857, induced Floyd to accept, as Secretary of War, drafts of theirs in anticipation of their earnings; he also wrote to various banks and individuals, urging the purchase or discount of these drafts. This practice began in 1858; it was brought to the notice of the President, probably in the early part of the year 1860; he told Floyd that it was improper and should be discontinued; Floyd promised not to accept another draft (Curtis, vol. ii. p. 407), but did not keep his promise. From time to time the contractors retired the acceptances. But their affairs apparently went from bad to worse, and so many of the acceptances of the Secretary of War were afloat that it became difficult to negotiate them, and in July, 1860, the contractors needed additional help to prevent some of them from going to protest. At this juncture, Bailey, a clerk in the Interior Department, having charge of trust funds, who came to Washington "a bankrupt in fortune, and a political adventurer seeking office," but who had good recommendations from Alabama and South Carolina, saved Floyd's credit by letting Russell have $150,000 of Indian trust bonds, he taking in their place a similar amount of Floyd acceptances: this he did, as he said, to prevent Floyd's "retirement in disgrace from the cabinet." (Bailey was a connection of Floyd.) From time to time more bonds were needed and obtained, the Floyd acceptances being substituted for them, until the deficit reached $870,000. December 22 the President was informed of this theft, and he requested Floyd's resignation. A special committee of the House of Representatives was appointed to investigate the affair in the usual way. It was composed of one anti-Lecompton and one administration Democrat, two Republicans, and one American. It took a large amount of testimony and made a unanimous report. It exonerated fully Thompson, the Secretary of the Interior; it ascertained that nearly $7,000,000 in acceptances had been issued, a record of which had been mostly kept on loose pieces of paper, and of which a large amount was still outstanding. It declared that these acceptances were "unauthorized by law and

deceptive and fraudulent in their character;" "that Russell, Majors
& Waddell not only absorbed all the sums earned by them under
their contracts, and sold all the bonds they received from Bailey,
but also raised very large sums of money upon the acceptances
issued by the Secretary of War;" and that Floyd's action could not
be reconciled "with purity of private motives and faithfulness to
public trusts."—See House Report No. 78, 36th Cong., 2d Sess.
The President ordered Floyd to be indicted for malversation in
office.—Essays and Speeches of J. S. Black, p. 266. The indictment, however, against him was quashed on a technicality.—New
York *Tribune*, March 21, 1861; Appletons' Annual Cyclopædia,
1861, p. 701. It is not surprising that Floyd was then, and has
since been, written down a thief, but the statement of C. F. Black,
which undoubtedly represented the opinion of his father, is conclusive evidence to the contrary. "There is no evidence," he
writes, "against him of anything worse than reckless imprudence;
not a cent from any money proceeding from these premature acceptances could be traced to his hands, and it is very clear that he
had no connection whatever, in thought, word, or deed, with the
abstraction of the Indian trust bonds from the Interior Department.
He left Washington empty-handed—so poor that he had to borrow
the money which paid the expenses of taking his family to Virginia."—See C. F. Black, p. 13.

Another charge against Floyd must be examined. It is that, an-
ticipating the war between the sections, he sent to the Southern arsenals in the spring of 1860 to aid the South in her preparation a
large quantity of muskets and rifles, and that in the same year he
was instrumental in making an unfair distribution, and one favorable to the South, of the arms for which an annual appropriation
was made by Congress to equip the militia of the several States.
At the North, this charge was generally believed in 1861 and during the war; and it met with much credence on account of General
Scott's support of it in his controversy with Buchanan in 1862.
See *National Intelligencer*, Nov. 13, Dec. 6, 1862. It occasionally
appears in the history books. It has been used as part of the
chain of the proof to show that the South was better prepared for
the war than the North, and it is sometimes employed to bolster a
theory of the secession, which I shall later carefully examine. Of
the 115,000 arms sent for storage to the Southern arsenals in the

spring of 1860, 105,000 were condemned muskets, not worth over
$2.50 each, and 10,000 were percussion rifles, calibre .54. The
Southern States, in 1860, did not apply for, nor get, their full quota
of new arms. These two facts plainly appear from the report of
the House Committee on Military Affairs and the evidence submitted with it, Report No. 85, 36th Cong., 2d Sess. The report was
made Feb. 18, 1861; Stanton, the chairman, was a Republican from
Ohio. The truth is more systematically stated in Buchanan's replies to General Scott, *National Intelligencer*, Nov. 25 and Dec. 18,
1862; in Buchanan's Defence, p. 223; in J. S. Black's open letter to
Henry Wilson, C. F. Black, p. 267; the subject is also treated with
detail by Curtis, vol. ii. p. 411. It is perfectly clear that before
the election of Lincoln Floyd was not a secessionist.

Between the November election and his resignation some of his
acts are suspicious, and seemed at the time treacherous to many steadfast Union men. November 14 he sold the State of Alabama 2500
of the condemned muskets; Nov. 24, 10,000 to a known agent of
South Carolina; 5000 each to Mississippi and Louisiana, all at $2.50
each. The last 10,000 mentioned, however, came from the arsenal
of Baton Rouge, La. See Report of Com. on Military Affairs; letter of Lamar to Floyd, and Floyd's reply, War Department Archives;
for the correspondence leading to the South Carolina purchase, see
Nicolay and Hay, vol. ii. p. 319 *et seq.*

Captain Foster of the Engineers, in charge of the work at Fort
Sumter and Castle Pinckney, had with some address, on Dec. 17,
obtained from the United States arsenal in Charleston forty muskets
to arm his two ordnance sergeants and his laborers in case of necessary defence. This transfer of arms occasioned much excitement in
Charleston and an official remonstrance. The matter was referred
to Floyd, who immediately ordered Foster to return the muskets to
the arsenal, in which at this time were stored over 21,000 muskets
and rifles. See report of Maynadier, Official Records, vol. i. p. 130.
For the correspondence relating to the forty muskets, ibid., p. 94 *et
seq.* The story is interestingly told by Nicolay and Hay, vol. ii.
chap. xxix.

October 20, Floyd directed verbally the Captain of Ordnance
Maynadier to send guns to the unfinished forts of Ship Island, Miss.,
and Galveston, Texas. When it was ascertained what the Pittsburgh
arsenal could furnish, Floyd gave the order (Dec. 20) to Maynadier

to have sent from there 110 columbiads and eleven thirty-two pounders. No guns could have been mounted at Ship Island for months. The Galveston fort would not have been in full readiness for its armament in less than five years. When preparations began to be made in Pittsburgh for this shipment, and the citizens came to know for what points the guns were destined, public feeling was strongly stirred up. Remonstrances were urged upon the President, with the result that he directed Holt, who was now acting Secretary of War, to rescind the order: the guns were not shipped. See report of House Com. on Military Affairs, Feb. 18, 1861; Buchanan in the *National Intelligencer*, Nov. 25, 1862; Buchanan's Defence, p. 224; Curtis, vol. ii. p. 416; New York *Tribune*, Dec. 27, 28, 29.

Buchanan states that Floyd was "an avowed and consistent opponent of secession" (Defence, p. 187) until receiving the request to resign, and Black's testimony is to the same effect. (Open letter to Henry Wilson, C. F. Black, p. 266.) It is now so commonly admitted that Buchanan was a very truthful, sincere, and honest man that I have not emphasized the fact; Black was scrupulously veracious and exact: their testimony, therefore, is of the highest value. But at the best Floyd was a Unionist of the Virginia States-rights school;[1] opposed to "the coercion of a sovereign State;" determined " not to reinforce the forts and not to allow them to be taken by an unlawful force " (Crawford, p. 59). Undoubtedly he thought, until the secession of South Carolina, that she had as much right to the arms belonging to the general government as had Massachusetts. Such a sentiment would explain all his acts except that connected with the transfer of the ordnance from Pittsburgh; and the perfected order for that was not given until after he had learned of the theft of the bonds from the Interior Department avowedly in his interest (see letter of Bailey to Floyd, Dec. 19; Report of Com. p. 95). Trescot had no such confidence in Floyd's devotion to Southern interests as he had in Cobb's and Thompson's (see his private and confidential letter to Drayton, Nov. 19, MS. Confederate Archives,

[1] "Union was a question of expediency, not of obligation. This was the conviction of the true Virginia school, and of Jefferson's opponents as well as his supporters; of Patrick Henry, as well as John Taylor of Caroline, and John Randolph of Roanoke."—Henry Adams's History of the United States, vol. i. p. 142.

cited by Nicolay and Hay, vol. ii. p. 322). No one can devote the least attention to Floyd's administration of affairs without being struck by his utter incapacity for the proper and systematic transaction of business. He had a poor conception of what he should do, and an imperfect understanding of what he had done.

My apology for devoting so much space to Floyd is for the reason previously mentioned, and furthermore for the desire to do entire justice to Buchanan, who has of course a certain responsibility for the acts of his secretaries. I am aware that it is a work of supererogation to defend Floyd from treachery which he and his friends boasted that he had committed. See his speech at Richmond, New York *Herald*, Jan. 17, 1861 ; Pollard's History of the First Year of the War, p. 67 ; Recollections of Mississippi and Mississippians, Reuben Davis, p. 395. Floyd afterwards served in the Confederate army, but not with honor.

I should have been glad to end this chapter and my account of the year 1860 with citations of the salient points of Benjamin's speech made in the Senate, Dec. 31, but the absolute need of compression forbade. It may be found on p. 212, *Congressional Globe*, and, as a strong presentation of the argument for the right of secession and for the injustice and inexpediency of coercion or of any attempt to enforce the laws in South Carolina, it may be read with profit. Benjamin was of Hebrew parents, wealthy, the ablest lawyer of the South in public life, and a fit representative of Louisiana, one of the more conservative of the cotton States. While sincerity does not inhere in his utterances as it does in so marked a degree in those of the South Carolina leaders, of Toombs, Stephens, and Jefferson Davis, this speech is an adroit plea of a clever attorney on behalf of a client for whom he held a brief.

CHAPTER XIV

THE administration had turned over a new leaf, and the personality of the man to whom this change was due becomes for us a matter of interest. Jeremiah Black, now nearly fifty-one, and in the maturity of his powers, was well fitted mentally and morally to bear the brunt of affairs. A good student from boyhood, fond of books, he submitted himself readily to the conditions of his life, and, recognizing that he had his own living to earn, he began in an attorney's office, at the age most boys go to college, the study of law. When a youth he chose as a gift from his father Shakespeare's plays, and this love clung to him through life, causing him to draw from that master lessons in expression and philosophy that influenced his literary style and affected profoundly his view of human concerns. Laying out his own course of study, Horace became the chief companion of his leisure and his relaxation after serious effort. Sincerely religious, he applied himself with diligence to the reading of the English Bible as the chart of his faith, acquiring a familiarity with the words and the turns of thought of our language in King James's time, that imparted terseness to the expression of his vigorous understanding. Admitted to the bar before he was of age, he received when thirty-two the appointment of judge of one of the district courts of his State. This position he held for ten years, until his election to the Supreme bench, from which, in the complete sense of the term, he was dispensing justice when called by Buchanan to the cabinet. Higher honors can come to no lawyer in America than to be revered as was Black by the bar of his own State, and by

the bar of the Supreme Court of his country as a learned
man and an upright judge. Pennsylvania, though rich in
legal talent, awarded to Black the palm in constitutional
law and in the whole field of jurisprudence. His ability and
correct training were fortified in mature years by laborious
studies and conscientious work; his lucid opinions cleared
up complicated points, and made simple abstruse ideas. He
was an intense partisan, and loyally supported Buchanan in
the policy of his administration, until the two came to
differ on the proper executive action to be taken in the
reinforcement of the Charleston forts, and in meeting the
threatened and accomplished secession of South Carolina.
They agreed, however, as to the powers of the States and the
limitations of the federal government. Black reverenced
the Constitution, and had a respect for law worthy of a
Roman statesman of noblest type. Socially, he was a genial
companion, and a man who hated shams and meanness of
all sorts. The crowning feature of his character, which
gave lustre to all his qualities, was his absolute and unquestioned purity. Of him it may truly be written, as he
himself said of Gibson, who sat on the Pennsylvania Supreme bench thirty-seven years, and who held the highest
place in the esteem of her bar until Black came to dispute
that eminence: " He was inflexibly honest. . . . I do not
mean to award him merely that commonplace integrity
which it is no honor to have, but simply a disgrace to want.
He was not only incorruptible, but scrupulously, delicately,
conscientiously free from all wilful wrong, either in thought,
word, or deed." [1]

Edwin M. Stanton, a personal friend of Black, had been
appointed Attorney-General for the reason that, having
been retained by the government in some cases, he, better

---

[1] I have drawn this characterization of Black from the biographical
sketch by C. F. Black; from the speeches of J. S. Black; from the Proceedings of the Bench and Bar of the Supreme Court of the United States
in memoriam J. S. Black, pamphlet, Washington, 1884.

than any one else, could proceed with them in the Supreme
Court. Stanton was a sound lawyer, an energetic man, and,
in the words of Black, a "quiet, unpretending, high-princi-
pled, Democratic gentleman." He had favored Buchanan's
Lecompton policy, had supported Breckinridge for President, and had endorsed Black's opinion of November 20,
and the annual message of December 3. He was devoted
to the President, even to the point of flattery, if we may accept without qualification a statement in one of Buchanan's
private letters.[1] After becoming a member of the cabinet,
he agreed implicitly with Black.[2] Joseph Holt was a distinguished lawyer of Kentucky, who had held office under
Buchanan from the commencement of his administration;[3]
he now used his influence and position in upholding the
national policy which, owing to the stand Black had taken,
became in the main the course of the government.

In harmony with his departure in the conduct of affairs,
the President, January 2, nominated for collector of the
port of Charleston, Peter McIntire of Pennsylvania, a man
fitted for the position by personal courage and decision of
character. The Senate never acted on this nomination.[4] As
the Republicans and Northern Democrats together had a
majority of this body, and as it does not appear that any
sustained effort was made to confirm the appointment of
McIntire, a certain measure of censure is their due for failing to co-operate with the President in his more energetic
policy.[5] Seven months later, Buchanan, in a private letter,

---

[1] Curtis, vol. ii. p. 523.

[2] See biographical sketch of J. S. Black ; open letters of Black to Judge
Hoar and Henry Wilson ; private letters of Stanton, printed by Curtis ;
McClure's Lincoln and Men of War Times.

[3] Crawford's Genesis of the Civil War, p. 25.

[4] Letter of Buchanan in *National Intelligencer*, Nov. 1, 1862 ; Buchanan's
Defence, p. 159.

[5] Jefferson Davis labored "to secure the defeat of the nomination of a
foreign collector for the port of Charleston."—Letter to Governor Pickens,
Jan. 13, Crawford, p. 263.

expressed the opinion that if the Senate had confirmed McIntire, the war would have begun in January.[1]

As we have seen, the President and General Scott had determined to send the powerful man-of-war *Brooklyn* with reinforcements to Sumter, but the general, averse to weakening the garrison at Fortress Monroe, and apprehensive that the *Brooklyn* would have trouble in crossing the bar at Charleston, changed the plan, and proposed to send a fast merchant steamer from New York, taking the troops from Governor's Island: this, he thought, would combine secrecy and quick despatch, and avoid the appearance of a coercive movement. To this alteration the President reluctantly consented.[2] The side-wheel steamship *Star of the West* was chartered. Taking on board two hundred men, with arms and ammunition, and four officers, she crossed the bar at Sandy Hook at nine o'clock on the night of January 5, and arrived about midnight, three days later, off Charleston harbor. All the coast lights being out, the steamer proceeded with caution, running slow and sounding until her captain discovered a light which he took to be on Fort Sumter, when she hove to and awaited daybreak. The Charlestonians, having received the day before from Secretary Thompson and Senator Wigfall advices of the expedition, were prepared for her.[3] A South Carolina guard-boat was on the watch. At daybreak, seeing the *Star of the West*, she burned colored signal-lights, and steamed rapidly up the channel, firing rockets as she went. The *Star of the West*, the soldiers all below, and the American flag flying at her flag-staff, now proceeded towards Fort Sumter. When within two miles of it, fire opened on her from a

---

[1] Letter of Sept. 18, 1861, to Horatio King, *Lippincott's Magazine*, April, 1872, p. 408. King was Buchanan's Postmaster-General after Holt's transfer to the War Department.

[2] Buchanan in the *National Intelligencer*, Nov. 1, 1862 ; Buchanan's Defence, p. 190 ; Nicolay and Hay, vol. iii. p. 95.

[3] Crawford, p. 178 ; Horatio King in *Lippincott's Magazine*, April, 1872, p. 409; Official Records, vol. i. p. 253.

masked battery on Morris Island, where was flying a red palmetto flag. At the first shot the *Star of the West* hoisted a large American ensign at the fore. Still proceeding towards Sumter, she remained ten minutes under the fire of this battery, which was five-eighths of a mile distant; she was struck once, but received no material damage. Observing the approach of a steamer towing a schooner supposed to be armed, and noting that, to reach Fort Sumter, they must pass under the guns of Moultrie, the captain of the *Star of the West*, and the lieutenant in command of the troops, after looking anxiously and in vain for some signal or for some evidence of support from Anderson, came to the conclusion that, their steamer being entirely unarmed, it would be useless and dangerous to proceed; therefore they turned about and steamed down the channel out to sea, returning directly to New York.[1]

Anderson had received no official advice of this movement, and had no orders to guide him. Early on the morning of January 9, Captain Doubleday of the Sumter garrison, gazing seaward, saw a large steamship, flying the United States flag, cross the bar, and the Morris Island battery fire a shot to bring her to. He hastened to wake Anderson, who gave orders to beat the long roll for the men to fall in and man the guns in the parapet: this was immediately done. A gunner was stationed at the eight-inch sea-coast howitzer with the lanyard in his hand ready to fire. Major Anderson, standing in the angle of the parapet, watched anxiously the movements of the steamship and the work of the battery. When the *Star of the West* hoisted the ensign to the fore, he took it as a signal, and endeavored to reply, but his flag, owing to the halyards being twisted about the staff, could not be used. Meanwhile Fort Moultrie opened fire on the steamer. Lieuten-

---

[1] See Capt. McGowan's report, New York *Times*, Jan. 14, cited in Moore's *Rebellion Record*, vol. i., Docs., p. 21; report of C. R. Woods, First Lieutenant, Official Records, vol. i. p. 9; account of a reporter of the New York *Evening Post* on board, cited in New York *Tribune*, Jan. 14.

ant Davis called Anderson's attention to the fact that their
guns could reach Moultrie but not the Morris Island battery.
Anderson, who had been held back by worthy hesitation, now
instructed Davis to "take command of a battery of two 42-
pounders which bore on Moultrie," and be in readiness for
action. Lieutenant Meade, a Virginian, earnestly entreated
that the order to fire, which would commence civil war,
should not be given. Just then the *Star of the West* turned
about, and Anderson said : "Hold on; do not fire. I will
wait. Let the men go to their quarters, leaving two at
each gun—I wish to see the officers at my quarters."[1]

The result of the council was that Anderson sent a note
to Governor Pickens, in which he asked if the firing on the
Star of the West had the official sanction, declaring that if
it were not disclaimed he "must regard it as an act of war,"
and he should not permit any vessels to pass "within range
of the guns" of his fort.[2] The governor replied that the
act of war was the sending of the reinforcement, that the
steamship had been fired upon in self-defence, and that he
perfectly justified the act.[3] Lapse of time and reflection
cooled the just anger of Anderson, who decided that, until
he had referred the matter to his government, he would not
carry out a threat which would assuredly light the torch of
civil war. To this effect he replied to Pickens, asking for
a safe-conduct for the bearer of his despatches. This was

---

[1] See Crawford, p. 185 *et seq.* His account is from his journal at the
time ; Doubleday's Fort Sumter and Moultrie, p. 101 *et seq.* Lieut.
Woods says specifically Moultrie did not fire. Neither Captain McGowan,
nor the reporter of the New York *Evening Post,* nor the Charleston correspondent of the New York *Tribune* mention the circumstance. The
Charleston *Courier* of Jan. 10 says Moultrie fired a few shots, Moore's
Rebellion Record, vol. i., Docs., p. 19. The Charleston *Mercury* of Jan. 10
says three shots were fired. Very satisfactory orders to Anderson from
Scott were written out Jan. 5, Official Records, vol. i. p. 132: these, according to Nicolay and Hay, vol. iii. p. 96, were on board of the *Star of the
West.*
[2] Anderson to Pickens, Jan. 9, Official Records,vol. i. p. 134.
[3] Pickens to Anderson, Jan. 9, ibid., p. 135.

courteously given, and Lieutenant Talbot of the garrison
was soon on his way to Washington.[1] Two days later the
governor sent to Anderson, under a flag of truce, Judge
Magrath, the Secretary of State of South Carolina, and
General Jamison, the Secretary of War, "to induce the delivery of Fort Sumter to the constituted authorities of the
State, with a pledge on its part to account for such public
property as is under your charge." [2] With this demand
Anderson refused to comply, but he proposed to send one
of his officers, in company with any messenger the governor
might name, to Washington in order to submit it to his
government.[3] This was agreed to, and Hayne, the attorney-
general of the State, and Lieutenant Hall of Fort Sumter
left for Washington, arriving there on the evening of January 13.[4]

From a military point of view, this abortive expedition
of the *Star of the West* is of little importance. Sending a
merchant steamer instead of a man-of-war was a mistake;
and there is yet another circumstance which might add to
the force of criticism upon the arrangements. The day that
the *Star of the West* sailed from New York, the War Department received a letter from Major Anderson advising
that a battery or batteries were being constructed on Morris
Island, and he added the assurance, "Thank God, we are
now where the government may send us additional troops
at its leisure. . . . We can command this harbor as long as
our government wishes to keep it." [5] On this account, an
order, concurred in by the President, General Scott, and
Secretary Holt, was telegraphed to New York to counter-
mand the departure of the steamship; but before the order
reached the proper officer, she had gone to sea.[6] January

---

[1] Anderson to Pickens, Jan. 9, Crawford, p. 190.
[2] Pickens to Anderson, Jan. 11, ibid., p. 192.
[3] Anderson to Pickens, Jan. 11, ibid., p. 194.
[4] Buchanan's Defence, p. 193.
[5] Anderson to Cooper, Dec. 31, 1860. Received A. G. O., Jan. 5.
[6] Holt, March 5, 1861, in *National Intelligencer*, cited by Buchanan,

7, an order was sent to Farragut, commander of the *Brooklyn*, to go in aid and succor of the *Star of the West*, but not to cross the bar at Charleston.[1] He did not find her, but, as we have seen, she had received no damage and needed no assistance in returning to New York.

Politically, this attempt to send reinforcements to Sumter was of the highest importance. In connection with the President's special message of January 8 to Congress,[2] it was an emphatic confirmation of the new policy which began with the reply to the South Carolina commissioners. The contemporary political literature and books treating of that time, written since by men of national views, attest in a striking manner the immense change of feeling at the North towards the President from that which had prevailed in November and December. The senators of the seceding States were no longer on a friendly personal and political footing at the White House.[3] Jefferson Davis, who had not visited the President for some time, immediately on hearing that the *Star of the West* had been fired upon, went to see him, and ineffectually entreated him to alter his course.[4] General Scott had become a trusted ad-

---

National Intelligencer, Nov. 1, 1862, and Horatio King, *Lippincott's Magazine*, April, 1872, p. 409.

[1] Buchanan's Defence, p. 191; Holt to Anderson, Jan. 10, Official Records, vol. i. p. 136.   [2] See Curtis, vol. ii. p. 433.

[3] Buchanan in *National Intelligencer*, Nov. 1, 1862.

[4] This was Jan. 9. Davis went to see the President before going to the Senate. Rise and Fall of the Confederate Government, vol. i. p. 218. That day the President's special message of Jan. 8, the first letter of the South Carolina commissioners, and Buchanan's reply were read. Davis criticised the President severely, and had a heated discussion with King of New York. The next day, in a set speech, he thus spoke : " The President's message of December had all the characteristics of a diplomatic paper, for diplomacy is said to abhor certainty as nature abhors a vacuum; and it was not within the power of man to reach any fixed conclusion from that message. When the country was agitated, when opinions were being formed, when we are drifting beyond the power ever to return, this was not what we had a right to expect from the Chief Magistrate. One policy or the other he ought to have taken. If a federalist, if believing this to

viser of the administration; this the North knew and rejoiced thereat, for it had implicit confidence in the general's capacity and patriotism.

The insult to the flag by South Carolina did not give rise
to as much indignation at the North as might have been expected.[1] Had Anderson, however, resented it by returning
the fire, that loyal uprising which took place three months
later would have occurred in January, and the civil war
would then have begun. Holt wrote Anderson that he had
rightly designated " the firing into the *Star of the West* as
'an act of war.' Had it been perpetrated," he continued, "by
a foreign nation, it would have been your imperative duty

---

be a government of force, if believing it to be a consolidated mass and
not a confederation of States, he should have said : no State has a right
to secede ; every State is subordinate to the federal government, and the
federal government must empower me with physical means to reduce to
subjugation the State asserting such a right.   If not, if a State-rights man
and a Democrat—as for many years it has been my pride to acknowledge
our venerable Chief Magistrate to be—then another line of policy should
have been taken.   The Constitution gave no power to the federal government to coerce a State ; the Constitution gave an army for the purposes of common defence, and to preserve domestic tranquillity ; but the
Constitution never contemplated using that army against a State.   A State
exercising the sovereign function of secession is beyond the reach of the
federal government, unless we woo her with the voice of fraternity, and
bring her back to the enticements of affection.   One policy or the other
should have been taken ; and it is not for me to say which, though my
opinion is well known ; but one policy or the other should have been pursued.   He should have brought his opinion to one conclusion or another,
and to-day our country would have been safer than it is."—*Congressional
Globe*, vol. i. p. 307.

" Benjamin thinks not otherwise nor any better of President Buchanan
than Mr. Douglas, though his opinion of Mr. Douglas is anything but flat-
tering."—Diary of a Public Man, entry Jan. 13.

[1] " I am surprised at the indifference, not to say apathy, with which this
overt defiance to the federal authority and this positive insult to the federal flag have been received by the people of the North and West.   Certainly, since we are not at this moment in the blaze of civil war, there
would seem to be little reason to fear that we shall be overtaken by it at
all."—Diary of a Public Man, entry Jan. 13 ; see also the file of the New
York *Tribune*.

to have resented it with the whole force of your batteries;"
but under the circumstances, "your forbearance to return
the fire is fully approved by the President."[1]

A gratifying result of the *Star of the West* expedition was
the bringing about the resignation of Secretary Thompson.[2]
The change of policy of the administration caused another
satisfactory resignation, that of Thomas,[3] Secretary of the
Treasury, a Maryland States-rights man, whose political
principles, joined to his lack of financial ability and standing, made him unable to win the confidence of the moneyed
magnates of the country, which the administration now
especially needed. In September, 1860, United States five-
per-cent. stock had sold at 103;[4] in December the government was obliged to pay twelve per cent. for a loan of five
millions,[5] at the same time that New York State sevens
were taken at an average of about 101¼.[6] A pressure by
the bankers and financiers of New York city was now
brought to bear upon the President; this resulted in the
offer of the Treasury portfolio to John A. Dix, which he
promptly accepted.[7] A fitter appointment could not have
been made. Dix had been a soldier for sixteen years, then
he engaged in the practice of law, went into politics and
held office, became a newspaper editor and a member of the
Assembly of the State of New York, and afterwards served
one term in the national Senate. Entering politics a Jack-

---

[1] Holt to Anderson, Jan. 16, Official Records, vol. i. p. 140.

[2] For the correspondence of Jan. 8 and 9, see Curtis, vol. ii. p. 401. The
impropriety of Thompson's remaining in the cabinet after the 1st of December was appreciated by the Washington correspondent of the Charleston *Mercury*, who wrote Dec. 6, "Thompson still holds on to his post to
the disappointment and chagrin of his friends."

[3] This was Jan. 11. See the correspondence in Curtis, vol. ii. p. 404.

[4] Report of Cobb, Secretary of the Treasury, Dec. 4, 1860.

[5] President's special message of Jan. 8; Knox's United States Notes, p.
76. This was from the issue of Treasury notes having one year to run.
The money was obtained between Dec. 28 and Jan. 1, 1861.

[6] New York *Evening Post*, Dec. 26. The amount desired and allotted
was $1,200,000; about $4,000,000 was bid for.

[7] Jan. 11, Curtis, vol. ii. p. 401; Memoirs of J. A. Dix, vol. i. p. 368.

son Democrat, he became a member of the Albany regency, was a Free-soiler in 1848, and supported Breckinridge in 1860. When called to the Treasury Department he held the office of Postmaster of New York city. Now almost sixty-three years old, a gentleman born and bred, a scholar, a good speaker, he was honest and systematic in his private money affairs, and had a public character without reproach.[1] Dix applied himself energetically to his task, and although by this time Mississippi, Florida, and Alabama had seceded, he soon obtained five millions of money at an average rate of $10\frac{5}{8}$ per cent.[2]

It is a mark of the feeling existing in the commercial circles of New York city, that Belmont, early in December, 1860, began urging Governor Sprague, of Rhode Island, to recommend to the legislature of his State a repeal of her Personal Liberty law.[3] Later, Belmont tells Sprague that the leading men of Boston and other parts of Massachusetts, and of New York, were working earnestly in the same direction.[4] In an address to the people of Massachusetts, the arguments for such a course were enforced over the signature of citizens who were of the highest character and position.[5] December 30, 1860, Belmont wrote Herschel V. Johnson, of Georgia, who united with Stephens in opposing secession, that a caucus of governors of seven Republican States had been held in New York city, and that they would recommend to their legislatures " the *unconditional* and *early* repeal of the Personal Liberty bills passed

---

[1] I have drawn this characterization from the Memoirs of J. A. Dix, by Morgan Dix.

[2] Knox's United States Notes, p. 76. This was Jan. 19, and the money was obtained on Treasury notes having one year to run.

[3] Belmont to Sprague, Dec. 6, 1860.   [4] Ibid, Dec. 19, 1860.

[5] Among the signers were: Lemuel Shaw, B. R. Curtis, H. J. Gardner, and George Ticknor, of Boston; Jared Sparks, Charles Theo. Russell, and Theophilus Parsons, of Cambridge; George Peabody, of Salem; J. G. Abbott, of Lowell; Levi Lincoln, of Worcester; and George Ashmun, of Springfield, New York *World*, Dec. 17, 1860; Life of Garrison, vol. iv. p. 2.

by their respective States."[1] This information was substantially correct. Washburn of Maine, Banks of Massachusetts, Morgan of New York, and Yates of Illinois
(Republicans), did make such recommendations; as did also
Sprague of Rhode Island, and Packer of Pennsylvania
(Democrats). Dennison, of Ohio (Republican), said that a
modification of the Fugitive Slave law would secure the
repeal of the obnoxious portions of the Personal Liberty
acts. Before the end of January, Rhode Island repealed
her Personal Liberty law; Massachusetts, in March, and
Vermont, in April, modified theirs. Ohio had no such act,
but her legislature recommended to her sister States to repeal any of their statutes "conflicting with or rendering
less efficient the Constitution or the laws," and thus restore
confidence between the States;[2] while the Wisconsin legislature took the preliminary steps towards revising her Personal Liberty act.[3] No doubt can exist that if it had been
believed possible to save the Union in this way, every
Northern State would by the 1st of May have repealed
these laws or satisfactorily altered them. Nothing is
clearer than that the South, after the first days of January,
was estopped from alleging as a grievance the making null
of the Fugitive Slave law.

Although the Senate committee had failed to agree on
any plan,[4] neither Crittenden nor Douglas despaired of securing an acceptable compromise. To an inquiry of some

---

[1] Belmont's Letters, privately printed, p. 27.   [2] Jan. 14.
[3] Harrisburg *Union*, cited by *National Intelligencer*, Jan. 15; New York
Tribune, Jan. 3, 8; Appleton's Annual Cyclopædia, 1861, pp. 436, 452,
556, 576 *et seq.*, 634; *Congressional Globe*, 2d Sess. 36th Cong., p. 44;
McPherson's Political History of the Rebellion, p. 44; Life of Samuel
Bowles Merriam, vol. i. p. 275; Memoirs of J. A. Dix, vol. i. p. 355; Life
of Colfax, Hollister, p. 169. The *National Intelligencer* of Dec. 11, in an
analysis of the Personal Liberty laws, stated that only those of Vermont,
Massachusetts, Michigan, and Wisconsin were "clearly unconstitutional."
Banks was the retiring governor of Massachusetts. Andrew, his successor,
sustained the Personal Liberty act of his State.
[4] Dec. 28. 1860. *Ante.* p. 178.

Georgia Union men concerning the prospect, they sent a joint telegraphic despatch saying, "We have hopes that the rights of the South and of every State and section may be protected within the Union. Don't give up the ship. Don't despair of the Republic." [1] January 3, Crittenden made to the Senate the novel proposition that the sense of the people should be taken by submitting his compromise to the popular vote.[2] Four days later he gave his reason for suggesting this extraordinary method ; it was because he doubted his ability to command in the Senate the two-thirds majority necessary to recommend his constitutional amendments to the States.[3] " The sacrifice to be made for the preservation of this government," he urged, " is comparatively worthless. Peace and harmony and union in a great nation were never purchased at so cheap a rate as we now have it in our power to do." [4] Douglas made a powerful argument in favor of Crittenden's proposal.[5]

---

[1] The telegram was dated Dec. 29, 1860. McPherson, p. 38. "I see some signs of hope, but it is probably a deceptive light."—John Sherman to General Sherman, Jan. 6, *Century Magazine*, Nov., 1892, p. 94.

[2] *Congressional Globe*, p. 237. For his compromise, see p. 150.

[3] *Globe*, p. 264.   [4] Jan. 3, ibid., p. 237.

[5] His speech was on Jan. 3. He said : " I hold that the election of any man, no matter who, by the American people, according to the Constitution, furnishes no cause, no justification, for the dissolution of the Union. But we cannot close our eyes to the fact that the Southern people have received the result of that election as furnishing conclusive evidence that the dominant party of the North, which is soon to take possession of the federal government under that election, are determined to invade and destroy their constitutional rights. Believing that their domestic institutions, their hearth-stones, and their family altars, are all to be assailed, at least by indirect means, and that the federal government is to be used for the inauguration of a line of policy which shall have for its object the ultimate extinction of slavery in all the States, old as well as new, South as well as North, the Southern people are prepared to rush wildly, madly, as I think, into revolution, disunion, war, and defy the consequences, whatever they may be, rather than to wait for the development of events, or submit tamely to what they think is a fatal blow impending over them and over all they hold dear on earth." Considering that Lincoln's " house-divided-against-itself " speech has been circulated as a campaign document, " is it

January 10, Jefferson Davis in a set speech gave expression to the views of the South. He argued the right of secession. "All that is not granted in the Constitution belongs to the States;" he said, "and nothing but what is granted in the Constitution belongs to the federal government; and keeping this distinction in view, it requires but little argument to see the conclusion at which we necessa-

---

surprising that the people of the South should suppose that he was in earnest and intended to carry out the policy which he had announced? . . . I do not, however, believe the rights of the South will materially suffer under the administration of Mr. Lincoln. . . . But this apprehension has become wide-spread and deep-seated in the Southern people. It has taken possession of the Southern mind, sunk deep in the Southern heart, and filled them with the conviction that their firesides, their family altars, and their domestic institutions are to be ruthlessly assailed through the machinery of the federal government. The Senator from Ohio (Wade) says he does not blame you, Southern Senators, nor the Southern people, for believing those things. . . .

"But we are told that secession is wrong, and that South Carolina had no right to secede. I agree that it is wrong, unlawful, unconstitutional, criminal. In my opinion, South Carolina had no right to secede; but *she has done it*. . . . *Are we prepared for war?* I do not mean that kind of preparation which consists of armies and navies and supplies and munitions of war; but are we prepared *in our hearts* for war with our own brethren and kindred? I confess I am not. . . . I prefer compromise to war. I prefer concession to a dissolution of the Union. . . . Why not allow the people to pass on these questions? If the people reject them, theirs will be the responsibility, and no harm will have been done by the reference. If they accept them, the country will be safe, and at peace. The political party which shall refuse to allow the people to determine for themselves at the ballot-box the issue between revolution and war on the one side, and obstinate adherence to a party platform on the other, will assume a fearful responsibility. A war upon a political issue, waged by the people of eighteen States against the people and domestic institutions of fifteen sister States, is a fearful and revolting thought. The South will be a unit, and desperate, under the belief that your object in waging war is their destruction, and not the preservation of the Union; that you meditate servile insurrection, and the abolition of slavery in the Southern States by fire and sword, in the name and under pretext of enforcing the laws and vindicating the authority of the government. You know that such is the prevailing, and, I may say, unanimous opinion at the South; and that ten million people are preparing for the terrible conflict under that conviction."— *Congressional Globe*, Appendix, p. 38 *et seq.*

rily arrive.   Did the States surrender their sovereignty to
the federal government?   Did the States agree that they
never could withdraw from the federal Union? . . . The
Constitution was a compact between independent States;
it was not a national government. . . . It was not adopted
by the mass of the people, as we all know historically; it
was adopted by each State."

Touching the present crisis, it devolves on the majority
section to consider now what it will do, "for with every
motion of that clock is passing away your opportunity.   It
was greater when we met on the first Monday in December
than it is now; it is greater now than it will be on the first
day of next week. . . . I would that it still remained to
consider what we might calmly have considered on the first
Monday in December — how this could be avoided; but
events have rolled past that point.   You would not make
propositions when they would have been effective.   I presume you will not make them now; and I know not what
effect they would have if you did.   Your propositions would
have been most welcome if they had been made before
any question of coercion, and before any vain boasting of
powers."

It pained Davis to think of quitting the Union.   "It may
be pardoned to me, sir," he said, " who, in my boyhood was
given to the military service, and who have followed under
tropical suns and over northern snows the flag of the
Union, suffering from it as it does not become me to speak
it, if I here express the deep sorrow which always over-
whelms me when I think of taking a last leave of that object of early affection and proud association, feeling that
henceforth it is not to be the banner which, by day and by
night, I am ready to follow, to hail with the rising and bless
with the setting sun. . . .

" Your platform," he said to the Republicans, " on which
you elected your candidate denies us equality.   Your votes
refuse to recognize our domestic institutions which pre-ex-
isted the formation of the Union, our property which was

guarded by the Constitution.   You refuse us that equality without which we should be degraded if we remained in the Union.   You elect a candidate upon the basis of sectional hostility; one who, in his speeches, now thrown broadcast over the country, made a distinct declaration of war upon our institutions. . . . What boots it to tell me that no direct act of aggression will be made?   I prefer direct to indirect hostile measures which will produce the same result.   I prefer it, as I prefer an open to a secret foe.   Is there a Senator upon the other side who to-day will agree that we shall have equal enjoyment of the territories of the United States?   Is there one who will deny that we have equally paid in their purchases, and equally bled in their acquisition in war?   Then, is this the observance of your compact?   Whose is the fault if the Union be dissolved? . . .

"Senators, I have spoken longer than I desired. . . . The time is near at hand when the places which have known us as colleagues laboring together, can know us in that relation no more forever.   I have striven to avert the catastrophe which now impends over the country, unsuccessfully; and I regret it.   For the few days which I may remain, I am willing to labor in order that that catastrophe shall be as little as possible destructive to public peace and prosperity.   If you desire at this last moment to avert civil war, so be it; it is better so.   If you will but allow us to separate from you peaceably, since we cannot live peaceably together, to leave with the rights we had before we were united, since we cannot enjoy them in the Union, then there are many relations which may still subsist between us, drawn from the associations of our struggles from the Revolutionary era to the present day, which may be beneficial to you as well as to us."[1]

It seemed as if the drama of 1850 would again be en-

---

[1] *Congressional Globe*, p. 308 *et seq.*, and the speech may also be found in Davis's Rise and Fall of the Confederate Government, vol. i. p. 603.

acted. It might be said that the mantle of Clay had fallen upon Crittenden, another son of Kentucky. Douglas spoke for the compromise on behalf of the Northern Democrats, even as he and Cass had spoken eleven years previously. Davis had succeeded to the leadership at that time held by Calhoun. Would the part then played by Daniel Webster be taken? Seward now filled the public eye as the greater statesman had done in 1850, and was the exponent of the Republicans as Webster had been of the Northern Whigs. Rumor's tongue busied itself with the New York senator's opinions and proposed action. It was constantly asserted and as uniformly denied that he would support the Crittenden compromise; and the denials came from better authority than the assertions.[1] Seward's potent influence and commanding position at this time is undoubted, but he had an overweening sense of his own importance; he thought that he held in his hands the destinies of his country. "I will try to save freedom and my country;" "I have assumed a sort of dictatorship for defence, and am laboring night and day with the cities and States;" "It seems to me that if I am absent only three days, this administration, the Congress, and the district would fall into consternation and despair; I am the only *hopeful, calm, conciliatory* person here;" "The present administration and the incoming one unite in devolving on me the responsibility of averting" civil war: these are his expressions when writing to the sympathetic home circle at Auburn.[2] December 28, 1860, he accepted Lincoln's offer of the secretaryship of State;[3] the Albany *Evening Journal* of January 9 gave this news to the world. Two days before he rose in the Senate to appease the anxiety of the people as to his position came the intelligence that

---

[1] See the files of the New York *Herald* and New York *Tribune* for Jan.

[2] The dates of these letters are respectively Dec. 28, 1860, Jan. 3, 18, 23— two written before his great speech, two after, Life of Seward, vol. ii, pp. 487, 491, 497.   [3] Ibid., p. 487.

the convention of Mississippi had passed an ordinance of secession; the morning newspapers of the day on which he spoke related that the conventions of Florida and Alabama had done likewise.[1]

January 12 Seward spoke to a packed Senate chamber, to lobbies and corridors filled with people straining their ears to catch any word that might give to them and to a waiting and distracted country an inkling of the plan of deliverance from disunion.[2] At first nearly every one was in some degree disappointed. Confidence in the power of one man to find a solution for the troubles that for so many years had been gathering to a head had risen too high. He proposed no concession to the South, beyond that which the Republicans had submitted in the Senate committee of thirteen.[3] He suggested, however, that when the secession movements had ended and the public mind had resumed its wonted calm—say in " one, two, or three years hence "—that a national convention should be called to consider the matter of amending the Constitution.[4] Of course Seward's speech met with no favor in the cotton States. The secessionists of Virginia maintained that it destroyed the last hope of compromise.[5] The feeling of the Union

---

[1] Mississippi passed her ordinance Jan. 9, Florida Jan. 10. Alabama Jan. 11. The New York *Tribune* did not have the news from Florida until its issue of Jan. 12.

[2] Washington correspondence New York *Tribune*, Jan. 12; Ben: Perley Poore's Reminiscences, vol. ii. p. 54.   [3] *Ante*, p. 175.

[4] I have not given an abstract or extracts from Seward's speech for the reason that it was important for its tone rather than for any plan proposed, and needs to be read as a whole to be comprehended. It may be found in Seward's Works, vol. iv. p. 651, as well as in the *Congressional Globe*, p. 341. A full and careful report of it was printed in the New York *Tribune* of Jan. 14. It was an able speech. The New York *Tribune* considered it "rhetorically and as a literary performance . . . unsurpassed by any of its author's earlier productions."—Editorial of Jan. 14. " I deplored Seward's speeches. [Those of Jan. 12 and 31.] The first he read to me and I supplicated him not to make it."—Sumner to Whittier, Feb. 5, Pierce's Memoir of Sumner, vol. iv. p. 17. Chase begged Seward "to give countenance to no scheme of compromise."—Schuckers, p. 202.

[5] Richmond *Enquirer*, Jan. 15.

men of the border States was one of bitter disappointment
and even profound grief.[1]   The conservative Republicans,
the Douglas Democrats, and the Bell and Everett men of
the North were, on reflection, well pleased, while the more
radical Republicans and the abolitionists did not like it.[2]
The tone of Seward's speech is admirable, and it undoubtedly had an effectual influence in making fidelity to the
Union, irrespective of previous party affiliations, a rallying-
point for Northern men.[3]

While Seward had not mentioned by name the Crittenden compromise, it was a decided inference from his statements that he could not be brought to support it ; and it
is a striking indication of the little confidence public men
and newspaper correspondents at Washington had in his
sincerity and constancy that the rumor that he would
come out for the compromise continually reappears.   But
he had a great hold on the Northern people ; their faith
in him was unbounded.   The Richmond *Whig* was not
far out of the way when it asserted that his vote in favor
of submitting the Crittenden propositions to the people
" would give peace at once to the country," meaning that
he would carry with him a majority of the Republican senators.[4]   The proposal to consult the people directly attracted much attention ; as we shall see later, it was the last
chance for averting civil war, and, to be effective, it should

---

[1] Richmond *Whig*, Jan. 17; Baltimore *Daily Exchange*, Jan. 14; New York
Herald, which was a good representative of this opinion, Jan. 13.

[2] See references of Douglas to Seward, Diary of a Public Man, *North
American Review*, Oct. and Nov., 1879; letter of August Belmont to Seward, Jan. 17; *National Intelligencer*, Jan. 15; New York *Tribune* Jan. 14;
New York *Evening Post*, Jan. 14; Life of Garrison, vol. iv. p. 10; Seward's
letter to his daughter, Jan. 23, Life, vol. ii. p. 497.

[3] Few men have received a nobler tribute for a speech than Seward had
on this occasion from Whittier.

[4] Issue of Jan. 18.   The bill spoken of was Bigler's, which submitted
constitutional amendments, substantially the same as Crittenden's, provided the machinery for taking the vote, and fixed Feb. 12 as the date for
it.   This was introduced Jan. 14.

have been adopted before the conventions of Georgia and Louisiana, soon to meet, had assembled and taken the virtually irrevocable step of secession. Seward afterwards [1] spoke of the scheme as "an unconstitutional and ineffectual way" of taking the "sentiments of the people." But it was never shown to be unconstitutional. The idea was that the vote should be informal; that it could be regarded only as an instruction to Congress, morally, not legally, binding; that afterwards Congress would still preserve full liberty of action. Yet it was clearly enough understood that a vote of the country in favor of the Crittenden compromise would impel a majority of the Republican senators and representatives to give it their support. No doubt can now exist, and but little could have existed in January 1861, that if it had been submitted to the people it would have carried the Northern States by a great majority; that it would have obtained the vote of almost every man in the border States; and that it would have received the preponderating voice of all the cotton States but South Carolina.[2]

---

[1] Jan. 30. Works, vol. iv. p. 678.

[2] "It was an indisputable fact at this time that the vote cast for Douglas, numbering 1,365,976, and that cast for Bell, numbering 590,631, and the vote for Breckinridge in the free States, numbering 284,422, making a total of 2,241,029, was unanimously in favor of a peaceful and reasonable settlement of all difficulties with any of the Southern States. The vote for Lincoln was 1,857,610, of which at least one fourth would have approved of such a peaceable settlement of the difficulties as might have been satisfactory to all the Southern States, whose complaints were founded upon questions connected with slavery. Of the vote given to Breckinridge in the slave-holding States, numbering 563,531, more than one fourth of it desired a peaceable settlement upon such terms as would have been satisfactory to the friends of conciliation and compromise in the Northern States. Thus the voice of the people of the country at this time was overwhelmingly in favor of conciliation, forbearance, and compromise."—Appleton's Annual Cyclopædia, 1861, p. 700. It must be noted that South Carolina, having cast no popular vote, is not included in this estimate. It is, of course, hazardous to reduce one's opinions to figures, but I really believe that this writer has guessed pretty nearly the way the popular vote would have gone on the Crittenden compromise.

This proposal to take the sense of the country never came to a vote in the Senate; had a majority of the Republican senators favored it, the bill which provided for it would have been reached and adopted. The question

---

"Let the question be submitted to the people . . . and I will venture the prediction that your own people (*i.e.*, the Republicans) will ratify the proposed amendments to the Constitution."—Douglas, Senate, Jan. 3. "The resolutions offered by you will be endorsed by the people of Pennsylvania by 200,000 majority if we can get a vote."—Conrad, of Philadelphia, to Crittenden, Jan. 5, Life of Crittenden, Coleman, vol. ii. p. 251. "I feel perfect confidence that New York would give 150,000 majority for this measure."—Horatio Seymour to Crittenden, Jan. 18, ibid., p. 254. The advocates of the Crittenden compromise, "with good reason, claimed a large majority of the people in its favor, and clamored for its submission to a direct popular vote. Had such a submission been accorded, it is very likely that the greater number of those who voted at all would have voted to ratify it."—Greeley's American Conflict, vol. i. p. 380, written in 1864. "If a popular vote could have been had on the Crittenden compromise, it would have prevailed by an overwhelming majority. Very few Republicans would have voted for it; but very many would have refrained from voting at all; while their adversaries would have brought their every man to the polls in its support, and carried it by hundreds of thousands."—Greeley's Recollections of a Busy Life, p. 397.

See the list of petitions from all parts of the North and from the border States in favor of the Crittenden compromise, printed in Coleman's Life of Crittenden, p. 240 *et seq.* It fills nine pages; see also *Congressional Globe*, pp. 634, 646, 670, 692, 710, 719, 729, 777, 792, 798, 822, 839, 862, 896, 985, 1094, 1126, 1148, 1186, 1225, 1243. Some of these petitions are worthy of notice: one was from 182 cities and towns of Massachusetts, signed by 22,315 citizens; another from the Boston City Council; four fifths of the people of Indiana were said to be in favor of the Crittenden compromise; one petition was from 14,000 women; 2000 citizens of Philadelphia who had voted for Lincoln signed another. Seward presented two petitions signed by 63,000 inhabitants of New York city, praying for some plan of adjustment.—Seward's Works, vol. iv. p. 670. "Many Northern men, even some Republicans, were willing to vote" for the Crittenden compromise. —Wilson's Rise and Fall of the Slave Power, vol. iii. p. 72. "There is a great pressure here from the business and high social circles of all our great cities for a compromise."—J. S. Pike, from Washington to New York *Tribune*, Feb. 3. A Faneuil Hall meeting, composed largely of the friends of Webster, endorsed the Crittenden plan.—New York *Tribune*, Feb. 8. The New Jersey legislature urged her senators and representatives in Congress to support the Crittenden compromise.—Appleton's Annual Cyclopædia, 1861, p. 515. The Virginia legislature gave by resolu-

arises : are the Republicans to be justified for their position ?
On those who affirm that they are, it is incumbent to show
that an agreement on the basis of the Crittenden compromise would have adjourned but for a short while the
Civil War; that this compliance with the South would have
made the slave-holders more arrogant in their future demands; that the real issue to be decided was absolute surrender or resistance; and that a better time than this to
try conclusions could never be looked for.   On Northern
men who aver that the Republicans ought to have accepted the Crittenden compromise, it is incumbent to show
that it would have postponed the civil conflict for at least
a decade, with a fair chance of ultimately avoiding it; that

---

tion substantially its approval.—Ibid., p. 178. "We have never entertained the slightest doubt that if the voice of the people could be fairly
heard in this time of our trouble, there would be a satisfactory and permanent settlement of existing differences between the two sections within
less than thirty days."—Richmond *Whig*, Jan. 17.   "There can be no
doubt that the people of the United States are anxious to preserve the
Union, and are perfectly willing to make reasonable concessions to secure its preservation.   It is certainly true in regard to the South, and
we believe it is equally true in regard to the North. . . . In every State
except South Carolina (and we doubt very much if that State should be
excepted) which has seceded, a very large majority of the people would
gladly preserve the Union, if they had not been led to believe that the
people of the North are their enemies. . . . There can be no doubt that
Crittenden's plan of adjustment, if submitted to a direct vote of the people,
would be adopted by such a vote as never was polled in this country.
Almost everybody in the South, including some of the bitterest disunionists among us, would willingly accept that compromise as a final settlement
of the questions which divide the country.   The Northern papers with
singular unanimity assert that the people of that section would gladly do
the same."—Ibid, Jan. 28.   "I believe that the South would accept the
propositions submitted by Mr. Crittenden."—Senator Pearce, of Maryland,
to B. T. Johnson, Jan. 9, Charleston *Mercury*, Jan. 19.   The Ohio Democratic
State convention, held Jan. 23, asserted they "would accept with joy"
the Crittenden compromise.—*Congressional Globe*, p. 646.   The New York
Democratic State convention, held Jan. 31, approved it.—Greeley's American Conflict, vol. i. p. 395 ; see Shaler's Kentucky, p. 241 ; Carr's Missouri, p. 283.   Only a very few petitions were presented against the Crittenden compromise.—See *Congressional Globe*, pp. 1126, 1243, 1300, 1301.

for such time the two sections, with the power of slavery in the South unimpaired, could have lived on tolerable terms; that the South would not have demanded Cuba, Mexico, or Central America as a condition for remaining in the Union; that Lincoln was wrong when he asserted, "There is in my judgment but one compromise which would really settle the slavery question, and that would be a prohibition against acquiring any more territory;"[1] in short, that for ten years the South would have quietly and submissively gazed upon the larger growth of the North by immigration and by development of manufactures and the arts, thus fitting itself for the conflict that must come; or that, on the other hand, repeated submissions would not have brought the North to the point where, its spirit being gone, it would have refused to fight.   Between these alternatives, one of which was civil war with its waste of blood and treasure, with its train of men's sacrifices and women's anguish, and with its failure to settle the race question in the South; and the other, which would have been an aggravated repetition of what took place between 1854 and 1860, with the possibility of a war to follow between more powerful contestants: between these an historian may well shrink from pronouncing a decided choice. The argument that this very question was determined at the presidential election does not seem to me decisive.[2] It is true, the proposed action, so far as American practice

---

[1] Letter to J. T. Hale, Jan. 11, Nicolay and Hay, vol. iii. p. 288.

[2] The Crittenden compromise (*i.e.*, the article relating to the territories) "is precisely the question submitted to the people at the late presidential election, and which the people in all parts of the nation have condemned by an overwhelming vote.   After having been debated by the newspapers and orators for the last ten years, and after having been practically determined by the voice of the people, Mr. Crittenden desires to debate it anew in Congress, and to review the popular determination by another appeal to the ballot."—New York *Evening Post*, Jan. 16.   "How many voters in the last election, before they went to the polls, had seriously thought out for themselves the real issue of the contest?" asked C. F. Adams, Jr., in the *Atlantic Monthly* for April, 1861, p. 452.

went, was unprecedented, and would have made a bad precedent; but the situation was extraordinary, and had Congress patterned after Athens, the parent State of democracy, freedom, and justice, it might have been justified in letting those men who had to do the fighting and furnish the money decide whether it should be compromise or civil war. Nor does it dispose of the matter to declare the South, as it plainly appears from my narrative, wrong and unreasonable. True, its whole claim was for additional safeguards to slavery. That this institution was condemned by Christianity and ethics I have more than once taken occasion to say, and I can now add the condemnation of science in the words of Darwin, its greatest master in this century, who says: " The greatest curse on earth [is] slavery." [1] The assertion that the South should not be treated with because it was wrong, is answered by the poet in fitter words than an historian can use:

> "Courage may be shown
> Not in defiance of the wrong alone;
> He may be bravest who, unweaponed, bears
> The olive branch, and, strong in justice, spares
> The rash wrong-doer, giving widest scope
> To Christian charity and generous hope." [2]

On the other hand, it is true that the regret for the war which characterizes the present speculation as to whether it might not have been avoided, is to a large extent based on the teaching of a widely accepted theory of the evolution of society in opposition to a view inspired by poetry and a poetic political economy. [3]

---

[1] Letter of June 5, 1861, Life and Letters, vol. ii. p. 166.

[2] Whittier's poem, " To W. H. Seward."—The succeeding lines, however, show that he did not intend his poem to be used as a justification of the Crittenden compromise.

[3] Compare chaps. xviii. and xix., vol. ii. of Spencer's Sociology with Fletcher's tribute to war in The Two Noble Kinsmen:

> "Oh, great corrector of enormous times,
> Shaker of o'er-rank states, thou grand decider

Failing to get a favorable response from the Republicans to his proposal to submit the question to the people, Crittenden labored to get a vote of the Senate on his constitutional amendments and resolutions. He had to contend with the usual attempts of senators to obtain precedence for their favorite measures, and with the opposition of some men who thought that by hampering him, the policy of masterly inactivity, on which most of the Republican senators had resolved,[1] was best furthered. At last, on January 16, he had hopes of getting a vote. Powell's amendment, providing that slavery should be recognized in territory hereafter to be acquired as well as in that now held south of the Missouri line, was adopted. The amendment of Clark, of New Hampshire, had next to be considered; this virtually declared that no compromise was necessary, and that the Constitution "needs to be obeyed rather than amended." Owing to the refusal of six Southern senators to vote, this amendment was carried,[2] having received the

---

> Of dusty and old titles, that heal'st with blood
> The earth when it is sick, and curest the world
> O' th' pleurisy of people !"   —Act v. sc. i.*

"Nations have always reached their highest virtue, and wrought their most accomplished works in times of straightening and battle ; as on the other hand, no nation ever yet enjoyed a protracted and triumphant peace without receiving in its bosom ineradicable seeds of future decline."— Ruskin, Modern Painters, vol. iii. p. 334. Wordsworth told Emerson in 1833 "that they needed a civil war in America to teach the necessity of knitting the social ties stronger."—English Traits, chap. i.

[1] Pike to the New York *Tribune*, Washington, Jan. 5.

[2] These were Benjamin and Slidell of Louisiana, Hemphill and Wigfall of Texas, Iverson of Georgia, and Johnson of Arkansas. All but Johnson had voted on the Powell amendment. The senators from Mississippi, Alabama, and Florida no longer took an active part. The vote was 25 to 23.

* Lowell wrote Mr. Hughes, "St. Shakespeare Day, 1860 " · "I believe that Shakespeare has expressed the true philosophy of war in those magnificent verses in 'The Two Noble Kinsmen,' which are as unlike Beaumont and Fletcher as Michael Angelo's charcoal head on the wall of the Farnesina is unlike Raphael." —Article of C. E. Norton, in *Harper's Magazine*, Sept., 1893, p. 558.

unanimous support of the Republicans.[1] Crittenden, with the laudable desire of staying the course of secession in North Carolina and in the border States, telegraphed to Raleigh that the failure of his resolutions was due to the action of six Southern men.[2] Though this statement was technically correct, the truth is that it was the Republicans who for a second time defeated, for weal or for woe, the Crittenden compromise. Crittenden furthermore said, "There is yet good hope of success."[3] Pike saw with a clearer and more prophetic vision when he apprised the New York *Tribune* that the scheme had received its death-blow.[4]

The pressure of the country upon Congress in favor of some compromise was strong. While the radical Republicans were powerful enough to stifle whatever leaning there was in their party towards the Crittenden plan, they could not bring all their associates to their own policy of no concessions whatever, nor prevent the House committee of thirty-three from reporting a plan of compromise, January 14, through its chairman, Thomas Corwin. This plan retained the constitutional amendment safeguarding slavery in the States, and the recommendation for the repeal of the Personal Liberty laws which Seward, acting for his Republican colleagues, had offered in the Senate committee of thirteen;[5] it also proposed the admission of New Mexico " with or without slavery," but it was well understood this would add a slave State, so far as laws could make one, to the Union.[6] This compromise was more liberal to the

---

[1] Seward and Cameron were present and voted for it.

[2] D..te of despatch Jan. 17, published in Raleigh *Register*, Jan. 19, *National Intelligencer* Jan. 22.   [3] Ibid.

[4] Despatch of Jan. 16.   [5] *Ante*, p. 175.

[6] See Corwin's report; Anthony's speech in the Senate, Jan. 16. Charles Francis Adams, a prominent member of the committee of thirty-three, gives an interesting account of some of the proceedings in committee and his own action in a private letter of April 8, 1861, to George H. Monroe. I am indebted to Mr. Monroe for the letter in MS. Adams writes : "In point of fact, the measures were not mine. They were carefully examined by the Republican members of the committee, at the time when some posi-

South than was the suggestion the Republicans had thrown out in the Senate committee, in that it did not propose as a counterbalance to New Mexico the erection of a free State out of the rest of the national territory. The other

---

tive action had been demanded of them, or the committee would have come to an end with their opponents consolidated against them. Two thirds of the Republicans agreed upon the two propositions [the constitutional amendment and the admission of New Mexico]. I had expressed my acquiescence in them as the only practical solution of the existing difficulty without essential sacrifice. The only thing left was to put them in the hands of some one to present them to the full committee. It was then that the chairman, Mr. Corwin, proposed my name, as one which would have more effect in checking the panic at the South than any other. I was greatly surprised, and declined the responsibility at once. But I could not be deaf to the arguments, presented in a purely public sense, or insensible to the ignominy of shrinking from a useful object merely on the score of personal hazard to myself. I stated my feelings frankly, and at last devolved the whole responsibility on my friends. If *they* would say my action would do any particular good, I would incur the risk, be it what it might. They did so say, and I went forward accordingly

" At that time there was no objection made on our side to one of the measures, the proposed amendment to the Constitution. The scruple raised was against the New Mexico proposition. Yet the only thing the other side manifested any satisfaction with was the amendment—and the other they declined to regard as a boon in any sense. I rested upon the ground that we conceded nothing ; that these measures were in no sense a compromise, because we asked for nothing and offered what we did solely as assurances of our good faith in the declarations constantly made by us when out of power. As to New Mexico, I declared very frankly that in making the offer I intended to destroy the claim of *protection* to slavery. It was that demand which made the entire basis of the Breckinridge platform. Of course the acceptance of the proposition would have disbanded the organization. They saw this clearly as I did. Hence the tenacity with which they clung to the clause about future territory. In comparison with this the presence of half a dozen slaves more or less in New Mexico seemed a trifle. Every proposition of a compromise line of latitude involved an implication of a future concession south of that line everywhere. On the contrary, my offer broke the charm of the magic line and restricted the question within the limits of a territory where slavery is not at home.

" The limit of my concession was then to give the slave-holders a chance to make New Mexico a slave State if they could. To that extent my offer was made in good faith. I did suppose they might make it such politically for a while. But the action of a new government in a different sense

resolutions and recommendations, and the proposed revision of the Fugitive Slave act reported by Corwin would probably have been satisfactory to the South, could an agreement have been reached on the territorial question. Had the senators and the representatives from the six cotton States still remaining in Washington acceded to this plan as a settlement, which indeed they ought to have done, it would undoubtedly have commanded a majority of Republicans and received the assent of Congress. While Lincoln could not have been brought to approve of the Crittenden compromise, he would have been satisfied with such an adjustment as Corwin offered. "I say now, however," he wrote Seward, February 1, "as I have all the while said, that on the territorial question — that is, the question of extending slavery under the national auspices—I am inflexible. I am for no compromise which assists or permits the extension of the institution on soil owned by the nation. And any trick by which the nation is to acquire territory, and then allow some local authority to spread slavery over it, is as obnoxious as any other. I take it that to effect some such result as this, and to put us again on the high road to a slave empire, is the object of all these proposed compromises. I am against it. As to fugitive slaves, District of Columbia, slave-trade among the slave States, and whatever springs of necessity from the fact that the institution is amongst us, I care but little, so that what is done be comely and not altogether outrageous. Nor do I care much about New Mexico, if further extension were hedged against." [1]

At this time another plan was proposed which received little heed, and naturally has attracted almost no attention from historians, yet was it eminently wiser and more philo-

---

would ere long counteract that influence, and the result would in the end be to make one more free State. That I was right in this idea is proved clearly enough by the final vote in the House which showed the slaveholders turning the scale *against* the bill."— *Vide infra*, note 2, p. 314.

[1] Nicolay and Hay, vol. iii. p. 260.

sophic than either the Crittenden or Corwin compromises, for they were makeshifts, only putting off the evil day, while this may be adjudged a real solution of the irrepressible conflict and the race question. The proposition was for gradual, compensated emancipation of the slaves in the border States, and colonizing them in Liberia or Hayti; it did not include the cotton States, since four of them had already seceded, and the other three were getting ready to follow. The project first appeared as a matter of discussion in Washington.[1] It then came up in the shape of a resolution offered in the State Assembly of New York, requesting the senators and representatives of that State to urge such a measure in Congress. The plan involved the consent of the States in question, and made the remuneration of the slave-holders and the expense of the colonization a charge upon the general government. The New York *Tribune* argued earnestly for a trial of it, reasoning with the free States that its money cost should be no objection, for, "One year of war would cost as much or more." To the slave States this journal addressed an argument that at this day[2] reads like prophetic inspiration. "Over the future of the South," it said, "impends, not far off, the black cloud of Africanization. Now is the time, if ever, to avert such a catastrophe. A little longer, and it may be too late."[3] McKean, a Republican representative from New York, offered a resolution in the national House providing for a select committee of five to inquire into the feasibility of such a project, and that was the end of it.[4] Instructed as we are by the experience of the generation which has succeeded, we cannot fail to see how many evils gradual and compensated emancipation would have avoided, and, from the economical point of view, what a saving it would have

---

[1] Pike to the New York *Tribune*, Jan. 15.   [2] 1895.
[3] *Tribune*, Jan. 24; see, also, Jan. 19. The resolution was introduced into the New York Assembly, Jan. 18, by Fullerton of Orange.
[4] Feb. 11, *Congressional Globe*, p. 854; see remarks on the subject in the House by representative Van Wyck, of New York, ibid., p. 631.

been!¹ There is no doubt whatever that the North would have been glad to agree to such a measure, and apply it to the cotton as well as to the border States. Had the Southern people known what the next four years were destined to bring forth, they would have voted for it to a man, but to urge a project of that kind upon men in their temper of mind in the winter of 1861 would have been to increase their irritation.²

Jefferson Davis and the senators from Florida and Alabama did not withdraw from the Senate until they had been officially notified of the secession of their States. It was January 21 when they made their formal leave-taking, and all spoke briefly. Davis, after a sleepless night caused by physical and mental distress, addressed the crowded chamber and galleries in a mournful and touching strain. Explaining the sincerity of his belief in the right of secession—for "it is," he asserted, "to be justified upon the basis that the States are sovereign"— he gave expression to his regret that the situation demanded that Mississippi should surrender the benefits of the Union, and sever the close and enduring ties of affection that bound her to it. For himself, as this was the last time he should ever speak in the Senate of the United States, he wished to say he had no feeling of hostility to the senators from the North; he wished them and their people well; he hoped that peaceful relations might continue with them, but, if they should choose otherwise, " we, putting our trust in God and in our own firm hearts and strong arms, will vindicate the right as best we may." Wishing to be forgiven for any pain he

---

¹ In round numbers there were in 1860 in all the slave States 4,000,000 slaves. A current and very high estimate of their value was $4,000,000,000. The New York *Tribune's* estimate of $400 each (instead of $1000 each), based on a sale at auction in Charleston of twenty-four cotton-plantation hands, at an average of $437 each, was too low (see New York *Tribune*, Jan. 19). The cost of the war, according to Edward Atkinson (The Industrial Progress of the Nation, p. 183), was $8,000,000,000.

² See New York *Times,* cited by the *Tribune,* Jan. 24.

had inflicted in the heat of discussion upon any senator, he
forgave whatever offence had been done himself.   To that
audience, affected to tears by the plaintive music of his
voice, the sincerity of his manner, and the pathos of his
words, the final farewell he bade his fellow-senators came
as the knell of the glorious Union.   That night Davis
wrestled in prayer, offering up more than once the supplication: "May God have us in his holy keeping, and grant
that, before it is too late, peaceful councils may prevail." [1]

Other parting addresses of senators and representatives
of the seceded States followed from time to time, until the
withdrawal of senators and members became a part of the
order of business of the day in the Senate and in the
House.   By February 3, Seward could write: "Either the
revolution grows more moderate, or we become more accustomed to it and society begins to resume its tone." [2]

Secession moved apace.   The conventions of Mississippi,
Florida, Alabama, Georgia, Louisiana, and Texas in quick
succession passed ordinances dissolving their bonds with
the federal Union. [3]   We shall better understand the ensu-
ing civil war if we study the movements in the four most
important of these States, in relation to a theory which asserts that the secession was a conspiracy whose central
cabal, composed of Southern senators and representatives
in Washington, dictated through its ramifications in the
States the inception and the course of the revolution.   The
most significant meeting of the junto was that of January
5, at which were present all of the senators, save one, of
these six cotton States. [4]   They resolved that each of the
Southern States should secede as soon as possible, and that
a Southern confederacy should be organized forthwith; and

---

[1] Memoir of Davis by his wife, vol. i. p. 69 *et ante;* Davis's Rise and
Fall of the Confederate Government, vol. i. p. 220 ; *Congressional Globe,*
p. 487.   [2] Life, vol. ii. p. 502.

[3] The dates were respectively Jan. 9, 10, 11, 19, 26, and Feb. 1.

[4] Fitzpatrick, of Alabama, was not present.   Johnson, of Arkansas, was
one of the number.

they asked instructions whether they and the representatives should remain in Congress until the 4th of March, for the purpose of defeating hostile legislation threatened against the seceding States. These resolutions were communicated to the conventions of Florida, Mississippi, and Alabama, then assembled or just about to assemble.[1] The authoritative action of this caucus, taken in connection with the array of Northern contemporary and later writers that support the conspiracy theory, will necessarily prevent the student of history from abandoning it, without careful investigation and proper reflection, to adopt the view held by nearly all of the Southern writers, that secession was the people's movement.[2] Before proceeding to consider the two different opinions, it is worthy of remark that if secrecy inheres in a conspiracy, that quality was not here preserved, for a substantially correct account of the caucus of senators on Saturday evening, January 5, was published in the Charleston *Mercury* of the following Monday.

In its public manifestations, secession had all the marks of a popular movement, proceeding in the regular manner which we should expect from a community accustomed to constitutional government and to delegate its powers to chosen representatives. Legislatures called conventions of the people.[3] Then, after animated canvasses in Alabama, Georgia, and Louisiana,[4] and after a full understanding by the electors in all of the States that they were voting for immediate secession or in favor of delay, delegates were

---

[1] Official Records, vol. i. p. 443 ; Washington despatch to Charleston *Mercury*, Jan. 6.

[2] I am acquainted with only one Southern writer who maintains the conspiracy theory, Pollard. See chap. vi. of his Life of Davis, published in 1869. I presume his support of it has had something to do with its being so commonly received at the North.

[3] Except in the case of Alabama, where by virtue of an authorization of the legislature the governor called the convention.

[4] The vote in Georgia was, for secession, 50,243, for delay, 39,123. Life of Toombs, Pleasant Stovall, p. 209 ; in Louisiana, 20,448 for secession, 17,296 for delay, Moore's Rebellion Record, Diary, vol. i. p. 20.

chosen to the conventions at popular elections. Soon after each convention met it adopted by an imposing majority its ordinance of secession.[1]

If this were the whole story, the conspiracy theory would not have so large a number of adherents. But other circumstances connected with the enactment of secession must be taken into account. In Alabama, Georgia, and Louisiana there was a large falling-off of the vote from that which had been cast at the presidential election. In Georgia a violent storm on election day cost the conservative party, in the opinion of Stephens, ten thousand votes.[2] In the conventions of Mississippi, Alabama, Georgia, and Louisiana a proposal in each one of them to submit the ordinance of secession to a popular vote was voted down.[3] In the Alabama convention the discussion of this project was attended with heat. Yancey denounced the people of northern Alabama, who were opposed to immediate secession, as "misguided, deluded, wicked men," who had entered on the path that led to treason and rebellion. He declared that they ought to be coerced into submission to the will of the majority.

---

[1] In Mississippi on the third day of the session by a vote of 84 to 15, Journal of the Convention, p. 14. In Florida on the sixth day by a vote of 62 to 7; in Alabama on the fifth day by a vote of 61 to 39, Appleton's Annual Cyclopædia, 1861, pp. 314, 10. In Georgia on the fourth day by a vote of 208 to 89, Journal of the Convention, p. 35. In Louisiana on the fourth day by a vote of 113 to 17, Journal of the Convention, p. 18. In Texas on the ninth day by a vote of 166 to 7, Appleton's Annual Cyclopædia, 1861, p. 688.

[2] Johnston and Browne, p. 378. According to the Richmond *Whig* of Feb. 5, the number of voters in New Orleans was 17,000; only 8000 went to the polls; majority in favor of secession, 300.

[3] In Mississippi by a vote of 70 to 29, Journal of the Convention, p. 14; in Alabama by a vote of 54 to 45, History and Debates of the Alabama Convention. The vote is not given in the Georgia Convention Journal. It was probably *viva voce;* see p. 46. In Louisiana, by 84 to 43, Journal of the Convention, p. 17. The Texas convention, owing to an irregularity in the proceedings that led to its choice, submitted by an almost unanimous vote the ordinance to the people. It was ratified Feb. 23, 34,794 for, 11,235 against, a falling-off from the vote at the presidential election.—Appleton's Annual Cyclopædia, 1861, p. 689.

Davis, of Huntsville, replied that if such an attempt were
made, the people of northern Alabama would meet the precipitators at the foot of their mountains and dispute the
question at the point of the bayonet.[1] In the conventions
of Mississippi, Alabama, Georgia, and Louisiana, motions
looking towards an attempt to get their grievances redressed in the Union, the adoption of which would have
caused delay in secession, were made, but failed to carry a
majority.[2] In the Georgia convention Herschel V. Johnson,
after consultation with Stephens, prepared a substitute for
the ordinance of secession, which provided for a convention
of the slave States and "the independent republics of South
Carolina, Florida, Alabama, and Mississippi," to be held at
Atlanta, February 16, to consider their relations with the
federal government and adopt the course that their interest
and safety might require.   This substitute, moreover, specified as the paramount grievance of Georgia the Personal
Liberty acts, and intimated that if they were repealed
she would be content to remain in the Union. The remarks of Stephens were powerful. "My judgment," he
declared, "is against secession for existing causes. I have
not lost hope of securing our rights in the Union and under
the Constitution. . . . I have been and am still opposed to
secession as a remedy against anticipated aggressions on
the part of the federal executive or Congress. I have held
and do now hold that the point of resistance should be the
point of aggression." Johnson's substitute, however, was
lost, receiving 133 votes in its favor to 164 against it.[3]

These facts, in the light of a full knowledge of the time
and a correct comprehension of the attitude taken by the
South, do not, however, prove that the course of the South-

---

[1] Smith's Debates of Alabama Convention, pp. 68–74.

[2] In Mississippi—ayes 21, nays 78, Journal of the Convention, p. 14.   In
Alabama—ayes 45, nays 54, Smith's Debates, p. 80.   In Louisiana—ayes
24, nays 106, Journal of the Convention, p. 15.

[3] Journal of the Convention, p. 32 ; Stephens's War between the States,
vol. ii. p. 300 *et seq. ;* Johnston and Browne, p. 380.

ern people was dictated by a dozen or by a hundred conspirators from whose secret conclaves in Washington and in the State capitals went forth decrees, nor that the politicians led the people by the nose. Davis and Toombs are always classed among the conspirators, yet Davis was in favor of delay;[1] and Toombs, in spite of his vehement talk at Washington,[2] could not keep pace with the secession movement in his State.[3] The South Carolina radicals murmured that the people were hampered by the politicians.[4] The secessionists would certainly have made their case stronger had they submitted the ordinance of secession to a popular vote, but there is no reason whatever for thinking that they feared the result; that plan, however, involved delay, and they were anxious above all to get the proposed

---

[1] See letter to Rhett, Nov. 10, 1860, Life of Davis, Alfriend, p. 222; Davis's Rise and Fall of the Confederate Government, vol. i. pp. 58, 201, 207, 208; Life of Davis by his wife, vol. i. p. 697; "By telegrams and letters to every Southern State he [Davis] endeavored to postpone their action."—Ibid., vol. ii. p. 3; New York *Times*, Jan. 23, cited in Moore's Rebellion Record, Rumors and Incidents, p. 20; Pike to New York *Tribune*, Washington, Feb. 12.

[2] See his Senate speech of Jan. 7.   [3] *Ante*, p. **213.**

[4] "My own opinion is," wrote William Gilmore Simms, May 21, 1860, "that the people of all the South are monstrously ahead of all their politicians."—Trent, p. 249. The Charleston *Mercury* said, Jan. 17, 1861: "If there is any one thing more than another disheartening and disgusting in the present juncture of affairs, it is the course of Southern politicians at Washington. . . . Southern senators upon the floor of Congress demean themselves by pitiable lamentations and lachrymose appeals to haughty, contemptuous, and openly threatening enemies — Republicans — Yankees. . . . Southern senators, representing directly sovereign States, must fall to begging, kneeling like very mendicants, for Yankee charity. . . . From first to last, in this great Southern movement for independence, the Southern politicians have been but stumbling-blocks in the way of Southern advancement. Vain schemes of compromise upon compromise they have labored, concocted, and offered to their scoffing enemies."

It also said, Feb. 7: "South Carolina warned the North, appealed to the South, still her prayers were in vain. *Too many Southern politicians had been bought up.* The people of the North judged the people of the South by the men they saw in the pestiferous atmosphere of Washington—a sad mistake."

Southern Confederacy speedily into operation. The course actually pursued had the best of precedents; the Constitution of 1787 had been ratified by conventions of the States without subsequent submission to the people, and it seemed fitting that the ties which its adoption had knit should be severed by similar sovereign bodies.[1] Nor were the secret sessions of the conventions, when matters of the highest importance were considered, an indication of a desire to repress the so-called union sentiment. In Milledgeville, the capital of Georgia, men who flocked there to exert a pressure on the convention were enthusiastic for immediate secession, and had they been admitted to the galleries they would heartily have cheered the precipitators and cried down Johnson and Stephens.[2] Revolutions always bring the radicals to the front, and we may safely presume that the element which was noted at Milledgeville preponderated in the other State capitals. The charge was freely made that intimidation bore a considerable part in the choice of a majority of delegates favoring secession, and that throughout the cotton States a veritable " reign of terror" held sway. While there may have been isolated cases of intimidation, the evidence does not show that this mode of carrying elections prevailed. The evolution of the secession movement proves that the employment of such a force would have been superfluous. A great leader had at the proper moment joined together the two ideas of the rightfulness of slavery and the sovereignty of the States, ideas which in that conjunction had been hitherto the property of agitators, of writers for the newspapers and the magazines. The ground being in a measure prepared, some at once received the doctrine gladly, while others accepted it because it was advocated by Calhoun. Then ensued in the cotton States the forming of a public opinion which, mak-

---

[1] South Carolina and Georgia, being of the original thirteen States, their secession ordinances were a repeal of the ordinances of the elder conventions which had ratified the Constitution of the United States.

[2] Milledgeville correspondence New York *Tribune*, Jan. 21.

ing allowance for certain differences between the two communities, was very like the development of the anti-slavery
sentiment at the North, and when the provocation of Lincoln's election came, this opinion shaped the course of these
seven States. It needed, as do all movements, leaders to
give it expression, but planters and lawyers of local influence, village attorneys, cross-road stump-speakers, journalists, and the people acted on the men of national reputation instead of being led by them. It is very doubtful
whether Davis, Toombs, Orr, and Benjamin, had they
agreed with Stephens, could have prevented secession, for
had they not headed the movement, the people would have
found other leaders. So striking were the manifestations
of public sentiment in the cotton States between November
6 and the date of the choice of delegates, that hardly a
doubt existed as to what would be the result of the elections and the action of the conventions. In the conventions
of four of the States a salutary minority existed, but when
the momentous act was consummated, nearly every one who
voted against secession signed the ordinances. Stephens
and Herschel V. Johnson thus united with the majority,
and the people by their demonstrations of joy showed that
they approved the action of their representatives.

The extent to which the conspiracy theory has been held
lies in a misconception of the nature of the so-called union
minority in Mississippi, Alabama, Georgia, and Louisiana.
Most of those who opposed immediate secession were against
it because they still hoped to obtain in the Union some such
guarantee as the Crittenden compromise ; others, like Stephens, would have been satisfied with the repeal of the Personal Liberty acts. Of unconditional Union men, who by
some writers are supposed to embrace all those voting for
Bell or Douglas in 1860,[1] the number was insignificant. It

---

[1] Partly, perhaps, for the reason that they rate too highly the influence
of Douglas and Bell on their former supporters in the cotton States. Bell
had spoken for the Union. See letter of Belmont to John Forsyth, Dec.
19, 1860.

was in the line, then, of a natural result that the people who constituted this minority, who believed that the South had grievances and that the States were sovereign, should bow themselves to the will of their States and devote their lives and fortunes to the carrying out of the policy now inaugurated.'

---

[1] On this subject see Life of Stephens, Johnston and Browne, p. 368 *et seq.;* Stephens's War between the States, vol. ii. pp. 127, 300 *et seq.;* Davis's Rise and Fall of the Confederate Government, vol. i. p. 200; letters of General Sherman to John Sherman from Alexandria, La., Dec. 1, 1860, Jan. 18, Feb. 1, 1861, *Century Magazine,* Nov., 1892, p. 93 *et seq.;* letter of Harris, Journal of the Convention of Mississippi, p. 197; letters to the New York *Tribune* from its correspondent at Macon, Jan. 1, Savannah, Jan. 5, 7, 11, Milledgeville, Jan. 19, 21; letter of Yancey, Jan. 12, New York *Tribune,* Jan. 19 ; Pike to the New York *Tribune,* Washington, Jan. 5, 22, 30 ; article of Basil L. Gildersleeve, *Atlantic Monthly,* Jan., 1892, p. 81. " In the South, the leaders were behind the people in their purposes and their feelings. The vote for secession was carried throughout the South by the greatest popular majority that ever endorsed any national policy."—Gen. D. H. Maury, Southern Historical Society Papers, vol. i. p. 426; Journal of the South Carolina Convention, p. 60. Per contra, see Greeley in the New York *Tribune,* Jan. 14 ; letter to the *Tribune* from Huntsville, Ala., March 9 ; American Conflict, vol. i. p. 351 ; Recollections of a Busy Life, p. 398 ; *National Intelligencer,* Dec. 22, 1860, Jan. 13, 18, 31, Feb. 6 ; Richmond *Whig,* Feb. 5 ; letter of Clemens, Feb. 3, Official Records, vol. i. p. 447; President Lincoln's Message of July 4, 1861; Pike's Prostrate State, p. 71 *et seq.;* Watson's Life in Confederate Army, p. 44 *et seq.;* The Iron Furnace, Aughey, p. 50 ; Roman's Beauregard, vol. i. p. 20. Bouligny, of Louisiana, elected by the American party, was the only representative from the cotton States who refused to withdraw from the House. His remarks showed a true devotion to the Union. Wigfall, of Texas, remained in the Senate, but he was a rank secessionist.

It is impossible for me to mention all the evidence I have considered before reaching the conclusion in the text. The different authorities pro and con are not always absolutely positive, and a satisfactory decision can only be arrived at after weighing them with circumspection. I feel an additional confidence in my statements for the reason that the careful historians Von Holst and Schouler have come to the same conclusion. Von Holst, vol. vii. p. 275 ; Schouler, vol. v. p. 509.

It is interesting to note that an hypothesis similar to the conspiracy theory prevailed in regard to the American Revolution. "Because statesmen like Dickinson and communities like Maryland were slow in believing that the right moment for a declaration of independence had come, the

If, after the evidence I have already adduced, any one doubts that slavery was the sole cause of the war, and that, had it not existed, the doctrine of States-rights would never have been pushed to the extreme remedy of secession, let him consider the proceedings of these conventions, and give especial attention to the justifications of Mississippi and Georgia. The convention of Mississippi declared that "Our position is thoroughly identified with the institution of slavery. . . . A blow at slavery is a blow at commerce and civilization. . . . There was no choice left us but submission to the mandates of abolition, or a dissolution of the Union." Toombs's report, adopted by the Georgia convention, was of the same tenor.[1]

In some cases before the adoption of the ordinances of secession, and in other cases afterwards, the forts, arsenals, and other property of the United States within their limits, were taken possession of by the cotton States.[2] To this there was one notable exception. Lieutenant Slemmer, with one company of artillery, had charge of Fort Barrancas near Pensacola, Florida, but, foreseeing the direction of events, he desired to throw his force into Fort Pickens, a large,

---

preposterous theory has been suggested that the American Revolution was the work of an unscrupulous and desperate minority, which, through intrigue mingled with violence, succeeded in forcing the reluctant majority to sanction its measures. Such a misconception has its root in an utter failure to comprehend the peculiar character of American political life."— John Fiske's American Revolution, vol. i. p. 195.

The features which I have found in the secession movement most inconsistent with this view are the suspicion of fraud concerning the Louisiana count (see Greeley's American Conflict, vol. i. p. 348 ; Watson's Confederate Army, p. 75 ; New York Tribune, April 4th), and the indefinite postponement in the Georgia convention by a vote of 168 to 127 of a resolution asking the governor "for information concerning the number of votes given by the people at the election for delegates to this convention." —Journal of the Convention, p. 27.

[1] Journal of the Mississippi Convention, p. 86 ; Journal of the Georgia Convention, p. 104. Gen. J. D. Cox in his article, "Why the Men of 1861 fought for the Union," makes an effective use of the Mississippi declaration, Atlantic Monthly, March, 1892.

[2] Official Records, vol. i. pp. 318, 326, 331, 489, 502.

strong work then unoccupied, which commanded the harbor. The day before Florida seceded he opportunely received an order from General Scott, which authorized such a movement, and on January 10, with the co-operation of the commander of the navy-yard, he spiked the guns of Barrancas and, with his company and thirty-one seamen, occupied Fort Pickens.[1]

In the meantime the cotton States, by their legislatures or by their conventions, and in some cases by enactments of both bodies, were putting themselves on a military footing.[2]

As previously mentioned, Hayne, Attorney-General of South Carolina, and Lieutenant Hall, an officer of Anderson's, arrived at Washington January 13, on a joint mission concerning Fort Sumter.[3] This concurrent act operated in the eyes of Anderson, of Governor Pickens, and of the President as a *quasi*-truce, during which South Carolina was in honor bound not to attack the fort, and the obligation rested on the United States government not to send reinforcements without notice. Hayne brought a demand from Pickens for the surrender of Sumter. The revolutionary senators now interfered, and a three-sided negotiation between themselves, Hayne, and the President followed. The senators aimed to restrain the impetuosity of South Carolina by urging her not to begin the war by striking the first blow, and to secure delay in order that the South might make adequate preparation for the conflict, if it were inevitable. They endeavored to bring about an agreement between the President and Pickens, by which he should promise not to send

---

[1] Official Records, vol. i. p. 333 *et seq.*

[2] McPherson, p. 3 *et seq.;* Appleton's Annual Cyclopædia for 1861, pp. 314, 427 ; report of Adjutant-General of Mississippi, Journal of the Convention, p. 221 ; Journal of the Georgia Convention, pp. 376, 390, 396 ; Journal of the Louisiana Convention, p. 247; Davis's Rise and Fall of the Confederate Government, vol. i. p. 228 ; Recollections of Mississippi and Mississippians, Reuben Davis, p. 404; Life of Jefferson Davis by his wife, vol. ii. p. 8.   [3] See p. 248.

reinforcements, and the governor should agree not to attack Sumter, but should permit Anderson to obtain necessary supplies from Charleston, and have free communication with his government. Buchanan declined to enter into such an engagement, but assured the senators that as Anderson was now making no request for more troops and felt secure in his position, an additional force would not for the present be sent; yet at the same time he plainly told them that he should make every effort to reinforce the Sumter garrison if Anderson's safety required it. Still, the senators advised Hayne not to present the demand for the surrender of the fort until he had submitted the whole correspondence to Charleston: this counsel he followed. Receiving fresh instructions January 30, Hayne delivered the next day to the President South Carolina's demand dated January 12, for the possession of Fort Sumter. February 6 the President gave his answer through a communication of the Secretary of War to Hayne. Holt refused to deliver up the fort, and ended his letter with an emphatic and true statement. "If," he said, "with all the multiplied proofs which exist of the President's anxiety for peace and of the earnestness with which he has pursued it, the authorities of that State shall assault Fort Sumter, and peril the lives of the handful of brave and loyal men shut up within its walls, and thus plunge our common country into the horrors of civil war, then upon them, and those they represent, must rest the responsibility." [1] In answer to this commu-

---

[1] See Letters of Jefferson Davis to Pickens, Jan. 13, 20, Crawford, pp. 263, 265; letter of Wigfall, Hemphill, Yulee, Mallory, Davis, Clay, Fitzpatrick, Iverson, Slidell, and Benjamin to Hayne, Jan. 15; Hayne's reply, Jan. 17; Slidell, Fitzpatrick, and Mallory to the President, Jan. 19; Holt's reply, Jan. 22; Hayne to the senators, Jan. 24; Slidell to the President, Jan. 28; Hayne to the President, Jan. 31, submitting with it Pickens's demand of Jan. 12; Holt's reply, Feb. 6. This correspondence may be found in Report No. 91, 2d Sess. 36th Cong., p. 58 et seq.; Judge Magrath to Hayne, Jan. 26, Crawford, p. 222; conversation of Senator Clay with the President, Jan. 16, Buchanan's memorandum, Curtis, vol. ii. p. 452; Buchanan's Defence, p. 194 et seq. Pickens in his demand says the pledge of the State will be

nication of Holt, Hayne sent an insulting reply addressed
directly to the President, which he refused to receive.[1]

Buchanan was disposed to regard sacredly the *quasi*-
truce agreed upon between Anderson and Pickens; yet had
not the advices from Anderson and Foster at this time
been against sending reinforcements,[2] there is no question
but that the pressure exerted upon him by Black, Stanton,
Holt, and Dix would have caused him to terminate the
truce by the proper notice, and to follow up the policy
which he had begun with the new year. Anderson now
received the warm approval of his government for having
transferred his force from Moultrie to Sumter; he was enjoined to continue "to act strictly on the defensive," but
was told in a despatch from Holt: "Whenever, in your
judgment, additional supplies or reinforcements are necessary for your safety, or for a successful defence of the fort,
you will at once communicate the fact to this department,
and a prompt and vigorous effort will be made to forward
them."[3] Somewhat later the President ordered an expedi-

---

given that the valuation of the public property of the United States within
Fort Sumter "will be accounted for by this State upon the adjustment of
its relations with the United States." Holt in his reply treated it as an
offer "to buy Fort Sumter and contents." Hayne indignantly repudiated
such a construction.

[1] Buchanan made on the letter the following endorsement : "The character of this letter is such that it cannot be received. Col. Hayne having
left the city before it was sent to the President, it is returned to him by
the first mail."—Buchanan's Defence, p. 205. The letter is printed by
Crawford, p. 231.

[2] "I shall not ask for any increase of my command, because I do not
know what the ulterior views of the government are. We are now, or
soon will be, cut off from all communication, unless by means of a powerful fleet, which shall have the ability to carry the batteries at the
mouth of this harbor."—Anderson to Cooper, Jan. 6. "I do not consider it
good policy to send reinforcements here at this time. We can hold our
own as long as it is necessary to do so."—Foster to Totten, Jan. 14. "I do
hope that no attempt will be made by our friends to throw supplies in;
their doing so would do more harm than good."—Anderson to Cooper, Jan.
30, Official Records, vol. i. pp. 133, 139, 159.

[3] Holt to Anderson, Jan. 10, 16, ibid., pp. 137, 140. "Had I demanded

tion for the reinforcement of Sumter to be prepared at New York, to sail on telegraphic notice from the Secretary of War;[1] but the order was not sent, as the effort of Virginia to heal the breach between the two sections, which resulted in the Peace Convention, made such an attempt undesirable. While from a military point of view it might have been better to send additional troops to Charleston in January, since the federal government could then have held Sumter throughout the war, yet, as the sequel shows, from a political point of view everything was gained by retaining possession of the fort until the 4th of March. The revolution had progressed with such rapidity that the clearly-defined policy of November and December had in many aspects now become questionable.

As soon as the news of Lieutenant Slemmer's exploit in occupying Fort Pickens and of the seizure, by Florida troops, of the other forts and navy-yard in Pensacola harbor reached Washington, the government sent from Fortress Monroe, as a reinforcement, the *Brooklyn*, with a company of artillery, military stores, and provisions.[2] Previously the Secretary of the Navy had ordered other ships of war to Pensacola, but before any of them reached there, through the instrumentality of Senator Mallory, of Florida, and other senators, a *quasi*-truce was entered into with the President, by which he agreed not to disembark the troops on the *Brooklyn*, and the commander of the Florida forces promised not to attack the fort. It was a part of the agreement that the provisions should be landed; at the same time an order was given that the men-of-war should remain on

reinforcements while Mr. Holt was in the War Department, I know he would have despatched them at all hazards. I did not ask them, because I knew that the moment it should be known here that additional troops were coming, they would assault me and thus inaugurate civil war."--Anderson to a lady friend, Crawford, p. 290.

[1] The first suggestion of this that I find from the President was on Jan. 30, Curtis, vol. ii. p. 474; see Buchanan's Defence, p. 209.

[2] This was Jan. 24.

the station, exercising the utmost vigilance, and in the event of an attack be prepared to reinforce the fort and co-operate with Slemmer in repelling it.[1] This agreement, having the approval of a part of the cabinet, and of General Scott, was carried out.[2]

While Buchanan's administration of affairs after January 1 deserves commendation, the merit of it was largely, if not entirely, due to Black, Stanton, Holt, and Dix. A man of sixty-nine rarely makes so thorough-going a change unless over-mastered by altered influences. His irresolute conduct of November and December, 1860, chiefly resulted from his anxious desire to avoid the commencement of the Civil War so long as he remained President. Although this was mingled with the eminently statesmanlike opinion that the North ought to keep from firing the first shot, yet the contrast between the period before and after January 1 brings to mind

---

[1] Curtis, vol. ii. p. 461; Buchanan's Defence, p. 214; Toucey's testimony, cited by Nicolay and Hay, vol. iii. p. 164.

[2] Buchanan says, of all the members of his cabinet, Defence, p. 216. This is probably a mistake. Buchanan's Defence, or, as he entitled it, "Buchanan's Administration on the Eve of the Rebellion," was written shortly after the beginning of the Civil War, and parts of it, if not the whole, submitted to Stanton, Black, and Dix. Stanton wrote him, July 16, 1861, regarding this part of it, that their recollection was that this Fort Pickens *quasi*-truce was opposed by them, Curtis, vol. ii. p. 558; see, also, C. F. Black, p. 17. Stanton said that the exception was of "no material consequence," and added: "I do not know that there is now any reason to question the wisdom of the measure; it may have saved Pickens from immediate attack at that time; and I have understood that General Scott says that Pickens could not have been successfully defended if it had then been attacked, and that he speaks of this as a blunder of the confederates. In this view the wisdom of the measure is fully vindicated; and at the time it was supported by the Secretary of War and Secretary of the Navy, to whose departments the subject appertained." The fact that Fort Pickens was held by the United States during the whole of the war of secession adds force to Stanton's statement of July, 1861.

Reinforcements in January were sent to Fort Taylor, Key West, and Fort Jefferson, Tortugas Island; this made them secure against capture, Buchanan's Defence, p. 218. These two, with Sumter and Pickens, were all the military posts in the cotton States that remained in the possession of the federal government March 4.

the difference between lame and apologetic measures and the policy of a vigorous defence prompted by strong patriotic and national sentiments. We may easily imagine frequent conversations, in which Buchanan, showing a disposition to falter, was nerved to pursue the correct course by the decided opinions of his four efficient advisers. Especially potent must have been the influence of Black and of Dix, whose personal and social relations with the President bordered on intimacy. Dix was his guest at the White House, and rarely did the two before going to bed fail to have a confidential conversation on the questions of the day. He has left his impression of Buchanan gained from this familiar intercourse. " I was strongly impressed with his conscientiousness," he wrote ; " but he was timid and credulous. His confidence was easily gained, and it was not difficult for an artful man to deceive him." [1]   Black's friendly letter of January 22 to the President is a whole chapter of pleading for a more resolute disposition and prompter action in coping with the secessionists. [2] In many of Holt's despatches and letters one seems to detect words and sentences added, on Buchanan's suggestion, to qualify an otherwise energetic paper. [3] Black, Stanton, Holt, and Dix were strong counsellors for a President in so trying a time, and any one of them would have guided the ship of state with a firmer hand than Buchanan. In executive matters, when prompt action is needed, there is a great difference between being in a position where one can act and where one can only advise. Black, in his letters to a friend, to General Scott, and to the President, showed the stuff of which he was made, and what he would have done had he been able to take the reins. [4] Stanton's after-career demon-

[1] Letter of March 31, 1865, Life of Dix, vol. i. p. 372.   This letter, in obedience to Dix's request, was not published until after Buchanan's and his own death.   [2] This is printed by Crawford, p. 241.

[3] A good example of Buchanan's extreme care in the use of a warlike force is seen in Holt's letter to General Scott, Jan. 26, Official Records, vol. i. p. 354.

[4] Letter to Parsons, Jan. 17, C. F. Black, p. 21 ; to Gen. Scott, Jan. 16, Official Records, vol. i. p. 140 ; to the President, Jan. 22, Crawford, p. 241.

strated the latent executive ability in a man then regarded
as only an able lawyer.   Dix came to the front by sending
to a treasury official at New Orleans a despatch that thrilled
the Northern heart : " If any one attempts to haul down
the American flag, shoot him on the spot." [1]   Partisanship
seems to have been sunk by these four members of the
cabinet.   Upon them had devolved the care of their country's honor, and worthily did they acquit themselves.[2]   Black
conferred publicly with Seward.[3]   Stanton, through an intermediary,[4] also had confidential communication with him,
and once at midnight had a secret consultation with Sumner.[5]   The country now had gained confidence in the administration.   New York, Massachusetts, and Maine, the
governors and legislatures of which were Republican, tendered to the President their entire resources of men and
money to uphold the authority of the federal government.[6]

Although the Crittenden compromise received its death-
blow on January 16, by the vote of the Senate, it did not
so appear to Douglas, Crittenden, and other of its advocates.[7]
The basis of this hope was that a number of Republicans

---

[1] Dix sent this without submitting it to the President.   On a point involved he did consult Stanton and General Scott.   For a very interesting
account of the sending of the despatch, see Life of Dix, vol. i. p. 370.

[2] " It undoubtedly would be a great party move as between Democrats
and Black Republicans to let the latter have a civil war of their own making. . . . Is not the business altogether beyond party considerations ?
For South Carolina compels us to choose between the destruction of the
government and some kind of defence.   They have smitten us on one
cheek ; shall we turn the other ?"—Black to Parsons, Jan. 17, C. F. Black,
p. 21.   [3] Black to Wilson, ibid., p. 279.

[4] Peter H. Watson, afterwards Assistant Secretary of War.

[5] Letters of Seward and Sumner, printed by Henry Wilson in article
" Black and Stanton,"*Atlantic Monthly*, Oct., 1870; Life of Seward, vol. ii.
p. 492.   "Sumner . . . conferred often with General Scott, . . . Stanton,
Holt, and Dix."—Edward L. Pierce, vol. iv. p. 23.

[6] Appletons' Annual Cyclopædia, 1861, pp. 436, 452, 519; *Congressional
Globe*, p. 597.

[7] See letter of Douglas, Crittenden, Boteler, and Harris, Jan. 25, and
letter of Millson, both to Barbour, Richmond *Whig*, Jan. 29, cited by
National Intelligencer.

under the leadership of Seward, sufficient to carry it, would
come to its support. " We have positive information from
Washington," declared the *Tribune*, January 29, in a double-leaded editorial, "that a compromise on the basis of
Mr. Crittenden's is sure to be carried through Congress
either this week or the next, provided *a very few more Republicans* can be got to enlist in the enterprise. We say a
very few more, for we have reason to believe that several
gentlemen who have hitherto enjoyed the confidence of the
Republican party are actively engaged in the endeavor to
convert their colleagues to their new faith." [1] Weed in his
journal was advocating with renewed strength the Crittenden plan, and the rumor that Seward favored it could not be
killed.[2] Yet in no public utterance nor private letter which
has been printed did he assert that he would sustain it.
In fact, denials, apparently authoritative, appeared in the
press.[3] But the story could be scotched only ; and this seems
to suggest either a wavering mind on Seward's part, or else

---

[1] " My apprehension has been that the Crittenden measure would find
favor among our friends. At one time there was a little danger of it.
There is little or none now."—C. F. Adams to F. W. Bird, Feb. 11, MS.
I am indebted to Edward L. Pierce for a copy of the letter from which
this extract is made.

[2] " Senator Seward, in his speech of Thursday last, declares his readiness to
renounce Republican principles for the sake of the Union."—Editorial, New
York *Tribune*, Feb. 4. The speech referred to is that of Jan. 31, a strong
argument, which ought to be read by all students of the period, Works,
vol. iv. p. 670 ; *Congressional Globe*, p. 657. " The Republican party . . . is
threatened by betrayal. It is to be divided and sacrificed if the thing can
be done. We are boldly told it must be suppressed, and a Union party rise
upon its ruins."—New York *Tribune*, Feb. 5. See, also, the article in the
same issue on the backing down of Seward, where the writer asks, " Has he
forgotten the 7th of March and the fate of Daniel Webster?" " Weed goes
with the Breckinridge Democrats. . . . The same is true, though less decidedly, of Mr. Seward."—Ibid., Feb. 6. " Oily Gammon Seward, aware
that intimidation will not do, is going to resort to the gentle powers of se-
duction."—Washington correspondent of Charleston *Mercury*, Feb. 19.

[3] See anecdote first appearing in the Boston *Daily Advertiser*, Feb. 2, in
a Washington letter of Jan. 31, and copied in the Albany *Evening Journal*,
presumed to be correct by the New York *Tribune* of Feb. 15.

that intimations, given out, perhaps, in the exuberance of after-dinner conversation, received a more positive interpretation than he meant to convey.[1] His own defence of his conduct should receive attentive consideration. "Twelve years ago" (1850 was the year he had in mind), he wrote, "freedom was in danger, and the Union was not. I spoke then so singly for freedom that short-sighted men inferred that I was disloyal to the Union. ... To-day, practically, freedom is not in danger, and union is. ... With the attempt to maintain union by civil war, *wantonly* brought on, there would be danger of reaction against the administration charged with the preservation of both freedom and union. Now, therefore, I speak singly for union, striving, if possible, to save it peaceably; if not possible, then to cast the responsibility upon the party of slavery. For this singleness of speech I am now suspected of infidelity to freedom."[2]

The motive now for a compromise was to retain the border States. The border States' proposition, which varied but little from the Crittenden plan, preserving its essential feature of a division by the Missouri line of the territory between slavery and freedom, attracted considerable attention.[3] With the prospect of keeping the border States went the hope that the cotton States might return. Laudable as may have been the aim of the compromisers, their hopes were illusory. Nothing less than the Crittenden compromise could have kept the cotton States from seceding, and something might be said in favor of it as an agreement between the North and the South; a good argument, too, could be made for its submission to a popular vote; but to

---

[1] The "Public Man," in his entry of Feb. 8, speaks of the singular confidence of Seddon of Virginia (afterwards Secretary of War of the Southern Confederacy) "in Mr. Seward, and his mysterious allusions to the skilful plans which Mr. Seward is maturing for an adjustment of our difficulties."—*North American Review*, Aug., 1879, p. 135.

[2] Letter of Seward to Dr. Thompson of the *Independent*. Life of Seward, vol. ii. p. 507.

[3] See *Harper's Magazine*, March, 1861, p. 547; McPherson, p. 73; Pike to the New York *Tribune*, Jan. 31; Letter of Belmont to Seward, Jan. 17.

offer it to seven seceded States to chew upon would indeed have been base. While satisfactory to Virginia, Tennessee, and North Carolina, the composition to be effective involved consent to peaceable separation of the cotton States, since, otherwise, at the first stroke of war, Virginia, Tennessee, and North Carolina would certainly join the section to which they were united by ties of blood, and by the bond of a common interest. The majority of the Republicans, who were fitly represented by Chase and Sumner, were consistent, and after the middle of January, apparently, pursued in the main the only wise and possible course. Sumner, having withstood the pleading of Edward Everett for compromise,[1] declared in the Senate: "There is but one thing now for the North to do. It is to stand firm in their position."[2] "The election of Lincoln," said Chase, in the Peace Convention, "must be regarded as the triumph of principles cherished in the hearts of the people of the free States. . . . Chief among the principles is the restriction of slavery within State limits; not war upon slavery within those limits, but fixed opposition to its extension beyond them. . . . By a fair and unquestionable majority we have secured that triumph. Do you think we, who represent this majority, will throw it away ? Do you think the people would sustain us if we undertook to throw it away?"[3]

Virginia, whose share in forming the Union had been greater than that of any other one State, was loath to see that great work shattered, and now made a supreme effort to save it. Her general assembly by joint resolutions invited the other States, whether slaveholding or non-slaveholding,

---

[1] Speech of George William Curtis, Boston *Herald*, Aug. 26, 1889; Pierce's Memoir of Sumner, vol. iv. p. 18.

[2] Feb. 12. See, also, extracts from his letters printed in Pierce's Memoir, vol. iv. pp. 16, 17.

[3] Chittenden's Report of the Proceedings, p. 428. A previous observation of Chase drew from ex-President Tyler, the president of the convention and a fit representative of Virginia, the remark, "You have, at all events, established your character as an honest and frank man."—Letters and Times of the Tylers, vol. ii. p. 605.

to send commissioners to meet hers in convention at Washington, February 4, to make an attempt "to adjust the present unhappy controversies;" and it gave formal notice that the Crittenden compromise "would be accepted by the people of this commonwealth." [1] It named ex-President Tyler as the head of the Virginia delegates; and it also appointed him a commissioner to the President and Robertson a commissioner to South Carolina, with the intent to preclude a collision of arms pending the convention proposed. These gentlemen repaired to their posts of duty and used their influence and that of their State to maintain the *status quo*.[2] Twenty-one States accepted the invitation of Virginia and sent commissioners, appointed either by their legislatures or by their governors, to the Peace Convention.[3]

On the same day, February 4, that the Peace Convention met at Washington, delegates from six cotton States [4] assembled at Montgomery to form a Southern confederacy, making it evident, could the country then have grasped the event as we can do, that an attempt at compromise was futile, and that the North must choose one of the alternatives: peaceable separation, or war. South Carolina, first in secession, also took the initiative in proposing this congress.[5] Constant communication between the governors,

---

[1] These resolutions are printed in the *Congressional Globe*, p. 601. One important addition to the Crittenden compromise, suggested, had already been made by the Powell amendment; another, indicated, is for our purpose unimportant.

[2] For an account of Tyler's mission see Letters and Times of the Tylers, vol. ii. p. 587; Buchanan's Defence, p. 206; Curtis, vol. ii. p. 472; see despatches of Tyler to Robertson and Pickens, Official Records, vol. i. pp. 253, 254.

[3] The States not represented were the seven cotton States, Arkansas, Michigan, Wisconsin, Minnesota, California, and Oregon. See Chittenden pp. 18, 453.

[4] South Carolina, Mississippi, Florida, Alabama, Georgia, and Louisiana. Texas did not pass her ordinance until Feb. 1, and was now waiting the submission of it to the people, the appointed day being Feb. 23.

[5] The resolutions of invitation were offered Jan. 3. Journal of the Con-

legislatures, and conventions of the seceding States had been maintained by commissioners with mandates passing to and fro, and the sympathy between the communities being complete, this obvious mode of procedure was at once adopted. The deputies received their appointment from the conventions;[1] each State had the same number as it had electoral votes under the Federal Constitution. Alexander H. Stephens, himself a delegate, after the experience of a month, wrote: "Upon the whole, this congress, taken all in all, is the ablest, soberest, most intelligent, and conservative body I was ever in. . . . Nobody looking on would ever take this congress for a set of revolutionists."[2] The absence of Yancey would seem to denote that the revolution had arrived at the point where agitators were thrust aside and statesmen rose to take direction of the movement. The congress selected Howell Cobb as its presiding officer, and one of its rules provided that questions should be decided by a vote of the States, each State being entitled to one vote.[3] February 8, a constitution for the provisional government of the Confederate States[4] was adopted, and on the next day, by a unanimous vote of the six States present, Jefferson Davis was elected president and Alex-

---

vention, p. 173 ; Charleston *Mercury*, Jan. 8, and New Orleans *Crescent* cited by it, Jan. 3.

[1] Journal of Mississippi Convention, pp. 39, 51 ; Journal of Georgia Convention, pp. 55, 63 ; Journal of Louisiana Convention, pp. 19, 21 ; Appletons' Annual Cyclopædia, 1861, pp. 11, 314.

[2] To his brother, March 3, Johnston and Browne, p. 392. This is inconsistent with Stephens's statements of Feb. 2 and March 1, see pp. 384, 391, but as he endorses the opinion cited in the text in his second volume of The War Between the States (p. 325), finished in 1870, we may regard these inconsistent expressions as the indulgence merely in a pessimistic strain to which he was given. Among the noted deputies were : Toombs, Martin J. Crawford, and Howell Cobb, of Georgia ; R. B. Rhett, R. W. Barnwell, L. M. Keitt, J. Chesnut, C. G. Memminger, W. P. Miles, and W. W. Boyce, of South Carolina. For a list of all the deputies, ibid., p. 324.

[3] For the rules, ibid., p. 710.

[4] This is printed by Davis, vol. i. p. 640, and by Stephens, vol. ii. p. 714.

ander H. Stephens, vice-president. Toombs, Cobb, and Stephens had also been talked of for the chief place, but after a short consideration of the merits and failings of each man proposed, the selection of the ablest statesman of the South fitly issued to meet the conditions confronting the new government.[1] Although Davis had always held the doctrine of states-rights in its extreme form, yet at this time he was looked upon by his Southern associates, when from theory they must proceed to action, as eminently conservative.[2] When he writes that he did not want the presidency we need not think that he affected the part of Cincinnatus, but may readily believe him sincere, and that he would have much preferred a high rank in the army.[3] Receiving his summons while at work on his Brierfield plantation,[4] he went promptly to Montgomery, and at the formal ceremony of his inauguration, February 18, delivered a carefully prepared address. It was, he averred, " wanton aggression on the part of others," that justified the action of the Southern people. "We have vainly endeavored to secure tranquillity and obtain respect for the rights to which we were entitled. As a necessity, not a choice, we have resorted to the remedy of separation."[5] With remarkable astute-

---

[1] See Johnston and Browne, pp. 385, 389 ; Stephens, vol. ii. p. 328 ; Davis, vol. i. p. 236. For an objection to Toombs, see Life of Toombs, Pleasant Stovall, p. 218 ; to Cobb, see Stephens, vol. ii. p. 331. A private letter of Stephens, written Feb. 8, shows clearly his position at this time, Cleveland, p. 161.

[2] See Stephens's testimony, vol. ii. p. 333. Stephens, however, thought Toombs, of all proposed, the best fitted for the position ; as to Davis's conservatism, see Campbell's and Kenner's testimony, Davis, vol. i. pp. 238, 239 ; Life by Mrs. Davis, vol. ii. p. 11.

[3] See Davis, vol. i. p. 230 ; testimony of Clayton and Campbell, ibid., p. 237 ; Stephens, vol. ii. p. 328 ; Mrs. Davis, vol. ii. p. 18.   [4] Ibid.

[5] Moore's Rebellion Record, vol. i., Docs., p. 31 ; Davis, p. 232. "The inaugural address . . . has been hailed with satisfaction throughout the length and breadth of the South. Let the people accord to his administration a hearty, united, and generous support."—Charleston *Mercury*, Feb. 21. "The United States of America are dissolved forever. 'Alas, poor Yorick! I knew him well.' But a sad rogue he was."—Montgomery Correspondent, ibid., Feb. 18.

ness he made not the slightest allusion to slavery.   By a section of the provisional constitution, the African slave-trade had been prohibited.[1] Thus did the cotton States and their president show that they realized that the public opinion of Christendom[2] must be taken into account, and that they must not let slip the slightest chance to justify their attempt at revolution and to belie its real character.

The Confederate provisional congress, having constituted a government, proceeded in a systematic way to provide for its orderly administration.   Executive departments were created, and, looking to the possibility of a war with the United States, acts providing military means were passed.   "An act to raise money for the support of the government" authorized the president to borrow on bonds of the Confederate States $15,000,000 at eight per cent., and imposed an export duty of one eighth of one cent per pound on raw cotton, pledging this tax to the payment of the interest and principal of the loan.[3]   By a general statute the United States Tariff act of 1857 was continued in force.[4]   A

---

[1] The Charleston *Mercury* of Feb. 12 did not like this provision being incorporated in the constitution, but was willing to prohibit the foreign slave-trade by legislative enactment.

[2] "One of their chief motives for seceding is to be able to renew the slave - trade." — London *Economist*, cited by New York *Tribune*, Feb. 6. Davis had clearer ideas of policy than his congress.   Feb. 25, in secret session, the congress passed a bill in relation to the slave - trade, and to punish persons offending therein, by the votes of Alabama, Florida, Georgia, Louisiana, and South Carolina ; Mississippi voting nay.   Davis vetoed this, as the provisions were not as stringent as the constitution required. Florida, Georgia, and South Carolina voted to pass the bill over the veto, while Alabama, Louisiana, Mississippi, and Texas sustained their president.—Journal of the Provisional Congress, MSS. War Department Archives.   For Davis's veto message, see Appletons' Annual Cyclopædia, 1861, p. 160.

[3] Approved Feb. 28.   Statutes at Large, Provisional Congress, C. S. A., p. 42.

[4] Adopted Feb. 9, ibid., p. 27.   This was not liked by the Charleston *Mercury*.   It said: "The tariff of '57 is odious and oppressive in its discriminations. . . . Free-trade is the true policy of the Confederate States" —Feb. 12.   Some other statutes passed were : An act to buy munitions of

resolution to assume all questions between the States of the Confederacy and the federal government relating to forts, arsenals, and other property acquired from the United States was adopted,[1] and at once communicated by telegraph to Governor Pickens.[2] The Congress also declared its opinion that "immediate steps should be taken to obtain possession of forts Sumter and Pickens . . . either by negotiations or force," and authorized Davis to carry the resolution into effect.[3] February 22, in accordance therewith, Davis, on the part of the Confederate government, took charge of the military operations in Charleston harbor.[4] Another resolution was passed which provided for the appointment by the president of three commissioners to be sent to Washington for the purpose of negotiating a treaty of amity with the federal government.[5] Davis appointed A. B. Roman, of Louisiana, Martin J. Crawford, of Georgia, and John Forsyth, of Alabama, supporters in 1860, respectively, of Bell, Breckinridge, and Douglas.[6]

Davis selected for his cabinet Toombs, of Georgia, as Secretary of State; Memminger, of South Carolina, for the Treasury; L. P. Walker, of Alabama, for the War, and Mallory, of Florida, for the Navy departments; J. H. Reagan, of Texas, as Postmaster-General; and Benjamin, of Louisiana, for Attorney-General.[7]

---

war, Feb. 20, Statutes at Large, Provisional Congress, C. S. A., p. 28; an act to provide the rates of postage, Feb, 23, p. 34; an act looking to the control of the military operations in all of the States, to receive from the States the arms and munitions of war acquired from the United States, and to receive into the service forces of the States for any time not less than twelve months, Feb. 28, ibid., p. 42.   Texas was admitted into the Confederacy, March 2, ibid., p. 44.   [1] Feb. 12, ibid., p. 91.

[2] See letter of Pickens to Cobb, Feb. 13, Official Records, vol. i. p. 254.

[3] Passed, Feb. 15, ibid., p. 258.   This is not printed in Statutes at Large.

[4] See letter of Pickens to Davis, Feb. 27, Davis to Whiting, Feb. 23, ibid., p. 258.

[5] Adopted Feb. 15, Statutes at Large, Provisional Congress, C. S. A., p. 92.

[6] Davis desired Stephens to head the commission, but he declined. Johnston and Browne, p. 389.

[7] Davis would have preferred Barnwell for the State and Toombs for

In the once proud Union there were now two established governments. The Southerners at Montgomery had proceeded in an orderly manner, and made evident that they shared with the North the political aptitude which is the peculiar attribute of Americans. In spite of the strained relations between the sections, no formal check had been given to their business or other intercourse; mail communication was uninterrupted.[1] The Northwest believed this severance of the Union a blow to its own prosperity, perhaps depriving it of the important outlet of the Mississippi River for its products. The South, considerate of the West, now declared by its congress the free navigation of the Mississippi River.[2] While one may note in the Southern literature of this period a particular animosity towards New England, there is evident a feeling of friendliness to the West, in some instances going so far as to express the extravagant hope that some of the Western States might join the Southern Confederacy.

Pausing for a moment to reflect that the people of the North and the South were both God-fearing—that they professed the same religion,[3] spoke the same language, read the same literature, venerated the same Constitution, had similar laws, and, with one exception, the same institutions —we may echo the regret of many men of 1861, What a

---

the Treasury departments. The South Carolina delegation having previously recommended Memminger for the Treasury, Barnwell declined the offer, see Davis, vol. i. p. 242. Toombs at first declined his appointment, but afterwards accepted, Johnston and Browne, p. 387.

[1] "The postal service generally throughout the South was continued under the direction of the government of the United States up to the 31st May, 1861, when it was suspended by a general order of the department;" Horatio King, Postmaster-General, Jan. and Feb., 1861, in *Lippincott's Magazine*, April, 1872, p. 411. The date of discontinuance was May 27.— See Postmaster-General Blair's letter to Speaker of the House, July 12th, *Congressional Globe*, p. 115.   [2] Feb. 25; Statutes at Large, p. 36.

[3] "The morality and religiousness of the Southern population were, on the average, not inferior to those of any other people."—Von Holst, vol. vii. p. 272.

pity that they should separate! What force must such a
feeling have had during the usual celebrations of the 22d
of February, as one thought that the memory of Washington belonged, beyond a possible blotting out, to both sections! This feeling was signally illustrated at Charleston,
where the revolution had commenced, and where the war
was to begin. At sunrise Castle Pinckney, under the palmetto banner, fired thirteen guns to honor the birthday of
the father of the common country; at noon Fort Sumter,
with the Stars and Stripes waving, gave a national salute.

From the point of view of political expediency, it is difficult to find in the annals of constitutional government such
mingled folly and rashness as the Southern people were
now displaying. In the event of war they would have
against them the odds of numbers, wealth, industries that
could be used for producing war material, and the machinery and the prestige of the national government; while remaining in the Union they would have three of the four
points of the game. The Republicans were in the minority
in both the Senate and the House,[1] and they had only one
judge of the Supreme Court.[2] The paramount tangible
grievance of the South was, as we have seen, the alleged
exclusion of its peculiar property from the common territories. But no satisfactory answer was ever made, or could
be made, to Charles Francis Adams's trenchant questions
in his speech in the House, January 31, except the one he
himself gave. "Who excludes the slave-holders with their
slaves?" he demanded. "Have they not obtained an opinion from the Supreme Court which will, in effect, override
any and every effort of Congress against them? They can,
if they choose, now go wherever they like on the public

---

[1] See vol. ii. p. 501, note 2. "If the Southern States had not run
away, we had both houses of Congress, and Lincoln could have done
nothing."—Richmond *Whig*, Jan. 28.

[2] McLean. The other judges were Taney, Wayne, Catron, Campbell,
Democrats from the slave States; Grier, Nelson, and Clifford, Democrats
from the free States. There was one vacancy.

domain.   There is no majority in Congress itself to prevent
their going, even if it had the power.   Why do they not use
that right?   The reason is plain.   It is not for their interest
to go so far north.   They will not leave the rich bottom-lands,
still open for the profitable cultivation of the cotton-plant in
the South, to go to a comparatively arid region farther off." [1]
The Supreme Court was now stronger for the principle laid
down in the Dred Scott decision than when it was promul-
gated. [2]   Curtis had resigned, and Clifford, a Democrat of
Maine appointed by Buchanan, had his place.   Daniel, indeed, was dead, but had there been no secession the Senate
would have confirmed the President's nomination of Black
for the vacancy; [3] and Black was in thorough sympathy with
Taney's Dred Scott opinion. [4]   Does it not seem strange that
a brave people should be sufficiently alarmed at a party
platform and at declarations of party leaders to throw away
such substantial advantages as they had in the Union?   No
truer word in this whole controversy was spoken than that
by Charles Francis Adams, when he termed the alleged
grievances of the South "mere abstractions." [5]   For the purpose even of saving slavery secession was a suicidal policy.
Many thinking men in the North told the Southerners, in a
strain of the utmost sincerity, that if civil war resulted slavery would have to go; and while Jefferson Davis made no
public declaration to that effect, he saw with prophetic soul

---

[1] *Congressional Globe* Appendix, p. 125. The same point is touched upon
by C. C. Washburn and M. W. Tappan, radical Republicans, in their minority
report of the House committee of thirty-three.   See Report, No. 31, p. 10.

[2] For the composition of the court then, see vol. ii. p. 250.   C. F. Adams
wrote F. W. Bird, Feb. 16: "As to the Dred Scott case, I regard it as yet
only a dictum, . . . but every man of sense knows that it will be affirmed in
the first case that may be brought up, and that in the meantime slaves are
held under it in the various territories.   And no action of the government
will effectually prevent it."—MS.

[3] Black was appointed Feb. 6, but the appointment was never acted on.
—C. F. Black, p. 24.

[4] Reply to Senator Douglas (1859), ibid., pp. 214, 215 ; see vol. ii. p. 374.

[5] *Congressional Globe* Appendix, p. 125.   "For what, then, are we about
to plunge into civil war ?   An abstraction."—Richmond *Whig*, Jan. 3.

that such would be the end.[1]   Had the Southern people followed Stephens, or had they adopted the plan of delay urged by Davis, the course of history might have been different. But the variance between that impetuous majority in the cotton States[2] and these far-seeing statesmen arose largely from the way in which they envisaged the future.   Some looked upon secession as a shrewd political move, which would enable the South to extort larger concessions than it could get while in the Union;[3] but a larger number believed that they could form a Southern Confederacy, and enforce to the fullest extent the sovereign rights of the States, without armed resistance from the North.[4]   Neither Davis nor Stephens had such illusions.   "War I look for as almost certain," wrote Stephens, February 21, from Montgomery.[5]   Prepare yourselves for a long and bloody war, was the burden of Davis's speeches in his progress from Washington to the capital of his State; a great war is impending over the country of which no man can foresee the end, was his constant inculcation

---

[1] "He said, 'In any case, I think our slave property will be lost eventually.'"—Mrs. Davis, vol. i. p. 11.   This was in Feb., just before going to Montgomery.

[2] Cobden wrote Sumner, Feb. 23: "The conduct of the South has disgusted everybody.   I do not mean their desire to disunite—*that* they may have a right to do, and it may be for the interest of all parties. But they have shown a measure of passionate haste and unreasoning arrogance which has astonished all lookers-on.   They have gone about the work of dissolving the Union with less gravity or forethought than a firm of intelligent drapers or grocers would think necessary in case of a dissolution of partnership."   Edward L. Pierce has kindly placed at my disposal a large part of the Sumner correspondence from 1860-65, in which is the letter containing the above extract.   I shall refer to it as the Pierce-Sumner papers, MS.

[3] This view was represented in Georgia by Thomas R. R. Cobb, and according to Stephens the wavering scale in the Georgia convention was turned by his remark, "We can make better terms out of the Union than in it."—War Between the States, vol. ii. p. 321; Davis, vol. i. p. 227; Report of H. P. Bell, Georgia Commissioner to Tennessee, Journal of Georgia Convention, p. 368; J. D. Cox, in *Atlantic Monthly* for March, 1892, p. 390.

[4] Davis, vol. i. p. 227; Roman's Beauregard, vol. i. p. 16; Life of Davis, Alfriend, p. 250.   [5] Johnston and Browne, p. 387.

while at Jackson. The war will be long, he said to Judge Sharkey, on his way to Montgomery to be inaugurated, and it behooves every one to put his house in order.[1]

The last formal step in the election of Lincoln—the counting of the electoral votes in the presence of both houses of Congress—was looked forward to with a certain amount of apprehension, as fears prevailed that a conspiracy existed to prevent it, and also the inauguration of the President-elect, by seizing the Capitol and other buildings, with the archives of the government.[2] General Scott, Black, Holt, Seward, and Governor Hicks, of Maryland, partook of this solicitude.[3] A conspiracy to take the capital "has been actually formed," wrote Black to the President, "and large numbers of persons are deeply and busily engaged in bringing the plot to a head at what they conceive to be the proper time."[4] "Treason is all around and amongst us;" said Seward in a confidential letter, "and plots [exist] to seize the capital and usurp the government." "One friend came in this morning to tell me," he wrote, later, "that there are two thousand armed conspirators in the city, and the mayor is secretly with them."[5] Considering the progress which the revolution had made, and the suggestion of the Richmond *Enquirer*, "Can there not be found men bold and brave enough in Maryland to unite with Virginians in seizing the Capitol at Washington?"[6] it is not surprising that anxiety was felt by

---

[1] Mrs. Davis, vol. ii. pp. 6, 8 ; Davis, vol. i. p. 230.   He left Washington the latter part of Jan.

[2] "It is as well for the people of the free States to wake up to the fact that this country is in full revolution, and this capital in undoubted peril." —Pike to New York *Tribune*, Jan. 5 ; New York *Times*, Jan. 2, cited in Moore's Rebellion Record, vol. i. Diary, p. 8.   For an animated account of this alarm, see Chittenden's Lincoln, chaps. vi. and vii.

[3] As to Scott and Hicks, see their testimony before the House committee, Report 79, pp. 52, 166; as to Holt, see his letter to the President, Feb. 18, cited by Nicolay and Hay, vol. iii. p. 147 ; Wilson's Rise and Fall of the Slave Power, vol. iii. p. 167.   [4] Jan. 22, Crawford, p. 241.

[5] Letters to his wife, Dec. 29, 1860, Jan. 18, Life of Seward, vol. ii. pp. 488, 497.   [6] Dec. 25, 1860.

these men who held positions of high responsibility. Yet
such fears had, in fact, little foundation. Washington was
abundantly secure so long as Virginia and Maryland remained in the Union.[1] They were towers of defence, and
Maryland recognized a special guardianship, as the capital
city stood on what was once her own soil. She had not
made the slightest move towards secession. Her governor,
Hicks, had been elected as an American, had owned slaves
since he was twenty - one years old, and sympathized
with the South; yet he declared that he desired to live
and die in the Union, and absolutely declined, although
urged to it, to.convoke the legislature, which, being Democratic, might have called a convention of the people.[2]
In this he was sustained by the public sentiment of his
State.[3] Virginia's governor, Letcher, had summoned in
special session the legislature, which passed a convention
bill. The election of delegates, taking place February 4, resulted in a signal Union victory, which determined that Virginia should not secede before the 4th of March, and al-
layed any still remaining fears of violence in the federal

---

[1] A House special committee of five was requested to investigate this
subject. It consisted of Howard (chairman), Dawes, Republicans; Reynolds, a Douglas Democrat; Cochrane and Branch, of North Carolina, Democrats. Hickman was first appointed, but he seems to have declined, Reynolds serving in his place. Howard, Dawes, and Reynolds left no stone
unturned to discover the conspiracy, if any such existed, and they took a
large amount of interesting and valuable testimony. Their report, Feb. 4,
was: "If the purpose was at any time entertained of forming an organization, secret or open, to seize the District of Columbia, attack the Capitol,
or prevent the inauguration of Mr. Lincoln, it seems to have been rendered
contingent upon the secession of either Maryland or Virginia, or both, and
the sanction of one of those states."—Report of committee, p. 2; see letter
of Howard to E. R. Hoar, Feb. 7, 1870, cited by Henry Wilson, *Atlantic
Monthly*, October, 1870, p. 467; also *Congressional Globe*, p. 316.

[2] See his testimony before the House committee, p. 166; Greeley's American Conflict, vol. i. p. 349.

[3] Hicks's letter to Handy, commissioner from Mississippi; his testimony;
Appletons' Annual Cyclopædia for 1861, p. 443; Baltimore *American*, cited
in Moore's Rebellion Record, vol. i. Diary, p. 9.

City.[1]   Indeed, a fortnight previous, Seward, whose private
letters had been those of an alarmist, had written Weed
that "the plots against the city are at an end." [2]   The President's judgment in this matter proved to be sounder than
that of Black and Holt, for he did not share their apprehensions, but, appreciating the wisdom of taking precautionary
measures, he authorized General Scott to bring several companies of United States troops to Washington to assist, if
need be, the civil functionaries in the preservation of peace
and order.[3]   February 13 the counting of the electoral votes
took place in a quiet and regular manner.

Two days before his election was officially declared
Lincoln started on his journey from Springfield to Washington.   Having received many invitations from States
and cities offering their hospitality, he stopped frequently,
and made many speeches as he proceeded along his cir-
cuitous route.   Greeted everywhere with enthusiasm, and
listened to with profound respect, he may at this time
have laid the foundations of that hold on the plain people
which was to be of such rich benefit to him and to his
country in the years that were to come.[4]   But if the purpose in view was to convince the reflecting Union men of
the North that he was equal to the task before him which
he himself thought "greater than that which rested upon
Washington," [5] the journey can only be looked upon as a
sad failure, and his speeches, except his touching farewell
to his old friends and neighbors at Springfield, and his
noble address in Independence Hall, Philadelphia, had bet-

---

[1] See Pike to New York *Tribune*, Feb. 5.   The Union majority was
estimated at 40,000, New York *Tribune*, Feb. 6.

[2] Jan. 21.   Life, vol. ii. p. 497; see, also, Pike to the New York *Tribune*.

[3] See the President's messages of Jan. 8 and March 2; General Scott's
testimony.   House Report 79, p. 61.   Seven or eight companies, 420 to 480
men, were in Washington at the time of the electoral count, ibid.; 653 men
and 32 officers at the time of the inauguration, Curtis, vol. ii. p. 494.

[4] Nicolay and Hay, vol. iii. chap. xix.; Herndon, p. 488.   The edition
referred to is the first, that of Belford, Clarke & Co.

[5] Farewell remarks at Springfield, Nicolay and Hay, vol. iii. p. 291.

ter not have been delivered. To acquit himself with dignity
in that position were difficult for any man ; and Lincoln,
now the cynosure of all eyes, did not have the knack of saying the graceful nothings which are so well fitted for the occasions on which he spoke. In his speeches the commonplace abounds, and though he had a keen sense of humor,
his sallies of wit grated on earnest men who read in quiet
his daily utterances. The ridiculous, which lies so near the
sublime, was reached when this man, proceeding to grave
duties, and the great fame that falls to few in the whole
world, asked at the town of Westfield for a little girl correspondent of his, at whose suggestion he had made a
change in his personal appearance, and when she came, he
kissed her, and said, "You see I have let these whiskers
grow for you, Grace."[1] The next day's journal headed the
account, "Old Abe Kissed by a Pretty Girl."[2]

Lincoln could indeed have spoken well of the serious
matters of which his mind was full, but prudence and propriety forbade that he should anticipate his inaugural address, which had been already prepared.[3] At Indianapolis,
while declining to commit himself, he threw out intimations
indicating that he saw a clear distinction between the coercion of a State on the one hand, and the holding and
retaking the United States forts and the collection of
duties on the other ; but his comparison of a Union on the
Southern theory to a "free-love arrangement," differing
from the true relation of a "regular marriage," while it
might have been effective in private conversation, was not
a dignified illustration for the President-elect to use when
addressing the people of a nation chaste in thought and
prudish in expression. Lincoln enounced many good ideas,
but it was one of the hardships of his position that his
misses were dwelt upon, and his hits ignored. His remarks
at Columbus: "There is nothing going wrong. . . . There

[1] Herndon, p. 487, note ; Raymond, p. 141.
[2] New York *Tribune*, Feb. 18.   [3] Herndon, p. 478.

is nothing that really hurts anybody;" and that at Pittsburgh, when, his features lighting up with a smile, he said:
" There is no crisis but an artificial one," [1] created a painful
impression; yet such utterances were dictated by a worthy
motive; he really felt more anxiety about the outlook than
he deemed it wise to show. [2] His declaration in Independence Hall ought to have compensated for all such slips.
" There will be no bloodshed," he assured the country, " unless it be forced upon the government. The government
will not use force unless force is used against it." [3]

Lincoln's ignorance of the ways of the fashionable world
told against him in New York city, where the tendency of
refined people is to judge new men at first rather by their
manners than by their qualities, and his wearing black kid
gloves at the opera on a gala night gave rise to sarcastic
comment. [4] Receiving warnings at Philadelphia which he
could not afford to disregard from General Scott, Seward, and
two other friends that a plot had been concocted to assassi-
nate him in Baltimore, he deviated from the published plan
of going through that city by day, and proceeded secretly
to Washington by night. [5] This drew ridicule from his enemies, and expressions of sincere regret from many of his
well-wishers, and augmented the prejudice against him
which he must surmount. Nor did his bearing in Washington between his arrival and the inauguration do anything to

---

[1] For the Indianapolis and Columbus speeches, see Nicolay and Hay,
vol. iii. pp. 294, 296 ; for the Pittsburgh and Cleveland speeches, when he
termed the crisis artificial, see Raymond, pp. 138, 140. Nicolay and Hay
print the most important speeches, and Raymond prints them all.

[2] Diary of a Public Man, entry Feb. 20.

[3] Nicolay and Hay, vol. iii. p. 300.

[4] Diary of a Public Man, entry Feb. 20.

[5] For a detailed account of this, see Nicolay and Hay, vol. iii. chap. xx.;
Lamon, p. 512; Lincoln and Men of War Times, McClure, p. 43 ; see, also,
Blaine's Twenty Years of Congress, vol. i. p. 280 ; Washburne's article in
Reminiscences, by North American Publishing Company, p. 34 ; Chitten-
den's Lincoln, pp. 58, 65. Lincoln arrived at Washington on the morning
of Feb. 23.

dispel the unfavorable impression that especially prevailed in the East touching his ability to cope with the difficulties he must meet.   When Bowles, in a private letter to Dawes, wrote, " Lincoln is a 'Simple Susan,' " [1] he expressed a silent but a commonly held opinion.   The hearts of many thoughtful persons must have failed as they contrasted Jefferson Davis, with his large public experience and high reputation, with this untried man from Illinois.   Curiously enough, Thurlow Weed, whose grief at the nomination of Lincoln had been of surpassing bitterness, was now one of the few in the East who seemed to have full faith that he would prove adequate to the duty imposed upon him. [2]

Meanwhile the Peace Convention at Washington, sitting with closed doors, ex-President Tyler being in the chair, was with patriotic purpose laboring diligently to save the Union.   Among the delegates were many men of character, ability, and distinction. [3]   While the proceedings were not

---

[1] Feb. 26, Life of Bowles, Merriam, vol. i. p. 318.   See, also, Springfield *Republican*, cited by *National Intelligencer*, Feb. 21.

[2] Weed on his return from Springfield wrote as an editorial in his journal, Dec. 22, 1860, as follows : "An interview with Mr. Lincoln has confirmed and strengthened our confidence in his fitness for the high position he is to occupy ; of his eminent qualifications for the great trust reposed in him; of his enlightened appreciation of the difficulties and dangers that surround us. . . .

"The American people will not have cause, so far as the head and heart of Abraham Lincoln are concerned, to regret the confidence they have reposed in him.   He is not only ' honest and true,' but he is capable—capable in the largest sense of the term.   He has read much and thought much of government, ' inwardly digesting' its theory and principles.   His mind is at once philosophical and practical.   He sees all who go there, hears all they have to say, talks freely with everybody, reads whatever is written to him, but thinks and acts by himself and for himself."

[3] For example: Fessenden and Morrill, of Maine; Charles Allen and George S. Boutwell, of Massachusetts; D. D. Field, J. S. Wadsworth, Erastus Corning, Francis Granger, William E. Dodge, General Wool, of New York; F. T. Frelinghuysen, of New Jersey; Wilmot, of Pennsylvania; Reverdy Johnson, of Maryland; Tyler, W. C. Rives, G. W. Summers, J. A. Seddon, of Virginia; Guthrie, of Kentucky; Chase, W. S. Groesbeck, Thomas Ewing, of Ohio; Caleb B. Smith, of Indiana; S. T. Logan, J. M. Palmer, of Illinois; Harlan and Grimes, of Iowa.   For a complete list of

published and secrecy was enjoined upon the members, the points of the important debates and the doings leaked out from time to time and — such was the shrinking of the country from civil war — occupied a larger space in the public mind than a due regard for historical proportion can accord to them.   February 27, the nineteenth day of its session, the convention recommended to Congress a constitutional amendment as a plan of adjustment; but the important section, that relating to slavery in the territories, had been carried, the convention voting by States, by a majority of one only, the votes of three States which were divided not being counted.   Moreover, several prominent members publicly announced their dissent from the prevailing voice of their respective delegations.[1]   The plan, being less favorable to the South than the Crittenden compromise and yet not satisfactory to the radical Republicans, lacked the support of a homogeneous majority, and went to Congress with no force behind it.   On the morning of March 4, in the last hours of the Senate session, Crittenden offered the project of the Peace Conference.   It came to a vote, receiving, however, only seven yeas, Crittenden and Douglas and two Republicans being among the number. [2]

The radical Republicans had from the first been opposed to the Peace Convention.   Lowell represents well a phase of thoughtful sentiment.   " The usual panacea of palaver was tried," he wrote ; " Congress did its best to add to the general confusion of thought ; and, as if that were not enough, a convention of notables was called simultaneously to thresh the straw of debate anew and to convince thoughtful persons that men do not grow wiser as they grow older."[3]   Those who represented Michigan at Washington and at

the delegates, see Debates and Proceedings of the Peace Convention, by Chittenden, himself a delegate from Vermont, p. 465.   The convention met Feb. 4.

[1] See Chittenden, p. 440 *et seq.*, for proceedings of the nineteenth day.

[2] The congressional day was March 2, see *Congressional Globe*, p. 1405; New York *Tribune*, March 5.

[3] See article, " The Pickens-and-Stealin's Rebellion," *Atlantic Monthly*,

her State capital were opposed to compromise, therefore she had not appointed commissioners to the Peace Convention ; but after it had been in session a week, her senators, at the request of Massachusetts and New York, advised her governor to send delegates. Senator Chandler's letter, which was made public before the convention adjourned, may be reckoned as one of the influences of the time. "I hope you will send," he wrote, " *stiff-backed* men or none. The whole thing (*i.e.*, the convention) was gotten up against my judgment and advice, and will end in thin smoke. . . . Some of the manufacturing States think that a fight would be awful. Without a little bloodletting this Union will not, in my estimation, be worth a rush." [1] This letter affected painfully the Unionists of the border States and the conservative Republicans, but some hard-headed Northern men had arrived at this conviction, although few thought there was wisdom in giving vent to it.

Virginia voted in the Peace Convention against the section relating to slavery in the territories, her senators opposed the plan in the Senate, and ex-President Tyler, who had much to do with bringing about this conference, repudiated its action in a public speech at Richmond. [2] The plan not being satisfactory to Virginia, it was idle to think that North Carolina, Tennessee, and Arkansas would consider it a sufficient guarantee for their remaining in the Union, or that it would bring back the cotton States.

The historical significance of the Peace Convention consists in the evidence it affords of the attachment of the border slave States to the Union, and the lingering hope of

---

June, 1861, p. 758.   Pike called it the "fossil convention."—New York *Tribune*, Feb. 9.

[1] Powell had this read in the Senate, Feb. 27, but it was published in the Detroit *Free Press*, a Democratic newspaper, several days before ; see, also, Life of Chandler, by Detroit *Post and Tribune*, p. 189.

[2] Letters and Times of the Tylers, vol. ii. pp. 608, 616, 622. Tyler's suggestion, however, was to limit the conference to the border States, ibid., p. 579.

readjustment in North Carolina and Tennessee. The different ways in which it was regarded brings out the contrast between the sentiment of these communities and that of the cotton States. The commissioner of Georgia, who had been sent to Maryland to persuade her to join the secession movement, was discouraged to find Governor Hicks believing that the Peace Conference would agree upon a compromise that should be entirely acceptable to his State.[1] A great obstacle, reported the commissioner, whose mandate had taken him to Raleigh, "to the immediate co-operation of North Carolina with the Confederate States was the belief entertained by the larger number of her citizens that the Peace Conference" would compose the dissension between the two sections.[2] The Union men of Tennessee cherished the hope that the border State convention, as they called this body, would adopt a plan that would satisfy the slave States on the border and bring back into the Union those which had seceded.[3]

The precipitate action of the cotton States helped the Union cause in the slave-holding communities farther north. Governor Hicks's loyalty to the federal government was more decided in February than in December.[4] He had uniformly refused to summon his legislature, and the lukewarm response by the people to the irregular convention which assembled at Baltimore in February showed that he was steadily gaining adherents.[5] The election in Virginia for

[1] Report of A. R. Wright of his visit of Feb. 25, at Annapolis, Journal of Georgia Convention, p. 330.

[2] Report of S. Hall of his visit of Feb. 13, ibid., p. 343.

[3] Report of H. P. Bell, Commissioner to Tennessee, ibid., p. 368. As to Missouri, see The Fight for Missouri, Snead, p. 60. On the desire for compromise in Kentucky, see Shaler's Kentucky, p. 235, and his article "The Border State Men of the Civil War," *Atlantic Monthly*, February, 1892, p. 253.

[4] Compare his letter to the Mississippi commissioner, Dec. 19, 1860, Journal of Mississippi Convention, p. 181, and his conversation with the Georgia commissioner Feb. 25, Journal of Georgia Convention, p. 330; also Baltimore *Daily Exchange*, Jan. 11.

[5] Journal of Georgia Convention, pp. 328, 330.

members of her State convention had much significance.¹
The 152 delegatès chosen were, with substantial correctness,
classed as 30 so-called secessionists, 20 Douglas men, and 102
Whigs; which proves, asserted the Richmond *Whig,* a journal
which argued strenuously for delay, that " the conservative
victory in Virginia is perfectly overwhelming," the precipitators having sustained " a Waterloo defeat." ² Nevertheless, it said, the meaning of this election must not be misap-
prehended. An impression obtained in the North that Virginia had "determined to remain in the Union *as matters now
stand,* to submit to the rule of the new dynasty *under the Chicago programme.*" This was a " pernicious error." Unless
security were given that her constitutional rights would be
respected, she would end her connection with the Northern
States. Of the Virginia delegates elected to the convention
only a half-dozen were "actual submissionists—that is, men
in favor of the preservation of the Union under any and all
circumstances." ³ The convention bill passed by the legislature of North Carolina provided that at the same time
the people chose delegates they should vote on the desir-
ability of the convention assembling. Eighty-two conservatives and 38 secessionists were elected; but the majority
against the convention was 651.⁴ The high hopes of North
Carolina, which the disunionists of the cotton States had
entertained in December, were dashed by this election of
January 28.⁵ Tennessee voted against a convention by
nearly 12,000 majority, while the sentiment indicated in the
choice of delegates was yet more decided against taking

¹ This took place Feb. 4.
² Issue of Feb. 12. Lyon G. Tyler says the secessionists numbered only
25, vol. ii. p. 621.
³ Richmond *Whig,* Feb. 8, 12; see also Summer's remarks in the Peace
Convention, Chittenden, p. 153.
⁴ *Tribune* Almanac, 1862, p. 59 ; Appletons' Annual Cyclopædia, 1861,
p. 538.
⁵ Compare Jacob Thompson's report of his visit at Raleigh, Dec. 18,
1860, Journal of Mississippi Convention, p. 184, with S. Hall's report of his
visit of Feb. 11, Journal of Georgia Convention, p. 343.

any present steps towards secession.[1] Even Arkansas had not responded to the disunion movement with the fervor that had been anticipated. While her people had voted for a convention, the conservatives had elected a majority of the delegates.[2] Missouri, in its election for members of a convention, February 18, decided by a majority of 80,000 against secession, and not one secessionist delegate was chosen.[3] Kentucky's legislature refused to call a convention, and adjourned before the middle of February.[4]

These elections, together with the peaceful electoral count, strengthened the uncompromising Republicans.[5] Little doubt can exist that at this time a majority of the party was opposed to so wide a concession as the Crittenden compromise involved.[6] Yet the public sentiment in the North was chameleon-like, and the compromisers, deriving hope from the elections, redoubled their efforts to meet the border-State men half-way. Feeling the public pulse with the sensitiveness of genius, the brilliant essayist told its beats

---

[1] Report of Commissioner Bell, Journal of Georgia Convention, p. 368; Appleton, pp. 677, 678. The so-called Union delegates had a majority of 64,000. On this vote see, also, Nicolay and Hay, vol. iv. p. 250, note 1.

[2] Appleton, p. 22, date of election, Feb. 18; Report of Commissioner Fall, Dec. 25, 1860, Journal of Mississippi Convention, p. 194.

[3] Carr's Missouri, p. 284 et ante; Snead's The Fight for Missouri, p. 66.

[4] Shaler's Kentucky, p. 240; Appleton, p. 395.

[5] "It is sadly evident that the border States of the South are going to content themselves with much less than the Crittenden amendment. . . . The Republicans are so stiffened up by the late wonderful exhibition of Union sentiment that they will now grant only the promise of a national convention."—Washington correspondence, Feb. 14, of Charleston *Mercury*. "The returns from Arkansas and Missouri are very encouraging to the Republicans, who now more than ever are convinced that the border States 'can't be kicked out.' They are not far wrong. Certainly nothing short of a steady kicking can do it."—Ibid., Feb. 21. See, also, the Mobile *Advertiser*, cited by the *National Intelligencer*, Feb. 26.

[6] See New York *Tribune* for Feb., especially Pike's letters from Washington, the double-leaded editorial of Feb. 18, with citations from the Republican press.

to the great historian across the sea, who was watching
events with the eye of a philosopher, but with the anxious
heart of a patriot. In a letter to Motley written from Boston, February 16, Holmes spoke of "the uncertainty of
opinion of men. I had almost said of principles," he continued. "From the impracticable abolitionist, as bent on
total separation from the South as Carolina is on secession
from the North, to the Hunker, or submissionist, or whatever you choose to call the wretch who would sacrifice
everything and beg the South's pardon for offending it, you
find all shades of opinion in our streets. If Mr. Seward or
Mr. Adams [1] moves in favor of compromise, the whole Republican party sways like a field of grain before the breath
of either of them. If Mr. Lincoln says he shall execute the
laws and collect the revenue though the heavens cave in,
the backs of the Republicans stiffen again, and they take
down the old revolutionary king's arms and begin to ask
whether they can be altered to carry minie bullets. . . . The
expressions of popular opinion in Virginia and Tennessee
have encouraged greatly those who hope for union on the
basis of a compromise." [2] The conservative Republicans
appreciated better than the radicals the meaning of these
elections. While the political reason of Virginia, Maryland,
and Kentucky inclined them to the North, their heartstrings
drew them towards the South. On Virginia, especially,
much depended. Her legislature by a unanimous vote of
both houses had declared that if reconciliation failed, honor

---

[1] "I have rejoiced, as you of New York must certainly have done, in
the spirit of conciliation which has repeatedly been manifested, during
the present session of Congress, by your distinguished senator Governor
Seward. I listened with no less gratification, while recently at Washington on an errand of peace, to the admirable speech of our Massachusetts
representative, Mr. Adams. I might have been glad if both of them could
have gone still further in the path of concession."—Robert C. Winthrop
to the Constitutional Union Committee of Troy, Feb. 17, Winthrop's Addresses and Speeches, vol. ii. p. 701.

[2] Motley's Correspondence, vol. i. p. 360 ; see, also, Pike's despatch of
Feb. 5.

and interest demanded that she should unite her destiny
with the cotton States.[1] Seddon told the Peace Convention
that Virginia was "solemnly pledged to resist coercion;"[2]
and by coercion he meant retaking the forts or collecting
the duties in the Confederate States. It was certain that
if Virginia seceded, North Carolina and Tennessee would
follow. The disunionists also had hopes that her action
would control that of Maryland and Kentucky.[3]

After the withdrawal of the senators and the representatives of the seceded States from Congress, the Republicans
had a good working majority in the House, and, as against
the combined opposition of Southern and Northern Democrats and South Americans,[4] were in the Senate in a minority of only one. As a delayed measure of justice, the Senate
passed the House bill of the previous session for the admission of Kansas as a State under the Wyandotte Constitution.[5] The course of legislation was conciliatory and
forbearing. Bills for the organization of the territories of
Colorado, Dakota, and Nevada were passed without a proposal from any Republican senator or representative to in-
corporate in them a section prohibiting slavery. Nor did
any Republican senator express the desire to take up the
House bill repealing the slave code of New Mexico, which
had been passed at the first session of this Congress.[6] Such
action in either case would have been superfluous. The
law of physical geography dedicated Colorado, Dakota, and
Nevada to freedom, and an act of Congress was not needed.

---

[1] Adopted Jan. 21, Letters and Times of the Tylers, vol. ii. p. 605.

[2] Feb. 19, Chittenden, p. 147.

[3] Reports of Commissioners Wright, Hall, and Bell, Journal of Georgia
Convention, pp. 328, 343, 368; Report of Commissioner Featherston, Journal of Mississippi Convention, p. 195.

[4] The members of Congress of the American party from the Southern
States were called South Americans.

[5] Passed Jan. 21, 36 to 16. The nays were all from the slave States, and
all but one Democrats. The senators from Louisiana and Texas, and Iverson of Georgia were present and voted nay, *Congressional Globe*, p. 489.

[6] See Douglas's remarks in the Senate, March 2, ibid., p. 1391.

All that propagandism, positive legislation, and executive compliance during the last seven years could do had been done to make New Mexico a slave territory, with the result that there were now twenty-two slaves within her borders.[1] Two bills to strengthen the arm of the President by furnishing him military means, and two bills intended to provide specifically for the collection of duties in such a case as existed in Charleston—all of them called by the Southerners "force bills"—were introduced into the House, but were not passed.

Although the House, by 113 nays to 80 yeas, refused to submit the Crittenden compromise to the people,[2] and although the Senate defeated it by 20 to 19 on a direct vote on the joint resolution proposing certain amendments to the Constitution,[3] Congress, by a two-thirds vote of each House, recommended to the States a constitutional amendment which, as bearing on the question on whom rests the blame for the Civil War, is of the highest importance. The proposed Thirteenth Amendment was as follows: "No amendment shall be made to the Constitution which will authorize or give to Congress the power to abolish or interfere, within any State, with the domestic institutions thereof, including that of persons held to labor or service by the laws of said State." This was carried by the conservative Republicans voting with the Democrats.[4] By this amendment, which Lincoln in his inaugural address approved, the North said to the South, We will forever respect your peculiar in-

---

[1] Speech of C. F. Adams, House, Jan. 31, *Congressional Globe* Appendix, p. 125.

[2] Feb. 27, *Congressional Globe*, p. 1261.

[3] March 2 officially, really March 4, ibid., p. 1405. The votes in favor of it were the two South Americans, Crittenden and Kennedy, and the rest were Democrats. All against it were Republicans. Seward's name is not recorded. Cameron was not present, but would have voted nay.

[4] The vote in the House, Feb. 28, was 133 to 65, ibid., p. 1285. In the Senate, March 2, 24 to 12. The nays were: Bingham, Chandler, Clark, Doolittle, Durkee, Foot, King, Sumner, Trumbull, Wade, Wilkinson, and Wilson. Seward's and Cameron's names are not recorded, ibid., p. 1403.

stitution in the States where it now exists.[1]   But it was not considered a sufficient concession by Virginia, North Carolina, and Tennessee, and it had no effect whatever on the States which constituted the Southern Confederacy.[2]

---

[1] If it would have cemented the divided Union, it would undoubtedly have received the ratification of the requisite number of States.   The legislatures of Maryland and Ohio agreed to it promptly, McPherson, p. 60, note.

[2] Two propositions, reported by the House Committee of Thirty-three, which were a compromise, were passed by the House, but not considered by the Senate, see *Congressional Globe*, pp. 1261, 1328.   The proposition to admit New Mexico as a State was laid on the table by a vote of 115 to 71.   Republicans and Democrats were mixed promiscuously in both the majority and minority.   The admission of New Mexico as a State was first proposed by the Republicans as a concession; but the South, after examining all the conditions, being obviously afraid it would become a free State, did not consider it as such.   This action is well summarized by McPherson, p. 58 *et seq.*

A minority in Tennessee, North Carolina, and Virginia were disposed to be satisfied.   Thos. A. R. Nelson, South American member of Congress from Tennessee, represented well this sentiment.   In a letter to Brownlow of March 13 he gave his reasons.   He wrote : "The proposition to amend the Constitution of the United States so [as] forever to prevent any amendment of that instrument interfering with the relation of slavery in the States we passed by a two-thirds vote in both houses of Congress.   This proposition, if carried out by the States, will remove the only real ground of apprehension in the slave States.   It blows the irrepressible-conflict doctrine moon-high, and received the sanction of the author of that doctrine himself.

"The territories of Dakota, Colorado, and Nevada were created without the Wilmot proviso which accompanied these bills at the long session. . . . Though extreme Republicans deny that there can be property in man, this provision, with the Dred Scott case, leaves the territories open to occupation with slavery, and effectually yields the doctrine of protection in favor of the South.

"Although the Republicans, at the long session, when they had not the power, endeavored to repeal the New Mexican laws allowing slavery, yet, at the short session, when, by reason of secession, they had a majority in both houses, they left the matter untouched.   Consequently slavery may exist and be protected in all the territories possibly open to slavery.

"At and for some time after the commencement of the last session of Congress a large majority of the Republicans had no idea of the true condition of things in the South.   They looked upon the threats made by South Carolina and other cotton States as mere gasconade, such as they had listened to for thirty years, and supposed it would soon pass away.   But after the secession of several of the cotton States they began to realize the danger, and a majority of their representatives were earnestly in favor of conciliation, though the extremists among them, as among us, were utterly opposed to anything of the kind. . . .

It has sometimes been asserted that the passage by the
Senate of the Morrill tariff bill, which had been enacted by
the House at the previous session, was a contributing cause
to the secession of Virginia, North Carolina, and Tennessee.
While it is true that objections were raised to the bill from
this quarter,[1] yet if it had any effect at all it was as a drop
in the bucket.[2] More important was its influence on English
opinion. " I know on the very highest authority and from
repeated conversations," wrote Motley from London to his
mother, March 15, " that the English government looks with
deepest regret on the dismemberment of the great American
republic. . . . At the same time I am obliged to say that
there has been a change, a very great change, in English
sympathy since the passing of the Morrill tariff bill. That
measure has done more than any commissioner from the
Southern republic could do to alienate the feelings of the
English public towards the United States, and they are much
more likely to recognize the Southern Confederacy at an
early day than they otherwise would have done. If the tariff
people had been acting in league with the secessionists to
produce a strong demonstration in Europe in favor of the

"Under the circumstances, why should not the seceding States come back
into the Union if the course of the Republican party on the slavery question is the true cause of their separation ? Although they have not received all they demanded, yet they have a guarantee on the vital question,
and their own doctrine of protection has been legally and practically acknowledged. The indications given by the last session of Congress are
decidedly in favor of peace and compromise, and warrant the belief that,
if anything is now wanted, it will, in due time and upon a proper appeal,
be granted by the North. Why, then, should there be civil war, unless the
secession leaders are determined to precipitate it, as they have already pre-
cipitated revolution ? The people in the border States ought to be satisfied, or at least to acquiesce, in what has already been done."—Knoxville
Whig, cited by *National Intelligencer*, March 25.

[1] See, especially, Clingman, Speeches and Writings, p. 545; Richmond *Dispatch*, Feb. 9 ; Baltimore *Daily Exchange*, Feb. 8. The New York *Times*
also opposed it, editorial of Feb. 15, as did the New York *Evening Post*,
cited by the *Tribune*, March 14.

[2] The bill was passed Feb. 20, see chap. xii.

dissolution of the Union, they could not have managed better." [1]

Jefferson Davis in his book intimates that the South would gladly have welcomed a general convention of the States for the consideration of differences and the amendment of the Constitution, but that this boon was denied them by the representatives of the North.[2] This is obviously an error in memory, not unnatural considering the way in which Davis's work was written,[3] and it would be unfair to assume that it was one of the arguments officially put forth to justify disunion, since the statement is so palpably untrue that no Southern writer would urge it after he had examined the evidence. Seward, Chase, and Lincoln advocated a national convention.[4] The leader of the conservative Republicans, the exponent of the radicals, and the President-elect all agreed on this point, and such a project would have met with unanimous favor in the North. But the cotton States would not listen to it.

On the 4th of March Lincoln was peacefully inaugurated. His address, to which careful heed was given by an anxious and eager crowd, had been carefully prepared at Springfield. With the Constitution, Henry Clay's speech of 1850, Jackson's proclamation against nullification, and Webster's reply to Hayne as authorities, " he locked himself up in a room up-stairs over a store across the street from the state-house," [5] and amidst dingy surroundings wrote an immortal state-paper. He submitted it to friends for approval and

---

[1] Motley's Correspondence, vol. i. p. 364.   Compare article in London *Economist* of Jan. 29, cited by New York *Tribune*, Feb. 13, with London *Times*, cited by Charleston *Mercury*, April 4.   The latter said: "Strange to say, the Southern congress enters bravely upon a policy of free-trade, whilst the North cuts itself off from every European sympathy by the introduction of an ultra-protectionist tariff."   Lowell wrote: "Nearly all the English discussions of the 'American crisis' which we have seen have shown far more of the shop-keeping spirit than of interest in the maintenance of free institutions."—*Atlantic Monthly*, June, 1861, p. 758.

[2] Rise and Fall of the Confederate Government, vol. i. p. 227.

[3] See Derby's Books, Authors, and Publishers, p. 493.

[4] Seward's speech of Jan. 12; speech of Chase in the Peace Convention, Chittenden, p. 432; Lincoln's inaugural.   [5] Herndon, p. 478.

advice; from Seward he received many suggestions, some of which he adopted.[1] Lincoln now proclaimed to the country that he had no purpose to interfere directly or indirectly with slavery in the States; he intimated that he should enforce the Fugitive Slave law;[2] he held " that in contemplation of universal law and of the Constitution, the union of these States is perpetual." "No state," he continued, "upon its own mere motion, can lawfully get out of the Union; resolves and ordinances to that effect are legally void; and acts of violence within any State or States, against the authority of the United States, are insurrectionary or revolutionary, according to circumstances. . . . To the extent of my ability I shall take care, as the Constitution itself expressly enjoins upon me, that the laws of the Union be faithfully executed in all the States. . . . In doing this there need be no bloodshed or violence; and there shall be none, unless it be forced upon the national authority. The power confided to me will be used to hold, occupy, and possess the property and places belonging to the government, and to collect the duties and imposts; but beyond what may be necessary for these objects there will be no invasion, no using of force against or among the people anywhere. . . . The mails, unless repelled, will continue to be furnished in all parts of the Union. . . .

" One section of our country believes slavery is right and ought to be extended, while the other believes it is wrong and ought not to be extended. This is the only substantial dispute. . . .

" Physically speaking, we cannot separate. . . . In your hands, my dissatisfied fellow-countrymen, and not in mine, is the momentous issue of civil war. The government will

---

[1] A very interesting relation of the story of this inaugural will be found in chap. xxi. vol. iii. of Nicolay and Hay.

[2] "When," asked Douglas, at Springfield, April 25, "was the Fugitive Slave law executed with more fidelity than since the inauguration of the present incumbent of the presidential office?"—Chicago *Tribune*, June 6; New York *Tribune*, May 1.

not assail you. You can have no conflict without being yourselves the aggressors. . . . We are not enemies, but friends. We must not be enemies. Though passion may have strained, it must not break our bonds of affection. The mystic cords of memory, stretching from every battle-field and patriot grave to every living heart and hearth-stone all over this broad land, will yet swell the chorus of the Union, when again touched, as surely they will be, by the better angels of our nature." [1]

Purposely conspicuous on the platform where Lincoln stood was Senator Douglas, for he wished to give notice to his followers and the country that he proposed to support the President in his efforts to maintain the Union.[2] The inaugural was generally satisfactory to the Northern peo-ple. Conservative and radical Republicans and Douglas Democrats alike approved it. Its power to win popularity lay in its being a straightforward and not uncertain expres-sion of the predominating Union sentiment of the North. It was a paper such as Jackson, Clay, and Webster would have sanctioned had they been living, and nearly every voter at the North owned one of these statesmen as his political teacher and guide. But in the Confederate States Lincoln's inaugural was construed to mean war.[3] It was similarly regarded in Virginia, and only the unconditional Unionists liked it in Maryland.[4] This feeling was reflect-

---

[1] It is hardly necessary to say that the entire inaugural deserves reading by the general reader as well as by the student of history. It is printed by Nicolay and Hay, Raymond, Holland, and Greeley.

[2] Diary of a Public Man, entry of March 4; Nicolay and Hay, vol. iii. p. 326.

[3] See despatch of Wigfall to Pickens, March 4, Official Records, vol. i. p. 261; letter of L. Q. Washington to Walker, Secretary of War, March 5, ibid., p. 263; Charleston *Courier*, March 8; Montgomery despatch to New York *Tribune*, March 4 and 5; Pike from Washington, March 4, ibid.

[4] The policy indicated in the Lincoln inaugural "will meet with the stern and unyielding resistance of a united South."—Richmond *Whig*, March 5. "Civil war must now come. . . . No action of our convention can now maintain the peace. Virginia must fight. . . . War with Lincoln or with Davis is the choice left us."—Richmond *Enquirer*, March 5. See, also, despatch to the New York *Tribune*, Richmond, March 5. "The meas-

ed in Wall Street in a decided downward movement of stocks.[1]

On the next day after the inauguration the President sent the names of his proposed cabinet to the Senate. Seward was named for the State Department and Chase for the Treasury; Simon Cameron, of Pennsylvania, as Secretary of War; Gideon Welles, of Connecticut, as Secretary of the Navy; Caleb B. Smith, of Indiana, as Secretary of the Interior. Edward Bates, of Missouri, was appointed Attorney-General, and Montgomery Blair, of Maryland, Postmaster-General. As the intentions of Lincoln in regard to his cabinet became known the war of factions raged. The most important contest turned on Seward and Chase, for it was one in which opposing opinions in the Republican party clashed. Seward stood for a policy of peace, of conciliation, perhaps of compromise. Chase had made no secret of his opinion—"Inauguration first, adjustment afterwards." To Seward himself little or no objection was made. All conceded that his position in the party, his ability, his fitness entitled him to the first place in the cabinet. But he was hit by the fight made against his follower Cameron, and by the failure of his friends to prevent the appointment of Chase. Cameron agreed with Seward that conciliation was the correct policy. On this account the radicals opposed him. Governor Curtin and A. K. McClure, of Pennsylvania, strenuously objected to him on account of his personal character and a long-standing factional feud. Many were the considerations for and against Cameron, but in the end the scale was probably turned in his favor by the powerful advocacy of Weed and Seward. Seward's friends, however, were not successful in the exclusion

---

ures of Mr. Lincoln mean war."—Baltimore *Daily Exchange*, March 5. See citations from the press, Moore's Rebellion Record, vol. i., Docs., p. 39. In the Senate, March 6, Douglas spoke of the apprehensions which the inaugural had given rise to in the slave States, and declared "It is a peace-offering rather than a war message."—*Congressional Globe*, p. 1436.

[1] Money articles, New York *Tribune*, March 6 and 7.

of Chase, and on that account, two days before the inauguration, Seward withdrew his acceptance of the position of Secretary of State. "The President is determined that he will have a compound cabinet," he wrote to his wife. "I was at one time on the point of refusing—nay, I did refuse for a time to hazard myself in the experiment."[1] Nicolay and Hay have told of the infinite tact with which on this occasion Lincoln treated Seward;[2] and if talent, as Chateaubriand said, is only long patience, what a talent for political affairs this inexperienced man from Illinois displayed at the outset of his executive career!

Pennsylvanians protested against the appointment of Chase, for in their view he was not sound on the tariff question. Conservatives objected to Blair, because he was radical and uncompromising, and because, being a true disciple of Andrew Jackson, he was ready to fight at once if need be for the restoration of the national authority. Lincoln listened to all objections and all protests ; he gave heed to all arguments, and though at times he hesitated and was on the point of changing his mind in regard to some of the appointments, the names he finally sent to the Senate made up the cabinet substantially as he had framed it in his mind the night of his election.[3]

Meanwhile the Confederate congress[4] and executive were

---

[1] Letter of March 8, Life of Seward, vol. ii. p. 518.

[2] March 5, Seward withdrew his letter of resignation.

[3] See chap. xxii. vol. iii., Nicolay and Hay ; Life of Seward, vol. ii.; chapter on Lincoln and Cameron in McClure's Lincoln and Men of War Times; Lincoln and Seward, Welles; Diary of a Public Man, entries of Feb. 28, March 2 and 3; Schuckers's Life of Chase, p. 206 ; Pike to New York *Tribune*, March 3; editorial, ibid., March 2, 7 ; Crawford, p. 320 ; Life of Thurlow Weed, vols. i. and ii. "In the Senate Simon Cameron declared himself desirous to preserve the Union 'by any sacrifice of feeling, and I may say of principle.'"—Life of Lincoln, Morse, vol. i. p. 197. A prevalent opinion was that Seward would be the master-spirit of the administration. "Seward is a necessity," wrote Bowles to Dawes, Feb. 26 ; "Chase or Banks ought to be ; but let the New-Yorker, with his Illinois attachment, have a fair trial."—Life of Bowles, vol. i. p. 318.

[4] "The members of the Confederate congress are **extraordinary workers.**

diligently at work at Montgomery. Beauregard had been made a brigadier-general, and sent to Charleston to take charge of the military operations in the name and by the authority of the Confederate States.[1] On the day of Lincoln's inauguration the Confederate flag was raised over the Montgomery capitol, and two days later it was displayed from the Charleston custom-house. It had three broad stripes—the one in the centre white, the others red, with a blue union containing seven white stars. Davis was reluctant to give up the old national flag, asserting that in the event of war a different battle-flag would make a sufficient distinction between the combatants.[2] The Confederate provisional congress remained in session until March 16. It authorized the raising of a military force of 100,000 volunteers to serve for twelve months, and the issue of $1,000,000 in treasury notes, bearing interest at the rate of one cent per day per $100, redeemable after one year. It passed acts to organize and support a navy; to organize a post-office department; to establish judicial courts. It passed the necessary appropriation bills.[3] A commission of three, with Yancey at its head, was sent to Europe to obtain recognition for the new government, and to make treaties of amity, commerce, and international copyrights.[4] The different States turned over to the Confederacy the property of the national government which they had taken, the State of

Their sessions average about ten hours daily, and very little of the time is consumed in buncombe speeches."—Montgomery despatch to New York *Tribune*, March 6.

[1] He arrived there March 1, Roman's Beauregard, vol. i. p. 25.

[2] See Montgomery despatches of March 4 to New York *Tribune ;* Montgomery *Advertiser*, March 5, cited by the New York *Tribune*, March 11; Foster to Totten, March 7, Official Records, vol. i. p. 192 ; Mrs. Davis, vol. ii. p. 36; Appleton, p. 156: Diary of a Public Man, entry March 6. The provisional congress met in the Senate Chamber of the Montgomery capitol.

[3] The Statutes at Large, Provisional Government of C. S. A., pp. 45, 47, 54, 57, 69, 70, 75.

[4] Appleton, p. 131; Life of Yancey, Du Bose, pp. 588, 594, 600, 604; Statutes at Large, p. 93.

Louisiana receiving a special vote of thanks from the Confederate congress for the transfer of $536,000 in coin, which she had seized in the United States mint and custom-house at New Orleans.[1]

Before the Confederate congress adjourned it adopted a permanent constitution.[2] It was the Constitution of the United States, with but three essential differences. It expressly affirmed the right of property in negro slaves; it made the recognition and protection of slavery in any new territory that might be acquired mandatory on congress; and in the different provisions touching the peculiar institution, seeking no refuge in the ingenious circumlocution of the federal Constitution, it used the words "slave" and "slavery." In the preamble it asserted the doctrine of the sovereignty of the States. It forbade congress to lay duties on foreign importations for the purpose of fostering any branch of industry. In two of these changes lay the essence of the secession ; the other change gave expression to a largely held construction of the Constitution of the United States. Still another alteration was made, which, in view of the strong sentiment existing in the cotton States in 1859 favorable to the reopening of the African slave-trade,[3] may seem extraordinary. The Confederate constitution prohibited the importation of negroes from any foreign country except the slave-holding States of the old Union.[4] This clause was adopted by the vote of four States to two, South Carolina and Florida opposing it.[5] It showed the re-

---

[1] Appleton, pp. 130, 430; Statutes at Large, p. 94.

[2] The government of the Confederacy was carried on for one year under the provisional constitution, and the legislative body was called the provisional congress. The first congress under the permanent constitution met Feb. 18, 1862.

[3] See vol. ii. under Slave-trade, African; letter of Robert C. Winthrop, May 20, 1859, Winthrop's Addresses and Speeches, vol. ii. p. 698.

[4] For the provision of the federal Constitution, see vol. i. p. 18.

[5] Appleton, p. 161 ; *National Intelligencer*, March 28. To confirm this vote I had a search made in the journal of the Confederate congress, but it is silent on the subject. Mr. Thian, chief clerk of the adjutant-

spect Southern statesmen had for the opinion of the enlightened world, and was thrown out as an allurement to foreign powers for their recognition, and as an inducement for the border slave States to join the Confederacy. It is probable that Southern senators and representatives would have objected to such a provision in the old Constitution, for, although urged to it by Winthrop, Crittenden did not deem it wise to make the article of his compromise that dealt with the foreign slave-trade a constitutional amendment, but offered it as one of the joint resolutions.[1] Further alterations were made, all of which are of great interest to students of political science, and which are generally considered by them as improvements on the Constitution of 1787.[2]

The religious character of the people manifested itself in the preamble to their organic instrument by "invoking the favor and guidance of Almighty God."

The permanent constitution was adopted on March 11, by a unanimous vote of the seven States represented,[3]

general of the army, to whom I desire here to express my thanks for assistance rendered, informs me that owing to press of other work this journal was not written out during the sessions. The clerk kept bills with the votes and other memoranda, and after the war J. J. Hooper, secretary of the congress, took these papers to his plantation with the intention of writing up the journal, but this he never did. When the papers came into the possession of the government, this work was done in Washington. Mr. Thian assures me that the journal is absolutely correct. I also wish to acknowledge my indebtedness to Joseph W. Kirkley, of the War Department, for important assistance.

[1] Letter of Winthrop to Crittenden, Dec. 24, 1860, Life of Crittenden, Coleman, vol. ii. p. 239; Journal of Committee of Thirteen, p. 7. It must, however, be stated that every Southern senator in committee voted for the resolution.

[2] In Jefferson Davis's book the constitutions of the United States and the Confederate States are printed in parallel columns, the changes being plainly shown, see vol. i. p. 648; see also p. 259, and Stephens's War between the States, vol. ii. p. 335. An excellent brief analysis of the Confederate constitution is given by Woodrow Wilson, Division and Reunion, p. 242.

[3] Roll-call of convention, March 11, War Department Archives, MS.; extract from the Journal of the Congress, Statutes at Large, C. S. A., p. 28.

and was promptly ratified by the different State conventions.[1]

When one thinks of the many fruitless attempts of peoples to devise wise systems of government, and of the many admirable constitutions on paper which have been adopted, but which have failed to find a response in the character and political habits of the men for whom they were intended, one might be lost in admiration at the orderly manner in which the Southerners proceeded, at the excellent organic instrument they adopted, at the ready acceptance of the work of their representatives, were it not that they were running amuck against the civilized world in their attempt to bolster up human slavery, and in their theory of governmental particularism, when the spirit of the age was tending to freedom and to unity. The sincerest and frankest public man in the Southern Confederacy, Alexander H. Stephens, told the true story. " The new constitution has put at rest forever," he declared, " all the agitating questions relating to our peculiar institution—African slavery as it exists amongst us—the proper status of the negro in our form of civilization. This was the immediate cause of the late rupture and present revolution. . . . The prevailing ideas entertained by Jefferson and most of the leading statesmen at the time of the formation of the old Constitution were, that the enslavement of the African was in violation of the laws of nature ; that it was wrong in principle socially, morally, and politically. . . .

" Our new government is founded upon exactly the opposite idea ; its foundations are laid, its corner-stone rests, upon the great truth that the negro is not equal to the white man ; that slavery — subordination to the superior

[1] South Carolina, April 3, by a vote of 138 to 21, Journal of South Carolina Convention, p. 248 ; Georgia, March 16, by yeas 276, nays none, Journal, p. 187 ; Mississippi, March 29, yeas 78, nays 7, Journal, p. 35 ; Louisiana, March 21, yeas 101, nays 7, Journal, p. 75 ; Texas, March 23, yeas 128, nays 2, Constitution of the State of Texas, etc., p. 36 ; Alabama, March 13, yeas 87, nays 5, Stephens's War between the States, vol. ii. p. 355, see, also, p. 339 ; Florida, April 22, by yeas 54, nays none. Proceedings of the Convention of the People of Florida at Called Sessions, pp. 31–38.

race—is his natural and normal condition. This, our new government, is the first in the history of the world based upon this great physical, philosophical, and moral truth. . . .

" The great objects of humanity are best attained when there is conformity to the Creator's laws and decrees, in the formation of governments as well as in all things else. Our confederacy is founded upon principles in strict conformity with these laws. This stone, which was rejected by the first builders, 'is become the chief of the corner'— the real 'corner-stone'—in our new edifice." [1]

It is obvious that when Lincoln took the oath of office he had two distinct purposes in his mind : to hold forts Sumter and Pickens, and to use all means short of the compromise of principle to retain the border slave States and North Carolina, Tennessee, and Arkansas in the Union. On going to his office the morning of March 5 he found that the Sumter question was more perplexing than he had imagined. A letter from Holt, still acting as Secretary of War, gave the information that Anderson had written that his provisions would last only a few weeks longer, and that to reinforce the fort successfully with a view to holding it would require an army of 20,000 disciplined men. [2] While the federal government, waiting the issue of the Peace Convention, had pursued a policy of inaction, the South Carolinians had been steadily at work on the islands in Charleston harbor, erecting batteries and strengthening the forts which bore on

---

[1] This speech was made in the Athenæum, in Savannah, March 21. I have made the citations from the speech as printed in Cleveland's Stephens, pp. 721, 723. That is taken from the report in the Savannah *Republican* made at the time. I have compared the quoted portions with the speech as printed in the New York *Tribune* of March 27, and in Moore's Rebellion Record, vol. i., Docs., p. 44, and they agree. The *Tribune* gives the date of the speech as March 22. Johnston and Browne make an attempt to explain away the parts of the speech I have cited, see pp. 394, 396. "The Confederate States are confederates in the crime of upholding slavery." —London *Punch*, Moore's Rebellion Record, vol. i., Poetry, etc., p. 24.

[2] Nicolay and Hay, vol. iii. p. 376 ; Official Records, vol. i. pp. 197, 202. Anderson's letter was received March 4.

Sumter. The President turned to General Scott for counsel, receiving the opinion that "evacuation seems almost inevitable." He was in a trying situation; there had been so
many defections in the military and civil service that he did
not know on whom he could depend.[1] Lincoln suspected
even Anderson, and sending for Holt took him into a private room, and asked whether he had ever had reason to
doubt the loyalty of the commander of Sumter. The President was relieved to learn that Holt had entire confidence
in Anderson's fealty. What made the situation almost intolerable was "the scramble for office," which Stanton wrote
"is terrific."[2] "Solicitants for offices besiege the President," said Seward in a private letter, "and he of course
finds his hands full for the present. My duties call me
to the White House one, two, or three times a day. The
grounds, halls, stairways, closets are filled with applicants,
who render ingress and egress difficult."[3] Lincoln himself

---

[1] On the 1st of March, by direction of President Buchanan, General
Twiggs had been "dismissed from the army of the United States for his
treachery to the flag of his country, in having surrendered on the 18th of
February, on the demand of the authorities of Texas, the military posts
and other property of the United States in his department and under his
charge."—Order of Secretary of War, Official Records, vol. i. p. 597; see
Buchanan's letter to Dix of April 19, where he calls Twiggs a "hoary-
headed rebel," Curtis, vol. ii. p. 542. General Dix wrote Anderson,
March 4, that in the extreme Southern States there had been "a demoral-
ization in all that concerns the faithful discharge of official duty, which,
if it had pleased God, I could have wished never to have lived to see.
The cowardice and treachery of General Twiggs is more disheartening
than all that has transpired since this disgraceful career of disloyalty to
the government commenced."—Curtis, vol. ii. p. 495. Anderson replied:
"The faithful historian of the present period will have to present a record
which will sadden and surprise. It would seem that a sirocco charged
with treachery, cunning, dishonesty, and bad faith had tainted the atmosphere of portions of our land; and, alas! how many have been prostrated
by its blast!"—Letter of March 7, Curtis, vol. ii. p. 496. The adjutant-
general of the army, Cooper, a native of New Jersey, resigned his position
on March 7, and went to Montgomery to take a similar office in the Confederate States.

[2] To Buchanan, March 10, Curtis, vol. ii. p. 530.

[3] Letter of March 16, Life of Seward, vol. ii. p. 530.

said, "I seem like one sitting in a palace, assigning apartments to importunate applicants, while the structure is on fire and likely soon to perish in ashes."[1]

Yet whenever the President could get away from the ceaseless clamor for office and recognition, the question what to do about Sumter occupied his mind. March 9 he held his first cabinet council and exposed the situation to his advisers. Thereupon ensued consultations with military and naval officers in regard to the feasibility of relieving the fort. March 12 General Scott formally gave his opinion that Anderson should be instructed to evacuate Sumter. Captain Gustavus V. Fox, of the navy, submitted a plan of reinforcement which to the President and a majority of the cabinet seemed practicable. Narrowing now the question to the matter of provisioning the fort and assuming that it was possible, Lincoln asked his cabinet at the meeting of March 15 whether, as a political measure, it were wise to attempt it. Seward, Cameron, Welles, Smith, and Bates said no; Seward made a plausible argument in support of his position. Blair emphatically answered yes, and Chase gave a conditionally affirmative reply.[2] Lincoln held his decision in abeyance. For the purpose of gaining more light he sent Fox to Charleston, who, through the influence of an old comrade now in the South Carolina service, obtained admit-

---

[1] McClure's Lincoln, p. 56. "It makes me heart-sick. All over the country our party are by the ears, fighting over offices worth one hundred to five hundred dollars." — Colfax to his mother, two weeks after the inauguration, Life of Colfax, Hollister, p. 173. The Diary of a Public Man, entry of March 7, speaks of "the strange and uncouth appearance of a great proportion of the people . . . lounging about the steps of the Treasury Department and the lobbies of the hotels. . . . Certainly, in all my long experience of Washington, I have never seen such a swarm of uncouth beings. The clamor for offices is already quite extraordinary, and these poor people undoubtedly belong to the horde which has pressed in here to seek places under the new administration, which neither has nor can hope to have places enough to satisfy one-twentieth part of the number." — North American Review, Nov., 1879, p. 488.

[2] Nicolay and Hay, vol. iii. chap. xxiii.; Crawford, chap. xxvii.; Official Records, vol. i. p. 196; Warden's Life of Chase, p. 370.

tance to Sumter, and had a conversation with Anderson.[1] To ascertain whether there was, as Seward had maintained, a latent Union feeling in South Carolina, the President induced Hurlbut, of Illinois, a personal friend, to visit his native city of Charleston, and learn the public opinion of the city and of the State from Petigru[2]—now the only Union man of prominence in the city—in whose office he had for four years studied law. Ward H. Lamon, a confidential companion of Lincoln, accompanied him. Hurlbut reported that the sentiment of South Carolina was unanimous for lasting separation, and that there was no attachment to the Union.[3] Fox's visit confirmed him in the notion that his plan was entirely feasible.[4] In the meantime, by direction of the President, an order had been sent by the war-steamer *Mohawk* to Captain Vogdes on board the sloop-of-war *Brooklyn*, lying off Fort Pickens, to land his company of artillery and reinforce that fort.[5]

Two of the Confederate commissioners[6] having arrived at Washington the early part of March, an attempt was made by them, through the influence of Senator Hunter, of Virginia, to get an informal interview with Secretary Seward. They knew that his policy was conciliatory, and that he was supported by Cameron and probably by General Scott, and they were aware that he believed that moderation would save the border States, and in the end induce the people of the Southern Confederacy to rebel against their leaders and return to the Union. While Seward's hopes were illusive, the commissioners thought it well he should indulge in them, for up to a certain point they could travel along together, he hugging his vain dreams while they paved the way for the surrender of Forts Sumter and Pickens and a peaceful sepa-

---

[1] Crawford, p. 370.   [2] *Ante*, p. 124, note 3.

[3] Nicolay and Hay, vol. iii. p. 391 *et ante*.

[4] Ibid., p. 389 ; Crawford, p. 371.

[5] The order was given March 11, the *Mohawk* left March 12, Nicolay and Hay, vol. iii. p. 393; Official Records, vol. i. p. 360 ; *ante*, p. 284.

[6] *Ante*, p. 295. These were Forsyth and Crawford.

ration.[1] Seward told Senator Hunter that if the commissioners made a formal demand and pressed for a reply, the result might be unfavorable.   This being communicated to Forsyth and Crawford, they prepared a memorandum in which they agreed not to bring forward the object of their mission, provided the United States government should preserve the present military status in every respect.[2] This paper Hunter presented to Seward, at the same time asking that he would grant the commissioners an informal interview. The secretary was "perceptibly embarrassed and uneasy," and answered that before giving his consent he must consult the President.   The next day, March 12, he wrote a note to Hunter, saying, "It will not be in my power to receive the gentlemen of whom we conversed yesterday."[3] Forsyth and Crawford then formally asked the Secretary of State to receive them as delegates of "an independent nation, *de facto* and *de jure* . . . with a view to a speedy adjustment of all questions growing out of this political separation upon terms of amity and good-will." Seward did not reply in the form of a letter, not deeming it wise to go even that far in an official recognition of the commissioners, but he prepared a memorandum which he placed on the files of the State Department, with instructions to furnish them a copy should they call for it; in this he declined official intercourse with Forsyth and Crawford.[4]

Justice Nelson, of New York, a man loyal to the core, and Justice Campbell, of Alabama, both of the United States Supreme Court, which had just ended its session, now appear in the negotiations.   Campbell had been opposed to

---

[1] Forsyth and Crawford to Toombs, March 8, MS. Confederate Archives, Treasury Department, Washington.

[2] Memorandum A to accompany Despatch No. 3, ibid.

[3] Confederate Diplomatic Correspondence, MS. Treasury Department; see also Crawford, pp. 323, 324 ; Nicolay and Hay, vol. iii. p. 402.

[4] The letter of the commissioners is dated March 12, the memorandum of the secretary March 15, Moore's Rebellion Record, vol. i., Docs., pp. 42, 43; Crawford, p. 325.

the secession of his State, was "anxiously and patriotically earnest to preserve the government," and still had hopes of the restoration of the Union.[1] He and Nelson after a careful examination had become convinced that the policy of coercion—and to them coercion had come to mean the retaking of the public property and the collection of the duties—could not be carried out "without very serious violation of the Constitution and statute."[2] March 15, Nelson called on Seward, Chase, and Bates, and gave them his opinion, with the reasons for it. Seward, after listening to him with warm interest, confided in him his own embarrassment at the demand for recognition of the Confederate commissioners. Nelson suggested that it might be well to consult Campbell, and later brought him to the Secretary of State. The two justices advised Seward to reply to the letter of the commissioners, announcing that the desire of the government was for peace, and that it would pursue a policy of conciliation and forbearance. Seward rose from his seat and said: "I wish I could do it. See Montgomery Blair, see Mr. Bates, see Mr. Lincoln himself; I wish you would: they are all Southern men. Convince them! No; there is not a member of the cabinet who would consent to it. If Jefferson Davis had known the state of things here he would not have sent those commissioners; the evacuation of Sumter is as much as the administration can bear."[3] Campbell had been unaware that the withdrawal of Anderson was under consideration, and he quite agreed with Seward as to its effect; rejoicing that so im-

---

[1] Crawford, pp. 326, 345. Campbell "has been as anxiously and patriotically earnest to preserve the government as any man in the United States, and he has sacrificed more than any Southern man rather than yield to the secessionists."—Stanton to Buchanan, May 19, 1861, *North American Review*, November, 1879, p. 478; Curtis, vol. ii. p. 549; see, also, Thurlow Weed's article in Albany *Evening Journal*, cited by New York *Tribune*, May 24; also *Tribune*, May 3.

[2] Campbell to Southern Historical Society, Dec. 20, 1873, Crawford, p. 326.

[3] Campbell's MS. Facts of History, Crawford, p. 328.

portant a move towards adjustment would be taken, he proposed to see the commissioners and to write to Jefferson Davis at Montgomery. " And what shall I say to him upon the subject of Fort Sumter ?" he asked. " You may say to him," replied the secretary, " that before that letter reaches him — how far is it to Montgomery ?" " Three days," answered Campbell. " You may say to him that before that letter reaches him the telegraph will have informed him that Sumter will have been evacuated." " And what shall I say as to the forts on the Gulf of Mexico ?" Seward replied, " We contemplate no action as to them ; we are satisfied as to the position of things there." [1]

On the same day, March 15, Campbell had his first interview with Commissioner Crawford. He told Crawford that the opinion prevailed at Washington that " the secession movements were short-lived, and would wither under sunshine." The commissioner replied that he " was willing to take all the risks of sunshine . . . but that the evacuation of Sumter was imperative, and the military status must remain unchanged." [2] Campbell left with Crawford a memorandum stating that he felt perfect confidence that Fort Sumter would be evacuated in the next five days ; that the existing military status would not be altered ; that an immediate demand for an answer to the communication of the commissioners would be productive of evil ; and he earnestly asked that they would delay ten days before pressing for a reply.[3] Campbell declined to say on whose authority he was giving these assurances, but Crawford correctly guessed it was on Seward's.[4] That evening Camp-

[1] Crawford, p. 328, note ; Campbell to Davis, April 3, Nicolay and Hay, vol. iii. p. 407 ; Crawford, Roman, and Forsyth to Toombs, March 22, MS. Confederate Diplomatic Correspondence, Treasury Department.

[2] Campbell MS., Crawford, p. 329 ; the commissioners to Toombs, March 22.

[3] MSS. United States Treasury Department, Crawford, p. 330 ; Campbell to Seward, April 13, Moore's Rebellion Record, vol. i., Docs., p. 427 ; the commissioners to Toombs, March 22.

[4] Campbell's MS., Crawford, p. 329.

bell communicated to the secretary, by letter, the substance
of the memorandum he had left with Crawford.[1] The five
days went by without the evacuation of Sumter. Under
pressure from the commissioners, Campbell and Nelson saw
the Secretary of State, and as a result of the interview
Campbell gave them, March 21, a memorandum saying,
" My confidence in the two facts stated in my note of the
15th is unabated."[2] On the next day Campbell had another
conversation with Seward, the gist of which he made a
memorandum of and submitted it to the Secretary of State,
afterwards leaving it with the commissioners. This paper
ran thus : " As a result of my interviewing of to-day, I have
to say that I have still unabated confidence that Fort Sumter will be evacuated, and that no delay that has occurred
excites in me any apprehension or distrust ; and that the
state of things existing at Fort Pickens will not be altered
prejudicially to the Confederate States."[3] Accounts of the
several interviews with Campbell and his memoranda were
transmitted by the commissioners to the authorities at Montgomery.[4] After March 22 Justice Nelson retired from the
negotiations and left Washington.[5]

Meanwhile the country and senators in session at Washington were anxious and eager to know what would be
done in regard to Sumter. The *National Republican*,
which Stanton called the " Lincoln organ," announced that
at the cabinet meeting of March 9 it was determined that
both Sumter and Pickens should be surrendered. That at
least Anderson would be withdrawn was the universal impression in Washington.[6] The news spread quickly through

---

[1] Campbell to Seward, April 13, Moore, vol. i., Docs., p. 426.

[2] J. A. C., MS. Confederate Archives, Treasury Department.

[3] J. A. C., March 22 ; ibid., letter of Campbell to Seward, April 13.

[4] March 22, MS. Confederate Diplomatic Correspondence.

[5] Crawford, pp. 332, 333.

[6] " As one of the editors of the *National Intelligencer* in 1861, I was
authentically informed of this purpose [the evacuation of Sumter] by Secretary Seward, not only for my guidance as a public journalist, but with

the country. Outside of New York city the Republicans and many other Union men heard it with dismay. Douglas, however, argued in the Senate that South Carolina was entitled to Sumter and Florida to Pickens, and that "Anderson and his gallant band should be instantly withdrawn." The report caused an excited and buoyant stock-market in Wall Street.[1] The Charleston *Mercury* and the Charleston *Courier* stated, March 12, that Sumter would be obtained by South Carolina without a fight.[2] Lamon, who was regarded at Charleston as a "confidential agent of the President," told Governor Pickens that he had come to make arrangements for the withdrawal of the garrison.[3] He gave Anderson to understand that the order would soon be sent

---

the request that I should communicate the fact to George W. Summers, the recognized leader of the Union majority in the Virginia convention." —James C. Welling, in the *Nation*, Dec. 4, 1879 ; Stanton to Buchanan, March 12, 14, Holt to Buchanan, March 14, Curtis, vol. ii. pp. 531–33 ; *National Republican*, March 11 ; Pike and other Washington correspondents to New York *Tribune*, March 10 and 11.

[1] " The people are now agitated by the intelligence that Fort Sumter is to be abandoned. Here I think there will be no decided demonstration of disapproval. But in the country it will be different. The disappointment will be very great, and it will go far to turn the current against the new administration."—Dix, from New York, to Buchanan, March 14, Curtis, vol. ii. p. 533 ; Weed to Seward, Crawford, p. 328 ; editorials in New York *Tribune*, March 11 and 12 ; Pike to New York *Tribune*, March 11 ; Douglas's speech, March 15, *Congressional Globe*, p. 1461 ; money article, New York *Tribune*, March 12. The report March 11 was that it would require 10,000 men and a strong naval force to reinforce Sumter ; by March 19 Anderson's despatch, received by Holt March 4, was substantially known to the public, see New York *Tribune*.

[2] Cited by New York *Tribune*, March 15.

[3] " I know the fact from Mr. Lincoln's most intimate friend and accredited agent, Mr. Lamon, that the President of the United States professed a desire to evacuate Fort Sumter, and he (Mr. Lamon) actually wrote me, after his return to Washington, that he would be back in a few days to aid in that purpose."—Letter of Governor Pickens, Aug. 3, Charleston *Courier*, Aug. 6 ; also Pickens's Message, Nov., 1861, Crawford, p. 373 ; Davis's Rise and Fall of the Confederate Government, vol. i. p. 272 ; Beauregard to Anderson, March 26, Official Records, vol. i. p. 222; Beauregard to Walker, ibid., p. 282.

for the evacuation of the fort,[1] and on his return to Washington he said to Stanton that he was satisfied Sumter could not be successfully reinforced.[2]   The Russian minister assured Commissioner Roman that Seward was averse to war, and tried to bring about a meeting between the two over a cup of tea at the Russian legation, but the secretary did not deem it wise to accept the informal invitation.[3] Both the British and Russian ministers manifested their sympathy with the aim of the Confederate commissioners.[4]

By March 28 the perplexities which environed Lincoln had thickened.   That day General Scott advised the abandonment of Pickens as well as of Sumter.   The President that evening gave his first state dinner,[5] and just before

---

[1] Anderson to Thomas, Adjutant-General, April 1, 4, Official Records, vol. i. pp. 230, 237 ; Crawford, p. 374.   Lamon's visit to Sumter was made March 25.

[2] Stanton to Buchanan, April 3, *North American Review*, Nov., 1879, p. 475.   Anderson had no confidence in Fox's plan, see Crawford, p. 371.

[3] Crawford and Roman to Toombs, March 26, MS. Confederate Archives, Treasury Department.   April 4, Secretaries Chase and Smith met Forsyth at dinner at the house of Senator Douglas, Russell's Diary, p. 62.

[4] Crawford and Roman to Toombs, March 26.

[5] W. H. Russell, correspondent of the London *Times*, was present at this dinner, and has given an interesting account of it, Diary, p. 41.   General Scott had been invited, and had come to the White House, but on account of an indisposition was unable to remain.   Russell relates : " In the conversation which occurred before dinner, I was amused to observe the manner in which Mr. Lincoln used the anecdotes for which he is famous. Where men bred in courts, accustomed to the world or versed in diplomacy, would use some subterfuge or make a polite speech or give a shrug of the shoulders as the means of getting out of an embarrassing position, Mr. Lincoln raises a laugh by some bold west-country anecdote, and moves off in the cloud of merriment produced by his joke.   Thus, when Mr. Bates was remonstrating apparently against the appointment of some indifferent lawyer to a place of judicial importance, the President interposed with, ' Come now, Bates, he's not half as bad as you think.   Besides that, I must tell you he did me a good turn long ago.   When I took to the law, I was going to court one morning, with some ten or twelve miles of bad road before me, and I had no horse.   The judge overtook me in his wagon. "Hallo, Lincoln !   Are you not going to the court-house ?   Come in, and I'll give you a seat."   Well, I got in, and the judge went on reading his papers.   Presently the wagon struck a stump on one side of the road ;

the members of the cabinet left for their homes, he imparted to them privately the general's last recommendation. All, with the possible exception of Seward, were amazed. Blair expressed in hot words his indignation at Scott's course, and aimed his shafts indirectly at the Secretary of State.[1] The next day a formal cabinet council took place. Lincoln again asked his advisers their opinion about Sumter. Only Seward and Smith were now in favor of abandoning the fort. Chase, Welles, and Blair decidedly maintained that it should be relieved. Bates was non-committal.[2] The manifestations of public sentiment and the protests of the radical Republican senators, joined perhaps to a clearer comprehension of the public duty, had had their effect.[3] At the close of the cabinet meeting, the President directed that the Secretary of War and the Secretary of the Navy prepare an expedition which should be ready to move by sea as early as the 6th of April.[4] Still he had not positively decided that he would send supplies to Sumter. This expedition was to be "used or not according to circumstances."[5]

then it hopped off to the other. I looked out and I saw the driver was jerking from side to side in his seat, so says I, "Judge, I think your coachman has been taking a little drop too much this morning." "Well, I declare, Lincoln," said he, "I should not wonder if you are right, for he has nearly upset me half a dozen times since starting." So putting his head out of the window, he shouted, "Why, you infernal scoundrel, you are drunk!" Upon which, pulling up his horses and turning round with great gravity, the coachman said, "By gorra! that's the first rightful decision you have given for the last twelvemonth."' While the company were laughing, the President beat a quiet retreat from the neighborhood of the attorney-general."

[1] Nicolay and Hay, vol. iii. p. 394 ; Official Records, vol. i. p. 200 ; Lincoln and Seward, Welles, pp. 57, 65.

[2] Nicolay and Hay, vol. iii. p. 429 *et seq.*

[3] The opinion of the radical Republicans was expressed in Trumbull's resolution of March 28, although they did not deem it prudent to take a vote on it, which the Democrats were anxious to do, *Congressional Globe*, p. 1519.

[4] Official Records, vol. i. p. 226; Nicolay and Hay, vol. iii. p. 433.

[5] Lincoln's message to Congress, July 4, 1861.

When Lamon was at Charleston he told Governor Pickens that he hoped to return in a few days for the purpose of arranging the removal of Anderson and his garrison.[1] South Carolina had long been impatient at the occupation of a fort commanding the harbor of her chief city by the force of what she regarded a foreign nation; her governor shared this impatience, and March 30, unquiet at hearing nothing from Lamon and seeing no move towards the evacuation of Sumter, he communicated by telegraph to the Confederate commissioners Lamon's statements and his own disappointed hopes. This despatch, through Justice Campbell, went to the Secretary of State, who in turn showed it to the President. April 1 Seward informed Campbell that "the President was concerned about the contents of the telegram—there was a point of honor involved; that Lamon had no agency from him, nor title to speak, nor any power to pledge him by any promise or assurance"; and so anxious was he that Governor Pickens should know this that he preferred a request to Campbell to question Lamon in a private interview, which the justice declined to do. On this same day Seward and Campbell had two conferences, and after the first one, on the main point involved, the secretary went to consult the President. On his return he wrote on a piece of paper, which he handed to Campbell, "I am satisfied the government will not undertake to supply Fort Sumter without giving notice to Governor Pickens." "What does this mean?" asked Campbell; "does the President design to attempt to supply Sumter?" "No, I think not," answered Seward. "It is a very irksome thing to him to surrender it. His ears are open to every one, and they fill his head with schemes for its supply. I do not think that he will adopt any of them. There is no design to reinforce it."[2] Campbell thought the

---

[1] Pickens's message, Nov., 1861, Rise and Fall of the Confederate Government, vol. i. p. 272 ; *ante*, p. 333, note 3.

[2] Campbell's MS., Crawford, p. 338 ; see also Davis's Rise and Fall of the Confederate Government, vol. i. p. 278.

writing "was a departure from the pledges of the previous month," but, as interpreted by the verbal explanation, he " did not consider it a matter then to complain of." Still feeling that his mediation had not been fruitless, he wrote Jefferson Davis, April 3: "I do not doubt that Sumter will be evacuated shortly, without any effort to supply it; but in respect to Pickens I do not think there is any settled plan. . . . All that I have is a promise that the status will not be attempted to be changed prejudicially to the Confederate States without notice to me. It is known that I make these assurances on my own responsibility. I have no right to mention any name or to pledge any person." [1]

As early as April 4 the President decided to send to the succor of Fort Sumter the expedition which, March 29, he had ordered to be got ready.[2] For several days there had been unusual stir in the War and Navy departments. It was known that they were preparing an expedition at the Brooklyn Navy-yard. It took air that the government had decided not to withdraw Anderson, that Sumter would be provisioned and Pickens reinforced.[3] These reports coming to the ears of Campbell, he asked Seward by letter, April 7, whether they "were well or ill founded." The secretary replied, "Faith as to Sumter fully kept — wait and see," meaning that the government would not make an attempt to supply the fort without giving notice to Governor Pickens.[4] April 6, Robert S. Chew, a clerk in the State De-

---

[1] Cited by Nicolay and Hay, vol. iii. p. 411.

[2] Cameron to Anderson, April 4, Cameron to Fox, April 4, Official Records, vol. i. p. 235; *ante*.

[3] See New York *Tribune* and its Washington despatches, April 1 to 6; Russell's Diary, entry April 3, p. 59; Stanton to Buchanan, April 3, Curtis, vol. ii. p. 538; various despatches of the commissioners to Toombs, cited by Nicolay and Hay, vol. iv. p. 2 *et seq.*

[4] MSS. cited by Crawford, p. 340, and Nicolay and Hay, vol. iv. p. 36; Campbell to Crawford, April 7, MS. Confederate Diplomatic Correspondence; see, also, Campbell's letter to Seward, April 13. Seward's answer to Campbell was made April 8. That day the commissioners called for and received a copy of the memorandum on the files of the State Department,

partment, was sent to Charleston with instructions draft-
ed by Lincoln's own hand to give the proper notification.[1]
Arriving there the evening of April 8, and being at once
accorded an interview, he read to Governor Pickens what
the President had written: "I am directed by the President of the United States to notify you to expect an attempt will be made to supply Fort Sumter with provisions
only; and that if such attempt be not resisted, no effort to
throw in men, arms, or ammunition will be made without
further notice, or in case of an attack upon the fort."[2]

I have related with considerable detail the story of the
Seward-Campbell negotiations, for the reason that Jefferson
Davis and Alexander H. Stephens in their books have urged
the duplicity of the Washington authorities in this affair
as a contributing justification to the Confederate attack
on Fort Sumter,[3] and for the further reason that Justice
Campbell, whose sincerity and straightforwardness cannot
be questioned, averred that "the equivocating conduct of
the administration" was the "proximate cause" of the commencement of the war in Charleston harbor.[4] If, as these
gentlemen more or less distinctly assume, the President
consented to this negotiation, and knew of the assurances
which Seward gave, his course cannot successfully be defended. Nicolay and Hay do not tell us in set terms how
far he was privy to the quasi-promises of his secretary, but
from their narrative it is a reasonable inference that he
knew little or nothing about them. Secretary Welles,
writing in 1873, says emphatically that the President did
not know of Seward's assurance that Fort Sumter would
be evacuated, and never gave it his sanction.[5] Considering

---

which Seward had caused to be placed there March 15, *ante*, p. 329; to it
they made a reply. For the correspondence, see Moore's Rebellion Records, vol. i., Docs., p. 42; Rise and Fall of the Confederate Government,
vol. i. p. 675.   [1] Nicolay and Hay, vol. iv. p. 43.
  [2] Official Records, vol. i. p. 291; Nicolay and Hay, vol. iv. p. 35.
  [3] Davis, vol. i. p. 268 *et seq.;* Stephens, vol. ii. p. 351.
  [4] Letter to Seward, April 13.   [5] Lincoln and Seward, p. 56.

Lincoln's character and manner of action, nothing but the most positive evidence should convince us that he was in any way a party to this negotiation, and of this there is none. His disturbance at the effusive and unauthorized representations of Lamon [1] goes to show that if he had become aware of the lengths to which his secretary was going, he would have called a halt and insisted that those who had been misled should be undeceived. The truth is that the assurances to Campbell were simply those of an officious Secretary of State whose vanity had grown by what it fed on, until now he deluded himself with the idea that he and not another was the executive of the nation. He had strenuously objected to the part of Lincoln's inaugural which asserted, "The power confided to me will be used to hold, occupy, and possess the property and places belonging to the government;" [2] he seemed to see so clearly the political wisdom of giving up Sumter that, when he came to have on his side General Scott and the majority of the cabinet, he did not for a moment suppose that the President would act contrary to counsel of such preponderating weight, and in his expressions to Campbell he was absolutely sincere. [3] But Jefferson Davis was not deceived. He knew Seward through and through, for when in the Senate the two had been intimate; [4] and although at this time he fell into the mistake of regarding the secretary as the power behind the throne, he was not misled in the affair of Sumter. At this time Davis worked in his office from nine to six, [5] and having been used to executive business, we may be sure that no important despatch went out from Mont-

---

[1] *Ante.*   [2] Nicolay and Hay, vol. iii. p. 319.

[3] See article of Thurlow Weed in the Albany *Evening Journal*, copied by New York *Tribune* of May 24, and cited by McPherson, p. 111 ; see, also, New York *Tribune*, May 18.

[4] See Mrs. Davis, vol. i. pp. 571, 579 ; conversation of Thomas Starr King and Davis, 1859, article of J. M. Gitchell, San Francisco *Call*, Feb. 26, 1893. For Seward's opinion of Davis at this time, see Russell's *Diary*, entry March 27, p. 40.   [5] Mrs. Davis, vol. ii. p. 40.

gomery the substance of which he did not know. "The government," wrote Walker, Secretary of War, to Beauregard, April 2, "has at no time placed any reliance on assurances by the government at Washington in respect to the evacuation of Fort Sumter, or entertained any confidence in the disposition of the latter to make any concession or yield any point to which it is not driven by absolute necessity."[1] The secret instructions from Montgomery to the commissioners were "to play with Seward, to delay and gain time until the South was ready."[2] The commissioners were little if at all deceived. They, like every one who had facilities for getting correct information, were aware that there was a decided difference of opinion in the cabinet, and that if the peace party prevailed, the Confederacy would obtain Fort Sumter without firing a shot;[3] they thought, as did Stanton and many others, that the Seward faction would carry the day,[4] but regarding the Secretary of State as unscrupulous,[5] they did not place absolute reliance on his assurances. Justice Campbell, believing that Seward was the President in fact, and trusting him implicitly, was the only sufferer on the part of the South.[6]

Whether in private conversation with Lincoln Seward received any intimation which with rash assumption he construed into an adoption of his own views, neither the biographies of Lincoln nor of Seward disclose. Douglas said that the President had assured him that Sumter would be evacuated as soon as possible;[7] but as he was eager for

---

[1] Official Records, vol. i. p. 285 ; see also Toombs to commissioners, March 28, cited by Crawford, p. 333.

[2] Statement of Forsyth to Crawford, 1870, p. 333.

[3] Forsyth to Walker, March 14, Nicolay and Hay, vol. iii. p. 404.

[4] Stanton to Buchanan, March 16, Curtis, vol. ii. p. 534.

[5] "We rely for his [Seward's] sincerity upon his wisdom, and not upon his integrity."—Forsyth and Crawford to Toombs, March 26.   March 22 the commissioners had referred to the possible "treachery of Secretary Seward," MSS. Treasury Department; see their conversation with Russell, entries April 3, 5, Diary, pp. 59, 63.   [6] Crawford, pp. 333, 345.

[7] Diary of a Public Man, entry March 11.   Douglas at this time stood on

such action,[1] we may readily believe that he gave to some indirect or qualified statement of Lincoln a positive interpretation. I feel quite sure that the President gave to no one a more certain expression of his thoughts than he did to Francis P. Blair, to whom, after the cabinet meeting of March 15, he said that it had not been fully determined to withdraw Anderson, but he thought such would be the result.[2] Between March 5 and March 29 the President hesitated; he looked on both sides of the question, heard all arguments, and weighed every consideration. The difficulties of the situation were great, and they were made greater because the three men, General Scott, Seward, and Chase, in whose experience or ability he had great confidence, and on whom he was disposed to lean, proved, so far as concerned the important question in March, broken reeds. General Scott again tried his hand at state-craft, and proposed to Seward four alternative policies. The two which he thought the most desirable were to offer the Crittenden compromise to the South, or to say, "Wayward sisters, depart in peace."[3]

Of the impracticable and optimistic notions of the Secretary of State we have seen much. "Seward is infatuated," wrote Sumner; "he says in sixty days all will be well."[4] But all that I have related is as nothing in folly compared to the "Thoughts for the President's consideration," submitted April 1. "We are at the end of a month's administration," Seward wrote, "and yet without a policy, either domestic or foreign." For the home policy he proposed: "Change the question before the public from one upon slavery or about slavery for a question upon union or dis-

---

a friendly footing with the President. "Lincoln and the family at the White House are represented to be greatly elated at Douglas joining in defence of the new administration."—Stanton to Buchanan, March 12, Curtis, vol. ii. p. 531.   [1] See his Senate speech of March 15.

[2] Statement of Blair to Crawford, p. 364.

[3] Letter to Seward, March 3, 1861, *National Intelligencer*, Oct. 21, 1862.

[4] To John Jay, March 27, Memoir of Sumner, Pierce, vol. iv. p. 17.

union;" evacuate Fort Sumter; "defend and reinforce all
the forts in the Gulf."

For the foreign policy: "I would demand explanations
from Spain and France categorically at once. I would seek
explanations from Great Britain and Russia. . . . And if
satisfactory explanations are not received from Spain and
France, would convene Congress and declare war against
them. But whatever policy we adopt, there must be an energetic prosecution of it. . . . Either the President must do
it himself . . . or devolve it on some member of his cabinet.
. . . It is not in my especial province. But I neither seek
to evade nor assume responsibility." [1] Egregious folly this
seems to us to-day. Wild, erratic, and indefensible would
such a policy have been in 1861. Yet it is true that a popular
notion then prevailed to some extent—though it was not, so
far as I know, held by any able public man except Seward
—that if a foreign war were brought about, the alienated sections would unite in amity, and like brothers fight the common foe under the old flag.[2] The President's reply showed
Seward that Lincoln was determined to be the master; yet
he argued kindly the question of domestic affairs, ignored
with rare consideration the wild foreign policy suggested,
and with magnanimity kept secret this correspondence.[3]

[1] Nicolay and Hay, vol. iii. p. 445.

[2] Russell got some conception of this feeling. After a long interview
with Seward at the State Department, April 4, he wrote: " It was matter
for wonderment that the foreign minister of a nation which was in such
imminent danger in its very capital, and which, with its chief and his cabinet, was almost at the mercy of the enemy, should hold the language I
was aware he had transmitted to the most powerful nations of Europe.
Was it consciousness of the strength of a great people, who would be
united by the first apprehension of foreign interference, or was it the peculiar emptiness of a bombast which is called buncombe ? In all sincerity
I think Mr. Seward meant it as it was written."—Diary, p. 61. In England there existed "an apprehension that the reunion may be cemented
upon the basis of hostile measures against Great Britain."—Charles Francis
Adams to Seward, June 21, Message and Docs., p. 109.

[3] Nicolay and Hay, vol. iii. p. 448 ; on this subject see remarks of Morse,
Life of Lincoln, vol. i. p. 275 et seq.

Chase clearly comprehended the situation. He saw there were but two alternatives, war or peaceable separation. But while he estimated aright the horrors of civil war, he did not perceive that it was practically impossible for the two governments to remain long at peace even if disunion were now agreed to. When, therefore, of the two evils he preferred to recognize "the organization of actual government by the seven seceded States as *an accomplished revolution*," [1] he put himself out of sympathy with the policy the President had set forth in the inaugural address. It is not probable that Lincoln thought out the only two alternatives as logically as did Chase.[2] With true greatness he did not shake his own judgment by peering into a future full of trouble.[3] As a result of mature reflection he had declared, "Physically speaking we cannot separate." To this truth

---

[1] Letter of Chase to Taft, April 28, Life of Chase, Warden ; see, also, McClure's Lincoln, p. 52 ; Russell's Diary, p. 55 ; Cox's Three Decades, p. 63 ; Diary of a Public Man, entry March 3. It is worthy of note that one of England's leading statesmen, and a friend of the North, thought the problem could be best solved by peaceful separation. Cobden wrote Sumner, Feb. 23 : " I am watching with intense interest the conflict which is raging on your continent. Were I a citizen of a free State in your Union, I should hold up both hands for peaceful and prompt separation. My earnest prayer is that you may avoid civil war, from which no advantage to any party can accrue. Let your voice be raised for peaceful separation."—Pierce-Sumner papers, MS.

[2] " The writer revisited Washington for a day or two, some two weeks or more after Mr. Lincoln's inauguration, and was surprised to hear and see on every hand what were to him convincing proofs that an early collision with the Confederates was not seriously apprehended in the highest quarters."—Greeley's American Conflict, vol. i. p. 429, note.

[3] " Men of genius who accomplish great things in this world do not trouble themselves with remote and visionary aims. They encounter emergencies as they rise, and leave the future to shape itself as it may."—Froude's Cæsar, chap. xiii. " It was not in Cromwell's nature to look far into the future. . . . 'No one rises so high as he who knows not whither he is going.' In these words Cromwell revealed the secret of his life—the refusal to adopt any definitely premeditated plan of action, and the resolution to treat each occurrence as it arose in the light vouchsafed to him when the need of action was felt."—Gardiner's History of the Great Civil War, vol. iii. pp. 290, 316.

he was determined to hold, and in conformity with it he proposed to conduct the affairs of the nation. Yet, for the very reason that in his dealings with the seceded States he was inflexible in his purpose to preserve the Union, so, with the aim of retaining Virginia, he was willing to go to the utmost verge of conciliation. He fully appreciated that to save her from secession would insure Maryland and Kentucky, and bring a lever to bear upon North Carolina and Tennessee. Virginia's convention had met February 13.[1] It was plainly apparent that while a majority of the delegates were opposed to the secession of their State, they were equally strong in their resistance to a policy of coercion on the part of the federal government towards the Confederate States. After the declaration of policy in the President's inaugural address, the sentiment favorable to secession increased in Virginia.[2] What Lincoln called the execution of the laws, the Virginians denominated coercion. Seward, however, thought much good could be accomplished by working on the Union men of the convention. In this he had the approval of the President, who, knowing that the Unionists were anxious for the withdrawal of Anderson, probably intended to use the evacuation of Sumter, if he should be forced to it by military necessity, as an inducement for them to adjourn the convention *sine die*, which would retard for a while the secession movement.[3] The report that the troops were to be withdrawn from Charleston harbor was good news to the Union men of Virginia, though unwelcome to the precipitators, and caused a reaction of

---

[1] *Ante*, pp. 301, 309.

[2] On the reception of the inaugural, *ante*, p. 318; see proceedings of the convention, Appleton, p. 731 : "All accounts here represent the secession feeling in Virginia to be rapidly strengthening and extending. It would not surprise me to see Virginia out in less than ninety days, and Maryland will be close at her heels."—Stanton to Buchanan from Washington, March 12, Curtis, vol. ii. p. 531 ; see, also, Richmond *Whig*, March 26.

[3] See the testimony of J. B. Baldwin, J. M. Botts, and J. F. Lewis, before the Joint Committee on Reconstruction, 1st Sess. 39th Cong.; The Great Rebellion, J. M. Botts, p. 194 *et seq.;* Dabney's Narrative, Southern Hist. Soc. papers, vol. i. p. 445 *et seq.;* Nicolay and Hay, vol. iii. chap. xxv.

sentiment friendly to the North.[1] But when it became apparent that Sumter would not be evacuated the secession wave rose again.[2] Nevertheless, as late as April 4 the convention voted down by 89 to 45 a resolution to submit an ordinance of secession to the popular vote.[3]

March 31 the President determined to send an expedition from New York to reinforce Fort Pickens, in conformity with a plan submitted to him by Captain Meigs.[4] Captain Fox was busy preparing the Sumter expedition, and while Lincoln had virtually decided, April 4, to send it, yet, as the earliest moment that it could be ready was the 6th, he reserved in his mind the privilege of countermanding it or changing its destination, should he hear that his former order touching Fort Pickens had been executed.[5] For what was needed for the effect it would have on the North and on Europe was a vigorous assertion at some point of the national authority. The question naturally arose, Could not this be done at Pickens, and the tender susceptibilities of the Virginia Unionists nursed by the withdrawal of the troops

---

[1] " The removal from Sumter [*i.e.*, the intention to evacuate it stated in a letter from Welling, on the authority of Seward, *ante*, p. 332] acted like a charm—it gave us [*i.e.*, the Union men] great strength. A reaction is now going on in the State. The outside pressure here has greatly subsided. We are masters of our position here, and can maintain it if left alone."—Geo. W. Summers to J. C. Welling, Richmond, March 19, 1861, the *Nation*, Dec. 4, 1879 ; Richmond *Whig*, March 14, 26 ; Holt to Buchanan, March 14, Curtis, vol. ii. p. 532.

[2] P. S. to letter cited in preceding note: " What delays the removal of Major Anderson ? Is there any truth in the suggestion that the thing is not to be done after all ? This would ruin us." See, also, Richmond *Whig*, April 8 and 9. April 3 Russell wrote in his Diary : " It is stated, nevertheless, that Virginia is on the eve of secession, and will certainly go if the President attempts to use force in relieving and strengthening the federal forts."—p. 60. " The rumors from Richmond are very threatening ; secession is rapidly gaining strength there."—Stanton to Buchanan, April 3, Curtis, vol. ii. p. 538 ; also Baldwin's account of his interview with the President, April 4, in his testimony.

[3] Appleton, p. 733 ; New York *Tribune*, April 5.

[4] Nicolay and Hay, vol. iii. p. 436.

[5] *Ante*, p. 328; Lincoln's message of July 4.

from Sumter ? April 6 the President heard that the order of
March 11 for the reinforcement of Fort Pickens had not been
carried out.[1] He no longer hesitated. As he said later, when
he took the people of the North into his confidence, " The
strongest anticipated case for using it (the expedition to supply Fort Sumter) was now presented, and it was resolved to
send it forward." [2] The President's decision was right. It
would have been also right had Vogdes landed his company
at Pickens ; and while, all the circumstances considered, no
blame can attach to him for being tardy, it would have been
better if he had come sooner to this determination. It was
apparent that public opinion at the North would sustain the
administration in any measure for the relief of Major Anderson.[3] Since the night when he transferred his force from
Moultrie to Sumter he had been her hero. That movement
represented the time when the government had ceased to be
swayed by Southern ideas and influences, and had come under the direction of men of national opinions. Moreover,
South Carolina had begun the revolution ; Charleston was
its centre. For its influence on the North and on Europe
one expedition to Sumter were worth a dozen to Pickens.
Lincoln had to contend with a united people in dealing with
the Southern Confederacy ; but he had not a united North
at his back. Clearly the best chance of uniting the North
lay in some just assertion of national authority in the harbor
of Charleston. He had been elected President of the United
States, and with his view of the indissolubility of the Union,
he owed it to his country to make the attempt to keep its flag
waving where the revolution had commenced. He owed it to
himself as well, for the world does not forgive the man who,
when the extremity comes, will not fight for the throne or
the chief power of the State to which his title is clear.

---

[1] The reason of this is clearly related by Nicolay and Hay, vol. iv. p. 7.

[2] Lincoln's message of July 4.

[3] The President's interview with Governors Curtin of Pennsylvania,
Morton of Indiana, and Washburn of Maine, must have confirmed him in
his decision, New York *Herald*, New York *World*, April 5.

To a hard-headed thinker like Lincoln it must have been patent that the surrender of Sumter would only adjourn the difficulty. Sumter obtained, the Confederate States would demand Pickens; Pickens in their possession, they would ask for the recognition of their government. The Virginia, North Carolina, and Tennessee Unionists would urge the giving up of Pickens, and in case the North did not make concessions which she had already repeatedly refused, they would press the policy of peaceful separation, and thus shaking a rod over Lincoln's head,[1] make his position intolerable, and lose him the respect of the North and of Europe.[2]

April 6, Judge Magrath, of Charleston, was advised by a friend in Washington that an attempt would be made to supply Fort Sumter. On the next day Anderson's purchases of fresh provisions were stopped by General Beauregard, who at the same time called out the rest of the contingent troops. April 9 the Sumter mails were taken possession of, and the official letters sent to Montgomery.[3] The President's formal notification of his design to send provisions to Anderson was immediately telegraphed by Beauregard to the Confederate Secretary of War. Jefferson Davis and his cabinet now had a momentous question to decide, and they gave it a long and profound consideration. Toombs at first said, "The firing upon that fort will inaugurate a civil war greater than any the world has yet seen; and I do not feel competent to advise you."[4] Later during the council he opposed the attack. "Mr. President," he declared, "at this time it is suicide, murder, and will lose us every friend at the North. You will wantonly strike a hornet's nest which extends from mountain to ocean, and legions now quiet will swarm out and sting us to death.

[1] Lincoln's own expression according to the testimony of Botts.

[2] How it appeared to the average Englishman is well illustrated by Russell's notes of April 8, Diary, p. 69.

[3] Official Records, vol. i. pp. 287, 289, 292.

[4] Walker's statement to Crawford, p. 421.

It is unnecessary; it puts us in the wrong; it is fatal."[1]
Yet the Confederate States, as they had assumed the position of an independent nation, could not brook it that a
foreign power should retain a strong fortress commanding
one of their important harbors.   To South Carolina this occupation of territory over which she held sovereignty was
intolerable, and to the people of Charleston the flaunting of
the Stars and Stripes before their eyes was a daily insult.
The pressure of the State and the city on the Confederate
government for the possession of Fort Sumter had already
been importunate, and now that the hope of obtaining it by
negotiation was gone, Davis could no longer resist the current; but in allowing himself to be carried along with it,
he committed a stupendous blunder.

Two days after Governor Pickens had received notice of
the intention to send supplies to Anderson, Davis ordered
Beauregard to demand the evacuation of Fort Sumter, and,
if it was refused, to proceed "to reduce it."[2]   In accordance
with this order Beauregard sent, on the afternoon of April
11, three aides to make the demand of Anderson, who, after
consultation with his officers, refused compliance; but when
he handed the aides his written reply he said, "Gentlemen,
if you do not batter the fort to pieces about us, we shall be
starved out in a few days."[3]   This remark was deemed by
Beauregard so important that he telegraphed it to Montgomery in connection with Anderson's formal refusal to
evacuate Sumter.   Walker, the Secretary of War, by direction of Davis, immediately replied: "Do not desire needlessly to bombard Fort Sumter.   If Major Anderson will
state the time at which, as indicated by him, he will evacuate, and agree that in the meantime he will not use his
guns against us unless ours should be employed against
Sumter, you are authorized thus to avoid the effusion of
blood.   If this or its equivalent be refused, reduce the fort

---

[1] Life of Toombs, Stovall, p. 226.
[2] Official Records, vol. i. p. 297.   [3] Ibid., pp. 13, 59.

as your judgment decides to be most practicable."[1] Four
aides at once took this proposition to Anderson, handing
it to him three-quarters of an hour after midnight of April
11. He had a long conference with his officers, and gave
his answer at 3.15 on the morning of the 12th. "I will,"
he wrote, . . . "evacuate Fort Sumter by noon on the
15th instant, and I will not in the meantime open my fires
upon your forces unless compelled to do so by some hostile
act against this fort or the flag of my government, . . .
should I not receive prior to that time controlling instructions from my government or additional supplies."[2] The
aides, in accordance with their instructions from Beauregard, read the letter, promptly refused Anderson's terms,
and notified him that in an hour their batteries would open
fire on the fort. The four men who in the last resort made
the decision that began the war were ex-Senator Chesnut,
Lieutenant-Colonel Chisolm, Captain Lee, all three South
Carolinians, and Roger A. Pryor, a Virginia secessionist,
who two days before in a speech at the Charleston Hotel
had said, "I will tell you, gentlemen, what will put Virginia
in the Southern Confederacy in less than an hour by
Shrewsbury clock. Strike a blow!"[3] The aides went immediately to Fort Johnson and gave the order to fire. At
4.30 A.M. a shell fired from a mortar of that battery "rose
high in air," writes Crawford, who was standing on the
parapet of Sumter, "and, curving in its course, burst almost
directly over the fort."[4] This was the signal for the bombardment to begin.

With Anderson's last response before them, would General Beauregard or Jefferson Davis have given the word to

---

[1] Official Records, vol. i. p. 301 ; Davis's message to the Confederate
Congress, April 29, Moore's Rebellion Record, vol. i., Docs., p. 171.

[2] Ibid., pp. 14, 60.

[3] Foster's Diary, Official Records, vol. i. p. 18, also ibid., pp. 31, 60 ;
Crawford, p. 424 ; Doubleday's Sumter and Moultrie, p. 141 ; Charleston
Mercury, cited by McPherson, p. 112 ; Pollard's Davis, p. 109.

[4] Crawford, p. 427; see Official Records, vol. i. p. 60.

commence the attack? As affairs turned out it was an
equivalent of Davis's conditions. As things were, it was
an endeavor of Anderson to meet Beauregard half way, for
he disapproved of the Fox expedition, and on both military
and political grounds believed that his government ought to
give him the order to evacuate the fort.[1] It was impetuosity, not sound judgment, which impelled Chesnut and
his companions to make a peremptory decision instead of
consulting their chief, which would have involved only an
hour's delay.

Beauregard, his officers, and Governor Pickens were
needlessly alarmed about the relief expedition.[2] It was
three days late in getting off from New York. Fox had
arranged that it should consist of the war-ships *Powhatan*,
Pawnee, *Pocahontas*, and *Harriet Lane;* the steam-tugs
Uncle Ben, *Yankee*, and *Freeborn ;* and the merchant steamer *Baltic*, with two hundred men and the necessary supplies on board. The *Powhatan* carried the armed launches
and the sailors to man them ; the tugs were intended to
convey the provisions to the fort and tow the launches.
The *Baltic*, on board of which was Fox, arrived off Charleston at three o'clock on the morning of April 12, and found
there only the *Harriet Lane*. The two stood in towards
the bar to make, under a flag of truce, an offer of provisions to the fort, but as they drew near they observed
that the bombardment of Sumter had commenced. Though
the *Pawnee* arrived at seven, war having actually begun,
nothing could be accomplished without the tugs and the
Powhatan. One tug had been detained in New York by
her owner. By a heavy northeast gale the *Uncle Ben* had
been driven into Wilmington, and the *Yankee* as far south
as the entrance to Savannah. Owing to a confused and un-

---

[1] See his letter to Thomas, April 8, Official Records, vol. i. p. 294.
[2] Beauregard to Cooper, Adjutant-General C. S. A., April 27, Official
Records, vol. i. p. 30 ; Pickens to Walker, April 9, ibid., p. 292 ; Reports to
and Orders of Beauregard, ibid., p. 299 *et seq.*

systematic administration of affairs at Washington and to the meddling of Seward the *Powhatan* had been detached from the Sumter expedition and had joined that destined for the reinforcement of Pickens. It was impossible even to attempt the execution of Fox's plan. The expedition was a failure. Fox and his companions watched the bombardment, chafing at their powerlessness to render their brothers-in-arms any assistance.[1]

Had Chesnut brought Anderson's last communication to Beauregard, he, being a careful man, might have submitted it to Davis, and it is more than probable that the Confederate President would have said, Wait. That the Montgomery government was solicitous to avoid the attack is evident from the anxious inquiry of Walker the morning of April 12, "What was Major Anderson's reply to the proposition contained in my despatch of last night?"[2] For it must not be forgotten that the primary object of the Sumter expedition was not to bring troops and munitions of war, but merely to furnish the garrison with a necessary supply of food. By this time both Lincoln and Davis undoubtedly felt that war was inevitable, and on account of the influence on public sentiment at the North both were anxious to avoid striking the first blow, and disposed to proceed with the utmost caution. Davis had good reason to regret that matters so fell out that the South became the aggressor; while Lincoln might well thank his stars for that blunder, since it gave him in his time of trouble a united North.[3]

---

[1] Fox to Cameron, April 19, Official Records, vol. i. p. 11 ; Crawford, p. 416 *et seq.;* Nicolay and Hay, vol. iii. p. 383, vol. iv. chaps. ii. and iii.

[2] Official Records, vol. i. p. 305.

[3] Beauregard, of course, in his report assumes the action of his aides as his own, Official Records, vol. i. p. 31, and Davis defends the attack on Sumter, message of April 29. In his book he argues that the South was not the aggressor, vol. i. p. 292. Stephens maintains that the attack on Sumter was rendered necessary in self-defence, vol. ii. p. 39. "I heard many discussions during the war between parties of Northern and Southern soldiers, when opportunities offered, such as at truce meetings

Half an hour after Fort Johnson gave the signal the fire from the Confederate batteries became general. Sumter remained silent for two hours. The garrison were on half-rations; their bread exhausted, they breakfasted on pork and damaged rice. At seven o'clock they began returning the fire of the Confederates. An artillery duel followed. There being no great disparity in the armament of the two forces, the contest would not have been unequal had Anderson possessed a full garrison. His force of officers, privates, musicians, and non-combatant laborers was a total of 128. Opposed to him was the South Carolina army of from 5000 to 6000 men. It was made up largely of the best blood of the State. Planters and their sons, men of wealth and family of Charleston, did not scruple to serve in the ranks.[1] In the gray of the morning, when the roar of the cannon was heard, the city poured out its people. They thronged to the wharves and the Battery. On no gala occasion had the reporter seen so many ladies on this favorite promenade as now turned out to witness the opening scene of the great tragedy of the Civil War.[2] As they gazed upon their beautiful bay what a spectacle they beheld! Fort Johnson, Fort Moultrie, the Cumming's Point, and the other batteries were firing continuously at Sumter. When

or with prisoners of war. When the Southerners asserted that all they wanted was to be let alone, the invariable reply was, Who began the war? Who struck the first blow? Who battered the walls of Fort Sumter?"—Life in the Confederate Army, Watson, p. 98; see, also, conversation reported by W. H. Russell, Diary, p. 204.

[1] Roman's Beauregard, vol. i. p. 29; Charleston correspondence New York *Tribune*, Jan. 11, 12, 16; Charleston Under Arms, by J. W. De Forest, *Atlantic Monthly*, April, 1861; Russell's Diary, pp. 100, 105. "Many of those who serve in the ranks are worth from £5000 to £10,000 a year —at least, so I was told; and men were pointed out to me who were said to be worth far more. One private feeds his company on French pâtés and Madeira, another provides his comrades with unlimited champagne . . . ; a third . . . purchases for the men of his 'guard' a complete equipment of Enfield rifles."—Russell to the London *Times*, from Charleston, April 21.

[2] Charleston *Courier*, April 13; Roman's Beauregard, vol. i. p. 43.

Anderson began, he replied first to Cumming's Point, then to the enfilade battery on Sullivan's Island, and "next opened on Fort Moultrie, between which and Fort Sumter a steady and almost constant fire was kept up throughout the day." [1] What war ever had a more dramatic beginning! Charleston, reflecting on the history of South Carolina in union with the other states since 1776, and on the crowded hours of stirring events from the November election of 1860 to this 12th day of April, now saw the "circumstance of glorious war," and heard in hostile array

> "the mortal engines whose rude throats
> The immortal Jove's dread clamors counterfeit."

The duel continued all day. In the afternoon, owing to an insufficient supply of cartridges, the fire of Sumter slackened; after dark it entirely ceased. The Confederate mortars threw shells at intervals of a quarter of an hour during the whole of the night. The night was dark and rainy, the wind and tide were high. Beauregard, afraid that troops and supplies might be thrown into Sumter from the fleet, commanded the utmost vigilance at the channel batteries and on Morris and Sullivan's islands. Early on the morning of the 13th the bombardment was renewed. "Fort Sumter," wrote Moultrie's commandant, "opened early and spitefully, and paid especial attention to Fort Moultrie." [2] At about nine o'clock the officers' quarters in Sumter took fire from the shells or hot shot of the Confederates, who thereupon redoubled the rapidity of their fire. The flames spread to the barracks; by noon they had enveloped all of the wood-work, and made it evident that the powder-magazine would have to be closed. Anderson gave the order to remove as much powder as possible, and by great exertion fifty barrels were taken out and distributed around in the casemates. The doors of the magazine were shut

---

[1] Beauregard's report, Official Records, vol. i. p. 31.
[2] Official Records, vol. i. p. 41.

and earth was packed against them. But now the fire
spread with such swiftness that the powder in the casemates was in danger, and all but five barrels were thrown
into the sea. The cloud of smoke and cinders almost suffo-
cated the men; they threw themselves upon the ground
and covered their faces with wet cloths, or crept to the
embrasures for a breath of fresh air. The flames reached
the magazine of grenades, and explosion after explosion
followed. The fire of Sumter ceased; that of the Confederates came thick and fast. To show that the Union soldiers were undaunted, Captain Doubleday ordered that a
few rounds be fired. At each discharge the Confederates
"cheered the garrison for its pluck and gallantry, and
hooted the fleet lying inactive just outside the bar." [1] At
1.30 in the afternoon the flag-staff was shot away and fell
to the ground; with all possible promptness the flag was
raised again. In the interval the fire of the Confederates
slackened. The disappearance of the flag prompted ex-Senator Wigfall to go from Cumming's Point to Sumter in a
small boat, under a flag of truce, with a request for the suspension of hostilities, and, leading Beauregard to think that
Anderson was in distress, caused him to send three other
aides with an offer of assistance. These visits resulted in
terms of evacuation being offered by Beauregard and accepted by Anderson. The story is told in the report of
Anderson, written on board the steamship *Baltic*, off Sandy
Hook: "Having defended Fort Sumter for thirty-four
hours, until the quarters were entirely burned, the main
gates destroyed by fire, the gorge walls seriously injured,
the magazine surrounded by flames, and its door closed
from the effects of heat, four barrels and three cartridges
of powder only being available, and no provisions remaining but pork, I accepted terms of evacuation offered by
General Beauregard, being the same offered by him . . .
prior to the commencement of hostilities, and marched out

---

[1] Beauregard's report, Official Records, vol. i. p. 32.

of the fort Sunday afternoon, the 14th instant, with colors flying and drums beating, bringing away company and private property, and saluting my flag with fifty guns."[1]

Judged by loss of life, no battle could be more insignificant; not a man on either side was killed. Judged by the train of events which ensued, few contests in our history have been more momentous.

Charleston gave itself up to joy. The Confederate flag waving over Sumter seemed to its people a glorious sight. The churches were crowded. At the Catholic cathedral a *Te Deum* was celebrated with great pomp. The venerable Episcopal bishop at St. Philip's and the rector at St. Michael's attributed "this signal and bloodless victory to the infinite mercy of God, who specially interposed his hand in behalf of their righteous cause."[2] During the week rejoicing of a more profane character was prolonged.[3] Montgomery cele-

---

[1] Anderson to Cameron, April 18, Official Records, vol. i. p. 12. For accounts of the bombardment of Sumter see especially Foster's Journal and Beauregard's reports, Official Records, vol. i. pp. 16, 28 *et seq.*; Crawford, chap. xxxii. The reports of the subordinate Confederate officers are of interest, Official Records, vol. i. p. 35 *et seq.* Also see Nicolay and Hay, vol. iv. chap. iii.; Doubleday's Sumter and Moultrie, chaps. x. and xi. On the number of South Carolina troops see Pickens's despatches, Official Records, vol. i. p. 292. "We had 7000 men along the shores of our two sea islands. Of these 6000 men never lifted weapon at Fort Sumter."—Charleston *Mercury*, May 14. The official return furnished Russell, April 21, was as follows:

Morris Island	2625
Sullivan's Island	1750
Stone and other points	750
Charleston	1900
	7025

—Letter to London *Times*.

[2] Roman's Beauregard, vol. i. p. 49; Charleston despatches to New York *Tribune*, April 15; letter of April 14: Charleston *Mercury*, April 15.

[3] Russell writes under date of April 18: "The streets of Charleston present some such aspect as those of Paris in the last revolution. Crowds of armed men singing and promenading the streets, the battle-blood running through their veins — that hot oxygen which is called 'the flush of victory' on the cheek; restaurants full, revelling in bar-rooms, club-rooms crowded, orgies and carousings in tavern or private house, in tap-room,

brated with enthusiasm the first triumph of the Confederate arms.[1]

The expedition to Fort Pickens was successful. After the reinforcement it had a garrison of eleven hundred soldiers and laborers and six months' supplies, and it remained in the possession of the Union forces during the entire Civil War.[2]

---

from cabaret—down narrow alleys, in the broad highway. Sumter has set them distraught; never was such a victory; never such brave lads; never such a fight. . . . It is a bloodless Waterloo or Solferino."—Diary, p. 98.

[1] Montgomery despatch to Richmond *Examiner*, April 13; New York *Tribune*, April 15; Pollard's Davis, p. 112.

[2] For an account of this expedition see Nicolay and Hay, vol. iv. chap. i.

CHAPTER XV

THE people of the North, to the last praying and hoping that actual hostilities might be averted, were profoundly moved by the news that civil war had begun. The shot at Sumter convinced nearly every one that the time of argument and compromise, of speech and entreaty, had given way to rude action; that the difficulty could not be composed by Congress, by conventions, or solved at the ballot-box, and that this peace-loving people must interrupt their industrial civilization and gird on the activity of war.[1] With excitement and with sorrow they followed the course of the bombardment; with stern determination their minds accepted the policy which this grave event portended; and when on Monday, April 15, they read of the President's call for 75,000 militia to suppress combinations obstructing the execution of the laws in seven of the Southern States, they gave with one voice their approval of the policy foreshadowed, and rose almost as one man to the support of their chief magistrate.[2] The blood of this people was stirred

---

[1] The most interesting and instructive parallel to this period of our history is the great Civil War in England. The history of this, by Gardiner, furnishes many suggestions of value to the student in the way of illustration and guidance. Of the opening he writes : "The Civil War, the outbreak of which was announced by the floating of Charles's standard on the hill at Nottingham, was rendered inevitable by the inadequacy of the intellectual methods of the day to effect a reconciliation between opposing mor il and social forces which derived their strength from the past development of the nation."—Vol. i. p. 1.

[2] "That first gun at Fort Sumter which brought all the free States to their feet as one man. That shot is destined to be the most memorable

as it had not been stirred since the days of the Revolution.[1] The sentiment of patriotism rose supreme in all hearts. The service of the country superseded bread-winning labor and business, and called for the sacrifice on its altar of parental feeling and wifely tenderness. It was the uprising of a great people. Militia regiments and military companies, formed merely for the exercise of the drill, for social intercourse, and for Fourth-of-July parades, made haste to get ready for the conflict. Men who had never dreamed of a soldier's life hurried to enlist. Laborers, mechanics, clerks, students and professors of the colleges, many sons of wealthy and influential families, enrolled themselves for the common cause. Men of position in civil life went out as officers of companies and regiments, but when such places were lacking, they shouldered muskets and served in the ranks. Individuals, towns, cities, and States offered money freely. Patriotism spake from the pulpit, the platform, the stump, and with the mighty voice of the press, urging able-bodied men to devote their lives, and wealthy citizens to give of their abundance to their country in its time of need. The passions then kindled at the North inspired with a magnificent energy a people who, it was thought, were given over to money-getting and sordid calculation. "At the darkest moment in the history of the republic," Emerson wrote, "when it looked as if the nation would be dismembered, pulverized into its original elements, the attack on Fort Sumter crystallized the North into a unit, and the hope of mankind was saved."[2] The feeling that

---

one ever fired on this continent, since the Concord fowling-pieces said, 'That bridge is ours, and we mean to go across it.'"—J. R. Lowell, article The Pickens-and-Stealin's Rebellion, *Atlantic Monthly*, June, 1861, p. 762.

[1] "The heather is on fire. I never before knew what a popular excitement can be. . . . Indeed, here at the North there never was anything like it ; for if the feeling were as deep and as stern in 1775, it was by no means so intelligent or unanimous ; and then the masses to be moved were as a handful compared to our dense population now."—George Ticknor to Sir Edmund Head, April 21, Life of George Ticknor, vol. ii. p. 433.

[2] Cabot, p. 605.

the South had been precipitate and unreasonable, and that she was clearly in the wrong, was almost universal. That she had wickedly rebelled, and without just and sufficient cause had begun a civil war, well expressed the sentiment of those who, stirred by passionate speech at the public meetings, went thence and enrolled themselves as volunteers. The speakers asserted that the people must preserve the Union and maintain the government; and this was clearly the purpose in the minds of the men who enlisted during the first months of the war. With all this enthusiasm and excitement in unison with a plain perception of duty, grave care sat on the brows of serious men, and their days of concern were followed by nights of unrest,[1] for they saw that American nationality was at stake, and that the struggle for the right might be severe and prolonged.

The President in his proclamation called for 75,000 State militia. The War Department, in communicating the particulars to the governors, requested that they detail from their militia their respective quotas to serve as infantry or riflemen for three months, and stated that as soon as practicable after assembling at each appointed rendezvous they would be mustered into the service of the United States. The designation of this short period was not in any way an expression of a belief by the President or his cabinet that the war would last only ninety days; the authority

---

[1] General J. D. Cox writes : "The situation hung upon us like a nightmare. Garfield and I were lodging together at the time (in Columbus) . . . and when we reached our sitting-room after an evening session of the Senate [of the Ohio legislature], we often found ourselves involuntarily groaning, 'Civil war in our land!' The shame, the folly, the outrage seemed too great to believe, and we half hoped to wake from it as from a dream. Among the painful remembrances of those days is the ever-present weight at the heart, which never left me till I found relief in the active duties of camp-life at the close of the month. I went about my duties (and I am sure most of those with whom I associated did the same) with the half-choking sense of a grief I dared not think of ; like one who is dragging himself to the ordinary labors of life from some terrible and recent bereavement."—Century War Book, vol. i. p. 87.

for the call was the Act of 1795, which permitted "the use of the militia so to be called forth" only for "thirty days after the commencement of the then next session of Congress."[1] "Deeming that the present condition of public affairs presents an extraordinary occasion," the President had summoned Congress to meet on the 4th of July, and, in accordance with the act, he commanded the combinations opposing the execution of the laws "to disperse and retire peaceably to their respective abodes within twenty days." The governors of the free states and the legislatures which were in session went to work with energy and zeal. "The response of the country," said the President in his Fourth-of-July message, "was most gratifying, surpassing in unanimity and spirit the most sanguine expectation." In answer to the call of April 15, and a subsequent one for three-years troops, there were in the field on the 1st of July, at the command of the government, 310,000 men.[2]

The response of the Republicans was most natural. Seward and Chase, conservatives and radicals, were at one. Party fealty combined with love of country to influence their action. The organization and the drill of the Wide-awakes in the presidential campaign may have contributed to the result. Yet in fact party lines seemed to be obliterated. No party cry was heard. Men apparently forgot that they had been Republicans or Democrats. The partisan was lost in the patriot. On the evening of the Sunday on which Fort Sumter was evacuated, Douglas, at his own request, had a long confidential interview with Lincoln.[3]

---

[1] For the legal question involved in this call see *National Intelligencer*, April 16. One section of the Act of 1795 expressly provided that the militia should not be compelled to serve more than three months in any one year.

[2] Report of Secretary of War, July 1. But according to the report of the Provost-Marshal-General there were in the service, July 1, 1861, of both regulars and volunteers, but 186,751 men, Phisterer's Statistical Record, p. 62.

[3] Nicolay and Hay, vol. iv. p. 80.

The journals of the next morning, which published the call
for troops, informed the country that the great leader of
the Democrats had spontaneously pledged himself " to sustain the President in the exercise of all his constitutional
functions to preserve the Union, maintain the government,
and defend the federal capital." [1] He represented and led
more than a million Northern voters. It was known the
next day that Buchanan sympathized heartily with the
North.[2] Everett, who had been a friend of the South and
held by her in high esteem, charged her with " acts of treason and rebellion," described the firing on Fort Sumter as
an " unutterable outrage upon the flag of the Union," and
declared that she had inaugurated "the unprovoked and un-
righteous war." [3]

Walker, the Confederate Secretary of War, in a public
speech at Montgomery the evening after the bombardment
of Sumter had commenced, said, " The flag which now
flaunts the breeze here will float over the dome of the old
Capitol at Washington before the 1st of May." [4] Northern people read this threat in the same issue of the journal
that printed the President's call for troops, and their fears
for the safety of Washington, which were already great on
account of the probable secession of Virginia and the doubt
as to the position of Maryland, were thereby intensified.

---

[1] Associated Press despatch, April 14.

[2] New York *Tribune*, April 16. Buchanan was positive in his letter to
Dix, April 19: " The present administration had no alternative but to accept the war initiated by South Carolina or the Southern Confederacy.
The North will sustain the administration almost to a man; and it ought
to be sustained at all hazards."—Life of Curtis, vol. ii. p. 543; see, also,
p. 541.

[3] Boston *Evening Transcript*, cited in Moore's Rebellion Record, vol. i.,
Docs., p. 206; see, also, p. 161.

[4] New York *Tribune*, April 15; *National Intelligencer*, May 9. Stephens
throws some doubt as to the correctness of this report, and further argues
that if these words were really used they are susceptible of a different
construction from that commonly given, War between the States, vol. ii.
p. 421.

"The immediate apprehensions of the government are for this city," wrote Lord Lyons, the British minister.[1] The first efforts of the administration were directed towards making safe the capital, "the heart," as Everett termed it, "of the body-politic."[2] The national and State authorities combined with the people to hurry forward soldiers for the defence of Washington. But one Northern State was fully ready for the emergency, and that was Massachusetts. Her governor, John A. Andrew, immediately after his inauguration in January, had caused the militia of the State to begin drilling actively and regularly in their armories. Five thousand men, of whom three thousand were armed with Springfield rifles, were in some measure prepared for war. On Tuesday, April 16, they commenced to muster in Boston. On Wednesday the Sixth Massachusetts Regiment armed with rifles started for Washington.[3] On the 19th, in passing through Baltimore from the Philadelphia to the Washington railroad depot, they were violently attacked by a mob. The soldiers fired upon their assailants. Several companies had to fight their way through the city. Four soldiers, a number of the mob, and a prominent citizen of Baltimore, a mere looker-on, were killed, but the regiment succeeded in getting to their train on the Baltimore and Washington Railroad, and soon afterwards were in the capital city. On the same train with the Massachusetts Sixth had come one thousand Pennsylvania volunteers who had neither arms nor uniforms, but expected to get them at Washington; as it would have been madness for them to make the attempt to pass through the city, they were, by advice of the governor and the mayor and by direction of the railroad authorities, sent back as far north as the Sus-

[1] Despatch to London, cited in Life of Seward, vol. ii. p. 545. Russell wrote to the London *Times* from Montgomery, May 8, "I have no doubt in my mind that the government here intended to attack and occupy Washington."   [2] Moore's Rebellion Record, vol. i., Docs., p. 206.
[3] Schouler's Massachusetts in the Civil War, pp. 33, 51, 72; Appleton.

quehanna River. Baltimore was in a frenzy.[1] The secessionists and Southern sympathizers were rampant; stifling
the Union sentiment of the city, they carried everything
before them with a high hand and dictated the action of
the constituted authorities. " The excitement is fearful.
Send no more troops here," telegraphed Governor Hicks
and Mayor Brown to the President. So great was the
commotion that the State and city military were called out
to assist the police in preserving the peace. In Monument
Square a mass-meeting assembled whose sentiment was
decidedly opposed to any attempt at coercion of the Confederate States. More troops were on the way, and the
order from the War Department was, " Send them on prepared to fight their way through if necessary."[2] Appre-
hending "a terrible collision and bloodshed" and fearful
consequences to Baltimore if the troops were not stopped,
Mayor Brown and Marshal Kane consulted together and
came to the decision that it would be wise to burn some of
the bridges on the Philadelphia, Wilmington and Baltimore Railroad, and on the Northern Central Railroad,
which went to Harrisburg. Receiving a very reluctant assent from Governor Hicks, the order was given at midnight
of the 19th and carried out.[3] At the same time a committee of citizens was sent by special train to Washington

---

[1] The Baltimore *Daily Exchange,* in speaking of "the affair which has
plunged our city in gloom and roused our people almost to madness,"
said: "The conduct of the troops who are guilty of this massacre will be
regarded by impartial men everywhere with disgust and reprobation; for
whatever differences of opinion there may be in regard to the extent and
character of the provocations offered to the soldiers, it is an indisputable
fact that they bore themselves like cowards in wantonly firing upon citizens who were congregated at places far away from the points at which
any collision occurred."

[2] This order was telegraphed in cipher to Felton, president of the Philadelphia, Wilmington and Baltimore Railroad, and was not known to the
Baltimore authorities. It was nevertheless patent to them that no troops
would be able to get through the city without a fight.

[3] Governor Hicks denied that he gave his consent. See his letter to the
people of Maryland, Moore's Rebellion Record, vol. ii., Docs., p. 181.

with a letter from the mayor, approved by the governor, begging that the President should send no more troops through Baltimore. Early on Saturday morning, April 20, the committee had an interview with Lincoln, who, after consultation with General Scott, wrote a letter to Hicks and Brown saying that troops must be brought to Washington, but that if it were practicable and proper in the judgment of the general, they would be taken around Baltimore, and not through it. Such an arrangement was substantially agreed to the next day between Mayor Brown—who had been summoned to Washington by Lincoln—the President, the Secretary of War, and General Scott. To this Governor Hicks had given his assent.[1]

The seven days since the evacuation of Sumter had been crowded with events which gave rise to deep anxiety. April 17 the Virginia convention, in secret sitting, passed an ordinance of secession, and this was known the next day to the President.[2] As an answer to Lincoln's call for 75,000 troops, Jefferson Davis by proclamation invited applications for letters of marque and reprisal against the merchant marine of the United States.[3] As a rejoinder, the President on the 19th proclaimed a blockade of Southern ports from South Carolina to Texas inclusive, and declared that privateers acting " under the pretended authority " of the Confederate States would be treated as pirates.[4] On the 18th the commander at Harper's Ferry, deeming his position untenable, abandoned it, demolished the arsenal, and burned the armory building.[5] On the 20th the Gosport navy-yard was partially destroyed by the Union forces and left to the

---

[1] My authorities for this account are official despatches, letters, statements, and reports in Official Records, vol. ii. p. 7 et seq., p. 578 et seq.; Moore's Rebellion Record, vol. i., Docs., p. 123 ; Congressional Globe, 1st Sess. 37th Cong., p. 201; Nicolay and Hay, vol. iv. chap. vi.

[2] Moore's Rebellion Record, vol. i., Docs., p. 70; Nicolay and Hay, vol. iv. p. 104 ; Washington despatches to New York Tribune, April 17 and 18; Letters and Times of the Tylers, vol. ii. p. 641.

[3] Moore's Rebellion Record, vol. i., Docs., p. 71.   [4] Ibid., p. 78.

[5] Official Records, vol. ii. p. 3 et seq.

possession of the Virginians.[1] It seemed to Chase, as he querulously stated it to the President, "that the disunionists have anticipated us in everything, and that as yet we have accomplished nothing but the destruction of our own property." [2] April 20 Robert E. Lee, who was esteemed by Scott the ablest officer next to himself in the service, and who had been unofficially offered the active command of the Union army,[3] resigned his commission. The situation de-

---

[1] Official Records, vol. ii. p. 21.

[2] Letter of April 25, Life of Chase, Schuckers, p. 424.

[3] Francis P. Blair stated on the 14th day of April, 1871 : "In the beginning of the war Secretary Cameron asked me to sound General Robert E. Lee, to know whether his feelings would justify him in taking command of our army. His cousin, John Lee, sent him a note at my suggestion. Lee came. I told him what President Lincoln wanted him to do. He wanted him to take command of the army. Lee said that he was devoted to the Union. He said, among other things, that he would do everything in his power to save it, and that if he owned all the negroes in the South, he would be willing to give them up and make the sacrifice of the value of every one of them to save the Union. We talked several hours on the political question in that vein. Lee said he did not know how he could draw his sword upon his native State. We discussed that matter at some length, and had some hours of conversation. He said he could not decide without seeing his friend General Scott. He said he could not, under any circumstances, consent to supersede his old commander. He asked me if I supposed the President would consider that proper. I said yes. Then had a long conversation on that subject. He left the house and was soon after met by a committee from Richmond. He went with them, as I understood from some friends afterwards, to consult the Virginia convention as to some mode of settling the difficulty. I never saw him afterwards.

"The matter was talked over by President Lincoln and myself for some hours on two or three different occasions. Secretary Cameron and myself talked some hours on the same subject. The President and Secretary Cameron expressed themselves as anxious to give the command of our army to Robert E. Lee. I considered myself as authorized to inform General Lee of that fact. I do not believe that Secretary Chase was consulted on the subject or that there was any regular cabinet consultation, for the reason that Lee did not agree to take command of the army."

Statement made by Captain James May, of Rock Island, Ill., to Chief-Justice Chase, April 28, 1871, in Washington.—Chase Papers, MS. In this manner I shall refer to the private papers of Salmon P. Chase which have been kindly placed at my disposal by his daughters, Mrs. Chase and Mrs. Hoyt, through the instrumentality of Professor Albert Bushnell Hart.

manded correct apprehension and prompt decision. The
gravity of it was heightened by the severance of communications between the national capital and the North as a
result of the trouble in Baltimore. The burning of the
bridges had cut off all railroad communication. Sunday
night (April 21) the telegraph ceased to work.[1] The only
connection the government now had with its loyal territory
and people was by means of private couriers; these made
their way with difficulty through Maryland, where for the
moment an unfriendly element reigned. Correct information
was hard to get and rumors of all sorts filled the air. The
government and the citizens were apprehensive of an attack
on the city. They feared that Beauregard's South Carolina

See, also, Montgomery Blair to Bryant, *National Intelligencer*, Aug. 9, 1866,
cited by Nicolay and Hay, vol. iv. p. 98. Lee himself wrote to Reverdy
Johnson, Feb. 25, 1868, as follows : "I never intimated to any one that I
desired the command of the United States army, nor did I ever have a
conversation but with one gentleman, Mr. Francis Preston Blair, on the
subject, which was at his invitation, and, as I understood, at the instance
of President Lincoln.

"After listening to his remarks I declined the offer he made me to take
command of the army that was to be brought into the field, stating, as
candidly and courteously as I could, that, though opposed to secession and
deprecating war, I could take no part in an invasion of the Southern States.

"I went directly from the interview with Mr. Blair to the office of General Scott—told him of the proposition that had been made to me and my
decision. Upon reflection, after returning home, I concluded that I ought
no longer to retain any commission I held in the United States army, and
on the second morning thereafter I forwarded my resignation to General
Scott.

"At the time I hoped that peace would have been preserved—that some
way would be found to save the country from the calamities of war ; and I
then had no other intention than to pass the remainder of my life as a
private citizen.

"Two days afterwards, on the invitation of the governor of Virginia,
I repaired to Richmond, found that the convention then in session
had passed the ordinance withdrawing the State from the Union, and
accepted the commission of commander of its forces which was tendered
me. These are the simple facts of the case."—*Life of Lee*, Long,
p. 93.

[1] Official Records, vol. ii. p. 586 ; Nicolay and Hay, vol. iv. p. 138; Life
of Seward, vol. ii. p. 550; New York *Tribune*.

army, flushed with victory, would be transported north as fast as the railroads could carry it, and that it would be joined by a large enough force of Virginia troops to make the capture of Washington an easy matter. Preparations were made to stand a siege. Panic seized the crowds of office-seekers, and they fled to the North. Many of the secessionists, afraid that the whole male population of the city would be impressed for its defence, departed for the South. This place, wrote General Scott, April 22, is "now partially besieged, threatened, and in danger of being attacked on all sides in a day or two or three." [1] On the same day, Northern soldiers having arrived at Annapolis, Governor Hicks advised the President "that no more troops be ordered or allowed to pass through Maryland"; he suggested, moreover, "that Lord Lyons be requested to act as mediator between the contending parties of our country." [2] Another project was to have the five ex-Presidents beseech the federal government to grant an armistice. [3] Lincoln clearly stated his position on this Monday (April 22), in his reply to a delegation from the Young Men's Christian Association of Baltimore, who prayed that no more troops be sent through Maryland : "You express great horror of bloodshed, and yet would not lay a straw in the way of those who are organizing in Virginia and elsewhere to capture this city. . . . I have no desire to invade the South ; but I must have troops to defend this capital. Geographically it lies surrounded by the soil of Maryland, and mathematically the necessity exists that they should come over

---

[1] Official Records, vol. ii. p. 587.

[2] Hicks to the President. Official Records, vol. ii. p. 588. For Seward's reply of April 22 see Moore's Rebellion Record, vol. i., Docs., p. 133. It was printed in the New York *Tribune*, April 24.

[3] "I know the fact that the administration would have been requested by the five ex-Presidents to grant an armistice but for the hesitancy of Mr. Van Buren, who declined to unite until he should be assured that the administration desired to be approached in that way."—William D. Kelley to Chase, Philadelphia, April 29, Chase Papers, MS. ; see, also, editorial in New York *Tribune*, April 29.

her territory." [1] Having a keen appreciation of how much depended on his holding the capital, the President was alarmed for its safety and nervously apprehensive at the outlook. As Tuesday the 23d passed by and no soldiers came, he paced the floor of the executive office in restless anxiety and thinking himself entirely alone, he exclaimed in tones of anguish, " Why don't they come! Why don't they come!" [2] That same day had brought a mail from New York three days old, containing newspapers which told that the uprising of the North continued with waxing strength and unbounded enthusiasm, giving the news of the departure of the Seventh New York Regiment and the sailing of Governor Sprague's Rhode-Islanders. It was the bitterness of hope deferred that led Lincoln, in his speech on Wednesday to the wounded soldiers of the Sixth Massachusetts, to burst out ironically : " I begin to believe that there is no North. The Seventh Regiment is a myth. Rhode Island is another. You are the only real thing." [3]

Nowhere may the uprising of the Northern people be better studied than in New York city, where on a grand scale might be witnessed the manifestations of that spirit which animated every city, town, and village from Maine to Kansas. The people and the press, with insignificant exceptions, showed a hearty loyalty to the Union. From the day that the news of the bombardment of Sumter

---

[1] Nicolay and Hay, vol. iv. p. 139. R. Fuller, a prominent Baptist minister of Baltimore, who was the spokesman of the Young Christians, thus wrote Chase from Baltimore, April 23: " From Mr. Lincoln nothing is to be hoped, except as you can influence him. Five associations, representing thousands of our best young men, sent a delegation of thirty to Washington yesterday . . . and asked me to go with them as the chairman. We were at once cordially received. I marked the President closely. Constitutionally genial and jovial, he is wholly inaccessible to Christian appeals, and his egotism will forever prevent his comprehending what patriotism means."—Chase Papers, MS.

[2] Nicolay and Hay, vol. iv. p. 152.

[3] J. H., Diary. Nicolay and Hay, vol. iv. p. 153. L. E. Chittenden, in chap. xviii. of his Recollections of President Lincoln, gives an animated account of " The Isolation of the Capital."

came, when the Stock Exchange resounded with enthusiastic cheers for Major Anderson, every indication showed
that the weight of the financial and trade centre of the
country would be on the side of the national government.
Party ties here as elsewhere were sunk in the common devotion to the flag. This was especially disappointing to the
South since, owing to her business connection and social
intercourse with New York city, and to the large Democratic majority which it always gave, she had reckoned
upon the friendship of the metropolis,[1] and regarded it as
an important factor in dividing the North, a result which
she had confidently expected. The mayor, Fernando Wood,
had proposed that, in the event of disunion, New York
should constitute itself a free city, retaining its commerce
with both sections,[2] and, unless John Forsyth was wofully
deceived, a conspiracy had gathered head to carry out that
purpose.[3]   William H. Russell, the correspondent of the

---

[1] "Will the city of New York 'kiss the rod that smites her' and at the
bidding of her Black Republican tyrants war upon her Southern friends
and best customers ? Will she sacrifice her commerce, her wealth, her population, her character, in order to strengthen the arm of her oppressors ?"—
Richmond *Examiner*, April 15.

[2] Mayor's message, New York *Herald*, Jan. 8.

[3] Forsyth, one of the Confederate commissioners to the United States,
wrote Jefferson Davis from Washington, April 4: "While in New York
last week, I learned some particulars of a contemplated revolutionary
movement in that city. . . . I was called upon by a gentleman by the name
of ——, who asked to speak confidentially to me. Leave granted, he proceeded to inform me that a movement was on foot to relieve New York city
and 'its surroundings' of the ruin with which that city was threatened. The
people of New York, he said, were living under a double tyranny—the one
located at Albany and reaching their domestic affairs, and the other at
Washington, breaking up their foreign trade. The evil was so great as to
justify a revolution for relief. To this end 200 of the most influential and
wealthy citizens of New York had been approached, and were then arranging the details of a plan to throw off the authority of the federal and State
governments, to seize the navy-yard at Brooklyn, the vessels of war and
the forts in the harbor, and to declare New York a free city. The military
of the city had been felt and found responsive; the mayor of the city, while
not taking a leading part from considerations of policy, will at the proper

London *Times*, was, in March, struck by the indifference
with which prominent men of the metropolis regarded the
impending trouble.[1]   But now the voice of its people gave

---

time throw his whole power into the movement. Several army officers are
in it, two of the principal ship-builders and the leading merchants and capitalists of the city. The movement is to be divested of everything like
party aspects, and among the conspirators are several who, although never
Republicans, voted for Lincoln under the then Northern delusive idea that
a sectional President might be elected with safety to the Union. The night
of the day I left the city a private meeting was to be held, and a circular
which was read to me in manuscript and which has since been forwarded
to me in print, . . . was to be distributed for signatures. There was no
doubt that 30,000 or 40,000 signatures would be obtained to it in a week.
The plan is to procure a powerful demonstration of public feeling, and to
follow up the demonstration by a *coup d'état* to be arranged beforehand. The
forts are to be possessed by furnishing the recruits from the ranks of the
conspirators who are daily being collected and sent to those forts by the
government. ——, the ship-builder, and his associates say that they can
convert enough of the merchant marine in the port of New York into a
naval force to drive the United States ships out of the harbor at very short
notice. Being on an island they can resist attack, and in a few hours concentrate 50,000 men at any point of assault.

"The object of the interview with me was to learn what would be the disposition of the Confederate States government towards such a movement.
. . . The circular enclosed was read to me by Dr. ——, a distinguished prac-
titioner and a gentleman of high position and large fortune in that city—a
man heretofore devoted to science, and one of the men least likely to take
part in a revolution. Such, I am assured, is the class of men who have
taken hold of it.

"The tone of the gentleman who conversed with me was one of deep earnestness and firm resolve. They say that New York is being punished for
its large Democratic vote, that they have no confidence in the ability of the
Black Republican administration to govern them wisely or justly, and that
the great masses only need to be shown the way to rush into the revolution. They speak with confidence of success at an early day. . . . Mr. Russell, the Crimean correspondent of the London *Times*, is here. He goes
south to study this revolution. We are cultivating him, and give him a
dinner to-morrow."—MSS. Confederate Diplomatic Correspondence, Treasury Department. I have suppressed the names in this despatch, as they do
not add materially to its force.

[1] Dining with a New York banker, Russell " was astonished to perceive
how calmly he spoke of the impending troubles. His friends, all men of
position in New York society, had the same *dilettante* tone, and were as
little anxious for the future, or excited by the present, as a party of *savants*

no uncertain sound.   The tone was the same as that heard
in New England and the West.   The flag waved everywhere.   The resoluteness with which those suspected of
Southern sympathies were warned to raise the sign of loyalty, and their speedy compliance, were a certain indication
of the prevailing sentiment.   In twenty - four hours the
New York *Herald*, a journal of wide influence with a Southern leaning, though apt to go with the popular current,
changed its tune, clearly demonstrating the opinion of the
Democratic majority.[1]   The New York Seventh Regiment,

---

chronicling the movements of a ' magnetic storm.' "—Entry March 17, Diary,
p. 14.   Later Russell dined with Horatio Seymour, Samuel J. Tilden, and
George Bancroft, and wrote, "The result left on my mind by their conversation and arguments was that, according to the Constitution, the
government could not employ force to prevent secession, or to compel
States which had seceded by the will of the people to acknowledge the
federal power."—Ibid., p. 20.   July 2, when, after a trip through the South,
he returned to New York, he was amazed at the change.   "As long as
there was a chance that the struggle might not take place, the merchants
of New York were silent, fearful of offending their Southern friends and
connections, but inflicting infinite damage on their own government and
misleading both sides.   Their sentiments, sympathies, and business bound
them with the South ; and, indeed, till 'the glorious uprising' the South
believed New York was with them, as might be credited from the tone of
some organs in the press, and I remember hearing it said by Southerners in
Washington that it was very likely New York would go out of the Union!
When the merchants, however, saw the South was determined to quit the
Union . . . they rushed to the platform—the battle-cry was sounded from
almost every pulpit—flag-raisings took place in every square, like the planting of the tree of liberty in France in 1848, and the oath was taken to trample
secession under foot and to quench the fire of the Southern heart forever.

" The change in manner, in tone, in argument, is most remarkable.   I met
men to-day who last March argued coolly and philosophically about the
right of secession.   They are now furious at the idea of such wickedness."
—Ibid., p. 370.

[1] " The people of this metropolis owe it to themselves, to their material
and political interests, to their social security, and to the country at large
to make a solemn and imposing effort in behalf of peace."— New York
Herald, April 15.   " The time has passed for such public peace meetings
in the North as were advocated, and might have effected some beneficial
result, a few weeks since.   War will make the Northern people a unit.
Republicans look upon it as inevitable, and Democrats have been becom-

the corps of the *élite*, offered its services to the government, and when it left for Washington, Friday the 19th, the heart of the metropolis went with it. As those fine fellows marched down Broadway, an enormous crowd with true sympathy and hearty accent bade them godspeed. " It was worth a life, that march," wrote Theodore Winthrop, who fifty days later laid down his own life on Virginia soil for the cause of the Union. " Only one who passed, as we did, through that tempest of cheers two miles long, can know the terrible enthusiasm of the occasion." [1] Patriotism fitly ended the week by a grand demonstration. With the city a mass of the national colors, a quarter of a million people [2] met in and about Union Square to hear Union speeches, to do homage to Major Anderson, and to pledge themselves to the maintenance of the Union and the defence of the Constitution. Distinguished men of all the political parties spoke in the same strain ; clergymen of various denominations offered up prayers of like tenor. The Catholic archbishop, Hughes, kept at home by illness, wrote a letter expressing his full sympathy with the object of the meeting. Mayor Fernando Wood declared : " I am with you in this contest. We know no party now." [3]

The New York Seventh Regiment left for Washington the day that the Massachusetts Sixth was attacked in Baltimore. It was learned on their arrival at Philadelphia early on the morning of Saturday the 20th that it would be impossible to reach the capital city by the usual route. Colonel Lefferts of the Seventh telegraphed the Secretary of War for orders. [4] There was considerable delay in the trans-

ing gradually disgusted at the neglect and ingratitude with which they have been treated by a section for which they have faithfully borne the heat and the burthen of conflict for so many years."—Ibid., April 16.

[1] Winthrop in *Atlantic Monthly*, June, 1861, p. 745. See, also, Fitz-James O'Brien in New York *Times*, Moore's Rebellion Record, vol. i., Docs., p. 148.

[2] A newspaper estimate.

[3] New York *Times*, New York *Herald*, April 21 ; New York *Tribune*, April 22; Moore's Rebellion Record, vol. i., Docs., p. 82.

[4] Official Records, vol. ii. p. 582.

mission of messages, and before he received a reply he chartered a steamer to take his regiment direct to Washington. He embarked his troops Saturday afternoon, but deciding that it was not prudent to attempt the passage of the lower Potomac, he directed the course of the transport up Chesapeake Bay to Annapolis, arriving there Monday morning the 22d. There he found, under the command of General Butler, the Massachusetts Eighth, which had gone from Philadelphia to Perryville by rail and thence by boat, but had not yet disembarked. Governor Hicks was at his capital earnestly advising Butler not to land the troops, and counselling the President to send them elsewhere.[1] Both of the regiments landed Monday afternoon under the governor's protest. Every one was eager to get to Washington. But much of the railroad track from Annapolis to the junction with the main line from Baltimore to Washington had been torn up. Experienced track-layers were called for, and these stepped forth from the ranks of the Massachusetts Eighth, and began to relay and spike the rails. Massachusetts machinists repaired a disabled locomotive which they had built in the days of peace. Wednesday morning the march to Annapolis Junction began. Some rickety cars attached to the locomotive carried the brass howitzers of the Seventh, and served as a baggage, supply, ambulance, and construction train. All sorts of rumors in regard to an attack from secessionists in force along the route were afloat, and it was deemed necessary to proceed with caution. The march was along the railroad. "The kid-gloved New York dandies," the "military Brummels," fraternized with the Massachusetts mechanics; the gourmets who had partaken of many a dinner at Delmonico's ate their scanty campaign fare with good-humor and relish. They shared their rations with their Massachusetts compatriots, and gave them assistance in laying track. "Our march," wrote O'Brien, "lay through an arid, sandy, tobacco-growing

---

[1] Official Records, vol. ii. pp. 586, 588.

country. The sun poured on our heads like hot lava." A
furious wind-storm and a heavy shower which wet them
through were among the trials they had to endure. Eight
miles from Annapolis they came to a broken bridge. A
working party was called for. At twilight the bridge
could be crossed. Night fell, but the capital was thought
to be in danger and the troops must press on. Although
moonlight, the march was monotonous and fatiguing. The
little army struggled manfully against their difficulties, and
by the early morning of Thursday, April 25, had reached
Annapolis Junction, completing their march of twenty
miles.[1] There they found a train which took them quickly
to Washington. The Seventh Regiment arrived first. Forming as soon as they left the cars, they marched up Pennsylvania Avenue to the White House. To the people who
noted their military bearing, and to the President who reviewed them, they were a goodly sight. Their actual presence, and the fact denoted by their arrival—that a route
from the loyal North to its capital was open, and that other
regiments were on the way soon to arrive—insured the
safety of Washington. "Ten thousand of our troops are
arrived here," wrote Seward, April 27, "and the city is considered safe." [2]

The alarm in regard to Washington was natural, but not
well-founded. During these eventful eleven days (from the
evacuation of Sumter to the arrival of the New York
Seventh) the capital had been in no danger of capture. The
Northern authorities and people looked at the situation
wholly from a military point of view, and from that view
an attempt to take it was feasible, and would probably have
met with success. Beauregard could have transported by
railroad his army of 5000 to 6000 [3] from Charleston to Alex-

---

[1] For lively descriptions of this march see Theodore Winthrop in *Atlantic Monthly*, June, 1861; letter of Fitz-James O'Brien, April 27, in the
New York *Times*, May 2.   [2] Life of Seward, vol. ii. p. 560.
[3] I think this a low estimate of his effective force. The official return
of the South Carolina army shown to Russell, April 21, was: in Charles-

andria in three or four days.[1] Six to fifteen thousand Virginia militia,[2] though all had not the best of equipment, were available to join him. The number of troops in Washington is variously given.[3] The only assurance that General Scott could give the President, Monday, April 22, was that he could defend "the Capitol, the arsenal, and all the executive buildings against 10,000 troops not better than our district volunteers."[4] The military conditions of capture were fulfilled. Beauregard's army had something like three months of discipline, and, supported by the Virginia militia,

---

ton harbor and Charleston, 7025 men; in Columbia, 1950; in the field, 3027; total, 12,002.—Letter to London *Times*.

[1] The time of express trains from Charleston to Washington was about forty-one hours. On the facilities for the transportation of troops see Bird, railroad superintendent, to Walker, Official Records, vol. ii. p. 771. Leaving Charleston April 23, a detachment of 450 South Carolina troops was transported from Charleston to Richmond in about thirty-six hours, Richmond *Examiner*, April 25. A. K. McClure writes that General Scott said to him, April 15, "General Beauregard commands more men at Charleston than I command on the continent east of the frontier," and that Beauregard could transport his army to Washington in three or four days. Lincoln said to Scott, "It does seem to me, General, that if I were Beauregard I would take Washington."—McClure's Lincoln and Men of War Times, p. 60.

[2] Various statements are made about this number. Virginia's "armed soldiery numbers now some 10,000 men, of which not more than 6000 are completely equipped."—Scott, a delegate in the Virginia convention, April 13, Richmond *Examiner*, April 15. "It will be seen by the proclamation of the governor . . . that the entire military force of the State has been ordered to hold itself in readiness to march at a moment's warning. The equipped force of volunteers in this State—by which we mean armed and equipped—is now between 6000 and 7000 men."—Ibid., April 18. April 25 Stephens, then in Richmond, reported 15,000 troops there, Johnston and Browne, p. 399. All but 450 of these were Virginians. April 21 there were 2000 at Harper's Ferry, Official Records, vol. ii. p. 772.

[3] "We have some four to five thousand men under arms in the city." —Personal Memorandum, April 19, J. G. N., Nicolay and Hay, vol. iv. p. 125. "Until the day before yesterday we had not 2500 men here under arms."—Cameron to Thomson, April 27, Official Records, vol. ii. p. 604; see General Scott's reports, Nicolay and Hay, vol. iv. p. 66 *et seq.*

[4] Nicolay and Hay, vol. iv. p. 144. As to the District of Columbia militia, ibid., pp. 66, 106.

could, had he made a dash upon Washington, have probably taken it. The moral effect of the seizure of the nation's capital by the revolutionists would have been so momentous, in all likelihood insuring the immediate recognition of the Southern Confederacy by the European powers, that it is no wonder the President and his cabinet were preyed upon by deep anxiety. Stanton, in his emphatic way, expressed the general feeling. " The state of affairs here," he wrote Dix, April 23, is " desperate beyond any conception. If there be any remedy—any shadow of hope to preserve this government from utter and absolute extinction — it must come from New York without delay." [1] As a matter of fact, however, with the exception of the reckless and unmeaning boast of the Confederate Secretary of War,[2] nothing has been disclosed showing that any design existed, or that any movement had been set on foot during these eleven days by the Confederate States or by Virginia towards the capture of Washington. " There is no truth whatever," wrote Stephens, confidentially, from Montgomery, April 17, " in the telegraphic despatches that the President intends to head an expedition to Washington." [3] The newspapers, indeed, flashed out threats, and in their sanctums the taking of the federal capital was seriously considered and planned;[4] there was a popular feeling that it might be and

---

[1] Life of Dix, vol. ii. p. 13.   [2] *Ante*.

[3] Johnston and Browne, p. 396. " Whether Mr. Walker did make such a speech as reported by that telegram, or not, I do not know. . . . I do know that such were not the views of the cabinet or of the people generally of the Confederate States."—Stephens's War Between the States, vol. ii. p. 421.

[4] "Attention, volunteers! Nothing is more probable than that President Davis will soon march an army through North Carolina and Virginia to Washington. Those of our volunteers who desire to join the Southern army, as it shall pass through our borders, had better organize at once for the purpose, and keep their arms, accoutrements, uniforms, ammunition, and knapsacks in constant readiness."—Richmond *Enquirer*, April 13. " Washington is to be the seat of war. Washington is the great prize in dispute, and if Southerners will rush instantly upon it the war will soon be ended."—Richmond *Examiner*, April 20. " The capture of Washington

ought to be done.¹ Stephens, on his arrival at Richmond, April 22, found "a strong inclination on the part of some here to make an attack upon Washington;" he added, "What course and policy will be adopted is not yet determined upon." ² A movement on the capital must have depended on Beauregard's army as the nucleus of the attacking force. No part of it reached Richmond until the evening of the 24th;³ and at mid-day of the 25th the New York Seventh was in Washington. While Lincoln feared the Charleston army, Beauregard was "apprehensive of an attack by the Northern ' fanatics ' before the South is prepared." ⁴ The panic in Washington was matched by the panic in Richmond. On Sunday, April 21, about noon, the report spread that the United States steamer *Pawnee*, having a large force of troops on board, was steaming up James River with the intention of attacking Richmond. The bell on the Capitol rang out the alarm. Men rushed from the churches and, seizing their weapons, hastened to the wharf to oppose the landing of the federal soldiers. Not until evening were the unfounded fears entirely dissipated.⁵

City is perfectly within the power of Virginia and Maryland, if Virginia will only make the proper effort by her constituted authorities. . . . The entire population pant for the onset; there never was half the unanimity amongst the people before, nor a tithe of the zeal upon any subject that is now manifested to take Washington, and drive from it every Black Republican who is a dweller there. . . . Our people can take it—they will take it—and Scott the arch-traitor and Lincoln the beast, combined, cannot prevent it."—Ibid., April 23; see citations from Southern newspapers in *National Intelligencer*, May 9; Richmond *Whig*, cited by Moore, vol. i., Diary, p. 74.   ¹ Richmond *Examiner*, April 24.
    ² Johnston and Browne, p. 399.
    ³ Richmond *Examiner*, April 25; letter from "Stonewall" Jackson, Biography, by his wife, p. 149.
    ⁴ Entry, April 25, Russell's Diary, p. 136.
    ⁵ Richmond *Enquirer*, April 22; Richmond *Examiner*, April 22; Life in the South, by a Blockaded British Subject (Catherine C. Hopley), vol. i. p. 278; Richmond During the War, Sarah A. Putnam (1867), p. 24. Down South, by Samuel Phillips Day, vol. i. p. 100. Stephens wrote, April 22: "The people are in apprehension this city will be attacked by the forces

Although the capture of Washington was from a military point of view feasible, the political obstacles to a dash upon it were insurmountable. The doctrine of state-rights, which was sincerely held in the Southern States, not only furnished the theory of secession, but it was maintained in a certain degree as against each other.[1] North Carolina not yet having seceded, the Confederate troops could not have been transported over her territory without her consent; that, indeed, was easily obtained, but consumed somewhat of time. The great difficulty lay with Virginia. The government of the State was now in the hands of the convention, which in the early part of April had voted against secession,[2] and of the governor, Letcher, who had not sympathized with the secessionists of his State.[3] When the convention passed the ordinance resuming the "rights of sovereignty" of Virginia, which they did April 17, the vote of 88 in its favor to 55 against it, and the submission of it to the popular vote at an election to be held on the fourth Thursday of May, did not indicate that those in authority had any notion of proceeding with rashness or without some

---

now in the Chesapeake and Potomac below. There are no forts on the James River to prevent armed ships from coming up. The *Pawnee*, *Cumberland*, and others, with a large force of soldiers at Old Point, are below." See, also, A Rebel's Recollections, Eggleston, p. 22.

[1] "We sincerely hope that no effort will be made by citizens of the South to take possession of the city of Washington and to expel the officials of the government of the United States from their abodes or offices. If any such effort be made before Virginia and Maryland shall have seceded from the Union of the United States it will be very disastrous to the cause of secession. It will raise the State pride of the citizens of these proud commonwealths, who will not be able to see with indifference their territories lawlessly invaded and used for an unlawful purpose. And when these States have seceded it will be for them to settle their relations towards Washington."—Charleston *Mercury*, April 19; see, also, A Rebel War Clerk's Diary, Jones, p. 27.

[2] *Ante*, p. 345.

[3] Note his action the day the news of the taking of Sumter was received at Richmond, Richmond *Enquirer*, April 16; Richmond *Examiner*, April 18.

respect for the forms of law.¹ No great significance, however, need be laid upon the proviso that the ordinance required ratification by the people before taking effect, since matters proceeded on the assumption that they would make it valid;² yet the course of the Virginia authorities precluded the prompt military action which was indispensable for the capture of Washington; and it is clearly evident that without her spontaneous consent and active co-operation no movement could have been made. April 19, Governor Letcher telegraphed to Montgomery, asking that a commission from the Confederate States be sent at once to Richmond, in order that the two governments might act conjointly. Stephens, the Vice-President of the Confederacy, was selected for this duty.³ Three days after his arrival he complained of the tardy disposition of Virginia. "The Virginians *will* debate and speak," he wrote, "though war be at the gates of their city. . . . The convention acts slowly —they are greatly behind the times."⁴ Nevertheless on that day, the 25th, the convention ratified the offensive and defensive alliance between Virginia and the Confederacy, which its committee and Stephens had agreed to, and it also adopted the constitution of the provisional government of the Confederate States, though declaring that this act should have no effect if the people at the appointed time rejected the ordinance of secession.⁵ It was not until this

¹ Jones, in A Rebel War Clerk's Diary, makes the following entry, April 19: "From the ardor of the volunteers already beginning to pour into the city, I believe 25,000 men could be collected and armed in a week, and in another they might sweep the whole abolition concern beyond the Susquehanna. . . . But this will not be attempted, nor permitted, by the convention, so recently composed mostly of Union men."

² "The ordinance of secession will be submitted as a matter of course to a vote of the people. But it will be a mere formality. The ratification will be carried by one almost unanimous shout."—Richmond *Whig*, April 23. Likewise the Richmond *Enquirer*, April 19, and Richmond *Examiner*, April 26.   ³ Johnston and Browne, p. 397.

⁴ Letter of April 25, ibid., p. 399.

⁵ Stephens's War between the States, vol. ii. pp. 378, 387; Johnston and Browne, p. 399.

agreement had been concluded that the Virginian and Confederate forces could legally unite in a military movement,
and by that time the alarm about Washington had come to
an end. On the 24th there were but three hundred Virginians at Alexandria fit for duty, while the force in Washington was greatly overrated by their general.[1] Robert E. Lee,
who had been appointed commander-in-chief of the Virginia
forces, instructed him that he should " let it be known that
you intend no attack, but invasion of our soil will be considered an act of war."[2]

The only indication I have found which, before April 25,
looked towards co-operation between the Confederate government and Virginia, and which might have eventuated in
an attack on Washington, is a despatch from Davis to Letcher of the 22d, saying, " Sustain Baltimore if practicable. We
reinforce you."[3] On the same day the Advisory Council of
Virginia recommended the governor to deliver 1000 of the
arms taken at Harper's Ferry to General Stewart at Baltimore, and to loan from the arsenal at Lexington 5000 muskets to the Maryland troops, to enable them to resist the
passage of Northern troops to Washington.[4] Two thousand of these arms were actually delivered.[5]

The doctrine of state - rights, rigidly adhered to as it
was by many Southerners, required the consent of Maryland for an attack on the national capital, for the District
of Columbia was considered her soil.[6] Hoping that she

---

[1] Cocke to Lee, Official Records, vol. ii. p. 776. He estimated the army
in Washington as numbering 10,000 to 12,000. The Richmond *Examiner*
was nearer right. "Exclusive of the District militia," it said, April 26,
"Lincoln's whole force now at his immediate command does not probably
exceed 500 regulars and 4000 raw militia."

[2] Lee to Cocke, April 24, Official Records, vol. ii. p. 777. Lee accepted
the command of the Virginia forces April 23, Life of Lee, Long, p. 98.

[3] Official Records, vol. ii. p. 773.

[4] Ibid.; see, also, Richmond *Enquirer*, April 25.

[5] McPherson's History of the Rebellion, p. 394.

[6] Speaking of Walker's speech, the Baltimore *American* said: "This is a
threat, not to the Republican party, but to the nation — to Virginia and

would cast in her lot with the South, the Virginians proceeded towards her with delicacy, and, even had they been ready, would not have made an attack on Washington, except at her request, comprehending that in such an event the fury of violated sovereignty and soil, now directed at the Northern troops, might be turned against the Southern invader. When they threatened Harper's Ferry and the Gosport navy-yard, they simply made an effort, according to their theory, to recover what was their own. But to cross the Potomac was an entirely different affair. "Your intention to fortify the heights of Maryland," wrote General Lee, May 10, to Thomas J. Jackson, then in command of the Virginia volunteers at Harper's Ferry, "may interrupt our friendly arrangements with that State, and we have no right to intrude on her soil unless, under pressing necessity, for defence." [1] Nor was this right assumed until the Virginians had come to regard Maryland as remaining one of the United States, and being therefore in "open and avowed hostility" to them. [2]

The Confederate States were full of joy at the bombardment and evacuation of Sumter. When Lincoln took up the gage of war by his call for troops, or, as the secessionists said, threw it down, the martial ardor which lay constantly in the Southern breast, and the belief that they must arm for the defence of their property and their liberties, prompted these people to rise as one man. The uprising of men and the proffers of money matched that which was

---

North Carolina, still in the Union, through whose territory the Southern invading army must pass, and to Maryland, upon whose soil the Capitol stands."—Cited by *National Intelligencer*, April 18. "No troops of the Confederate States, or of any other State, can with propriety assail Washington before Maryland has seceded from the Union and shall request their aid and intervention."—Charleston *Mercury*, April 23.

[1] Official Records, vol. ii. p. 825.

[2] See letter of J. M. Mason to General Lee, May 15, and his reply, May 21, ibid., pp. 849, 860.

going on at the North. All hearts were in the cause.
Stephens, who had travelled from Montgomery to Richmond, said on his way back, at Atlanta : " I find our people everywhere are alive to their interests and their duty
in this crisis. Such a degree of popular enthusiasm was
never before seen in this country."[1] "The anxiety among
our citizens," declared Howell Cobb, " is not as to who shall
go to the wars, but *who shall stay at home.*"[2] As at the
North, so in the Confederate States, the best blood was
offering itself to fight for country and rights which were
prized.[3] Nor was the feeling less hearty in eastern North
Carolina and eastern Virginia. " North Carolina," wrote
Stephens, " is in a blaze from one extremity to the other.
Yesterday, Sunday as it was, large crowds were assembled
at all the stations along the railroad—at Wilmington five
thousand at least, the Confederate flag flying all over the

---

[1] Moore's Rebellion Record, vol. i., Docs., p. 176.
[2] Ibid., p. 268.
[3] See, for example, Charleston *Mercury*, April 18, 19, 20, 22, May 4 ;
private letter from Montgomery, printed in Baltimore *Daily Exchange*,
April 16 ; private letter from a prominent merchant of New Orleans, ibid.,
April 25 ; *National Intelligencer*, April 25 ; opinions of the New Orleans
press, cited by Moore, vol. i., Docs., p. 138 ; also ibid., pp. 164, 179 ; vol.
i., Diary, pp. 41, 68 ; *Atlanta Commonwealth*, April 25, May 2. "Our
troops are composed of rich and poor, learned and unlearned. Our best
and most respected citizens fill the ranks as common soldiers."—Richmond
Examiner, April 26. "The flower of the Southern youth, the prime of
Southern manhood, are collected in the camps of Virginia. Some of the
most remarkable of these are here in the close neighborhood of Richmond.
Genius, learning, and wealth, enough to furnish the aristocracy of an empire, wear the coarse gray of the common soldier and learn the use of the
soldier's common weapon."—Ibid., April 30. "In the South, the volunteers who spring to arms with so much alacrity are men of substance and
position, wealthy farmers and planters with their sons, professional men,
merchants and their clerks, intelligent and industrious mechanics, and
indeed from every art, trade, profession, and occupation ; the wealth, intelligence, industry, and backbone of society have rallied for the defence
of their homes, and for the assertion of constitutional liberty."—Richmond
Enquirer, April 25. For the constitution of the Stonewall brigade, see
Life of "Stonewall" Jackson, by his wife, p. 160. I may add as authori
ties nearly all Southern writers since the war.

city." [1] "All Virginia is in arms," he wrote from Richmond. [2] Requisitions were made on Virginia and North Carolina for their quota of militia under the President's call of April 15, as they were still in the Union. Governor Letcher and Governor Ellis each sent a defiant refusal. [3] Ellis at once called a special session of the North Carolina legislature. It met May 1, and one hour after assembling unanimously passed an act providing for a convention which should have unrestricted powers, and the action of which should be final. It also voted men and money for the war. May 13 the people elected delegates, who one week later came together in convention. On the first day of the meeting, having voted down a motion that they should sit with closed doors, they passed unanimously an ordinance of secession, and after deciding in the negative a proposition to submit the constitution of the provisional government of the Confederate States to a popular vote, they ratified it without one voice of dissent. [4]

In answer to the President's call for State militia, Tennessee's governor peremptorily refused to "furnish a man for purposes of coercion." [5] April 18 a number of her prominent citizens, one of whom was John Bell, united in an address to the people, in which they averred that "the present duty of Tennessee" was to preserve her independence both of the North and the South—to take sides with neither. "Her position should be to maintain the sanctity of her soil from the

---

[1] Letter from Richmond, April 22, Johnston and Browne, p. 398.

[2] Letter of April 25, Johnston and Browne, p. 399 ; for enthusiasm over taking of Sumter see Richmond *Examiner*, April 15 ; Richmond *Dispatch*, April 15; Richmond *Enquirer*, April 16, also April 23, 26 ; Richmond *Whig*, April 16 ; see also editorials in Richmond *Examiner*, April 25 and 26, and proclamation of Governor Letcher, same date ; letter of Mrs. John Tyler to her mother, April 18, Letters and Times of the Tylers, vol. ii. p. 646 ; A Rebel's Recollections, Eggleston, p. 19.

[3] Official Records, Series iii., cited by Nicolay and Hay, vol. iv. pp. 90, 91.

[4] Journal of North Carolina Convention, 1861, pp. 15, 17. The vote against a secret session was 59–54 ; against submission of the constitution to the people, 72–34 ; see, also, Appletons' Annual Cyclopædia, 1861, p. 539.   [5] Ibid., p. 678.

hostile tread of any party." Less than a week later, Bell, in a public speech, declared that he was "for standing by the South," and that his "voice was clear and loud to every Tennesseean—to arms! to arms!"[1] May 7 the legislature in secret session made an offensive and defensive military league with the Southern Confederacy. It also adopted a declaration of independence, and passed an ordinance ratifying the constitution of the provisional government of the Confederate States, subject to the result of their submission to a popular vote. June 8 the people at the ballot-box approved the action of their representatives, giving a majority of nearly 58,000 for separation from the Union.[2]

---

[1] Moore's Rebellion Record, vol. i., Docs., pp. 72, 137. T. D. Winter, who had spent several months in the South, made, June 10, a report to Secretary Chase, which is a substantially correct description of Tennessee sentiment. But as he wrote before the result of the election was known, he overrated the Union strength and the salutary effect of a federal invading army. Winter wrote : "After the presidential election . . . the Union men and the Union press . . . strongly opposed the feeling of secession that seemed to be gaining ground, and though they felt no sympathy with the administration, yet they strongly recommended that the administration have a fair commencement, and that if the just rights of the South were conceded, they could live as well under a Republican administration as any other. This position was maintained until even after all the other States had gone out with the exception of Virginia, and when she seceded and the evacuation of Fort Sumter took place, and still later, until Mr. Bell made his wonderful leap into the secession ranks, when the Union press placed the secession flag at the head of their column, with all the array of the press of Tennessee against the Union. I do not think it has changed the sentiment of a large number of its patrons. . . . My firm belief is, that should an army formidable enough to control as they went march into the South, and show to the masses that they came only to execute the laws and protect their slave property, the current of [secession] feeling would change materially."—Chase Papers, MS.

[2] Moore's Rebellion Record, vol. i., Docs., p. 202; Appletons' Annual Cyclopædia, 1861, p. 678. The vote was as follows:

	For separation.	No separation.
East Tennessee	14.780	32,923
Middle Tennessee	58,265	8,198
West Tennessee	29,127	6,117
Military camps	2,741	
	104,913	47,238
Majority for separation		57,675

May 6 the convention of Arkansas reassembled and, with but one dissenting vote, immediately passed an ordinance of secession.[1]

Fifty-five out of one hundred and forty-three delegates of the Virginia convention had voted against the ordinance of secession,[2] and, indeed, the day before its adoption John Tyler, one of the influential members, who believed that Virginia had no alternative but war, and that it was a choice between "submission or resistance," doubted whether the ordinance would be passed.[3] The ardent secessionists complained that the convention by no means represented the people. The politicians may be divided, but "the people of Virginia are henceforth united," declared the Richmond *Examiner* on the day that the President's call for troops reached Richmond.[4] Immediately after the vote on the

Proclamation of Governor Harris, June 24, Moore's Rebellion Record, vol. ii., Docs., p. 169 ; see, also, *Tribune* Almanac, 1862, p. 59. The total vote was 6818 more than at the presidential election of 1860. For the charge of intimidation at this election, see Greeley's American Conflict, vol. i. p. 483.

[1] Appletons' Annual Cyclopædia, 1861, p. 23.

[2] The vote was kept secret, but was published in detail in Richmond *Examiner*, June 17. It is also printed by McPherson, p. 7, note.

[3] Letter to his wife, April 16, Letters and Times of the Tylers, vol. ii. p. 640 ; see, also, the debate in the convention, April 13, Richmond *Examiner*, April 15.

[4] April 15. See, also, the *Examiner* of April 17, 25. "In the latter days the convention had secret meetings. The women and children are not admitted, and it is from them and the press that the little practical sense hitherto exhibited by its members has been derived. No one who has not witnessed it can conceive the amount of outside pressure to which, from the first day of its session, the convention has been subjected. But for this it would hardly have taken ground against coercion."—Ibid., May 2. Likewise the Richmond *Enquirer*, April 13, and the Richmond *Dispatch*, April 15. But the Richmond *Whig*, May 3, said the convention "was fully abreast, if not ahead, of public sentiment. . . . An ordinance of secession in the month of February would have met a prompt rejection at the polls." "The masses of the people were really ahead of their leaders" in Virginia as well as in Georgia.—Stephens's War between the States, vol. ii. p. 389. "In Virginia the 'leaders' of the people had been opposed to the secession of the State."—General D. H. Maury, Southern Historical Society Papers, vol. i. p. 426.

ordinance had been taken nine delegates changed their votes from the negative to the affirmative, and six who had not answered to their names obtained leave to record their voices for secession. The final vote then stood 103 to 46.[1] The proceedings were not unattended with emotion. One delegate when speaking against the ordinance broke down in impassioned and incoherent sobs. Another, who voted for it, at the thought of rending the ancient ties wept like a child.[2] Many delegates who had strenuously opposed secession now bowed to the will of the majority, and were ready to devote their lives and their fortunes to their State. Such an one was Stuart, who in a public letter urged all good citizens " to stand together as one man." [3] Another was Baldwin, who, when asked by a Northern politician, " What will the Union men of Virginia do now?" replied : " There are no Union men left in Virginia. We stand this day a united people, ready . . . to make good the eternal separation which we have declared. . . . We will give you a fight which will stand out upon the page of history." [4] For the eastern part of the State Baldwin spoke truly.[5] The mountains were the dividing line between union and secession. Many of the delegates from west of the Alleghanies remained loyal to the national government and began organizing a movement to hold their section with the North. East of the mountains sympathy with the States farther

---

[1] For the names in detail see Richmond *Examiner*, June 17 ; see, also, Letters and Times of the Tylers, vol. ii. p. 641; Richmond *Whig*, June 14, which states that one half of the 46 signed the original parchment copy of the ordinance.　　　　　　　　　　[2] Richmond *Examiner*, April 17.

[3] Cited in Greeley's American Conflict, vol. i. p. 478.

[4] John B. Baldwin to G. B. Manley, May 10, Richmond *Dispatch*, May 16 ; see, also, article of R. L. Dabney, Southern Historical Society Papers, vol. i. p. 443.

[5] " Eastern Virginia is a unit for instant and eternal resistance."—Richmond *Whig*, April 18, also April 19. " The expression of sentiment is wellnigh unanimous in favor of the maintenance of Southern rights."—Richmond *Enquirer*, April 17, also April 19; likewise Richmond *Examiner*, April 17, 18.

south determined the action of a majority, while the sentiment that patriotism meant devotion to one's State carried
along the rest.[1] In Virginia the opinion that the States
were sovereign was strongly held; but many, denying that
she had the constitutional right to secede, placed her action
on the ground of justifiable revolution.[2] The popular vote
on the ordinance of secession of May 23 resulted as might
have been expected, a majority of 96,750 being given for its
ratification; the 32,134 votes cast against it came mostly
from the western counties.[3]

---

[1] "The unanimity of the people was simply marvellous. So long as the
question of secession was under discussion, opinions were both various
and violent. The moment secession was finally determined upon, a revolution was wrought. There was no longer anything to discuss, and so
discussion ceased. Men got ready for war, and delicate women with equal
spirit sent them off with smiling faces."—Eggleston's A Rebel's Recollections, p. 47.

[2] See Baldwin's letter of May 10; also his testimony before a congressional committee in 1866, Reports of committees, 1st Sess. 39th Cong., vol.
ii. p. 107.

[3] Governor Letcher's proclamation of June 14, with returns of the counties appended thereto, Richmond Enquirer, June 18; Richmond Whig,
June 17. This was a total vote of 161,018 against 167,223 at the presidential election of 1860. The Richmond Whig said: "This is the largest popular vote ever cast in the State for any proposition." For the charge of
intimidation in this election see New York Tribune, May 24, and Greeley's
American Conflict, vol. i. p. 479, which compare with the following from
the Richmond Examiner of May 24 and 25: "The latest accounts from
northwestern Virginia lead us to apprehend that a very heavy vote was
yesterday cast in that country against the ordinance of secession. It was
intimated that the feeling was so strong in particular portions of that district that the secession vote would not be allowed to be cast at all. . . .
When the judges of election are all on one side, when the popular feeling
is so excited as to stifle the freedom of suffrage, when the moral sense is
likely to be corrupted by the contaminating contact of Pennsylvania and
Ohio, we may very reasonably expect that great frauds may have been prac-
tised upon the ballot-box. Abolitionism knows no law in its war upon the
South. Its 'higher law' authorizes all the maxims of morality, religion,
honesty, justice, and honor to be set aside. If, therefore, any point of advantage can be gained by ballot-box stuffing and kindred election frauds,
we are apprehensive that these pernicious arts of Northern chicanery and
malice had their advent in Virginia in yesterday's election." "Had a few

In Baltimore and in Maryland the frenzy of opposition to
the efforts of the national government to insure the safety
of its capital did not last for a week after the attack on the
Massachusetts Sixth; from the date of the arrival of the
New York Seventh at Washington it began rapidly to sub-
side.[1] The railroad from Annapolis to the Junction was put
in good repair, and the line through to Washington guarded;
by this route troops were daily transported. Soon the capital was secure against any possible attack, but the increase
of its army went on,[2] with the design in view of making, at
the proper time, the forward movement demanded by the
President's proclamation. Thoroughly loyal to the Union
and distrusting his legislature, Governor Hicks was loath to
convene it; but during the excitement, either because he
could not resist the pressure or because he was forced to a
choice of evils, he summoned it to meet April 26; afterwards,
for the reason that Annapolis, the capital, was occupied by
federal troops, he changed the place of meeting to Frederick City, discreetly selecting a town where Union sentiment
dominated, instead of Baltimore, the more natural meeting-
point.[3]   "I honestly and most earnestly entertain the con-

_____

regiments of Southern troops been sent to the Northwest, the result there
would have been very different.   The majority of the citizens, even in
that section, are certainly true to Virginia.   But they were frightened.
They believed that Lincoln and his myrmidons would instantly seize them
if they appeared at the polls.   It was a sense of insecurity, not abolitionism, that carried the Northwest against the ordinance."

[1] Baltimore *Sun*, cited by New York *Times*, April 27; New York *Courier
and Enquirer*, April 28; Moore's Rebellion Record, vol. i., Diary, pp. 46, 47;
Appletons' Annual Cyclopædia, 1861, p. 446.

[2] The city "begins to be a camp."—Seward to his wife, April 27, Life of
Seward, vol. ii. p. 560.

[3] See Appletons' Annual Cyclopædia, 1861, p. 445; Moore's Rebellion
Record, vol. i., Docs., p. 175.   Reverdy Johnson, in writing from Frederick
City, May 8, to Secretary Chase (Chase Papers, MS.), says, "The envelope
(the only one I can obtain) will show the Union feeling."   Reference is made
to one of the envelopes, very common at the beginning of the war, which
had designs and mottoes printed upon them exhibiting strong Union sentiments.   An interesting and instructive collection of these, containing also
envelopes testifying to the Southern cause, the gift of Miss Wing, is in the

viction," he said in his message, "that the only safety of
Maryland lies in preserving a neutral position between our
brethren of the North and of the South." [1] The legislature adopted a policy of neutrality; it decided that it had
no constitutional power to pass an ordinance of secession;
nevertheless, it called no convention; at the same time the
House protested against the war, implored the President
to make peace, and declared that Maryland desired the
" immediate recognition of the independence of the Confederate States." [2] The legislature adjourning without having made one step towards secession, Maryland remained
officially attached to the federal government, with the result that here the doctrine of state-rights operated on the
side of the Union, by influencing its adherents to abide by
the action of their State. But the governor and the people
more than the legislature sympathized with the North.
" The Union sentiment gets stronger and stronger," wrote
Reverdy Johnson. [3] May 9 federal troops on their way to
Washington passed unmolested through Baltimore; these,
the first to make the attempt since the trouble of April 19,
were brought by transports from Perryville. Four days
later the first train from Philadelphia arrived at the capital,
and shortly afterwards regular railroad communication with
the Northern cities, for passengers as well as for the military,
was re-established. [4] Whittingham, the Episcopal bishop of
Maryland, rebuked clergymen who had omitted the prayer
for the President of the United States, and admonished
them that the offence must not continue. [5] It became evident that the secessionists, although an influential minority,
were losing their hold on the waverers, who waited before

Boston Athenæum.   I desire here to acknowledge my indebtedness to Miss
Wyman, of that library, for her intelligent aid.
    [1] Appletons' Annual Cyclopædia, 1861, p. 446.
    [2] Ibid.; McPherson, p. 9.   [3] To Chase, May 8, Chase Papers, MS.
    [4] Nicolay and Hay, vol. iv. p. 172 ; National Intelligencer, May 16.
    [5] Circular of May 15, New York Times, cited by Moore, Rebellion Record,
vol. i., Docs., p. 252.

declaring themselves, to see on which side were the strongest
battalions.[1] By the middle of May Maryland was actively on
the side of the North. Pursuant to the President's proclamation of April 15, and by a subsequent arrangement with
the Secretary of War, Governor Hicks called for four regiments to serve within the limits of Maryland or for the defence of the capital, under the orders of the commander-in-
chief of the United States army ; the response to this call
was prompt.[2] The election for members of Congress in
June, when Union men were chosen in all of the six districts, put to rest any doubts regarding the position of
Maryland.[3] This happy issue out of the trouble and gloom
which proceeded from the collision of the Baltimore populace with the Massachusetts troops was in a large degree
due to the wisdom with which the President, pursuing a
conciliatory but firm policy, had handled affairs ; it was his
generals who, when left to a certain discretion, overstepped
the limits he had marked out for himself, as did Butler in
occupying Baltimore by the military, a course inexpedient
in the opinion of Reverdy Johnson, a true Union man,[4] and
one which brought forth a rebuke from General Scott ; and
as did Cadwallader in suspending the privilege of the writ

[1] The columns of the Baltimore *Daily Exchange*, which argued that both
sympathy and commercial interest should impel Maryland to join the
South, reflect in a striking manner the fading of the hopes of those who
ardently sympathized with the Southern Confederacy.

[2] The date of the governor's call was May 14, New York *Times*, cited
by Moore, Rebellion Record, vol. i., Docs., p. 245 ; see, also, Nicolay and
Hay, vol. iv. p. 174.

[3] *Tribune* Almanac, 1862, p. 59 ; Baltimore *Daily Exchange*, June 17.

[4] Johnson said, in a private letter to Chase of May 8, giving him permission to show it to the President : " In the present condition of Baltimore
and the State, the governor thinks (and I concur with him) that even one
company of United States soldiers in the city would be more mischievous
than otherwise. Indeed, he does not believe, nor do I, that it is necessary
to the protection of the government property, or the assertion of any of
its rights, to have any such force there, and I should advise against it. If
the troops pass through the city without resistance, as it is thought they
will, it will be evident that no such force would be required."—Chase
Papers, MS.

of habeas corpus at Baltimore, and in causing a conflict between the President and Chief Justice Taney.[1]

In answer to the President's call for State militia, Governor Magoffin telegraphed, "Kentucky will furnish no troops for the wicked purpose of subduing her sister Southern States," and at once summoned his legislature to meet in special session on the 6th of May. So far Magoffin represented the sentiment of his State, but in his desire of having her secede and join the Southern Confederacy, he was no true exponent of that sentiment. Like her mother Virginia, Kentucky was drawn in two ways. Sympathy, blood, and the community of social feeling growing out of slavery, inclined her to the South; her political faith, which Clay more than any other man had inspired her with, and which Crittenden now loyally represented, held her fast to the Union. While there were unconditional secessionists and unconditional Union men, a majority of the people, though believing in state-rights, thought that the grievances of the Southern States were not grave enough to justify secession; at the same time they opposed coercion, and since a re-cemented Union by compromise was plainly impossible, they would have solved the difficulty by peaceable separation. The course of public sentiment was very like that of Virginia up to the parting of the ways; and as most of the political leaders of ability were with the South, it is easy to see that a little change in circumstances, a little alteration of the direction of feeling, might in the end have impelled Kentucky to take up arms for the Confederacy instead of for the Union. By the 6th of May, when the legislature met, there had been evolved out of conflicting opinions and purposes the idea that the proper course for the commonwealth was neutrality. This imported that her soil should be held sacred against invasion by either of the contending parties, and the House, by resolution, gave an official stamp to the sentiment. Impracticable as this course turned out to be, it

---

[1] Tyler's Taney, p. 420.

deserves respect as an attempt to adhere to principle without breaking the heartstrings. In the succession of events neutrality was found to be impossible, and Kentucky chose the Union side; yet we may honor her the more that she retained a tenderness for the mother and sister States, and felt the bitterness of regret that events had so fallen out that she must make so hard a choice. President Lincoln knew his native State well. Selecting several of her well-known and honest citizens to co-operate with him, and holding himself amenable to counsel, he guided the Union movement, now openly, now with an unseen hand; at other times waiting with patience and refraining from direction, he had in the end the gratification of seeing, as a result of his policy, Kentucky actively on the Northern side. In June nine out of ten anti-secession congressmen were elected, the Union majority in the State being 54,700; in August a strong Union legislature was chosen, which, in response to the invasion of the State by the Confederate forces in September, ordered the United States flag raised over the Capitol at Frankfort, and, by resolutions that affirmed distinctly, though indirectly, the doctrine of state-rights, placed Kentucky in political and military association with the North.'

---

[1] For the account of public sentiment in Kentucky I have relied mainly on Shaler's Kentucky, and have also drawn several of the facts stated from that work, of which, in this connection, the whole of chap. xv. should be read. On Lincoln's action see Nicolay and Hay, vol. iv. chap. xii. The speeches of Guthrie and Dixon, and the resolutions adopted at the public meeting in Louisville, April 18, may be read with profit, Moore's Rebellion Record, vol. i., Docs., p. 72 ; Magoffin's proclamation of May 20, ibid., p. 264 ; see, also, Appletons' Annual Cyclopædia, 1861. Garrett Davis, afterwards senator from Kentucky, wrote General McClellan, June 8, twelve days before the congressional election : " The sympathy for the South and the inclination to secession among our people is much stronger in the southwestern corner of the State than it is in any other part, and as you proceed towards the upper section of the Ohio River and our Virginia line it gradually becomes weaker, until it is almost wholly lost. . . . I doubt not that two-thirds of our people are unconditionally for the Union. The timid and quiet are for it, and they shrink from convulsion and civil war, whilst all the bold, the reckless, and the bankrupt are for secession."—Official Records, vol. ii. p. 678.

The Missouri convention had in March declared against secession by a vote of 89 to 1 ; this was then a fair index of public sentiment, but after Sumter and the President's call for troops, when war became inevitable, there were many of her citizens who thought that Missouri should espouse the cause of the Confederacy. This was not from any special devotion to slavery, for in Missouri the institution had not the political and social power that it had in nearly all the other slave States, the ratio of her slave population to the whole being less than in any of them except Delaware ; it was rather from the friendly, family, and political ties binding her to the South. Southern sympathy moreover exhibited strength, for the reason that it found a head in Governor Jackson, who gave it expression in speech and action. To the President's call for State militia he answered, " Your requisition, in my judgment, is illegal, unconstitutional, and revolutionary in its object, inhuman and diabolical, and cannot be complied with." [1] The leader of the Union men was Francis P. Blair, Jr., a man of extraordinary physical and moral courage, of high social position in St. Louis, and possessing great personal popularity. In conjunction with Captain Lyon he had already organized four regiments as a home guard ; these were largely constituted from the companies of Wide-awakes of the previous political campaign, and were mainly composed of Germans— a large element in the population of St. Louis—who in their opposition to slavery and devotion to the Union were not, like many Missourians, troubled as to whether their paramount allegiance was due to their State or to the national government. Blair now offered these four regiments to the Secretary of War as Missouri's quota; five regiments were sworn in and the command of them given to Lyon. The story of Missouri for the next four months is of a contest between Blair and Jackson—a contest of political

---

[1] April 17, Official Records, Series iii., cited by Nicolay and Hay, vol. iv. p. 90.

management, of martial proceeding, and of battle. Blair showed great political ability, and assisted by Lyon, who had military talent and whose forces constantly increased, made steady progress. St. Louis was soon gained and the Union sentiment in the State grew rapidly. July 30 the convention, sitting at Jefferson City, the capital, deposed Governor Jackson, appointed Gamble, a Union man, in his stead, and in other ways brought the machinery of the State government to the support of the Union cause. Though this did not end the fight for Missouri, yet she was henceforward officially as well as in dominant sentiment on the side of the North.[1]

There was at no time any fear of the secession of Delaware. Her interest in slavery was small. Slaves formed but an insignificant fraction of her population, and since 1830 had steadily declined in number and in ratio to the whites. Her governor, not deeming that he had legal authority to offer her militia to the President, recommended the formation of volunteer companies to comply with his requisition. Accordingly one regiment, her quota, was promptly formed and mustered into the service of the United States.

The days in which the President was shut up in Washington, cut off from communication with the States which were his support, were days when the task that had been forced upon him seemed heavy indeed. But he was fast learning the lessons of war. He began making preparations for a long conflict. More volunteers offering than were necessary to fill the call for 75,000, and more than were desired for only three months' service, he determined to utilize this outburst of patriotism by enlisting men for three years, and sent advices to that effect to the governors of the different States.[2] May 3 he issued a proclamation calling for 42,034

---

[1] In this account I have mainly followed Carr's Missouri, of which, in this connection, chaps. xiii. and xiv. should be read. See, also, The Fight for Missouri, Snead ; Nicolay and Hay, vol. iv. chap. xi.

[2] Official Records, Series iii., cited by Nicolay and Hay, vol. iv. p. 255;

volunteers, to serve for three years unless sooner discharged; he directed an increase of the regular army of 22,714 men and the enlistment of 18,000 seamen for the naval service.[1] Such action, though clearly beyond the President's constitutional authority, received the approval of the North. Previously to this he had extended the blockade to Virginia and North Carolina.[2]

" The declaration of war against this Confederacy," issued by the President of the United States, said Jefferson Davis, in his message to his congress, referring to the call for 75,000 troops, " prompted me to convoke you " in special session.[3] Accordingly, the delegates met April 29 at Montgomery. Their legislation was bellicose. They passed an act recognizing the existence of war between the United States and the Confederate States, and authorizing their president to issue letters of marque and reprisal.[4] Davis

---

see correspondence between Chandler and Cameron, Life of Chandler, Detroit *Post and Tribune*, p. 205.

[1] Moore's Rebellion Record, vol. i., Docs., p. 185.   Filling these calls made the army establishment as follows :

Regular army (Report, April 5)	. .	17,113	
Call of May 3	22,714		39,827
Volunteers—Call of April 15 . . .	75,000		
Call of May 3 . . .	42,034		117,034
Regular navy (March 4) . .	7,600		
Call of May 3	18,000		156,861
	25,600		

Nicolay and Hay, vol. iv. p. 255, note.

[2] Moore's Rebellion Record, vol. i., Docs., p. 161.   [3] Ibid., p. 171.

[4] Statutes at Large, Provisional Government C. S. A., p. 100, passed May 6.   W. H. Russell wrote the London *Times* from Montgomery, May 7: " Already numerous applications have been received from the ship-owners of New England, from the whalers of New Bedford, and from others in the Northern States for these very letters of marque, accompanied by the highest securities and guarantees! This statement I make on the very highest authority." I question the truth of this statement.   A search in the Confederate Archives in the Treasury Department, Washington, discloses sixty-seven applications for letters of marque and reprisal.   The owners, captains, and bondsmen of the vessels asking these letters are from Texas, North and South Carolina, Virginia, Louisiana, Tennessee,

informed them that he had in the field in various localities 19,000 men, that 16,000 more were on the way to Virginia, and that it was proposed to organize an army of 100,000,[1] for which volunteers were offering in excess of his wants. Five days after Lincoln by proclamation had decreed an increase of the Union force, the Confederate congress authorized Davis to accept without limit volunteers " to serve for and during the existing war." [2]   It also authorized a loan of fifty million dollars, which might be raised by the sale of eight per cent. bonds, or twenty millions of it might be obtained by the issue of treasury notes without interest; the notes should be receivable for all debts and taxes due the Confederate States except the export duty on cotton; the bonds were " to be sold for specie, military stores, or for the proceeds of sales of raw produce or manufactured articles." [3]   It prohibited, pending the war, all persons from paying their debts to individuals or corporations in the United States, except in Delaware, Maryland, Kentucky, Missouri, and the District of Columbia, and it authorized them to pay the amount of their indebtedness into the treasury of the Confederate States, receiving therefor a treasurer's certificate, redeemable on the restoration of peace.[4]   It prohibited the export of cotton except through the seaports.[5] It admitted Virginia, North Carolina, Tennessee, and Arkansas into the Confederacy, and, accepting an invitation from the Virginia convention, made Richmond the capital of the new government, adjourning to meet there July 20.[6]

Florida, Georgia, Alabama, and three from Baltimore, and one from Wilmington, Delaware, but none from farther north.   The New York *Tribune* of June 17 denied the story.

[1] This was under the authority of an act passed at the first session of the provisional congress, *ante*, p. 294.

[2] Statutes at Large, Provisional Government C. S. A., p. 104, passed May 8.   [3] Ibid., p. 117, passed May 16.

[4] Ibid., p. 151, passed May 21.   [5] Ibid., p. 152, passed May 21.

[6] Ibid., pp. 104, 118, 119, 120, 165.   As to the action of the Virginia convention see Richmond *Examiner*, April 30.   This congress enacted a strictly revenue tariff which possesses little interest, as the federal block-

The Union of twenty-three States and the Confederacy of eleven [1] were now arrayed against each other. Twenty-two million people confronted nine million, and of the nine million three and a half million were slaves.[2] The proportion was nearly that of five to two. The Union had much greater wealth, was a country of a complex civilization, and boasted of its varied industries; it combined the farm, the shop, and the factory. The Confederacy was but a farm, dependent on Europe and on the North for everything but bread and meat, and before the war for much of those. The North had the money market, and could borrow with greater ease than the South. It was the iron age. The North had done much to develop its wealth of iron, that potent aid of civilization, that necessity of war; the South had scarcely touched its own mineral resources. In nearly every Northern regiment were mechanics of all kinds and men of business training accustomed to system, while the Southern army was made up of gentlemen and poor whites, splendid fighters, of rare courage and striking devotion, but as a whole inferior in education and in a knowledge of the arts and appliances of modern life to the men of the North.[3]

---

ade was so effective that it brought little revenue. The duties on all articles but two were *ad valorem*, ranging from 5 to 25 per cent. The free list was largely made up of articles of food, war materials, and other things of necessity for the prosecution of the war. For the tariff, see Statutes, p. 127.

[1] South Carolina, Georgia, Florida, Alabama, Mississippi, Louisiana, Texas, Arkansas, Virginia, North Carolina, Tennessee.

[2] These are the totals of population of the seceding and non-seceding States by the census of 1860; but the computation is not absolutely exact, for western Virginia remained with the Union. But western Virginia, Maryland, Kentucky, and Missouri furnished more soldiers for the Confederates than western North Carolina and eastern Tennessee gave to the Union. The subject of relative population and wealth is clearly discussed by Professor A. B. Hart in the *New England Magazine* for November, 1891, reprinted in Practical Essays on American Government.

[3] What Everett said of the volunteers of Massachusetts may be applied to the whole Northern army. "They have hurried from the lawyer's office, from the counting-room, from the artist's studio, in instances not a

The Union had the advantage of the regular army and
navy, of the flag, and of the prestige and machinery of
the national government:[1] the ministers from foreign countries were accredited to the United States; the archives
of what had been the common government were also in
the possession of the Union.[2] The aim of the Confederacy
was to gain its independence. Davis, in the message of
April 29 to his congress, expressed the sincere purpose of
the Southern people. "We feel that our cause is just and
holy," he declared. "We protest solemnly in the face of
mankind that we desire peace at any sacrifice save that
of honor. In independence we seek no conquest, no ag-
grandizement, no cession of any kind from the States with
which we have lately confederated. All we ask is to be
let alone—that those who never held power over us shall
not now attempt our subjugation by arms. This we will,
we must resist, to the direst extremity."[3] The aim of the
North was to save the Union, to maintain the integrity of
the nation. The Confederates, the President said in his
Fourth-of-July message, "forced upon the country the distinct issue 'immediate·dissolution or blood'. . . It was with
the deepest regret," he further declared, "that the executive found the duty of employing the war power in defence

---

few from the pulpit; they have left the fisher's line upon the reel, the plough
in the furrow, the plane upon the work-bench, the hammer on the anvil,
the form upon the printing-press—there is not a mechanical art nor a useful handicraft that has not its experts in these patriotic ranks."—Moore's
Rebellion Record, vol. i., Docs., p. 206.

[1] "It is worthy of note, that while in this the government's hour of trial
large numbers of those in the army and navy who have been favored with
the offices have resigned and proved false to the hand which had pampered them, not one common soldier or common sailor is known to have
deserted his flag."—Lincoln's Fourth-of-July message. "Of 4470 officers
in the public service, civil and military, 2154 were representatives of States
where the revolutionary movement was openly advocated and urged, even
if not actually organized."—Seward to Adams, April 10.

[2] That these advantages were appreciated by some in England is seen
by an article in the London *Times* of April 27, Moore's Rebellion Record, vol. i., Docs., p. 228.   [3] Ibid., p. 174.

of the government forced upon him. He could but perform this duty or surrender the existence of the government." From Davis's message we may clearly see that
the doctrine of state - rights would not have been carried
in 1861 to the point of secession, had it not been for the
purpose of repelling what was considered an aggression on
slavery. No one knew this better than Lincoln,[1] but in
his message there is not a word concerning the subject, and
the reason is apparent. Restricting the object of the war
to the restoration of the Union, he had with him Democrats and Bell and Everett men, as well as Republicans;
a mention of slavery would at once have aroused the contentions of party.

Many at the South thought that when it came to the
supreme test the North would not fight. Assuming even
that the Republicans might be ready to take up arms, they
believed that the Democrats and conservatives would earnestly oppose an attempt to conquer the seceding States,
and so hamper the dominant party that it would be unable to carry out its designs.[2] These became disenchanted
as they witnessed the uprising of the North, and bewildered
as they saw man after man of distinction on whom they
had counted giving in his adherence to the Lincoln government because of the attack on the flag.[3] Had the Con-

---

[1] See Lincoln's pregnant statement to John Hay, May 7, Nicolay and
Hay, vol. iv. p. 258.

[2] Many Democratic newspapers and the speeches and resolutions of several Democratic meetings had given a certain support to this notion.

[3] "The North seems to be thoroughly united against us. The *Herald* and
the *Express* both give way and rally the hosts against us. Things have
gone to that point in Philadelphia that no one is safe in the expression of a
Southern sentiment."—Ex-President Tyler to his wife, April 18, Letters
and Times of the Tylers, vol. ii. p. 641. "Where are Messrs. Fillmore,
Everett, Winthrop, Cushing, Butler, and Hallet, of Boston; Van Buren,
Cochran, McKeon, Weed, Dix, and Barnard, of New York ; Ingersoll, Wilkins, Binney, Black, Bigler, and ex-President Buchanan, of Pennsylvania;
Douglas *et id omne genus*—Democrats and Whigs of all stripes, hues, and
conditions—where are they in the bloody crusade proposed by President
Lincoln against the South? Unheard of in their dignified retirement! or

federates foreseen that they would at the very first confront
a practically united North, they would have hesitated more
than they did to strike the irrevocable blow. Nevertheless, as a large majority believed in the constitutional right
of secession, the war on the part of the national government seemed to them a war of subjugation. The North
had fastened a stigma on their property, and when they
availed themselves of that safeguard of the minority which,

---

hounding on the fanatic warfare, or themselves joining 'the noble army
of martyrs for liberty' marching on the South. The New York *Herald*,
but yesterday denouncing the 'bloody disunionism of President Lincoln's
administration,' now declares triumphantly that 'the whole North is of
one party, and that party is to conquer and subdue the South.'"—Charleston *Mercury*, April 23. "The North is a unit for the Union."—Richmond
correspondence, ibid., May 7. "We are told the whole North is rallying
as one man; Douglas, veering as ever with the popular breeze, conferring
cheek by jowl with Lincoln; Buchanan lifting a treacherous and time-
serving voice of encouragement from the icy atmosphere of Wheatland;
well-fed and well-paid Fillmore, eating up all his past words of indignation
for Southern injuries, and joining in the popular hue-and-cry against his
special benefactors; and even poor old Cass, with better heart than them
all, but with mind spent with age, doting over recollections of Jackson
and the Force bill, mistaking the Baboon of '61 for the Lion of '32, and
shouting the hurrahs of thirty years ago."—Richmond *Examiner*, April 22.
"It can no longer be denied that the North is a unit against the South.
They are not only as one man for upholding Lincoln, but as one man
for invasion and conquest. The proposition to *subjugate* comes from the
metropolis of her boasted conservatism, even from the largest beneficiary
of Southern wealth, New York City."—Ibid., April 24. "The sentiment
which pervades the Northern Republican press is most ferocious towards
the South. . . . The tone of the conservative press, too, has undergone
a very marked change. Most of them have caved in—not exactly to approbation of the war policy of the Republicans, but to an admission,
which amounts to the same thing, of the necessity of sustaining the
government."—Richmond *Whig*, April 17. "The statesmen of the North,
heretofore most honored and confided in by the South, have come out
unequivocally in favor of the Lincoln policy of coercing and subjugating
the South."—Richmond *Enquirer*, April 26. Mention is made of Fillmore,
Cass, Buchanan, Douglas, B. F. Butler. See, also, ibid., April 30, article
entitled "Our Northern Allies," where Everett, Cushing, and D. S. Dickinson are spoken of. It ends with: "The Northern politicians have all left
us. 'Let them fly—all, false thanes!'"

according to their view, was intended by the fathers, it
tried to compel them by force to remain in the Union.
The Southern literature of this period is pervaded with two
notions which were fused into the public sentiment: that
their fight was for their property and their liberties, and
that it was against spoliation and conquest. This sentiment, sincerely held by the statesmen, politicians, and
journalists, was translated into vituperative language to
excite the populace.[1] All held the opinion that the North

---

[1] "The soldiery of New England, carrying out the decrees of that miserable despot who, without the character of George the Third, would doom
the people from the Capitol at Washington, . . . fire upon the populace at Baltimore, having penetrated in armed bands to the heart of a
Southern city for the purpose of subjugating the South."—Charleston
Mercury, April 23; Pickens in a proclamation speaks of "Northern
Goths and Vandals."—Ibid., April 27; "The Northern people were
mere plunderers in peace; and now become murderers in war. From
persecutors they have become bloody tyrants, ready to destroy us to sub-
serve the foul purposes of their sectional domination. . . . Their arms
must be weakened by a consciousness of injustice and criminality. Let
yours be strengthened by the holy conviction that you strike for your
homes, your institutions, your all."—Ibid., May 7; "Let the fathers,
mothers, sons, and brothers of Richmond and Charleston, Raleigh and
Savannah, Mobile and New Orleans, look to the treatment of the women
and the people of Washington and Baltimore, at the mercy of the gross-
est ruffians from the stews of New York, Philadelphia, and Boston.
Hearken to their *cri de guerre*, 'Beauty and Booty.' Hear them declare
that the war is one of conquest, spoil, and extermination."—Ibid., May
16; "The Northern troops, like Falstaff's ragged regiment, are made up
of 'the canker of a bad world and a long peace;' of ignorant unem-
ployed foreigners, loafers, criminals, and desperadoes. . . . But if conquered and subjugated, we should soon be massacred, and another St.
Domingo tragedy would darken the pages of history. . . . The troops of
our enemies are composed of men without honor, honesty, or morality,
and are impelled to fight by not a single worthy or respectable motive.
They possess no other courage except that desperation which crime,
poverty, and misfortune sometimes endow bad men with, and who, like the
murderer in Macbeth, become willing for the moment to 'set their life on
any chance to mend it or get rid on it.'"—Richmond *Examiner*, April 26;
"The war which the Lincoln administration has begun upon the Southern
States is the most unnecessary and wicked war which ambition or lust
has ever inaugurated."—Richmond *Whig*, April 15; the Richmond *En-*

was unconstitutionally and unjustly attempting to make
sovereign States do that which they had deliberately resolved not to do. With such an idea thoroughly diffused
among an Anglo-Saxon people, one might have known that
resistance would be long and stubborn. The Confederates
were by no means dismayed at the realization of the united
North and the appreciation of the odds of number and
wealth against them. "The numbers opposed to us are
immense," wrote ex-President Tyler; "but twelve thousand
Grecians conquered the whole power of Xerxes [*sic*] at
Marathon, and our fathers, a mere handful, overcame the
enormous power of Great Britain."[1] "Has the strongest
nation in capital and population always prevailed in the
contest between nations?" asked the Charleston *Mercury*.
"Did Philip of Spain or Louis XIV. of France subdue
Holland? Did Great Britain subdue our ancestors in
1776?"[2] Nevertheless, in making the effort to gain their
independence the Confederates had undertaken a stupendous task; they had started out on a road the end of which

quirer, April 25, thus describes the Northern army: "Discharged operatives, street loafers, penniless adventurers, and vagrants fill up the ranks
of the Yankee regiments. The 'solid men' of the North, their sons and
relations, prudently keep out of the reach of danger, while they send the
floating scum of free society to do the work of vandals and marauders."
"War . . . has been forced upon us by the folly and fanaticism of the
Northern abolitionists, whose sole end and aim it is to aggress upon the
rights and property of the people of the South. . . . We fight for our
liberties, our independence, our altars, our firesides, our wives, and our
children."—Atlanta *Weekly Intelligencer*, May 11. These are fair ex-
amples of journalistic utterances. Stephens said at Atlanta, May 23
(Moore's Rebellion Record, vol. i., Docs., p. 271): "The acts of Lincoln
exhibit the spirit of anarchy which is abroad in the North, and total
disregard of all constitutional obligations and limits by the abolition
despot now in power. The North is fast drifting to anarchy and an
established despotism." Davis said, June 1, at Richmond: "To the
enemy we leave the base acts of the assassin and incendiary, to them we
leave it to insult helpless women; to us belongs vengeance upon man."
—Moore's Rebellion Record, vol. i., Docs., p. 323.
[1] Letter of April 18, Letters and Times of the Tylers, vol ii. p. 641.
[2] May 10.

was at best doubtful; they had gone to an extreme, before proceeding to which it had been better to endure somewhat of grievance. Their fight, they averred, was made for liberty, and yet they were weighted by the denial of liberty to three and one half million human beings. They had the distinction of being the only community of the Teutonic race which did not deem negro slavery wrong; in their social theory they had parted company with England, France, Germany, and Italy, and were at one with Spain and Brazil.

On the other hand, what a great work had the Northern men set out to do![1] They had undertaken to conquer the wills of five and one half million people—a community equal to themselves except, owing to their peculiar institution, in the arts and manufactures, in business training, and in scientific thought. There was undoubtedly a basis for the Southern opinion that in certain qualities which go to make up the soldier the men of the South were superior to those of the North. An intelligent observer who left Mississippi early in June, and travelled through Tennessee, expressed the belief to Garrett Davis " that the Southern men had much greater skill in the use of small-arms, superiority in horsemanship, and were more alert and spirited than Northern men, and that when they were anything like equal in numbers they would be victorious, especially in the early

---

[1] Russell wrote the London *Times* from Montgomery, May 16: "I expressed a belief in my first letter, written a few days after my arrival, March 27, that the South would never go back into the Union. The North thinks that it can coerce the South, and I am not prepared to say they are right or wrong ; but I am convinced that the South can only be forced back by such a conquest as that which laid Poland prostrate at the feet of Russia;" and from New Orleans, May 24: "It is impossible to resist the conviction that the Southern Confederacy can only be conquered by means as irresistible as those by which Poland was subjugated. The South will fall, if at all, as a nation prostrate at the feet of a victorious enemy. There is no doubt of the unanimity of the people. If words mean anything, they are animated by only one sentiment, and they will resist the North as long as they can command a man or a dollar."

battles." [1]   The nature of the case made it an offensive warfare on the part of the North.   " The first service assigned
to the forces hereby called forth," declared the President in
his proclamation of April 15, " will probably be to repossess
the forts, places, and property which have been seized from
the Union."   To perform this service the national troops
must march into the States of the Confederacy ; the fighting must be on Southern soil.   Not the defence of Washington, but the taking of Richmond, was their task.   For such
warfare the proportion of five to two in population was
none too great, the odds of wealth and industrial activities
were none too large.   Had they been less the North might
have failed.   In truth, the expectation of the South that
by an exchange of its cotton with Europe it would be able
to supply itself with the implements and munitions of war
and the necessaries of life, was not extravagant.[2]   Had the
North thoroughly understood the problem ; had it known
that the people in the cotton States were practically unanimous; that the action of Virginia, North Carolina, and Tennessee was backed by a large and genuine majority, it
might have refused to undertake the seemingly unachiev-
able task.   For while hardly a man at the North assented
to the constitutional right of secession, all acknowledged the
right of revolution ;[3] and had they been convinced that the
action of the Southern States represented the free and un-
trammelled will of the Southern people, many would have
objected to combating that right ; arguing that even if the
action of the men of the South was unjust and founded upon
a wrong, it was not incumbent on the North to war upon

[1] Garrett Davis to General McClellan, June 8, Official Records, vol. ii.
p. 677.   This was also Russell's opinion, Diary, p. 340.

[2] The efficiency of the blockade in making this hope vain was a mighty
instrument on the Northern side.   This is well stated by Professor A. B.
Hart in a thoughtful article on the subject in the *New England Magazine*
for November, 1891, p. 369.

[3] Many in Virginia justified her action on the right of revolution, *ante*.
The Declaration of Independence of Tennessee was based on the right of
revolution.

them because they would not see the light and walk in it. In such a case the national idea, the feeling that the country must not physically be dismembered, would have lost much of its force.

It is impossible to escape the conviction that the action of the North was largely based on a misconception of the strength of the disunion sentiment in the Confederate States. The Northern people accepted the gage of war and came to the support of the President on the theory that a majority in all of the Southern States except South Carolina were at heart for the Union, and that if these loyal men were encouraged and protected they would make themselves felt in a movement looking towards allegiance to the national government.[1] By the 4th of July Lincoln knew the

---

[1] A similar view began to be advocated with great earnestness by Greeley in the New York *Tribune* as early as Jan. 14, and was urged with frequency. He held that notion during the war. In the first volume of the American Conflict, written between July, 1863, and April, 1864, he said: "No rational doubt can exist that, had time been afforded for consideration and both sides been generally heard, a free and fair vote would have shown an immense majority, even in the slave [cotton?] States, against secession."—p. 515, but compare p. 510. I have already discussed this question at length, and do not consider it necessary to offer evidence in rebuttal; but, as showing that the sentiment of the South at this time was brought to the notice of one of the most distinguished men of the administration in a forcible and sincere manner, I will quote extensively from a letter of May 30 from Mrs. R. L. Hunt, of New Orleans, to Secretary Chase: "Do not delude yourself or others with the notion that war can maintain the Union. Alas, I say it with a heavy heart, the Union is destroyed; it can never be restored. If, indeed, the federal government had frowned upon the first dawning of disunion, things might have been different. But the United States suffered South Carolina to secede without opposition, and with scarcely a murmur of disapprobation. . . . All the Southern States, with the exception of Kentucky, Missouri, and Maryland, have joined in the secession, and have formed themselves into a powerful confederacy of States, with a government possessing all the usual powers of sovereignties, exercising entire and exclusive sway, legislative, executive, and judicial, within the limits of those States, and dissolving all connection with the United States. Having thus by a revolution hitherto almost bloodless assumed and exercised the right of self-government, the Confederate States are now threatened with war and desolation if they do not abjure the government they have formed, and

sentiment of the Northern people as well as any ruler has
ever known a nation's feeling, and he spoke with sincerity
when he addressed the public.   In his message to Congress

renounce forever the right of altering or abolishing that **government**—no
matter how oppressive or despotic it may become.

"The time has passed for a discussion about the territories and fugitive
slaves and the constitutional right of a State to secede.   Secession has
proved to be a revolution, the overthrow of the Constitution, the dissolution of the Union.   Still secession is *un fait accompli*.   Disunion is a fixed
fact.   It is worse than useless to deny or attempt to evade this truth.

"The question, then, to be determined is not, Shall the Union be maintained? but, Shall the Confederate States be allowed to govern themselves?   And this is a question of liberty and free government.

"And how do the statesmen of the North, how do you, my dear brother,
who should recognize facts as they are, propose to deal with this question?
With sword and buckler, the rifle, the bayonet, and the musket, the cannon, and all the dread instruments of war, with infantry and cavalry and
ships and navies and armies!

"With these you propose to subjugate the entire free people of the South,
while you mock them with the declaration that your object is to maintain
a Union which no longer exists.   Is this wise, just, quite in keeping with
the spirit of Christianity and of liberty, and with the lofty character of
the United States?   Would you desire a union of compulsion, a union to
be maintained by the bayonet, a union with hatred and revenge filling the
hearts of the North and of the South?   I hope you would not.   But if
you would, the thing is impossible.   You can never subjugate the South
—never.   Her people are high-spirited, martial, and intelligent.   Educated
in the school of American liberty, they value the right of self-government
above all price. . . .   They view the attempt to conquer them and to compel them to submit to the government of their victors as an effort of
high-handed tyranny and oppression.   You may for the moment have an
advantage in wealth and numbers.   But . . . the North is fighting for subjugation and domination, the South for liberty and independence.   It is
precisely like the great revolutionary struggle of '76 against the tyranny of
Great Britain—a struggle for liberty on one side and for despotism on the
other.   How can you expect victory in such a cause? . . .   Surely eight
millions of people, armed in the holy cause of liberty in such a country as
they possess are invincible by any force the North can send against them.
. . . The South is now united to a man.   There is no division among
the people here.   There is but one mind, one heart, one action.   Do not
suffer yourself to be misled with the idea that there are Union men in
the South.   There is not a man here who will not resist the arms of the
North.   The action of Mr. Lincoln and his cabinet has made them all of
one mind.

at the beginning of the special session, he expressed his own opinion and that of the mass of men whose unreserved support he had. "It may well be questioned," he said,

"I will tell you what I see here in the city. Every night the men are drilling. Young and old, professional men and laborers, lawyers, doctors, and even the ministers are all drilling. The shops are closed at six that the clerks may go to their drilling. The ladies hold fairs, make clothes, lint, etc., for the army, and animate the men by appeals to their chivalry and their patriotism to resist the enemy to the death. What is seen in New Orleans pervades the whole South. Never were a people more united and more determined."—Chase Papers, MS.

Other testimony relating to this time corroborates that of Mrs. Hunt. Garrett Davis wrote General McClellan, June 8, that an intelligent friend just from the South had told him that "the whole Southern people were animated by the most intense hatred against the Northern States and Lincoln's administration."—Official Records, vol. ii. p. 677. William H. Russell, an impartial observer, travelled from April 14 to June 18 through the South. May 11 he wrote the London *Times* from Mobile : "Let there be no mistake whatever as to the unanimity which exists at present in the South to fight for what it calls its independence, and to carry on a war to the knife with the government of the United States." May 12 he set down in his diary: "I have now been in North Carolina, South Carolina, Georgia, Alabama, and in none of these great States have I found the least indication of the Union sentiment or of the attachment for the Union which Mr. Seward always assumes to exist in the South. If there were any considerable amount of it, I was in a position as a neutral to have been aware of its existence."—Diary, p. 192. June 18, having in addition travelled through Mississippi, Louisiana, and Tennessee, he summed up his impressions thus: "So far I had certainly no reason to agree with Mr. Seward in thinking this rebellion was the result of a localized energetic action on the part of a fierce minority in the seceding States, and that there was in each a large, if inert, mass opposed to secession, which would rally round the Stars and Stripes the instant they were displayed in their sight. On the contrary, I met everywhere with but one feeling, with exceptions which proved its unanimity and its force. To a man the people went with their States and had but one battle - cry, 'state - rights, and death to those who make war against them!'

"Day after day I had seen this feeling intensified by the accounts which came from the North of a fixed determination to maintain the war."—Diary, p. 315.

Schleiden, "minister from the Hanseatic towns, well versed in European affairs and a shrewd observer of public men and passing events" (Pierce, vol. iii. p. 601), wrote Sumner May 11: "You foretell in your kind note of the 5th inst. the subjugation of the rebels, and the exile of Jefferson Davis,

"whether there is to-day a majority of the legally qualified voters of any State, except, perhaps, South Carolina, in favor of disunion. There is much reason to believe that the Union men are the majority in many, if not in every other one, of the so-called seceded States." He repelled the notion that had taken hold of the Southern mind. The aim of the government, he declared, was its preservation, and not coercion, conquest, or subjugation.[1]

Much stress was laid by Lincoln and other exponents and leaders of Northern public opinion upon the assertion that the Southern movement was rebellion and the acts of the leaders treason; this, indeed, seems a natural corollary from the hypothesis that the work of secession had been that of a minority. The difference of meaning now attached to the same words in each section[2] is an illustration of the intensity of feeling that existed.[3] General Scott was by Virgin-

---

Toombs, and *hoc genus omne.* I have my doubts whether your predictions will be speedily fulfilled, and whether the final settlement of the present differences will be materially changed by the war now about to begin. All news I have received from the South go to prove that the South is nearly, if not quite, as unanimous, enthusiastic, and confident of the result as the North is. That the power and most of the other advantages are on the side of the North is undeniable. But the South has two great allies, its climate and sickliness, and the prospect of fighting on its own soil for its independence. One State a month seems to be Mr. Seward's programme. Maryland is to be pacified in May, Virginia in June, Tennessee or Arkansas in July, and so forth. The task will not be an easy one. . . . The North will, no doubt, gain the respect of the South, so long denied, and satisfy its thirst of revenge. As to the principal object of the war, the reconstruction of the Union, I am, I am sorry to say, not quite as confident as you seem to be."—Pierce-Sumner Papers, MS.

[1] Sumner, who may be looked upon as the exponent of the radical Republicans, spoke of the contest differently. He wrote, May 5: "This generous uprising of the North is a new element of force, which foretells the subjugation of the rebels."—To Schleiden, Pierce's Memoir, vol. iv. p. 37.

[2] Lieber had noted this in 1860, see vol. ii. p. 489.

[3] June 20, when Russell had arrived at Cairo, Ill., he wrote: "The space of a very few miles has completely altered the phases of thought and the forms of language.

"I am living among 'abolitionists, cutthroats, Lincolnite mercenaries,

ians called "the archtraitor," because he had not followed the fortunes of his State;[1] Governor Hicks was termed a traitor, for the reason that he would not co-operate with the secessionists of Maryland.[2] General Lee, who was moderate and accurate in the use of language, referred to the Union men of western Virginia as traitors.[3] Since the firing on Sumter and the President's call for troops the quality of vindictiveness had increased strikingly.[4] The religious press on both sides of the line was not behind the secular in urging on the war.[5]

Of arms belonging to the national government the Confederate States possessed, from the seizure of the different arsenals within their borders, substantially what would have been their due had a distribution been made *pro rata* to the population.[6] Touching government armories there was

---

foreign invaders, assassins, and plundering Dutchmen.' Such, at least, the men of Columbus tell me the garrison at Cairo consists of.   Down below me are 'rebels, conspirators, robbers, slave - breeders, wretches bent upon destroying the most perfect government on the face of the earth in order to perpetuate an accursed system, by which, however, beings are held in bondage and immortal souls consigned to perdition.' "—Diary, p. 332.

[1] Richmond *Examiner*, April 23.   A report that General Scott had resigned and would offer his sword to Virginia, had previously gained wide currency, see letter of ex-President Tyler to his wife, April 16, Letters and Times of the Tylers, vol. ii. p. 640; letter of Stephens, Johnston and Browne, p. 397; New York *Tribune*, April 24; Russell's Diary, pp. 163, 193; Russell to the London *Times*, Mobile, May 11.

[2] Richmond *Examiner*, April 20; Richmond *Enquirer*, May 18.

[3] Official Records, vol. ii. p. 874.

[4] On vindictiveness at the South, see Russell's letters to the London *Times* from South Carolina, April 30, Montgomery, May 8; Russell's Diary, pp. 154, 225, 236, 315.   "There is certainly less vehemence and bitterness among the Northerners; but it might be erroneous to suppose there was less determination."—Entry of July 3, ibid., p. 375.   On vindictiveness at both the North and the South, see letter of George Ticknor, Life and Letters, vol. ii. p. 442.

[5] See citations from a large number of religious journals in the Baltimore *True Union*, cited by Moore, Rebellion Record, vol. i., Docs., p. 181.

[6] The Confederate States had 145,154 muskets, 18,652 rifles.   The Union

no signal inequality. The Virginians saved the machinery at Harper's Ferry, which was erected at Richmond and Fayetteville, and may be said to have offset the Springfield armory. But in workmen the North had the superiority. Numerous private establishments for the manufacture of warlike implements, open communication with Europe, money and credit for the purchase of arms—all these increased its advantage; although late in the year the Confederates received Enfield rifles from England. The appeals of the governors of Georgia and Mississippi to the people for the loan of country rifles and double-barrelled shot-guns show to what straits they were reduced.[1] In powder and facilities for making it the South was ill off as compared with the North; while in the discipline obtained by life in camp and daily drill the Confederacy was, with a goodly portion of its force, at least three months in advance of the Union.

During these first months of preparation, while the best blood of the North and of the South were making ready to slay one another, the remark of Captain Granger, of the

---

had 416,246 muskets, 30,210 rifles. Computed from the statement from the ordnance office by General Ripley to the President, July 4, War Department Archives, MS. Jefferson Davis gives substantially the same number of arms in the Confederacy, Rise and Fall of the Confederate Government, vol. i. p. 471. The arms in the Confederacy stated by the Columbia *Democrat and Planter* were: Arms seized, 243,000; purchased by the States, 417,000; cannon, 8000, cited by Atlanta *Southern Confederacy*, May 9. This is an exaggeration, as was also the estimate of the Memphis *Appeal*, cited by Richmond *Dispatch*, June 17, and the statement of the Memphis *Avalanche*, "In arms, large or small, the South at this moment is better off than the North," cited by the Atlanta *Commonwealth*, May 21. "The haul of heavy cannon that was made at the Norfolk navy-yard was one of the most valuable acquisitions ever made by a people. . . . A Norfolk correspondent of the Columbia *Times* remarks, 'For six weeks every train that leaves has been loaded with guns.' "—Richmond *Dispatch*, June 17.

[1] Proclamation of Governor Brown, of Georgia, July 26. He estimated the people had 40,000 good country rifles and 25,000 good double-barrelled shot-guns, Atlanta *Weekly Intelligencer*, July 31; proclamation of Governor Pettus, of Mississippi. He estimated there were in private hands arms sufficient for 25,000 men, Moore's Rebellion Record, vol. ii., Docs., p. 195.

regular army, when mustering the Fourth Ohio into service, must have expressed the feeling of many souls in both sections, when contemplating for what purpose were these arrays of men. "Looking down the line of a thousand stalwart men, all in their Garibaldi shirts" (not yet having received their uniforms), he turned to General Cox and exclaimed, "My God! that such men should be food for powder!"[1]

The Confederates had an advantage in that Robert E. Lee espoused their cause; to some extent appreciated at the time, this in reality was an advantage beyond computation. Had he followed the example of Scott and Thomas, and remained in service under the old flag, in active command of the army of the Potomac, how differently might events have turned out!

Lee, now fifty-four years old, his face exhibiting the ruddy glow of health and his head without a gray hair, was physically and morally a splendid example of manhood. Able to trace his lineage far back in the mother-country, he had the best blood of Virginia in his veins. The founder of the Virginia family, who emigrated in the time of Charles I., was a cavalier in sentiment; "Light-horse Harry" of the Revolution was the father of Robert E. Lee. Drawing from a knightly race all their virtues, he had inherited none of their vices. Honest, sincere, simple, magnanimous, forbearing, refined, courteous, yet dignified and proud, never lacking self-command, he was in all respects a true man. Graduating from West Point, his life had been exclusively that of a soldier, yet he had none of the soldier's bad habits. He used neither liquor nor tobacco, indulged rarely in a social glass of wine, and cared nothing for the pleasures of the table. He was a good engineer, and under General Scott had won distinction in Mexico. The work that had fallen to his lot he had performed in a systematic manner and with conscientious care. "Duty is the

---

[1] Century War Book, vol. i. p. 97.

sublimest word in our language," he wrote to his son. Sincerely religious, Providence to him was a verity, and it may be truly said he walked with God.

A serious man, he anxiously watched from his station in Texas the progress of events since Lincoln's election. Thinking "slavery as an institution a moral and political evil," [1] having a soldier's devotion to his flag and a warm attachment to General Scott, he loved the Union, and it was especially dear to him as the fruit of the mighty labors of Washington. Although believing that the South had just grievances due to the aggression of the North, he did not think these evils great enough to resort to the remedy of revolution, and to him secession was nothing less. "Still," he wrote, in January, 1861, "a Union that can only be maintained by swords and bayonets, and in which strife and civil war are to take the place of brotherly love and kindness, has no charm for me. . . . If the Union is dissolved and the government is disrupted, I shall return to my native State and share the miseries of my people, and, save in defence, will draw my sword on none." [2] Summoned to Washington by his chief, Lee had arrived there a few days before the inauguration of Lincoln, and he had to make the decision, after the bombardment of Sumter and the President's call for troops, whether he should serve the national government or Virginia. The active command of the federal army with the succession to the chief place was virtually offered to him, [3] but, with his notion of state-rights and his allegiance to Virginia, his decision, though it cost him pain to make it, could have been no other than it was. He could not lead an army of invasion into his native State, and after the ordinance of secession had been passed by the Virginia convention he resigned his position and accepted the command of the Virginia forces. [4]

---

[1] Letter of Dec. 27, 1856, Life of Lee, Long, p. 83.
[2] Life of Lee, Long, p. 88.   [3] *Ante.*
[4] See letter to General Scott, April 20; also to his sister, same date, Life

Northern men may regret that Lee did not see his duty in the same light as did two other Virginians, Scott and Thomas, but censure's voice upon the action of such a noble soul is hushed. A careful survey of his character and life must lead the student of men and affairs to see that the course he took was, from his point of view and judged by his inexorable and pure conscience, the path of duty to which a high sense of honor called him. Could we share the thoughts of that high-minded man as he paced the broad pillared veranda of his stately Arlington house, his eyes glancing across the river at the flag of his country waving above the dome of the Capitol, and then resting on the soil of his native Virginia, we should be willing now to recognize in him one of the finest products of American life. For surely, as the years go on, we shall see that such a life can be judged by no partisan measure, and we shall come to look upon him as the English of our day regard Washington, whom little more than a century ago they delighted to call a rebel. Indeed in all essential characteristics Lee resembled Washington, and had the great work of his life been crowned with success or had he chosen the winning side, the world would have acknowledged that Virginia could in a century produce two men who were the embodiment of public and private virtue.

The contemplation of Lee's course at the parting of the ways has another lesson for us of the North : it should teach us to regard with the utmost charity other officers in the army and men in civil life who either did not believe in the constitutional right of secession or in the expediency of exercising it, yet who deemed it the path of duty to follow the fortunes of their States when they, in the parlance of the day, resumed their full sovereign powers.[1]

---

of Lee, Cooke, p. 29. Most of this characterization of Lee and many of the facts I have drawn from the biographies of Lee by Long and Cooke; see, also, Recollections of a Rebel, by George Cary Eggleston.

[1] In a thoughtful article in the *Atlantic Monthly* for Jan., 1892, Professor Basil L. Gildersleeve refers to an expression in private conversation

"The loss of Stephen A. Douglas at this crisis must be regarded as a national calamity," wrote Greeley, while Douglas was lying on his death-bed in Chicago.[1] Leaving Washington soon after pledging his support to the President, he had on his way home spoken words of wise and pure patriotism to the citizens of Wheeling, to the people of Columbus, and to the legislature of his own State. The last time that he addressed his countrymen from the platform, always a labor of love, was on his arrival, the 1st day of May, at Chicago, when a concourse of all parties met him at the depot and escorted him to the wigwam in which Lincoln had been nominated, now, as then, crowded with ten thousand people. In his emphatic way Douglas declared: "There are only two sides to the question. Every man must be for the United States or against it. There can be no neutrals in this war; *only patriots—or traitors.* . . . It is a sad task to discuss questions so fearful as civil war, but sad as it is, bloody and disastrous as I expect it will be, I express it as my conviction before God that it is the duty of every American citizen to rally round the flag of his country."[2] His work, however, was done. Worn out and sick, he took to his bed to die. His last thoughts were of his country; his dying message to his sons came with a full voice. "Tell them," he said, "to obey the laws and support the Constitution of the United States."[3] With all his fail-

---

of Lowell's "touching Lee's course in turning against the government to which he had sworn allegiance," and he shows that he himself, who served in the Confederate army, regards Thomas much in the same light as Lowell did Lee. We must not, however, ignore that many Southerners have paid feeling tributes to Lincoln. A noteworthy one was the Phi Beta Kappa poem of Maurice Thompson, read at Cambridge, June 29, 1893.

[1] New York *Tribune,* June 1.
[2] Ibid., June 13; for an abstract of his speech at Columbus, ibid., April 26; his speech at Springfield, ibid., May 1; Chicago *Tribune,* June 6; his remarks at Bellaire, Ohio, Moore's Rebellion Record, vol. i., Rumors and Incidents, p. 41; his last public letter, May 10, Ibid., vol. ii., Docs., p. 126. For a graphic account of his impromptu speech at Columbus, article of J. D. Cox, Century War Book, vol. i. p. 86.
[3] Chicago *Journal,* cited by Moore's Rebellion Record, vol. i., Rumors

ings he lacked not patriotism. His ambition had wrecked himself and his party; but he had done much to retrieve his great error, and the nation, in sorrowing at his loss, forgot the Kansas-Nebraska bill or forgave its author.[1]

The solidarity of Christendom is such that the nations across the water could not look on the struggle in America unmoved. The North and the South appealed to Europe, the one for sympathy, the other for material aid ; and such was the connection between the English-speaking peoples,[2] that to each the attitude of all the rest of Europe together was unimportant compared with what they expected from England. The people of the Confederacy not only asked her assistance, but confidently believed that the want of cotton would compel her recognition of their independence and the eventual breaking of the federal blockade;[3] that

---

and Incidents, p. 110. My father, who was with Douglas during his last days, has often told me that this was the word he sent to his two boys, then at Georgetown college. Douglas died June 3 ; his age was 48.

[1] Two tributes given Douglas, one from each side of Mason and Dixon's line, are worthy of recall. Greeley wrote, in Recollections of a Busy Life, p. 359, published in 1868: "Our country has often been called to mourn severe, untimely losses; yet I deem the death of Stephen A. Douglas, just at the outbreak of our great Civil War and when he had thrown his whole soul into the cause of the country, one of the most grievous and irreparable." Alexander H. Stephens wrote, in The War between the States, vol. ii. p. 421, published in 1870: "His [Douglas's] death, at the time, I regarded as one of the greatest calamities, under the dispensations of Providence, which befell this country in the beginning of these troubles."

[2] "Of the whole foreign trade of the United States more than three fifths, of the foreign tonnage entering American ports more than four fifths, were contributed by this kingdom [Great Britain] and its colonies. From the Western States of the Union we drew every year large supplies of food, and from the Southern the raw material for our most important manufacture."—The Neutrality of Great Britain during the American Civil War, Bernard, p. 122.

[3] "By the end of this summer the stock of cotton and tobacco in Europe will be exhausted. Europe must have more, or witness the commencement of the most terrible of revolutions at home—a revolution arising from starvation. It is therefore a matter of compulsion that they should break through the blockade and obtain our crop under the right of their neutral flag."—Richmond *Examiner*, July 2. Aug. 9 the same jour-

she would not hesitate to adopt that policy when she comprehended the situation, and knew that the South offered
her cotton in exchange for her manufactured goods, which
would be subject only to a·simple revenue tariff.   Nor, indeed, in their opinion, had she a choice in the matter; for
so many of her operatives were dependent for bread on a
constant supply of the Southern staple that if it were not
to be had a revolution would break out in Great Britain.[1]
"'Look out there,' a Charleston merchant said to William
H. Russell, pointing to the wharf on which were piled some
cotton bales; 'there's the key will open all our ports, and
put us into John Bull's strong-box as well.'"[2]   "Rhett,"
Russell wrote, "is also persuaded that the Lord Chancellor
sits on a cotton bale.   'You must recognize us, sir, before

---

nal commended united voluntary withholding of cotton from the market.
Action by the Confederate government would be ill advised from a diplomatic standpoint; comp. Charleston *Courier* of July 30.   The Charleston *Courier* declared, Sept. 21, "that honor and duty and policy and
patriotism require that not a bale of cotton should leave a Southern
port . . . until it can be exported legally and regularly after a recognition of the Confederacy."   "The American crop is grown and gathered, but its proprietors threaten to withhold it from our markets."—
London *Times*, Sept. 19.   "The Confederate States have presumed upon
their monopoly so far as to make it an engine of coercion.   They
have declared, though perhaps without much sincerity, that they will
hold back their crops and leave Europe to see what can be done without
them."—Ibid., Sept. 21.   The Richmond *Dispatch*, Oct. 1, 1861, expressed
surprise that a single man in the South could entertain the notion "that it
would be good policy to permit England to purchase the entire cotton
crop."   Professor Sumner says in regard to this view, which seems to have
had more currency at this time in private circles than among the Confederate statesmen: "Perhaps the grandest case of delusion from the fallacy
of commercial war which can be mentioned is the South in 1860.   They
undertook secession in the faith that 'cotton is king,' and they had come
to believe that they had a means to coerce the rest of the world by refusing
to sell cotton.   As soon as they undertook secession their direst necessity
was to sell cotton.   Their error came down to them in direct descent from
1774 and Jefferson's embargo."—Alexander Hamilton, p. 65.

[1] W. H. Russell's Diary, entries of April 18 and 19, pp. 118, 123; Russell's letters to the London *Times*, from Montgomery, May 8, Cairo,
June 20.   [2] Diary, p. 123.

the end of October.'"[1]   Jefferson Davis did not share the overweening confidence of his people. The *Times* correspondent, arriving at Montgomery early in May, noted his anxious expression, his "haggard, care-worn, and paindrawn look," and set down in the diary that the Confederate President "was quite aware of the difficulty of conquering the repugnance which exists (in Europe) to slavery."[2] Benjamin, the attorney-general of the Confederacy, felt sure, however, that cotton would prove to be the king over Great Britain. "All this coyness about acknowledging a slave power will come right at last," he declared with a jaunty air.[3]

Both the North and the South were disappointed at the action of England. Lord John Russell, the foreign minister, received unofficially the Confederate commissioners, but gave them no encouragement.[4] In May the British government decided that a due regard to the commercial interests of its subjects required that it should take notice of affairs in America,[5] and accordingly it issued, May 13, "The Queen's Proclamation of Neutrality." "Whereas," it said, "hostilities have unhappily commenced between the government of the United States of America and certain States styling themselves the Confederate States of America," it declared the "royal determination to maintain a strict and impartial neutrality in the contest between said contending parties."[6] The proclamation, modelled after that issued in 1859 on the commencement of the war between Austria and France and Sardinia, with the usual

[1] Russell's Diary, p. 148.
[2] Ibid., pp. 173, 174; see, also, letter to the London *Times*, May 7.
[3] Ibid., p. 176.
[4] Lord Russell to Lord Lyons, May 11, British and Foreign State Papers, 1860–61, p. 186; Adams to Seward, June 14, Message and Documents, 1861, p. 104. Yancey and Mann gave Toombs, May 21, a full account of this interview, Confederate Diplomatic Correspondence, MSS. Treasury Department.   [5] Bernard, p. 129 *et seq.*
[6] The proclamation is printed by Bernard, p. 135, and from the *Gazette*, in Moore's Rebellion Record, vol. i., Docs., p. 245.

whereases, recitals of statutes, warnings, and commands—an official matter-of-course on the occasion of a war between two friendly nations—derived now great importance for the reason that its issuance and the nature of its terms were the recognition of the Confederacy as a belligerent power. To regard the Confederate States as a belligerent conflicted with the theory of the Lincoln administration that the Southerners were insurgents, and with the largely prevailing notion at the North that they should be treated as rebels and traitors; and it placed in the eyes of nations— for all the important powers of Europe substantially followed the example of Great Britain — the vessels that should accept letters of marque from the Confederate government on the level of privateers, instead of considering them pirates and the men on board amenable to punishment for piracy, as the President's proclamation of April 19 had declared them to be. By Davis's inviting applications for letters of marque, and by Lincoln's proclamation of blockade, it seemed probable to the English government that a maritime war would result;[1] and the declaration of neutrality appeared necessary for the protection of British interests on the high seas as well as "an endeavor, so far as possible, to bring the management of it (*i.e.*, 'a war of two sides') within the rules of modern civilized warfare."[2] It was a decided disadvantage to the Union that the probable Confederate cruisers were at once given the quality of privateers instead of having the hand of every maritime power raised against them as pirates; but

---

[1] Bernard, pp. 134, 144 *et seq.*

[2] Lord John Russell's statement in conversation to Adams, Adams to Seward, May 21. Russell also stated : "The fact was that a necessity seemed to exist to define the course of the government in regard to the participation of the subjects of Great Britain in the impending conflict. To that end the legal questions involved had been referred to those officers most conversant with them, and their advice had been taken in shaping the result. Their conclusion had been that, as a question merely of *fact*, a war existed."—Message and Documents, p. 92 ; see, also, Bernard, p. 127 *et seq.*

the English then, and have since, made out a good case.[1]
It was a stubborn fact that the United States had, in 1856,
refused its unconditional assent to a proposition, agreed to
by the larger number of civilized nations, that "privateer-
ing is and remains abolished." [2] Nevertheless, the American government and people felt honestly aggrieved at this
action of Great Britain. Seward wrote that the queen's
proclamation was "exceptionable," on account of its being
issued on the very day of the arrival in England of Charles
Francis Adams, the minister to the Court of St. James appointed by President Lincoln, and also for the matter of
it; [3] and Adams, in a conversation with Lord John Russell,
"conducted in the most friendly spirit," after hearing his
assignment of the reasons for the government's course, re-

---

[1] Lord Russell, in conversation already cited and in that reported by
Adams to Seward, June 14 ; Lord Russell to Lord Lyons, May 21, June 21,
British and Foreign State Papers, 1860–61, pp. 192, 198 ; debate in the
House of Lords, May 16. The London *Times* of May 15 said : "Being no
longer able to deny the existence of a dreadful civil war, we are compelled
to take official notice of it. . . . Our foreign relations are too extensive, the
stake we hold in the commerce of the world is too vast, and, we may add,
our attitude is a matter of too much importance for us to allow ourselves
the gratification of saying 'Peace, when there is no peace,' so largely indulged in up to the very latest moment by the statesmen of America herself. Yes, there is war. . . . Eteocles and Polynices are confronting each
other with hostile weapons, and England, like the venerable queen of
Thebes, stands by to behold the unnatural combat of her children. From
acknowledging the state of war the next step is to acknowledging the belligerent rights of the contending parties. . . . As belligerents they are as
equal in our eyes as Trojan or Tyrian was in the eyes of Queen Dido. We
are bound equally to respect their blockades and equally to abstain from
any act which may violate the conditions of the most impartial and undis-
criminating neutrality ;" see, also, Earl Russell to Adams, Aug. 30, 1865 ;
Bernard, p. 162 *et seq.;* Goldwin Smith's article, "The Case of the Alabama," *Macmillan's Magazine,* Dec., 1865 ; McCarthy's History of Our Own
Times, vol. ii. p. 193.

[2] Bernard, chap. viii.; Nicolay and Hay, vol. iv. p. 277 *et seq.* On the
negotiations in 1861 respecting this subject see the same and the diplomatic correspondence, printed in Message and Documents, 1861–62 ; also
Henry Adams's article, "The Declaration of Paris, 1861," printed in his
Historical Essays.   [3] Seward to Adams, June 3, 8.

marked "that the action taken seemed . . . a little more
rapid than was absolutely called for by the occasion."[1]

Northern men, feeling in every nerve that slavery was

---

[1] Adams to Seward, May 21 ; see, also, his despatch of June 14. Motley,
who was well known in English society and loved it, came to America in
June after an absence abroad of ten years, and wrote his wife from Washington, June 18, "Had the English declaration been delayed a few weeks
or even days, I do not think it would ever have been made, and I cannot
help thinking that it was a most unfortunate mistake."—Correspondence,
vol. i. p. 380.

The charge that the English government was precipitate merits some
attention. "It" (recognizing the Confederates as belligerents), said John
Bright in the House of Commons, March 13, 1865, "was done with unfriendly haste and had this effect : that it gave comfort and courage to the
conspiracy at Montgomery and Richmond, and caused great grief and irritation among that portion of the people in America most strongly desirous
of maintaining amicable and friendly relations between their country and
England."—Cited on p. 63 of The Case of the United States, to be laid before the Tribunal of Arbitration at Geneva ; Rogers's edition of John
Bright's Speeches, vol. i. p. 132. Woolsey, who in the main is favorable to
the English side of the dispute, writes that the advisers of the queen's
proclamation "are chargeable with haste, bad judgment, and a certain un-
statesmanlike indifference to results."—New Englander, July, 1869, p. 579.
After a careful consideration of much of the evidence and many of the
arguments, I have arrived at the conclusion that the English government
was not in May actuated by any particular unfriendliness to the North.
The sentiment of England and the disposition of the government at that
time must not be confounded with what they were later. If we may
judge by the proceedings in the House of Commons, American affairs occupied only a very small share of the attention of the ministry, and it is
possible that, if the political as well as the legal points had been carefully
considered, the proclamation might have been delayed, which it obviously
could have been without harm to British interests. Yet those who contend earnestly for the American position will, it seems to me, find it difficult to answer two questions in a way to support their reasoning :

1. Could the Proclamation of Neutrality have been by any possibility
delayed after the battle of Bull Run ?

2. What greater damage resulted to the United States from having the
proclamation issued May 13 instead of the 1st of August ?

The American argument is strongly put by Adams in his letters to Earl
Russell of April 7, May 20, and Sept. 18, 1865; and the English position is
equally well maintained by Earl Russell in his replies of May 4 and Aug.
30, 1865, though not, I think, with equal consistency.

The United States "regard the concession of belligerency by Great

the single cause of the trouble, and deeming it impossible that England could shut her eyes to the patent fact that the peculiar institution was the corner-stone of the Confederacy, looked to her, on account of her honorable and praiseworthy position towards negro slavery since 1833, for generous sympathy. The apparently undue haste, therefore, with which her government placed the Confederate States on an equality with the Union as to belligerent rights was galling; and it seemed to presage the recognition of their independence at the earliest opportune moment. There is, wrote Motley from his home, June 14, "a deep and intense feeling of bitterness and resentment towards England just now in Boston. . . . The most warm-hearted, England-loving men in this England-loving part of the country are full of sorrow at the attitude taken up by England. It would be difficult to exaggerate the poisonous effects produced by the long-continued, stinging, hostile articles in the *Times*. The declaration of Lord John Russell that the Southern privateers were to be considered belligerents, was received, as I knew and said it would be, with great indignation. . . . This, then, is the value, men say to

---

Britain as a part of this case [the case before the Tribunal of Arbitration at Geneva] only so far as it shows the beginning and animus of that course of conduct which resulted so disastrously to the United States." I have not been able to find anything in the opinions of the three unbiassed arbitrators which indicates that this assertion, or the argument on which it was based, added aught of strength to our case. On the contrary Count Sclopis distinctly declared, "I am far from thinking that the animus of the English government was hostile to the federal government during the war."

It is a plain inference from the arguments of two of our best authorities on international law that England's acknowledgment of the belligerent rights of the Confederacy was justifiable, R. H. Dana's note to Dana's Wheaton, § 23 ; Woolsey's International Law, § 180, also his article in *New Englander*, July, 1869. The United States Supreme Court, at its December term of 1862, decided that the President's proclamation of blockade of April 19, 1861, was "itself official and conclusive evidence to the Court that a state of war existed ;" see, also, Snow's Cases of International Law, pp. xvi. 254.

me every moment, of the anti-slavery sentiment of England, of which she has boasted so much to mankind. This is the end of all the taunts and reproaches which she has flung at the United States government 'for being perpetually controlled by the slavery power, and for allowing its policy to be constantly directed towards extending that institution." [1] The irritation at the North came largely from the belief that the Queen's Proclamation represented an evident desire on the part of the ruling classes of Great Britain to aid the South. The sending of the *Great Eastern* with troops to Canada fostered this impression. [2] The concession of belligerent rights to the Confederates raised their hopes, and seemed to them to imply that they had not reckoned in vain on the support of England. [3]

---

[1] Correspondence, vol. i. p. 372. August Belmont, a Democrat, wrote from New York, May 28, in a similar strain, to Baron Rothschild, a member of Parliament representing the city of London, and " a very intimate friend of Lord John Russell, and on equally friendly relations with Lord Palmerston," the prime-minister. He said : " It would be difficult for me to convey to you an idea of the general feeling of disappointment and irritation produced in this country by this manifesto of the British government, by which a few revolted States are placed, in their relations with Great Britain, upon the same footing as the government of the United States. . . . England's position threatens to prolong the war by giving hope and comfort to the rebels." Belmont also speaks of "the short-sighted policy of the gentlemen of Manchester, who now allow cotton to outweigh their anti-slavery professions."—Belmont's Letters and Speeches, privately printed, pp. 36, 38. Belmont wrote, June 3, to Lord Dunfermline, of the House of Lords, who had intimate relations with Lord John Russell : " The people of the North see now revealed to them, in all their horrid nakedness, the treasonable schemes of the slavery oligarchy, who, while pretending to battle for their threatened constitutional rights," really purpose " to fasten *slavery* as a *political element* upon this country."—Ibid., p. 42. Belmont wrote, June 7, to N. M. Rothschild & Sons, London: "Lord Palmerston's organ, the *Morning Post*, hints at a recognition of the Southern Confederacy as a *de facto* government. . . . It seems almost incredible to see England, the great advocate and leader of negro emancipation, give now her aid and influence to a most criminal rebellion, got up for no other purpose than that of fastening slavery not only upon our country, but also upon Mexico and Central America." See, also, his letter to Seward, June 6, ibid., p. 45.   [2] Adams to Seward, June 14, 28.

[3] Ibid., June 14 ; Russell's Diary, entry June 18, p. 319. But Russell

It cannot be averred that at this time our Secretary of State conducted foreign affairs with tact and wisdom. His despatch of May 21, even in the shape that it reached Adams, might, in the hands of a less competent and prudent minister, have led to serious difficulty; but had it been sent as Seward first wrote it — without the modifications and suggestions of the President, with the instruction to deliver to the British foreign minister a copy of it if he continued even unofficial intercourse with the Confederate commissioners;[1] menacing, as it did, Great Britain for this and her presaged acknowledgment of the Southern privateers as lawful belligerents;[2] threatening her categorically with war if she should recognize the Confederacy, and intimating that "the result of the debate in which we are engaged" may be war "between the United States and one, two, or even more European nations," in which the United States will come out of it very much better than Europe—the game would then have been in England's hands.[3] To repel Seward's reckless language would be easy; to carry out the policy of acknowledging the independence of the Confederate States or of breaking the blockade, demanded by what then would have grown to be an irresistible sentiment, would have been grateful work

writes that the Southerners overestimated the value to them of the declaration.

[1] At this time Seward did not know that Lord John Russell had seen the Confederate commissioners; he had told Dallas, the retiring minister, that he was not unwilling to see them unofficially. Adams wrote, June 14, that Russell said that "he had seen the gentlemen once some time ago, and once more some time since; he had no expectation of seeing them any more."

[2] The Queen's Proclamation was May 13, and, of course, Seward did not know of it when this despatch was sent. The news was published in the New York *Tribune* of May 25, having been received by telegram from Cape Race, from a steamship leaving Queenstown the 16th. Between the date of despatches at Washington or London and their reception a fortnight seems to have elapsed.

[3] Compare the despatch as sent, Message and Documents, p. 87, and as first submitted to the President, Nicolay and Hay, vol. iv. p. 270.

for the English government.   In turn, Northern public
opinion might have exacted a declaration of war against
Great Britain, which would also mean war with France,
as the two European nations were then on a friendly footing and were acting together in American affairs.[1]   The
infatuation of Seward is hard to understand; it shows that
the notion which had prompted the " Thoughts for the President's consideration"[2] still lodged in his brain, and that
he dreamed that if the United States made war on England
because she helped the Confederacy, the Southerners, by
some occult emotional change, would sink their animosity
to the North, and join with it for the sake of overcoming
the traditional enemy.[3]   His unconcern at the prospect of
serious trouble with England was not courage, but a reck-
lessness which made him oblivious of what all discerning
Northern statesmen knew—that the people devoted to the
Union had undertaken quite enough, in their endeavor to
preserve the nation from destruction by its internal foes.
" Great Britain," Seward wrote to his wife, " is in great
danger of sympathizing so much with the South, for the
sake of peace and cotton, as to drive us to make war against
her as the ally of the traitors.   If that comes, it will be
the strife of the younger branch of the British stock for
freedom against the older for slavery.   It will be dreadful,
but the end will be sure and swift."[4]   It is no wonder that
Thurlow Weed, his friend and mentor, apprehended that

---

[1] Yancey and Rost to Toombs, Paris, May 10; Yancey and Mann to
Toombs, London, May 21 ; Yancey, Rost, and Mann to Toombs, London,
June 1; Yancey and Mann to Toombs, London, July 15 ; Yancey to
Hunter, Paris, Oct. 28, Confederate Diplomatic Correspondence, MSS.
Treasury Department.   [2] *Ante*, p. 341.

[3] This inference might be drawn from the concluding portion of his
despatch to Adams of May 21, and from his private letters to Weed of May
23 and to his wife of June 5, Life of Seward, vol. ii. pp. 576, 590; see p.
342, note 2.   The New York *Herald* of July 4 proposed that the North
and South unite to wage war on England and France.   The Richmond
Dispatch of July 15 called it a " preposterous lunatic" suggestion.

[4] Letter of May 17, Life of Seward, vol. ii. p. 575.

he was "too decisive" with the European powers.[1] The
course of Seward was all the more dangerous in that it represented the defiant sentiment of many Northern people,
and one can hardly exaggerate the evil it might have brought
upon us had he not been restrained by the President, whose
native good sense was instructed by the intelligence and
discretion of Sumner.[2] It produced mischief in England,
where, sympathy being divided between the North and the
South, it tended to make the position of the friends of the
Union more difficult to maintain. "I earnestly entreat,"
wrote to Sumner the Duke of Argyll, a member of the
British cabinet, and thoroughly friendly to the North, "that
you will use your influence and official authority to induce
your government, and especially Mr. Seward, to act in a
more liberal and a less reckless spirit than he is supposed
here to indicate towards foreign governments, and especially towards ourselves. I find much uneasiness prevailing here lest things should be done which would arouse a
hostile spirit in this country. . . . I believe there is no desire
stronger here than that of maintaining friendly relations
with America. But there are points on which our people
are very sensitive; and if they saw themselves touched on
these points in honor or interest, the irritation would be
extreme and could not be controlled."[3] Fortunately, the
position of minister to England was filled by a man who
had extraordinary qualifications for the place. Charles

---

[1] See letter to Weed, May 23, Life of Seward, vol. ii. p. 576. While glad
Count Gurowski had been appointed private secretary to Secretary Seward,
Schleiden wrote Sumner, June 5: "I feel rather uneasy in regard to the influence he will try to exercise—and, perhaps, really exercise—upon your relations with Great Britain. I think the fire already burns briskly enough
in the State Department and requires no stirring."—Pierce-Sumner Papers, MS.

[2] See Pierce's Sumner, vol. iv. pp. 31, 117 (Sumner was chairman of the
Committee on Foreign Relations of the Senate); also Russell's Diary, entry
of July 3, p. 377. Russell apparently had intimate relations with Lord
Lyons, the British minister at Washington.

[3] Letter of June 4, Pierce's Sumner, vol. iv. p. 31.

Francis Adams—the selection of Seward,[1] and thoroughly loyal to his chief—whose distinguished ancestry gave him especial welcome in a country where birth is highly esteemed, translated the harsh language of the Secretary of State into courteous but forcible reasoning: menace became remonstrance, and without taking a radical, or what might have proved an untenable, position, he persistently urged the claims of his government. If it be good diplomacy to see your own side of the question intensely, and your opponent's side with sufficient distinctness to repel his arguments, but not clearly enough to sympathize in the least with his standpoint, and, moreover, to present your case with candor and firmness, then Adams, in these first negotiations with Lord John Russell, showed himself a good diplomat, winning admiration from his own countrymen and respect from England.

While Adams was exhibiting our position in the most favorable light to the government and to "persons of weight in Great Britain,"[2] sober second thought had come to the administration and people in America. "There has nothing occurred here," wrote Schleiden from Washington, June 5, to Sumner, "in regard to Great Britain; and the President, who last night entertained the whole diplomatic body at dinner, told me, when I alluded to these relations, in a very sensible manner, that it appeared to him as if this government had no reason to complain of any European power in this contest, all of them having, by the long-continuing want of any distinct policy on the part of the United States, been induced more or less to believe the Union weaker, and the seceded States stronger, than was really the fact. He seemed not, at least, to be apprehensive, neither was Lord Lyons."[3] A leading article in the New York *Tribune* of June 3, when compared with preceding expressions of opinion, showed either that it was

---

[1] Life of Seward, vol. ii. p. 525.

[2] Adams, June 14.

[3] Pierce-Sumner Papers, MS.

inspired in high official quarters and was an effort to lead opinion, or else that it represented a changing public sentiment. This journal argued that the "evident desire" of the western European powers to maintain amicable relations with us had not been fairly met on this side of the water;[1] defending England in some measure for her recognition of the belligerent rights of the Confederate States, it excused the unofficial reception of their commissioners by Lord John Russell. Returning to the subject the following day, it said that even if Great Britain or France should open one of the blockaded ports and load a merchant fleet with cotton, we had better pocket the insult for the supreme reason of necessity, for our war with the South was a "life-and-death struggle." As the scope of the Queen's Proclamation of Neutrality came to be more clearly understood, sentiment in the Union certainly grew more favorable towards Great Britain. The letters of Belmont and of Motley, representing as they did a wide range of opinion, reflect this improved feeling.[1] Motley, while in Washington, had an hour's talk with Lincoln, and he spoke out of his large knowledge of the subject with friendliness and warm sympathy of the English government and people — to good purpose, he thought.[2] The President's remark in his Fourth-of-July message was a sincere expression, and stated with reasonable exactness the sentiment of the public. "The sovereignty and rights of the United States," he declared, "are now everywhere practically respected by foreign powers, and a general sympathy with the country is manifested throughout the world."

With the change of feeling towards England, opinions altered touching the treatment of the Confederates. That severe punishment should be visited upon them had been the common desire. "I have seen it placarded in the

---

[1] See Belmont's letter to Baron Rothschild of June 18; Motley's of June 23.   [2] See letter of June 23.

streets of Boston," wrote George Ticknor, " that we should hang the secession leaders as fast as we can get them into our power. I have found this course openly urged in lead. ing papers of New York and Boston. It is even said that the government at Washington is now considering the expediency of adopting it." [1] No one, indeed, had seriously proposed that a traitor's doom should be meted out to the rank and file; and by the 4th of July it became apparent that prisoners taken in battle must be exchanged, and the war in other respects conducted on the same principles as war with a foreign nation. It was then seen that executions of the leaders would be revolting to humanity, and, moreover, that the Confederate States were strong enough to make reprisals. While I have not been able to trace the matter, it seems reasonable to believe that the declarations of the European powers had an influence in modifying public sentiment in this regard. Not that these declarations affected the law in the case, for legally as well as according to the popular notion the Confederates were rebels and traitors,[2] but the nations of Europe expressed the opinion that they had shown sufficient strength to have conceded to them the rights of belligerents. Chase accurately described the course of the administration when, as chief-justice, he afterwards said, in a judgment delivered from the bench, " The rights and obligations of a belligerent were conceded to it [the Confederacy] in its military character very soon after the war began, from motives of

---

[1] He added, " I have, indeed, little fear that my government, or its military chief, will seriously consider such a suggestion—none that they will adopt it."—Life of George Ticknor, vol. ii. p. 442. The New York *Tribune* of May 27 was specific: " Davis, Toombs, Rhett, Yancey, Mason, Stephens, Cobb. Letcher, Hunter, Benjamin, Pickens, and civilians of that class, and Twiggs, Bragg, Beauregard, Lee, Johnston, Magruder, Pillow, and soldiers like them, with thousands of other men of high repute and great influence, must succeed in this rebellion, or either sue for pardon or be put to death as traitors or flee from their native land forever."

[2] According to a decision of the Supreme Court of the United States at the December term of 1862, Miller's Decisions, vol. iv. p. 876.

humanity and expediency, by the United States."¹ A fair
statement of Northern sentiment by the 4th of July is
that, although most of the rebels would be pardoned by
a gracious government, Jefferson Davis and the men captured on board of vessels bearing his letters of marque
should be hanged.²

Adams wrote from London, May 31 : " The feeling towards the United States is improving in the higher circles
here. It was never otherwise than favorable among the
people at large." ³ Of the same tenor were his despatches
of a week and a fortnight later. June 1 the English government interdicted the armed ships and privateers of both
parties from carrying the prizes made by them into any British ports.⁴ This order in its operation would hurt the
Confederacy, but not the Union, which had commissioned no
privateers ; it caused expostulations from the Confederate
agents in London, and drew from Seward the remark that
" it would probably prove a death-blow to Southern priva-
teering." ⁵ So much pressure was brought to bear upon
Gregory, a member of the House of Commons, that he
withdrew, June 7, his motion " to call the attention of the

<hr>

¹ Wallace's Reports, Supreme Court, Dec., 1868, p. 10.

² It was impossible to put this sentiment in force regarding so-called
pirates. The crew of the *Savannah*, a Southern privateer captured June 3,
were tried, but the jury was unable to agree upon a verdict. William
Smith, one of the crew of the *Jeff Davis*, was convicted, but never executed. Retaliation was threatened by the Confederate government. The
crew of the *Savannah* were at first put in irons, but afterwards were
treated as prisoners of war, Nicolay and Hay, vol. v. p. 10 ; Bernard, p. 99 ;
Stephens's War between the States, vol. ii. p. 430 ; Belmont to Baron
James de Rothschild, June 18 ; New York *Tribune*, June 18, 19 ; New
York *Times*, June 16, cited in Moore's Rebellion Record, vol. i., Docs., p.
375 ; Wharton's International Law Digest, § 381.

³ Adams had heard with pleasure Lord John Russell's and Gladstone's
friendly references to the United States in the House of Commons, May 30,
for which see Hansard, vol. clxiii. pp. 278, 331.

⁴ Statement of Lord John Russell in the House of Commons, June 3,
Bernard, p. 136.

⁵ Cited by Bernard, p. 133, and in Woolsey's International Law, § 180.

House to the expediency of the prompt recognition of the
Southern Confederacy." [1] The true nature of the conflict
and the embarrassment to British interests from it were at
this time clearly understood by the English government.
" The taint of slavery," wrote Lord Lyons from Washington,
" will render the cause of the South repugnant to the feelings of the civilized world. On the other hand, commercial
intercourse with the cotton States is of vital importance to
manufacturing nations." [2] Lord John Russell declared in
the House of Commons that the trouble had " arisen from
that accursed institution of slavery." [3] " The commercial
protectionism of the North," wrote the Duke of Argyll to
Sumner, " is doing you infinite mischief here ; but still I
think it is seen by the press generally and by the public
that other and deeper issues are at stake in your domestic
quarrel." [4] " The intelligence received from the United
States," wrote Adams, June 21, " of the effect produced by
the reception of the Queen's Proclamation has not been
without its influence upon opinion here. Whilst people of
all classes unite in declaring that such a measure was unavoidable, they are equally earnest in disavowing any infer-
ences of want of good - will which may have been drawn
from it. They affect to consider our complaints as very unreasonable, and are profuse in their professions of sympathy
with the government in its present struggle. This is certainly a very great change from the tone prevailing when I

---

[1] Hansard; Adams's despatch of June 14.
[2] Cited in Life of Seward, vol. ii. p. 546.
[3] May 30, Hansard.   The London *Times* of May 22 said : " A slave-holding community under an almost tropical sun has separated itself—perhaps
unjustifiably, but still quite naturally—from the traders and shippers and
mechanicians and farmers of a northern land." The London *Daily News*
of May 22 said : " The only object the South have in separating is that
slavery, hitherto limited by counteracting principles, may henceforth become sovereign, expanding itself, and pervading and moulding every institution of government." " The insolence of the slave-owners has at last
produced its natural effect."—The *Saturday Review*, cited by New York
Tribune, June 3.
[4] Letter of June 4, Pierce-Sumner Papers, MS.

first arrived. It is partly to be ascribed to the accounts of the progress of the war, but still more to the publications in the London *Times* of the letters of its special correspondent." [1] This is a reference to William H. Russell's graphic and impartial letters describing his journey through the Southern States, in which he told the English public in unmistakable terms that the cause of the South was the cause of the slave power. [2] Nevertheless there was a divided sen-

---

[1] Message and Documents, 1861–62, p. 109.

[2] Russell wrote from Charleston, April 21 : " The State [South Carolina] is but a gigantic Sparta, in which the helotry are marked by an indelible difference of color and race from the masters." From Montgomery, May 6, he states the position of South Carolina, "which has been the *fons et origo* of the secession doctrines, and their development into the full life of the Confederate States, thus : ' We hold that slavery is essential to our existence as producers of what Europe requires ; nay, more, we maintain it is in the abstract right in principle ; and some of us go so far as to maintain that the only proper form of society, according to the law of God and the exigencies of man, is that which has slavery as its basis.' " Under the shadow of the Capitol in which the Confederate Congress was sitting Russell had an object-lesson, which he presented to his readers in a graphic and sympathetic manner. He wrote from Montgomery, May 8 : " My attention was attracted to a group of people to whom a man was holding forth in energetic sentences. . . . ' Nine h'un'nerd and fifty dollars ! Only nine h-hun'nerd and fifty dollars offered for him !' exclaimed the man. . . . . ' Will *no one* make any advance on nine hundred and fifty dollars ?' A man near me opened his mouth, spat, and said, ' Twenty-five.' ' Only nine hundred and seventy-five dollars offered for him ! Why, 'at's radaklous—only nine hundred and seventy-five dollars ! Will no one,' etc. Beside the orator auctioneer stood a stout young man of five-and-twenty years of age, with a bundle in his hand. He was a muscular fellow, broad-shouldered, narrow-flanked, but rather small in stature ; he had on a broad, greasy old wide-awake, a blue jacket, a coarse cotton shirt, loose and rather ragged trousers, and broken shoes. The expression of his face was heavy and sad, but it was by no means disagreeable, in spite of his thick lips, broad nostrils, and high cheek-bones. On his head was wool instead of hair. I am neither sentimentalist nor Black Republican nor negro-worshipper, but I confess the sight caused a strange thrill through my heart. I tried in vain to make myself familiar with the fact that I could, for the sum of nine hundred and seventy-five dollars, become as absolutely the owner of that mass of blood, bones, sinew, flesh, and brains as of the horse which stood by my side. There was no sophistry which could persuade me the man was not a man ; he was, indeed, by no means my

timent, and Belmont, who went to England in July, and saw, perhaps, more of commercial and financial people than did Adams, was struck at the lack of any real sympathy for

brother, but assuredly he was a fellow-creature. I have seen slave-markets in the East, but somehow or other the Orientalism of the scene cast a coloring over the nature of the sales there which deprived them of the disagreeable harshness and matter-of-fact character of the transaction before me. For Turk or Smyrniote or Egyptian to buy and sell slaves seemed rather suited to the eternal fitness of things than otherwise. The turbaned, shawled, loose-trousered, pipe-smoking merchants, speaking an unknown tongue, looked as if they were engaged in a legitimate business. One knew that their slaves would not be condemned to any very hard labor, and that they would be in some sort the inmates of the family and members of it. Here it grated on my ear to listen to the familiar tones of the English tongue as the medium by which the transfer was effected, and it was painful to see decent-looking men in European garb engaged in the work before me. Perchance these impressions may wear off, for I meet many English people who are the most strenuous advocates of the slave system, although it is true that their perceptions may be quickened to recognize its beauties by their participation in the profits. The negro was sold to one of the bystanders, and walked off with his bundle, God knows where. ' Niggers is cheap,' was the only remark of the bystanders." See, also, his letters of April 30 and May 22, the latter from New Orleans. A later letter, from Natchez, June 14, gives his further unfavorable impressions concerning slavery, and concludes by averring that if the South is successful the African slave-trade will be reopened. See article in New York *World*, July 30, testifying Russell's impartiality, and article of Richmond *Examiner*, of Aug. 7, and of Memphis *Appeal*, cited by *Tribune*, Aug. 13, condemning Russell.

Punch understood the meaning of the contest, and composed "The National Hymn of the Confederate States."

> " When first the South, to fury fanned,
>   Arose and broke the Union's chain,
>   This was the charter, the charter of the land,
>   And Mr. Davis sang the strain:
>   Rule Slaveownia, Slaveownia rules, and raves,
>   Christians ever, ever, ever have had slaves.

> .   .   .   .

> " And trade, that knows no god but gold,
>   Shall to thy pirate ports repair;
>   Blest land, where flesh—where human flesh is sold,
>   And manly arms may flog that air. . . ."

the North. After an hour's interview with Lord Palmerston, he thought that the prime-minister summed up in one pithy remark the reason of the government's action and the sentiment of the public. " We do not like slavery," Palmerston said, " but we want cotton, and we dislike very much your Morrill tariff." [1] Adams was convinced that the de-

Of state-rights Russell said, in his letter from Savannah, May 1 : " To us the question is simply inexplicable or absurd." See, also, letter from Montgomery, May 7. Russell set down in his Diary, June 18 (p. 315): " Day after day . . . the impression on my mind was strengthened that 'state-rights' meant protection to slavery, extension of slave territory, and free trade in slave produce with the outer world." The London *Times* in a leader of May 22 said : " There can be no doubt that secession was never contemplated by the parties to the Union of 1787." And, " If the North prevails, it will prove that the Union was a nationality ; if the South makes good its independence, it will prove that the Union was a partnership during pleasure ;" see a mournful article in the Richmond *Examiner* of July 13, to the effect that foreigners do not fully comprehend the character of the war.

[1] Letter of Belmont to Seward, July 30. It must be remembered that the English had not yet the news of the battle of Bull Run. Belmont added: " I am more than ever convinced that we have nothing to hope from the sympathy of the English government and people in our struggle. Because this war is not carried on for the abolition of slavery in the Southern States, they try to maintain that the war has nothing to do with slavery ; wilfully shutting their eyes to the fact that the attitude of the North with regard to introducing slavery into the territories is the main ground upon which the secessionists justify their action. As a distinguished lady, wife of a prominent liberal in Parliament, told me last evening, 'I am sorry to say we have been found wanting in the present emergency, and principles have to yield to interest.' . . . I hope that by the time this reaches you our troops have been victorious in Virginia ; one or two battles now will very soon change the tone and feeling of our English cousins."

Punch gave expression to the same idea:

> "Though with the North we sympathize,
>   It must not be forgotten
> That with the South we've stronger ties,
>   Which are composed of cotton.
> Whereof our imports mount unto
>   A sum of many figures;
> And where would be our calico
>   Without the toil of niggers?.

velopment of an active sympathy and the gaining over of
the waverers depended on military successes and an exhibition of federal strength that would seem to promise a
speedy termination of the war.¹ Such, then, was the sentiment of the English people when they heard the news of
the battle of Bull Run.

The President, when possible, adhered literally to the provisions of the law ; therefore, in his proclamation of April
15, he commanded the insurgents " to disperse and retire
peaceably to their respective abodes in twenty days."
Naturally no forward movement would take place until the
expiration of that time. Then the question of marching
United States troops with hostile intentions into a State
had to be considered. The necessities of geographical position required the advance to be made into Virginia, but
she did not consummate the act of secession until May 23,
the day of the popular vote on the ordinance. After that
election she constituted in a complete manner one of the
Confederate States, and the repossession of the Richmond
custom-house came within the purview of the President's

> "The South enslaves those fellow-men,
>   Whom we love all so dearly;
> The North keeps Commerce bound again,
>   Which touches us more nearly.
> Thus a divided duty we
>   Perceive in this hard matter:
> Free-trade, or sable brothers free ?
>   Oh, won't we choose the latter!"

¹ Adams said, in his despatch to Seward of June 21: "Neither party
would be so bold as to declare its sympathy with a cause based upon the
extension of slavery, for that would at once draw upon itself the indignation of the great body of the people. But the development of a positive spirit in the opposite direction will depend far more upon the degree in which the arm of the government enforces obedience than upon
any absolute affinity in sentiments. Our brethren in this country, after
all, are much disposed to fall in with the opinion of Voltaire, that ' Dieu
est toujours sur le côté des gros canons.' General Scott and an effective
blockading squadron will be the true agents to keep the peace abroad, as
well as to conquer one at home."—Message and Documents, p. 110.

proclamation as much as the retaking of the forts in
Charleston harbor. On the administration theory of the
war, an advance into Virginia was entirely proper; so, in
the early morning of the 24th, the federal soldiers crossed
the Potomac River, and occupied Arlington Heights and
the city of Alexandria. Even this was primarily a move
for the protection of the capital; while a sentiment of
nationality prompted the eager desire to take possession
of Alexandria, for from the windows of the Executive
Mansion could be plainly seen a Confederate flag flying
over its principal hotel.[1] The invasion of Virginia, the
pollution of her sacred soil as it was termed, called forth a
vigorous proclamation from her governor and a cry of
rage from her press.[2] General Beauregard, then in command "of the troops in the Alexandria line," issued a proclamation which showed a strange misapprehension of the
character of the Northern soldiers, unless it was conceived
with the dexterous purpose of firing the Virginian heart
with anger. "A reckless and unprincipled tyrant has invaded your soil," he declared. "Abraham Lincoln, regardless of all moral, legal, and constitutional restraints, has
thrown his abolition hosts among you, who are murdering
and imprisoning your citizens, confiscating and destroying
your property. . . . All rules of civilized warfare are abandoned, and they proclaim by their acts, if not on their banners, that their war-cry is 'Beauty and booty.'"[3]

The people of western Virginia, by reason of their character, occupations, and small ownership of slaves, were
more closely connected with Pennsylvania and Ohio than

---

[1] Nicolay and Hay, vol. iv. p. 311.

[2] Richmond *Examiner*, May 25, June 5; Richmond *Enquirer* and Richmond *Whig*, May 25; Russell's Diary, entry of May 25, p. 235.

[3] Date of proclamation, June 5. Official Records, vol. ii. p. 905. For
a defence of this proclamation, see Roman's Beauregard, vol. i. p. 73. On
a current notion at the South that "beauty and booty" were the aim of
the Northern troops, see Richmond *Enquirer*, June 13; New York *Tribune*,
July 20 ; Greeley's American Conflict, vol. i. p. 508, note.

with the eastern part of their State, and their vote on the
ordinance of secession made evident their wish to adhere
to the Union.[1] Before the election a movement began
which had for its object the erection of an independent
commonwealth west of the Alleghanies. Hoping to check
this movement, Governor Letcher sent troops from the
eastern part of the State beyond the mountains. General
McClellan, commanding the Department of the Ohio, having already organized a considerable force, had been invited by Union men to march into western Virginia, but
this he would not do until he had heard the result of the
popular vote. May 26 he ordered a detachment to cross
the Ohio River, and co-operate with the loyal volunteers in
driving the Confederates from their territory. Under this
protection and encouragement the Union men proceeded
rapidly in constituting themselves a State; they assembled
in convention at Wheeling, adopted a declaration of independence, passed ordinances requisite to the occasion, and
elected a governor. Shortly after the convention adjourned
a legislature, composed of members from the western counties, met, enacted necessary legislation, and chose United
States senators, who were permitted to qualify and take
their seats in the Senate as senators from Virginia at the
special session. The reception which General McClellan's
troops met on their march through upper western Virginia,
and that General Cox had in his progress through the valley
of the Kanawha, showed that the election returns represented the true sentiment of that part of the State. The
Union forces met the Confederates at Philippi[2] and defeated
them. June 22 McClellan took command in person and
issued a bombastic proclamation to his army, in which he
rated the secessionists as wicked as Beauregard had pronounced the Northern soldiers. "Your enemies have violated every moral law," he declared; "neither God nor
man can sustain them." The campaign continued to be an

---

[1] *Ante,* p. 387.   [2] A small town in western Virginia.

advance on his part, and a retreat on the part of the Confederates.[1]

In eastern Virginia there had been several skirmishes, mainly to the disadvantage of the federal troops, but with results of no importance. As the army in the neighborhood of Washington grew in numbers and discipline, a fierce desire arose in the Northern people that it should advance, defeat the secessionists in one great battle, and make an end of the war. Business was bad, financial distrust prevailed, and, on account of the uncertain condition of the country, better times could not be seen ahead. "The Nation's War-cry" of the New York *Tribune* gave utterance .to this sentiment, and at the same time fostered it. June 26 this journal declared, at the head of its editorial columns, with all the emphasis that type could give : "*Forward to Richmond! Forward to Richmond! The Rebel Congress must not be allowed to meet there on the 20th of July!* BY THAT DATE THE PLACE MUST BE HELD BY THE NATIONAL ARMY!"[2]

Congress met in Washington July 4. On the next day the President's message was read in the Senate and the House, the representatives testifying their approval of many parts of it by enthusiastic applause.[3] The President asked Congress for at least 400,000 men and $400,000,000, in order to make "this contest a short and decisive one." Congress gave him authority to accept the services of 500,-000 volunteers, and, carrying out substantially the more detailed recommendation of the Secretary of the Treasury, authorized a loan of $250,000,000 ; it also increased the tariff duties, provided for a direct tax of $20,000,000, appor-

---

[1] See Appletons' Annual Cyclopædia, 1861; Official Records, vol. ii.; Moore's Rebellion Record, vol. ii.; J. D. Cox's article, "McClellan in West Virginia," Century War Book, vol. i. p. 126; McClellan's Own Story ; New York *Tribune*.

[2] This was printed in several succeeding issues. The war-cry, however, was not Greeley's, see *Tribune* of July 25.

[3] Portions of this important state-paper have already been referred to when discussing matters of which it treated, see pp. 346, 398, 405–408, 427.

tioned to all the States and territories, and imposed an income-tax, hoping from this legislation to get a revenue of
about $75,000,000 for the fiscal year.[1]

The President spoke in his message of his extraordinary
acts since Sumter fell. He believed that the call for 75,000
militia and the proclamation of the blockade were strictly
legal. The call for three-years troops and the increase of
the regular army and navy were measures which, if not
strictly legal, he trusted then and now that Congress would
readily ratify. He had ,deemed it necessary to the public
safety to authorize the commanding generals to suspend the
privilege of the writ of *habeas corpus*, in justification of
which he made the argument of necessity, but he also rea-
soned that it was no violation of the Constitution. This
subject from the first engaged the attention of Congress,
and a joint resolution was introduced to approve and confirm these several acts.[2] The extreme Democrats opposed
this violently ; but though their arguments were forcible,
they had the defect of applying to a state of war considerations mainly applicable only to a condition of peace.[3] It
was more important, however, that Republicans and the
Democrats who were disposed to co-operate with them in all
measures for the vigorous prosecution of the war to restore
the Union differed in regard to these points. There was a
concord of opinion that the call for 75,000 militia and the
proclamation of blockade were strictly legal, but able jurists out of Congress and lawyers and statesmen of the Senate did not agree about the suspension of the privilege of

---

[1] The notable increases of the tariff which gave a revenue were the duties
of four cents per pound on coffee and fifteen cents per pound on tea—both
of which, in the Morrill tariff, were on the free list—and the considerable
augmentation of the duty on sugars. The direct tax was allotted to the
disloyal as well as the loyal States, and would not yield over $15,000,000.
The income-tax was three per cent. on incomes over $800, and was to be
levied after Jan. 1, 1862, on incomes of the preceding year.

[2] For this see *Congressional Globe*, p. 40 ; see p. 457.

[3] See Vallandigham, *Congressional Globe*, pp. 58, 130; Powell, of Kentucky,
p. 66 ; Breckinridge, p. 137 ; Pearce, of Maryland, p. 332; Bayard, *Globe*
Appendix, p. 14.

the writ of *habeas corpus*.[1] The notion prevailed that the
call for three-years volunteers and the increase of the army
and the navy by proclamation was an assumption of powers by the executive which the Constitution strictly and
unmistakably vested solely in Congress, and that the argument that they did not involve a violation of the organic
act was strained.[2] In the last days of the session there
was tacked to the bill for the increase of the pay of the
privates in the army a section ratifying the acts and proc-
lamations of the President respecting the regular army and
navy and the militia and volunteers from the States. This
passed the Senate with only five negative votes, all five
being from the border slave States. On a test vote in the
House nineteen opposed it.[3]

Lincoln, in his message, spoke not only to Congress, but
to the people—the " plain people," as he called them ; and
no one understood them better than he. He told them
how he regretted the war, and made it clear that it had
been forced upon him. He related, by the aid of a familiar illustration, the course of the secessionists, combated
their argument, and gave, in emphatic and easily understood words, the theory on which the resistance of the government to the " rebellion " was based. He told them the

---

[1] Chief Justice Taney, in the Merryman case, declared that "the President, under the Constitution of the United States, cannot suspend the privilege of the writ of *habeas corpus*, nor authorize a military officer to do it."
Congress alone has that power, Tyler's Taney, p. 645 *et seq.* Reverdy
Johnson, between whom and Taney there had been thorough sympathy in
regard to the Dred Scott opinion (see vol. ii. p. 269), totally differed now
with the chief justice, and wrote an elaborate reply, declaring that "the
President's conduct was perfectly constitutional."—See Moore's Rebellion
Record, vol. ii., Docs., p. 185. As to disagreement of Republicans in the
Senate, for Browning's opinion see *Congressional Globe*, p. 188; Trumbull's,
p. 337; Sherman's, p. 393; Howe's, p. 393; Fessenden's, p. 453.

[2] For the reasoning of Morrill, of Maine, see *Congressional Globe*, p. 392.

[3] For the vote in the Senate see *Congressional Globe*, p. 442; in the House,
p. 449. The bill passed the Senate Aug. 5; the House, Aug. 6. For an explanation why the Senate did not also ratify the suspension of the *habeas
corpus*, see letter of Grimes, Sept. 16, Life of Grimes, p. 150.

meaning and the purpose of the conflict; he explained the reason of the war. "This is essentially a people's contest," he declared. "The leading object of the government for whose existence we contend" is "to afford all an unfettered start and a fair chance in the race of life." Such a government the secessionists aim to overthrow, and "the plain people understand and appreciate this." Many of the officers of the army and the navy in high station have "proved false to the hand which had pampered them," but "not one common soldier or common sailor is known to have deserted his flag. . . . This is the patriotic instinct of plain people. They understand without an argument that the destroying the government which was made by Washington means no good to them." They have therefore rushed to its defence. "One of the greatest perplexities of the government," he said, "is to avoid receiving troops faster than it can provide for them. In a word, the people will save their government, if the government itself will do its part only indifferently well." "And having thus chosen our course, without guile and with pure purpose," he concluded, "let us renew our trust in God, and go forward without fear and with manly hearts."

No demagogue ever made a more crafty appeal, and yet nothing could be further from the appeal of a demagogue. In manners, habits of life, to a large extent in tastes, Lincoln was himself one of the "plain people;" he was separated from the mass only by his great intellectual ability. The people of the North felt him to be one of them, and since the 4th of March it had come to them, at first dimly, but steadily, though by slow degrees, that their President was a man of power, fitted to guide the nation in its crisis, and they knew that when he proclaimed anything it was the truth as he saw it. They felt that Lincoln was their true representative; that when he acted, their will was expressed. Their hearts went out to him. The relation was one of mutual confidence. He felt he had their trust. They knew their trust lay in worthy hands.

The cabinet were beginning to see that Lincoln would be the master. "Executive skill and vigor are rare qualities," privately wrote Seward. "The President is the best of us."[1] The discussions in Congress and the action of that body show what a change of opinion had been wrought since the 4th of March concerning him in the minds of the politicians and statesmen of the nation. No ruler could hope to have his wishes more fully met by his legislature than were Lincoln's by the Congress which deliberated from July 4 to August 6. As one of its members afterwards wrote, the "session was but a giant committee of ways and means."[2] In the Senate were 12 Democrats and 4 Unionists[3] from the border slave States, and of these one half co-operated faithfully with the Republicans in the important measures for the vigorous prosecution of the war.[4] The House was composed of 106 Republicans, 42 Democrats, and 28 Unionists;[5] but on the resolution offered by McClernand, a Democrat, that the House pledge itself "to vote for any amount of money and any number of men which may be necessary to insure a speedy and effectual suppression of the rebellion," there were only 5 nays.[6] This substantial unanimity of Congress, its members bred in an atmosphere of liberty and having a profound respect for the law, was the more remarkable inasmuch as the acts of the President since April 15 had been the acts of a Tudor rather than those of a constitutional ruler. He had encroached on the legislature, a department of our govern-

---

[1] June 5, Life of Seward, vol. ii. p. 590.

[2] Riddle, Life of Wade, p. 291. Riddle was a representative from Ohio.

[3] There were 32 Republicans.

[4] Two of the opposition, Breckinridge, of Kentucky, and Polk, of Missouri, joined the Confederacy before the next session.

[5] This is the classification of the *Tribune* Almanac of the House which met Dec., 1861, but it is substantially correct for the special session.

[6] *Congressional Globe*, p. 131. The yeas were 121. On the National Loan bill the vote was larger, there being 150 yeas, but only 5 nays, ibid., p. 61. Burnett, of Kentucky (who afterwards joined the Confederacy), Vallandigham, of Ohio, Benjamin Wood, of New York, were among the nays.

ment always jealous for the limits of its authority. "One of the most interesting features of the present state of things," wrote Schleiden to Sumner, "is the illimited power exercised by the government. Mr. Lincoln is, in that respect, the equal, if not the superior, of Louis Napoleon. The difference consists only in the fact that the President rests his authority on the unanimous consent of the people of the loyal States, the emperor his on the army."[1] Lincoln was strong with Congress; he was stronger still with the people. The country attorney of Illinois had assumed the power of a dictator. Congress agreed that the times needed one, and the people backed their President. Yet there was method in this trust, for never had the power of dictator fallen into safer and nobler hands.

July 16 the House voted General McClellan thanks for "the series of brilliant and decisive victories" which he had achieved in western Virginia. Since taking command in person he had defeated the Confederates in the affairs of Rich Mountain and Beverly. General Scott telegraphed him, "The general-in-chief, and what is more the cabinet, including the President, are charmed with your activity, valor, and consequent successes."[2] On the same day that he received this despatch McClellan gained the combat of Carrick's Ford, and sent word to Washington, "Our success is complete, and secession is killed in this country."[3] Although these engagements were small affairs, they secured the important result of freeing upper western Virginia from organized bands of Confederates, and they made McClellan the military hero of the North. He displaced in the popular favor Major Anderson and General Scott.

Northern public opinion demanded that the Union soldiers force a battle in eastern Virginia. It was an intelligent sentiment, and the administration was right in yielding to it. For a battle gained now would be of immense value.

---

[1] Letter of May 11, Pierce-Sumner Papers, MS.
[2] Despatch of July 13, Official Records, vol. ii. p. 204.
[3] Despatch of July 14, ibid.

To maintain that unanimity of feeling at the North which had prevailed since the firing on Sumter success was needed. A short war would keep patriotism at the high-water mark; a long one would breed differences of opinion and foster an opposition party. Europe, now beginning to regard with good-will the efforts of the national government to preserve its authority, would feel sympathy with the North, could it show that it had the stronger battalions. Moreover, the time of the three-months men was fast expiring, and as they were eager to fight, it seemed injudicious to disband an army which represented the best blood and noblest purpose of the North without giving it a chance to feel the enemy. The President was wise, therefore, in calling a council of war of his cabinet and of the prominent military men, in order that the political aim might be considered in the light of technical skill. June 29 this council met at the White House. By request, General McDowell, a graduate of West Point, who had served with credit in the Mexican War, submitted a plan of attack on Beauregard, who had at Manassas Junction and within easy distance an effective force of 21,900.[1] McDowell said he would make the movement, provided Joseph E. Johnston, who was in the Shenandoah valley with nearly 9000 available men,[2] could be prevented from joining Beauregard. General Scott, who did not approve of the plan of fighting a battle in Virginia, but who set himself loyally at work to carry out the wish of the President,[3] said, "If Johnston joins Beauregard, he shall have Patter-

---

[1] To avoid considerable detail in this account I give this army as it was the day of the battle of Bull Run. This is a statement in 1884 of Beauregard's adjutant-general (Century War Book, vol. i. p. 195), and almost exactly agrees with Beauregard's official report of Oct. 14, 1861, Official Records, vol. ii. p. 487. Manassas was the junction of the railroad from Alexandria to Richmond with that which went to the Shenandoah valley.

[2] Johnston's Narrative, p. 31.

[3] McDowell's Testimony, Report on the Conduct of the War, part ii. p. 37; Richardson's statement in the House, July 24, of a declaration of Scott to the President, McClernand, Logan, Washburne, and himself, *Congressional Globe*, p. 246.

son on his heels." [1] General Patterson, a veteran of the War
of 1812 and of the Mexican War, held command of 18,000
to 22,000 troops [2] at Martinsburg, and had been instructed
to beat Johnston, or, if not strong enough, to detain him in
the Shenandoah valley. [3]

War on a large scale was a new business for Americans;
to handle and move troops expeditiously was an art to be
learned. The advance was not made as soon as intended, but on the afternoon of July 16 McDowell's " Grand
Army," about 30,000 strong, composed of nearly 1600 regulars, [4] and the rest for the most part three-months volunteers, marched to the front. The Confederates retired before him, and by the 18th he had occupied Centreville.
" The march," writes William T. Sherman, who commanded
a brigade, "demonstrated little save the general laxity of
discipline." [5] On the 18th a reconnoissance was made by
one of the brigades of Tyler's division at Blackburn's Ford
of Bull Run ; a skirmish ensued, in which the Union troops
got the worse of it, and although the material damage was
not great, the effect on the morale of the army was considerable.

Informed of the movement of the federal army, Beauregard ordered his advanced brigades to withdraw within the
lines of Bull Run. This was accomplished without interruption. At the same time he begged Davis for reinforce-

[1] McDowell's Testimony.

[2] His army, after being reinforced by General Sandford July 8. Sandford
says it was 22,000, Testimony, p. 56.   Patterson admits 18,225, ibid., p. 99.

[3] Scott to Patterson, July 13, Official Records, vol. ii. p. 166.

[4] I am under obligations to Joseph W. Kirkley, member of War Records Publication Board, War Department, Washington, for having calculated for me from the official returns the number of men in five companies
of artillery and in the battalions of infantry and marines. For four companies of artillery there is no return, and at the suggestion of General J.
D. Cox I have estimated their number at the average of the five companies,
and the battalion of cavalry at 200. This makes a total of 1561 regulars.
For the number of guns in McDowell's army and the number that went
into action, see James B. Fry's statement, Century War Book, vol. i. p. 195.

[5] Memoirs, vol. i. p. 181.

ments.[1] The Richmond government telegraphed Johnston to join Beauregard if practicable.[2] Johnston received the despatch at one o'clock on the morning of July 18, and he at once determined to make the movement. To do this it seemed necessary to defeat Patterson or elude him. Elusion was thought the more speedy and certain, but Johnston could not know that his artifice would be as successful as if the Union army were fifty miles away. Patterson's mind had fed upon rumors and false reports until he had magnified Johnston's 9000 into a force of 35,000.[3] Nevertheless, July 15, he advanced to Bunker Hill, being then within nine miles of Johnston's camp at Winchester; but instead of remaining where he was, approaching nearer, or, as one of his generals proposed, throwing his large force between the Confederates and the Shenandoah River, he marched directly away from them, moving on the 17th to Charlestown, twenty-two miles from Winchester, thus giving Johnston as good an opportunity for escape as if he had actually planned to do it.[4] While the time of many of the three-months men had nearly expired and they were anxious to return home, yet the army was a fine body of men, largely made up of New York and Pennsylvania militia, who were willing to stay over time for a fight, but, when ordered to march away from the enemy, clamored for discharge to the moment.[5] General Scott's anxiety lest Patterson should not perform his part became alarm on July 18, when he telegraphed: "I have certainly been expecting you to beat the enemy. If not, to hear that you had felt him strongly, or at least had occupied him by threats and demonstrations. You

---

[1] Beauregard to Davis, July 17, Official Records, vol. ii. p. 439.
[2] Ibid., p. 478.
[3] Patterson to Townsend, July 20, Official Records, vol. ii. p. 172.
[4] Official Records, vol. ii. p. 166; Sandford's, Stone's, and Cadwalader's testimony before the Committee on the Conduct of the War. These were officers under Patterson.
[5] Sandford's, Doubleday's, and Patterson's testimony before the Committee on the Conduct of the War.

have been at least his equal, and I suppose superior, in numbers. Has he not stolen a march and sent reinforcements towards Manassas Junction?" "The enemy has stolen no march upon me," promptly replied Patterson. "I have kept him actively employed, and by threats and reconnoissances in force caused him to be reinforced."[1] While Patterson was sending this and another complacent report, Johnston was leaving Winchester on his way to Manassas. "The discouragements of that day's march," he writes, "are indescribable."[2] The delays, the lack of discipline, made him despair of reaching Beauregard in time. At Piedmont, therefore, he took the railroad, and by noon of Saturday, July 20, arrived with 6000 troops at Manassas Junction. On that day Patterson first learned that Johnston had left Winchester with his whole force, and so telegraphed to Washington.[3]

McDowell's subsistence train having arrived, he deemed his information of the country and of the enemy sufficiently exact, and determined to make the attack on Sunday, July 21, his intention being to turn the Confederate left. At half-past two in the morning the troops were in motion. The officers were inexperienced and the men green, so that delays in marching and manœuvring were inevitable. Tyler's division was slow in getting out on the road, and hindered the divisions which were to make a long detour by the right flank. It marched on the Warrenton turnpike to the stone bridge over Bull Run, and at 6.30 fired a signal gun to show that it was in position. Hunter's division turned off from the turnpike to the right, marched through the woods to the ford at Sudley Springs, crossed Bull Run, and met the Confederates at ten o'clock, three hours later than had been planned, on a hill north of Young's Branch. The Union troops engaged outnumbered the enemy, and drove them back across the Warrenton turnpike and Young's Branch,

---

[1] Official Records, vol. ii. p. 168.   [2] Narrative, p. 36.
[3] Official Records, vol. ii. p. 172.

a distance of one and a half miles, gaining possession of the road and uncovering the stone bridge. The Confederates were in full retreat, but as they ran up the slope of the plateau, about the Henry House, Thomas J. Jackson's brigade stood there in line calmly awaiting the onset. General Bee, who commanded a Confederate brigade, cried out in encouragement to his retreating troops, "Look at Jackson! There he stands like a stone wall," an exclamation that gave him the name by which he has since been known.[1] McDowell had with promptness pushed across Bull Run two other divisions, and soon had 18,500 men with twenty-four pieces of artillery[2] advancing on the Confederates, and the day seemed gained.

Beauregard, thinking it advisable to assume the offensive before Patterson could effect a junction with McDowell, had formed the plan of crossing Bull Run by his right, and attacking the Union troops; for both he and Johnston supposed that the Union general, who had actually retired to Harper's Ferry in fear of an attack, was now making all haste to meet McDowell. Johnston, the ranking officer, approved the plan, but the orders miscarried, and before this could be remedied he and Beauregard, though four miles away, divined, from the sound of cannon in the direction of Sudley Springs, that McDowell was trying to turn their left. They rode furiously to the scene of action. "We came not a moment too soon," writes Johnston.[3] The Confederates were demoralized. A disorderly retreat had begun. It needed all the influence and force of will of the commanding generals to rally them. "General Johnston impressively and gallantly charged to the front with the colors of the Fourth Alabama Regiment by his side,"[4] and

---

[1] Daniels (1863), Dabney (1866), Cooke (1866), Mrs. Jackson (1891) relate this circumstance. General D. H. Hill, in the *Century Magazine* for Feb., 1894, says the tale was "a sheer fabrication."

[2] James B. Fry's statement, Century War Book, vol. i. p. 195.

[3] Official report, Oct. 14.

[4] Beauregard's official report of Oct. 14.

5 Genl. Smith shot
6 Lieut.-Col. Law wounded
7 Maj. Wheat "
8 " Gardner "
" Adj. Branch fell
" Capt. Cooper "
" Barlow's horse killed
9 Capt. Howard fell
10 Col. Jones "
11 Mr. Wilkins "
12 Beauregard's horse killed
13 Cameron's grave
O Capt. Kemper taken prisoner

2d Regt. Va. Vols.
17—1st Pos.

4th Regt. Va. Vols.
16—1st Pos.

5th Regt. Va. Vols.
14—1st Pos.
9—2d "
50—3d "
10—4th "

18th Regt. Va. Vols.
25—1st Pos.
13—2d "

19th Regt. Va. Vols.
24—1st Pos.
25—2d "
44—3d "

27th Regt. Va. Vols.
15—1st Pos.

28th Regt. Va. Vols.
27—1st Pos.
20—2d "
29—3d "

33d Regt. Va. Vols.
18—1st Pos.

49th Regt. Va. Vols.
23—1st Pos.
19—2d "

Wheat's Battalion
38—1st Pos.
33—2d "
41—Tiger's skirm.

Hampton Legion
4—1st Pos.
50—2d "
11—3d "

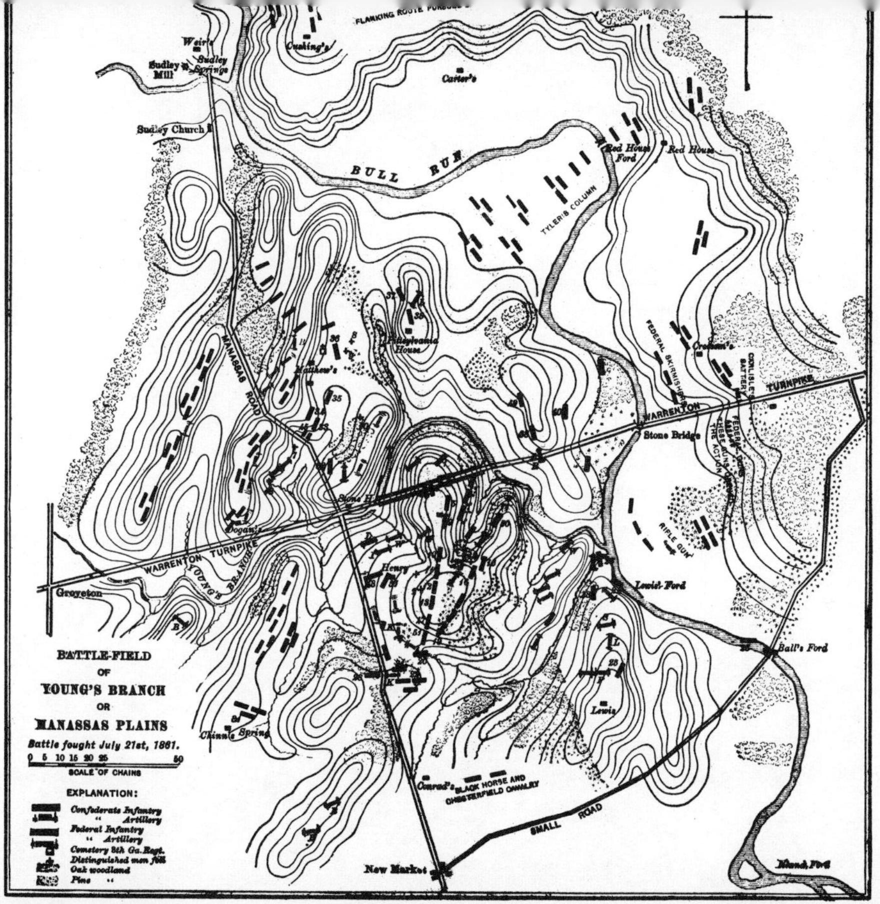
BATTLE-FIELD
OF
YOUNG'S BRANCH
OR
MANASSAS PLAINS
Battle fought July 21st, 1861.
0 5 10 15 20 25 50
SCALE OF CHAINS
EXPLANATION:
Confederate Infantry
" Artillery
Federal Infantry
" Artillery
Cemetery 8th Ga. Regt.
Distinguished men fell
Oak woodland
Pine "
BULL RUN
Weir's
Sudley Mill
Sudley Springs
Sudley Church
Cushing's
Carter's
Red House Ford
Red House
TYLER'S COLUMN
MANASSAS ROAD
Matthew's
Pittsylvania House
WARRENTON TURNPIKE
YOUNG'S BRANCH
Groveton
Dogan's
Henry
Chinn's Spring
Conrad's
BLACK HORSE AND CHESTERFIELD CAVALRY
SMALL ROAD
New Market
Stone Bridge
FEDERAL SKIRMISHERS
Crossman's
CARLISLE'S BATTERY
RIFLE GUN
Lewis' Ford
Ball's Ford
Lewis
Island Ford

8th Regt. Va. Vols.
48—1st Pos.
11—2d "

4th Regt. S. C. Vols.
49—1st Pos.
37—2d "
32—3d "
33—4th "
1—5th "
7—6th "
5—7th "
14—8th "
10—9th "

2d Regt. S. C. Vols.
21—1st Pos.

7th Ga. Regt. Vols.
43—1st Pos.
3—2d "
2—3d "
8—4th "
58—5th "
51—6th & last Pos.

8th Regt. Ga. Vols.
26—1st Pos.
43—2d "
36—3d "
1—4th "
6—5th "
11—6th "

4th Regt. Ala. Vols.
35—1st Pos.
8—2d "
13—3d "
44—4th "

2d Regt. Miss. Vols.
32—1st Pos.
41—2d "
46—3d "
45—Companies Skirm.

Elzey's Brigade
22—1st Pos.
30—2d "

Early's Brigade
31—1st Pos.

40 Capt. Kilpatrick
42 " Anderson

then all the men obeyed the order to form on the line of
their colors. Beauregard remained, in the thick of the fight,
in command of the troops there engaged, while Johnston
regretfully rode to the rear to hurry forward reinforcements.

It was high noon when the two Confederate generals
appeared on the field. From this hour until three the battle surged. The hottest part of the contest was for the
possession of the Henry plateau. The Union troops had
seized it, brought forward Ricketts' and Griffin's batteries
of regulars, and placed them in effective position. Through
a mischance they were captured, but were retaken, then
taken again. At two o'clock Beauregard gave the order
to advance to recover the plateau. The charge was made
with spirit. Jackson's brigade pierced at the bayonet's
point the Union centre. The other parts of the line moving forward with equal vigor, the federal lines were broken
and swept back from the open ground of the plateau. The
Union troops rallied, recovered their ground, and drove the
Confederates entirely from the plateau and beyond it out
of sight. McDowell, who had this part of the field immediately under his own eye, thought this last repulse final,
and that the day was his. Although the numbers of available troops were substantially equal,[1] McDowell seems to
have disposed his men better than did Johnston, for up to
three o'clock he had a superior force engaged. Johnston
with remarkable candor admits it was "a great fault" on
his part that he did not order two brigades into action earlier, and that he failed to bring the largest part of three
other brigades on to the field of battle at all.[2]

---

[1] McDowell's 30,000 had been reduced to less than 29,000 by the withdrawal of the Fourth Pennsylvania and the battery of volunteer artillery
of the Eighth New York. Their time had expired, they had insisted on
their discharge, and they "moved to the rear to the sound of the enemy's
cannon."—McDowell's report. Beauregard's army of 21,900, and Johnston's reinforcement of July 20, of 6000, brought the Confederate force
nearly to 28,000.   [2] Johnston's Narrative, p. 57.

Thus stood affairs at three o'clock. McDowell had possession of the plateau, hoping the fight was over. His men
had been up since two in the morning, one division having
had a long, fatiguing march. The day was intensely hot.
They had been fighting five hours. Many of the men had
thrown away their haversacks and canteens. They were
choked with dust, thirsty, hungry, and tired. Beauregard
ordered forward all of his force within reach, including his
reserve, with the purpose of making a last supreme effort
to regain the plateau, and he intended to lead the charge
in person. Then cheers of fresh troops were heard. It
was the remainder of the army of the Shenandoah, which
had followed Johnston as expeditiously as the railroad could
bring them. Twenty-three hundred soldiers led by Kirby
Smith, directed by Johnston, threw themselves upon Mc-
Dowell's right. From mouth to mouth of the Union men
went the word, "Johnston's army has come." At the
same time Beauregard moved forward his whole line. The
federal troops broke and retired down the hill-side. All
order was soon lost. In vain did McDowell and his officers attempt to rally them. The battalion of regular infantry alone obeyed commands. It covered the volunteers'
retreat, which became a rout and then a panic. The troops
crossed the fords of Bull Run and crowded the Warrenton
turnpike, a confused mass of disorganized, frightened men.
The Confederates pursued them as far as Cub Run ; the road
there becoming blocked with artillery and wagons, the
panic increased. McDowell intended to make a stand at
Centreville.[1] There and somewhat nearer the scene of action were a crowd of congressmen and civilians who had come
out to witness the expected victory of "the grand army."
The panic in an aggravated form was communicated to
them, and also to the drivers of the ambulances and of the

---

[1] The stone bridge at Bull Run was one half mile from Cub Run,
and four miles from Centreville. Manassas Junction is seven miles southwest of Centreville. Centreville is twenty-seven miles from Washington.

commissariat and ammunition wagons. It was a save-him-
self-who-can, a disorderly flight towards Washington, an
impetuous rush for the shelter of the federal capital. It
was found impossible to make a stand, either at Centreville
or Fairfax Court-House. " The larger part of the men,"
telegraphed McDowell from Fairfax Court-House, " are a
confused mob, entirely demoralized." " They are pouring
through this place in a state of utter disorganization." ¹
The flight of the troops was not stopped until they reached
the fortifications south of the Potomac, and many of the
soldiers crossed the Long bridge into Washington. The
alarm had been utterly baseless. The men were frightened
by a shadow. The Confederates made no effective pursuit.²

---

¹ Official Records, vol. ii. p. 316.

² The loss of the Union army was : 16 officers and 444 men killed, 78
officers and 1046 men wounded, 50 officers and 1262 men missing. J. B. Fry,
assistant adjutant-general to McDowell, Century War Book, vol. i. p. 193.
Compare Official Records, vol. ii. p. 327. The Confederate loss was 378
killed, 1489 wounded, and 30 missing. "Twenty-eight pieces of artillery,
about 5000 muskets, and nearly 500,000 cartridges, a garrison flag, and 10
colors were captured on the field or in the pursuit. Besides these we
captured 64 artillery horses with their harness, 26 wagons, and much camp
equipage, clothing, and other property abandoned in their flight."—Johnston's official report. The literature of the Bull Run battle is volumi-
nous. The best authorities are, of course, the official reports of both sides,
published in vol. ii. of Official Records. I have made up my account almost
wholly from the reports of McDowell, Johnston, Beauregard, Jackson, W.
T. Sherman, and Tyler, and from McDowell's and Patterson's testimony,
and that of several of their officers before the congressional Committee on
the Conduct of the War. It is worthy of note that McDowell's report was
made Aug. 4, while Johnston's and Beauregard's were not fully prepared
until Oct. 14. I feel quite sure General Sherman is right when he says,
"The reports of the opposing commanders, McDowell and Johnston, are
fair and correct."—Memoirs, p. 181. General Johnston and General Sherman's accounts in their books are very interesting. Johnston's, Beauregard's, and James B. Fry's articles in vol. i. Century War Book aid one
to understand the battle if carefully compared with the official reports.
Swinton's account is picturesque, and I should have been glad to incorpo-
rate in my narrative some incidents he mentions, for I presume they are
true, but I could not find warrant for them in the Official Records. His book
was published in 1867, before the government began to print the Official

"It is now generally admitted," writes William T. Sherman, "that Bull Run was one of the best-planned battles of the war, but one of the worst fought."[1] Detracting as this fact must from its value as a lesson to the military man, it is to the student of men one of the most interesting of battles. In the one view it was an encounter between two fighting mobs; in the other, as the result of the uprising at the North and the South, it was the meeting on a bloody field of their best. Without discipline and experience, without knowledge of the art of war, those men fought bravely and died heroically, both armies feeling that they were contending for a sacred principle. The available forces were substantially equal in number. The arms of the Northern infantry were little if any superior. The Southerners were more expert in the use of the rifle. Beauregard had in his army five South Carolina regiments, and the Hampton Legion, which had been under discipline more than six months; but as an offset to them must be reckoned the reg-

---

Records. Roman's Beauregard, the biographies of "Stonewall" Jackson by his wife and by Cooke, Dabney's Life and Campaigns of Jackson, and General J. A. Early's account (Rise and Fall of the Confederate Government, vol. i. p. 392) add something of interest to the story. William H. Russell, in his Diary, gives an interesting and accurate account of the panic on the road. General Patterson made an elaborate defence before the Committee on the Conduct of the War, and James B. Fry makes a generous defence of him in Century War Book, vol. i. p. 182, note, neither of which has modified the judgment I expressed in the text. I do not know that civilian criticism of military matters is of much value, but it seems to me that the Committee on the Conduct of the War told the true story in their report—"the movement was made too late rather than too soon. . . . The principal cause of the defeat . . . was the failure of General Patterson to hold the forces of Johnston in the valley of the Shenandoah." General McDowell hoped to make the attack Saturday, but he was prevented by delays for which he was not responsible. He had heard rumors that Johnston's army had joined Beauregard's, but did not fully credit them ; see Official Records, vol. ii. p. 308, his testimony before the Committee on the Conduct of the War, and Century War Book, vol. i. p. 183. Scott telegraphed McDowell the day of the battle that Johnston had strongly reinforced Beauregard, but then the fight was on. Official Records, vol. ii. p. 746 ; Century War Book, vol. i. p. 182.   [1] Memoirs, p. 181.

ulars in the Union army and, in a degree, three Massachusetts regiments which since January had had somewhat of
drill. The federal artillery was superior. There were nine
companies of regulars, and they had better guns than the
enemy. But on the whole the two armies were evenly
matched in this first contest. At the council of war called
by the President, McDowell had asked for longer time to
discipline his men. The reply was made, " You are green,
it is true; but they are green also." [1] This was correct. If
McDowell had had only Beauregard's army to meet, he
would undoubtedly have gained a signal victory. If the
2300 fresh troops that came into battle at three o'clock had
been from Patterson's instead of from Johnston's army,
there would still have been a retreat, a rout, and a panic,
but the flight would have been towards Richmond instead
of Washington. When Jefferson Davis arrived at Manassas
Junction the afternoon of the battle, he found many stragglers who had left the field in a panic and who told " fearful stories " of the defeat of the Confederate army. A gray-
bearded man calmly said, " Our line was broken, all was
confusion, the army routed, and the battle lost." [2]

A curious game is war. In his official report General
Beauregard exults over the supposed enormous loss in killed
and wounded of his adversaries, and yet, when he made his
final charge, not yet absolutely sure that victory was his,
seeing Captain Ricketts, whom he had known in the old
army, lying on the ground badly wounded, he paused in his
" anxious duties to ask him whether he could do anything
for him;" and he sent his own surgeons to care for the
Union soldier.[3]

Into the controversy between Johnston and Beauregard,
and between those generals and Jefferson Davis, we need
not go. Johnston and Beauregard, who worked harmoni-

---

[1] McDowell's Testimony.
[2] Rise and Fall of the Confederate Government, vol. i. p. 349.
[3] Beauregard's article, Century War Book, vol. i. p. 213.

ously together the day of battle, who showed courage and
fertility of resource in the hour of danger, and who deserved
well of the South for their action, have since fought over in
print the question as to who was actually in command of
the Confederate army.[1]   Jefferson Davis, whose conduct
was such as a civil ruler's in consultation with his victorious
generals should have been, felt so keenly the later strictures
that to him must be imputed the failure to follow up the
victory by the capture of Washington, that he, too, entered
into an undignified controversy.   The Southern memories
of the battle of Bull Run would have been more grateful if
the final word concerning it had been the judgments at the
time of Johnston and Davis.   " Our victory was as complete as one gained by infantry and artillery can be," wrote
Johnston.[2]   " Enough was done for glory, and the measure
of duty was full," said Davis in a letter of August 4 to
Beauregard.[3]   Touching the pursuit of the federals, and the
notion that McDowell's army and Washington might have
been taken, all three are agreed that it was impossible.[4]
" The Confederate army was more disorganized by victory
than that of the United States by defeat," writes Johnston.[5]
The Confederate generals were unquestionably right in attempting no pursuit.   While to Edwin M. Stanton and William H. Russell it seemed clear that the capital might be
easily taken,[6] McDowell and his generals in the fortifications on the south bank of the Potomac knew that they
could make a stubborn resistance to any attack.[7]   It was
not a deceitful reassurance, but a well-sustained confidence,

---

[1] An excellent statement of this controversy and a decision of it by a
military critic is given in General J. D. Cox's review of Beauregard's
"Battle of Manassas" in the *Nation* of June 11, 1891.

[2] Official report.

[3] Rise and Fall of the Confederate Government, vol. i. p. 365.

[4] See Johnston's and Beauregard's reports; Johnston's Narrative, p. 61;
Davis, vol. i. p. 352.   [5] Narrative, p. 60.

[6] Stanton to Buchanan, July 26, *North American Review*, Nov., 1879;
Russell to the London *Times*, July 29 ; Diary, p. 170.

[7] Official Records, vol. ii. p. 755 ; Sherman's Memoirs, p. 188.

that led Cameron to telegraph to New York, Monday, July
22: "Our works on the south bank of Potomac are impregnable, being well manned with reinforcements. The capital
is safe." [1]

On the night of July 21 no man in America had greater
need of pity than the commander of the defeated army
which was fleeing from the enemy; but as the mists clear
away he seems, in the historical view, to have come out of
the events of that terrible day the best of all. He did
bravely and well. McDowell was a victim to the mismanagement of others, but few now will question the general
verdict that he was a true soldier and a magnanimous man.

The defeat was a dreadful blow to Lincoln, the more so
that the first news had been favorable. Having reason to
believe from the despatches that the Union troops had
gained a victory, he went out for his afternoon drive, during which he undoubtedly ruminated on the course he
should adopt as a fitting sequel to his success. On his return to the White House he was told the last word which
had come: "General McDowell's army in full retreat
through Centreville. The day is lost. Save Washington
and the remnants of this army." [2] He heard the crushing
news with fortitude and without moving a muscle. He met
this adversity with dauntless spirit, and in the sleepless
night that followed he busied his mind with plans to retrieve the disaster.[3] Tuesday, July 23, he visited the camps
on the south side of the Potomac, and made a speech full of
feeling to the soldiers, many of whom had been panic-strick-
en the Sunday previous.[4]

The Northern people read in their journals of Monday
morning that their army had gained a signal victory; but
as the day wore on, and the truth came with overwhelming

[1] Official Records, vol. ii. p. 756.
[2] Ibid., p. 747.
[3] Nicolay and Hay, vol. iv. pp. 353, 355, 367.
[4] Sherman's Memoirs, vol. i. p. 189; Official Records; Nicolay and Hay.

force, dismay was in every heart, proceeding not from the loss of the battle nor from the retreat, but from the rout and the senseless panic that made all hang their heads for very shame. The result seemed to imply that Northerners were cowards, and that, as the South had boastingly asserted, they would not fight. The hope that the army would be on its triumphant way to Richmond gave place to fears for their own capital. Various reasons and explanations of the disaster were popularly current. It is worth while to refer to one of them as showing the literal hold the Jewish Scriptures had upon the Northern people. It was asserted that since the attack on the Confederates had been made on the Sabbath, God, on account of the desecration of his holy day, had given the victory to the enemy.

The bitter discouragement was of short duration. Only a few proposed to give up the contest, but it was perceived that instead of one short campaign the war would be long and severe, and that training as well as enthusiasm was needed to win. A second uprising of the North took place. Recruiting went on with vigor, and the time for which men engaged themselves was three years or during the war. In a week the North had recovered from its dejection, and girded itself anew for the conflict.[1]

The South received her great victory with a quiet sense of triumph and with expressions of profound gratitude to Jehovah, the God of battles, who had wrought so powerfully in her behalf. The manifestation of sentiment was

---

[1] New York *Times*, July 22, 23; *Evening Post*, July 22, 23, 25; *Tribune*, July 22, 23, 24, 25, 27; *Herald*, July 22, 23, 24; *World*, July 22, 23, 24, 29. Letter of Greeley to Lincoln, July 29, Nicolay and Hay, vol. iv. p. 365; Stanton to Buchanan, July 26, *North American Review*, Nov., 1879; Seward to Judd, July 26; Motley to his wife, July 23, 28. Touching the allegation that the defeat resulted from fighting on the Sabbath, see New York *Herald*, July 24, 30. I remember well hearing a sermon at Racine, Wis., the Sunday after the battle, in which this reason for the Confederate victory was emphatically maintained. Richmond thanked "the merciful God, who, on the precious and solemn day of his service, had been pleased to bless our arms with victory."—*Examiner*, July 22.

that of a deeply religious people who felt that they had a cause hallowed by duty and honor. The Confederate congress by resolution recognized "the hand of the King of kings and Lord of lords" in the "mighty deliverance" of their people. I have not been able to find evidence of loud exultation and boisterous rejoicing such as took place after the taking of Sumter. Richmond had many of her sons in battle, and the loss in killed and wounded tempered the general joy. As full tidings of the rout and panic became known, there were keen regrets that the Confederate army had not pushed on to Washington. The Southern newspapers began to boast. The battle had been between the cavaliers and "the roundhead bullies;" it was a fight between the game-cock and the dunghill; it demonstrated that the Southern soldiers could beat the Yankees two to one. With arrogance it was asserted, " Our social institutions are right," and we must show the rest of the enlightened world that theirs are wrong. The Confederates fully expected recognition from the European governments and the breaking of the blockade, but they did not think that the war was over. They had no idea that the North would give up the contest, and felt that their own exertions must be unremitting and energetic, although they hoped to carry the war into Maryland, and threaten, and perhaps take, Washington. " I have no idea that the North will give it up," wrote Stephens in a private letter. " Their defeat will increase their energy." This was unquestionably the view of the Confederate government.[1]

---

[1] Johnston and Browne, p. 407; for Davis's opinion see Richmond *Dispatch*, July 24, Mrs. Davis's book, vol. ii. p. 165. On Southern sentiment generally see Richmond *Examiner*, July 22, 23, 24, 25, 26, 29 ; Richmond *Whig*, July 24, 26 ; Richmond *Dispatch*, July 22, 24, 25 ; Charleston *Courier*, July 30; Atlanta *Weekly Intelligencer*, July 31; Pollard's First Year of the War, p. 116. Johnston, however, writes in his Narrative, p. 60: "The Southern volunteers believed that the objects of the war had been accomplished by their victory, and that they had achieved all that their country required of them. Many, therefore, in ignorance of their military obligations, left the army—not to return."

The result of Bull Run was a heavy blow to the Union cause in so far as the North longed for the sympathy of England in its hour of trial. "The ill news of last week," wrote Adams to Seward, August 8, "has had the effect of bringing to light the prevailing feeling in Great Britain. . . . The division of the Union is now regarded as a *fait accompli*."[1] The government, however, maintained strict neutrality. August 14 the Confederate commissioners addressed a long letter to Earl Russell praying for recognition, and using Bull Run as one of the strongest arguments. Ten days later Russell replied, and said positively that her majesty declined to acknowledge the independence of the Confederate States.[2] "The relations with England," wrote Schleiden from Washington, August 24, to Sumner, "appear to be for the moment more friendly than they have been for a long while."[3]

---

[1] MSS. State Department Archives.

[2] British and Foreign State Papers, 1860–61, pp. 219, 231 ; see, also, letter from the Duke of Argyll to Mrs. Motley, Aug. 20, Motley's Correspondence, vol. ii. p. 31.   [3] Pierce-Sumner Papers, MS.

NOTE TO PAGE 438. — Lincoln's order to General Scott of April 27, 1861 : "If at any point on or in the vicinity of any military line which is now or which shall be used between the city of Philadelphia and the city of Washington you find resistance which renders it necessary to suspend the writ of *habeas corpus* for the public safety, you personally, or through the officer in command at the point at which resistance occurs, are authorized to suspend that writ." — Works, II. 39.

CHAPTER XVI

THE battle of Bull Run demonstrated that in the Confederate army were two generals, Joseph E. Johnston and Thomas J. Jackson, who had military talents of a high order. Johnston was fifty-four years old; of the same age as Lee, he was graduated from West Point in the same class.[1] The two ablest commanders of the South, of the first families of Virginia, formed while at the Military Academy a fast friendship which was never impaired. They served under General Scott in the Mexican War, when the youthful intimacy had ripened into the mellow attachment of manhood, the sympathy between them remaining complete. At Contreras Johnston's nephew—whom, having no children of his own, he regarded as a son—was killed, and it fell to Lee to break the news. Finding his friend standing on captured intrenchments, flushed with victory at the success of a seemingly desperate assault, Lee, with the tenderness of a woman, told him of the sad fate of his nephew, and their tears, mingling together, cemented a friendship that helps to light up the dark story of the carnage and the waste of energy of our Civil War.

With the exception of one year, Johnston, since his graduation from West Point, had served constantly in the army, being quartermaster-general at the time Sumter was taken. Like Lee he was opposed to secession, but he made no question of his duty. Five days after the secession of Virginia he resigned his commission in the federal army and offered

---

[1] Lee stood second, Johnston thirteenth, in a class of forty-six.

his services to his native State; he was the officer highest
in rank who espoused the Southern side.

While in the Shenandoah valley, he and Jefferson Davis
were on the best of terms, and their correspondence was of
the most friendly nature.   Davis addresses him, " My dear
General," "may God bless and direct you," and assures
him, "My confidence and interest in you, both as an officer
and as a friend, cause me to turn constantly to your position
with deepest solicitude." [1]   On the battle-field of Bull Run
their relations seem to have been cordial.   But immediately after a quarrel arose between them, which boded no
good to the Southern cause.   A conflict of authority between the Richmond War Office and Johnston occurred,
and he wrote Adjutant - General Cooper two letters, displaying acerbity and combativeness; these Davis endorsed
as " insubordinate." [2]   For this or for some other personal
reasons the Confederate President, in sending the nominations of five generals to Congress, determined Johnston's
rank as fourth.   This drew from him an emphatic letter, in
which he maintained that by his previous rank in the
United States army and by the acts of the Confederate
Congress he still rightfully held the rank of first general in
the armies of the Southern Confederacy.   Davis replied:
The language of your letter " is, as you say, unusual; its
arguments and statements utterly one-sided, and its insin-
uations as unfounded as they are unbecoming." [3]   The
breach was never healed.   Had Johnston been less sensitive to an affront to his personal dignity, had he been in
temper like Lee, and had Davis shown such abnegation of

---

[1] June 22, July 10, 13, Official Records, vol. ii. pp. 945, 974, 977.

[2] Johnston's letters are July 24, 29, and are printed in Mrs. Davis's
Memoir, vol. ii. p. 139.

[3] The Confederate Congress confirmed, Aug. 31, the nominations of
Cooper, A. S. Johnston, Lee, J. E. Johnston, Beauregard.   J. E. Johnston
dated the letter referred to Sept. 12, but had thought it over two days before sending it.   Davis's reply is of Sept. 14, see Mrs. Davis's Memoir, vol.
ii. p. 144 et seq. ; Johnston's Narrative, p. 70 et seq.

self as did Lincoln in his dealings with his generals, blame
and recrimination would not be written on every page of
Southern history in the endeavor to explain why the Southern cause was lost.[1] We now begin to discern the inferiori-
ty of Davis to Lincoln in the conduct of the large affairs of
men and of state.

The most striking figure of the war on the Southern
side, "Stonewall" Jackson, has the fascination of a character of romance. No characterization of him has fully satisfied his admirers. To some he seems made up of contra-
dictions; to others a rare consistency appears to run
through his mature life. Growing up in a community of
western Virginia where morals were loose and where the
sentiment was irreligious, he developed in manhood a piety
which, had it not been so manly and consistent, would seem
extreme and fanatical. As a youth, racing horses with a
jockey's skill, and an eager frequenter of merry-makings, a
gay young officer in the City of Mexico after its capture,
eating dinners prepared by Parisian art, and participating
with the dark-eyed señoritas in the wild delights of the
dance, he took, after making a public profession of his
faith, the attitude towards worldly amusements of a New
England Puritan. No man was more devout. With an
unquestioning faith in a God who directed by continual in-
terposition human affairs, his religion became a part of his
being, influencing every act. When misfortune and sorrow
came, his comfort lay in the reflection, "We know that all
things work together for good to them that love God."
His communion with his Maker seemed complete. He
prayed without ceasing, supplicating the throne of grace for
the most common things and asking divine guidance in the

<hr>

[1] I have drawn this characterization of Johnston from his Narrative;
General J. D. Cox's review of same in the *Nation*, May 21, 1874; Cox's
Obituary of Johnston, the *Nation*, March 26, 1891; Sketch of Johnston,
by Judge Robert W. Hughes, in Lee and His Companions in Arms; Life
of Johnston, Great Commander Series, R. M. Hughes; letter of Johnston's, printed in Long's Lee, p. 71.

most trivial affairs of life. He said that the habit of prayer
had become with him almost as fixed as the habit of
breathing. His reverence for ministers of the gospel, his
thoughtful analysis of their sermons, his profound respect
for their exposition of Bible texts, call to mind the regard
paid the preacher in the colonial days of Massachusetts,
when he was, indeed, the wisest man in the community.
These traits were a rightful inheritance from Jackson's
Scotch-Irish ancestry. His observance of the Sabbath was
extremely rigorous, yet he was no Pharisee, for it was in
full keeping with the rest of his life.

He imposed upon himself the severest bodily discipline,
having always the same care of his physique as an athlete
in training. He loved liquor, but would not drink it. " I
am more afraid of it," he said, during the war, "than of
federal bullets." In his mental operations he was rigidly
methodical. Not well prepared at the time of his entrance
to West Point, he made up in industry what, owing to his
poverty and the necessity that compelled him to work on
an uncle's farm, he had lacked in opportunity. Inexperienced for his professional duties at the Virginia Military
Institute, he fitted himself for his daily tasks by diligent
study, and acquired by his habit of reflection a remarkable
concentration of mind. Morally he was conscientious to a
nicety that appears extreme, but his exact truthfulness and
ready self-denial were traits of a noble soul. Had the war
not occurred, had his own prayer and the prayers of righteous men averted, as he at one time hoped they would,
the conflict between Christian peoples, Jackson would have
been remembered in a small circle of Virginia as an eccentric professor, unpopular with his students and respected
by serious men. But he was a born fighter, and the war
breaking out when he was only thirty-seven, gave him his
opportunity. One great principle of his life had been to
obey orders, and such discipline he imposed on his men.
Yet he won from them a love and devotion such as no other
Southern general except Lee obtained.

Jackson had no love for slavery, but, believing that the
Bible taught that it was ordained of God, he had no question that it was the best actual relation for the two races.
A strict but kind master to his own slaves, he requested his
wife to teach two of their negro boys to read, and he himself organized a Sabbath-school for the instruction of the
colored people of Lexington, in which, until the war broke
out, he labored with interest and zeal. He was present in
command of his cadets at the execution of John Brown.
" Awful was the thought," he wrote to his wife, "that John
Brown might, in a few minutes, receive the sentence, ' Depart, ye wicked, into everlasting fire.' I sent up a petition
that he might be saved." Jackson was opposed to secession, but, being a thorough state-rights man, he had no
difficulty about his duty after the decision of Virginia, and,
firmly believing in the justice of the Southern cause, he
threw himself into it with the ardor of a crusader.[1]

It is easy to understand why both Davis and Lincoln
were so anxious for the adhesion of Virginia. Her worth
was measured by the quality as well as the number of her
men. Reflect that her secession gave to the Confederate
army the three generals, Lee, Johnston, and Jackson! Had
Virginia remained with the Union, it is unlikely that any
of them would have commanded a Confederate army; it is
possible that Lee and Johnston might have served under
the old flag.

While Lincoln had not lost confidence in McDowell[2]—
and, as affairs turned out, it would have been better had he
remained at the head of his army—yet, after the battle of
Bull Run, military judgment, political opinion, and public
sentiment, dominated by the successes in western Virginia,
combined to mark McClellan as a great soldier. To place
him in command of the army at Washington was the un-

---

[1] I have drawn this characterization of Jackson from his Life by R. L.
Dabney, D.D. ; his biography by his wife; Life, by John Esten Cooke ;
Eggleston's Recollections of a Rebel.

[2] Lincoln to Buell, Jan. 13, 1862, Official Records, vol. vii. p. 928.

questioned course to pursue. He was immediately summoned to the capital, and, July 27, he assumed command of the troops in and about the city,¹ going diligently to work to reorganize the armies of McDowell and Mansfield, and to drill systematically in camps of instruction these soldiers, as well as the fresh recruits constantly arriving. By his untiring exertions and power of organizing he soon had them under some degree of discipline.

McClellan, now thirty-four years old, had graduated from West Point in the same class as "Stonewall" Jackson, and immediately afterwards had seen active service in Mexico. In 1855, being one of a commission sent by the government to Europe to report on the art of war, he saw something of the operations in the Crimea. Two years later he resigned from the army to take the position of chief engineer of the Illinois Central Railroad, of which he became the vice-president. When the war broke out, he was president of the eastern division of the Ohio and Mississippi Railroad, living in Cincinnati, and in receipt of an annual salary of ten thousand dollars. Made in May a major-general in the United States army, and placed in command of the Department of the Ohio, he displayed from the start the personal qualities that gave him such a hold on the men with whom he came in contact. His "intercourse with those about him was kindly, and his bearing modest," writes General Cox, who had much to do with McClellan in the early days of the war. In daily life and conversation he was a "sensible and genial man."² "His unusually winning personal characteristics," write the private secretaries of Lincoln, contributed in a large degree to inspire "a remarkable affection and regard in every one, from the President to the humblest orderly who waited at his door."³

¹ Official Records, vol. ii. p. 763; vol. v. p. 11.
² Century War Book, vol. i. p. 135.
³ Nicolay and Hay, vol. iv. p. 444. The other authority I have drawn from in this characterization is McClellan's Own Story.

In no apparent trepidation, Congress met at the usual hour the day after the battle of Bull Run. It transacted the ordinary amount of business, and the House adopted a resolution of Crittenden's, introduced two days previously, which gave expression to the common sentiment of the country touching the object of the war. This resolution declared that the war was not waged for conquest or subjugation, or to overthrow or interfere with the rights or established institutions of the Southern States, but to maintain the supremacy of the Constitution and to preserve the Union.[1] It passed the House with only four dissenting voices, and the Senate three days later, the vote standing 30 to 5.[2] Congress also passed an act confiscating all property used in aid of the " insurrection." One section of it caused considerable opposition in the House, since it was the beginning of legislation concerning slavery.[3] This provided that the claims of owners should be forfeited to those slaves whom they should require to take up arms against the United States, or to labor in forts or intrenchments, or whom they should employ in any military or naval service whatsoever against the national government.

The Confederate provisional Congress, in session at Richmond from July 20 to August 31, sitting most of the time with closed doors, passed, in retaliation for the Confiscation act, a law providing for the sequestration of the estates and property of alien enemies; it brought within its operation debts due Northern merchants by the Southern people.[4] The Congress by statute had previously defined as alien enemies all citizens of the United States, except those residing in the Confederacy, who should declare their intention to become citizens of it and who should acknowledge the

---

[1] *Congressional Globe*, p. 222.   [2] Ibid., p. 265.
[3] The Confiscation bill passed the House Aug. 3 by 60 to 48, ibid., p. 431.
[4] Approved Aug. 30, Statutes at Large of the Provisional Government, p. 201 ; see article of Richmond *Examiner*, Sept. 3.

authority of its government.¹ The Confederate district
courts of Richmond, Charleston, Savannah, and New Orleans were largely occupied during the fall of 1861 with
proceedings under the Sequestration act, which appear to
have been conducted in as orderly a manner and with as
great safeguards for the privilege of the defendant as would
have obtained in similar cases at the North.²

---

¹ Approved Aug. 8, Statutes at Large of the Provisional Government,
p. 175. Citizens of Delaware, Maryland, Kentucky, Missouri, and of the
District of Columbia were put on a somewhat different footing from the
citizens of the free States.

² See Richmond *Examiner*, Oct. 9, 11, 16, 18, 31 ; Richmond *Whig*, Oct.
8, 29 ; Richmond *Enquirer*, Oct. 31 ; Savannah *Republican*, Oct. 8, 16,
Nov. 27, Dec. 9, 21 ; Charleston *Courier*, Sept. 10, Oct. 8, 10, 21 ; New
Orleans *True Delta*, Oct. 6, 8, 9, 12, 25, Dec. 5. The question of the constitutionality of the Sequestration act was submitted to the Confederate
district courts, see Richmond *Examiner*, Oct. 19, Nov. 7 ; Richmond
Whig, Nov. 8; Savannah *Republican*, Dec. 21. Judge Magrath, of Charleston, decided that the act was constitutional, Charleston *Courier*, Oct. 25.

"We have seen it estimated that under the operation of the Sequestra
tion act of the Confederate Congress, from fifteen to thirty millions of
dollars will pass into the custody of the Confederate receivers in Virginia.
The estimate strikes us as moderate. It is well known that nearly all the
merchants of our cities, towns, and villages were in the habit of purchas-
ing their stock at the North. Even though a small portion of the merchants of the interior laid in their goods in Richmond, still, inasmuch as
the Richmond merchants bought the largest portion of their goods from
New York, the result was the same as if the country merchants had all
gone directly to the city. The war came on in April, just after the season
when the merchants had laid in their spring supplies of goods from the
North. Very few of these goods were purchased for cash. The custom
of trade was to buy on credit, and nearly all these goods were bought on
the usual terms of six months' time. Thus the war opened on an indebtedness from Virginia (and doubtless the case was the same with all
the Southern States) to the North, equal to the total of the spring purchases of her merchants. This indebtedness was augmented by the whole
amount of old debts of prior standing, which had resulted from a course
of business that had existed for a long train of years. From these considerations we are inclined to put the indebtedness from Virginia to the
North on mercantile account at a very high figure. We do not think it
can be less than twenty millions. For that portion of the State not overrun by the enemy we suppose it to be at least fifteen millions."—Richmond *Dispatch*, Sept. 24. The New Orleans *Delta* "estimated the amount
of property which will be liable to sequestration at twelve millions of dol-

Despite the efforts of the Lincoln administration and the majority of the Northern people to keep the slavery question in abeyance; despite the wish of Jefferson Davis that it might not obtrude, and the emphatic assurances of the Confederate commissioners to Lord John Russell that slavery was not the cause of the war,[1] the negro in bondage was a stubborn fact, and as the federal armies advanced into slave territory, his condition and his status had to be dealt with. Three negroes who had come to Fortress Monroe were, on May 24, the day after Virginia had ratified by popular vote the ordinance of secession, claimed by an agent of their owner. General Butler, who was in command, refused to deliver them up, on the ground that, as they belonged to a citizen of a State offering resistance to the federal government and had been employed in the construction of a battery, they were "contraband of war."[2] Although the application of this phrase had not, as Butler himself admits, high legal sanction, it was at once taken up by the popular mind as an admirable and effective solution of a vexing question, and the policy of the government towards the "contrabands" who flocked into Fortress Monroe became a subject of great interest. May 27 General Butler reported to the War Department that he had within his lines negro men, women, and children to the value of $60,000, as they were rated in good times. He had determined to feed them, to put the able-bodied at work, keeping an account of the value of their services and the cost of maintenance of the whole number.[3] The

---

lars."—Richmond *Enquirer*, Oct. 15. These extravagant estimates were not justified. I find no mention of receipts from sequestration until Secretary Memminger's report of Dec. 7, 1863, where the amount is set down as $1,862,550.21; May 2, 1864, he notes the receipts under this head as $3,000,787.37. Capers's Life of Memminger, pp. 457, 477; see, also, Pollard's Davis, p. 183; J. C. Schwab, The Finances of the Confederacy, *Political Science Quarterly*, March, 1892.

[1] British and Foreign State Papers, 1860–61, pp. 186, 226.

[2] Butler's Book, p. 256 *et seq.;* correspondence of New York *Tribune*, May 25, editorial, May 28.

[3] Butler to Scott, Official Records, vol ii. p. 53.

government formally approved this course.[1] At first, some
of the fugitive slaves became the servants of officers, while
others were employed in storing provisions landed from vessels; but, as they continued to increase in number, many
were set to work on the intrenchments, under the superin-
tendence of Edward L. Pierce, an attorney of Boston, who
had written a law book of authority, who was a strong
anti-slavery Republican, active in politics, and who, prompted by patriotism, had come to Fortress Monroe as a private
in the Massachusetts Third.[2] July 30 General Butler reported that he had under his control 900 negroes, and asked
further instructions.[3] August 8 Cameron replied in a letter
which indicated the carefully-thought-out policy of the administration : " It is the desire of the President that all existing rights in all the States be fully respected and maintained; in cases of fugitives from the loyal slave States,
the enforcement of the Fugitive Slave law by the ordinary
forms of judicial proceedings must be respected by the military authorities; in the disloyal States the Confiscation act
of Congress must be your guide."[4] This act, which the
President had signed with reluctance,[5] did not, however,
make provision for fugitives escaping from loyal masters in
disloyal States. Cameron instructed that care should be
taken to protect the interests of such owners. As affairs
turned out, this was of little practical moment to them or
to their slaves, but it is important as showing Lincoln's
carefulness and regard for vested rights when the question
was thrust upon him. Practice differed in the military departments, depending largely upon the respective opinions
of the commanding generals; but in the main the Confisca-

---

[1] Cameron to Butler, May 30, cited by Nicolay and Hay, vol. iv. p. 389.
[2] See Pierce's article, "The Contrabands at Fortress Monroe," *Atlantic
Monthly*, Nov., 1861.
[3] Moore's Rebellion Record, Docs., vol. ii. p. 437.
[4] Ibid., p. 493.
[5] Chase to Green Adams, of Kentucky, Sept. 5, Schuckers, p. 428; New
York *Evening Post*, Sept. 16.

tion act of Congress and the instructions of Cameron to Butler determined the course towards fugitive slaves who came within the lines of the Union armies.[1] Public opinion at the North was gradually developing to the point at which it would support the President in striking at the root of the trouble should the war be prolonged;[2] but, in spite of the murmurs of the abolitionists and some radical Republicans, a large majority of the Northern people had acquiesced in his policy as a wise temporary expedient, when General Frémont opened the question afresh by his proclamation in Missouri.

Frémont, "the pet and protégé of the Blairs,"[3] at their earnest solicitation had been made a major-general and placed in command of the Western Department, which included Missouri. The appointment was immensely popular in the country; it seemed fitting that the first presidential candidate of the Republican party, who was supposed to possess military talent, should have a prominent place in the armies of the North. Frémont arrived from Europe about the 1st of July, but remained in New York three weeks, though he was sorely needed in St. Louis. Arriving there July 25, he found the confusion incident to the organization and supply of an army before a proper administrative system has been established. He had neither business training nor military ability, and affairs went from bad to worse. Lyon was in the field, begging for reinforcements, his entreaties fortified by the urging of well-in-

---

[1] Nicolay and Hay, vol. iv. p. 395.

[2] "Slavery is a doomed institution."—New York *Times*, July 29; see New York *World*, July 30. "If it shall appear that either slavery or this government must perish, then the voice of a united people will declare, let slavery perish."—Dixon, of Connecticut, in Senate, July 15, *Congressional Globe*, p. 119; see, also, remarks of Browning, of Illinois, and Sherman, July 18, ibid., pp. 187, 190. These are utterances of conservative newspapers and conservative senators. The New York *Tribune* and Sumner, representing a reasonable radical sentiment, were eager to strike at slavery, see *Tribune, passim ;* Pierce's Sumner, vol. iv. p. 41.

[3] Lincoln's statement, 1863, Nicolay and Hay, vol. iv. p. 415.

formed Union citizens. Troops were in reach that could
have been sent to him in time, but Frémont refused to give
the order. At the battle of Wilson's Creek, August 10,
Lyon was outnumbered by the Confederates, his army
defeated, and he himself killed.[1]

This disaster turned the attention of those who were in
a position to get at the truth to the Western Department.
Less than one month had sufficed to demonstrate that Frémont was intellectually a weak man, utterly unfit for a
responsible command; before the 1st of September serious
charges were made against him. It was averred that he
was over-fond of display; that he had surrounded himself
with dishonest and bad men, some of whom were on his
staff; that, although he maintained the state of a European
monarch, and allowed high military and civil officers and
honest Union citizens to wait days in his ante-room for an
interview, in many cases making himself inaccessible, his
door was always open to his intimates, most of whom had
neither character nor standing. It was also charged that
his time, instead of being occupied with the proper duties
of a commanding general, was taken up in giving out contracts; that he was recklessly extravagant; that some of
his officers were interested in the fat contracts, and that
the Department of Missouri seemed to be managed rather
for the purpose of making private fortunes than for the
country's weal.[2] Surrounded though he was by speculat-

---

[1] Adjutant-General Thomas's report, Official Records, vol. iii. p. 545.

[2] See the report of the House Committee on Government Contracts, and
the testimony taken by them, Reports of Committees, 2d Sess. 37th
Cong., vols. i. and ii. The members of this committee who went to St.
Louis and took the testimony implicating Frémont and his friends in corrupt transactions were Elihu B. Washburne, of Illinois, the friend of Lincoln and of Grant, a gentleman of strict integrity, who later acquired the
name of the "Watch-dog of the Treasury"; William S. Holman, winning
afterwards the title of the "Great Objector"; Henry L. Dawes, of Massachusetts, and W. G. Steele, of New Jersey. The report said: "In furnishing supplies in the Western Department the commanding general was
peculiarly unfortunate in the character of the men by whom he was sur-

ing flatterers, Frémont must have got an inkling of the opinion in which he was held by many people of worth and influence; he could hardly have been persuaded by his sycophants that his administration of military affairs was so far successful. He undoubtedly had some conception of the smouldering anti-slavery sentiment at the North, and it may have occurred to him that a way was open by which he might commend himself to the radical Republicans, and detract attention from the gross mismanagement of his department. At all events, his action is susceptible of such an explanation. August 30 Frémont issued from his headquarters at St. Louis a proclamation confiscating the property "of all persons in the State of Missouri who shall take up arms against the United States, or who shall be directly proven to have taken an active part with their enemies in the field," and declaring their slaves freemen.[1] He then "set up a bureau of abolition,"[2] and issued deeds of manumission to slaves.[3] The first knowledge which Lincoln had of the proclamation was gained from the newspapers. Although the act was one of insubordination, and a major-general of two months' standing, with no careful survey of the whole field, with no appreciation of the important and various interests involved, had, on a sudden impulse[4] assumed to solve a question which the President, his cabinet, and Congress were only approaching in a careful and

rounded. The system of public plunder which pervaded that department was inaugurated at the very beginning and followed up with untiring zeal; the public welfare as entirely overlooked and as effectually ignored as if the war was gotten up to enable a mammoth scheme of peculation at the expense of the people to be carried out."—p. 55. See also testimony of Francis P. Blair, Jr., before the Committee on the Conduct of the War, part iii. of report; editorial in New York *Times*, Sept. 20.

[1] Official Records, vol. iii. p. 467.

[2] Lincoln's remark, 1863, Nicolay and Hay, vol. iv. p. 415.

[3] Moore's Rebellion Record, vol. iii. p. 129.

[4] "In the night I decided upon the proclamation. . . . I wrote it the next morning and printed it the same day. I did it without consultation or advice with any one."—Frémont to Lincoln, Sept. 8, Official Records, vol. iii. p. 477.

tentative manner, Lincoln's letter to Frémont of September 2 was as full of kindness as of wisdom. "I think there is great danger," he wrote, "that the closing paragraph, in relation to the confiscation of property and the liberating slaves of traitorous owners, will alarm our Southern Union friends and turn them against us; perhaps ruin our rather fair prospect for Kentucky. Allow me, therefore, to ask that you will, as of your own motion, modify that paragraph so as to conform to the" Confiscation act of Congress, approved August 6. "This letter is written in a spirit of caution and not of censure." [1]

The President had his finger on the pulse of Kentucky; he felt that after much trembling her sentiment was now distinctly favorable to the Union, [2] and he was loath to see it in any way disturbed. "The proclamation of General Frémont reached here yesterday," wrote Garrett Davis, September 3, from Frankfort, where he was in attendance on the session of the legislature, "and is most inopportune for the Union party. It fell amongst us with pretty much the effect of a bombshell. The slavery feature is greatly objected to by our friends, and has greatly disconcerted, and, I fear, has scattered us. We should have passed all our measures but for it. . . . There is a very general, almost a universal, feeling in this State against this war being or becoming a war against slavery. The position of the secessionists here has been all the time that it is, and this proclamation gives them the means of further and greatly pushing that deception. . . . I wish it had not been made until this legislature had done its business and adjourned." [3] Joseph Holt wrote Lincoln that the Union-loving citizens of Kentucky had read the proclamation with "alarm and consternation," and that the approval of it by the administration

---

[1] Official Records, vol. iii. p. 469. Lincoln requested the modification of another point, which is now relatively unimportant, but it shows his extreme caution in dealing with weighty matters.

[2] *Ante.*   [3] To Chase, Chase Papers, MS.

would chill "the power and fervor of the loyalty of Kentucky."[1]

Frémont was unwilling to retract the objectionable part of his proclamation, and suggested that the President should openly direct him to make the correction.[2] Lincoln, therefore, by letter of September 11, ordered him to modify the clause "in relation to the confiscation of property and the liberation of slaves" so as to conform to the Confiscation act of Congress.[3]

The first impression of a majority of the Northern people, on the publication of Fremont's proclamation, was decidedly favorable to it; generally regarded as a wise and effective move, it aroused enthusiasm on the part of many.[4] When the President modified it, so sound were his reasons, so strong a hold had he himself on the people, so determined were the mass of Republicans and war Democrats to support the administration in the prosecution of the war, that Lincoln carried with him an efficient public opinion.[5] The mischief of Frémont's action was that it brought out a factional difference in the Republican party, which, since the firing on Sumter, had had but little to excite it. Sumner grieved at this manifestation of Lincoln's policy.

---

[1] Sept. 12, Moore's Rebellion Record, vol. iii. p. 127.

[2] Frémont to the President, Sept. 8, Official Records, vol. iii. p. 477.

[3] The President to Frémont, ibid., p. 485.

[4] See New York *Times*, Sept. 2 ; New York *Evening Post*, Sept. 2; New York *World*, Sept. 4; New York *Tribune*, Sept. 1, 2, 3 ; Boston *Evening Transcript*, Sept. 2; Boston *Advertiser*, Sept. 7; New York *Herald*, Sept. 1; Life of Bryant, Godwin, vol. ii. p. 161.   " Even such Democratic papers as the Boston *Post*, Detroit *Free Press*, Chicago *Times*, and New York *Herald* approved of it, while it stirred and united the people of the loyal States during the ten days of life allotted it by the government far more than any other event of this war."—George W. Julian in the House of Representatives, Feb. 18, 1863; see also his Political Recollections, p. 199.

[5] See, for example, New York *World*, Sept. 19; New York *Times*, Oct. 9, Boston *Herald*, Boston *Advertiser*, Sept. 17.   The result of the fall elections, and the canvass preceding them, and the trend of thought from Sept. 15, the day the President's letter of modification was published, to Dec. 31, warrant the statement in the text.

"Our President," he wrote, "is now dictator, imperator—which you will; but how vain to have the power of a god and not to use it godlike!" [1] October 1 he delivered a carefully prepared speech before the Massachusetts Republican Convention at Worcester, maintaining that emancipation was our best weapon, and, while he did not in direct words applaud Frémont or condemn Lincoln, that was the tenor of his discourse. [2] Sumner in Congress and Chase in the cabinet stood for the radical anti-slavery sentiment of the country; they gave a sympathetic ear to the earnest and unreserved expression of that opinion, and their private correspondence shows how strong the tendency was with many good people to abase Lincoln and exalt Frémont. [3]

---

[1] To Dr. Lieber, Sept. 17, Pierce's Sumner, vol. iv. p. 42.

[2] See his Works, vol. vi.; Pierce's Sumner.

[3] Since his acceptance of the Treasury Department Chase had won golden opinions. "You have taught Massachusetts men to rely upon you for counsel and aid," wrote to him Dr. Samuel G. Howe, May 14. "You were never so highly appreciated in Ohio as at this moment," wrote Rutherford B. Hayes, from Camp Chase, in Ohio, June 29. "The good things done at Washington people are disposed to place to your credit. The errors are charged to others."—Chase Papers, MS. At this time Chase's Ohio friends tried to impress upon him that the administration had made a mistake in regard to Frémont. George Hoadly, an eminent lawyer of Cincinnati and judge of the Superior Court, afterwards governor, wrote, Sept. 18: "Our people are in a state of great consternation and wrath on account of the quarrel between Frémont and the administration, public opinion being entirely with General Frémont; . . . no word describes popular sentiment but 'fury.' I have heard men of sense, such as are called conservative, advocate the wildest steps, such as the impeachment of Mr. Lincoln, the formation of a party to carry on the war irrespective of the President and under Frémont, etc., etc. For myself, I must say that if the letters of Mr. Lincoln to Magoffin and Frémont are any fair indication of his character and policy, I pray God to forgive my vote for him. Loyal men are giving their lives and means like water to no end, if the imbecility of Buchanan's administration is to be surpassed thus. I cannot, cannot think that your wise head and true anti-slavery heart have consented to this abasement of the manhood and honor of our nation. Let Mr. Lincoln, while he is conciliating the contemptible State of Kentucky, a State which ought to have been coerced long ago, bear in mind that the free States may want a little conciliation,

Chase himself, however, agreed with the President, and in
a private communication stated with force the legal posi-

---

that they are not wasting their substance to secure the niggers of traitors."
Hoadly was so full of the subject that he wrote the following day: " I
have never heard wilder or more furious denunciation than yesterday and
day before found expression from the lips of cool men.   Three times I
was applied to to join in getting up a public meeting to denounce the administration and support Frémont; and while no such disturbance will be
permitted, I am nevertheless certain that there is here a perfect and, I am
sorry to say, very angry unanimity in support both of Frémont's proclamation and of his action at St. Louis in other respects, expensive though it
may have been. . . . General Frémont is thus far the favorite of the
Northwest, because he has come up to the standard.   And if the election
were next fall, to displace him would be to make him President. . . .
The bitterest attacks I have heard upon the cabinet in this matter have
been based upon the theory that a jealousy of Frémont as a presidential
candidate is the root of all the trouble.   My wife expresses the common
feeling about Lincoln's letter to Frémont, by saying it seems to her to be
the old conflict of Mr. Feeble-Mind and Mr. Ready-to-Halt with Mr. Great-
heart." James Monroe, a member of the Ohio legislature from 1855
to 1862, afterwards consul to Rio de Janeiro for eight years and member of Congress for ten years, wrote Chase, Sept. 17, from Oberlin: "After
having attended our State convention, and after having enjoyed many
opportunities there and elsewhere for an interchange of sentiment with
men of all parties, and from all parts of the State, I am fully convinced
that Frémont's proclamation, without ' modification,' is universally endorsed by all Union-loving men in this State.   It is evident to me and to
all men here that the great free North is fully prepared for the course
which General Frémont proposes in regard to the emancipation of the
slaves of rebels." C. N. Olds, a leading lawyer of central Ohio, wrote from
Columbus, Sept. 17: " I was deeply impressed by the effect on the public
mind of Frémont's late proclamation. . . . I saw men, who were never
suspected of any anti-slavery tendencies, meet on the street to shake
hands over it, in mutual congratulations—' Now the administration is in
earnest,' 'That looks like work,' 'Now our army will have some heart
for the fight,' 'Now the war means something.' The modification of this
proclamation by Mr. Lincoln produces great disappointment.   The moral
effect is worse than that of the battle of Bull Run.   I suppose it was
modified in deference to the delicate position of Kentucky, but that has always been a false position, that has greatly protracted and complicated our
struggle.   Kentucky has no right to be coaxed into a slow and reluctant
loyalty, at the risk of crippling the hearty and spontaneous loyalty of the
entire North."—Chase Papers, MS.
	James Chestney, in writing to Sumner from Washington, Oct. 1, men-

tion, and indignantly disclaimed that "aspirations for the
presidency" had in this affair any influence on Lincoln or

---

tioned the President's "disposition to listen to the demands of slavery. . . .
The New York *Herald* is the organ and oracle now." Frank W. Ballard,
a member of the executive committee of the Young Men's Republican
Union of New York city, spoke in a letter of Oct. 1 of the "infernal idea
of carrying on a war for the Union *upon border-State specifications* and dic-
tation." Moncure D. Conway wrote from Cincinnati, Oct. 7: "Mulligan
surrendered to Price only because the President surrendered to the slave-
holders of Kentucky."—Pierce-Sumner Papers, MS. Ballard, who was
active in arranging for a speech from Sumner at Cooper Institute, New
York, Nov. 27, wrote him Oct. 26: "I think we can make the meeting endorse the principles of the Frémont proclamation as a gentle hint to Mr.
Lincoln that the 'modification' was a mistake. Let me add that *strong
meat* will be quite acceptable to all who hear you this time."—Ibid. The
meeting did adopt such a resolution, which is printed in Sumner's Works,
vol. vi. p. 114; but the New York *Tribune*, which published the speech
Nov. 28, neither printed nor mentioned the resolution.

Sumner's speech at Worcester, Oct. 1, had a large circulation, being printed
in full by the New York *Tribune* and the New York *Independent*, and brought
forth a large expression of public opinion touching slavery in press comments and in private letters. Many of these are printed in Sumner's
Works, vol. vi. pp. 33–64. I will cite extracts from several letters. Carl
Schurz, though at Madrid as our Minister to Spain, understood well the
feeling of his countrymen who had become American citizens, and wrote:
"Let me thank you for the glorious speech you have delivered before the
Massachusetts Convention. I agree with you on every point, and expect
shortly to fight by your side." Montgomery Blair, Postmaster-General,
wrote from Washington: "Your speech is noble, beautiful, classical, sensible. I would have timed it differently; but I will take it now rather than
lose it."—p. 56. George H. Monroe, editor Norfolk County *Journal*, wrote
Sumner, Oct. 26: "Events every day are tending to induce the conviction
in my mind that your position is the right one, and I scarcely doubt that
it will be generally acknowledged such in the future."—Pierce-Sumner
Papers, MS. Schleiden wrote from New York, Oct. 28: "Apart from the
Evening Post and the *Tribune*, I have not yet discovered an echo of your
views in the press. It is true all seem to agree that if slavery or the Union
must fall, then let slavery perish and not the Union; but I cannot help
thinking that the great majority of the people do not believe that the
time for a change of the programme of the war has already arrived."—
Ibid.; see, also, Pierce's Sumner, vol. iv. p. 45. "Does the war go on to
suit you?" asked William H. Herndon, Nov. 20, from Springfield, Ill.
"It does not suit me. Frémont's proclamation was right. Lincoln's
modification of it was wrong."—Pierce-Sumner Papers, MS.; see, also,

his cabinet.[1] Lincoln, in a confidential letter to his friend
Browning, senator from Illinois, who was a conservative,
and, to his astonishment, approved Frémont's proclamation,
fully justified his own course from policy as well as on principle. "The Kentucky legislature," he wrote, "would not
budge till that proclamation was modified. . . . I think to
lose Kentucky is nearly the same as to lose the whole
game. Kentucky gone, we cannot hold Missouri, nor, as I
think, Maryland. These all against us, and the job on our
hands is too large for us. We would as well consent to
separation at once, including the surrender of this capital."[2]

If Frémont had been able, honest, and patriotic, the an-
nulment of his decree touching the emancipation of slaves
and the confiscation of property would have ended the
matter, and he would have remained in command of the

New York *Evening Post*, Sept. 16; Life of Bryant, Godwin, vol. ii. p. 161;
Boston *Evening Transcript*, Sept. 17; Grimes to Fessenden, Sept. 19, Life
of Grimes, Salter, p. 153.

[1] Letter to Simeon Nash, Sept. 26; see, also, letter to Green Adams, Sept.
5, Schuckers, pp. 277, 428. In an article in *National Intelligencer*, of Oct.
8, the authorship of which is disclosed by a private letter of James C. Welling, its editor, to Chase, Chase Papers, MS., Chase made a clear exposition of the administration policy, with which, it is obvious, he sympathized fully. He wrote: "We have already taken occasion to express our
general approval of the policy adopted by the administration, and set forth
in the letter of Secretary Cameron to Major-General Butler, in respect to
slaves employed or involved in the existing insurrection. It is a policy in
full harmony with the act of Congress on the subject, and equally remote
from that of emancipation by proclamation, and that of heedless inaction
in regard to a matter of great consequence. The leading principle of Mr.
Cameron's letter is that the existing war has no direct relation to slavery.
It is a war for the restoration of the Union under the existing Constitution.
. . . The whole subject of slavery in loyal States [is left] to the civil authorities . . . in insurrectionary States the military authorities are directed to refrain from all interference with servants lawfully employed in
peaceful pursuits. . . . Mr. Cameron's instructions . . . simply direct that
those who come within the lines and offer their services to the government
be received and employed. . . . In using these services the national government will only follow the example of the Confederate rebels. Slaves
and free negroes have been pressed into the service of the insurrection."

[2] Sept. 22, Nicolay and Hay, vol. iv. p. 422.

Western Department. There was neither the slightest disposition nor the most remote design on the part of the administration to shear his lawful powers or to remove him because in this affair he had transcended his authority.[1] But the mismanagement and corruption at St. Louis imperatively demanded correction. Francis P. Blair the younger, though he was loath to lose faith in the man whose appointment had given him exceeding gratification, could not fail, on his return home from the special session of Congress, to appreciate the alarming condition of affairs and the loss which the Union cause had suffered,[2] though he found no fault with the proclamation freeing the slaves, except that it should have been sooner issued. September 1 he wrote his brother, the Postmaster-General, that it was his decided opinion that Frémont "should be relieved of his command, and a man of ability put in his place."[3] On seeing this letter, the President directed that Montgomery Blair, and Meigs, the Quartermaster-General of the army, should go to Missouri for the purpose of making a thorough inquiry. They arrived at St. Louis September 12, and remained there long enough for the Postmaster-General to make up his mind that the good of the country required the removal of Frémont; this he recommended.[4] In a confidential letter to Sumner, with whom he was on the best of terms, he gave his own and his brother's opinion of affairs in the Western Department. "Frank[5] is a fearfully earnest man," he wrote. "The blood of the old ship-building Covenanters who fought James at Londonderry, which flows in his veins, speaks in all his acts. He cannot tolerate trifling in a great cause,

---

[1] Letter of Lincoln to Browning, before cited; Chase to Cable, Oct. 23, Schuckers, p. 432.

[2] Testimony before Committee on the Conduct of the War, part iii. p. 170.

[3] Cincinnati *Enquirer*, copied in New York *Tribune*, Oct. 7.

[4] Testimony before Committee on the Conduct of the War, part iii. p. 154.

[5] Francis P., familiarly called Frank. He frequently signed his name Frank P.

and when he discovered that Frémont was a mere trifler, he was not to be reconciled to seeing the State overrun by pro-slavery myrmidons, by an empty proclamation threatening to deprive them of their negroes. It was a bitter sarcasm on the cause of emancipation at the time it was issued. The truth is, with Frémont's surroundings, the set of scoundrels who alone have control of him, this proclamation setting up the higher law was like a painted woman quoting Scripture." [1]

While Montgomery Blair and Meigs were in St. Louis, Jessie Benton Frémont, the devoted wife of the general, was at Washington pressing his cause with zeal. " She sought an audience with me at midnight," Lincoln afterwards related, " and taxed me so violently with many things that I had to exercise all the awkward tact I have to avoid quarrelling with her. She surprised me by asking why their enemy, Montgomery Blair,[2] had been sent to Missouri. She more than once intimated that if General Frémont should decide to try conclusions with me, he could set up for himself." [3] She sent the President a written demand for a copy of Francis P. Blair's letter of September 1. This he respectfully declined to furnish, and at the end of his note he said, "No impression has been made on my mind against the honor or integrity of General Frémont, and I now enter my protest against being understood as acting in any hostility towards him." [4]

Meanwhile the contest at St. Louis increased in heat. Frémont placed under arrest Francis P. Blair, who was colonel of the First Missouri Regiment of light artillery ; he in turn made formal charges against his commanding general.[5]

---

[1] Letter of Oct. 16, Pierce-Sumner Papers, MS.

[2] Lincoln sent him because he had been the stanch friend of Frémont.

[3] Nicolay and Hay, vol. iv. p. 415.

[4] This and Mrs. Frémont's letter were printed by the Cincinnati *Enquirer*, and copied in the New York *Tribune* of Oct. 7.

[5] Blair was first arrested Sept. 15. He was released Sept. 25, and the next day wrote Adjutant-General Thomas that he should make formal

The rumor gained ground that Frémont would be removed. Besides his hold on the officers to whom he had given commissions, many of which were irregular, and on his satellites who were making money out of the government, he was genuinely popular with the Germans, of whom there were a large number in St. Louis and other parts of Missouri. B. Rush Plumly, general appraiser in the Philadelphia Custom-house, an appointment due to Chase's influence, had, with his knowledge, and perhaps with his commission as a secret agent of the Treasury Department, gone to St. Louis.[1] Plumly was a friend of Frémont, and, arriving there, heartily espoused his cause. Indignant at the President for the modification of the proclamation freeing the slaves, Plumly reported to Chase the dire results which would ensue should the general be removed. " I despatched to you the day of Frémont's rumored removal," he wrote, " for in thirty years of participation in popular commotions, I have never seen such desperate and deadly feeling as then existed. The ' Headquarters' were thronged with committees of inquiry and opposition to his removal ; great numbers of officers were preparing to resign ; companies threw down their arms or dashed them to pieces. Mass-meetings were extemporized, and a general revolt seemed inevitable. Had the report been true, the army would have been virtually disbanded. I am sure that Colonel Blair would have been killed in the street. I think that will be the end of him, sooner or later, so fearful is

charges against Frémont, New York *Tribune*, Oct. 8.   He was then rearrested, when he prepared his charges and specifications, Cincinnati *Enquirer*, copied in *Tribune*, Oct. 9.

[1] In requesting leave of absence and designation as a secret agent of the Treasury Department, Plumly wrote Chase, Aug. 29 : "If I could tell you what I know, not what I imagine, about this contract-and-supply practice, you would do as I do, despair, not only of the government, but of human nature. I cannot turn ' informer,' but I could be a sentinel." Chase, Aug. 4, had warned Frémont against extravagance, and from a letter to a friend, Oct. 23, it is evident he had feared financial mismanagement on the part of the general, Schuckers, pp. 275, 432.

the hostility to him. . . . Since the publication of his charges against Frémont the sentiment has strengthened against Blair, because some of the charges are the ' eating his own words,' and others are flatly false." [1]

Lincoln had thought well of Frémont,[2] and obviously hoped to continue him in command, for it was worth much to conciliate the sentiment in his favor in St. Louis and in the rest of the country, where he had become the idol of the radical Republicans. The President sought fuller knowledge, and sent Secretary Cameron and Lorenzo Thomas, the Adjutant-General of the army, to investigate affairs in Missouri.[3] General David Hunter and General Samuel R. Curtis, who were serving under Frémont, told Cameron that he was not fit for the command, and the letters of General Pope to Hunter were of the same purport.[4] Before Cameron returned to Washington, Plumly was there. He went to see the President, and thus relates his interview : " I said to him at once that I had called out of respect to him, having never seen him ; that I should say very little of the West, as I would not forestall General Cameron's report, whom I expected to find here. He asked me some questions and . . . then spoke of the West, and especially of the threatened tumult there in the event of Frémont's removal, and added, ' You yourself have written and telegraphed this, Mr. Plumly.' ' Certainly, sir,' said I, ' I did, at the request of Colonel Scott, write and despatch a state of facts, and the inference, made by the very friends of the administration on the spot.' ' I did not,' said he, 'attribute these despatches and letters to General Frémont in any way, but to a set of speculators who would be disturbed if General

---

[1] Letter of Oct. 9 from St. Louis, Chase Papers, MS.; see, also, despatches of Plumly to T. A. Scott from St. Louis, Oct. 3, 16, Official Records, vol. iii. pp. 516, 535.

[2] Nicolay and Hay, vol. iv. p. 415.

[3] They arrived there Oct. 11.

[4] Nicolay and Hay, vol. iv. pp. 430, 432; Report of the Committee on the Conduct of the War, part iii. p. 246.

Frémont was removed.' 'I hope, sir, you do not include me in that category.' 'I do, sir,' said he. 'Mr. President, I am not of them; I have no interest, remote or immediate, in contracts, and no other interest but to serve the government by sending the exact state of things; do you accept my statement, Mr. President?' 'I think I cannot; nobody has said anything to me against you, but my opinion was formed from your letters and despatches.' 'Power needs the truth,' said I, 'and I sent the truth to the power, at its own request; if it was disagreeable, it was no fault of mine.' 'Why, sir,' said he, 'as soon as I saw your card, the thought arose that you had come here post-haste, to be ahead of General Cameron.'"[1]

October 21 Cameron and Adjutant-General Thomas arrived at Washington. The result of their investigations was embodied in Thomas's report; this contained three statements, which afforded sufficient ground for the removal of Frémont: General Curtis "deemed General Frémont unequal to the command of an army, and said that he was no more bound by law than by the winds;" "General Hunter expressed to the Secretary of War his decided opinion that General Frémont was incompetent and unfit for his extensive and important command;" "It is the expressed belief of many persons that General Frémont has around him on his staff persons directly and indirectly concerned in furnishing supplies."[2] The President could no

---

[1] Letter to Chase from Washington, Oct. 19, Chase Papers, MS. Plumly assured the President, "General Cameron knew of my coming; he invited me to accompany him," and he explained to Chase, "I am out of pocket by going west. I have refused what seemed to be proper modes of profit, because I could not participate in them, much as I need a few thousand dollars to release my property from the grip of judgments." He also wrote, "The removal of Frémont will justify the statements I made, either by elevating Frémont into a political martyr, or by dividing the nation, disaffecting the West to the administration, and dissipating that grand enthusiasm which has poured into Missouri an army of 50,000 men in sixty days."

[2] Official Records, vol. iii. pp. 541, 542, 547. Thomas's report is also

longer hesitate, and, October 24, made an order for Frémont's removal, to be delivered to him with all reasonable
despatch unless, when reached by the messenger, he should
have "fought and won a battle," or should "then be actually in a battle," or should be "in the immediate presence
of the enemy in expectation of a battle." None of these
conditions obtaining, the order was given to General Frémont, and, November 2, he turned over his command to
Hunter.[1]   The change occasioned neither trouble in the
army nor an outbreak at St. Louis.

It was indeed time that Frémont should be removed.
Elihu B. Washburne, who was at the head of the sub-committee on government contracts that spent two weeks in
St. Louis taking a large amount of testimony relating to
the procedure of Frémont and his friends,[2] wrote Secretary
Chase from Cairo, October 31: "I was on the point of writing you from St. Louis several times, but the situation of
things there was so terrible and the frauds so shocking, I
did not know where to begin or where to end; and then
again it appeared that everything communicated by our
best men there in regard to Frémont and the condition of
matters in the city and State was utterly disregarded. Our
committee labored for two weeks, and our disclosures will
astound the world and disgrace us as a nation. Such rob-
bery, fraud, extravagance, peculation as have been developed in Frémont's department can hardly be conceived of.
There has been an organized system of pillage, right under

---

printed in the Report of the Committee on the Conduct of the War. The
newspapers published it Oct. 30. Frémont made an elaborate defence in
his testimony, Jan., 1862, before the Committee on the Conduct of the
War. The majority of the committee, who were its leading men, were
friendly to him, and their report, made in April, 1863, was distinctly favorable.   [1] Official Records, vol. iii. pp. 553–556.

[2] For the members of this sub-committee *vide ante*, p. 469. Their first
report was made Dec. 17, when they had examined 265 witnesses, and
the testimony covered 1109 pages; a subsequent report was based on 1600
printed pages of testimony of 350 witnesses. A large part of this had reference to Frémont's department.

the eye of Frémont. Governor Chase, what does the administration mean by permitting this state of things to exist in the Western Department? It cannot be ignorant of what the situation of matters is. I fear things have run on so far there is no remedy, and that all has gone. Frémont has really set up an authority over the government, and bids defiance to its commands. The government, in failing to strike at Frémont and his horde of pirates, acknowledges itself a failure. The credit of the government is ruined. Everybody knows there has been such an extent of swindling that payment ought not to be made, and people are now afraid to trust anybody who acts for the government. I am utterly discouraged and disheartened. A people so blind, so corrupt, and so dishonest and unpatriotic are not deserving a free government." [1]

The evidence I have presented and indicated justifying the removal of Frémont is more than the men of the North had when the news came, November 6, that the removal had finally been made. Yet they were in possession of facts enough to be aware that the President had acted wisely, and it is probable that a majority of them so believed. It is, however, one of the melancholy reflections of history that many worthy people have been led by a charlatan for the sole reason that he knew how to play upon the one idea dearest to their hearts. We have an example of this in the case of Frémont, whose removal was regarded by a goodly number as martyrdom in the anti-slavery cause. "Is it known to the administration that the West is threatened with a revolution?" asked Richard Smith, the editor of the Cincinnati *Gazette*, in a letter to Chase of November 7. "Could you have been among the people yesterday and witnessed the excitement, could you have seen sober citizens pulling from their walls and trampling under foot the portrait of the

---

[1] Chase Papers, MS. Washburne did not then know that the order had been sent for the removal of Frémont.

President, and could you hear to-day the expressions of all classes of men, of all political parties, you would, I think, feel as I feel, and as every sincere friend of the government must feel, alarmed. What meaneth this burning of the President in effigy, by citizens who have hitherto sincerely and enthusiastically supported the war? What mean these boisterous outbursts of indignation, and these low mutterings favorable to a Western confederacy that we hear? Why this sudden check to enlistments? Why this rejection of Treasury notes by German citizens? Why is it that on the 6th of November, 1861, not one dollar was subscribed here to the national loan? Why is it that it would not be safe to go into places where the Germans resort, and publicly express an opinion favorable to the President? Why this sudden, this extraordinary, this startling change in public sentiment, on 'change, in the street, in the banking-house, in the palace and the cottage, in country and city? Is it not time for the President to stop and consider whether, as this is a government of the people, it is not unsafe to disregard and overrule public sentiment, as has been done in the case of General Frémont? The public consider that Frémont has been made a martyr of. . . . Consequently he is now, so far as the West is concerned, the most popular man in the country. He is to the West what Napoleon was to France ; while the President has lost the confidence of the people." [1]

----

[1] Chase Papers, MS. O. Follet, president of the Sandusky, Dayton, and Cincinnati Railway, wrote Chase, Nov. 6 : "You have no idea of the deep and all-pervading excitement that pervades all classes of people—men, women, and children. It is not loud, but deep and threatening. You know my means of information, and I can say I do not know half a dozen men, not in office, that justify the course of the administration ; most of them loudly condemn. Now that the removal has been made, I fear a sad reaction at the West on the war question. God grant that patriotism may keep the bad spirits in subjection." Ex-mayor Senter, of Cleveland, who supported the President, told Chase, Nov. 17, of a war meeting in Cleveland, at which "members of Congress sought to prejudice the people against

Lincoln's policy in dealing with the question of freeing the slaves, raised by Frémont, made the Democratic opposition to him less active than it otherwise would have been, and it bound to the Republican Union party those waverers, composed of conservative Republicans and of Democrats, who, in the emergency, had been willing to give up their party allegiance. But Democrats who revered their name, who looked upon the yearly conflict with the Republicans as an integral part of their life, and who were determined to maintain their organization, were sure to create some issue before election day came. " Do not, my friend," wrote Washington McLean, editor of the Cincinnati *Enquirer*, to Chase, "mistake the clamor of the mob for the real sentiment of the people, who would hail the return of peace with rapturous joy. In the strictest confidence I assure you that nine tenths of the Democrats are at heart bitterly opposed to the war." [1] Immediately after the firing

the administration for displacing Frémont, backed up by editors, office-holders, etc." Professor C. E. Stowe wrote from Andover, Mass., Nov. 6: " I do not know that you have either time or inclination to listen to a word from the common people; but I wish you could hear the voice of surprise, indignation, disgust, and contempt which now everywhere finds utterance at the removal of Frémont. The feeling is frightfully earnest."—Chase Papers, MS. Henry Ward Beecher said in his church, Oct. 20 : "I cannot but express my solemn conviction that both our government, and in a greater degree the community, have done great injustice to the cause in Missouri, in the treatment which has been bestowed upon that noble man, General Frémont. I have narrowly watched the course of things, not unacquainted with the reality of facts in the case ; and it is my settled judgment that, partly from private ambition, partly from political reasons, and partly from calculating aspirations of rivals, the most unjust influences have been permitted to issue against this heroic man."—New York *Tribune*, Oct. 22. See also editorial in New York *Evening Post*, Nov. 5; letters of Grimes to his wife and to Fessenden, Nov. 13, Life, p. 154. For comment on the abolition opposition to the administration, see New York *Herald*, Nov. 9.

[1] Letter of June 30, Chase Papers, MS. In this letter McLean also said: "Be assured, my friend, that the country looks to you as the responsible head of this administration, and all calamities growing out of the same will be charged (justly or not) against you, while any glory that may be

on Sumter, Democrats and Republicans, as we have seen, acted together without distinction of party, and nearly all the Democrats, at the special session of Congress, were willing to vote men and money freely for the prosecution of the war; although, at the same time, most of them thought that it should be waged with the sword in one hand and the olive-branch in the other. Samuel S. Cox, a representative from Ohio, was able to get in the House forty-one votes for his motion to suspend the rules in order that his peace propositions might be considered.[1]

As the time for holding party conventions approached, the Republicans, in most of the important States where fall elections were to take place, asked the Democrats to co-operate with them in naming a ticket on which both parties should be fairly represented; the platform of the coalition was simply to be the vigorous prosecution of the war for the restoration of the Union. Those who had authority to speak for the Democratic organization declined the invitation, but many individuals shook off their party trammels and entered heartily into the plan proposed. Daniel S. Dickinson, a Breckinridge Democrat, and David Tod, a Douglas Democrat, headed respectively the Union tickets of New York and Ohio. The Democrats who adhered to the regular organization held conventions, formulated declarations of principles, and placed candidates in nomination. They generally approved of prosecuting the war with vigor, but criticised the President for the suspension of the writ of *habeas corpus*; the Democrats of New York and Ohio fa-

---

reaped from it will inure to the military political leaders who are so clamorous for the prosecution of the war." William Gray, a Boston merchant of high standing and a good representative of business men, wrote Chase, Sept. 4: "I have had a conversation, this morning, with a prominent Democrat, who is entirely devoted to sustaining the government in the present struggle. He informs me that the leaders and committee men generally of that party are opposed to the war and sympathize with the South; that they keep quiet because it will not advance their views to move just now."
—Chase Papers, MS.   [1] July 29, *Congressional Globe*, p. 331.

vored a national convention, in the view that it might lead to a settlement of the difficulties. The action of the Northern Democrats gave a certain degree of comfort to the Confederates, and it led to a revival of the hope with which the South had entered on the path of revolution—that she would have a divided North to contend against. But the result of the elections gave her little encouragement. Although the vote was everywhere small, Governor Andrew in Massachusetts overtopped his competitor by 34,000; Dickinson carried New York city by over 17,000 majority and the State by 107,000; and Tod, in Ohio, had 206,000 votes for governor to his competitor's 151,000.[1]

In the Confederacy the people were, for the first time, to choose a President and Vice-President in accordance with their permanent Constitution. The mode of election was the same as that in force in the United States. But there was no contest. The symptoms of opposition to the administration shown in the Richmond Congress at its July session were, after its adjournment, no longer seen. One voice went up from all the States that Davis should be chosen. The Confederates " believe in no other man," wrote William H. Russell to Sumner,[2] and the tone of the Southern press at this time confirms this opinion. Some muttering there had been against Stephens, but this was quickly overborne. Conventions were not generally held for the purpose of nominating electors; the electoral tickets were in most cases the suggestion of self-constituted committees of prominent and trusted men through the medium of the press. Although the President and Vice-President were to be

---

[1] See New York *Tribune*, Aug. 9, 31, Sept. 6; *National Intelligencer*, Aug. 10; Columbus correspondence Cincinnati *Commercial*, Aug. 7, Sept. 5; Boston *Advertiser*, Sept. 19; New York *World*, Nov. 5, 7; New York *Times*, Nov. 5; New York *Evening Post*, Nov. 6; New York *Herald*, Sept. 1, 8, Nov. 20; Richmond *Examiner*, Aug. 13, Sept. 7, Oct. 15; Richmond *Enquirer*, Aug. 2, 30, Oct. 22 ; Richmond *Whig*, Aug. 2, Sept. 7 ; *Tribune* Almanac. The vote in New York city was remarkable, as it had gone against Lincoln in 1860 by 29,000.

[2] Letter of Sept. 5, Pierce-Sumner Papers, MS.

chosen for a term of six years from February 22, 1862, one journal complained that the coming election hardly drew as much notice as an ordinary contest for members of the State legislature or for county officers.[1] For many of the other positions there was some strife, yet it turned on no difference of principle or of policy, but merely on a preference as to men. The place of representative was competed for in all of the congressional districts of Virginia, and in the Richmond district an animated contest took place, in which ex-President Tyler polled more votes than both of his opponents. In Arkansas and Mississippi ballots were necessary for the choice of Confederate senators, and the struggles for the senatorship in the North Carolina, Georgia, and Louisiana legislatures called to mind the contests of the days of peace. The people of Alabama divided in an election for governor. Only after a hard struggle in Georgia did Brown defeat his opponent, the difference being personal, heightened by the point made against him that it was unprecedented to choose a man governor for a third term. In none of these elections were voters marshalled under political banners that had been raised when these States were in the Union; men were no longer Democrats, Whigs, or Americans. The grounds of controversy of the preceding year, which had found expression in the support of Breckinridge, Bell, or Douglas, had been entirely lost sight of. In Virginia it was at one time said that the submissionist, or, as the North called it, the Union, party still lived; yet its influence was not felt in the elections. On the first Wednesday of November, electors in the several States were chosen; and at the proper time, and in accordance with the statute, they cast a unanimous vote for Davis and Stephens as President and Vice-President of the Confederacy.[2]

---

[1] Richmond *Examiner*, Sept. 16.

[2] Ibid., Aug. 6, 10, 29, Sept. 5, 12, Oct. 2, 8, 17, Nov. 4, 5, 7, 11, 30, Dec. 10 ; Richmond *Whig*, Sept. 10, Oct. 1, 18, Nov. 8, 19 ; Richmond *Enquirer*, Aug. 13, Sept. 13, 14, 16, 25, Oct. 8, 29, Nov. 6, 12, 26; Atlanta *Southern Confederacy*, Sept. 15, 21, 22, 24, 26, 29, Oct. 1, 4, 12,

The war of bullets went on but slowly. General Cox drove Wise out of the Kanawha valley. Rosecrans as ranking officer succeeded McClellan in western Virginia. Owing to a lack of harmony between Wise and Floyd—the latter at the head of a brigade he had raised in his own section of his State—Robert E. Lee was sent to take command of the Confederate forces, but he was not able to wrest from Rosecrans and Cox the ground which the Union forces had gained. Their operations, following McClellan's earlier successes, secured western Virginia for the Union, and made the Alleghanies the line between the Confederacy and the United States.[1]

The navy at the outbreak of the war was small. Many of the ships were on distant cruises, and their orders to return were long in reaching them. Through the indefatigable exertions of Secretary Welles and his assistant Gustavus V. Fox, and by the purchase and charter of merchant steamers, a navy was improvised which was powerful enough to maintain a reasonably effective blockade.[2] By the end of the summer this department could assist in offensive movements. August 26 a joint army and naval expedition, under the command of General Butler and Flag-officer Stringham,

---

Nov. 7; Atlanta *Intelligencer*, Sept. 3, 12, 14, 20, 26, Oct. 3; Atlanta *Commonwealth*, Oct. 22; Letters and Times of the Tylers, vol. ii. p. 662. Many expressions of praise of Davis from the press might be given. I will cite the strongest I have found: "The President has never yet committed a blunder or neglected to achieve a practicable advantage for the South." —Richmond *Whig*, Aug. 13. "The South Carolina legislature has passed resolutions, with only one dissenting voice, expressive of confidence in the patriotism and ability of President Davis and the administration."—Richmond *Enquirer*, Dec. 2. The Richmond *Examiner* of Sept. 16 made a severe attack on Stephens. He was defended in the Richmond *Enquirer* of Sept. 16, the Richmond *Whig* of Sept. 20, the Atlanta *Southern Confederacy* of Sept. 24, the Charleston *Courier* of Sept. 25.

[1] These operations continued from July to October inclusive; see Cox's article, Century War Book, vol. i. p. 137; Davis's Rise and Fall of the Confederate Government, vol. i. chap. x.

[2] See Yancey, Rost and Mann to Earl Russell, Nov. 30, 1861, British and Foreign State Papers, 1860–61.

sailed from Fortress Monroe and took Forts Hatteras and Clark, which commanded Hatteras Inlet, on the coast of North Carolina, a point of importance for the blockading fleet. Its capture caused considerable joy to the people of the North, who were in a condition to be cheered by the slightest successes, and it occasioned some dismay at the South.[1] November 7 another expedition, under General Thomas W. Sherman and Captain Du Pont, took Port Royal, South Carolina, the finest harbor on the Southern coast, thirty miles from Savannah and fifty miles from Charleston. This created alarm in South Carolina, and tended to hold back troops for home defence which otherwise would have been sent to Virginia.[2]

Meanwhile McClellan was at work with energy and talent, erecting fortifications around Washington and organizing the " Army of the Potomac," as he christened it soon after assuming command. He had good executive ability, an aptitude for system, and, being in robust health, an immense capacity for labor. All these qualities were devoted without stint to the service. In the saddle a large part of the day, he visited the several camps, mixed with the different brigades and regiments, and came to know thoroughly his officers and his men. Himself a gentleman of sterling moral character, having come to Washington with the respect and admiration of these soldiers, he soon gained their love by his winning personality, and inspired an attachment such as no other Northern general of a large army, with one exception, was ever able to obtain. He was called " the young Napoleon," being believed by the army, the administration, and the country to have military genius such as entitled him to the name. In these first days he was on excellent terms with every one save the veteran of the army, General Scott, whom he began to ignore soon after his ar-

---

[1] Nicolay and Hay, vol. v. chap. 1.; Butler's report, Official Records, vol. iv. p. 581 ; New York *Tribune*, Sept. 2 ; Richmond *Examiner*, Sept. 4.
[2] Nicolay and Hay, vol. v. chap. i.; Charleston *Courier*, Nov. 9, 13, 29.

rival at Washington. Scott had a full sense of his own importance, and with age had grown irascible, but he deserved
better treatment from the young officer whose star was rising. We may imagine with what respect and tenderness
Robert E. Lee, under similar circumstances, would have treated the older man, and we may recognize thus early a defect
in McClellan's character. In the first open difference with
Scott, he exhibited the failing which made his splendid opportunities go for naught. Personally courageous himself,
he had great fear for his army, and was full of apprehension
that his movements would not be attended with success.
Joined to this, his intelligence of the enemy was either defective or his judgment on the facts he possessed radically
unsound. In August he was pursued by the phantom that
the Confederates largely outnumbered him, and that they
would attack his position on the Virginia side of the Potomac and also cross the river north of Washington.[1] At this
time, however, Johnston did not purpose either movement,
and was chafing at the smallness of his force, the large
amount of sickness and the lack of discipline in his army,
and the defects of the commissariat.[2] Scott divined that he
would not attack, and wrote the Secretary of War, August
9 : " Major-General McClellan has propagated in high quarters the idea . . . that Washington was not only 'insecure,'
but in 'imminent danger.' . I have not the slightest apprehension for the safety of the government here." [3] Since
the beginning of the war the old general's despatches and
letters had, on the whole, shown good business and military

---

[1] Letter of Aug. 8 to Scott, Official Records, vol. xi. part iii. p. 3. "I have
scarcely slept one moment for the last three nights, knowing well that the
enemy intend some movement. and fully recognizing our own weakness.
If Beauregard does not attack to-night I shall look upon it as a dispensa-
tion of Providence. He ought to do it."—Letter of McClellan to his wife,
Aug. 8, McClellan's Own Story, p. 84.

[2] Roman writes that Beauregard wished to make an offensive movement
the first part of August, but Johnston did not approve of the plan, Roman's Beauregard, vol. i. p. 131.

[3] Official Records, vol. xi. part iii. p. 4.

ability and judgment, and his opinion at this time, as the
sequel has shown, was entitled to more weight than McClellan's;[1] but the younger general had cast a glamour over every one and gained a reputation for infallibility. Although
Scott felt hurt at his treatment, and showed it in a letter of
sensitive dignity which he wrote Cameron, he acknowledged
that his " ambitious junior " had " unquestionably very high
qualifications for military command." [2]

While McClellan was working with diligence, every one was
co-operating with him in a way to give his talent for organization the widest scope. The President, the Treasury and the
War departments, the Secretary of State, the governors of
the Northern States assisted him faithfully with their full
powers. The officers under him displayed zeal and devotion. He had the sway of a monarch. Such complete harmony produced fertile results. Troops poured in from the
enthusiastic North, swelling the army of 52,000 men of July
27 to one of 168,318 three months later.[3]

There was no time at which the Confederate army was
as large as the Union force, but McClellan's fears prevented
him from correctly envisaging the situation. August 16 he
wrote his wife: " The enemy have from three to four times
my force." [4] As time wore on and he was not disturbed he
gained confidence and wrote, August 25: " Friend Beauregard has allowed the chance to escape him. I have now
some 65,000 effective men ; will have 75,000 by the end of
week. Last week he certainly had double our force. I feel
sure that the dangerous moment has passed." [5] At this
time the effective total of the Confederate army was less

---

[1] "I am leaving nothing undone to increase our force, but the old general always comes in the way. He understands nothing, appreciates nothing."—Letter of McClellan to his wife, Aug. 8, McClellan's Own Story,
p. 84.   [2] Official Records, vol. xi. part iii. p. 6.
[3] Present for duty, 147,695. These are McClellan's figures from his report to the Secretary of War, Oct., 1861, and from his general report of
Aug. 4, 1863, Official Records, vol. v. p. 10.
[4] McClellan's Own Story, p. 87.   [5] Ibid., p. 89.

than 41,000. September 6 he wrote: "I feel now perfectly secure against an attack; the next thing will be to attack him." [1] William H. Russell wrote Sumner, September 5: "Washington is, I feel, quite safe from a direct attack, and a turning movement into Maryland the only thing to be feared. Such an operation would be attended with extreme hazard, but the Confederates must do something. I think if they do attack they will be beaten." [2]

McClellan himself, and experienced observers, began to believe that he was creating an efficient army. William H. Russell wrote the London *Times*, September 2: "Never perhaps has a finer body of men in all respects of *physique* been assembled by any power in the world, and there is no reason why their *morale* should not be improved so as to equal that of the best troops in Europe." [3] Three days later he wrote Sumner: "McClellan is working hard and is doing much good. The enemy must be greatly embarrassed by his inaction, which is really hard work, drilling and the like;" [4] and September 10 he said: "McClellan is doing his best to get his troops into order. Hard work." [5] The outposts of the Confederate army were at Munson's Hill, six and a half miles from Washington; their flag could be seen from the federal capital. The lower Potomac was blockaded, and McClellan would not furnish troops to co-operate with the navy in silencing the Confederate batteries and taking possession of points that would secure an uninterrupted communication by water between the North and Washington. Having a vivid remembrance of Bull Run,

[1] McClellan's Own Story, p. 90.

[2] Pierce-Sumner Papers, MS.

[3] In a letter to the London *Times* of Nov. 10 this enthusiastic opinion is modified, perhaps owing to the fact that, as events progressed, the tone of Russell's letters became less favorable to the North But it must be remembered his judgment is always based on a comparison with well-disciplined European armies. See on this point The Civil War in America, Comte de Paris, vol. i. p. 407; same author in Century War Book, vol. ii. p. 113; Webb's Peninsula, p. 169.

[4] Pierce-Sumner Papers, MS.   [5] Ibid.

the country looked on patiently, and did not complain at the daily news, "All quiet on the Potomac," deeming the period of inaction a necessary incident of the work of disciplining an army, which would, when ready, bring the civil war to an end.

The last of September, Johnston, considering his advanced position hazardous, withdrew his outposts from Munson's Hill.[1] At his request Jefferson Davis came to the army headquarters at Fairfax Court-house the 1st of October, and had, with Beauregard, General Gustavus W. Smith, and himself, a council of war in reference to taking the offensive. All agreed that the Confederate army was in better shape to fight now than, unless arms could be obtained from abroad, it would be in the spring, and that if inactive it would retrograde in discipline during the winter; it was also clearly understood that the federal army was constantly augmenting in number and efficiency. Smith then asked: "Mr. President, is it not possible to increase the effective strength of this army, and put us in condition to cross the Potomac and carry the war into the enemy's country? Can you not, by stripping other points to the last they will bear, and even risking defeat at all other places, put us in condition to move forward? Success here at this time saves everything; defeat here loses all."

"The President asked me," wrote Smith, who related the story of the council, "what number of men were necessary, in my opinion, to warrant an offensive campaign, to cross the Potomac, cut off the communications of the enemy with their fortified capital, and carry the war into their country. I answered, 'Fifty thousand effective, *seasoned* soldiers,' explaining that by *seasoned* soldiers I meant such men as we had here present for duty. . . . General Johnston and General Beauregard both said that a force of *sixty thousand* such men would be necessary, and that this force would

---

[1] McClellan was jubilant at obtaining possession of Munson's and Upton's hills, letter to his wife, McClellan's Own Story, p. 92.

require large additional transportation and munitions of war, the supplies here being entirely inadequate for an active campaign in the enemy's country even with our present force."

With regret Davis declared that "want of arms was the great difficulty," and that it would be impossible to furnish the army with the reinforcements and supplies asked for.[1] The alternative, therefore, was that the Confederates must remain on the defensive, awaiting the action of McClellan. October 19 Johnston drew his army back from Fairfax Court-house to Centreville and Manassas Junction—a much stronger position.[2]

Meanwhile McClellan was perfecting his organization. Neither he nor any one else apparently had any other idea than that at some time during the fall he would attack Johnston's army. When he and McDowell were riding together from camp to camp on the south side of the Potomac, he used to point towards Manassas and say: "We shall strike them there."[3] In October he declared to the Secretary of War that the object of the government should be to "crush the army under Johnston at Manassas."[4] "With the great increase in numbers of men," wrote William H. Russell to Sumner, October 14, "and above all with his preponderance in artillery, McClellan ought to be able to overcome all the obstacles of the enemy, and to overlap and beat them, in spite of their advantages in position, for I believe they are inferior in number and in guns and in all but perhaps the craft of their leaders and the animosity of their men. There is still to a European a woful lack of real discipline in this

[1] G. W. Smith's account, probable date Oct. 1, 1861. Beauregard and Johnston wrote, Jan. 31, 1862, that their recollections agreed fully with his statement, Official Records, vol. v. p. 884. See also Johnston's Narrative, p. 75; Hughes's Johnston, p. 92; criticism of Smith's account, Davis's Rise and Fall of the Confederate Government, vol. i. p. 450, and the examination of this criticism, Roman's Beauregard, vol. i. p. 139; Confederate War Papers, G. W. Smith   [2] Johnston's Narrative.
[3] Swinton's Army of the Potomac, a book friendly to McClellan, p. 69.
[4] Webb's Peninsula, also favorable to McClellan, p. 168.

Conrad's Ferry

Poolesville

Dawsonville

Long

M O N T G O

Leesburg

Edwards Ferry

P O T O M A C

Darnestown

Seneca Creek

M E R Y

Good Road to Georgetown

Ohio Canal

Washington R.

Belmont P.O.

Rushville

Frankville

Bottom Land

No Timber

Old Channel

Woolington

Farmwell Sta.

Turnpike

Dranesville

Springvale

Loudoun

Farmwell

Church Road

Guilford Sta.

Herndon Sta.

Thornton Sta.

Hampshire

Difficult Run

Broad

Hog Pen Run

Frying Pan

Hunter's Mills

Gum Spring

Little River Turnpike

F A I R F A X

Freedom Hill

Centreville Road

Pleasant Valley

Chantilly Church

Ox Road Junction

Vienna

Saunders' Toll Gate

Chantilly

Flint Hill

Mill Lick Run

Cub Run

Flat Lick Run

Ox Run

Germantown

Thornton

Fairfax C.H.

Little River

Sudley Springs

Bull Run

Centreville

Brimston

Battle-field at Bull Run

Stone Bridge

July 21st 1861

Manassas

Sangster's Sta.

Groveton

New Market

Blackburn's

McLean's Fd.

Fairfax

Burke's Sta.

Brimstone Hill

Manassas Gap R.R.

Manassas Sta.

Woodyard's Fd.

Bull's Ford

MAP OF

NORTHEASTERN VIRGINIA

AND

VICINITY OF WASHINGTON

[From the Map compiled at Division Headquarters of General Irvin McDowell, Jan. 1862, and corrected from later surveys and reconnaissances under direction of the Bureau of Topographical Engineers.]

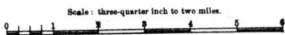

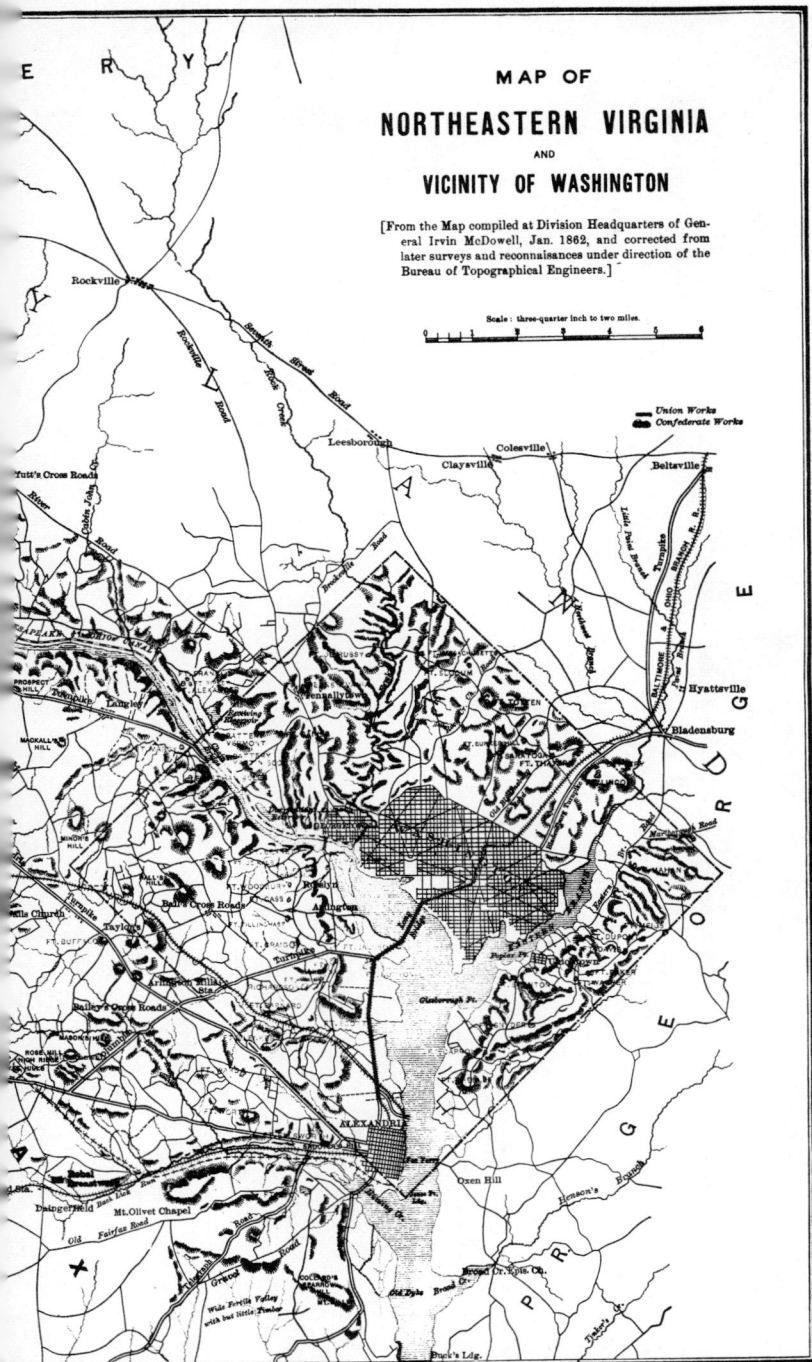

Scale : three-quarter inch to two miles.

Union Works
Confederate Works

Rockville

Leesborough

Colesville

Claysville

Beltsville

Tutt's Cross Roads

Hyattsville

Bladensburg

PROSPECT HILL

MACKALL HILL

MINOR'S HILL

Bull's Cross Roads

Arlington

Falls Church

Taylor's

Bailey's Cross Roads

ROSS HILL

Oxen Hill

ALEXANDRIA

Daingerfield

Mt. Olivet Chapel

COCHRAN'S

Wide Fertile Valley with but little Timber

Broad Cr. Epis. Ch.

Buck's Ldg.

army, and the country is so difficult that no general can control or oversee the movements of the enormous mass once it is set in motion. . . . I am not sure of the result if the Confederate States army be nearly equal."[1]

Three months had passed by with McClellan in command. Although the country was becoming impatient that there were no signs of a forward movement, it did not for a moment lose faith in its general. Could the Northern people, however, have known him as well as we now do through the publication of his private correspondence, they would have been amazed and their confidence shaken. Rapid advancement and hero-worship had swollen him up with conceit. As early as October he had arrived at the conviction that all the ability needed for the conduct of the war centred in himself and in a few of his favorite generals, and that no one else in responsible position had any wisdom whatever.[2] October 21 occurred on the Potomac, above Washington, the affair of Ball's Bluff, in which, owing to mismanagement, the Union forces were defeated. Measured by subsequent battles, the casualties were not large; but the death of Colonel Baker, a dear friend of Lincoln and a popular senator and officer, and the loss to New York, Massachusetts, and Pennsylvania of some of "the very pride and flower of their young men,"[3] caused a profound feeling of discouragement all over the North; still, there was little

---

[1] Pierce-Sumner Papers, MS.; see, also, The Civil War in America, Comte de Paris, vol. i. p. 407.

[2] Oct. —: "I can't tell you how disgusted I am becoming with these wretched politicians." Oct. —: "I presume I shall have to go after them when I get ready ; but this getting ready is slow work with such an administration. I wish I were well out of it." Oct. 2: "I am becoming daily more disgusted with this administration—perfectly sick of it. If I could with honor resign, I would quit the whole concern to-morrow." Oct. 10: "There are some of the greatest geese in the cabinet I have ever seen—enough to tax the patience of Job."—Letters of McClellan to his wife, McClellan's Own Story, pp. 167, 168, 169.

[3] Roscoe Conkling's speech in the House of Representatives, Jan. 6, 1862.

tendency to impute this disaster to McClellan, although it occurred in his department.

The friction between Scott and McClellan increased, resulting in the voluntary retirement with due honors of the elder soldier. This took place October 31, and McClellan succeeded him in the command of all the armies of the United States. A few days earlier Senators Trumbull, Chandler, and Wade had urged upon the President the importance of immediate action, but Lincoln and Seward maintained that McClellan was right not to move until he was ready.[1] Yet for financial as well as for political reasons it was eminently desirable that some progress should be made in the work which the North had set out to perform. The expenses of the government were now $1,750,000 a day.[2] From a military point of view it would seem as if the conditions were favorable for an advance. October 27, according to McClellan's own figures, the aggregate strength of the Army of the Potomac was 168,318, and the force present for duty 147,695; of these 13,410, from various causes, were unfit for the field, reducing his effective force to 134,285.[3] At the same time Johnston's "effective total"—soldiers "capable of going into battle"—was 41,000.[4] McClellan had substantially three to one, and his force was constantly increasing. December 1 he had 198,000 men, of whom 169,000 were present for duty.[5] During the same period Johnston had gained 6200.[6] The discipline, experience, and fighting qualities of the two armies were equal. The federal artillery

---

[1] Nicolay and Hay, vol. iv. p. 467.

[2] Letter of Chase to Larz Anderson, Oct. 2, Schuckers, p. 430.

[3] Official Records, vol. v. p. 10.

[4] Johnston's Narrative, p. 81. Northern writers have generally accepted the statements of Johnston as correct, but on his method of computation see J. D. Cox in the *Nation*, May 21, 1874, p. 334. Nevertheless, after all allowances, the statement frequently made that McClellan had three men to Johnston's one is true. See Webb's Peninsula, p. 169 ; The Civil War in America, Comte de Paris, vol. i. p. 407 ; Swinton's Army of the Potomac, p. 72.   [5] Official Records, vol. v. p. 12.

[6] Johnston's Narrative, p. 83.

was superior ; the infantry had better arms. The workshops
of the North and of Europe were busy in supplying the
Union army, and money, or the credit of the government,
was used lavishly for this purpose.   The manufacture of
arms and ordnance in the public armories and private establishments of the Confederacy was attended with difficulty
and discouragement, largely owing to the lack of skilled
workmen.[1] Munitions of war from Europe could be brought
only in vessels which were able to run the blockade, and so
rarely did such a cargo arrive at a Southern port that it
afforded a day of rejoicing.[2] The health of the Union army
was good, that of the Confederate bad.[3] The weather was
fine and dry ; up to Christmas the roads were in condition
for military operations. The officers and men of the Army
of the Potomac were devoted to McClellan, were eager to
fight, and would have been glad to follow where he led.
It only remained for the commanding general to give the
word.

McClellan, however, could neither make up his mind to
advance nor to abandon all idea of offensive operations
until spring. On account of the affair of Ball's Bluff,
writes the Comte de Paris, " a fatal hesitation took possession of McClellan."[4] But in truth he was by nature irresolute, and he did not study his enemy with good results.
He deluded himself as to the size and efficiency of the Confederate army, magnifying Johnston's force of 41,000 into
one of 150,000,[5] and such was the weight attached to his

---

[1] Davis's Rise and Fall of the Confederate Government, vol. i. p. 473 ;
Life of Albert Sidney Johnston, W. P. Johnston, p. 417.

[2] Richmond *Examiner*, Aug. 30, Nov. 15 ; Richmond *Enquirer*, Nov. 14.

[3] McClellan's Own Story, p. 126 ; Johnston's Narrative, p. 65 ; The Civil
War in America, Comte de Paris, vol. i. p. 407 ; Richmond *Dispatch*, Aug.
27 ; Pollard's First Year of the War, p. 218 ; A Rebel War Clerk's Diary,
Jones, vol. i. p. 81 ; Down South, Samuel Phillips Day, vol. ii. p. 109.

[4] Century War Book, vol. ii. p. 114.

[5] " All the information we have from spies, prisoners, etc., agrees in
showing that the enemy have a force on the Potomac not less than 150,-
000 strong, well drilled and equipped, ably commanded, and strongly in-

opinion that he impressed upon nearly every one the correctness of his judgment. In a speech to a delegation of Philadelphians, he said : " The war cannot last long. It may be desperate. I ask in the future forbearance, patience, and confidence. With these we can accomplish all." [1] The country gave him what he asked,[2] but the sequel will show that he was not worthy of the unconditional trust reposed in him. Although McClellan was a good organizer and had a high degree of patriotism, he lacked the brains to command a large army in the field. As Lowell expressed it, " Our chicken was no eagle, after all." [3] Yet he himself had no conception of his own limitations. To save the country he was willing to accept the dictatorship.[4] Recognizing " the weakness and unfitness of the poor beings who control the destinies of this great country," the impulse came to him that he must give Lincoln and Seward counsel respecting a grave diplomatic question.[5]

Johnston, by means of spies, knew almost accurately the size of the federal army.[6] McClellan likewise should have known that he only had 40,000 or 50,000 troops to contend against, instead of three times that number as he persisted in believing. Had Johnston been in McClellan's place, we may be reasonably certain that a battle in Vir-

---

trenched."—McClellan to Secretary of War, latter part of Oct., Official Records, vol. v. p. 9.   Seward and Meigs estimated the enemy at 100,000, Life of Seward, vol. ii. p. 621 ; testimony of Meigs before the Committee on the Conduct of the War.   [1] New York *Tribune*, Nov. 4.

[2] " General McClellan asked . . . ' forbearance, patience, and confidence.' He has a right to them all, and he enjoys them all at the hands of those to whom the appeal is made. . . . The people have all the confidence in General McClellan which it would be safe for any man in his position to enjoy."—New York *Times*, Nov. 6; see, also, New York *Herald*, Nov. 9.

[3] Political Essays, p. 94 ; *North American Review*, April, 1864.

[4] Letter to his wife, Aug. 9, McClellan's Own Story, p. 85.

[5] Letter to his wife, Nov. 17, ibid., p. 175; but see Lothrop's Seward, p. 327.

[6] Johnston's Narrative, p. 81.

ginia, perhaps as momentous in its results as Gettysburg,
would have been fought before Christmas day of 1861;
with a great commander, "that rare son of the tempest,"[1]
the capture of the Confederate army or of Richmond was
in the range of possibilities. But McClellan dallied with
opportunity, seeing phantoms in the shape of an immense
army before him and powerful enemies behind him.[2] Had
he decided, as did Johnston, in spite of clamors of the press,[3]
not to take the offensive that autumn, but to wait until he
had his army under better discipline, military authorities
might justify him; but on such a policy he could not resolve. Some time in November he wrote his wife, "I am
doing all I can to get ready to move before winter sets in,
but it now begins to look as if we were condemned to a
winter of inactivity;" and November 25 he shows a manifest joy at a "driving snow-storm," and a hope that the
roads will be bad enough to render a decision against a
forward movement unmistakably clear.[4] Let us not, however, overlook one fine trait in McClellan, which, united to
a greater ability, would have been of significant service to
himself and his country. "Our George," he wrote, the

---

[1] Parkman, Montcalm and Wolfe, vol. i. p. 181.

[2] "I am concealed at Stanton's to dodge all enemies in shape of 'brows-
ing' Presidents, etc. . . . I have a set of men to deal with unscrupulous
and false. . . . The people think me all-powerful. Never was there a
greater mistake. I am thwarted and deceived by these incapables at every
turn."—Letter of McClellan to his wife, Nov. —, McClellan's Own Story,
pp. 176, 177.

[3] "All over the South, in every State from the Rio Grande to the Potomac, the desire is universal that our brave army shall go forward. . . .
We believe that McClellan's army could on a fair field be defeated by
twenty-five thousand Southern soldiers. . . . Our army once across [the
Potomac], we do not fear the result. . . . The enemy would have to quit
his intrenchments and fight at a disadvantage with an army paralyzed
with apprehension, and exceedingly anxious to get back to the land of
pumpkin-pies and scraggy-faced females."—Richmond *Examiner*, Sept.
20, see also Sept. 25 ; also Richmond *Dispatch*, Sept. 23.

[4] McClellan's Own Story, p. 177, also p. 199, and testimony before the
Committee on the Conduct of the War.

soldiers "have taken it into their heads to call me. I
ought to take good care of these men, for I believe they
love me from the bottom of their hearts; I can see it in
their faces when I pass among them." [1]

It is impossible to contemplate McClellan's treatment of
the President with patience. Misled, as many indeed were,
by Lincoln's lack of society manners, by his want of systematic attention to the details of administration, by his
neglect to exact punctiliousness in official intercourse, the
young general of thirty-five failed to see beyond these
things his capacity for dealing with men and large affairs,
and summed up his character with, " the President is honest
and means well." [2] So anxious was Lincoln about the progress of military operations that it was his custom to call
often at the house of the general, sometimes coming before
breakfast, but more frequently in the evening. On the
evening of November 13 he came with Seward, and was
told that McClellan had gone to an officer's wedding, but
would soon return. They waited. The general entered,
and, though informed by the orderly of his visitors, went
directly up-stairs. The President, thinking there must be
some misunderstanding, sent a servant to announce him
again; this brought the information that the general had
gone to bed. Lincoln probably asked no explanation of
this incident, for personal slights, in view of the magnitude
of the cause which engaged him, were of no moment. On
another occasion, when the general failed to meet an appointment with him, he said, " Never mind; I will hold
McClellan's horse if he will only bring us success." [3] Such
occurrences cannot fail to suggest a comparison with

[1] McClellan's Own Story, p. 172.
[2] Letter to his wife, Nov. 17, McClellan's Own Story, p. 176.
[3] Nicolay and Hay, vol. iv. p. 468. "Officers of McClellan's staff tell
that Mr. Lincoln almost daily comes into McClellan's library and sits
there rather unnoticed. On several occasions McClellan let the President wait in the room, together with other common mortals."—Count
Gurowski's Diary, Nov., 1861, p. 123.

Davis's treatment of Joseph E. Johnston;[1] they make manifest to us that Lincoln had the magnanimity of a great mind.

In December McClellan fell ill with typhoid-fever. The Army of the Potomac, the administration, the country waited on his recovery.[2]

As has been shown, English sentiment up to late in the summer was favorable to the federal government. " I have not seen or heard of a soul," wrote Darwin, June 5, to Asa Gray, " who is not with the North."[3] But when the detailed news of the battle of Bull Run became fully understood, when the full effect of it was comprehended, a marked revulsion of feeling took place. It is easy to classify the many manifestations of opinion, from the day that the tale of Bull Run was told in England to that on which London heard of the capture of Mason and Slidell.[4] There were outspoken friends of the North, and men distinctly favorable to the South ; but the dominant sentiment was that of the main body of the aristocracy and middle class, who, seeing clearly, as they thought, that the Union could not conquer the Confederacy, earnestly longed for the war to cease. The aristocracy had no tears to shed that the great and powerful democracy, rent by internal feud, was going the way of all democracies ; they felt that a divided Union would be less of a moral menace than a compact democratic federal government to the intrenched rights on which most European governments, and particularly that of Great Britain, were based. The middle class, devoted

[1] *Ante.*

[2] Besides authorities specifically quoted, I have used the report of the Committee on the Conduct of the War, and the testimony before it of McClellan, Franklin, McCall, Fitz-John Porter, Heintzelman, McDowell, Wadsworth, and Meigs ; also McClellan's Military Career Reviewed and Exposed, Swinton, pamphlet, 1864 ; General J. D. Cox's review of McClellan's Own Story, the *Nation*, Jan. 20 and 27, 1887 ; John C. Ropes's review of the same, *Atlantic Monthly*, April, 1887.

[3] Life and Letters, vol. ii. p. 166.

[4] Aug. 5 to Nov. 28.

to commerce and manufactures, were disturbed that the
supply of cotton was cut off. Business became deranged.
Hunger stared thousands of laborers in the face. Higher
in the social scale, the fear of curtailed incomes and of the
sacrifice of luxuries and necessaries may be plainly seen.
Goldwin Smith, a friend to the North, described the situation in terms none too strong: " The awful peril, not only
commercial but social, with which the cotton famine threatened us, and the thrill of alarm and horror which upon
the dawning of that peril ran through the whole land." [1]
Peace would open the Southern ports, would restore comfort to the British householder ; and as it seemed to him
that the South was in the end certain to gain her independence, the sooner the fact was acknowledged by the
North, the sooner would the disturbed equilibrium be restored. This was the opinion of the great body of voting
Whigs and of such Conservatives as did not distinctly sympathize with the South,[2] and it found fitting representation

---

[1] *Macmillan's Magazine*, Dec., 1865, p. 167. See detailed figures in London *Times* of Sept. 7. " The reports from Lancashire apprise us that the
first mutterings of the long-expected storm are already heard. Mills are
working short time, manufacturers are reducing wages, and operatives
assembling in trouble and alarm to discuss the prospects before them.
. . . The fact is that our stocks of cotton are rapidly sinking, while the
supplies on the road to us are of uncertain quality and insufficient
amount. . . . So a manufacture which pays upward of £11,000,000 in
wages, and supports a fifth part of our whole population, is coming gradually to a stand."—London *Times*, Sept. 19. " Lancashire calls for so many
million bales of cotton, but these bales are paid for with so many millions
of pounds. In fact, it is a trade of some £40,000,000 a year."—Ibid., Sept.
21. " To a man whom books or travel have made familiar with the great
features of nature throughout the earth, it must seem strange that Manchester should be shaking in her shoes, and that Liverpool should be in a
fever of speculative excitement, on account of the non-arrival of a few
ship-loads of cotton."—Ibid., Nov. 2.
[2] John Stuart Mill speaks of " the rush of nearly the whole upper and
middle classes of my own country, even those who passed for Liberals,
into a furious pro-Southern partisanship : the working classes and some of
the literary and scientific men being almost the sole exceptions to the
general frenzy."—Autobiography, p. 268.

in Palmerston and Russell, the two leading men of the cabinet. Earl Russell, in a speech at Newcastle in October, told the British public that the American civil war did not turn on the question of slavery, "though that, I believe," he added, " was the original cause of the quarrel;" neither was the strife about free trade or protection ; but the two parties were " contending, as so many States in the old world have contended, the one for empire and the other for independence." To what good result, he asked, can the contest lead? He answered his own question, to the effect that a separation of the two sections was the only logical and permanent settlement of the controversy.[1] The notion that the Union could never be restored found expression in the *Times* and the *Saturday Review*, which, gravitating naturally to the representation of the opinion of the majority of the English public, made, by reason of the ability with which they hammered away, many converts from among the waverers.[2] The laboring class, so far as they

---

[1] London *Times,* Oct. 16 ; on this speech see the *Spectator* of Oct. 19. Many speeches in the same tone as Russell's were made. Bright said publicly, Dec. 4: " Of all the speeches made since the end of the last session of Parliament by public men, by politicians, the majority of them have either displayed a strange ignorance of American affairs, or a stranger absence of that cordiality and friendship which, I maintain, our American kinsmen have a right to look for at our hands."—Speeches, vol. i. p. 180.

[2] " The South is not absolutely so strong as the North, but it has hitherto been stronger in the field, and it will always be strong enough, in all human probability, to resist subjection, if not to enforce its will."—London *Times*, Sept. 17. " Slavery counts for little in the quarrel, commercial antagonism for much. . . . The watchword of the South is ' Independence,' of the North ' Union,' and in those two war-cries the real issue is contained."—Ibid., Sept. 19. " The contest is really for empire on the side of the North, and for independence on that of the South, and in this respect we recognize an exact analogy between the North and the government of George III., and the South and the thirteen revolted provinces. These opinions may be wrong, but they are the general opinions of the English nation."—Ibid., Nov. 7. See W. H. Russell's letter from Washington, Oct. 17. " It continues to be improbable that the South should be conquered, and impossible that it should be held in subjection."—*Sat-*

thought at all, sympathized with the United States. They
saw clearly, as did the aristocracy, that the cause of the
North was the cause of democracy in England; but they
counted little in making up the sum of public sentiment,
for parliamentary representation was based upon the reform bill of 1832, which gave them no share in the suffrage.

It is not the least of the glories of England that when
public opinion veers strongly in one direction, she has men
who see clearer than the mass, and set themselves at work
to stem the current; who speak boldly and with no uncertain sound; whose boldness, whose resistance to the tyranny .of the majority, if joined to ability and honesty,
rarely if ever—such is the wholesomeness of English political life—compel them to retirement. Most conspicuous of
these men, who at this time were unreservedly on the side
of the North, was John Bright. September 6 he wrote
Sumner from Rochdale, giving his own opinion and an exposition of the sentiment of the country. " The *Times*
newspaper, as you know," he said, " will willingly make
mischief if its patrons want mischief, and on your side you
have the New York *Herald* doing Southern work when it
dares to do it, and stirring up ill-blood with England as the
best mode of helping its Southern friends. Public opinion
here is in a languid and confused state. The upper and
ruling class have some satisfaction, I suspect, in your
troubles — they think two nations on your northern continent more easy to deal with than one, and they see, without
grief, that democracy may get into trouble and war and

---

urday Review, Sept. 28. " The belief of foreigners that the Union can
never be restored by force contradicts the language rather than the convictions of American speakers and writers." —- Ibid., Oct. 12, see, also,
Nov. 23. I have seen many extracts from the London *Morning Post*,
which was the accredited organ of Lord Palmerston ; this was more
friendly to the South than the *Times* and *Saturday Review*. I have not
consulted the files of the London *Standard* and *Herald*, conservative
journals, but from frequent references to them I observe that their sympathy with the Confederacy was warm.

debt and taxes, as aristocracy has done for this country. The middle class wish abolition to come out of your contentions, but they are irritated by your foolish tariff, and having so lately become free-traders themselves, of course they are great purists now, and severely condemn you.   In this district we have a good many friends of the South — the men who go South every year to buy cotton for our spinners, and those among our spinners and merchants who care little for facts and right, and go just where their interest seems to point.   I have not, so far, seen any considerable manifestation of a disposition to urge our government to interfere in your affairs; and yet with some, doubtless, there is a hope that France and England will not permit their cotton manufacture to be starved out by your contest.   There is a great anxiety as to what is coming.   Our mills are just now reducing their working time to four days and some of them to three days in the week; this is not universal or general, but it is spreading, and will soon become general, I cannot doubt.   Working half-time we can go on till April or May perhaps, but this will cause suffering and discontent, and it is possible pressure may be put upon the government to take some step supposed likely to bring about a change.   I preach the doctrine that the success of the North is our nearest way to a remedy, but there are those who hold a contrary opinion. . . . With our upper-class hostility to your country and government, with the wonderful folly of your tariff telling against you here, and with the damage arising from the blockade of the Southern ports, you will easily understand that the feeling here is not so thorough and cordial with you as I could wish it to be." [1]

Bright was the ablest and best-known exponent of the friendly feeling towards the North, but he had many sympathizing friends.   Cobden,[2] William E. Fors-

[1] Pierce-Sumner Papers, MS.
[2] Cobden wrote Sumner, Nov. 27 : "My respect and admiration for your

ter,[1] the Duke of Argyll, and Thomas Hughes are not only
men of grateful memory to the North, but they reflect
honor on their own land. The *Daily News* and the *Spectator* urged the cause of the North without ceasing, with signal ability uniting large information to correct judgment.[2]
The sentiment towards America in England depended to
some extent on differences of political opinion. The war
and the Northern conduct of it were used with effect
by the *Times* and the *Saturday Review* to point the moral of the failure of the great democracy to realize the
hopes of its English advocates. " Help us to a breath of
generous strengthening sympathy from Old England,"
wrote Sumner to William H. Russell, " which will cheer
the good cause, and teach everybody that there can be no
terms of any kind with a swarm of traitors trying to build

---

free States is so great that I have regretted you did not let the vile in-
cubus of slavery slip off your back. And yet I confess the almost insu-
perable difficulty of making two nations of the United States. The geographical obstacles alone seem insurmountable. . . . Be assured that we
are deeply sympathetic with you and all earnest friends of peace and freedom."—Pierce-Sumner Papers, MS.

[1] Forster made a warm speech for the North in Oct., see Life, by Reid,
p. 337. See comment on same by London *Daily News*, Oct. 4. " I wish
success to the North," he said, " because I love freedom and hate slavery."

[2] " We believe, as we always did, that the South cannot hold out."—
Daily News, Sept. 17. " The Southern States are, according to their
own formal declaration, fighting not only to perpetuate, but to extend
the institution of slavery."—Ibid., Oct. 10 ; see, also, Sept. 18, Oct. 2, 3, 4.
" The news of every succeeding mail from America makes it more and
more evident that the slavery issue is the practical hinge of the civil
war. . . . The view taken by the conservatives, whether avowed or concealed under the cloak of moderate liberalism, is . . . that the North are
fighting for an impossibility. . . . This impossibility is rather a new invention ; it dates from the battle of Bull Run. . . . To talk of the endeavor [of the North] as an impossibility is an abuse of human language."
—London *Spectator*, Sept. 14; see, also, Sept. 28, Nov. 16. The London *Star*
was also strong in its sympathy with the North. I have read many extracts
from it, but have not consulted its files, for the reason that, as it was the
reputed organ of Cobden and Bright, I have preferred to show this phase
of sentiment by their private letters.

a State on human slavery." [1]   "I do not approve," wrote
Russell in reply, " of the tone of many papers in Great
Britain in reference to American matters ; but do not forget,
I pray you, that in reality it is Brightism and republicanism
at home which most of those remarks are meant to smite.
America is the shield under which the blow is dealt." [2]   In
the light of succeeding events and the well-rounded career
of John Bright, we may venture to assert that he had high
moral and political wisdom and chose the right side, and
that the dominant English opinion was wrong and did
harm to Great Britain, to America, and to civilization.
"Some friends of mine in this town," he wrote Sumner
from Rochdale, November 20, "have invited me to a public dinner on the 4th of December. I intend to take that
opportunity for saying something on your great political
earthquake, and I need not tell you that I shall not abandon the faith I have in the greatness of the free North. It
has been a misfortune here that so little has been said to
instruct the public on the true bearings of your question, for
it is incredible almost how densely ignorant even our middle and upper class is with regard to your position. The
sympathies of the great body of the people here are, I
think, quite right, although some papers supposed to be
read by them are wrong. I suspect there has been some
tampering with a certain accessible portion of the press.
I am very anxious that your affairs should take some more
decided turn before our Parliament meets about the 1st
of February. When a mob of 650 men get together with
party objects and little sympathy for you or for the right
anywhere, there is no knowing what mischief may come
out of foolish and wicked speeches, with a ministry led by

---

[1] Sept. 16, Pierce's Sumner, vol. iv. p. 42.
[2] Letter of Oct. 2, Pierce - Sumner Papers, MS.; see the London *Times*
of Aug. 19. " The real secret of the exultation which manifests itself in
the *Times* and other organs over our troubles and disasters, is their hatred,
not to America so much as to democracy in England."—Motley to his
mother from England, Sept. 22, Correspondence, vol. ii. p. 35.

such a man as the present Prime Minister of England. However, I will hope for the best." [1]

If, with the results before us, we extol the political perceptions of the few, fairness demands that we examine the contemporary evidence to ascertain what may excuse the mistake of the majority. That Earl Russell, the *Times*, and the *Saturday Review* made out an apparently good case, hardly needs stating. The iterated and reiterated argument ran that, as the Confederacy was certain to gain its independence, the sooner the disturbance was put an end to the better. "The people of the Southern States," declared the *Times*, "may be wrong, but they are ten millions." [2] This summed up the political philosophy of the British public; yet the notion that the North could not conquer the South was shared by many of our friends. "Judging from this distance," wrote Bright to Sumner, September 6, "I confess I am unable to see any prospect of reunion through a conquest of the South, and I should grieve to see it through any degrading concessions on the part of the North. I confess I am surprised at the difficulties you meet with even in the border States. It would seem that the separation in regard to feeling and interests had made a fatal progress before secession was openly proclaimed; for surely, if there was a large and preponderating sympathy for the Union

---

[1] Pierce-Sumner Papers, MS.

[2] Oct. 9, in the same article, it was said: "The one great fact which swayed English opinion was the decided and multiform antagonism between North and South, which time and events combined to disclose. . . . We think the policy of the federal government wrong. If the whole case of the war is to be analyzed, we must needs say the Northerners have the right on their side, for the Southerners have destroyed without provocation a mighty political fabric, and have impaired the glory and strength of the great American Republic." The London *Daily News* of Oct. 10 said, in reply: "The Confederate States may be ten millions, but they are wrong—notoriously, flagrantly wrong." William H. Russell wrote the London *Times* from Washington, Oct. 17: "The history of the world cannot point out two countries now more divided than North and South—two governments, two nations, two policies. Is it possible that the broken vase can ever be restored? Thousands of able men think it can."

in those States, the Northern forces would have great advantages over the South in the conduct of their operations which they do not now appear to have. . . . I cannot see how the South, with its vast territory, is to be subdued, if there be any of that unanimity among its population which is said to exist, and of which there are some proofs. If it be subdued, I cannot see in the future a contented section of your great country made up of States now passing through the crisis of a civil war, with every ferocious passion excited against the North ; and the prospect being so dark, looking through the storm of war, I am hoping for something that will enable you to negotiate." [1]   " The belief is largely held," he wrote, November 20, that the subjugation of the South " is barely, if at all, possible, and that a restoration of the Union is not to be looked for." [2]   Cobden did not believe that the North and the South could " ever lie in the same bed again." [3]   " I hope to God," wrote Darwin, " we English are utterly wrong in doubting whether the North can conquer the South." [4]   On our side of the water the letter of William M. Evarts to Thurlow Weed, purporting to give " about the staple of opinion and conversation when men talked freely," breathed out despair of the Union being able to conquer the Confederacy. [5]

It was frequently asserted that if the North, in 1861, had avowed the war to be against slavery, we should have had the warm sympathy of the British public. [6]   The proclamation

---

[1] Pierce-Sumner Papers, MS.   [2] Ibid.

[3] Morley's Cobden, American edition, p. 572.

[4] To Asa Gray, Sept. 17, Life and Letters, vol. ii. p. 169. Dec. 11 he wrote, " How curious it is that you seem to think that you can conquer the South ; and I never meet a soul, even those who would most wish it, who think it possible—that is, to conquer and retain it."—Ibid., p. 174.

[5] Letter of Feb. 2, 1862. Weed was in London. Life of Weed, vol. ii. p. 410.

[6] " If the issue of forcible and total emancipation is raised, the United States will have no reason hereafter to complain of a want of popular sympathy in England."—London *Saturday Review*, Sept. 28 ; see, also, Oct. 5, Nov. 9. " That the doctrine of emancipation, if always and sincerely

of emancipation, if issued a year earlier, would undoubtedly
have increased the enthusiasm of our English friends,[1] and

---

professed by the Northern States, would have strongly commended their
cause to the sympathies of this country, is not for a moment to be doubted.
. . . The public in this country would rejoice to see an end made of
slave-holding, and so far the North might gain."—London *Times*, Sept. 30.
" There would perhaps be an overwhelming sentiment of popular sympathy with the North in this conflict if they were fighting for freedom ; but
the pretence that this is an anti-slavery war cannot be sustained for a moment, and is sedulously disavowed by the government itself."—W. H.
Russell to Sumner, Oct. 14, Pierce-Sumner Papers, MS.; see also New
York *Tribune*, Aug. 11.

[1] Bright wrote Sumner, Sept. 6 : " Many console themselves with the
hope that the great question of the future condition of your four million
negroes is about to be solved. I do not see how you can move for emancipation within your Constitution, or without giving to the South a complete case in favor of their insurrection ; but if necessity or the popular
feeling should drive you to it, then there will, I think, be no power in this
country able to give any support to the South. Many who cavil at you
now say, ' If the war was for liberating the slave, then we could see something worth fighting for, and we could sympathize with the North.' I
cannot urge you to this course. The remedy for slavery would be almost
worse than the disease, and yet how can such a disease be got rid of without some desperate remedy ?" Harriet Martineau wrote Sumner, Nov.
14 : " Whenever the anti-slavery view is adopted and acted upon at Washington in any preponderant way, you will have no reason to complain of
coldness on this side of the water. . . . I need not explain that I, with my
American friendships and sympathies, am eager and constant in speaking
up for what you and I consider the right, and in hoping for the best ; but
the pottering at Washington is infinitely damaging here to your cause."—
Pierce-Sumner Papers, MS. Darwin wrote Asa Gray, June 5 : " Some
few, and I am one of them, even wish to God, though at the loss of millions
of lives, that the North would proclaim a crusade against slavery. In the
long-run, a million horrid deaths would be amply repaid in the cause of
humanity."—Life and Letters, vol. ii. p. 166. " We can wait till the
occasion arises for showing how England can sympathize with a people
who have a purpose to abolish slavery."—London *Daily News*, Sept. 17.
" We have no hesitation in saying that we believe the boldest course would
be the wisest. The Union can never be restored again with the old canker
at the roots."—London *Spectator*, Oct. 5.

Carl Schurz, our minister to Spain, wrote Seward from San Ildefonso,
Sept. 14, a careful exposition of the sentiment of Europe generally. As
it was not printed, I insert the greater part of it: " It is my conviction,
and I consider it a duty to communicate it to you, that the sympathies of

lent augmented potency to their arguments; but the course
of English opinion after September, 1862, may well raise

---

the liberal masses in Europe are not as unconditionally in our favor as
might be desired, and that unless the war end soon or something be done
to give our cause a stronger foothold in the popular heart, they will, in the
end, not be decided and powerful enough to control the actions of those
governments whose good-will or neutrality is to us of the greatest importance.   When the struggle about the slavery question in the United States
assumed the form of an armed conflict, it was generally supposed in
Europe that the destruction of slavery was to be the avowed object of the
policy of the government, and that the war would, in fact, be nothing less
than a grand uprising of the popular conscience in favor of a great human-
itarian principle.   If this opinion had been confirmed by the evidence of
facts, the attitude of Europe, as determined by popular sentiment, could
not have been doubtful a single moment.   But it was remarked, not without a feeling of surprise and disappointment, that the federal government,
in its public declarations, cautiously avoided the mentioning of the slavery
question as the cause and origin of the conflict; that its acts, at the beginning of the war at least, were marked by a strikingly scrupulous respect
for the sanctity of slave property, and that the ultimate extinction of an
institution so hateful to European minds was most emphatically denied to
be one of the objects of the war.   I do not mean to question the wisdom
of the government under circumstances so difficult and perplexing, but I
am bearing witness to the effect its attitude produced upon public opinion in
Europe. . . . It is exceedingly difficult to make Europeans understand,
not only why the free and prosperous North should fight morally for the
privilege of being reassociated with the imperious and troublesome slave
States, but, also, why the principle, by virtue of which a population, sufficiently strong for establishing and maintaining an independent national
existence, possesses the right to have a government and institutions of its
own choice, should be repudiated in America, while it is almost universally
recognized in monarchical Europe.   I have had to discuss this point with
men whose sympathies were most sincerely on our side, and all my constitutional arguments failed to convince them that such a right can be consistently denied, unless our cause was based upon principles of a higher
nature.   I know that journalists, who in their papers work for us to the
best of their ability, are secretly troubled with serious scruples on that
point.   The agents of the South, whose footprints are frequently visible
in the public press, are availing themselves of this state of things with
great adroitness.   While they carefully abstain from alluding to the rights
of slavery, they speak of free trade and cotton to the merchant and the
manufacturer, and of the right of self-government to the liberal.   They
keep it well before the people that the same means of repression which are
of so beneficial a memory to most European nations—the suspension of the

the doubt whether it would have helped us with the aristocracy and the bulk of the middle class.[1]

---

writ of *habeas corpus*, arbitrary imprisonments, the confiscation of newspapers, the use of armed force—are now found necessary to prop the federal government; and that the latter, in its effort to crush the independent
spirit of eight millions of people, is with rapid strides approaching the line
which separates democratic government from the attributes of an arbitrary
despotism. The incidents of the war, so unfavorable to our arms, could not
fail to give weight and color to these representations. . . . And if opinions
like these could gain ground among our natural friends, what have we to
expect of those who secretly desire a permanent disruption of the Union ?
. . . And what will the federal government have to oppose to this plausible reasoning ? A rupture of relations, which would undoubtedly be more
disagreeable to us than to them ? Fleets and armies, which so far have
been hardly able to close some Southern ports and to protect the President
from capture in his capital ? The resentment of the American people,
which has ceased to be formidable ? There are, in my opinion, but two
ways in which the overwhelming perplexities can be averted which a rupture with foreign powers, added to our troubles at home, would inevitably
bring upon us. The one consists in great and decisive military success
speedily accomplished, and the other in such measures and manifestations
on the part of the government as will place the war against the rebellious
slave States upon a higher moral basis, and thereby give us the control of
public opinion in Europe. . . . It is my profound conviction that as soon
as the war becomes distinctly one for and against slavery, public opinion
will be so strongly, so overwhelmingly in our favor that, in spite of commercial interests or secret spites, no European government will dare to
place itself, by declaration or act, upon the side of a universally condemned
institution. Our enemies know that well, and we may learn from them.
While their agents carefully conceal from the eyes of Europeans their only
weak point, their attachment to slavery, ought we to aid them in hiding with
equal care our only strong point, our opposition to slavery ? While they,
well knowing how repugnant slavery is to the European way of feeling,
do all to make Europeans forget that they fight for it, ought we, who are
equally well acquainted with European sentiment, to abstain from making
Europeans remember that we fight against it ? In not availing ourselves
of our advantages, we relieve the enemy of the odium attached to his cause.
It is, therefore, my opinion that every step done by the government towards the abolition of slavery is, as to our standing in Europe, equal to a
victory in the field."—MSS. State Department archives.

[1] This is foreshadowed by the *Spectator* of Oct. 5, in an acute analysis of
the indifferent and unfriendly sentiment of the London press to the North.
The article is entitled "Ambiguous Counsels to the Northern States."
See, also, *Saturday Review* of Nov. 30, 1861, Jan. 4, 1862.

The articles in the *Times* and the *Saturday Review* were eagerly read on our side of the water, and they caused much irritation. The sneers at the panic and cowardice of the Northern troops at Bull Run were hard to bear. The criticism of the arbitrary measures of our government, the assertion that we had cut loose from the moorings of the Constitution, the comparison continually drawn between the despotism in France and the despotism in America, between the *coup-d'état* of Louis Napoleon and the *coup-d'état* of Abraham Lincoln, were galling.[1] Few of the English

---

[1] "The arrest of the newly elected members of the legislative assembly [of Maryland] before they had had any time to meet, without any form of law or prospect of trial, merely because President Lincoln conceived that they might in their legislative capacity do acts at variance with his interpretation of the American Constitution, was as perfect an act of despotism as can be conceived. . . . It was a *coup-d'état* in every essential feature. Every argument by which it can be justified will justify the Second of December."—*Saturday Review*, Oct. 19.   "Northern orators and such Northern journalists as are allowed to write still love to celebrate their country as 'the land of the free and the home of the brave.' Its title to the latter designation has been conclusively established at Leesburg [Ball's Bluff] and Bull Run. . . . 'The land of the free' is a land in which electors may not vote for fear of arrest, and judges may not execute the law for fear of dismissal—in which unsubmissive advocates are threatened with imprisonment and hostile newspapers are suppressed."—Ibid., Nov. 23. The *Spectator* of Oct. 12 also criticised the arbitrary measures of the administration.

"I recollect arguing once with a Northern gentleman, whose name as an author is known and honored in this country, about what seemed to me his unreasonable animosity towards England.   After a concession on his part that possibly his feelings were morbidly exaggerated, he turned round and pointed to the portrait of a very near and dear relative of his—a brave, handsome lad, who had been killed a few months before when leading his men into action at the fatal defeat of Ball's Bluff.   'How,' he said to me, 'would you like yourself to read constantly that that lad died in a miserable cause, and, as an American officer, should be called a coward?' And I own to that argument I could make no adequate reply.   Let me quote, too, a paragraph from a letter I received the other day from another friend of mine, whose works have been read eagerly wherever the English tongue is spoken [probably O. W. Holmes].   'I have,' he wrote, 'a stake in this contest, which makes me nervous and tremulous, and impatient of contradiction.   I have a noble boy, a captain in one of our regiments,

understood how earnestly we craved their sympathy. Darwin, who saw both sides of any question as well if not better than any man living, and whose lightest word deserves respect,[1] wrote Asa Gray: "I heartily wish I could sympathize more fully with you, instead of merely hating the South. We cannot enter into your feelings; if Scotland were to rebel, I presume we should be very wrath; but I do not think we should care a penny what other nations thought."[2] True enough is it that if the United States had had behind them England's splendid history, and had given birth to her splendid literature, the Northern people might have pursued their course, caring little what other nations thought, so long as they kept within the strict letter of international law.[3]

---

which has been fearfully decimated by battle and disease, and himself twice wounded within a hair's-breadth of his life.' If you consider that in almost every Northern family there is thus some personal interest at stake in the war, it is not to be wondered at if the nation itself is also unduly impatient of contradiction."—Dicey's Federal States, vol. ii., pp. 12, 13; see, also, vol. i. p. 170.

[1] "I have a great respect for Mr. Darwin, as almost the only perfectly disinterested lover of truth I ever encountered."—J. R. Lowell, Sept. 1, 1878, Letters, vol. ii. p. 230.

[2] March 15, 1862, Life and Letters, vol. ii. p. 178; see, also, the London *Daily News* of Sept. 17.

[3] Thomas Hughes looked at the matter differently from Darwin, and in a strong letter to the *Spectator*, published Sept. 21, said: "Let any Englishman try to put himself honestly in the place of an American, and then read such articles as the one to which I have alluded ["Mrs. Beecher Stowe's Wounded Feelings," in the *Saturday Review*], and which is by no means an unfavorable specimen of the class, and I venture to say he will no longer wonder at the effect they have had in the United States. They are remarkable for two characteristics: first, for the deliberate imputation of mean motives, and, secondly, for the cruel spirit in which they are written. It may have been right to say unpleasant things, but it cannot be right to say them in the way, of all others, which will give most pain. To a nation or a man engaged in a struggle for life or death, the tone of flippant and contemptuous serenity is the worst we can adopt, if we must speak. . . . As to the imputation of the worst motives to the Northerners by the *Times* and the *Saturday Review*, from the first outbreak of hostilities till now, could anything have been more unfair or more needless? . . . We

The irritation caused by the ungenerous criticism of the London journals was cast back by the recrimination of our own press. Chief in truculence was the New York *Herald*. "We first unmasked," it said, "and then spiked the battery which English aristocrats were preparing against this country and its liberties. . . . We notified the English government and aristocracy that we were prepared to resent the insults they seemed disposed to offer us, and have thus far kept England in abeyance;" and seven weeks later it declared, "Let England and Spain look well to their conduct, or we may bring them to a reckoning."[1] Such writing did harm to our cause. "It is unfortunate," said John Bright, in a letter to Sumner of November 20, "that nothing is done to change the reckless tone of your New York *Herald*; between it and the *Times* of London there is great mischief done in both countries."[2] As friends of the North

---

all know that the North has not put the slavery question forward officially. All of us who care to study the subject know why this has not been done. Many of us think the policy unwise, and the reasons wholly insufficient. We may think and say that, if persisted in, it will ruin the cause of the North ; that it has already given an enormous advantage to the secessionists. But this is quite another thing from crying out, over and over again, ' It is naught, it is naught. The Yankees are, after all, only fighting for tariff and hurt vanity.' It was our duty, as the nation which has taken the lead in the abolition of slavery, to have borne all things from, and hoped all things for, those who had gone down into the lists with the great slave power ; to have given them credit for what they could not, or dared not, yet avow ; to have encouraged them to go bravely on in the path they had taken, let it lead them where it might. We have not done this. Our press has chosen to take the other course : to impute the lowest motives, to cull out and exult over all the meanness and bragging and disorder which the contest has brought out, and, while we sit on the bank, to make no allowances for those who are struggling in the waves. The consequence is the state of feeling we see now in all loyal Americans towards England." Dr. G. E. Ellis, in an article entitled " Why Has the North Felt Aggrieved with England?" in the *Atlantic Monthly* for Nov., 1861, gave an excellent description of the feeling in America excited by the criticism of the English press.

[1] Sept. 18 and Nov. 9. See the New York *Herald passim* between these dates.   [2] Pierce-Sumner Papers, MS.

in England endeavored to depreciate the influence of the
London *Times*,[1] so did friends of England in America un-
derrate the power of the New York *Herald*.[2] But, in truth,
this journal spoke for a potent public sentiment outside of
New England. By its large news-gathering agencies, and
by its unvarying support of the administration, it had a
large and increasing circulation. Men who were eager for
the latest and fullest news from the field, and who wished
to stand loyally by Lincoln against the fault - finding of
peace Democrats on one side and of Frémont radicals on
the other, read it gladly.[3] It had a body of devoted readers whom it could influence, and in working up animosity
towards England it played upon an oft-used string. The
American voter of 1861 had learned at school, from his
crude historical study of the Revolution and the War of
1812, that England was a natural enemy; and failing now,
in his own country's death-grapple, to make proper allowance for the difficulties of her situation, he was ready and
apt to misjudge her. Thus censure and recrimination went
on between the two countries.[4]

---

[1] " After I have read something very ugly in the *Times* I have a sort of
longing to tell you how full one feels of sympathy for all you are going
through."—Duchess of Argyll to Sumner, Oct. 22. "I most certainly
agree with you as to the odious spirit of some of the newspaper articles.
. . . I think you rate the importance of the *Times* very high."—Ibid., Dec. 1.
Pierce-Sumner Papers, MS. See letter of Motley of Jan. 13, 1862, and letter
of Lord Wensleydale to Motley, Feb. 7, Correspondence, vol. ii. pp. 52, 59.

[2] For a just appreciation of what the London *Times* and New York
Herald represented, see Edward Dicey's Federal States, vol. i. pp. 27, 273.
Dicey was in the United States a large part of 1862 as correspondent of the
Spectator and *Macmillan's Magazine*.

[3] " Mr. Lincoln . . . reads no paper . . . the New York *Herald* excepted.
So at least it is generally stated."—Count Gurowski's Diary, Aug., 1861,
p. 81. John Hay wrote Herndon from Paris, in 1866, Lincoln "scarcely
ever looked into a newspaper unless I called his attention to an article on
some special subject."—Herndon's Lincoln, p. 516.

[4] " The North was learning to hate England, and day by day the feeling
grew upon me that, much as I wished to espouse the cause of the North,
I should have to espouse the cause of my own country."—Anthony Trollope, speaking of Nov. and Dec., 1861, in North America (1862), vol. i. p. 317.

The English public had facts enough for a correct judgment. The *Times* and *Daily News* were full of trustworthy information,[1] and a careful reading of them, with a fairly enlightened judgment, ought to have led to the conviction that, although the success of the North would not necessarily bring about the abolition of slavery, it was certain to deprive that institution of its political and social power, and eventually destroy it, while the success of the South was sure to extend negro slavery and reopen the African slave-trade. To deny this was to shut the eyes to patent facts. Yet the English would not believe there was a moral question involved in the contest,[2] because, under the influence of their hatred of democracy and their desire for good trade and prosperous manufactures, they did not wish to believe it; and the thought that the South would probably succeed developed into a wish for its success. Nevertheless, it may not be becoming for an American to pass condemnation, for, being true children of the mother-country,[3] it may be suspected that, in similar circumstances, we should have likewise erred; that, had England been engaged in a war in which justice, supported by the monarchy and the aristocracy, was on one side, and American dollars and a plausible case on the other, the dominant sympathy

---

[1] "As to interest in the war," the Americans "may assure themselves it is the one absorbing topic. It fills the *Times*, as they may see. It is the grand theme of conversation, as they may be easily assured." — London *Saturday Review*, Oct. 5.

[2] Edward Dicey wrote: "I have often heard it asserted, and I have seen the statement constantly repeated in the English press, that slavery had nothing to do with the questions at issue between the North and the South. I can only say that during my residence in Washington [the early part of 1862] I heard little talked about except the question of slavery."—Federal States, vol. i. p. 190. Anthony Trollope wrote: "It is vain to say that slavery has not caused secession, and that slavery has not caused the war. That, and that only, has been the real cause of this conflict, though other small collateral issues may now be put forward to bear the blame."—North America (1862), vol. ii. p. 61.

[3] See Dicey's Federal States, vol. i. pp. 80, 273.

in our country would have been with the cause which seemed linked with our commercial prosperity.

Great Britain preserved a strict neutrality. What Motley wrote from Paris may, in the light of the later evidence, be affirmed as true up to the last of November. " The present English government," he said, " has thus far given us no just cause of offence." [1] Louis Napoleon, the emperor of the French, though in his American policy he did not represent the intelligent and liberal sentiment of his country, had officially asked England to co-operate with him in recognizing the Confederacy and breaking the blockade, but this she had refused to do. [2] Motley saw the English Foreign Secretary in September, and gave to Holmes an account of his visit. " I think I made some impression on Lord John Russell," he wrote, " with whom I spent two days soon after my arrival in England ; and I talked very frankly and as strongly as I could to Lord Palmerston. . . . For this year there will be no foreign interference with us, and I do not anticipate it at any time, unless we bring it on ourselves by bad management. . . . Our fate is in our own hands, and Europe is looking on to see which side is the strongest. When it has made the discovery, it will back it as also the best and the most moral." [3] The impression which Motley made was not lasting. In October Earl Russell suggested to Palmerston that England unite with France in an offer of mediation between the North and the South, with the implied understanding that a refusal of it by the United States would make these two European countries her enemies. Palmerston did not agree with

---

[1] Letter of Oct. 18. He added : " Moreover, although we have many bitter haters in England, we have many warm friends. . . . No man in England more thoroughly understands American politics than Mr. Forster does. There are few like him."—Correspondence, vol. ii. p. 37.

[2] Yancey and Rost to Hunter, Paris, Oct. 5 ; Yancey to Hunter, Paris, Oct. 29 ; Rost to Davis, Paris, Dec. 24, 26 ; Slidell to Benjamin, Paris, April 14, 1862, Confederate Diplomatic Correspondence, MSS. Treasury Department.   [3] Correspondence, vol. ii. p. 43.

Russell, but thought their true policy was to keep clear of the conflict;[1] his opinion determined the course of the government, which was in harmony with the prevailing sentiment of the country, although the disposition of the Emperor Napoleon was a matter of public knowledge.[2]

Such was the state of public sentiment in England, and of feeling in the United States in regard to it, when an overzealous American naval commander brought the two countries to the brink of war. James M. Mason and John Slidell, who had been appointed commissioners from the Southern Confederacy to Great Britain and France, reached Cuba on a little steamer which had successfully run the blockade; at Havana they embarked on the British mail packet *Trent*, on their way to Southampton. November 8, the next day after she left Havana, she was overhauled in the Bahama Channel by the American man-of-war *San Jacinto*, under the command of Captain Wilkes. He fired a shot across her bow without result, and then a shell; this brought her to. The lieutenant of the *San Jacinto* with a number of sailors and marines boarded the *Trent*, and took from her by force Mason, Slidell, and their secretaries, in spite of their appeal to the British flag for protection, and in spite of the protest of Commander Williams, of the royal navy, in charge of the mails.[3] The prisoners were taken to Fort Warren in Boston harbor.

The news of this transaction was received in New York November 16. The country went as wild with jubilant delight as if it had gained a signal victory in the field. The Northern people had waited and watched so long for some result from the immense levies of men and of money that

[1] The letter of Earl Russell was written Oct. 17 ; Palmerston replied the next day, Walpole's Life of Russell, vol. ii. p. 344 ; Ashley's Life of Palmerston, vol. ii. p. 216.

[2] See London *Times*, Nov. 5; London *Saturday Review*, Oct. 26, Nov. 2, 9.

[3] Reports of Captain Wilkes and Lieutenant Fairfax ; protests of Mason and Slidell and Captain Williams ; statement of the purser of the *Trent*, Moore's Rebellion Record, vol. iii., Docs., p. 321 *et seq.*

it is no wonder they gave way to extravagant joy when
the two men, who of all the Confederates except Davis and
Floyd were hated the worst, were delivered into their
hands. Blended with the feeling that Mason and Slidell
would now be prevented from doing us mischief abroad [1]
was the thought that they would serve as important host-
ages. Fourteen federal officers, prisoners of war at Richmond and Charleston, had been selected by lot to be
hanged in case the pirate's doom should be meted out to
the same number of privateersmen confined at the North,
and carrying out the plan of treating them as common
felons, they had been incarcerated in the county jail.[2] It
was now proposed that, in retaliation, Mason and Slidell be
sent to the Tombs, and that if the hanging began, it should
not end until these men of distinction had died on the scaffold. It was understood that Great Britain had to be reckoned with, but in the flush of excitement war with her was
looked at without trepidation; for the belief existed that if
half a million men could be raised to battle for the Union,
double that number would enlist to fight the traditional
enemy. As representing the prevalent sentiment, Secretary
Welles sent a congratulatory letter to Captain Wilkes;
Boston gave him a banquet at which Governor Andrew
and the Chief Justice of the Massachusetts Supreme Court
spoke with enthusiasm; he was a guest at the dinner of the
Boston Saturday Club; and the National House of Representatives on the first day of its session thanked him. It also
requested the President to confine Mason as a convicted
felon. Edward Everett, Caleb Cushing, and Richard H.
Dana, Jr., justified the act of Wilkes. The press teemed
with discussions of the legal points involved, and with citations from the authorities on international law tending to

---

[1] "The government would give a good deal to seize upon such an
able and dangerous man as Slidell."—W. H. Russell to London *Times*,
Sept. 2.

[2] Ely's Journal in Richmond, p. 211 *et seq.*

show that the American captain had acted within proper limits.[1]

Secretary Welles is authority for the statement that all the members of the cabinet, except Blair, shared his own jubilation and that of the House and the country at the arrest of Mason and Slidell.[2]   Lincoln was not carried away by the general joy.   He knew that the act of Wilkes was not in line with principles for which we had contended, and for this reason, and for the further one that it might be hard to resist the popular clamor for their summary punishment, he feared that they would " prove to be white elephants." [3]   Of all the men in responsible positions Sum-

---

[1] New York *Tribune*, Nov. 18, 19 ; New York *Herald*, Nov. 17, 19, 22 ; New York *Times*, Nov. 18 ; New York *Evening Post*, Nov. 16 ; Boston *Evening Transcript*, Nov. 18; Boston *Advertiser*, Nov. 18 ; Boston *Herald*, Nov. 18, 27 ; Edward Everett, in New York *Ledger*, cited in New York *Tribune*, Dec. 24 ; W. H. Russell's letters to London *Times*, Nov. 19, Dec. 27 ; Moore's Rebellion Record, vol. iii., Docs., p. 330 ; Pierce's Sumner, vol. iv. p. 51 ; Adams's Dana, vol. ii. pp. 167, 259 ; Life of Bowles, vol. i. p. 332.   " What you complain of in the Boston dinner was indeed lamentable; such men should not have talked bosh, even at a little private ovation, and we have reason to know some of them were heartily ashamed of it as soon as they saw it in print."—Asa Gray to Darwin, Feb. 18, 1862, Gray's Letters, p. 476.   For action of the House, see *Congressional Globe*, p. 5.   The proposed treatment of Mason was in retaliation for that to which Colonel Corcoran had been subjected.

Anthony Trollope wrote in his North America, vol. i. pp. 264, 317 : " It was pretty to hear the charming women of Boston, as they became learned in the law of nations.   ' Wheaton is quite clear about it,' one young girl said to me.   It was the first I had ever heard of Wheaton, and so far was obliged to knock under."   " ' We are quite right,' the lawyers said.   ' There are Vattel and Puffendorf and Stowell and Phillimore and Wheaton,' said the ladies."

After Mason and Slidell had been surrendered, General George W. Morgan, of Ohio, still regarding war with Great Britain inevitable, wrote Chase: " A war with England would inspire our people with the fierce passion necessary to successful war.   It is what our army and people now stand in need of."—Letter of Jan. 6, 1862, Chase Papers, MS.

[2] Lincoln and Seward, Welles, p. 184.   Nicolay and Hay partly substantiate this, vol. v. p. 26.

[3] Lossing's Civil War, vol. ii. p. 156 ; Nicolay and Hay, vol. v. p. 26; Welles, in the *Galaxy*, May, 1873.

ner and Blair saw the clearest; they were in favor of at
once surrendering to England the Confederate commissioners.[1] Had Lincoln understood international law as well as
Sumner, and had he felt that confidence of public support
which he did later, he might have directed this, for in doing
a rightful act he was capable of breasting popular sentiment. His sense of the feeling of the people was keener
than his knowledge of international law, and knowing he
had alienated the radicals by his treatment of Frémont, he
held back with his habitual caution from a peremptory
move which might also lose him the support of that body
of conservative Republicans and war Democrats whose
ideas were fairly espoused by the New York *Herald*. Yet
at this time four men could have led public opinion. If
Lincoln, Seward, Chase, and Sumner had declared that the
act of Wilkes was contrary to the law of nations and our
own precedents, that Great Britain had been wronged, and
that the injury could be atoned only by the surrender of
Mason and Slidell, the country would have acquiesced in it.
Policy as well as justice dictated such a course. It was
true, as the London *Times* affirmed, that "the voices of
these Southern commissioners, sounding from their captivi-
ty, are a thousand times more eloquent in London and in
Paris than they would have been if heard at St. James's
and the Tuileries."[2] The American government, not being
able to rise to the height of giving up these captives before
they were demanded, did the next best thing. If, as
Welles asserts, Seward was at first as elated as any one,[3]
reflection changed his mind, for his despatch to Adams of
November 30 was prudent, and seems to indicate that he

---

[1] Pierce's Sumner, vol. iv. pp. 52, 61 ; Lincoln and Seward, Welles, p.
186. This opinion was shared by others of prominence and authority,
W. H. Russell to the London *Times*, Dec. 10, 27. It was clear from the
first to Charles Francis Adams that the act was not justifiable, see his Address on Seward, April, 1873.

[2] Nov. 28 ; likewise the London *Saturday Review*, Nov. 30.

[3] Chittenden denies this, Recollections of President Lincoln, p. 148.

believed the surrender of Mason and Slidell to be the probable solution of the difficulty.[1] The secretary informed
Adams that Captain Wilkes had acted " without any instructions from the government," and gave him permission
to impart this fact, and to read the whole of his friendly,

---

[1] It seems to me clear from Seward's letters to Weed (Dec. 27, 1861, and
Jan. 22, 1862, Life of Seward, vol. iii. pp. 34, 43) that he was determined,
after he had carefully considered the matter, to urge the surrender of the
commissioners, if Great Britain demanded them ; and although his letter to
Weed of March 7, 1862 (*Galaxy*, March, 1870), is somewhat inconsistent
with this view, it does not necessarily contravene it. This is all the more
creditable to Seward on account of the Jingo policy he had pursued, and
on account of his bitterness towards England. His confidential letter
to Sumner of Oct. 11, which he wished to be shown to Bright, exhibits his
personal feeling. "Many thanks, my dear Sumner," he wrote, " for the
perusal of this noble letter from John Bright [that of Sept. 6]. How sad
for the cause of humanity, yet how honorable to John Bright, that he is the
only Englishman having public position or character who has written one
word of favor to or desire for the preservation of the American Union !
Tell him that I appreciate his honesty, his manliness, his virtue. Tell him
the American question is not half so difficult of solution as he thinks. The
rebellion is already arrested. Henceforward it will drag, languish, perish ;
that it owes all the success it attained to the timidity, hesitation, and indirect favor of British statesmen and the British press ; that our interest
in regard to it is Great Britain's interest—nothing different. Both countries were wrong. Both feared it too much and thereby made it formidable. Both have been impatient of the continuance of civil war, and sought
to extinguish it by convulsive demonstration against it, when it was only
to be accepted as inevitable and treated as such. But we have passed that
stage and we shall soon see the war successful. Great Britain has reached
a period when she can reflect, and reflecting she cannot fail to see that if
she wishes, and will only declare the sentiment, that the government may
triumph, the emissaries of faction will retire from her shores, and its authorities here, no longer sustained by false hopes from abroad, will flee
before the returning allegiance of the misguided people."—Pierce-Sumner
Papers, MS. R. H. Dana, Jr., to whom this letter was shown, wrote: " Mr.
Seward's was for British consumption evidently, and well adapted to the
needs there."—Ibid. The Secretary of State appears to advantage in a
controversy had with Lord Lyons in October. It drew from the *Spectator*
the remark : " Mr. Seward has for once made a hit. In his recent correspondence with Lord Lyons he has developed, possibly from a novel consciousness of being in the right, an unexpected self-restraint, and writing
like a gentleman, is victorious as a diplomatist."—Nov. 9.

confidential note to Earl Russell and Lord Palmerston. In
his annual message the President made no allusion to the
affair. November 27 England received the news of the
arrest of Mason and Slidell. The opinion was general that
it was an outrage to her flag. Liverpool, strong in sympathy with the South, held a crowded and influential indignation meeting. It "has made a great sensation here,"
wrote John Bright to Sumner from London, "and the
ignorant and passionate and ' Rule Britannia' class are
angry and insolent as usual. The ministers meet at this
moment on the case."[1] The next day Bright wrote from
Manchester : "A cabinet council was held yesterday. The
chancellor, attorney, and solicitor-general were agreed, and
decided that you have done an illegal act in seizing the
commissioners. . . . I have urged that . . . nothing should be
asked from your government that you could not easily
comply with. The tone of the ministers is not violent, and
I hope they will be moderate."[2] At that meeting the
cabinet decided that the act of Captain Wilkes was "a clear
violation of the law of nations, and one for which reparation must be at once demanded."[3] Earl Russell prepared a
despatch to Lord Lyons, the language of which was soft-
ened and made more friendly on the suggestion of the
Queen and the Prince Consort; but as modified, the British
government demanded the liberation of Mason, Slidell, and
their secretaries, and "a suitable apology for the aggression." Seward was to have seven days, if necessary, to
make a reply; but if at the end of that time no answer or
an unfavorable one should be received, Lord Lyons was instructed to leave Washington and "to repair immediately
to London."[4] On Sunday, December 1, a Queen's messenger
bearing this despatch was on his way to Washington.[5] The

[1] Nov. 29, Pierce-Sumner Papers, MS.

[2] Nov. 30, Ibid. ; see, also, London *Times*, Nov. 29.

[3] Ibid., Nov. 30.

[4] British Blue-Book ; Walpole's Russell, vol. ii. p. 346 ; Martin's Life of
the Prince Consort, vol. v. p. 422.   [5] London *Times*, Dec. 2.

admiralty began making extensive naval preparations; eight thousand troops were sent to Canada; the Queen by proclamation prohibited the export of arms and ammunition.[1]

"England's attitude," wrote Martin Farquhar Tupper, a friend of the North, "is that of calm, sorrowful, astonished determination."[2] This well expresses the sentiment of the majority of Englishmen who had property and intelligence.[3] They felt that the United States "had invaded the sanctuary which England extends to all political exiles who seek her protection,"[4] and that it had, moreover, insulted her flag. Though averse to war, they agreed that if adequate reparation were not made they must resort to the ultimate argument of nations. War meant the decimation of families and increased taxation, yet while Great Britain could inflict injury on the United States, such a war could bring no glory. Neither could it be ignored that she would be the ally of a slave power, nor that her merchant marine could be harmed beyond measure by American privateers. The longing that the Washington government would so act that this public woe might be averted was earnest and sincere. That such a war would open the Southern ports and give them the much-needed supply of cotton,[5] was far from being deemed a sufficient compensation for the damage to

---

[1] Annual British Register, cited in Life of Thurlow Weed, vol. ii. p. 368 ; Martin's Life of the Prince Consort, vol. v. p. 419 ; London *Gazette Extraordinary*, Dec. 4, cited in New York *Tribune*.

[2] To Sumner, Dec. 3, Pierce-Sumner Papers, MS.

[3] This opinion was represented by the London *Times, Daily News, Saturday Review*, and *Spectator*. With one or two exceptions, this was the sentiment of the press of the provinces, see *Daily News*, Nov. 30. It also appears in much of the private correspondence of the time.

[4] Expression of London *Times*, Jan. 9, 1862.

[5] "There should have arrived by this time at the Southern ports of America, for shipment to England, from 500,000 to 1,000,000 bales of last year's cotton crop. By the latest estimate it was calculated that not 1000 bales had been sent down, and it was known indeed that small stocks of cotton remaining over from the preceding year's crop had been removed from the ports to the interior of the country."—London *Times*, Jan. 9, 1862.

England which would ensue. The question still pending made the usual merry Christmas a gloomy festival.[1]

A certain set in England, however, strong in social influence and position, had so ardent and active a sympathy with the South that they were for war at any price, and they did their best to embroil the two countries. "The excitement here has been and is great," wrote John Bright to Sumner, December 5, "and it is fed, as usual, by newspapers, who seem to imagine a cause of war discovered to be something like 'treasure-trove.'"[2] Two days later he said: "There is more calmness here in the public mind—which is natural after last week's explosion—but I fear the military and naval demonstrations of our government point to trouble, and I am not sure that it would grieve certain parties here if any decent excuse could be found for a quarrel with you. You know the instinct of aristocracy and of powerful military services, and an ignorant people is easily led astray on questions foreign to their usual modes of thought."[3] In his letter of December 5 he described the sentiment of a majority of his countrymen much as it seems to me to have been from a study of the London press and the other evidence. "Our law officers," he wrote from Rochdale, "are agreed and strong in their opinion of the illegality of the seizure of the commissioners. . . . All the people here, of course, accept their opinion as conclusive as to the law of the case. . . . Now, notwithstanding the war spirit here, I am sure, even in this district where your civil strife is most injuriously felt, that all thoughtful and

---

[1] "Christmas comes this year on a country bright with sun and frost, but on a people oppressed with a national loss and threatened with a formidable war. Already closed mills and short time have given some part of our population an earnest of what they may hereafter expect; already speculation is more careful than it has been for many years, and the sombre appearance of our churches and chapels last Sunday portends a bad season next spring for the many trades concerned in female attire. The prospect of an aggravated income-tax sits like a nightmare on many households."— London *Times*, Dec. 27.   [2] Pierce-Sumner Papers, MS.

[3] Dec. 7, ibid.

serious men, and indeed the great majority of the people, will be delighted if some way can be found out of the present difficulty. . . . Nations *drift* into wars—as we drifted into the late war with Russia—often through the want of a resolute hand at some moment early in the quarrel. So, now, a courageous stroke, not of arms, but of moral action, may save you and us. . . . It is common here to say that your government cannot resist the mob violence by which it is surrounded. I do not believe this, and I know that our government is often driven along by the force of the genteel and aristocratic mob which it mainly represents. But now in this crisis I fervently hope that you may act firmly and courteously; any moderate course you may take will meet with great support here, and in the English cabinet there are, as I certainly know, some who will gladly accept any fair proposition for friendly arrangement from your side." [1]

An offset to the war-at-any-price faction was the group represented by Bright, Cobden, and Forster. They urged the treatment of the matter in an amicable way; should the federal government maintain that its act was legal and right, they were ready to accept arbitration, or even propose it, rather than go to war. [2] At Rochdale, December 4, Bright made a noble, sympathetic, and convincing speech, reaching a moral height which few public men ever attain. [3] "This steamer will take out a report of Bright's speech," wrote Cobden to Sumner, December 5, "and my letter of excuse for not being able to attend. You will see that we stand in the breach, as usual, to stem the tide of passion.

---

[1] Pierce-Sumner Papers, MS.

[2] Bright's letters to Sumner show this; Cobden to Sumner, Dec. 12, 19, Morley's *Cobden*, p. 574; Forster's speech at Bradford, London *Times*, Jan. 3, 1862.

[3] The whole speech should be read. It is printed in vol. i. of Rogers's edition of Bright's speeches. The comments of the London *Times* of Dec. 6, of the *Saturday Review* and the *Spectator* of Dec. 7, are interesting; see Motley's reference to it in his letter of Dec. 10, Correspondence, vol. ii. p. 48.

But you know that we don't represent all England at such a moment. . . . You will see a new feature in this disagreeable matter in the ardor with which the French press takes up the cry against you. Some of the papers most eager to push us to extremities are those which are conducted by parties who are supposed to be in the confidence of the emperor." [1]

_____

[1] Pierce-Sumner Papers, MS. As neither this letter nor any part of it was printed by Morley, I will add liberal extracts from it: "Spending as I did eighteen months in France, and always in close communication with the emperor's ablest advisers, and frequently having very free audiences with himself, I came to the conclusion that *the corner-stone of his policy was friendship with England.* . . . It was because I knew the inner policy of the French government that I could not see without mortification and disgust the shallow antics of some of your official representatives in Paris, at that most lamentable public meeting where individuals, *accredited by your government*, invited the emperor to join you against England to avenge Waterloo and St. Helena! These proceedings not having led to the recall or official rebuke of the parties, have done more harm in this country than all the ravings of your *Herald*. . . . From all that I hear from France the trade of that country is dreadfully damaged, and *I feel convinced the emperor would be supported by his people if he were to enter into alliance with England to abolish the blockade and recognize the South.* The French are inconvenienced in many ways by your blockade, and especially in their relations with New Orleans, which are more important to them in exports than to us. For ourselves in England, in spite of the bluster of the *Times*, the majority are anxious for peace. Do not overrate the powers of the *Times*. Seven years ago it had a monopoly of publicity. Now its circulation is not perhaps one-tenth of the daily press. The *Star* and Manchester *Examiner*, two admirable papers, circulate far more than the *Times*. But it cannot be denied that the great motives of hope and fear which kept us at peace, and inclined the English government always to recede in pinching controversies with you are gone. The English people have no sympathy with you on either side. You know how ignorant we are on the details of your history, geography, constitution, etc. There are two subjects on which we are unanimous and fanatical—*personal freedom and free trade.* These convictions are the result of fifty years of agitation and discussion. In your case we observe a mighty quarrel : on one side protectionists, on the other slave-owners. The protectionists say they do not seek to put down slavery. The slave-owners say they want free trade. Need you wonder at the confusion in John Bull's poor head ? He gives it up ! leaves it to the government. Which government, by the way, are the most friendly to your gov-

On the whole, the attitude of the majority of the English pending the difficulty was dignified,[1] although they showed some acerbity upon hearing the news of the way in which Wilkes's action had been received in the United States—"the outburst of hilarity," as the *Times* described it.[2] The Southern sympathizers, however, were active and aggressive, using arguments which had considerable power over the English mind. The pressure of the blockade,[3] the pro-

---

ernment which could be found in England, for although Palmerston is fond of hot water, he boasts that he never got us into a serious war. As for his colleagues, they are all sedate, peaceable men. God bless us! 'A mad world, my masters!'" Perhaps it is unnecessary for me to add that I do not agree with Cobden's depreciation of the influence of the *Times*, and that I feel sure of the correctness of my statements in the text. His remarks about the English government seem to me strictly accurate, and should be constantly borne in mind as the story of our relations with Great Britain goes on. Charles Francis Adams wrote from London, July 13, 1865 : " At the time when I first reached this country, in 1861, the character of the elections then taking place, to fill casual vacancies, was such, in consequence of the general impression that the 'bubble of democracy had burst in America,' as to fill the conservatives with hopes of what they denominated a strong reaction. It was this feeling which really lay at the root of all their views of our struggle. Had the Parliament been dissolved at any time prior to July, 1863, there can be little doubt that it would have had a considerable effect on the issue." The conservative leaders, Disraeli and Sir Stafford Northcote, were, however, opposed to any interference in the American war, see article of Lord Coleridge in *Macmillan's Magazine*, Jan., 1888, p. 165 ; Froude's Disraeli, p. 159. Lord Stanley had also spoken a friendly word for the North, see Bright's speech of Dec. 4, 1861.

[1] " I don't think the nation here behaved badly under the terrible evil of loss of trade and danger of starving under your blockade. Of course all privileged classes and aristocracies hate your institutions—that is natural enough."—Cobden to Sumner, Dec. 19, Pierce-Sumner Papers, MS.; Morley's Cobden, p. 574.

[2] Dec. 4 ; see, also, Cobden's letter of Dec. 19, ibid.

[3] Cobden wrote Sumner, Dec. 12: " I am afraid that we in England who are well-wishers to the North take a more accurate measure of the difficulties of your position than you who are in the heat of the turmoil can do; just as you took a more correct view of the Crimean war and its utter uselessness than the bulk of Englishmen did. We do not believe that the subjugation of the South can be a *speedy* achievement. Nobody doubts the power of the North ultimately, if it chooses to make the sacrifice, to ruin the South, and even to occupy its chief places. But this will take a very long time,

posal of the federal government to sink in the channels
leading to the Southern ports vessels laden with stone,[1] the
animosity of Seward to Great Britain, were urged as fortifying reasons to the outrage committed on board the steamer *Trent*, all of which together would justify a declaration
of war.   Seward's course had irritated English opinion, and
made the position of our friends and that of the larger number of Englishmen who desired to preserve a strict neutrality harder to maintain.   "There is a feeling among our
ministers," wrote Bright to Sumner, November 29, "that
Mr. Seward is not so friendly in his transactions with them
as they could wish."[2]   This feeling was shared by the public.   A remark he was said to have made to the Duke of
Newcastle, who accompanied the Prince of Wales to America in 1860, went the rounds.   Seward told the duke, at a
dinner given by Governor Morgan to the prince, that in the

---

and the world will not look on, I believe, patient sufferers during the
process. I am not justifying any interference on the part of Europe ; but
it is a fearful thing to have the whole civilized world undergoing privations
and sufferings which they lay at the door of the North, thus making it the
interest of their governments to interfere with you. Recollect that your
own government has condemned blockades of purely commercial ports ;
the world has in truth outgrown them. . . . The state of modern society,
where you have millions of laborers in Europe depending for the means of
employment on a regular supply of raw materials brought from another
continent, to say nothing of hundreds of millions of capital invested on the
same dependence, will necessitate a change in the law of blockade and
other belligerent rules. . . . I do not, I repeat, say that the rest of the world
has the right to force you to raise your blockade. But I do think you
ought to consider these tendencies of the world's opinion, and how much
you are acting in opposition to the spirit of the age ; and above all, in your
present state, weigh well the danger of putting yourself in the dilemma of
making all the world your enemies. The recognition of the independence
of the South, and the forcing of the blockade, will come to be viewed,
about next March, as a matter of life and death by many millions of
people in Europe, and as a question of high political urgency by the most
powerful governments of the world."—Pierce-Sumner Papers, MS.

[1] Report of Welles, Dec. 2 ; Cobden's letter of Dec. 19, Morley's Cobden,
p. 574 ; Life of Weed, vol. ii. p. 392.
[2] Pierce-Sumner Papers, MS.

next administration he should probably occupy high office;
that " it would become his duty to insult England, and that
he should insult her accordingly." [1] The remark—suppos-
ing that the duke understood it correctly—was probably an
attempt at facetiousness, but he took the very poor joke in
sober earnest, and gave the story to the ministry; afterwards it got into the newspapers, and at this time had considerable influence on public opinion.[2] The subsequent acts
of Seward seemed to confirm the accuracy of the report. It
was also believed that, soon after his accession to office, he
had proposed to the North and the South that they sink
their differences and unite in an attack on Canada. His
public circular of October 14 to the governors of all the
States on the seaboard and lakes, urging them to put their
ports and harbors in a condition of complete defence in
order to guard against attack from foreign nations,[3] when
joined to all the other circumstances, seemed to show that,
for his own behoof, he was determined to provoke a war
with Great Britain.[4] "There is general distrust and hostility to yourself," said Thurlow Weed, in a letter from London of December 6 to Seward.[5] "There is an impression,
I know, in high quarters here," wrote Cobden to Sumner,
November 29, "that Mr. Seward wishes to quarrel with
this country. This seems absurd enough. I confess I

[1] London *Times*, Dec. 14, 1861.

[2] See Thurlow Weed's letters from London to Seward, Dec. 6, 10 ; see
Seward's reference to it, letters of Dec. 27, 1861, Jan. 2, 1862, Life of Seward,
vol. iii. pp. 29, 30, 34, 37. George Peabody to Weed, Jan. 17, 1862, Life
of Weed, vol. ii. p. 365 ; also see p. 355, and Thurlow Weed's letter in the
London *Times* of Dec. 14.

[3] New York *Tribune*, Oct. 17. Chase wrote Jay Cooke, Oct. 19, that
there was no necessity for Seward's circular, Schuckers, p. 432. The
President, however, in his message of Dec. 3, and the Secretary of War in
his report of Dec. 1, advocated such a measure.

[4] London *Times*, Nov. 7, Dec. 14, 30 ; London *Saturday Review*, Dec. 14.

[5] Life of Seward, vol. iii. p. 29. Weed, Archbishop Hughes, and Bishop
McIlvaine had gone to Europe, at the request of the administration, in the
hope of influencing sentiment in England and France favorably to the
North, Life of Weed, vol. i. p. 634.

have as little confidence in him as I have in Lord Palmerston. Both will consult bunkum for the moment, without much regard, I fear, for the future."[1] We may, I think, accept as faithful this characterization.

Yet in the Mason and Slidell affair Seward behaved better than Palmerston. We have seen that the secretary wrote Adams, November 30, that he might assure Lord Palmerston and Earl Russell that Captain Wilkes had acted without any authority whatever from the government.[2] December 19 Adams imparted this to Russell, and although the American minister took great care that the despatch and his conference with the British foreign secretary should be kept strictly private, an inkling of them in some manner leaked out, and the funds rose one per cent. on the next day. In the meantime popular opinion took an admirable turn. The Bright and Cobden party had gained on the British public at the expense of the sympathizers with the Southern Confederacy. The feeling became strong that if agreement could not be reached by negotiation, arbitration were preferable to war.[3] The giv-

---

[1] Pierce-Sumner Papers, MS.; Morley's Cobden, p. 573; see Sumner's reply, Pierce's Sumner, vol. iv. p. 60. "The *Times* and other journals, but the *Times* chiefly, have sought to create the opinion that your government, and Mr. Seward principally, seeks war with England. . . . Unfortunately, while heretofore cotton has been the great bond of peace between the United States and England, *now* it is acting in a contrary direction."—Bright to Sumner, Dec. 21, Pierce-Sumner Papers, MS. Gray said to Darwin, in a letter written late in 1861 or early in 1862: "Seeman wrote me that the general belief at the clubs and in the City was that our government wanted to get into war with England for an excuse to give up the South."—Gray's Letters, p. 473.

[2] *Ante.*

[3] Bright wrote Sumner, Dec. 14, "There is less passion shown here than there was a week ago, and there has been a considerable expression of opinion in favor of moderate counsels and urging arbitration rather than war." Dec. 21 he wrote, "There has been more manifestation of opinion in favor of peace and of moderate counsels, and of arbitration in case your government cannot accept the opinion of our law officers on the unhappy *Trent* affair."—Pierce-Sumner Papers, MS. The *Daily News* of Dec. 27 said, "The principle of arbitration has excited during the last ten days an amount of public interest and received an amount of public

ing out of the virtual contents of Seward's despatch by
Palmerston would have been proper, and would have caused
joy in the financial and commercial circles of London. But
not only did he fail to confirm the pleasant rumor which
had obtained currency, but he suffered his accredited organ,
the *Morning Post*, to assert more than once, without correction, that while Adams had indeed communicated a despatch to the British government, it "in no way related to
the difficulty about the *Trent*." [1] It is possible that Palmerston, with an eye to his majority in the House of Commons,
soon to assemble, saw fit to cajole the war party, in which
were many members of Parliament, while other members
of the cabinet sympathized with the dominant opinion for
peace. [2] "I *suspect*," wrote Bright to Sumner, December
21, "there is a section of our government disposed for war,
but I *know* there is another section disposed for peace." [3]

support that could hardly have been anticipated at such a moment."
Adams wrote Seward, Dec. 27: "Although many of the leading presses
zealously continue their efforts to keep up the war feeling here against
the United States, I think the signs are clear of a considerable degree of
reaction, and a growing hope that the friendly relations between the two
countries may be preserved."—Diplomatic Correspondence, 1862, p. 12 ;
see Cobden's letter of Jan. 23, 1862, Morley's Cobden, p. 575.

[1] Adams to Seward, Jan. 17, 1862, Diplomatic Correspondence, 1862, p.
14. Goldwin Smith, in *Macmillan's Magazine* for Dec., 1865, speaks of
"the suppression of Mr. Seward's pacific note, and the positive denial of
the fact that such a communication had been received published in the
prime-minister's personal organ."

[2] Adams to Seward, Dec. 27, 1861, Jan. 17, 1862, Diplomatic Correspondence, 1862, pp. 13, 16. The *Observer*, a weekly paper, supposed to
represent Earl Russell, gave after the first denial of the *Post* the substance
of Seward's pacific despatch, see Diplomatic Correspondence, 1862, p. 15.
Russell had acted with dignity. The Confederate commissioners had
pressed for an interview which he declined, British and Foreign State
Papers, 1860–61, p. 261. See also Adams to Seward, Dec. 27, Diplomatic
Correspondence, 1862, p. 13 ; Bright's criticism of Palmerston in House
of Commons, Feb. 17, 1862, and Palmerston's reply, Hansard, pp. 379, 390.

[3] Pierce-Sumner Papers, MS. Bright had written, Dec. 14 : "The unfavorable symptom is the war preparations of the government and the
sending of troops to Canada and the favor shown to the excitement
which so generally precedes war. This convinces us either that this gov-

" We in England," said Cobden in a letter to Sumner, " have ready a fleet surpassing in destructive force any naval armament the world ever saw, exceeding greatly the British navy in the great French war in 1810. *This force has been got up under false pretences.* There is always a desire on the part of governments to use such armaments, by way of proving that they were necessary. *France* was the pretence, and now we have plenty of people who would be content to see this fleet turned against you." [1]

The Queen's messenger delivered Earl Russell's despatch of November 30 to the British minister at Washington at

---

ernment believes that you intend war with England, or that itself intends war with you. The first supposition is scarcely credible—unless the New York *Herald* be accepted as the confidential organ of your government (!), or that Lord Lyons has misrepresented the feeling of the Washington cabinet. The second supposition may be true—for it may be imagined that by a war got up on some recent pretence, such as your steamer *San Jacinto* is supposed to have given, we may have cotton sooner than by waiting for your success against the South. I know nothing but what is in the papers, but I conclude that this government is ready for war if an excuse can be found for it. I need not tell you that at a certain point the moderate opinion of a country is borne down by the passion which arises and which takes the name of patriotism, and that the good men here who abhor war may have no influence if a blow is once struck."—Ibid.

[1] Letter of Dec. 12, Pierce-Sumner Papers, MS. Cobden wrote, Jan., 1862 : " Palmerston ought to be turned out for the reckless expense to which he has put us. . . . Then came Seward's despatch to Adams on the 19th December, which virtually settled the matter. To keep alive the wicked passions in this country as Palmerston and his *Post* did was like the man, and that is the worst that can be said of it."—Morley's Cobden, p. 572; see, also, Goldwin Smith's article, *Macmillan's Magazine*, Dec., 1865. Besides authorities which have been mentioned from time to time, I have read all the leaders on American affairs pending the *Trent* difficulty in the London *Times, Daily News, Saturday Review*, and the *Spectator*, and several articles in the London *Morning Post* and *Morning Star*, printed in the New York *Tribune*. I desire to refer especially to the *Times* of Nov. 28, 29, 30, Dec. 2, 3, 4, 5, 6, 7, 13, 14, 16, 21, 24, 25, 30, 1861, Jan. 2, 1862 ; the *Daily News*, Nov. 28, 30, Dec. 4, 5, 11, 27 ; *Saturday Review*, Nov. 30, Dec. 7, 14, 28; the *Spectator*, Nov. 30, Dec. 7, 21, 28, 1861, Jan. 4, 1862. See the correspondence between Weed and Seward, Life of Seward, vol. iii. chaps. iii., iv.; also Life of Weed, vol. i. p. 634 *et seq.*, vol. ii. p. 348 *et seq.;* Motley's Correspondence, vol. ii. p. 45.

half-past eleven on the night of December 18. Lord Lyons saw Seward the next day, and, in accordance with private instructions, did not read Russell's despatch, but acquainted him with the tenor of it, saying that her majesty's government would be satisfied with nothing less than the liberation of the captive commissioners. The Secretary of State asked for a little delay. December 23 Lyons read to Seward England's formal demand, and left him a copy of it. It does not appear that the British minister stated that unless he received a satisfactory answer in seven days he should close his legation and leave Washington, nor that Seward asked what would be the consequence should the United States refuse compliance. In a private note from Russell to Lyons the desire of the English government " to abstain from anything like menace " was expressed. Courtesy and a conciliatory manner marked the conduct of the Englishman, dignity and gravity that of the American during these negotiations. On Christmas morning the President assembled his cabinet. Earl Russell's despatch was read. The Secretary of State submitted the draft of his answer proposing to surrender Mason and Slidell to the British authorities. Sumner came by invitation to the cabinet meeting, and read to the gentlemen assembled the letters of John Bright, and the most important of those from Cobden.[1] While the discussion to which these papers

---

[1] Bright's up to and including Dec. 14, Cobden's up to and including Dec. 12. I have already quoted freely from these letters, but I will add two more citations from Bright which bore directly on the point discussed. He wrote, Dec. 7 : " At all hazards you must not let this matter grow to a war with England ; even if you are right and we are wrong, war will be fatal to your idea of restoring the Union, and we know not what may survive its evil influences. I am not now considering its effects here—they may be serious enough—but I am looking alone to your great country, the hope of freedom and humanity, and I implore you not, on any feeling that nothing can be conceded, and that England is arrogant and seeking a quarrel, to play the game of every enemy of your country. Nations in great crises and difficulties have often done that which in their prosperous and powerful hour they would not have done, and they have done it without humiliation or disgrace. You may disappoint your enemies by the

gave rise was going on, a despatch from the Minister of Foreign Affairs of France to Mercier, her representative at Washington, was sent into the council-room. This asserted that England had made a just demand, and urged that the federal government comply with it. The despatch had been received only that morning by Mercier. Impressed by its importance he had hurried to the White House, and begged that it be submitted at once to Seward.[1] The discussion went on until two o'clock, and was continued the next day. Seward maintained that, Wilkes having clearly violated the law of nations, England had a right to ask for the restoration of the Confederate commissioners. Sumner, either in the cabinet meeting or out of it, strongly supported this view of the Secretary of State. The President and some members of the cabinet hesitated. Lincoln had entertained the notion of proposing arbitration; perhaps it had been suggested to him by one of Bright's letters.[2]

---

moderation and reasonableness of your conduct, and every honest and good man in England will applaud your wisdom. Put all the fire-eaters in the wrong, and Europe will admire the sagacity of your government." —Pierce-Sumner Papers, MS. Dec. 14 he said: " If you are resolved to succeed against the South *have no war with England;* make every concession that can be made ; don't even hesitate to tell the world that you will even concede *what two years ago no power would have asked of you,* rather than give another nation a pretence for assisting in the breaking up of your country. The time will probably come when you can safely disregard the menaces of the English oligarchy ; now it is your interest to baffle it, even by any concession which is not disgraceful. "—Ibid.

[1] The despatch was dated Dec. 3. The Austrian and Prussian governments were both friendly to the North. Their despatches did not reach Washington until after the affair was settled. Count Rechberg wrote from Vienna, Dec. 8, to Hülsemann that he thought England was in the right. Count Bernstorff wrote from Berlin, Dec. 25, to Baron Gerolt in a similar strain and said, " Public opinion in Europe has with singular unanimity pronounced in the most positive manner for the injured party." —British Blue-Book.

[2] Bright wrote, Dec. 5 : " If opinions on your side and ours vary and are not to be reconciled—I mean legal opinions—then I think your government may fairly say it is a question for impartial arbitration, to which they are willing to submit the case ; and, further, that, in accordance with

While he cared little about keeping Mason and Slidell, and was earnestly anxious to avoid war with Great Britain, he feared the sentiment of the people. In the end, however, from the considerations that the United States did not have a good case and that it could not afford a war with Great Britain, all came to Seward's position and approved his answer. His letter, dated December 26, was a lengthy discussion of the law, obviously written for its effect at home. The best and perhaps the only necessary parts were: This government cannot deny the justice of the claim presented by the British government, which " is not made in a discourteous manner," and " the four persons in question . . . will be cheerfully liberated." [1] Mason, Slidell, and their secretaries were delivered to an English steamer at Provincetown. The disavowal of the act was accepted as a sufficient apology. [2]

all their past course, they are willing to agree to such amendments of maritime or international law as England, France, and Russia may consent to. If I were minister or President in your country, I would write the most complete answer the case is capable of, and, in a friendly and courteous tone, send it to this country. I would say that if, after this, your view of the case is not accepted, you are ready to refer the matter to any sovereign or two sovereigns, or governments of Europe, or to any other eligible tribunal, and to abide by the decision, and you will rejoice to join with the leading European governments in amendments and modifications of international law in respect to the powers of belligerents and the rights of neutrals. I think you may do this with perfect honor, and you would make it impossible for the people of England to support our government in any hostile steps against you ; in fact, I think a course so moderate and just would bring over to your side a large amount of opinion here that has been poisoned and misled by the *Times* and other journals since your troubles began."—Pierce-Sumner Papers, MS. Compare Lincoln's MS. draft of a reply, Nicolay and Hay, vol. v. p. 32.

[1] Cobden wrote, Jan. 23, 1862 : " I regret that your foreign secretary did not give a word of sympathy in this direction instead of threats. However, he had his hands full at home, and I am bound to say there is much in his correspondence to inspire both admiration and respect."—Pierce-Sumner Papers, MS.

[2] My authorities for this account are three despatches of Russell to Lyons of Nov. 30 ; ibid., Dec. 19 ; Lyons to Russell, Dec. 19, 23, and two despatches of Dec. 27, British Blue-Book ; Walpole's Russell, vol. ii. p. 346 ;

The President had misread public sentiment. The outburst of exultation when the news of Wilkes's exploit was
first received had given way to sober reflection on the right
and policy of our act. " The decision of our government,"
wrote Asa Gray to Darwin, " will be as unitedly and thoroughly sustained by the whole people as if it had been the
other way." This is an accurate statement of popular
opinion.[1] Although the people of the North were impulsive,
they were generous and desired to be just ; they certainly
did not at this time wish a war with England, but they believed that she desired an excuse to interfere in their trouble
and help the South. If the *Trent* had been a Russian ship,
the people with one accord would have demanded that the
offer be immediately made for the surrender of the prisoners ; and had English opinion justified Earl Russell in sending words as kind and sympathetic as those which Russia
had sent in July, the same feeling would have existed towards Great Britain. That the hearts of Americans, in
spite of their griefs, beat warmly for those of their stock
across the sea was manifested when the intelligence of

Bates's MS. Diary, Nicolay and Hay, vol. v. p. 35 *et seq.;* Chase's Diary,
Warden, p. 393 ; Sumner's letters to Bright and Cobden, Pierce, vol. iv.
p. 57 *et seq.;* Seward to Weed, Jan. 22, 1862, Life of Weed, vol. ii. p. 409,
and other private letters of Seward printed in the biographies of Seward
and Weed ; Charles Francis Adams's address on Seward, April, 1873 ; for
an abstract of the legal points involved, see Snow's Cases of International
Law, p. 486.
 [1] Gray's Letters, p. 473 ; New York *Herald,* Dec. 21, 29 ; New York
World, Times, Dec. 16, 30 ; New York *Tribune, Evening Post,* Boston
Evening Transcript, Daily Advertiser, Dec. 30 ; Boston *Herald,* Dec. 29 ;
private correspondence of Sumner for Dec., Pierce-Sumner Papers, MS.
Edward L. Pierce wrote Sumner, Jan. 12, 1862 : ''When you asked me
how the surrender of Mason and Slidell would be received if determined
upon, I said it might meet with indignation in the morning, but would be
acquiesced in in the evening ; but it was acquiesced in universally in the
morning. All thought it wise." Ibid; Anthony Trollope's North America,
vol. ii. p. 35; Motley's Correspondence, vol. ii. pp. 45, 49, 53. Seward's despatch of Nov. 30 to Adams, Earl Russell's demand, Seward's reply, the
advice of the French minister of foreign affairs, were printed in the New
York *Tribune* of Dec. 30.

Prince Albert's death came.   The decision in the Mason and
Slidell case had not been reached, and it was not known
whether it would be for peace or for war, but New York
showed its respect for the good and capable man by lower-
ing to half-mast the flags of the ships in the harbor and
those on the buildings in the city.[1]

All England, with the exception of that party which sympathized so strongly with the South that they were ready to
go to war to aid her, received the news of the surrender of
Mason and Slidell with great thankfulness.[2]   Gladstone had

---

[1] New York *Evening Post*, Dec. 28.

[2] London *Times*, Jan. 9 ; London *Daily News*, Jan. 10; London *Saturday
Review* and *Spectator*, Jan. 11, 1862.   Lord Lyons wrote Sumner, Feb. 1,
1862 : " You will, I am sure, hear with pleasure that the queen has created
me a Knight Grand Cross of the Bath.   This is a great mark of the satisfaction with which the termination of the dangerous question is regarded
by her majesty and the government."—Pierce-Sumner Papers, MS.   The
leader in the *Times* of Jan. 11 is a striking illustration of English sentiment, and goes to prove that if our government had at once liberated
Mason and Slidell, and had taken pains to recall to the British public that
Mason was the author of the Fugitive Slave law, and that Slidell had been
the champion of filibustering, it would have been a master-stroke of policy.
I therefore quote largely from it : "The four American gentlemen who
have got us into our late trouble and cost us probably a million apiece,
will soon be in one of our ports. . . . How, then, are we to receive these
illustrious visitors ?. . . We may as well observe that Messrs. Mason and
Slidell are about the most worthless booty it would be possible to extract
from the jaws of the American lion.   They have long been known as the
blind and habitual haters and revilers of this country.   They have done
more than any other men to get up the insane prejudice against England
which disgraces the morality and disorders the policy of the Union.   The
hatred of this country has been their stock in trade.   On this they have
earned their political livelihood and won their position, just as there are
others who pander to the lower passions of humanity.   A diligent use of
this bad capital has made them what they are and raised them to the rank
of commissioners.   It is through their lifelong hatred and abuse of England that they come here in their present conspicuous capacity.   The nation under whose flag they sought a safe passage across the Atlantic, the
nation that has now rescued them with all her might from the certainty
of a dungeon and the chances of retaliatory murder, is that against which
they have always done their best to exasperate their countrymen.   Had
they perished in the cell or on the scaffold, amid the triumphant yells of

written Sumner, January 3: " I write in the interval, not, let us hope, a trough between the waves, when your answer to our demand in the case of Mason and Slidell is on the way. ... I must not enter into the gigantic question of the convulsion now agitating the North American continent. For British interests, I could heartily wish the old Union had continued. I will only further say that I am sure you have entered on this terrific struggle in good faith and good conscience, and that I do not believe even it can destroy your greatness." [1] After the action of the American government was known, Gladstone spoke in public with generous and friendly sympathy for the Union.[2] In a letter to Sumner of January 10 the Duke of Argyll said: " The news which came to us two days ago has been *indeed* a relief. I am sure I need not tell you how I *hated* what appeared the prospect before us. There were just two things which appeared to me certain : one was that if the act of the *San Jacinto* were defended, war was absolutely forced upon us; the other was that such a war, odious at all times, was doubly odious now." [3] Bright rejoiced and wrote, " The war - mongers here are baffled for the time, and I cannot but believe that a more healthy opinion is gradually extending itself on all matters connected with your great struggle." [4] Yet he was

---

the multitude, memory would have suggested that their own bitter tirades had raised the storm, and that their death was only the natural and logical conclusion of their own calumnies and sophistries. So we do sincerely hope that our countrymen will not give these fellows anything in the shape of an ovation. . . . Impartial as the British public is in the matter, it certainly has no prejudice in favor of slavery, which, if anything, these gentlemen represent. . . . They must not suppose, because we have gone to the very verge of a great war to rescue them, that therefore they are precious in our eyes. We should have done just as much to rescue two of their own negroes, and, had that been the object of the rescue, the swarthy Pompey and Cæsar would have had just the same right to triumphal arches and municipal addresses as Messrs. Mason and Slidell. So please, British public, let's have none of these things."

[1] Pierce-Sumner Papers, MS.   [2] London *Daily News*, Jan. 14, 1862.
[3] Pierce-Sumner Papers, MS.
[4] To Sumner, Jan. 11, ibid.; also his speech in the House of Commons, Feb. 17, Hansard, p. 386.

afraid of Palmerston. "I have a letter from a friend of mine in a government office," he added, "in which he expresses his confident belief that Palmerston and Louis Napoleon do intend at an early period to recognize the independence of the South and to repudiate or break the blockade."

It is a pity that this honorable settlement of the difficulty does not end the chapter of misunderstanding, of lack of sympathy, of irritation between England and the United States. The affair left a rankling wound. "You have made us sore," wrote Asa Gray to Darwin.[1] Lowell said, in 1869: "It is the *Trent* that we quarrel about, like Percy and Glendower. That was like an east wind to our old wound and set it a-twinge once more. . . . That imperious despatch of Lord John's made all those inherited drops of ill-blood as hot as present wrongs."[2] "I agree with you,"

---

[1] Feb. 18, Letters, p. 477 ; see, also, letter of W. C. Bryant to a friend in England, Life of Bryant, Godwin, vol. ii. p. 159.

[2] Letter to E. L. Godkin, May 2, 1869, Lowell's Letters, vol. ii. p. 29. This is a curious instance of the survival in a broad-minded man of a former intensity of feeling. Earl Russell's despatch and instructions were, as long as a peremptory demand had to be made, courteous and even considerate, and were so regarded at the time, see Seward's letter of Dec. 26; New York *World*, Dec. 30. Lowell's remark was possibly on the supposition that the demand for the surrender of Mason and Slidell was accompanied with the threat that, if they were not given up in seven days, Lord Lyons should close his legation and leave Washington. Although it is frequently stated that such a threat was made by Lyons to Seward, I have not been able to find any evidence of it. William Gray, writing Chase from Boston, Dec. 24, that the general opinion of the Law Club was that war with Great Britain must be avoided, added, "The conduct of England during the whole year has caused an estrangement in our people, the effect of which will outlive the present generation."—Chase Papers, MS. Richard H. Dana wrote Sumner, Feb. 12 : "I am glad to see the London *Times*' attack on you and your speech. [Sumner's speech on the *Trent* case, Senate, Jan. 9, 1862, see Pierce's Sumner, vol. iv. p. 55 ; Adams's Dana, vol. ii. p. 261.] It will make you feel to the quick what you did not seem to feel, or refused to admit—the intolerable insolence of England towards us, and the false and fraudulent manner in which they have treated this case. Those few semi-republican, semi-abolition, liberally inclined men in England whom few respect, and who command, perhaps, one

wrote Darwin to Sir Joseph Hooker, January 25, 1862; "the present American row has a very Torifying influence on us all." [1]

With military operations at a stand-still, the Southern people looked on the progress of the difficulty about the *Trent* with painful suspense, and they grieved at its settlement, for they felt that a war between Great Britain and the United States would be an absolute warrant of their independence. Nevertheless, at the close of 1861 it would have been difficult to find many Southerners who doubted, whether or not there was foreign interference in the struggle, eventual success. The battles of Bull Run and of Ball's Bluff seemed to show that they were more than a match in prowess for their assailants. In eight months the North had made no progress towards a restoration of the Union, or as the Southerners expressed it, towards the subjugation of the South. There was a triumphant note in Jefferson Davis's message to his congress, which met at Richmond November 18, as he spoke of their victories, the waxing strength of the Confederacy, and its well-regulated financial system. [2] The financiering extolled by Davis consisted in meeting the expenses of the war by loans and the issue of treasury notes. From July 1 to November 16 less than one per cent. of the receipts had come from customs and "miscellaneous

---

paper and one monthly, are a drop in the bucket. The mass of the English are determined to sever this republic, and all their pent-up jealousy, contempt, arrogance, revenges, and superciliousness are breaking out stronger and stronger. There is not one English paper that has not either suppressed or falsified the material facts of this case, because they foresee they could not bear the light. I am rejoiced that you are made to feel this! Talk not of the 'press' and of private letters! You might as well set up the Isle of Skye against London, as all that against the avalanche of the *Times, Herald, Post, Westminster, Blackwood, Quarterly, Edinboro, Punch, Saturday*, etc. If I were Secretary of State I would keep my temper as Seward does, I hope—and keep peace. But if this style of treating us goes on much longer there must be war. Human nature cannot endure it."—Pierce-Sumner Papers, MS.

[1] Life and Letters, vol. ii. p. 177.
[2] Davis's message, Moore's Rebellion Record, vol. iii. p. 404.

sources;" $20,400,000 had been raised by loans, $31,000,000 in treasury notes had been paid out.[1] A direct war tax had indeed been imposed by the Confederate congress in August, but it had not yet yielded anything. Such was the aversion of the people to taxation that most of the States assumed this tax, as they were allowed to do by the statute, and paid it to the Confederate government, raising the means by issuing State bonds and State treasury notes.[2] The expenditures for the two months previous to November 20, when the Secretary of the Treasury made his report, had averaged about twenty millions per month.[3] The banks in the Confederacy had suspended specie payments. Before the 1st of May gold was four per cent. premium in Atlanta; quoted in Richmond at 110 August 1, it sold at 120 by the end of the year.[4]

While there is not a glimmering of discouragement in Davis's message, in Memminger's report, or in the legislation of the Confederate congress,[5] the pressure of the blockade had begun to be felt severely. Salt, bacon, butter, coffee, tea, soap, candles, matches, starch, and glue had advanced enormously in price, and these articles were extremely scarce. The same may be said of dry goods. Highly bred young women of Charleston dressed in homespun, and the gentlemen of Richmond made a virtue of wearing last year's clothes. The blockade was teaching lessons of economy

---

[1] Memminger's report.

[2] J. C. Schwab, "Finances of the Confederacy," *Political Science Quarterly*, March, 1892, and "The Financier of the Confederate States," *Yale Review*, Nov., 1893; Davis's Confederate Government, vol. i. p. 495. For the tax law see Statutes at Large, Provisional Government C. S. A., p. 177.

[3] Memminger's report, which also gives total receipts and expenses from the organization of the government to Nov. 16, Life of Memminger, Capers, pp. 422-28.

[4] Atlanta *Commonwealth*, April 23; Richmond *Examiner*, Aug. 1; Schwab, *Political Science Quarterly*, p. 44; also Stephens's War between the States, vol. ii. p. 569.

[5] The last session of the provisional congress of the Confederacy lasted from Nov. 18, 1861, to Feb. 17, 1862, but its proceedings do not call for special notice.

to an extravagant people. The first cold weather of the
autumn made evident that coal was scarce and wood in
short supply; both had become luxuries for the well-to-do.
The supply of medicines was becoming low. The scarcity
of lint and surgical plaster was felt seriously by the surgeons in the hospitals, and the wounds of federal prisoners taken at Bull Run were for a time left undressed.
"Tell your master Lincoln to raise the blockade, and then
we will tend to you," the doctors frequently said. "We
have not lint enough for our own wounded, and they must
be served first." [1]

Shifts were made to get along without the comforts and
necessaries of life. To eke out their store of coffee people
mixed rye with it, and when the supply of rye ran short,
they found that wheat would answer as well. Drawing a
lesson from European experience, the use of chiccory, which
grew in profusion in Virginia, was recommended; the root,
it was said, when dried, roasted, and ground, would make
an excellent substitute for coffee, or a mixture with it, while,
being less irritating to the nerves than the pure coffee, it
would prove a wholesome as well as an economical bever-
age. The bark of the dogwood-tree in some measure supplied the want of quinine. The Confederacy affords an
example of the discomforts and inconveniences to which
a wholly agricultural people are subject when shut off from
intercourse with the inventive and manufacturing world.
Though it had been apparently more profitable to devote
particular attention to the cultivation of the peculiar Southern staples — cotton, tobacco, rice, and sugar — and to buy
food from the North, it was now perceived that the Southern States could raise bread and meat enough for their population. It happened fortunately for them that in the year
1861, before their system of planting had become adjusted
to the conditions of war, their crops of wheat and corn were
large. Distribution, however, is almost as important as

---

[1] Ely's Journal in Richmond, p. 101.

production. Excluded from commerce with the North and
England, the railroads of the Confederacy ran down, and
as their track and their rolling-stock could be neither renewed nor repaired, they were unable at times to do more
than the government work and keep the armies supplied.
Hence, we may note a great discrepancy in prices, remarkable in railroad days, in different parts of the Confederacy.
Whatever industrial capacity the South possessed was set
to work to manufacture implements of war, and in this
field accomplished important results, yet there was no over-
plus to devote to the arts of peace.   For example, a street
railroad had been constructed in Richmond, but the cars
ordered from the North could not be procured.   It was
humiliating, the Richmond *Whig* declared, to see the track
in Main Street unused because no one in the Confederacy
could make a car.[1] When at last one car was obtained, it
was a gratifying, almost a gala sight to the citizens of
Richmond to see it running from Ninth Street to Rocketts.[2]

The cutting off of the supply of paper was grievously
felt. The tightening of the pressure of the blockade may be
studied in the deterioration in the appearance of the daily
newspapers. The Richmond *Examiner* at the beginning of
the war was an admirably printed sheet, but as the days
wore on its paper became poorer and its print less legible.
The Richmond *Whig* and the Charleston *Courier* decreased
in size. The Atlanta *Southern Confederacy* and the Atlanta
Commonwealth appeared occasionally as half-sheets only,
since they could not procure sufficient paper for the whole
of their matter, and for several days they were obliged to
print their meagre issues on brown wrapping-paper.[3] When
Alfred Ely, a New York congressman captured at Bull Run
and held a prisoner for several months in Richmond, was
released, his passport was written on brown paper[4] of South-

---

[1] Aug. 9.   [2] Richmond *Enquirer*, Sept. 3.
[3] See the *Southern Confederacy* for Sept. 25, 28, Oct. 1, 2; the *Commonwealth* for Oct. 1, 2.   [4] A Rebel War Clerk's Diary, vol. i. p. 102.

ern manufacture. Unable to get the notes ordered from the American Bank Note Company, New York, the treasury operations of the new government were attended with inconvenience. It is sometimes said that the financiering of the Confederacy required only paper and a printing-press, but such a remark ignores that the manufacture even of its bonds and its notes was conjoined with difficulty. The first bank-note paper was brought from Baltimore, its special agents eluding the watch of the federal pickets. But no skilled engravers could be found. At last, by diligent search, Capers, Memminger's chief clerk, found in Richmond a clever German who was doing lithographing in a small way, and engaged him to prepare the treasury notes by his own process. Memminger called them "uncanny bills," but he recognized the exigency and that the people could not wait for artistic work. In truth, the first demand for the promises to pay of the Confederacy was so urgent that to provide for his daily wants he was forced to have recourse to the banks for a loan of their own notes.[1] Not until October did the Confederate government have its postage-stamps ready for distribution. Complaints of the administration of the Post-office department were frequent. In fact, after making allowance for all the difficulties that beset the new government, it cannot be denied that the management of affairs was defective. The reason of this has been explained in a word by a brilliant Southern writer. " The Southern mind," he said, " lacked the faculty of *business*." [2]

The cotton and tobacco crops of the year were ready for market. England and France wanted the cotton and France wanted the tobacco, and both stood ready to pay a high price for these staples, while they had the implements of war and

---

[1] Life of Memminger, Capers, pp. 317, 335, 430.

[2] Pollard's Davis, p. 166. It is perhaps unnecessary to say that, owing to Pollard's animosity to Davis and his inaccuracy as to details, his works must be used with caution, but if employed with proper care they are valuable. Pollard was editor of the Richmond *Examiner* during the war.

the comforts, conveniences, and luxuries of life which the
South so earnestly longed for.   The only barrier between
such a wished-for traffic was the federal blockade, which the
powerful navies of England and France could have broken
in a day.   Let Lincoln, Seward, and Adams have all the
credit which is their due that their management of affairs
did much to prevent self-interest and the might that makes
right from forcing the exchange of these desirable commod-
ities;[1] but underneath it all, disguised and misrepresented
as the contest was in England, the overpowering consideration that stayed the hand of the European powers was that
the South was fighting for slavery and the North contending against its extension.[2]

The whole story of the people of the Confederacy during
the war is one of such discomfort and privation that the de-
moralization prevalent, which seems to be an incident of all
war and of large expenditure of public money, is sometimes
lost sight of.   This decay became apparent in Richmond in
the year 1861.   Vice had increased.   Drunkenness and gam-

---

[1] In connection with this brief exhibit of the sufferings of the South
from the blockade I will quote from a letter to Sumner from Paris of John
Bigelow, our consul, to show the injury done Europe by it.   "So long as
the blockade lasts it will be impossible to make the European States look
with an impartial eye upon our situation or withhold a certain amount of
moral support from the South.   I fear you do not realize the force of the
political necessity which is operating here.   Our war has deranged the
financial calculations of the government and bankers of Europe to a greater degree than any of the wars or revolutions that have preceded it in Europe.   The statesmen are at their wits' end to know what to do.   Sources
of revenue are dried up upon which all their calculations have been heretofore based with the greatest confidence.   The capital of many States is in-
sufficiently employed; hundreds of thousands of people are becoming a
charge upon the governments for their daily bread, and the heavens seem
charged with some terrible convulsion from which they think nothing can
save them but raising our blockade."—Pierce-Sumner Papers, MS.

[2] "It was the fashion among English critics at the time I left England
to state that the whole secession question had no direct bearing on, no immediate connection with, the issue of slavery.   As to the letter, there was
some small truth in this assertion; as to the spirit, there was none."—
Dicey's Federal States, vol. i. p. 65.

bling were rampant.   The simple and refined Virginia city
had become an overgrown capital to which votaries of all
sorts of wickedness flocked.   The *Examiner* of October 22
spoke of "the rapid development of vice and vulgarity in
Richmond," and asked, sarcastically, "Are not these the
happy times of saturnalia?" [1]   With the wide-spread gambling went extravagance, and, if Pollard may be credited,
many defalcations of public money.[2]   The best women of
Richmond undoubtedly exhibited in the first year of the war
devotion to the Confederate soldiers and self-sacrifice; yet the
evidence appears to show that there was some love of display,
some extravagance, and some eagerness for gay excitement
among people of quality after the battle of Bull Run which
seemed to demonstrate that the Southerners would win their
independence.   Although commercial intercourse between
the Union and the Confederacy had been declared unlawful
by President Lincoln, under authority of an act of Congress,
and the merchandise subject to confiscation,[3] and although
the bringing in of such goods was denounced in the South
as a fraud on the Confederacy and as taking the gold out of
the country, yet there was considerable smuggling.   There
is much complaint of speculators and extortioners who obtained goods from the North and sold them at extravagant
profits.   Jewish merchants were said to travel at pleasure
between the Confederacy and the Union, wholly engaged in
this illicit trade.   The Richmond *Examiner* spoke of "the
extensive system of smuggling which the dishonored and

---

[1] Oct. 9 this journal had declared: "The city of Richmond is full of the
vilest licentiousness.   Among all the loathsome vices imported into it by
the harpies who prey upon the army, that of gambling has become so
prominent and brazen as to defy public decency as well as law, intruding
its allurements on the most frequented parts of our most public streets.
. . . The painted dens of San Francisco and 'hells' of the old federal city
were not a whit more diabolical than the 'saloons' on Main Street, Richmond. . . . There is said to be now in this city a sufficient number of
gamblers to form a regiment."

[2] Life of Davis, p.153.

[3] New York *Tribune*, Aug.17; see, also, Schuckers's Chase, p. 318.

disreputable merchants of the South are carrying on across the northern border," and declared that "the smuggler is a worse enemy of the South than the infamous Dutchman who engages to shoot our people for thirteen dollars a month." [1] There was considerable intercourse between the North and the South, much of which the commanding generals on each side probably winked at. Northern newspapers were freely received at the South, and Southern journals found their way North. Exchange on New York was for a long time quoted regularly in the financial columns of the Richmond journals. As late as October 19 the Adams Express Company advertised in the Richmond newspapers that it would collect "notes, drafts, and bills, with or without goods, at all accessible points throughout the United States," and guarantee "prompt returns;" it also carried letters under certain conditions. Later still there were private letter-carriers going between Richmond and Washington and Maryland, who gained a good livelihood by charging $1.50 postage and bringing from the North divers articles which were desired in the Confederacy. In spite of the many discomforts and inconveniences, life in Richmond, as pictured in the newspapers and other contemporary accounts, does not seem to have been especially severe in the last half of 1861. The banks and railroad companies continued to pay dividends; Virginia State stock and Richmond city bonds appeared to have a ready sale. Business activity characterized the early days of the capital of the Confederacy. The factitious prosperity produced by the issue of paper money by the government was further stimulated by a flood of "shinplasters" which, to supply the place of silver small change that had disappeared, had been let loose by the corporation of Richmond, by the regular banks, and by spurious banking associations. The civil and criminal courts held their appointed terms. The advertisements in the journals are substantially such as appear in the time of peace,

---

[1] Dec. 31.

and one notes with interest the usual announcements of run-away negroes. Most of the Southern cities celebrated the Fourth of July in the usual manner. Richmond had a merry Christmas. Its theatre was open and generally crowded ; there were also concerts and balls. Its annual fair and cattle show, however, did not take place, for the Hermitage fair grounds had been converted into a vast camp. " Ceres has been dislodged by Mars," the chronicler said.[1]

Charleston did not share the prosperity of the Confederate capital.[2] Its theatre was not open, and public amusements were almost entirely given up. Grinding necessity was the lot of that portion of the South the welfare of which depended on the marketing of the cotton crop. Cotton was kept in the interior and not sent forward to the shipping ports, for fear that by their capture it might fall into the hands of the enemy. When the federal forces took Port Royal and commanded the adjacent islands, on which was grown the sea-island cotton, the finest in the world, the planters without hesitation applied the torch to the year's product.[3] December 11 Charleston suffered from a large

---

[1] Richmond *Whig*, Oct. 1.

[2] "We have suffered severely, we are suffering now. Property represents painfully uncertain sums. Business of all kinds is prostrated, fortunes have been swept away, and we have been forced to restrict our wants within the limits of mere comforts."—Charleston *Courier*, Nov. 23.

[3] "The Fires of Patriotism!—At eleven o'clock last night the heavens towards the southwest were brilliantly illuminated with the patriotic flames ascending from burning cotton. As the spectators witnessed it they involuntarily burst forth with cheer after cheer, and each heart was warmed as with a new pulse." "Burning the Crops.—We learn with gratification that the patriotic planters on the seaboard are hourly applying the torch to their cotton and other produce and effects. Those who have not had the heart to enter upon this work of praiseworthy patriotism and destruction themselves, have authorized the military authorities, before yielding anything that can in the least minister to Yankee lust and greed, to make the destruction complete before them. Parties from North Edisto and the neighborhood unite in asserting that cotton and valuables on the plantations, which could not be readily removed, were involved in one common flame and ruin."—Ibid., Nov. 30. "The 'fires of patriotism' continue;

fire. Five churches, the theatre, and several public buildings were burned, the loss being estimated at from five to seven millions. At any time this would have been a severe infliction upon a city of 48,000 people,[1] but, following other grievous misfortunes, it was a hard blow to stand up under. But it did not daunt the spirit of the people. December 20 was the anniversary of the secession of South Carolina, and although St. Andrew's Hall, in which the ordinance had been passed, and Institute Hall, in which it had been ratified, were destroyed in the conflagration, the citizens of Charleston celebrated the return of the day, and gave mutual pledges that, in spite of their misfortunes, they had not a jot or tittle of regret for their action.[2]

Congress met December 2, and the next day heard the

thirteen cotton houses have been burnt on Port Royal Island, one on Paris, and one on St. Helena, since the Yankee occupation."—Charleston *Courier*, Dec. 9; see, also, letter from Charleston of Nov. 20 to the Manchester *Guardian*, cited in Life of Weed, vol. ii. p. 404.

[1] Census of 1861, Charleston *Courier*, Nov. 4.

[2] In addition to authorities specifically cited, I may say that in this account of life in the Confederacy I have studied the files of the Richmond *Examiner, Whig, Enquirer*, and *Dispatch;* the Charleston *Courier;* the Atlanta *Southern Confederacy, Intelligencer*, and *Commonwealth*. I refer particularly to the Richmond *Examiner* of June 5, 6, 20, 24, July 12, 23, 25, Aug. 1, 9, Sept. 6, 9, 20, 23, 27, Oct. 2, 8, 9, 10, 11, 12, 15, 21, 30, Nov. 6, 9, 11, 15, 22, Dec. 2, 4, 6, 9, 11, 16, 17; Richmond *Enquirer*, May 10, 15, 20-25, June 1, 5, 26, July 2, 4, 11, 25, 29, Aug. 1, 3, 6, Sept. 24, Oct. 19, 31, Nov. 1, 2; Richmond *Whig*, Aug. 9, 13, Sept. 3, 10, 20, 27, Oct. 4, 5, 18, 29, Nov. 1, Dec. 20, 21, 27, 31; Richmond *Dispatch*, July 5, 25, Aug. 6, 9, 10, 13, 18, 20, Oct. 1, 2, 3, 5,8, Nov. 12, 13; Charleston *Courier*, July 29, 30, Aug. 1, Sept. 2, 4, 5, 7, 11, 21, 24, 28, Oct. 2, 5, 8, 9, 18, 21, 22, 24, Nov. 11, 12, 13, 25, 26, 29, Dec. 12, 13,19, 20, 21 ; Atlanta *Commonwealth*, April 23, Oct. 2 ; Atlanta *Southern Confederacy*, Aug. 1, Oct. 8, 12; Atlanta *Daily Intelligencer*, May 11, Sept. 10 ; New Orleans *Picayune*, July 4, cited in Moore's Rebellion Record, vol. ii. p. 98; Pollard's First Year of the War (Richmond, 1862); Pollard's Life of Davis ; Davis's Confederate Government ; A Rebel War Clerk's Diary, Jones, vol. i.; Samuel Phillips Day's Down South ; Mrs. Davis's Memoir of J. Davis, vol. ii.; Ely's Journal in Richmond ; Richmond During the War, Sarah A. Putnam; Four Years in Rebel Capitals, T. C. De Leon; Life in the South, by a Blockaded British Subject (Catherine C. Hopley), vol. ii.

President's message. The reference in it to foreign affairs
differed much from that of the previous 4th of July; the
complacent tone had given way to one of sorrow and anxiety. Although Lincoln put the best face possible on the
situation in general, we may gather from his omissions, as
well as from his statements, that seven and one-half months
of war had accomplished nothing towards bringing back
into the Union a single one of the eleven Confederate States.
In fact, the shedding of blood had made the chasm wider.
The mention of that noble majority of Northern men on
whom he relied for support and of whom he was fitly the
representative served as a consolation. "It is gratifying to
know," he said, "that the expenditures made necessary by
the rebellion are not beyond the resources of the loyal people . . . that the patriotism of the people has proved equal
to the occasion, and that the number of the troops tendered
greatly exceeds the force which Congress authorized me to
call into the field." He made no allusion to the exercise of
extraordinary powers by the administration in which the
warrant of the law had been exceeded; perhaps because he
himself had misgivings about the necessity of many things
that had been done by his agents. But the charge that the
freedom of the press was materially abridged[1] is without
full justification. Some restrictions were placed upon newspapers in Maryland and the other border States; editors
were arrested in these States and also at the North; yet
the impression one gets from perusing the Northern newspapers is that the public prints were substantially untram-
melled.[2] The subject of arbitrary arrests may not, however,
be dismissed in a sentence. Fearing that the legislature of
Maryland, which was to convene in September, would pass
an ordinance of secession, the Secretary of War ordered the
arrest of all or any part of its members and several citizens
of Baltimore, if necessary, to prevent such action. Under

[1] See Russell's letter to the London *Times*, Sept. 10.
[2] This was also Dicey's opinion, Federal States, vol. i. p. 248.

this order General Dix apprehended ten members-elect of the legislature, the mayor of Baltimore, a congressman, and two editors; and at Frederick City, the meeting-place of the legislature, General Banks laid hold of "nine secession members." These men were subsequently confined in Fort Lafayette, New York, and in Fort Warren, Boston, where other state-prisoners arrested in Kentucky and Missouri were also incarcerated.[1] That these arrests were infractions of the Constitution need not for a moment be questioned. They were made on simple orders from the executive departments instead of on the proper warrants required by law. The prisoners were charged with no offence, were brought before no magistrate for examination, and the commandants of the military prisons were instructed to disregard any writ of *habeas corpus* issued in their behalf. Nevertheless, it would, it seems to me, be historical hypercriticism to find fault with the federal government for its exercise of these extraordinary powers in the border States. Maryland, Kentucky, and Missouri were high stakes which Lincoln and Davis were playing for, and that Lincoln won without lasting harm to the great rights of personal liberty must, in spite of some cases of injustice and many of hardship for opinion's sake, be a sufficient historical justification for his policy of precaution.[2] In truth, that Maryland, Kentucky, and Missouri were for the Union, having furnished 40,000 soldiers for its army, and that western Virginia had been reclaimed, were almost the sole justification for the

---

[1] Official Records, vol. v. p. 193 *et seq.;* Marshall's American Bastile; Frank Key Howard's Fourteen Months in American Bastiles; letters of C. S. Morehead to J. J. Crittenden, Coleman's Crittenden, vol. ii. p.333 *et seq.;* Debate in the Senate, Dec. 16, 1861, and April 29, 1862; My Imprisonment, Rose O'N. Greenhow, London (1863).

[2] See authorities cited in previous note; also Dicey's Federal States, vol. ii. p. 59. For Lincoln's statement regarding the Maryland arrests see Raymond's Lincoln, p. 378. Governor Hicks wrote General Banks, Sept. 20: "We see the good fruit already produced by these arrests. We can no longer mince matters with these desperate people. I concur in all you have done."—Official Records, vol. v. p. 197.

President's statement in his message: "The cause of the Union is advancing steadily and certainly southward."

But this is not the whole story.   Arbitrary arrests were made in the Northern States where the courts were open and where the regular administration of justice had not been interrupted by any overt acts of rebellion.   Among the arrests were those of two men at Malone, a village in the extreme northern part of New York; an editor of the New York *Daily News*, at Burlington, N. J.; two citizens of Maine; a Vermont farmer, being enticed from his farm to Bennington, two miles away; a crippled newsboy for selling the New York *Daily News* on the Naugatuck Railroad, Connecticut; several citizens of Connecticut for getting up "peace meetings."   There were many other similar cases. Most of these were apprehended by order of the Secretary of State, the others by that of the Secretary of War.   Sometimes the authority of the officer was a simple telegram; in no case was the warrant such as the Constitution required. Little wonder was it that the critics of the administration asseverated that these arrests were made on *lettres-de-cachet*. These men, like those arrested from the border States, were charged with no offence, they were examined by no magistrate, and they were confined in Fort Lafayette or Fort Warren as prisoners of state.'   The justification made in

---

[1] Marshall's American Bastile ; Debate in the Senate, Dec. 16. "The United States government assumes the right to arrest persons in any part of the country, and to keep them during its pleasure in confinement in charge of military officers.   The courts of law are unable to give any redress, as the officers of the army decline to make any return to writs of *habeas corpus*."—Lord Lyons to Earl Russell, Sept. 6, British Blue - Book. In a lecture delivered in New York and Boston, Dec., 1861, Wendell Phillips said: "Lieber says that *habeas corpus*, free meetings like this, and a free press are the three elements which distinguish liberty from despotism. All that Saxon blood has gained in the battles and toils of two hundred years are these three things.   But to-day, Mr. Chairman, every one of them —*habeas corpus*, the right of free meeting, and a free press—is annihilated in every square mile of the republic.   We live to-day, every one of us, under martial law.   The Secretary of State puts into his bastile, with a warrant as irresponsible as that of Louis, any man whom he pleases.   And you know

the Senate of these stretches of authority was that the persons apprehended were, by treasonable speaking and writing, giving aid and comfort to the enemy, and that their imprisonment was necessary for the safety of the republic. Yet the matter did not go unquestioned. Senator Trumbull introduced a resolution asking information from the Secretary of State in regard to these arrests, and in his remarks supporting it pointed out the injustice and needlessness of such procedure. " What are we coming to," he asked, " if arrests may be made at the whim or the caprice of a cabinet minister ?" and when Senator Hale asked, " Have not arrests been made in violation of the great principles of our Constitution ?" no one could gainsay it.

Public sentiment, however, sustained the administration in this action, and it was only from a minority in the Senate and in the country that the murmurs came.[1] Nevertheless,

---

that neither press nor lips may venture to arraign the government without being silenced. At this moment one thousand men at least are 'bastiled' by an authority as despotic as that of Louis, three times as many as Eldon and George III. seized when they trembled for his throne. . . . For the first time on this continent we have passports, which even Louis Napoleon pronounces useless and odious. For the first time in our history government spies frequent our great cities."

[1] "The applause with which each successive stretch of power is received by the people is a very alarming symptom to the friends of liberty and law."—Lord Lyons to Earl Russell, Sept. 16, British Blue - Book. Count Gurowski wrote in his Diary, Jan., 1862: "The thus called arbitrary acts of the government prove how easily, on the plea of patriotic necessity, a people, nay, the public opinion, submits to arbitrary rule. All this, servility included, explains the facility with which, in former times, concentrated and concrete despotisms have been established. Here every such arbitrary action is submitted to because it is so new, and because the people has the childish naïve, but to it honorable, confidence that the power intrusted by the people is used in the interest and for the welfare of the people. But all the despots of all times and of all nations said the same. However, in justice to Mr. Lincoln, he is pure and has no despotical longings, but he has around him some atomistic Torquemadas."

This is also evident from the debate and action of the Senate. Trumbull's resolution was referred to the judiciary committee, of which he was chairman, but there it slept. Late in the session a bill relating to state prisoners passed the House (*Congressional Globe*, pp. 3106, 3184). Trumbull

the protests were emphatic and couched in irrefutable logic.[1]
The criticisms were directed against Seward, who was
deemed responsible for this policy. The Secretary of State,
so Senator Pearce, of Maryland, asserted by implication, sits
in his office, and by "a dash of his pen" sets "the electric
fire in motion to order arrests at Cincinnati, at Chicago, at
Baltimore, or even in Connecticut."[2] In truth, the apprehension of men in Maine, Vermont, Connecticut, and northern New York on suspicion that they were traitors, instead
of leaving them to be dealt with by the public sentiment
of their thoroughly loyal communities, savored rather of
the capriciousness of an absolute monarch than of a desire
to govern in a constitutional manner. A clever journalist,
who had good opportunities for observation during the war,
maintains that Seward was intoxicated with power, loving
to exercise it with mere wantonness;[3] and such a conception of his character serves well to explain many of his
acts. The mischief of this policy was immediate, in that
it gave a handle to the Democratic opposition, probably
increasing its strength, and in that it furnished our critics
over the sea an additional opportunity for detraction. The
remote consequences which were feared—that our people
would lose some of their liberties, that we had begun to
tread the well-worn path from democracy to despotism—
have not been realized.

It is true that acts of a cabinet minister, unless disavowed
by the President, become his own acts, and in so far he
must be held responsible for these arbitrary arrests. Nevertheless, it is not probable that Lincoln of his own motion
would have ordered them, for although at times he acted
without warrant of the Constitution, he had a profound

pressed this in the Senate, but was unable to get it considered. See, also,
Raymond's Lincoln, p. 378; Trollope's North America, vol. ii. p. 205.

[1] See editorials in New York *Tribune*, Sept. 19, Oct. 21; Trumbull and
Hale's remarks in the Senate, Dec. 16.

[2] Dec. 16, *Congressional Globe*, p. 94.

[3] Donn Piatt's Memories of Men who Saved the Union, p. 79.

reverence for it, showing in all his proceedings that he
much preferred to keep within the strict limits of the letter
and spirit of the organic law of the land, and that he exercised or permitted others to exercise arbitrary power with
keen regret. It was undoubtedly disagreeable to him to
be called by Vallandigham the Cæsar of the American
Republic,[1] and by Wendell Phillips "a more unlimited
despot than the world knows this side of China,"[2] and
to be aware that Senator Grimes described a call at the
White House for the purpose of seeing the President, as
an attempt "to approach the footstool of the power en-
throned at the other end of the avenue."[3] The executive
order issued February 14, 1862, in the name of the Secretary
of War, is evidence that Lincoln had no love for arbitrary
arrests and cruel punishments and was willing to set limits
to his own power. He directed "that all political prisoners or state prisoners now held in military custody be
released on their subscribing to a parole engaging them to
render no aid or comfort to the enemies in hostility to
the United States;" to such as should keep their parole
he granted "an amnesty for any past offences of treason
or disloyalty which they may have committed;" the conclusion of the order was: "Extraordinary arrests will hereafter be made under the direction of the military authorities alone."[4] A commission which was at once appointed
to carry this order into effect released many prisoners from
custody.

The remark which Thucydides puts into the mouth of one
of his characters, "War is not an affair of arms, but of
money which gives to arms their use," fitly introduces a
record of our financial operations. The Secretary of the
Treasury reported that from July 1 to September 30, the
first quarter of the fiscal year, the actual expenses of the

[1] *Congressional Globe* Appendix, p. 46.
[2] Dicey's report of a speech he heard at Washington, Federal States,
vol. i. p. 180.
[3] *Congressional Globe*, p. 311.   [4] Raymond's Lincoln, p. 380.

government had been $98,000,000, of which $7,500,000,[1] or less than 8 per cent., had been derived from customs and miscellaneous sources, the receipts of revenue from duties not having come up to his expectations, and the taxation imposed at the special session of Congress yielding as yet no returns. Up to December 1 he had realized from loans $197,000,000. Of this amount there had been obtained $100,000,000 from the sale of three-years' bonds bearing 7.30 per cent. interest, and nearly $46,000,000 from the negotiation of $50,000,000 twenty-year 6 per cent. bonds on a 7 per cent. basis. The balance had come from the issue of United States notes payable on demand without interest,[2] and by the sale or by the payment to creditors of 6 per cent. notes, part of them running sixty days and part of them two years. The secretary estimated the expenses for the whole of the fiscal year at $543,000,000. He hoped the ordinary revenues would reach $40,000,000, and he recommended additional taxation to that provided by the act of August 5, so that an aggregate amount of $50,000,000 might be obtained. The balance must come from loans, some of which had been negotiated, but about $250,000,000 remained to be provided for by loans between December 9, 1861, the date of the secretary's report, and June 30, 1862, the close of the fiscal year. Chase would not recommend the further issue of United States notes, but advocated a national banking system, similar in its salient features to that of the present, which should work the gradual retirement of the notes of the State banks. The balance-sheet was not a cheerful one for a finance minister to present to the House of Representatives; there went with it an urging of retrenchment and reform in the public expenditures.

The only comfort which the secretary could find in the situation was that there had been "a considerable improvement in the condition of trade and industry." During the

---

[1] In treating of the financial operations round numbers are used.
[2] $24,550,325 of these had been issued.

first months of 1861, on account of the political troubles, business men had gasped for breath. The outbreak of the war paralyzed trade. The loss of Southern custom was grievously felt by Eastern merchants and manufacturers, and the prospect of it had much to do with the eagerness of New York city for compromise while the question of compromise was mooted. The practical repudiation of commercial debts due the North by the South, the amount being estimated as high as $200,000,000,[1] brought disaster and downfall. " The fabric of New York's mercantile prosperity," declared the New York *Tribune* of May 27, "lies in ruins, beneath which ten thousand fortunes are buried. . . . Last fall the merchant was a capitalist ; to-day he is a bankrupt."[2] Many men of wealth, apprehensive for the stability of the government, transferred their property to Europe,[3] but how the country's cause lay at the heart of the people is exemplified by Asa Gray. " My wife and I," he wrote, October 4, " have scraped up $550, all we can scrape, and lent it to the United States."[4] The financial pressure was severe. " I had a little Italian bluster of brushwood fire yesterday morning," said Lowell, in a private letter, " but the times are too hard with me to allow of such an extravagance except on the brink of gelation. The horror of my tax-bill has so infected my imagination that I see myself and all my friends begging entrance to the P. H. (From delicacy I use initials.)"[5] " The 1st of Janu-

---

[1] New York *Tribune*, Sept. 18 ; President's message of Dec. 3.

[2] The *Tribune* of Sept. 18 said: " New York was largely a creditor of the South, and rebellion was held by her debtors throughout the seceded States as a receipt in full for the amount of their obligations. Not that a part of them have not professed and perhaps cherished a vague intent to pay some time or other, but there was no solace in this for the present sufferings of our prostrated merchants. Not less than $200,000,000 of Southern indebtedness to our city was blotted out as in a night. . . . Trade, of course, for a season sank to zero." See, also, Trollope's North America, vol. ii. p. 76.

[3] Schuckers's Chase, p. 330 ; Hooper in House of Representatives, Feb. 3, 1862.   [4] Letters, p. 470.

[5] To Miss Norton, Sept. 28, Letters, vol. i. p. 315.

ary," wrote Emerson in 1862, " has found me in quite as
poor a plight as the rest of the Americans. Not a penny
from my books since last June, which usually yield five or
six hundred a year; no dividends from the banks or from
Lidian's Plymouth property. Then almost all income from
lectures has quite ceased, so that your letter found me in
a study how to pay three or four hundred dollars with
fifty. . . . I have been trying to sell a wood lot at or near
its appraisal, which would give me something more than
three hundred, but the purchaser does not appear. Meantime we are trying to be as unconsuming as candles under
an extinguisher, and 'tis frightful to think how many rivals
we have in distress and in economy. But far better that
this grinding should go on bad and worse than we be driven
by any impatience into a hasty peace or any peace restoring
the old rottenness." [1]

The loans, amounting to $146,000,000, which Chase had
negotiated, had been taken by the banks of New York,
Philadelphia, and Boston. To assist them in bearing the
burden, he had " caused books of subscription to be opened
throughout the country, and the people subscribed freely
to the loan." These transactions had been made on a specie
basis, involving the actual disbursement by the banks of a
large amount of coin. The secretary and the banks worked
together harmoniously, the banks appreciating that they
and the government must stand or fall together.[2] But these
loans exhausted their resources. Saturday night, December 28, 1861, the managers of the New York banks, after
a meeting of six hours, decided that they must suspend
specie payments. Gold soon brought a slight premium.
This condition had to be considered by the House committee
of ways and means, as, in conjunction with Chase, it matured its financial measure. The senators and representa-

---

[1] J. E. Cabot's Emerson, vol. ii. p. 612.

[2] An interesting account of some of these negotiations is given by Maun-
sell B. Field in chap. viii. of his Memories of Many Men and Some
Women.

tives, being in closer contact with the people than the Secretary of the Treasury, were aware of their willingness and even eagerness to be taxed, notwithstanding that this generation had not known the imposition of a direct tax, an excise, or internal duties by the federal government. In January, 1862, Congress passed a joint resolution declaring their purpose of raising from taxation and from the tariff on imports at least $150,000,000.[1] Thus there was a substantial agreement that any financial plan adopted must involve a material increase of taxation; accordingly a sub-committee of the ways and means went to work on a bill which should carry out the sentiment of Congress. To frame a tax-bill and get it through the House and the Senate would, however, require considerable time; when enacted, its operation would bring money into the Treasury but slowly. To devise immediate means to carry on the war was the province of another sub-committee of three, of which Spaulding, a bank president of Buffalo, was chairman. He went diligently to work as soon as the secretary's report was made. In a private letter of January 8, 1862, he stated the problem: " We must have at least $100,000,000 during the next three months, or the government must stop payment."[2] The question was, How should that sum be raised? Moreover, as Thaddeus Stevens, the chairman of the ways and means committee, said,[3] the expenses of the government were $2,000,000 a day; the banks had broken down under the last loan to the Treasury and suspended specie payments, and they would not receive the Treasury demand notes; the secretary had attempted to pay creditors in the 7.30 bonds, but

---

[1] On public sentiment favorable to large taxation see New York *World* and New York *Times*, Dec. 30, 1861; article of Bryant in New York *Evening Post* of Feb. 1, Godwin, vol. ii. p. 164; Hooper, Feb. 3, and Roscoe Conkling, Feb. 4, 1862, in the House of Representatives; letter of Asa Gray, Feb. 20, 1862, Letters, p. 471.

[2] History of the Legal-Tender Paper Money Issued during the Great Rebellion, E. G. Spaulding, p. 18.　　　　　　　　　　[3] Feb. 6.

they at once declined 4 per cent. Spaulding's plan was to issue $100,000,000 of non-interest-bearing Treasury notes, making them receivable for all debts and demands due the United States, and a legal tender in payment of all debts public and private; it also made a legal tender the $50,000,000 of Treasury notes authorized by the act of the previous July. The legal-tender notes were to be exchangeable at par for 6 per cent. twenty-year bonds, the issue of $500,000,000 of which should be authorized. This, in the form of a bill, the ways and means committee by a majority of one adopted, and Spaulding reported it to the House. Although in favor of the national banking scheme, he argued that it could not be adopted soon enough for immediate relief. Samuel Hooper, of Boston, a gentleman of large business experience, who had served on the sub-committee with Spaulding, and earnestly supported his plan, maintained that it was necessary to make the Treasury notes legal tender to render the government financially independent;[1] and Stevens asserted that without this quality the notes would not be taken by the banks or the people, and if forced upon the contractors and soldiers, they must "submit to a heavy shave before they could use them."[2] Spaulding, Hooper, and Stevens agreed that the only other way of providing the immediate means was to sell the bonds of the government on the market for what they would fetch, as had been done in the War of 1812. While money for commercial purposes could be had at 5 per cent., the government could not borrow at 7.30, and large quantities of bonds forced on the market would cause a ruinous discount. Spaulding and Stevens thought that the 6 per cent. bonds would not bring more than sixty cents on the dollar; and "even then," Stevens declared, "it would be found impossible to find payment in coin." Their argument was summed up in the few words in which they both stated it: "This bill is a measure of necessity, not of choice."

---

[1] House, Feb. 3.   [2] Ibid., Feb. 6.

The opponents of the section making the treasury demand notes legal tender had the best of the argument. It is, declared Justin S. Morrill, of Vermont, "a measure not blessed by one sound precedent, and damned by all;" you will "vastly increase the cost of carrying on the war" by the inflation of the currency; and you are exercising "an inferential or doubtful power" of the Constitution. Roscoe Conkling said that on the plea of necessity we were "invited to leave the trodden paths of safety, and seek new methods of 'coining false moneys from that crucible called debt';" he refuted the argument of necessity; he argued that the bill was "of very doubtful constitutionality," and that its moral imperfections were equally serious; "it will," he averred, "proclaim throughout the country a saturnalia of fraud, a carnival for rogues."[1]

After the Legal-tender bill had been reported, delegates from the banks of New York, Philadelphia, and Boston went to Washington to oppose its passage. They, with members of the boards of trade of several cities, met, January 11, the Secretary of the Treasury and several members of the ways and means committee of the House and of the committee of finance of the Senate. James Gallatin, a son of the great minister of finance, submitted a plan on the part of the banks, which was not satisfactory to the congressmen and senators present.[2] Four days later, however, Chase and the bank delegates agreed upon a scheme[3] which avoided making the Treasury notes a legal tender, and which comprised the passage by Congress, as soon as possible, of a National Banking act. The delegates then went home to urge the plan upon the bankers of their cities. January 20 the Boston delegate telegraphed that the Boston banks would not assent to the proposed arrangement; after which the Secretary of the Treasury no longer objected to the legal-tender

---

[1] House, Feb. 4.

[2] For the plan and objections see Spaulding, pp. 20, 21 ; also Gallatin's letter to Fessenden, printed in New York *Tribune*, Dec. 31, 1861.

[3] See Spaulding, p. 21 ; Warden, p. 406.

clause. January 22 he wrote a letter to Spaulding, expressing
his regret that the course proposed should be deemed necessary.[1] This being regarded as non-committal, the ways and
means committee formally asked his opinion as to the propriety and necessity of the immediate passage of the bill by
Congress. To this he replied January 29: "It is not unknown to the committee that I have felt, nor do I wish to
conceal that I now feel, a great aversion to making anything
but coin a legal tender in payment of debts. It has been my
anxious wish to avoid the necessity of such legislation. It is,
however, at present impossible, in consequence of the large
expenditures entailed by the war and the suspension of the
banks, to procure sufficient coin for disbursements; and it has,
therefore, become indispensably necessary that we should resort to the issue of United States notes. The making them a
legal tender might, however, still be avoided if the willingness
manifested by the people generally, by railroad companies,
and by many of the banking institutions to receive them and
pay them as money in all transactions were absolutely or practically universal; but, unfortunately, there are some persons
and some institutions which refuse to receive and pay them,
and whose action tends not merely to the unnecessary depreciation of the notes, but to establish discriminations in business against those who, in this matter, give a cordial support
to the government, and in favor of those who do not. Such
discriminations should, if possible, be prevented; and the provision making the notes a legal tender, in a great measure at
least, prevents it, by putting all citizens, in this respect, on the
same level, both of rights and duties."[2] This letter was read
in the House by Spaulding, and, the secretary's authority
being great, contributed much to the passage of the bill.

The Legal-tender act was passed by Congress for the reason that its supporters honestly believed the alternative to
be a wasteful and even ruinous method of conducting the
war. But they were mistaken. From the recommenda-

---

[1] Spaulding, p. 27.   [2] *Congressional Globe*, p. 618.

tions of the bankers and business men, and from their conferences with the Secretary of the Treasury and the senators and representatives, there was evolved a plan which
was introduced into the House by Morrill, as the report of
the minority of the ways and means committee, and which
would apparently have provided for the pressing exigency.
Recognizing that the government could not borrow for less
than 7.30 per cent., Morrill proposed to have $200,000,000 of
the $500,000,000 bonds issued at that rate, and, in addition,
$100,000,000 of Treasury notes bearing interest at 3.65 per
cent., payable in two years; these notes should be receivable for all debts and demands due the United States except
duties on imports, should be paid out for the government
salaries and supplies, and should be exchangeable at par for
the 7.30 bonds; they were not to be made a legal tender.[1]
This plan, if adopted, would probably have been followed
by the passage of a national banking act, instead of defer-
ring it, as was actually the case, to the next session of this
Congress.   In the light of the plain principles of finance,
and the results which followed our financial legislation, it
seems clear that making the Treasury notes a legal tender
was not a measure of economy, as it is conceded that our
war was one of the most expensive ever waged.   Spaulding
and Stevens were perturbed at the possibility of the government stock selling at sixty cents on the dollar, but in a
little more than two years they saw Europe buy our 6 per
cent. bonds at about thirty-five cents.[2]   Whether Morrill's
plan would have been less extravagant than Spaulding's
depended on the avoidance of continued issues of Treasury
notes, which was the result of the actual legislation, and on
the conduct of the war according to business principles, by

---

[1] For full text of this substitute see *Congressional Globe*, p. 693.   When
voted on, Feb. 6, it was slightly different from Morrill's statement of it,
Feb. 4, ibid., p. 632.

[2] Francis A. Walker and Henry Adams, Adams's Historical Essays, p.
301 ; see the discussion of the financial management of the war in Henry
C. Adams's Public Debts, p. 127 *et seq.*

selling the bonds on the market for what they would fetch. The choice lay between a forced loan without interest, as was the Legal-tender act,[1] or a voluntary loan from bonds and from interest-bearing Treasury notes not made a legal tender. It is an illusion to suppose that a government can in the long-run borrow on better terms by a forced than by a voluntary loan. There can be no doubt that if the committee of ways and means and Chase had set themselves resolutely to work to carry on the war on a policy of adequate taxation and voluntary loans, they would have succeeded as well as they did, and at a smaller cost than on the plan actually put in force. When the main factors of financial success were the resources and good-will of an energetic and fairly wealthy people, in conjunction with military achievements, it is ridiculous to maintain that the only feasible financial scheme was one at war with plain economic truths. If we arrive, then, at the conclusion—which it seems to me a careful consideration of all the facts must bring us to—that the Legal-tender act was neither necessary nor economical, what a pernicious piece of legislation it turned out to be![2] It was grossly unjust, in that it made pre-existing

---

[1] On legal-tender notes being a forced loan, see Henry C. Adams's Public Debts, pp. 144–46. He says: " When a government decides in favor of forced circulation, it takes a step leading inevitably to the inflation of general prices, and to the depreciation of its own obligations of every sort. . . . Voluntary loans must be accepted as the only permanent and satisfactory foundation of credit transactions."

Baron von Hock, the Austrian financier, in his valuable Die Finanzen und die Finanzgeschichte der Vereinigten Staaten (Stuttgart, 1867), regards the issue of paper money during the war as unavoidable (pp. 471–72). The issue of paper money, he says, is conceded to be justifiable when a State is involved in a struggle for its own existence after all resources as those of taxation and credit are exhausted; but it is, he declares, the most expensive and detrimental of all means of raising revenue (pp. 455–56). His work gives a detailed account of the actual processes of the financial administration of the war. See, also, London Economist, Jan. 18, May 17, June 28, 1862 ; Professor F. W. Taussig, ch. xii. vol. ii., of The United States of America, edited by N. S. Shaler (Appleton, 1894) ; Hugh McCulloch, Men and Measures of Half a Century, p. 175.

[2] Bryant, in an article in the Evening Post of Feb. 14, entitled " A Deluge

debts payable in a currency of less value than that in which
they had been contracted, and it debauched the public mind
by inculcating, on high authority, the notion that all requisite value could be given to money by decree.   Eight years
later, Chief Justice Chase said from his high seat that the
Legal-tender act violated justice, that it was inconsistent
with the spirit of the Constitution, and that it was prohibited by the Constitution.[1]   Francis A. Walker and Henry
Adams wrote shortly afterwards: " The law of legal tender
was an attempt by artificial legislation to make something
true which was false." [2]

We may regret that the good law, the good business
sense, and the correct economic principles which Chief Justice Chase enounced in his two opinions on the Legal-tender
act did not prevail with him in January and February,
1862.   Had Secretary Chase followed out his first impres-

---

at Hand," wrote, " The dikes of Holland were once pierced by a water-rat,
and, the opening made by the animal rapidly enlarging, the ocean rushed
in, sweeping away its barriers, and the land was laid under water," and he
suggested that the following lines be prefixed to the bill:

> "I hear a lion in the lobby roar ;
> Say, Mr. Speaker, shall we shut the door ?
> Or shall we rather let the lion in,
> And try if we can turn him out again ?"

[1] 8 Wallace, pp. 624, 625.

[2] *North American Review*, April, 1870; Henry Adams's Historical Essays,
p. 307.   This essay, entitled "The Legal Tender Act," is an interesting and
valuable historical review of this legislation, considered in the light of
economic truths.   In connection with it the article "The Bank of England Restriction," by Adams, in the same volume, is worthy of attention.
The experience of England in the long French wars from 1793 to 1815 was
appealed to by both sides in the debates in Congress.   Reasoning from
English experience, as shown in Adams's thorough and fair historical study,
it seems to me clear that the Morrill plan, with the necessary consequences,
would have proved more economical than the Spaulding scheme, for it is
probable it would have kept our paper money nearer to a specie basis, and
had it done so, it is obvious, the expense of the war would not have been
so great.   See a table calculated by Henry C. Adams, showing the gold
value of Treasury receipts from public obligations of all sorts during the
war, Public Debts, p. 131.

sion and vigorously opposed it, thus making himself a rallying-point for the Republican opponents, he could undoubtedly have defeated it, for he had much influence and a large
following.   When George Bancroft wrote him, "I am one
of those who repose confidence in your superior ability and
inflexible integrity,"[1] the historian spoke for thousands of
intelligent men, some of whom grieved sorely at Chase's
action.   "Let me say plainly," wrote William Cullen Bryant to Sumner, "Mr. Chase is wrecking himself in the course
he is steering, and I feel some solicitude that you should
not drive upon the same rock."[2]   While it is proper that
the economist should condemn the Secretary of the Treasury for his departure from the sound principles which he
understood, it is right that the historian should remember
that it is not so easy to arrive at a correct judgment in the
harassing office of a finance minister who has a bankrupt
treasury and large pressing obligations, as it is in the cool
seclusion of the study.   Nor must it be forgotten that the
business men and bankers of the country differed from one
another, and that their individual opinions fluctuated from
day to day.[3]

---

[1] Letter of Dec. 24, 1861, Chase Papers, MS.

[2] Letter of Feb. 13, Pierce-Sumner Papers, MS.

[3] Fessenden said in the Senate, Feb. 12 ? "I declare here to-day that in
the whole number of learned financial men that I have consulted, I never
have found any two of them who agree ; and, therefore, it is hardly worth
while for us to plead any very remarkable degree of ignorance when nobody is competent to instruct us ; and yet such is the fact.   I can state to
you, Mr. President, that on one day I was advised very strongly by a leading financial man at all events to oppose this legal-tender clause ; he exclaimed against it with all the bitterness in the world.   On the very same
day I received a note from a friend of his, telling me that we could not get
along without it.   I showed it to him, and he expressed his utter surprise.
He went home, and next day telegraphed to me that he had changed his
mind, and now thought it was absolutely necessary; and his friend who
wrote to me wrote again that he had changed his [laughter], and they
were two of the most eminent financial men in the country."—*Congressional Globe*, p. 766.   Blaine (Twenty Years of Congress, vol. i. p. 423) states
that these gentlemen were James Gallatin and Morris Ketchum of New

Chase explains his inconsistency in a frank manner,[1]
which excuses, but does not fully justify, his action as Secre-

York city. Ketchum had taken great interest in the subject, and, as a
letter of James C. Welling to Chase of Dec. 25, 1861, in the Chase Papers
discloses, had written two communications to the *National Intelligencer*,
discussing the new paper currency proposed by the secretary in his report.
William Gray, a representative of Boston manufacturers, business men,
and society, wrote Sumner, Jan. 20 : ''The truth is, quackery is the order
of the day ; self-interest is working with immense power at Washington.
Unpaid creditors of government, speculators, debtors, and many creditors
who believe their debtors will be more able to pay in paper depreciated
than in coin or specie equivalent,all urge disastrous measures. . . . There
is no safety but in sound principles ; events are too momentous for novel
experiments ; stand on the old landmarks of finance and we shall be safe."
Amos A. Lawrence wrote Sumner, Feb. 6 : '' There is great anxiety and
considerable distress here among those who have had contracts with government, owing to the large amount long since due and unpaid. On this account it would be impossible for government at this time to purchase in
this vicinity at a fair rate. When payment shall be made in the new issue
of Treasury notes, it is absolutely necessary that these notes shall be a
legal tender, however objectionable it may be in principle." C. H. Dalton,
a representative business man, wrote, Feb. 6, that half a dozen of the
leading houses of Boston engaged in domestic manufactures and representing transactions amounting to thirty-five to forty millions annually, had
united, in a letter to Representative Thomas, who opposed Spaulding's
bill, affirming that "the legal-tender clause is a sad but necessary expedient." Edward Atkinson wrote, Feb. 7 : ''In the accompanying letter I
state my belief in the legal - tender clause as a sad necessity. By this I
mean that I fear it must pass. I do not believe in the real necessity. You
cannot thus force a loan upon the people without depreciation. Nothing
but confidence will give the government its money, and taxes, direct, immediate, and large, will thus give confidence; then small and large notes
will pass freely, without the legal-tender clause." George Morey, a representative politician, wrote, Feb. 8 : '' It is considered essential to our salvation that this bill should go promptly through the Senate. I have taken
pains to converse with our most sagacious capitalists, bank men, and merchants, and they say that if this bill lags, and is not put through *straight*, we
are doomed." These letters are from Boston, Pierce-Sumner Papers, MS.
William M. Evarts wrote Weed, Feb. 2: '' Our finances are in disorder and the
administration in disgrace." A. T. Stewart wrote Weed, Feb. 4, that ''the
finances of the government [are] now wretchedly managed."—Life of Weed,
vol. ii. pp. 411, 412. Spaulding, in his book, prints many private letters to
him, largely from bankers, favoring the legal-tender provision, and (p. 18)
gives the opinion of the New York city press.

[1] 8 Wallace, 625; 12 Wallace, 575.

tary of the Treasury. He was not a trained financier, but he had a large, assimilating mind, and was able to learn the lessons of his new business fast.[1] Having arrived at the conviction that prompt and decided action was imperatively necessary, and that the only measure which could speedily get through Congress was the bill of the ways and means committee, he gave it an earnest support. "Mr. Seward said to me on yesterday," he wrote Spaulding, February 3, "that you observed to him that my hesitation in coming up to the legal - tender proposition embarrassed you, and I am very sorry to observe it, for my anxious wish is to support you in all respects. It is true that I came with reluctance to the conclusion that the legal-tender clause is a necessity, but I came to it decidedly and I support it earnestly. I do not hesitate when I have made up my mind, however much regret I may feel over the necessity of the conclusion to which I have come. . . . Immediate action is of great importance. The Treasury is nearly empty. I have been obliged to draw for the last instalment of the November loan; so soon as it is paid I fear the banks generally will refuse to receive the United States notes. You will see the necessity of urging the bill through without more delay."[2]

February 6 the Legal-tender act passed the House by a vote of 93 to 59. Most of the Democrats voted nay, but the Republicans who divided from the majority of their party were of the best and ablest members of the body.[3] The bill went to the Senate. Fessenden and Collamer opposed the legal - tender clause. Sumner[4] and Sherman ad-

---

[1] See Hugh McCulloch, Men and Measures of Half a Century, p. 185.

[2] Spaulding, p. 59; part of this letter was read in the House by Spaulding, Feb. 3; see, also, Chase's letter of Feb. 5, ibid., p. 71; also his letter to Bryant of Feb. 4, Godwin, vol. ii. p. 165.

[3] The nays were 29 Democrats, 13 Unionists, and 17 Republicans; 5 Democrats voted yea.

[4] W. C. Bryant wrote Sumner confidentially, Feb. 13: "I hope you do not mean to vote for the legal-tender clause in the Treasury-note bill, nor for the bill with that clause in it. It is clear to me that the framers

vocated it on the ground of necessity, and they both laid great stress on the point that it had the support of the Secretary of the Treasury. Without that, indeed, it would not have received the assent of the Senate. The crucial vote was on the motion to strike out the legal-tender clause, which was lost by 22 nays to 17 yeas.[1] The bill, with several amendments, then easily passed the Senate, but before it became a law it had to go to a committee of conference. The important amendment to the House bill there agreed to was that the $500,000,000 of bonds were made 5-20's, and the interest on them was required to be paid in coin. This was to be procured by exacting the payment of the duties on imports in the same currency.

President Lincoln approved the bill February 25, but before this time his hand does not appear in this legislation. His private secretaries write that the affairs of the Treasury engaged his attention less than those of some other departments.[2]

The Confederate States never made their treasury notes a legal tender. The policy began to be seriously advocated early in 1862, the argument of necessity being brought into service; it came up for consideration by the Confederate congress from time to time during two years, but the belief that such an act would be unconstitutional — the provisions of the Federal and Confederate constitutions relating to the ques-

---

of the Constitution never meant to confer upon the federal government the right of issuing Treasury notes at all, and the reason was that they meant to tie its hands from making them a legal tender. . . . The idea of a necessity for the measure is the shallowest of delusions. My friend Mr. John D. Van Buren, now at Washington in consultation with the ways and means committee on the taxation question—a better theoretical and practical political economist than any bank cashier or president in the country — can give you in ten minutes a scheme which will be sure to revive the credit of the country, and furnish the means of carrying on the war."—Pierce-Sumner Papers, MS.

[1] Eight Republicans, 7 Democrats, 2 Unionists made up the affirmative vote; 2 Democrats voted in the negative.

[2] Nicolay and Hay, vol. vi. p. 247.

tion were substantially the same — stood mainly in the way of its adoption.[1]

The Secretary of War, in his report to the President of December 1, estimated the strength of the army at 660,971 men; he had no doubt that a million troops might have been raised had not the number been restricted by Congress. Under instructions from the executive he had sent a special agent to Europe to purchase $2,000,000 worth of arms. He spoke highly of McClellan, who by energy and ability in the organization of the army had justly won "the confidence and applause of the troops and of the nation." The most important part of this report as originally written was omitted in the final revision. The secretary made the suggestion, in terms which could be construed to recommend it strongly, that the slaves should be armed, and when employed as soldiers should be freed. Without submission to Lincoln, the report as thus drawn had been mailed to the postmasters of the chief cities, with instructions to hand it to the press as soon as the President's message was read in Congress. When Lincoln ascertained this, he insisted that the copies which had been sent out should be recalled by telegraph, and that the report should be modified to accord with his own policy in regard to slavery.[2]

The astounding portion of Cameron's report was his reference "with great gratification . . . to the economical administration of affairs displayed in the various branches of the service." In many ways, owing to the executive ability of Thomas A. Scott, assistant secretary, and to the capacity and honesty of Montgomery Meigs, Quartermaster-General, the management of the War Department had been efficient and honest; but where the hand of its chief could be traced, a line of peculation followed. Instead of contracts, which mounted up to enormous sums, being awarded with an eye

---

[1] See J. C. Schwab, *Political Science Quarterly*, March, 1892; Richmond *Dispatch*, April 11; Charleston *Mercury*, April 10.

[2] Nicolay and Hay, vol. v. p. 125; *Congressional Globe*, 2d Sess. 37th Cong.

single to the advantage of the government, they were, in many cases, given out to Cameron's political followers and henchmen as a reward for past services or in anticipation of future work.   To cite the report of the committee on government contracts would profit us little, for it does not in set terms express the logical deductions which may be drawn from it; to analyze its testimony and point out special instances of apparent fraud would be tedious and might be inconclusive; but I venture the statement that no man of judgment can go over that report and that testimony, and check them by the opinions of honest and well-informed men of the day, without arriving at the conviction that the conduct of the Secretary of War was not that of a correct business man.   There is no evidence of which I am aware that any of the money which was made out of the government by exorbitant prices, commissions, and the delivery of inferior goods found its way into Cameron's pocket.   He had an ample fortune when he received the portfolio of the War Department,[1] and that he was rich when he gave it up cannot be urged against him, but the suspicion existed at the time that he had not been clear in his great office. From the nature of the case it is impossible for me to mention all the evidence that has led me to these conclusions; but it is such that I could have no hesitation, although I have had regret, in expressing them.   Some of the evidence to the extravagance and the worse than extravagance in the War Department I shall, however, adduce.   "The truth is," said Senator Grimes to Fessenden, in a letter from Washington, November 13, 1861, "we are going to destruction as fast as imbecility, corruption, and the wheels of time can carry us;" further on he referred to "the flood of corruption that is sweeping over the land and perverting the moral sense of the people.   The army is in most inextricable confusion, and is every day becoming worse and worse."[2]

---

[1] New York *Tribune*, Nov. 5, 1861.

[2] Life of Grimes, Salter, p. 156.

"The want of success of our armies," Chase wrote Cameron, November 27, 1861, "and the difficulties of our financial operations, have not been in consequence of a want or excess of men, but for want of systematic administration. If the lack of economy and the absence of accountability are allowed to prevail in the future as in the past, bankruptcy and the success of the rebellion will be necessary consequences."[1] "We are thinking of a public meeting in favor of rigid economy in the public expenditures," wrote George Bancroft to Chase, from New York, December 24, 1861; "there is no use in disguising the consequences of our present extravagance."[2] Nesmith, a Democrat from Oregon, and Hale declared in the open Senate that men high in office had been guilty of corruption;[3] and Powell, a Democrat of Kentucky, put the charge more precisely. "If the statements contained in the report of the committee of investigation of the other House on government contracts are true," he said, "the head of the War Department and the head of the Navy Department must be written down in public opinion as possessed of a very great degree of stupidity or knavery. From one or the other they cannot escape."[4] While it is true that one instance unearthed by the House committee reflected as severely on the Secretary of the Navy[5] as anything it brought to light against the Secretary of War, several senators were at once ready to declare their unbounded confidence in the honesty of Welles, but none of them during this debate spoke for Cameron.[6] The House

---

[1] Schuckers, p. 280.   [2] Chase Papers, MS.

[3] Jan. 7, 1862, *Congressional Globe.* p. 203.

[4] Ibid., p. 207. For other references to corruption in high places, see Conkling, pp. 35, 633, Dawes, pp. 298, 1382, 1840, Morrill, p. 632, Van Wyck, p. 711.

[5] See Report of Committee, pp. 21, 24, 31, 34; Trollope's North America, vol. ii. p. 148.

[6] Wilson, p. 205, Hale and Dixon, p. 246, *Congressional Globe.* In Sumner's private correspondence I find a letter from Montgomery Blair of Jan. 14, 1862, testifying to Welles's invariable honesty. A good many people were thinking as A. B. Ely expressed it in a private letter to Sumner of

of Representatives censured Cameron by a vote of 79 to 45, and refused to censure Welles by 72 nays to 45 yeas.[1]

January 11 the President sent Cameron a curt dismissal from the position of Secretary of War, and nominated him as Minister to Russia.[2] It was given out at the time, and has since been asserted on authority, that Lincoln removed him from office for the reason that the position he had taken in his report respecting the arming of the slaves and the manner of his taking it had destroyed their harmonious relations.[3] This seems to me, however, an inadequate explanation. Cameron's offence in this matter had not been as grave as that of Frémont, yet the President did not remove Frémont on account of his proclamation. The suppressed part of Cameron's report had been published in the newspapers and referred to in the House of Representatives, and the policy therein advocated met with favor from the radical anti-slavery people, who were now disposed to sym-

---

Jan. 14: "Cameron's report which contained the suppressed part about contrabands was got up by him and put out by him not because he cared anything about the slaves, but merely as a tub to the popular whale, so as to turn away inquiry from the corruptions of his department." Ely added, "Thad Stevens said Cameron would add a million to his fortune. I guess he has done it."—Pierce-Sumner Papers, MS.

[1] April 30, *Congressional Globe*, p. 1888.

[2] Nicolay and Hay, vol. v. p. 128; Chase's Diary, entry of Jan. 12, Field's Memories, p. 268; McClure's Lincoln, p. 150.

[3] This was the explanation given by the New York *Times*, *World* of Jan. 14, and *Herald* of Jan. 15; Trollope's North America, vol. ii. p. 152. The New York *Tribune* of Jan. 14, however, said: "The retirement of General Cameron will be attributed by some to his frankly expressed views on the contraband question, but (we are confident) incorrectly. . . . The truth is that General Cameron has had very unprofitable friends. Himself patriotic and devoted to the heart's core, he has been surrounded and pressed upon by troops of noisy well-wishers who would have scorned the idea of selling their God for thirty pieces of silver so long as there was the faintest hope of making it forty. These have bored him into signing contracts by which they have made enormous profits at his expense as well as the country's." The *Evening Post* of Jan. 14 took a similar view, and acquitted "Cameron of any participation in these robberies."

[4] *Congressional Globe*, p. 79.

pathize with him, as they had previously done with Frémont. John Bigelow across the sea detected this and asked
Sumner, "Are Cameron and Frémont to be canonized as
martyrs?"[1] Such a temper aided to cloud the real truth in
regard to this change in the cabinet. But all the circumstances seem to point to the conclusion that popular sentiment in Congress and in the country demanded the removal
of Cameron on account of a distrust of his efficiency and
his honesty, and that the President recognized it as an
opinion to which he must yield, enforced as it probably
was by his own conviction that the War Department had
been badly administered.[2]

Justice to Cameron demands mention of the special message of the President to Congress, in which he exculpated
Cameron from one count in the resolution of censure by
the House.[3] Chase also defended him. December 25, 1861,
he wrote to Halstead: "You are unjust to Cameron, and I
am bound as a man of honor to say so. I have seen him
closely as most men here, and I am sure he has acted hon-
orably and faithfully and patriotically. . . . He challenges
investigation of all his transactions on the score of corruption, and may do so, I believe, with entire safety."[4] Sumner moved the confirmation of Cameron as Minister to Russia without the customary reference, and obviously did not
believe the charges affecting his official integrity.[5]

---

[1] Jan. 30, Pierce-Sumner Papers, MS.

[2] Field in his Memories, p. 266, relates a conversation between Lincoln
and Seward which, if we could always rely on recollections, would directly substantiate this. I prefer, however, to rest my case on the natural
inference from all the contemporaneous evidence concerning the matter.

[3] May 26, *Congressional Globe*, p. 2383. The conventional correspondence between Lincoln and Cameron was not published until Feb. 10. It
was then dated back to Jan. 11. Read in connection with the real facts in
the case it would sustain the view I have taken in the text had not Lincoln
in his letter expressed his confidence in Cameron's "ability, patriotism,
and fidelity to public trust."—New York *Evening Post*, Feb. 10.

[4] Schuckers, p. 281.

[5] Pierce's Sumner, vol. iv. p. 63. Several members of the House of
Representatives also spoke in his favor.

The President appointed Edwin M. Stanton Secretary of War. Stanton, in his private correspondence of the summer of 1861, had expressed himself freely touching "the painful imbecility of Lincoln" and the impotence of his administration,[1] and as he was neither politic nor reserved, he had undoubtedly been equally free with his comments in conversation with his friends and acquaintances in Washington, where he was then living. If Lincoln cared to listen to Washington gossip he might have heard enough of this sort, but if any of these stories came to him when he began to consider the appointment of Stanton, they did not weigh with him a feather in making up his mind that from location, previous party association, and fitness this Democratic lawyer from Pennsylvania was the man for the place. The appointment was acceptable to Seward and Chase,[2] to Congress and to the country, for Stanton had gained the confidence of all by his sturdy patriotism when a member of Buchanan's cabinet.

The inaction of the Army of the Potomac, due at first to McClellan's incompetence, and afterwards to his illness during the fine weather and smooth roads of December and the first half of January,[3] was a deep disappointment to the people. The senators and representatives were full of it. "We are in a condition now where we must stir ourselves on account of the expense," said Senator Wade to General McDowell, December 26, 1861. "It is awful; and we are endeavoring to see if there is any way in God's world to get rid of the capital besieged, while Europe is looking down upon us as almost a conquered people."[4] "It is no wonder," declared Lovejoy in the House, January 6,

---

[1] Life of Dix, vol. ii. p. 19; *North American Review*, Nov., 1879, p. 482; also McClure's Lincoln.

[2] Chase's Diary, entry Jan. 12, 1862; letter to Zinn, Jan. 16, Schuckers, p. 363.

[3] Conkling in the House, Feb. 4, *Congressional Globe*, p. 634.

[4] Report of the Committee on the Conduct of the War, part i. p. 140.

1862, "that the people are growing impatient; it is no wonder that that impatience is becoming earnest in many portions of the country, and is almost reaching a point beyond that of passive emotion. The whole nation is waiting for the army to move forward. They have furnished the men and the money, and why does not the army move?"[1] Writing from the office of the *Evening Post*, New York, Parke Godwin asked Sumner, "what the awful and disastrous inaction of our military men means? People here are rapidly becoming disgusted," he added, "even the most patient are losing heart; and all see that unless some grand blows are struck the war is gone."[2] "When," asked John Bigelow, despairingly, from over the sea, "are we to stop hearing of the great things our army and our navy and our young Napoleon are *going to do*, and to begin to hear of what they *have done?*"[3] Anthony Trollope read public opinion correctly when he concluded that "belief in McClellan seemed to be slipping away."[4] Chase had lost confidence in the general of the army.[5] Lincoln stood by McClellan, but he was convinced that Seward's diplomacy, Chase's finance, and his own hold on the people could be sustained only by military victories, or at all events by an

---

[1] *Congressional Globe*, p. 194.

[2] Letter of Jan. 10, Pierce-Sumner Papers, MS.

[3] To Sumner from Paris, Jan. 30, ibid. Governor Morgan wrote Weed, Jan. 11: "There is a very strong disposition to complain of the inactivity of our generals, as well as the enormous expense of the army."—Life of Weed, vol. ii. p. 413; see remarks of Hale in the Senate, Dec. 16, 1861, *Congressional Globe*, p. 93; Wilson, Jan. 7, ibid., p. 205; Morrill and Conking in the House, Feb. 4, ibid., pp. 632, 634.

[4] North America, vol. ii. p. 27. Gurowski's Diary represents the development of a certain phase of sentiment. In Sept. he wrote: "The country is — to use an Americanism — in a pretty fix, if this McClellan turns out to be a mistake." In Dec. he set down: "The Congress appointed a war-investigating committee, Senator Wade at the head. There is hope that the committee will quickly find out what a terrible mistake this McClellan is, and warn the nation of him. But Lincoln, Seward, and the Blairs will not give up their idol."

[5] Letter of Jan. 5, Warden, p. 397.

earnest effort to win them.   January 10 he called a council at the White House of Generals McDowell and Franklin, Seward, Chase, and the assistant Secretary of War;
McClellan, not having yet recovered fully from his illness,
was not present.   The President said: "I am in great distress.   If something is not done soon, the bottom will be
out of the whole affair ; and if General McClellan does not
want to use the army I would like to *borrow* it, provided I
could see how it could be made to do something.   What
can be done with the army soon?" he asked McDowell.
The general replied that it was feasible to attack the
enemy at Centreville and Manassas, and he verbally out-
lined a plan of operation; this, further developed in writing, he read the next evening to the council.   His conclusion as then stated was: "It seems to me the army should
be ready to move in all of next week."   Monday, January
13, McClellan met at the White House these gentlemen and
also Montgomery Blair and General Meigs.   The President
explained how and why the advice of the two generals had
been demanded, and requested McDowell again to expose
his plan.   This he did, ending with a natural apology to
his superior officer for his action, which McClellan received
coldly.   The President then asked what and when anything could be done?   McClellan replied that "the case
was so clear a blind man could see it," and then, discussing
matters of detail, made difficulties and befogged the issue.
Chase, undoubtedly with impatience, put the direct question
to the general what he intended doing with his army, and
when he intended doing it?   A long silence ensued.   Mc-
Clellan broke it at last, saying that it was his intention to
have the general operations of the armies begin by a movement of Buell in Kentucky.   He paused; then resuming
speech said: "I am very unwilling to develop my plans, for
I believe that in military matters the fewer persons to
whom they are known the better.   I will tell them if *ordered* to do so."   The President asked: "Do you count upon
any particular time?   I do not ask what that time is, but

have you in your own mind any particular time fixed when a movement can be commenced?" McClellan replied, "I have." "Then," rejoined the President, "I will adjourn this meeting." [1]

A fortnight passed away, and still the story ran, "All quiet on the Potomac." January 27 the President issued his "General War Order Number 1;" this "ordered that the 22d of February, 1862, be the day for a general movement of the land and naval forces of the United States against the insurgent forces." He followed this up with his "Special War Order Number 1;" this directed "that all the disposable force of the Army of the Potomac . . . be formed into an expedition for the immediate object of seizing . . . Manassas Junction." [2]

Meanwhile General George H. Thomas defeated a superior force of Confederates at Mill Spring, Kentucky.[3] A little later General Burnside, in co-operation with Commodore Goldsborough, took Roanoke Island, North Carolina.[4] Eclipsing far, however, every success on the federal side, and in its importance and influence matching the Confederate victory of Bull Run, was an achievement of General Grant in Tennessee.

In the West the Confederate line of defence was from Columbus, on the Mississippi River, to Bowling Green. Both of these places were in Kentucky : the first was called a "Gibraltar," the second the "Manassas of the West." Two other important points on this line in the State of Tennessee were Fort Henry, which defended the Tennessee River, and Fort Donelson, which commanded the Cumberland, the two rivers here being but eleven miles apart. If these forts were capt-

---

[1] In this narrative I have faithfully followed McDowell's memorandum, which he gave to Raymond in the spring of 1864. Raymond submitted it to Lincoln, who substantially confirmed the account except in one unimportant particular, Raymond's Lincoln, p. 772. McClellan gives an account of the conversation of Jan. 13, Own Story, p. 156; see also Swinton's Army of the Potomac, p. 79.

[2] Official Records, vol. v. p. 41.   [3] Jan. 19.   [4] Feb. 7.

ured, two important gateways would be open to the heart of the Confederacy. The troops in this field of operation were under the command of Albert Sidney Johnston, then esteemed the ablest general of the South. Halleck, with headquarters at St. Louis, had control of the Union forces in this department; Grant, under him, was at Cairo. The notion that this line ought to be broken occurred to several federal generals; that it entered into the minds of Grant and Flag-officer Foote is of the highest moment, for by their position and character they were fit men to head an expedition to break it. Acting upon reconnoissances made by General C. F. Smith and Foote, Grant urged Halleck that he be permitted to capture Fort Henry, and in this request for authority he was joined by Foote January 28. January 30 Halleck telegraphed the desired permission. February 1 Grant received by mail the detailed instructions; on the 2d the expedition of iron-clad and wooden gun-boats, and transports carrying the troops, started from Cairo under his and Foote's command. On the 6th he telegraphed Halleck: "Fort Henry is ours. . . . I shall take and destroy Fort Donelson on the 8th." [1] The business had been done by Foote and his iron-clads. Owing to the badness of the roads, the troops were unable to make in time the march which was necessary for co-operation, and most of the Confederate garrison escaped to Donelson.

Albert Sidney Johnston heard with dismay of the fall of Fort Henry. "I determined," he afterwards wrote Davis, "to fight for Nashville at Donelson, and gave the best part of my army to do it, retaining only 14,000 men to cover my front, and giving 16,000 to defend Donelson." [2] On account of the heavy rains, which made the roads impassable for artillery and wagons, Grant was unable to carry out his prophecy to the letter; but having sent the gun-boats and some of the troops around by water, he left Fort Henry on the morn-

---

[1] Official Records, vol. vii. p. 124.
[2] Ibid. p. 259.

ing of February 12 with about 15,000 men, including eight
batteries and part of a regiment of cavalry, and marched
across the country towards Donelson, arriving in front of
the enemy about noon. " That afternoon and the next day,"
writes Grant, " were spent in taking up ground to make the
investment as complete as possible." [1]   On the 13th there
was some fighting, in which the Union troops got the worse
of it.   That night Foote with his gun-boats and reinforcements arrived.   " On the 14th," wrote Grant, " a gallant
attack was made by Flag-officer Foote upon the enemy's
works with the fleet.   The engagement lasted probably an
hour and a half, and bid fair to result favorably to the cause
of the Union, when two unlucky shots disabled two of the
armored boats, so that they were carried back by the current.   The remaining two were very much disabled also,
having received a number of heavy shots about the pilot-
houses and other parts of the vessels.   After these mishaps
I concluded to make the investment of Fort Donelson as
perfect as possible, and partially fortify and await repairs to
the gun-boats." [2]   Foote had been wounded.   Discouragement and discomfort were supreme in the Union ranks that
night.   When the soldiers quitted Fort Henry the weather
was springlike and warm ; many of them had left behind
their blankets and overcoats.   Now a storm of sleet and
snow prevailed.   They had no tents, they were so near the
enemy that they dared not light their fires, and their sufferings during that cold and pitiless night were intense.

The Confederate generals were Floyd—Buchanan's Secretary of War—Pillow, and Buckner.   They and their men
had been cast down by the fall of Fort Henry, but their
spirits had risen with the repulse of the gun-boats, which had
not cost them the injury of a battery or the death of a man.
They saw, however, the arrival of the federal reinforcements
with concern.   That evening they held a council of war,

---

[1] Personal Memoirs, p. 298.
[2] Official report, Feb. 16, Official Records, vol. vii. p. 159.

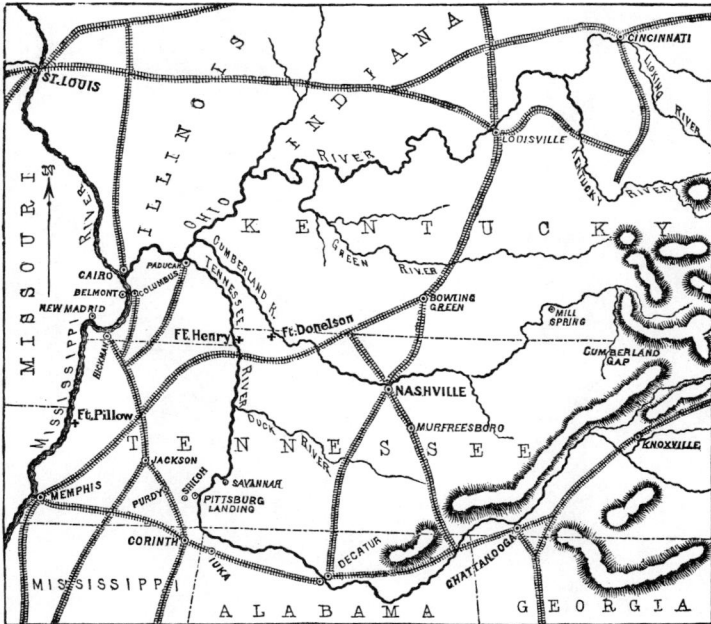

THE CAMPAIGN IN TENNESSEE

and they were of one mind that Grant, with a constantly
increasing force, would soon be able completely to beleaguer
the fort, and that nothing remained for them but to make
an attempt to cut their way through the besiegers and recover the road to Nashville.   They determined to attack
early the next morning.

Reinforcements had increased Grant's army to 27,000.
McClernand's division was on the right, holding the Nash-
ville road; Lew. Wallace's was in the centre, and C. F.
Smith's on the left.

Extending beyond the earthwork of Fort Donelson was
a winding line of intrenchments nearly two miles in length,
defended on the outside at some points with abatis.   These
intrenchments were fully occupied by the Confederates.
At five o'clock on the morning of February 15 Pillow's
division sallied out and fell upon McClernand.   The Union
troops were not surprised, and made a stubborn resistance.
The fight was hot, the snow was red with blood.   McClernand sent to Grant's headquarters and then to Lew. Wallace
for assistance, but Wallace decided that his instructions required him to maintain his actual position.   Meanwhile
Buckner, who commanded the Confederate right wing, had
sent troops to Pillow.   A second message reached Lew. Wallace, saying that McClernand's command was endangered.
So Wallace, having learned that Grant was on a gun-boat
more than five miles away, sent forward his first brigade,
which, however, being imperfectly directed by a guide, did
not reach a position to render effective help.   McClernand,
bearing the brunt of the battle, was outnumbered, his ammunition failed, and he was obliged to fall back.   The fugitives who crowded up the hill in the rear of Lew. Wallace's
line brought "unmistakable signs of disaster. . . . A mounted officer galloped down the road shouting ' We are cut to
pieces.'"[1]   The Confederates, having possession of the Nashville road, had a chance of escape, but they made no attempt

---

[1] Wallace's official report.

to avail themselves of it. They continued to advance on their retreating foes, when Lew. Wallace ordered his third brigade to check their onset; this was done with vigor; the charge of the enemy was repelled.

Early that morning Foote had requested Grant to come to his flag-ship for consultation, he himself being too badly injured to leave the boat. Complying with this request, the commanding general of the Union army was not, therefore, during this attack, on the field where he could direct operations. His conference with Foote terminated, he met, on going ashore, Captain Hillyer, of his staff, "white with fear . . . for the safety of the national troops."[1] The roads, which had been deep with mud, were now frozen hard. Travel on horseback was slow. The fight had been on the Union right of a line three miles long. Grant "was some four or five miles north of our left."[2] He made his way back with the utmost possible speed. "I saw everything favorable for us along the line of our left and centre," he says.[3] On the right, however, there was confusion. The fighting had ceased.

It was the intensest moment in Grant's life. The war had given him an opportunity to amend a broken career; should he fail in this supreme hour, another chance might never come to him. His unfortunate absence during the morning's battle would certainly be misconstrued. Yet he was equal to the emergency. He showed himself a true soldier and a compeller of men. "Wholly unexcited, he saluted and received the salutations of his subordinates," writes Lew. Wallace, who was in conversation with McClernand when Grant rode up. "It cannot be doubted that he saw with painful distinctness the effect of the disaster to his right wing. His face flushed slightly. With a sudden grip he crushed the papers (which looked like telegrams) in his hand. But in an instant these signs of disappointment

---

[1] Grant's Personal Memoirs, p. 305.
[2] Ibid., p. 306.   [3] Ibid.

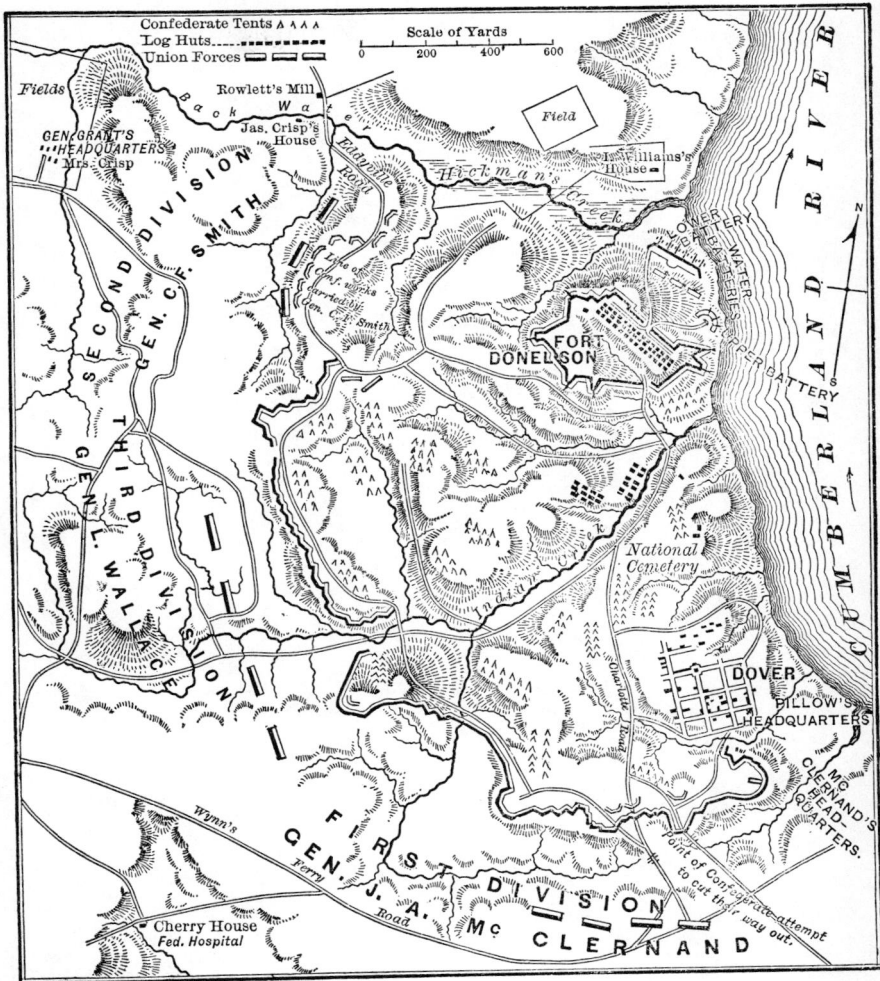

Confederate Tents ∧ ∧ ∧
Log Huts
Union Forces

Scale of Yards
0   200   400   600

Fields

Rowlett's Mill

GEN. GRANT'S
HEADQUARTERS
Mrs. Crisp

Jas. Crisp's
House

SECOND DIVISION
GEN. C. F. SMITH

THIRD DIVISION
GEN. L. WALLACE

Field

Hickman Creek

Jas. Williams's
House

FORT
DONELSON

LOWER WATER BATTERY
UPPER WATER BATTERY

CUMBERLAND RIVER

N
S

National
Cemetery

DOVER

PILLOW'S
HEADQUARTERS

McCLERNAND'S
HEAD-
QUARTERS.

FIRST DIVISION
GEN. J. A. McCLERNAND

Wynn's
Ferry
Road

Cherry House
Fed. Hospital

Point of Confederate attempt
to cut their way out.

MAP OF FORT DONELSON

or hesitation cleared away.   In his ordinary quiet voice he said, addressing himself to both officers, 'Gentlemen, the position on the right must be retaken.'" [1]

Grant tells in an unaffected manner the story of his action.   "I heard some of the men say," he writes, "that the enemy had come out with knapsacks and haversacks filled with rations. . . . I turned to Colonel Webster, of my staff, and said : 'Some of our men are pretty badly demoralized, but the enemy must be more so, for he has attempted to force his way out, but has fallen back; the one who attacks first now will be victorious, and the enemy will have to be in a hurry if he gets ahead of me.'   I determined to make the assault at once on our left. . . . I directed Colonel Webster to ride with me and call out to the men as we passed : 'Fill your cartridge - boxes quick and get into line; the enemy is trying to escape, and he must not be permitted to do so.'   This acted like a charm.   The men only wanted some one to give them a command.   We rode rapidly to Smith's quarters, when I explained the situation to him, and directed him to charge the enemy's works in his front with his whole division, saying at the same time that he would find nothing but a very thin line to contend with.   The general was off in an incredibly short time." [2]

It is seldom that a writer of the remarkable powers of description which Lew. Wallace possesses sees a decisive battle from the stand-point of a general; it is, therefore, fitting that he should tell the story of this glorious charge. "Taking Lauman's brigade," he writes, "General Smith began the advance.   They were under fire instantly.   The guns in the fort joined in with the infantry, who were at the time in the rifle-pits, the great body of the Confederate right wing being with General Buckner.   The defence was greatly favored by the ground, which subjected the assail-

---

[1] Century War Book, vol. i. p. 422.

[2] Grant's Personal Memoirs, vol. i. pp. 307, 308.

ants to a double fire from the beginning of the abatis.
The men have said that 'it looked too thick for a rabbit to
get through.' General Smith, on his horse, took position in
the front and centre of the line. Occasionally he turned in
the saddle to see how the alignment was kept. For the
most part, however, he held his face steadily towards the
enemy. He was, of course, a conspicuous object for the
sharp-shooters in the rifle-pits. The air around him twit-
tered with minie-bullets. Erect as if on review he rode on,
timing the gait of his horse with the movement of his
colors. A soldier said, ' I was nearly scared to death, but I
saw the old man's white mustache over his shoulder, and
went on.'

"On to the abatis the regiments moved without hesitation, leaving a trail of dead and wounded behind. There
the fire seemed to get trebly hot, and there some of the men
halted, whereupon, seeing the hesitation, General Smith put
his cap on the point of his sword, held it aloft, and called
out, 'No flinching now, my lads! Here—this is the way!
Come on!' He picked a path through the jagged limbs of
the trees, holding his cap all the time in sight; and the
effect was magical. The men swarmed in after him, and
got through in the best order they could—not all of them,
alas! On the other side of the obstruction they took the
semblance of re-formation and charged in after their chief,
who found himself then between the two fires. Up the
ascent he rode; up they followed. At the last moment the
keepers of the rifle-pits clambered out and fled. The four
regiments engaged in the feat planted their colors on the
breastwork. Later in the day Buckner came back with
his division, but all his efforts to dislodge Smith were
in vain." [1] That night a large part of Smith's division
bivouacked within the Confederate lines.

After he had commenced his advance Grant ordered a
charge on the enemy's left, which was undertaken by Lew.

[1] Century War Book, vol. i. p. 423.

Wallace. A hill had to be won. When he made known the desperate character of the enterprise to his regiments, the men "answered with cheers and cries of ' Forward, forward!' and I gave the word." [1]   The charge was successful, the hill was gained. The sortie had cost the Confederates about 2000 killed and wounded; the loss of the Federals was somewhat greater. The night closed with the Union troops in possession of the Nashville road. There was no way of escape from Fort Donelson except by the river and by a road submerged from the river's overflow. Grant made arrangements for an assault at daylight the next morning. Hardly a doubt of its success could exist.

Inside the fort there was dismay. An hour after midnight the three generals took counsel together. "I am confident," said Buckner, "that the enemy will attack my lines by light, and I cannot hold them for half an hour." "Why so; why so, general?" Pillow demanded. "Because I can bring into action not over 4000 men, and they demoralized by long and uninterrupted exposure and fighting, while they can bring any number of fresh troops to the attack." Pillow rejoined: "I differ with you. I think you can hold your lines; I think you can, sir." "I know my position," exclaimed Buckner, "and I know that the lines cannot be held with my troops in their present condition." Floyd, who outranked the others, broke in: "Then, gentlemen, a capitulation is all that is left us." This Pillow denied. "I do not think so," he said; "at any rate, we can cut our way out." Buckner replied: "To cut our way out would cost three-fourths of our men, and I do not think any commander has a right to sacrifice three-fourths of his men to save one fourth." To which Floyd replied: "Certainly not. We will have to capitulate; but, gentlemen, I cannot surrender; you know my position with the Federals; [2] it wouldn't do; it

---

[1] Lew. Wallace's official report.

[2] On account of Floyd's operations in Buchanan's cabinet he was regarded generally at the North as a thief and an aggravated traitor. Threats were common that he should hang did he fall into the hands of the Union

wouldn't do." "I will not surrender myself nor the command," declared Pillow, "will die first." "Then I suppose, gentlemen," said Buckner, "the surrender will devolve upon me." Floyd asked Buckner, "General, if you are put in command, will you allow me to take out by the river my brigade?" "Yes, sir," was the reply; "if you move your command before the enemy act upon my communication offering to capitulate." Then Floyd turned to Pillow and said, "I turn the command over, sir." Pillow replied, promptly, "I pass it." This drew from Buckner the remark: "I assume it. Give me pen, ink, and paper, and send for a bugler."[1]

Two small steamers, which arrived at the fort about daybreak, furnished Floyd and about 1500 of his Virginia troops a means of escape. Pillow crossed the river in a skiff. Colonel Forrest took out 500 of his cavalry and a number of men from the infantry and artillery regiments, mounted on the artillery horses, over the road which was submerged by the overflow of the Cumberland.

Early Sunday morning, February 16, Buckner sent the Union general a letter, which brought forth the famous reply that gave him, by a play upon his initials, the name of Unconditional Surrender Grant. "Yours of this date," he wrote Buckner, "proposing armistice and appointment of commissioners to settle terms of capitulation, is just received. No terms except unconditional and immediate surrender can be accepted. I propose to move immediately upon your works." The Confederate general was compelled to accept what he called "the ungenerous and unchivalrous terms." The surrender of Fort Donelson included 12,000 to 15,000 men, "at least forty pieces of artillery, and a large amount of stores, horses, mules, and other public property."[2]

army. From the extensive circulation of Northern newspapers South, Floyd must have been aware of these menaces.

[1] Sworn statements of Nicholson, Henry, and Haynes, March, 1862, Official Records, vol. vii. p. 296.

[2] Grant's official report of Feb. 16. My authorities for this account,

Men of the Northwest and men of the Southwest met here for the first time in battle on a large scale. Both armies were made up of raw troops; both fought well. The generalship on the Union side was distinctly superior. On account of their environment Western men were at the start better fitted to endure the hardships and adapt themselves to the conditions of soldiering in a rough country, than were men from the cities, the trim villages, and the rural districts, fairly provided with good roads, of New England and New York, and of such the Army of the Potomac was largely composed. But the main reason for the greater success of the Western armies cannot be found in any such slight differences in surroundings between peoples so homogeneous; and, making further allowance for the relief of the Western troops from the ever-present responsibility of defending the capital, we are forced to the conviction that in the chance of becoming skilled and self-reliant soldiers, the tremendous odds in favor of the three-years' men of the West over those of the East lay in their being led by Grant instead of by McClellan. Striking and refreshing to the student is it to turn from the excuses and subterfuges of McClellan's reports and letters to the direct and prompt manner in writing and action of Grant.

Ulysses S. Grant is one of the most interesting men whom the war brought out of obscurity. In his "Personal Memoirs" he has told with fascinating simplicity the story of his education and training in boyhood and youth. There was manual labor on the farm as well as attendance at the school; he broke horses and took care of them, he studied under the ordinary teachers, and in the crude text-books of

---

besides those specifically stated, are: official reports of Lieutenant-Colonel Jas. B. McPherson, A. H. Foote, General McClernand; reports of Gilmer, Floyd, Pillow, Buckner, and Forrest, of the Confederate army, Official Records, vol. vii. p. 161 *et seq.;* Swinton's Decisive Battles of the War; Life of Albert Sidney Johnston, by W. P. Johnston; J. D. Cox, in the *Nation,* July 30, 1885, Feb. 25, 1886; From Fort Henry to Corinth, Force; Hoppin's Life of Foote; Badeau's Military History of General Grant.

the day.   Matthew Arnold, attracted by his early history, makes the comment, "What a wholesome bringing up it was!" He had no desire to go to West Point, but went there because his father insisted on it. He took little interest in the studies or the life of the Military Academy, and showed aptitude for nothing but mathematics. Nevertheless he was graduated twenty-first in a class of thirty-nine, and went into the army. He was twenty-four years old when the Mexican War began, and served with credit through the whole of it under Taylor and Scott. Here we get glimpses of his self-education induced by contact with men and affairs. He was not a man who assimilated a variety of knowledge; he had, in fact, a mind the reverse of encyclopædic, but by careful observation and systematic thinking he made certain truths his own; these became ingrained in the fibre of his brain, guiding his action in the supreme moment of opportunity.

Returning from the Mexican campaign he married a woman whom he had long loved. Remaining in the army, he passed nearly four years at Detroit and Sackett's Harbor, when his regiment was ordered to the Pacific coast. This occasioned a separation from his family, and a cloud came over his life. He fell into habits of intemperance. In 1854 he resigned from the army and rejoined his family. "I was now to commence," he writes, "at the age of thirty-two, a new struggle for our support." On his wife's farm, near St. Louis, he endeavored to gain their livelihood. He lacked capital, but struggled on with indifferent success. One of the pictures of this time of his life is his loading of a cord of wood on a wagon, and taking it to the city for sale. At last he had a tedious attack of ague, which partially incapacitated him for work, and he gave up farming. He became a real-estate agent in St. Louis, but in this venture he did not prosper. When thirty-eight years old he came for advice and assistance to his father, who was in comfortable circumstances, and had a hardware and leather store in Galena, Illinois. "I referred him to

Simpson," the father writes, "my next oldest son, who had charge of my Galena business. . . . Simpson sent him to the Galena store to stay until something else might turn up in his favor, and told him he must confine his wants within $800 a year; that if that would not support him, he must draw what it lacked from the rent of his house and the hire of his negroes in St. Louis. . . . That amount would have supported his family then, but he owed debts at St. Louis, and did draw $1500 in the year, but he paid back the balance after he went into the army." Did it not throw light on his later career, it would be unnecessary to refer to a phase of his life in Missouri and in Galena. He had not thrown off the bad habits he had acquired in the army, and with them went impecuniosity and shiftlessness. Acquaintances in St. Louis and in Galena used to cross the street to avoid meeting Grant, and being solicited for the loan of small sums of money. "Among his old army acquaintances," says a well-informed writer in the *Nation* "and particularly in the staff corps, the impression was prevalent that his life was hopelessly wrecked." Breaking through this wretchedness, however, there were gleams of true manhood. He was honest and truthful, and he had the instincts of a gentleman, which prevented him from becoming a loafer. He never used profane language; he did not tell obscene stories; and this was not from refinement of taste, for that he lacked, but from his purity of soul.

Such was Ulysses S. Grant when he had reached the age of thirty-nine, and when, in April, 1861, after the firing on Sumter, he was called upon to preside over a war meeting in Galena. He declined to be a candidate for the captaincy of the company enlisted in his town, but he never went back to the leather store. He drilled these men and accompanied them to Springfield, remaining with them until they were mustered into the United States service. Governor Yates, of Illinois, then employed him in the adjutant-general's office of the State. In May he wrote

the adjutant-general of the army, offering his services to
his country, saying that he thought himself "competent to
command a regiment." "I felt some hesitation," he writes
in his book, "in suggesting rank as high as the colonelcy of
a regiment, feeling somewhat doubtful whether I would be
equal to the position." But no notice whatever was taken
of his letter. He then went to Cincinnati and called at
the headquarters of the Department of Ohio, on McClellan,
whom he had known slightly at West Point and in Mexico,
hoping he would be offered a position on the general's staff.
"I called on two successive days at his office, but failed to
see him on either occasion," is his record. In June he was appointed colonel of an Illinois regiment of three-years' men,
and in August a brigadier-general of volunteers. From a
military experience in Missouri he had learned a lesson
which always seemed beyond McClellan. Advancing on a
Confederate force, he was feeling much afraid of the enemy,
but kept on, and when he reached the camp found that they
had fled, showing that they had been equally afraid of him.
"From that event to the close of the war," he says, "I
never experienced trepidation upon confronting an enemy,
though I always felt more or less anxiety. I never forgot
that he had as much reason to fear my forces as I had his."
In November, 1861, he attacked a Confederate camp at
Belmont; a battle ensued which was without result, but it
served as an education for Grant and his soldiers, and
demonstrated his coolness in the time of danger. At
Donelson he showed intellectual qualities of a high order.
He knew Floyd was no soldier, he had a poor opinion of
Pillow's military ability, and made the disposition of his
forces accordingly. Had Buckner been in command, Grant's
plan of investment would have been different. His physical
courage was rare even among soldiers, who regard the virtue
as nothing extraordinary. "I can recall only two persons,"
writes Horace Porter, "who throughout a rattling musketry
fire always sat in their saddles without moving a muscle or
winking an eye; one was a bugler and the other was

General Grant." But the sight of a bull-fight in Mexico was sickening to him.[1]

The capture of Fort Donelson was indeed a great victory; it caused the Confederates to abandon Bowling Green[2] and Columbus, and to evacuate Nashville; it resulted in a Union advance of over two hundred miles of territory before the enemy could rally or reorganize. It set at rest all doubts, if any still existed, as to the permanent position of Kentucky in the civil conflict, and it was a step towards the recovery of Tennessee, in the eastern part of which a formidable Union sentiment existed. The North rejoiced with exceeding great joy.[3] "The underpinning of the rebellion seems to be knocked out from under it," wrote Chase.[4] In an article in the *Evening Post*, Bryant maintained that "the victories we have gained are equal at least to five hundred million dollars poured at once into the public exchequer;" and he therefore urged the President to veto the Legal-tender bill.[5] Holmes wrote Motley: "Never was such ecstasy, such delirium of excitement, as last Monday, when we got the news from Fort Donelson. Why, to give you an instance from my own experience, when I, a grave college professor, went into my lecture-room, the class, which had first got the news a little before, began clapping and clapping louder and louder, then cheering, until I had to give in myself, and flourishing my wand in the air, joined with the

---

[1] In this estimate of Grant I have been helped by his Personal Memoirs; by the articles of J. D. Cox in the *Nation*, July 30, 1885, Feb. 25, 1886; Life of Grant, by Dana and Wilson; Badeau's article, *Century Magazine*, May, 1885; James H. Wilson's article, ibid., Oct., 1885; General W. T. Sherman's article, ibid., Feb., 1888; Horace Porter's on the "Philosophy of Courage," ibid., June, 1888, and his articles on Grant in Appletons' Cyclopædia of Biography, and in *McClure's Magazine*, May, 1894.

[2] The evacuation of Bowling Green was ordered before the capture of Donelson, and was executed while the battle was being fought, Official Records, vol. vii. p. 259.

[3] See New York *Tribune, Times, Herald, World*, Feb. 18; *Congressional Globe*, pp. 846, 850.

[4] Warden, p. 416.   [5] Life of Bryant, Godwin, p. 169.

boys in their rousing hurrahs, after which I went on with my lecture as usual. The almost universal feeling is that the rebellion is knocked on the head ; that it may kick hard, even rise and stagger a few paces, but that its *os frontis* is beaten in." [1]

The capture of Fort Donelson was in England regarded as a victory of high importance, and helped much the cause of the North. Even before the news of it was received sentiment favorable to the Union had been growing. " Before our Parliament met," wrote John Bright to Sumner, February 27, "there was much talk of interference with the blockade, and much was still said in favor of the South. All that has passed away. In London all has changed, and it is difficult to find a noisy advocate of the secession theory. The press has become much more moderate, and the great party that was to have driven the government into hostilities with you is nowhere to be found. Even the hot Mr. Gregory, the Southern advocate in the House of Commons, is very slow at taking any step in the direction of his known sympathies, and has contented himself with a notice that, at some time not yet fixed, he will call the attention of the House to the state of the blockade." [2] When the particulars of Grant's victory became known, it could no longer be asserted that the South had a monopoly of competent officers and of good and brave soldiers. Confidence in the ability of the Confederates was shaken. The friends of the North felt that at last the United States had demonstrated that it had the stronger battalions.[3]

The fall of Donelson gave the South the bitterness of defeat which the North had felt after Bull Run, and it was doubly bitter, as the Confederates had begun to think that in the field they were invincible. No one appreciated the

---

[1] Motley's Correspondence, vol. ii. p. 68.

[2] Pierce-Sumner Papers, MS.

[3] See London *Times*, March 6; London *Daily News*, March 7; London *Spectator*, March 8; Debate in House of Commons, March 7, Hansard, p. 1158.

magnitude of the disaster better than the commanding general in the West. "The blow was most disastrous," wrote Albert Sidney Johnston to Davis, "and almost without remedy."[1] When the governor of Tennessee proclaimed that the troops must evacuate Nashville, and adjourned the legislature to Memphis, panic seized upon the people, and disorder, turbulence, and rapine ensued. At Richmond consternation reigned. The management of the campaign was on all sides found fault with, and Davis at once ordered that Floyd and Pillow be relieved from command. The pressure from the people and the Confederate congress upon Davis for the removal of Johnston was strong, but he resisted it and stood by his favorite general.[2] Shortly after the fall of Donelson came the day appointed for the provisional government to give place to the permanent government of the Confederacy, and for the inauguration of its president and vice-president for the term of six years. This was February 22, and one is struck with the emphasis that all the contemporary and subsequent accounts give to the dismalness of the day. The heavens were black and the rain poured down. Davis, pale and emaciated, delivered his inaugural address, at the foot of the Washington monument in Capitol Square, to a crowd of people, the gloom in whose hearts was fitly reflected by nature's sombre hue. All minds were full of the defeats suffered by the Confederate arms. "At the darkest hour of our struggle," their president declared, "the provisional gives place to the permanent government. After a series of successes and victories which covered our arms with glory, we have recently met with serious disasters. But in the heart of a people resolved to be free, these disasters tend but to stimulate to increased resistance. . . . With humble gratitude and adoration," he concluded, "acknowledging the Providence which has so visibly protected the

---

[1] March 18, Official Records, vol. vii. p. 260.

[2] Davis to Johnston, March 12, Official Records, vol. vii. p. 257; A. S. Johnston at Shiloh, Century War Book, vol. i. p. 550.

Confederacy during its brief but eventful career, to thee, O God! I trustingly commit myself, and prayerfully invoke Thy blessing on my country and its cause."

Reflecting in scathing terms on the arbitrary acts and violations of the Constitution and the law by the Lincoln government, Davis boasted " that, through all the necessities of an unequal struggle, there has been no act on our part to impair personal liberty or the freedom of speech, of thought, or of the press. The courts have been open, the judicial functions fully executed, and every right of the peaceful citizen maintained as securely as if a war of invasion had not disturbed the land." [1] This might Davis truthfully say on the 22d of February, but not for many days longer. The Confederates stood adversity no better than had the Federals. By authority of an act of Congress, passed in secret session,[2] the Confederate president, March 1, proclaimed martial law in the city of Richmond and the adjoining country to the distance of ten miles, and declared the suspension of the privilege of the writ of *habeas corpus*.[3] At first the law-abiding citizens were well pleased with this action. One morning, shortly after the inauguration, the walls in different parts of the city were " scrawled over with inflammatory and treasonable mottoes ;" these were interpreted to mean a call upon the Unionists to co-operate in resistance to the Confederate government, and caused alarm.[4] When, therefore, under the operation of martial law, several notorious Unionists, who were regarded in this time of distress as traitors, were arrested, the people applauded the vigor of their government. Moreover, the municipal administration and police system, which had served well the quiet and refined Virginia capital, had broken down under the growth of the city and the influx of soldiers, gamblers, and adventurers. General Win-

---

[1] Davis's inaugural is printed by Alfriend, p. 348.

[2] Passed Feb. 27, Acts of the First Congress, C. S. A., p. 1.

[3] Life of Davis, Mrs. Davis, vol. ii. p. 185.

[4] Richmond *Examiner*, Feb. 28; Appletons' Annual Cyclopædia, 1862, p. 239.

der, to whom was delegated practically unlimited power, positively prohibited the distillation of spirituous liquors, and ordered all the dram-shops closed.[1] He established a military police, and strictly enforced this and other orders, restoring peace to the city where had been confusion and turbulence. Rowdies, drunkards, and idle soldiers disappeared from the streets. Ladies could now walk out without fear of insult, and gentlemen could go out at night without danger of being robbed.

But the delight of the people was short-lived. General Winder did not use his arbitrary power with mildness and discretion. The well-grounded belief obtained that he employed it for private oppression and the gratification of personal malice. Extraordinary arrests of respectable citizens were made, capricious acts of tyranny were done, and it was impossible for the sufferers to get redress. A vexatious passport system was established. The Richmond *Whig*, on account of its criticisms of the administration, was obnoxious to Winder, and one day when an article appeared which he supposed to be a violation of one of his orders, he gave the command to arrest the editor and close the office. This order was not carried out, however, owing to the dissuasion of Jones, a clerk in the Confederate war-office, who maintained that no offence had been committed. Jones's entry of April 17 in his diary is: " The press has taken the alarm, and several of the publishers have confessed a fear of having their offices closed if they dare to speak the sentiments struggling for utterance. It is indeed a reign of terror! Every Virginian and other loyal citizens of the South— members of Congress and all—must now, before obtaining General Winder's permission to leave the city for their homes, bow down before the aliens in the provost-marshal's office and subscribe to an oath of allegiance, while a file of bayonets are pointed at their backs." [2] This much one may

---

[1] General Order No. 8, March 1, Richmond *Examiner*.
[2] A Rebel War Clerk's Diary, vol. i. p. 120, see, also, p. 115; Richmond

gather from the contemporary evidence, but Pollard asserts that the half was not told in the newspapers of the day, that Winder exercised the powers of a viceroy in a terrible manner. His police was largely composed of disreputable men; he gave employment to two hundred spies, on whose reports of private conversations good citizens were imprisoned, and then had to depend for their release on the whim of the tyrant. Not only men but women suffered indignities at his hands.[1] His rule was indeed a despotism of the worst kind. He was responsible to no one but Davis, who sustained him, or at all events kept him in his place. Public opinion, however, asserted itself so strongly that Congress modified the law under which the President had exercised these extraordinary powers.[2]

It was now that a party in opposition to Davis, with powerful exponents in Congress and in the press, was formed. Owing to changes in the cabinet, Benjamin now held both the state and war portfolios;[3] he was the chief adviser of the Confederate president and his confidential friend. The blame for the disasters of the early part of 1862 was largely imputed to Benjamin, and at the same time much criticism intended for Davis was showered upon the secretary's head. The permanent congress was composed of a Senate and House of Representatives, but, since the army attracted the best talent of the Confederacy, it was in ability not up to the level of the provisional congress, nor to the representation which the South used to send to the national legislature. "This is a very poor congress," Stephens said, confidentially. "There are few men of ability in the House. In the Senate not more than two or three."[4]

Examiner, March 3, 4, 7, 8; Richmond *Whig,* March 4, 25, 27, April 1; Richmond *Dispatch,* March 1, 8, 12, 17; Pollard's History of the First Year of the War.   [1] Pollard's Davis, p. 215.

[2] Passed April 19, Acts of the First Congress, C. S. A., p. 40. Not as much as it should have done according to Jones, Diary, vol. i. p. 120.

[3] Randolph, of Virginia, was afterwards appointed Secretary of War.

[4] Johnston and Browne, p. 414.

Lincoln's war orders were probably designed as much for assuring the people that something would be done as for commands to his generals. But as affairs turned out, his " Special War Order Number 1," issued January 31, which directed McClellan to begin a forward movement February 22, whose object should be the seizure of Manassas Junction, was the highest strategy. McClellan had an army three times as large as Johnston's, better equipped, better fed, in better health, and full of confidence on account of the victories which had been gained for the Union; while Johnston's army was almost as much demoralized as were the Richmond government and people, and the time of enlistment of a large number of his men had nearly expired. Had McClellan advanced February 22 a cheap victory awaited him. An intelligent study of the internal affairs of the Confederacy, a reasonable knowledge of the force of the enemy—which might have been easily gained—could not fail to convince a man who was fit to command an army that now was the supreme moment to strike a series of blows, that it was the time when the tide of affairs should be taken at its flood. Only one obstacle existed. The roads were bad, but not impassable. Edward Dicey saw them when they were at the worst, and his testimony is that " they were not worse than many of the roads in the south of Italy, over which the Sardinian army marched in 1860." [1] Moreover, McClellan would have had a railroad behind him to transport his supplies. Of the army of the Potomac, Dicey wrote: "I have seen the armies of most European countries, and I have no hesitation in saying that, as far as the average raw material of the rank and file is concerned, the American army is the finest." [2] These magnificent men, full of courage and desire to end the war speedily, panted to be led against the enemy; but their general, instead of giving the word, haggled with the President over a plan of campaign. It is certain that if the Grant of Don-

[1] Federal States, vol. ii. p. 19.   [2] Ibid., p. 7.

elson had been in command, he would have fought Johnston's army and beaten it, and it is possible he might have
captured it, or Richmond, or both, thus shortening the war
at least a year, and putting an end to the probability of
foreign interference.

Meanwhile the astute Confederate general, finding it impossible to conjecture that McClellan would not take advantage of the peculiarly favorable conditions, and aware
that in that event he stood in jeopardy, was making preparations to withdraw his army to a more secure position.
Beginning his preparations February 22, he commenced the
retreat March 7, and four days later had his army safely on
the south bank of the Rappahannock River.   Constantly
expecting an attack, he had deemed it impossible to remove
all the property accumulated at Manassas Junction, and
therefore a large amount of stores, provisions, clothing,
blankets, and baggage was burned.[1]   March 9 McClellan
heard of Johnston's movement, and immediately gave the
order for the occupation of Centreville and Manassas.   The
Union army found that they had been fronting phantom
ordnance as well as phantom soldiers.   Being deficient in
artillery, Johnston had made " rough wooden imitations of
guns," which were " kept near the embrasures in readiness
for exhibition "[2] — " Quaker guns," our newspapers called
them.   Hawthorne was in Washington at this time, and
has with exquisite skill described this advance.   " On the
very day of our arrival," he wrote, "sixty thousand men had
crossed the Potomac on their march towards Manassas, and
almost with their first step into Virginia mud the phantas-
magoria of a countless host and impregnable ramparts, before which they had so long remained quiescent, dissolved
quite away.   It was as if General McClellan had thrust his
sword into a gigantic enemy, and, beholding him suddenly
collapse, had discovered to himself and the world that he

---

[1] Johnston's Narrative; Mrs. Davis's Memoir, vol. ii.
[2] Johnston's Narrative, p. 78.

had merely punctured an enormously swollen bladder. . . .
The whole business, though connected with the destinies of
a nation, takes inevitably a tinge of the ludicrous. The
vast preparation of men and warlike material—the majestic
patience and docility with which the people waited through
those weary and dreary months—the martial skill, courage,
and caution with which our movement was ultimately made
—and, at last, the tremendous shock with which we were
brought up suddenly against nothing at all! The Southerners show little sense of humor nowadays, but I think
they must have meant to provoke a laugh at our expense
when they planted those Quaker guns. At all events, no
other rebel artillery has played upon us with such overwhelming effect." Hawthorne accurately describes a phase
of public opinion touching McClellan, upon which he comments in words of incisive criticism of the "young Napoleon." "There was and is a most fierce and bitter outcry,
and detraction loud and low, against General McClellan, ac-
cusing him of sloth, imbecility, cowardice, treasonable purposes, and, in short, utterly denying his ability as a soldier
and questioning his integrity as a man. Nor was this to be
wondered at, for when before, in all history, do we find a
general in command of half a million of men, and in presence of an enemy inferior in numbers and no better disciplined than his own troops, leaving it still debatable, after
the better part of a year, whether he is a soldier or no ?"[1]

While McClellan dallied, the Confederates recovered from
their reverses. Of the same blood, they went through the
same stages of feeling as did the Northern people after
Bull Run. After the first discouragement they resolved to
fight to the bitter end, and their congress expressed in defiant resolutions their stern determination.[2] From words
they proceeded to action. On the recommendation of Davis,
the Confederate congress passed a conscription act. This

---

[1] "Chiefly About War Matters," *Atlantic Monthly*, July, 1862.
[2] March 11, Acts of the First Congress, C. S. A., p. 53.

provided that all the white men of the Confederacy between the ages of eighteen and thirty-five, except those
legally exempted, should be called into the military service
for three years, and that those who had already enlisted for
twelve months should be continued in the service for the
date of three years from the term of their original enlistment.[1] The Governor of Virginia called out the whole
militia of his State, which was estimated to amount to
100,000 men.[2] The government had previously taken steps
to push the enlistment of troops,[3] and under the influence
of all of this action, the reorganization of the army went
on with vigor and a heartiness of spirit that resulted in an
earnest and efficient body. When McClellan at last allowed
his men to fight, instead of meeting an apathetic army
weakened by disease and diminished by a liberal system of
furloughs, which he would have encountered in February,[4]
he had to contend with a larger army, under Johnston and
Lee, increased by resolute, fresh recruits, yet with enough
of the leaven of disciplined soldiers to manœuvre and fight
like veterans.

The President and McClellan differed as to a plan of
campaign, and had much discussion concerning it. Lincoln
desired the Army of the Potomac to advance on Richmond
directly by the way of Manassas Junction, while McClellan
wished to transport his army by water to some point on
the lower Chesapeake, making that his base, and advancing
thence on the capital of the Confederacy. The advantage of
Lincoln's plan was, as we have seen, that it would have enabled the Union troops to strike a blow when Johnston was
ill prepared to resist it. Nevertheless Lincoln, although with

---

[1] Passed April 16, Acts of First Congress, C. S. A., p. 29 ; Alfriend's
Davis, p. 367.   [2] Richmond *Examiner*, March 12.

[3] See Davis's message to his Congress, Alfriend, p. 355.

[4] Chase appreciated this. He wrote, Feb. 17, "The time has now come
for dealing decisively with the army in front of us, weakened by sickness,
desertions, and withdrawals of troops, until a victory over it is deprived of
more than half its honor."—Warden, p. 416.

keen regret, yielded his preference and gave his consent to McClellan's plan. The retirement of Johnston to the south bank of the Rappahannock determined Fort Monroe as the point on the lower Chesapeake which should be made the base, and the advance upon Richmond would be up the Peninsula, between the York and James rivers.[1] With the evidences of the incompetence of McClellan which have been adduced, and the difference of opinion between him and the President, it might seem as if the public service would have been subserved by his removal. But the case then was not so plain as it is now. McClellan had the love and confidence of his soldiers, and a strong support in the country from the conservative Republicans and Democrats. While he had never taken much interest in politics, and had never voted but once and then for Douglas, he had manifested unmistakably his conservatism on the slavery question, so much so that the distrust of him by the radical Republicans, who mainly were his critics, was increased. Lincoln himself, although his confidence was shaken, could not but believe that McClellan would accomplish important results when once in the field. At that time no eminently fit successor to him was at hand. Had Chase been supreme in authority, he might have placed McDowell in command; but McDowell was not popular with the soldiers, and the unfortunate battle of Bull Run hung like a millstone around his neck; moreover, subsequent experience with commanders of the Army of the Potomac, when McClellan was finally displaced, demonstrated that there were greater evils than having him at its head.

On Sunday, the 9th of March, the day that the news of the evacuation of Manassas came, the President received the startling intelligence of the havoc done the day previous in Hampton Roads by the Confederate iron-clad *Merrimac*. On this Saturday began a new chapter in naval warfare, the introduction to which had come from the hands of two

---

[1] See Nicolay and Hay, vol. v.; McClellan's Own Story.

friendly but rival powers of Europe.   In 1858 France built
an armor-plated steam frigate, and speedily thereafter England had constructed another.   Their success was sufficient
to render "armor-plating an essential feature in the construction of vessels of war." [1]   In the dissolution of the

Union the Confeder-
acy got its share of
competent naval offi-
cers, and they at once
turned their attention
to this new invention.
In July, 1861, the Con-
federate Secretary of
the Navy gave the or-
der to raise the Unit-
ed States steam frig-
ate *Merrimac*—which
was one of the ships
burned and sunk at
the time of the de-
struction of the Gos-
port navy-yard—and
convert her into an
iron-clad; this work
proceeded as rapidly

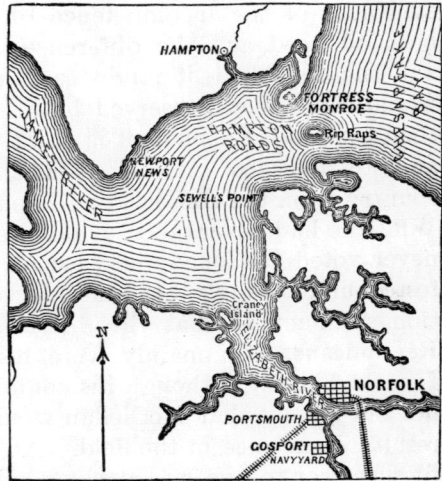

MAP OF HAMPTON ROADS

as could be expected under the imperfect manufacturing
and mechanical conditions which prevailed in the South.
Not until October did the Navy Department at Washington let the contract for the building of an iron-clad
on a plan submitted by John Ericsson.   The necessity
for rapid construction, that she might be ready as soon as
the *Merrimac*, on which he knew work was progressing,
the desire to have a vessel of light draught, together with
some other reasons, had induced Ericsson to design the peculiar type of the *Monitor*, instead of following the French

[1] Article of John Ericsson, Century War Book, vol. i. p. 730.

and English models.   Work on the *Merrimac* at Gosport
and work on the *Monitor* at Brooklyn went on; it was a
race to get ready first, and each side had an inkling of what
the other was doing.   The *Merrimac* appeared upon the
scene of action a few hours before the *Monitor*.

About noon on Saturday March 8, the *Merrimac* with
several tenders steamed into Hampton Roads.   The officers
of the blockading squadron knew her at once and prepared
for action.   The frigates *Minnesota, St. Lawrence*, and *Roanoke*, anchored at Fortress Monroe, headed for the enemy,
which to them looked "like a huge half-submerged croco-
dile," but the water being low, they grounded.   The sailing frigate *Congress* of fifty guns, and the *Cumberland*, a
sloop-of-war of twenty-four guns, at Newport News made
ready for the *Merrimac*, and as she approached discharged
their broadsides, the shore batteries opening fire immediately after.   The balls rebounded from her iron sides as if
they had been of india-rubber.   She reserved her fire until
within easy range, gave the *Congress* a broadside as she
passed, then, steering directly for the *Cumberland*, brought
her guns to bear upon the Union sloop-of-war killing and
wounding men at every shot, and proceeding on under full
headway, rammed the *Cumberland*, "knocking a hole in the
side near the water line as large as the head of a hogshead."
Backing clear she continued her fire.   The water rushed
into the hole in the *Cumberland*, but she kept up the fight,
discharging her cannon until they reached the water's edge,
and going down with colors flying.   The commander of
the *Congress*, seeing the fate of her sister ship, ran her
aground to escape destruction, but she was attacked vigorously by the *Merrimac* and the Confederate gun-boats.   The
fight was unequal, she being able to make little resistance;
at last hot shot from the *Merrimac* set her on fire and
completed her destruction.   The *Minnesota* was aground
and at the mercy of the iron-clad, but although there remained nearly two hours of daylight, the pilots were afraid
to attempt the channel at ebb tide, the *Merrimac* drawing

twenty-two feet; she therefore returned to Sewell's Point and anchored, to wait the light of the next day, when her officers expected to return and destroy the *Minnesota*.

That night the consternation in the Union fleet and among the Union troops was profound. The stately wooden frigates, deemed in the morning powerful men-of-war, had been shown to be absolutely useless to cope with this new engine of destruction. The next morning, in Washington, Seward, Chase, Stanton, and Welles hastened to the White House to confer with the President. Alarm pervaded their discussion; their prognostications were gloomy. Stanton was especially excited and declared: "The *Merrimac* will change the whole character of the war; she will destroy *seriatim* every naval vessel; she will lay all the cities on the seaboard under contribution. . . . I will notify the governors and municipal authorities in the North to take instant measures to protect their harbors." I have no doubt, he said, that the monster is at this moment on her way to Washington. Looking out of the window, which commanded a view of the Potomac for many miles, he continued, "not unlikely we shall have from one of her guns a shell or cannon-ball in the White House before we leave this room." [1] The despatches from the War Department reflect the same anxiety. Besides other measures of precaution, a fleet of canal-boats loaded with stone were sent down the Potomac to be sunk, if it was found necessary to obstruct the channel. [2] The terror, though natural, was extreme. The *Merrimac* had, however, broken the blockade at Norfolk, and she could do likewise at other ports—a consideration of the utmost importance.

While, on this Sunday morning, March 9, the President and the other authorities were a prey to keen anxiety, bounds were set to the *Merrimac's* power for ruin by John Ericsson's *Monitor*. Barely escaping shipwreck twice on her

[1] Gideon Welles, in the Annals of the War, p. 24.
[2] Official Records, vol. ix. p. 18 *et seq.*

voyage from New York, she arrived at Hampton Roads at ten o'clock on the evening of the 8th, and took a position which protected the *Minnesota*. Early on the morning of the 9th the *Merrimac* stood for the *Minnesota* and opened fire on her. The *Monitor*, which was commanded by Lieutenant John L. Worden, steered directly for the *Merrimac* and commenced firing. Then ensued, for four hours, a hand-to-hand fight. The *Monitor*, appropriately described as a "cheesebox on a raft," was of 900 tons, the *Merrimac* of 3500. The *Monitor* had two 11-inch Dahlgren guns, fired from a revolving turret; the other had six 9-inch Dahlgren guns and two 32-pounder Brooke rifles in broadside, and 7-inch Brooke rifles on pivots in the bow and stern. Men said at the time a pygmy strove against a giant; David had come out to encounter Goliath. Shot after shot struck the *Merrimac* and the turret of the *Monitor* without injury; the armor was superior to the projectiles. At one time Lieutenant Jones, who was in command of the *Merrimac*, inquired, "Why are you not firing, Mr. Eggleston?" "Why, our powder is very precious," was the reply; "and after two hours' incessant firing I find I can do her about as much damage by snapping my thumb at her every two minutes and a half." [1] The *Merrimac* tried to ram her antagonist, but she herself was unwieldy, and the *Monitor*, being easily handled, got out of her way without difficulty, receiving only a glancing blow which effected nothing. The *Monitor* then "came up on our quarter," Wood relates, "her bow against our side, and at this distance fired twice." The impact of the shots "forced the side in bodily two or three inches. All the crews of the after-guns were knocked over by the concussion, and bled from the nose or ears. Another shot at the same place would have penetrated." [2] At another time, Greene, who was in the turret of the *Monitor*, writes, the *Monitor* made a dash at the *Merrimac's* stern, hoping to disable her screw, which Worden thinks he missed

---

[1] J. T. Wood, C. S. A., Century War Book, vol. i. p. 702.   [2] Ibid.

by not more than two feet.[1] "Soon after noon," as Greene relates the story, "a shell from the enemy's gun, the muzzle not ten yards distant, struck the forward side of the pilot-house[2] directly in the sight-hole or slit, and exploded, cracking the second iron log and partly lifting the top, leaving an opening. Worden was standing immediately behind this spot, and received in his face the force of the blow, which partly stunned him, and filling his eyes with powder, utterly blinded him."[3] This caused the *Monitor* to withdraw temporarily from the action. The commander of the *Merrimac*, perhaps thinking that she had given up the contest, or because his own boat was leaking badly, steered towards Norfolk, and the struggle was over. Only a few had been wounded on the *Merrimac;* with the exception of the injury to Worden, there was no casualty of account on the *Monitor.*[4]

It had been a wonderfully picturesque fight. Holmes, in a letter to Motley, spoke of the *Monitor's* "appearance in front of the great megalosaurus or deinotherium, which came out in its scaly armor that no one could pierce, breathing fire and smoke from its nostrils; is it not the age of fables and of heroes and demigods over again?"[5] The relief of the Union government and people was great. The power of the *Merrimac* was broken; she did no further mischief.[6]

---

[1] Century War Book, vol. i. p. 723.

[2] The pilot-house was of iron logs, and constructed in the manner of a log cabin.   [3] Century War Book, vol. i. p. 726.

[4] My authorities for this account besides those already named are several articles in vol. i. Century War Book; reports of Flag-officer Marston, Captain Van Brunt, of the *Minnesota*, Lieutenant Morris, of the *Cumberland*, Lieutenant Pendergast, of the *Congress*, Lieutenant Jones, of the *Merrimac*, statement of the pilot of the *Cumberland*, Moore's Rebellion Record, vol. iv., Docs., p. 266 *et seq.;* report of Flag-officer Buchanan, of C. S. Navy, Official Records, vol. ix. p. 8; Nicolay and Hay, vol. v.; The Blockade and the Cruisers, Soley; Swinton's Decisive Battles of the War.

[5] Motley's Correspondence, vol. ii. p. 73.

[6] When Norfolk was evacuated in May by the Confederates, they destroyed the *Merrimac*. In Dec. the *Monitor* foundered off Cape Hatteras.

This first encounter between iron-clads determined that they alone would be of avail in the naval warfare of the future. The English government and people showed intense interest in the accounts of the contest, and it was the subject of a long debate in the House of Commons. The admirable performance of the *Monitor*, and the intelligence that the United States purposed building a fleet of such boats,[1] increased their respect for its blockade of the Southern ports.[2]

The President, having consented to McClellan's Peninsula plan of campaign, issued an order March 8, dividing the Army of the Potomac into four army corps, to be commanded, respectively, by Generals McDowell, Sumner, Heintzelman, and Keyes. General Wadsworth was to have command of the forces in and about Washington. March 11 another presidential order relieved McClellan of the command of all military departments except that of the Potomac. The

---

[1] Acts of Feb. 13 and April 17, Appendix *Congressional Globe*, pp. 336, 348; Report of the Secretary of the Navy, Dec. 1.

[2] Hansard, March 31, 1862. The London *Times* of March 25 said: "Who would have thought it possible that after England and France had theorized so long on iron-plated and iron-prowed vessels, the first real trial should be made by the inhabitants of the peaceful New World met in unnatural strife? . . . Nothing now remains for our Admiralty but to discontinue the building of wooden vessels, and to convert all that will bear it into machines of war resembling the Confederate frigate." See, also, the London *Daily News*, March 29, the London *Spectator* of March 29, April 5. The London *Saturday Review* of March 29 said: "Not more than a year ago the *Times* dwelt with much emphasis on the fact that the Americans had steadily refused to avail themselves of the new-fangled device of iron-plated ships. That a people so adventurous and skilful in mechanical appliances should have pronounced the new invention a chimera, was supposed to be a serious ground for doubting the wisdom of the course which France had initiated and England sluggishly followed. No one could then have imagined that the first real test of armor-plated ships in actual warfare would be furnished by America. It is only within a few weeks that either of the belligerents has had a plated ship ready for sea; and, as if to supply the crucial experiment which was wanting to build up the confidence of our naval architects, the *Merrimac* and the *Monitor* have exhibited their powers of attack and defence, and proved that even imperfect specimens (as they probably are) of their class are quite capable of sweeping from the ocean whole fleets of the old wooden liners."

ostensible reason for this was that the general would be actively engaged in the field; at the bottom it represented the waning confidence of Lincoln and Congress in him, for their trust had received a shock from his being outgeneralled by Johnston, when he allowed the Confederate commander to steal away from Manassas unimpeded and without harm. March 13 he and his corps commanders had a council at Fairfax Court-house, where they decided in favor of the Peninsula plan of campaign, provided—besides other conditions not necessary to be mentioned for our purpose — that the aid of the navy could be had in silencing the batteries of the enemy on York River, and determined that "the force to be left to cover Washington shall be such as to give an entire feeling of security for its safety from menace." When the plan was submitted to the President, he, in a communication from the War Department, made no objection to it, but stipulated again that Washington be left entirely secure. The embarkation of the troops began. McClellan himself reached Fortress Monroe on the afternoon of April 2. Part of his army was there, and the rest of it was on the way. Directly after his departure there cropped out a serious misunderstanding between the President and the War Department on one side, and McClellan on the other, in reference to what they understood to be necessary to make the capital entirely secure. It was not so much a difference regarding the number of troops needed, but McClellan counted Banks's army in the Shenandoah as part of the covering force required. The President did not so understand it, and, alarmed at the dispositions the general had made, directed that McDowell's corps be detained at Washington. This was an exceedingly unfortunate misunderstanding. Too much depended on the federal possession of Washington for Lincoln to take the slightest chance touching its safety, and yet the withdrawal of 35,000 men was naturally a serious disappointment to the general. He was more to blame, probably, than any one else for this misapprehension. The idea one gets of McClellan from his

book and reports is that of a man who does not think
straight and work out matters to a logical conclusion.
There is a lack of precision and an inconsistency in his
statements which indicate a want of clear and concentrated thinking.   Such men go through life victims to frequent and honest misunderstandings.   Possibly Lincoln
may have been at fault in not fully entering into the details with his general, for relations between Stanton and
McClellan had already become so inharmonious that no
efficient and generous co-operation between them could be
expected.

McClellan's plan was a good one, but in the execution
of it he showed neither promptness nor ability.   Magruder,
the Confederate general in command, held a fortified line of
thirteen miles from the York River to the James, to defend
which he had 11,000 men; 6000 of these were at Yorktown on the York River, and at Mulberry Island on the
James; 5000 were posted at the assailable points along his
front.   McClellan, with his overwhelming force, could easily
have broken the Confederate line within a week after the
arrival of his army on the Peninsula, and Yorktown would
have fallen into his hands.   Lincoln's letter of April 9,
urging immediate action, is pathetic in its display of his
yearning for his general's success, and his desire to furnish
abundant means to secure it.   "I suppose," he wrote, "the
whole force which has gone forward for you is with you by
this time, and if so, I think it is the precise time for you
to strike a blow.   By delay the enemy will relatively gain
upon you; that is, he will gain faster by fortifications and
reinforcements than you can by reinforcements alone.   And
once more let me tell you it is indispensable to you that
you strike a blow.   I am powerless to help this.   You will
do me the justice to remember I always insisted that going
down the bay in search of a field, instead of fighting at
or near Manassas, was only shifting, and not surmounting,
a difficulty; that we would find the same enemy and the
same or equal intrenchments at either place.   The country

will not fail to note, is now noting, that the present hesitation to move upon an intrenched enemy is but the story of Manassas repeated. I beg to assure you that I have never written you or spoken to you in greater kindness of feeling than now, nor with a fuller purpose to sustain you so far as, in my most anxious judgment, I consistently can. But you must act."[1] Instead, however, of piercing the Confederate line by assault, McClellan sat down before Yorktown, and began the siege of it in a deliberate and scientific manner, probably losing more men by disease in the swamps of Virginia than an assault would have cost him; meanwhile complaining of the lack of his expected co-operation of the navy and of the withdrawal of McDowell's corps, begging the President and the Secretary of War for more troops, and hugging the delusion that Stanton and the radical Republicans at heart desired the failure of his campaign. He gave the Confederates what of all things they most desired —time to recover from their early discouragement, time to bring about the recuperation which shattered the sanguine hopes of the North. While he was erecting most formidable-siege works before Yorktown, the Confederate congress, perhaps influenced by fears for the safety of their capital, passed the conscription act, giving an additional impetus to the reorganization of their army.[2]

Meanwhile at the West the cause of the Union was gaining ground. General Curtis had driven the Confederates out of Missouri into Arkansas. But the victory of Donelson had not been followed up to its full fruition. It was Grant's opinion that "if one general, who would have taken the responsibility, had been in command of all the troops west of the Alleghanies, he could have marched to Chattanooga, Corinth, Memphis, and Vicksburg with the troops we then had; and as volunteering was going on rapidly over

---

[1] Official Records, vol. xi. part i. p. 15.

[2] My authorities for this account are Official Records, vols. v., x. part ii., xi. part i.; Nicolay and Hay, vol. v.; Webb's Peninsula; McClellan's Own Story; Swinton's Army of the Potomac.

the North, there would soon have been force enough at all these centres to operate offensively against any body of the enemy that might be found near them." [1] Such an occupation would have precluded the operation of the Confederate conscription act in a large extent of territory, and prevented a considerable increase of the Southern army. His actual success pointed out Grant for such a command, and, considering what a tremendous advance the insignificant victories in western Virginia gained for McClellan, it might seem astonishing that his ability as a soldier, testified to by the capture of Donelson, was not sooner recognized. Such an arrangement, however, would have supplanted Halleck, which, as he shared with Grant and Foote the glory of Forts Henry and Donelson, would have been unnatural, and was probably not entertained by any one in authority at Washington. There was, moreover, a general distrust of Grant. Owing, probably, to defective means of communication, Halleck did not get as full and prompt reports from Grant as he deemed necessary, and he complained of this to McClellan, who still had command of all the Union armies. "I have had no communication with General Grant for more than a week," he telegraphed March 3. "He left his command without my authority and went to Nashville. His army seems to be as much demoralized by the victory of Fort Donelson as was that of the Potomac by the defeat of Bull Run. . . . I can get no returns, no reports, no information of any kind from him. Satisfied with his victory, he sits down and enjoys it without any regard to the future." "Do not hesitate to arrest him at once if the good of the service requires it, and place C. F. Smith in command," promptly replied McClellan. Halleck the next day rejoined: "A rumor has just reached me that since the taking of Fort Donelson General Grant has resumed his former bad habits. If so, it will account for his neglect of my often-repeated orders. I do not deem it advisable to arrest him at present, but

---

[1] Personal Memoirs, p. 317.

have placed General Smith in command of the expedition up the Tennessee." [1]   This was an injustice to Grant. Halleck condemned the victor of Donelson without a hearing and on insufficient and untrustworthy evidence, thus displaying a disposition to supersede him on a mere pretext. Grant was ordered to remain at Fort Henry. Hurt by the reprimands he received from Halleck, and also at being superseded, he asked, after explaining why his reports had not been regularly received, to be relieved from further duty in that department, a request which he twice repeated. Halleck was satisfied with his explanations, so advised the War Department, and sent Grant a despatch expressive of trust.   This was glad tidings to him, and he at once replied that he would "give every effort to the success of our cause." [2] General Smith, on account of an injury received at Pittsburg Landing, was incapacitated for active exertion, and this occurring at the time that Grant gained the favor of Halleck, he was restored to the command of the Army of the Tennessee. He arrived at Savannah, in western Tennessee, March 17, and soon had five divisions of his army in camp at Pittsburg Landing, nine miles above Savannah, on the Tennessee River and south of it ; Lew. Wallace's division was stationed at Crump's Landing, five miles below Pittsburg and on the same side of the river. The Army of the Ohio, under General Buell, which occupied Nashville and middle Tennessee, had been ordered to join the Army of the Tennessee at Savannah. The plan of campaign was an offensive movement against the Confederates, who were in force at or near Corinth, Mississippi.

After the battle of Mill Spring, Beauregard had been sent to the West to assist Albert Sidney Johnston in what was recognized as a grave situation, and now he had fixed upon Corinth as the base of operations. He used the utmost exertion to collect an army, calling upon the governors of

---

[1] Official Records, vol. vii. p. 679 *et seq.*
[2] Ibid., p. 683; vol. **x**. part ii, p. 3 *et seq.*

Alabama, Louisiana, Mississippi, and Tennessee, and the
generals of other departments, for help in the most earnest manner; he even appealed to the people of the Southwest to send their church-bells to be manufactured into cannon, an appeal which met with a prompt response. March
25 Johnston's army joined Beauregard's at Corinth, and the
Confederate generals determined to attack Grant before
Buell should join him, hoping by a quick movement to surprise his forces at Pittsburg Landing.   April 3 the Confederate army left Corinth, but the weather was stormy and
the roads were bad, causing the usual delays in the movement of troops, so that the attack planned for April 5 could
not be made until Sunday the 6th.

Grant was so bent on his projected offensive movement,
and so confident that Johnston would not assume the aggressive so soon after the long and apparently demoralized
retreat from Bowling Green and Columbus, that he had neglected all defensive measures; he had, indeed, some apprehension of an attack on Crump's Landing, but none for one
on Pittsburg Landing.   He was careless about the disposition of his forces; he threw up no intrenchments, although
he had been ordered by Halleck to fortify his position,[1] and
although he had a swollen river at his back which separated
him from his expected reinforcements, while he himself had
his headquarters at Savannah; but at this time he would
have moved them to Pittsburg Landing had he not expected
Buell at Savannah on the 6th.

The Confederates were now face to face with their foe.
Beauregard, disappointed at the delay, fearing that the
chance to surprise Grant had been lost and that Buell might
join him at any moment, favored giving up the attack and
retiring to Corinth.   Johnston overruled his second in command, and said to Beauregard and his corps commanders,
" Gentlemen, we shall attack at daylight to - morrow. I
would fight them if they were a million."   In the early

---

[1] Halleck to Grant, March 20, Official Records, vol. x. part ii. p. 51.

morning of April 6 the Confederates made the onslaught
with vigor.

Few if any battles of our Civil War have given rise to so
much controversy as this of Shiloh, for so the contest is
now generally known.   One of the points of dispute is
whether the federal troops were surprised.   That they were
surprised was the current opinion at the North, largely
based, it is true, on the accounts of newspaper correspondents.   Halleck, who went to Pittsburg Landing soon after
the battle, and had no desire to screen Grant, telegraphed
Stanton from there, May 2 : "The newspaper accounts that
our divisions were surprised are utterly false.   Every division had notice of the enemy's approach hours before the
battle commenced ;" and after "a patient and careful inquiry and investigation" he reiterated this in a letter of
June 15 from Corinth.[1]   Grant and Sherman have maintained the same.[2]   The evidence is, indeed, conflicting, but
it is clear enough that at least a portion of the Union army
was on the alert, and that a reconnaissance had been made
to discover the force of the enemy ; it seems equally clear
that few, if any, of the federal officers suspected that the
whole Confederate army of 40,000 men was before them.
That Johnston had not succeeded in effecting a complete
surprise was due to the vigilance of the division, brigade,
and regimental commanders, and not to the foresight of
the commanding general.   April 5 Grant telegraphed Halleck, "The main force of the enemy is at Corinth ;" and
later on the same day he said, "I have scarcely the faintest idea of an attack (general one) being made upon us, but
will be prepared should such a thing take place."[3]   Colonel
Ammen, who commanded a brigade of Nelson's division in
Buell's army, which division had arrived at Savannah at

[1] Official Records, vol. x. part i., p. 99.
[2] See Grant's Personal Memoirs. "Correspondence between General Sherman and John Sherman," Century Magazine, Jan., 1893, p. 428.
[3] Cited by Force, pp. 120, 121 ; see, also, Grant to Buell, April 5, Official Records, vol. x. part ii. p. 93.

noon of the 5th, saw Grant, as he recorded in his diary, at about three o'clock in the afternoon of that day, and said to the general that his troops could march on to Pittsburg Landing, if necessary.   Grant replied: "You cannot march through the swamps; make the troops comfortable; I will send boats for you Monday or Tuesday, or some time early in the week.   There will be no fight at Pittsburg Landing;

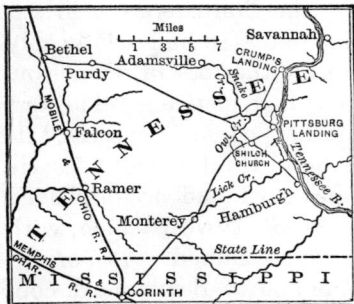

MAP OF SHILOH CAMPAIGN

we will have to go to Corinth, where the rebels are fortified. If they come to attack us we can whip them, as I have more than twice as many troops as I had at Fort Donelson."[1] Had Grant suspected that 40,000 Confederates confronted his army of 36,000, he certainly would have slept at Pittsburg Landing that night. In an air line Savannah was only six miles from Pittsburg Landing, and while eating his breakfast he heard the firing.   Sending an order to Nelson to march his division up the river to a point opposite Pittsburg Landing, the general took boat for the scene of action, stopping on the way at Crump's Landing, to tell Lew. Wallace to hold himself in readiness for an order to come to the assistance of the rest of the army.   Arriving at Pittsburg Landing, and finding a tremendous battle in progress, he sent the anticipated order to Wallace, and pressed Nelson to hasten. Although he visited the several divisions, and made perhaps the best disposition he could, it was a battle in which the commanding general on the Union side counted for little; the division, brigade, and regimental commanders did the work.   General William Tecumseh Sher-

---

[1] Official Records, vol. x. part i. p. 330.

man was the hero of the day. He was wounded twice, and had several horses shot under him. McClernand did valiant service. Hurlbut, W. H. L. Wallace, and Prentiss (these five led divisions) were equal to the demands upon them. Wallace and Prentiss were surrounded. Wallace, in attempting to cut his way out, fell mortally wounded. Prentiss, to save a useless and complete sacrifice, surrendered with 2200 men.

The most pathetic incident on the Confederate side was the death of Albert Sidney Johnston. He had felt keenly the strictures on his generalship for the loss of Donelson, and yet in a measure he admitted their justice. " The test of merit in my profession with the people is success," he wrote Davis. " It is a hard rule, but I think it right." [1] He could not help seeing that Beauregard had accomplished results in rallying the people of the Southwest which, with his loss of prestige, he could not have attained. At Corinth he proposed to turn over the command to Beauregard, confining himself to the duties of a department commander, an unselfish offer which Beauregard at once refused. When the battle began he left his second at the headquarters in the field, while he himself rode forward to the front, and cutting loose from communication with his corps commanders, fought as a volunteer of high rank in the line, without attempting to keep his hand on the general control of the army. His seeming disposition was to win a signal victory or die in the attempt. At a critical moment in the afternoon, while leading a charge of a Tennessee regiment, he received a ball in his leg which cut an artery ; he soon bled to death. The wound was not necessarily fatal, and had his surgeon, who had attended him most of the morning, been with him he might have been saved ; but seeing a large number of wounded men, he had ordered the surgeon to establish a hospital and care for them. His death was a severe blow to the Confederate army.

---

[1] March 18, Official Records, vol. vii. p. 261.

The battle of Shiloh was a fierce fight. It is described by Force as "a combat made up of numberless separate encounters of detached portions of broken lines, continually shifting position and changing direction in the forest and across ravines."[1] The contest of the first day lasted twelve hours and was a Confederate victory, in that the Union troops were driven back one mile and a half and lost Shiloh church, the point which, Grant writes, "was the key to our position."[2] Beauregard's headquarters on the night of April 6 were where Sherman's had been the night before. Nevertheless the result utterly failed to meet the expectations of Johnston and Beauregard; they had hoped to capture the Union army, or at any rate to drive it from the field in complete rout. Lew. Wallace's division, through a misunderstanding of orders, did not get to the field until Sunday's battle was over. Colonel Ammen's brigade of Buell's army reached the Landing in the afternoon and was ferried across the river, arriving in time to take part in the last minutes of the contest. Ten thousand stragglers from the Union army cowered under the high bank of the river. Many of the troops were raw and fled panic-stricken at the first charge; some of the officers showed cowardice as well as inefficiency. Stragglers from the Confederate ranks were numerous. Nearly ten thousand Union soldiers were killed, wounded, or captured; the Confederate loss in killed and wounded was as great as the Union, but the loss in prisoners was small. Through it all Grant preserved his imperturbability. "The tremendous roar to the left," writes Whitelaw Reid, who, as a newspaper correspondent, saw the battle, "momentarily nearer and nearer, told of an effort to cut him off from the river and from retreat. Grant sat on his horse quiet, thoughtful, almost stolid. Said one to him, 'Does not the prospect begin to look gloomy?' 'Not at all,' was the quiet reply. 'They can't force our lines around these batteries to-night—it is too late. Delay counts everything

---

[1] p. 124.   [2] Personal Memoirs, vol. i. p. 338.

with us. To-morrow we shall attack them with fresh troops, and drive them, of course.' " [1]

The night of the battle a heavy rain poured down on the unsheltered soldiers of both armies as they slept on their arms. The Union gun-boats fired at regular intervals heavy shells over the woods towards the point where the Confederates had bivouacked, for the purpose of disturbing their rest. Beauregard's disorganized and shattered army, worn out with the exertions of Sunday, was little fitted to cope with the body of fresh troops that had joined Grant. Lew. Wallace had arrived with 6500 men. The rest of Nelson's division, Crittenden's, and part of McCook's division of Buell's army, amounting in all to about 20,000, had reached the scene of action. Buell himself had been on the field of battle Sunday. He and Grant met that night, and determined to make a simultaneous attack on the Confederates early Monday morning. The onslaught was made and resulted in victory. At two o'clock, after eight hours of fighting, Beauregard gave the order to retire; this was accomplished in good order. That night again it rained heavily, making the bad roads worse. Owing to the fatigue of the Army of the Tennessee Grant ordered no immediate pursuit; the later pursuit was not effective. The loss of Grant's army was 1513 killed, 6601 wounded, 2830 captured or missing, a total of 10,944; the casualties in Buell's army were 241 killed, 1807 wounded, and 55 captured or missing, a total of 2103. The whole Union loss amounted to 13,047. In the Confederate army, as officially reported, there were 1728 killed, 8012 wounded, and 959 missing. Never before had a battle of such magnitude been fought in America. It was a desperate effort of the Confederates to retrieve what they had lost by the capture of Donelson, but their advance northward was for the time effectually repelled.

General C. F. Smith, who had done such heroic service at Donelson, did not share in the battle of Shiloh. He was in

---

[1] Ohio in the War, vol. i. p. 375. Reid heard this conversation.

bed at Savannah, owing to an abrasion on the leg received as he was getting into a small boat at Pittsburg Landing; the wound mortified, and he died April 25. In his death the Union army suffered a great loss. Grant writes that, at the time he was superseded by Smith, Halleck's opinion and that of the generality undoubtedly was that Smith had greater fitness for the command of the Army of the Tennessee than he himself had, and in fact he rather inclined to that opinion himself.[1]

The general notion at the North was that only the arrival of Buell's army saved Grant from a second and more disastrous defeat. Whether that judgment be correct has since become a matter of controversy. Grant and Sherman have affirmed that, with Lew. Wallace's division of fresh troops, they would on Monday have driven the Confederates from the field. Bearing on this dispute, the remarks of General Sherman, in his official report of April 10, 1862, are significant. At about ten A.M. Monday, he wrote, " I saw for the first time the well-ordered and compact columns of General Buell's Kentucky forces, whose soldierly movements at once gave confidence to our newer and less-disciplined forces. . . . I concede that General McCook's splendid division from Kentucky drove back the enemy along the Corinth road, which was the great central line of this battle." [2] It is safe, at all events, to say that the arrival of Buell converted what would have been at best a doubtful result into an almost absolute certainty. Considering the bad roads, the obstacles encountered, the orders received that haste was unnecessary, and that the soldiers were not veterans, Buell and his officers showed energy and celerity in their march from Nashville to Pittsburg Landing.[3]

---

[1] Personal Memoirs, vol. i. p. 328.

[2] Official Records, vol. x. part i. p. 251.

[3] My authorities for this account are, the reports of Grant, Buell, McClernand, Sherman, Prentiss, Nelson, and Ammen, of the Union army; of Beauregard, Polk, Bragg, and Hardee, of the Confederate army, Official Records, vol. x. part i.; the correspondence, ibid., part ii.; articles of Grant,

The laurels which Grant had won at Donelson were faded by his carelessness at Shiloh. That the battle had been a useless slaughter was the opinion of many of his officers and soldiers; and as the details of it became known, and as private letters began to be received from the army, the feeling towards him in the Western States, from which his troops came, was full of bitterness. The press faithfully reflected this sentiment, and members of Congress shared it. Elihu B. Washburne, in the House, and John Sherman, in the Senate, alone defended him. " You will see, from Harlan's remarks," wrote Sherman to his brother, the general, "there is much feeling against Grant, and I try to defend him, but with little success." [1] All sorts of charges against him were made; that he had been reckless could not be gainsaid with much show of reason. The pressure on the President for his removal was great. A. K. McClure relates that, carried along by the overwhelming " tide of popular sentiment," and backed by " the almost universal conviction of the President's friends," he urged this course upon Lincoln. Going to the White House at eleven o'clock one night, in a private interview of two hours, in which he did most of the talking, McClure advocated with earnestness the removal of Grant as necessary for the President to retain the confidence of the country. " When I had said everything that could be said from my standpoint," McClure proceeds with his story, " we lapsed into silence. Lincoln remained silent for what seemed a very long time. He then gathered

Buell, William Preston Johnston, Beauregard, and Jordan, Century War Book, vol. i.; also the composition, strength, and losses of the opposing forces at Shiloh, ibid.; J. D. Cox, in the *Nation*, July 30, 1885, Feb. 25, 1886 ; From Fort Henry to Corinth, Force ; Nicolay and Hay, vol. v. ; Swinton's Decisive Battles of the War. My thanks are especially due to General J. D. Cox for reading in MS. my account of the battle of Shiloh, and for making several critical suggestions, which, on revision, I incorporated in my narrative. I am also under obligation to him for a like attention to my descriptions of the battle of Bull Run and of the capture of Fort Donelson.

[1] *Century Magazine*, Jan., 1893, p. 429.

himself up in his chair and said, in a tone of earnestness that
I shall never forget, '*I can't spare this man; he fights.*' " [1]
The result demonstrated what a clear perception of military
ability Lincoln had in this case, when he determined to save
Grant from removal and disgrace.

April 7, the second day of the battle of Shiloh, General
John Pope, in conjunction with two of Foote's gun-boats,
captured Island No. 10 with 6000 or 7000 prisoners; this
was a fortress commanding the Mississippi River, and the
next one below Columbus. Halleck went to Pittsburg Landing, arriving there April 11, and ordered Pope and his army
to join him. Receiving also other reinforcements, he soon
had 100,000 effective troops. Appointing General Thomas
commander of the right wing, Buell of the centre, and Pope
of the left, he named Grant his second in command; but as
there went with it no precise duty, this assignment of position was really a displacement. Grant chafed under this,
asked several times to be relieved from duty, and would
have left the army had he not been dissuaded by Sherman,
with whom he had already begun that fast friendship which
endured throughout his whole life. Beauregard had been
reinforced, and had an effective strength of 50,000. Towards
the close of April Halleck began his move on Corinth, marching slowly and cautiously, and intrenching at every halt.
The enemy's outposts hovered near the advancing army, but
Halleck's orders to his subordinate commanders were to bring
on no engagement. He was more than a month advancing the
twenty-three miles from Pittsburg Landing to Corinth, and
as soon as he arrived before the Confederate intrenchments
Beauregard evacuated the place, of which the Union army
then took peaceful possession. Grant, Sherman, and Pope
had been anxious to fight the enemy, but Halleck discour-

---

[1] McClure's Lincoln and Men of War Times, p. 179. See Washburne's
speech of May 2; Sherman's speech in the Senate, Harlan's remarks, May
9; Cincinnati *Commercial*, April 15, 16, 18, 25, 28; New York *World*, April
10; Sherman's Memoirs, vol. i. p. 244.

aged all such suggestions and efforts. Corinth being a strategic point, on account of the junction there of the Mobile and Ohio Railroad running north and south, and the Memphis and Charleston Railroad running east and west, was worth having; but a victory over Beauregard's army would have been worth vastly more.[1]

In the last days of April New Orleans was surrendered to Flag-officer Farragut, and the Union flag waved over the city. This result had been attained by an expedition of men-of-war under the command of Farragut, and a fleet of mortar boats under David D. Porter, which had bombarded with effect Forts St. Philip and Jackson; these forts were depended on as the main defences of New Orleans, although seventy-five miles below it. After five days of bombardment without reducing the forts, Farragut decided to make an attempt to run by them, and at two o'clock, on the morning of April 24, he gave the signal to advance, Porter, in the meanwhile, opening fire with fury from his mortar boats. Farragut, returning vigorously the fire of the forts, succeeded in getting past them with the largest portion of his fleet; he then attacked the Confederate gun-boats, which disputed the passage of the river above the forts, and, owing to the superiority of his vessels and the better discipline of his men, he easily defeated them in the naval battle which ensued, consigning most of them to destruction. He then steamed up the river without further serious molestation. When the news spread in New Orleans that the federal fleet was coming, hundreds of drays were set to work to haul the cotton in the presses and the yards to the levee; here patriotism applied the torch to the staple so eagerly desired at the North and in Europe. May 1 General Butler with 2500 troops occupied the city; Forts St. Philip and Jackson had surrendered to Commander Porter three days previously.[2]

[1] See Force's From Fort Henry to Corinth; Nicolay and Hay, vol. v.; Grant's Personal Memoirs; Sherman's Memoirs.

[2] See Nicolay and Hay, vol. v.; D. D. Porter, G. W. Cable, W. T. Meredith, in Century War Book, vol. ii.

The taking of New Orleans, a city of 160,000 inhabitants, the chief commercial port and the largest city of the South, a place well known in Europe as an important trading point, had a profound effect on opinion in England and France. May 15 Slidell wrote Benjamin from Paris that a conversation with Thouvenel, the French Minister of Foreign Affairs, led him " fairly to infer that if New Orleans had not been taken, and we suffered no very serious reverses in Virginia and Tennessee, our recognition would very soon have been declared." On the next day he had a conversation with Billanet, " minister *sans* portfolio, especially charged to represent the government in the Chambers on all subjects connected with foreign affairs. . . . In reply to my suggestions," Slidell wrote, "that the war could only be brought to a close by the intervention of European powers, which should be preceded by our recognition and a renewed proffer of mediation, he said that France could not act without the co-operation of England, but that within the last few days there seemed to be a change in the tone of the English cabinet; that if New Orleans had not fallen, our recognition could not have been much longer delayed." Mason wrote Benjamin from London, " The occupation of the principal Southern ports by the enemy, and the increased rigor of the blockade of those remaining to us, resulting from it, give little hope now of any interference in regard to the blockade, and leave only the question of recognition." [1]

While the army and navy were winning victories, the President and Congress were grappling with the evil which had caused the war. In March Arnold, of Illinois, introduced a bill into the House, the purport of which was to render slavery sectional and freedom national; this resulted later in the passage of an act prohibiting slavery in all the

---

[1] Slidell's second despatch is dated June 1, and Mason's is June 23. These despatches are in the MS. Confederate Diplomatic Correspondence in the Treasury Department, Washington; see, also, London *Times*, May 12; *Daily News*, May 13; the *Spectator*, May 17; *Saturday Review*, May 17.

present territories of the United States, and in any that
should hereafter be acquired,[1] thus crystallizing in a formal
statute the cardinal principle of the Republican party, which
had constituted the reason of its existence. April 16 the
President approved an act of Congress, which went further
than it had been deemed prudent to go in either of the
Republican national platforms; this abolished slavery in
the District of Columbia, provided for the compensation
of the owners of slaves, and appropriated a sum of money
for the voluntary colonization of the negroes in Hayti or
Liberia.[2] In March the President had taken a step far beyond either of these measures. On the 6th he sent a special
message to Congress, asking it to adopt a joint resolution
"which shall be substantially as follows: *Resolved*, That
the United States ought to co-operate with any State which
may adopt gradual abolishment of slavery, giving to each
State pecuniary aid, to be used by such State in its discretion, to compensate for the inconveniences, public and
private, produced by such change of system." He enforced
his recommendation by argument. " The leaders of the existing insurrection," he said, "entertain the hope that this
government will ultimately be forced to acknowledge the
independence of some part of the disaffected region, and
that all the slave States north of such part will then say,
'the Union for which we have struggled being already gone,
we now choose to go with the Southern section.' To deprive them of this hope substantially ends the rebellion. . . .
The point is not that *all* the States tolerating slavery would
very soon, if at all, initiate emancipation, but that, while
the offer is equally made to all, the more northern shall, by
such initiation, make it certain to the more southern that
in no event will the former ever join the latter in their proposed confederacy. I say 'initiation' because, in my judgment, gradual, and not sudden, emancipation is better for
all. . . . War has been made and continues to be an indis-

---

[1] *Congressional Globe*, p. 1340, Appendix, p. 364.   [2] Ibid., Appendix, p. 347.

pensable means" for the preservation of the Union. "A
practical reacknowledgment of the national authority would
render the war unnecessary, and it would at once cease. If,
however, resistance continues, the war must also continue;
and it is impossible to foresee all the incidents which may
attend, and all the ruin which may follow it. Such as may
seem indispensable, or may obviously promise great efficiency towards ending the struggle, must and will come.
The proposition now made, though an offer only, I hope it
may be esteemed no offence to ask whether the pecuniary
consideration tendered would not be of more value to the
States and private persons concerned than are the institution and property in it in the present aspect of affairs." [1]
In private letters to Senator McDougall, who opposed the
plan, and to the editor of the New York *Times*, Lincoln
was earnest in urging this policy. To McDougall he wrote:
" As to the expensiveness of the plan of gradual emancipation with compensation, proposed in the late message,
please allow me one or two brief suggestions. Less than
one-half day's cost of this war would pay for all the slaves
in Delaware, at $400 per head. Thus:

All the slaves in Delaware, by the census of 1860, are 1798
$400

Cost of slaves................................. $719,200
One day's cost of the war..................... 2,000,000

Again, less than eighty-seven days' cost of this war would,
at the same price, pay for all in Delaware, Maryland, District of Columbia, Kentucky, and Missouri. Thus:

Slaves in Delaware........................... 1,798
"   " Maryland........................... 87,188
"   " District of Columbia................ 3,181
"   " Kentucky........................... 225,490
"   " Missouri........................... 114,965
432,622
$400

Cost of slaves................................. $173,048,800
Eighty-seven days' cost of war............... 174,000,000

[1] *Congressional Globe*, p.1102.

"Do you doubt that taking the initiatory steps on the part of those States and this District would shorten the war more than eighty-seven days, and thus be an actual saving of expense? A word as to the *time* and *manner* of incurring the expense. Suppose, for instance, a State devises and adopts a system by which the institution absolutely ceases therein by a named day — say January 1, 1882. Then let the sum to be paid to such State by the United States be ascertained, by taking from the census of 1860 the number of slaves within the State, and multiplying that number by 400; the United States to pay such sum to the State in twenty equal annual instalments, in six per cent. bonds of the United States. The sum thus given, as to *time* and *manner*, I think, would not be half as onerous as would an equal sum raised *now* for the indefinite prosecution of the war; but of this you can judge as well as I." [1] The President pressed the acceptance of this offer upon the members of Congress from the border slave States. [2]

No one, I think, instructed by the succeeding events, can rise from the reading of this message and this letter without being impressed by the wisdom of Lincoln when he dealt with a subject to which he had given much thought and which he fully understood. No man in the country comprehended the slavery question in all its bearings better than he. We have seen how, in the beginning of his administration, he did not attempt to forecast the future, but deemed it sufficient to meet each exigency as it arose; and although the year of office had given him confidence in himself, and the knowledge that he had won the trust of the people, he still proceeded with care, shaping his policy, in a large degree, by circumstances as they arose, and heedful not to lead faster than the North would follow. Yet he could not fail to see, as did all reflecting persons, whither events were tending. That if the North were successful in

---

[1] Letter of March 14, Nicolay and Hay, vol. v. p. 210.
[2] McPherson, History of the Rebellion, p. 210 *et seq.*

the conflict slavery was eventually doomed seemed to him
certain ; that it might be necessary to proclaim immediate
emancipation in the Confederate States as a means of military success was equally clear. That such a policy, decided
upon opportunely, would have the support of the people was
beginning to be apparent. It is interesting to trace the
course of public sentiment, by observing who of the afore-
time statesmen of the republic were made the popular heroes. In November and December, 1860, the pusillanimous
course of President Buchanan caused the men of the North
to cry with one accord, " Oh, for an hour of Andrew Jackson !" Later, when the Union sentiment crystallized around
the reconstructed cabinet of Buchanan, when the Confederate States fired upon Sumter, when everywhere the North
declared with one voice that the sole purpose of the war was
the restoration of the Union, the patriotic glow of Daniel
Webster animated all hearts, his fervent words were in all
mouths ; from nearly every platform and pulpit might be
heard, " Liberty and Union, now and forever, one and insep-
arable." As the war went on, and thinking men began to
see that the restoration of the Union was indissolubly connected with the doom of slavery, they began to study the
speeches of John Quincy Adams in the House of Representatives, in which he had laid down the principle that if the
slave States became the theatre of war, the President or
Congress might, under the war powers of the Constitution,
order the universal emancipation of the slaves.[1]

With a true regard for vested rights, and the Anglo-Saxon
aversion to violent social and political changes, Lincoln anticipated the future enough to devise a plan by which freedom
should come to the slaves gradually, and by which the own-

---

[1] Morse's Life of John Quincy Adams, p. 262; New York *Tribune*, June
3, 22, Sept. 1, 1861 ; New York *Evening Post*, Sept. 2, 1861 ; Sumner's
speech at Worcester, Oct., 1861 ; Pierce's Sumner, vol. iv. p. 44; Edward
L. Pierce, in the *Atlantic Monthly*, Nov., 1861, p. 629; Lecture of Wendell
Phillips in New York and Boston, Dec., 1861, Speeches and Lectures, p.
435.

ers should receive compensation for their loss. Although, as
a practical measure, it was not expected that any but the
border States would avail themselves of it, the offer — for
the House, March 11, and the Senate, April 2, adopted the
joint resolution proposed by the President—was open to all
of the slave States; and if the people of any and all of the
Confederate States had, in this hour of the military successes
of the North, agreed to lay down their arms and respect the
authority of the national government, not a reasonable doubt
can exist that they would have received, in a plan of gradual emancipation, about four hundred dollars for each slave
set free. The record of Lincoln and the Republican party
on slavery is clear; their course was conservative and in
line with the best traditions of America and England. Before Sumter was fired upon they had agreed, practically, to
guarantee in perpetuity the possession of slaves to their
owners in all of the slave States; now, after nearly a year
of war and in the hour of victory, when the logic of events
clearly showed that slavery must go, they were willing to
reimburse the slave-owners for the misfortune which they
had brought upon themselves. Lincoln, in this special message, exhibited a magnanimous statesmanship which is admirable, and the Republicans of Congress, in co-operating with
him so speedily, showed their confidence in his judgment
and their own desire to do justice.[1] All who have read my
description of sentiment at the South, and who comprehend
what was the meaning of the war to the Southern people,
will see at once that it would be impossible for the States
of the Confederacy to entertain this offer; in spite of all
the influence which Lincoln could bring to bear, it was,
unfortunately, not accepted by the border slave States which
remained in the Union. Bound up as was slavery with their

---

[1] The vote on the resolution offering compensation for the slaves was:
Senate, yeas, 28 Republicans, 1 Democrat, 3 Unionists; nays, 6 Democrats, 3 Unionists; total, 32 yeas, 9 nays. House, yeas, 83 Republicans,
1 Democrat, 5 Unionists; nays, 2 Republicans, 20 Democrats, 9 Unionists;
total, 89 yeas, 31 nays.

social and political life, they could not see that its doom had
come. Nevertheless we may rejoice that the offer was in all
sincerity made, and that the worth and the meaning of it
were appreciated by the friends of the North in England.[1]
This volume ends with the rejoicing of the North over its
military successes in the winter and spring of 1862. The
President, by proclamation, asked the people to show their
gratitude by giving, in their accustomed places of worship,
thanks for these victories to Almighty God.[2] Roanoke
Island, Mill Spring, Forts Henry and Donelson, the occupation of Nashville, the freeing Missouri of the Confederate
forces, Shiloh, Island No. 10, the taking of New Orleans,
made up a roll of victory that seemed to presage the end
of the war. Instead of discouragement at the North, as
there had been after its defeats in 1861, depression and gloom
now prevailed at the South. McClellan, with over 100,000
men, was approaching Richmond, and great things were
expected of him. McDowell with another army covered
Washington. Frémont and Banks were in the Shenandoah
valley. Halleck, with an army of 100,000 men, and with
subordinate commanders who had military talents of a
high order, was moving on Corinth. The general opinion
of those in authority, and of the people, was that the war
would be over by midsummer. The Secretary of War had
stopped recruiting.[3] While the movement against slavery

---

[1] "I have been watching with deep interest all that has served to indicate the better tendencies and most hopeful results of your great contest.
. . . Your cause has been steadily 'marching on' by the inevitable force of
events. I think that, whatever may be the fate of the Union, the fate of
slavery is settled. Yet I see you daily abused in the American correspondence for giving, consciously and intentionally, to the struggle, that one
great aim and object for which, more than for any other, it will be memorable in the history of the world."—Duke of Argyll to Sumner, June 12,
Pierce-Sumner Papers, MS. See a sensible article in the London *Spectator*
of March 22, entitled "The Beginning of the End;" also the London *Daily
News* of March 21. The London *Times* of March 21 had a leader very
unsympathetic in tone.

[2] Moore's Rebellion Record, vol. iv., Docs., p. 465.

[3] General Order No. 33, War Department, Adjutant - General's office

had not been rapid enough for the radical Republicans, it was reasonable to believe that the restoration of the Union, should it come in the year 1862, would comprise some scheme of gradual emancipation. In the little more than a year of war, the progress towards liberty had been swift. Slavery prohibited in the territories, abolished in the District of Columbia, the President and Congress making an offer to the States to compensate them for giving freedom to their slaves, when a resolution to that effect, introduced into the House in February, 1861, hardly attracted notice— these demonstrated with what rapidity events had hurried on in a time of revolution and war. We may well conceive with what gratulation Lincoln and the Republicans regarded these landmarks, in the establishment of which they had been the instruments. They were convinced that the end of the struggle was near, that their work was almost accomplished, and that, if their sanguine hopes should prove true, they had, in saving the Union and in giving deadly blows to slavery, wrought out their country's salvation.[1]

April 3, 1862; also cited in McClellan's Own Story, p. 258. General Sherman was one of the men who did not share the popular view. May 7 he wrote his brother, the senator: "That the war is ended, or even fairly begun, I do not believe;" and May 12: "I think it is a great mistake to stop enlistments. There may be enough soldiers on paper, but not enough in fact."—*Century Magazine*, Jan., 1893, p. 429.

[1] My thanks are due to Hon. Daniel S. Lamont, Secretary of War, for access to the Confederate archives in the War Department.

I have already acknowledged my indebtedness to Professor Edward G. Bourne for his assistance on Chapter XII. To this I must add that he read carefully in manuscript the four succeeding chapters, and that he made me many suggestions touching economic matters and literary expression. I am indebted to Dr. Titus Munson Coan for a literary revision of this volume, as well as of Volumes I. and II. I desire to recognize the intelligent aid of Thomas J. Kiernan, superintendent of circulation of the college library of Harvard University, and to acknowledge my indebtedness to Mrs. M. S. Beall for careful work done in the government archives at Washington.

The printer's preparation of this volume was so far along at the time of the publication of Volume I. of John C. Ropes's "Story of the Civil War" that I was unable to make any use of that work.

Note to p. 423: From a letter of Lyons to Russell on December 19, 1861, it appears that, at the first interview, he told Seward "privately and confidentially" that he must have the answer in seven days, and also that on the same day (December 19) he sent to the Secretary in confidence Russell's dispatch. The seven days did not begin to run however until the formal demand was made on December 23.

— *Life of Lord Lyons*, Newton (1913), I, 67.